Part biography and part literary history, this book is about the experience of the American modernist poet Wallace Stevens in the 1930s. Stevens is generally thought to have antagonized, even enraged, the young literary radicals of the period; his long poem "Owl's Clover" has been generally understood as a negative, even bitter response to leftist aesthetics. Using the archives of many little-known political poets, Alan Filreis offers a detailed description of various literary-political battles, in which the very texture of the positions taken up in the movement between left and right becomes available to us in the language of the participants. Filreis demonstrates that radicals knew and appreciated modernism more than has been recognized, and that Stevens's poetry – as well as that of other then-eminent modernists – was significantly influenced by poets and critics on the left. *Modernism from Right to Left* shows that the interactions between eminent modernists – Stevens, Marianne Moore, William Carlos Williams – and upstart radicals – Stanley Burnshaw, T. C. Wilson, Ruth Lechlitner, Kenneth Fearing, Muriel Rukeyser, Willard Maas, and others – were far more dynamic than has been acknowledged during and beyond the eras of anticommunism. This book is a contribution to the history of the American 1930s as well as a novel approach to an oft-studied figure.

CAMBRIDGE STUDIES IN AMERICAN LITERATURE
AND CULTURE

Modernism from Right to Left

CAMBRIDGE STUDIES IN AMERICAN LITERATURE
AND CULTURE

Editor: ERIC SUNDQUIST, University of California, Los Angeles
Founding Editor: ALBERT GELPI, Stanford University

Advisory Board

NINA BAYM, University of Illinois, Champaign-Urbana
SACVAN BERCOVITCH, Harvard University
ALBERT GELPI, Stanford University
MYRA JEHLEN, Rutgers University
CAROLYN PORTER, University of California, Berkeley
ROBERT STEPTO, Yale University
TONY TANNER, King's College, Cambridge University

Continued on page following the Index

Modernism from Right to Left:

Wallace Stevens, the Thirties, & Literary Radicalism

ALAN FILREIS
University of Pennsylvania

CAMBRIDGE
UNIVERSITY PRESS

Published by the Press Syndicate of the University of Cambridge
The Pitt Building, Trumpington Street, Cambridge CB2 IRP
40 West 20th Street, New York, NY 10011-4211, USA
10 Stamford Road, Oakleigh, Melbourne 3166, Australia

© Cambridge University Press 1994

First published 1994

Printed in the United States of America

Library of Congress Cataloging-in-Publication Data

Filreis, Alan, 1956–

    Modernism from right to left : Wallace Stevens, the thirties, &
literary radicalism / Alan Filreis.

        p.   cm. – (Cambridge studies in American literature and
culture)

    Includes bibliographical references (p.) and index.

    ISBN 0-521-45384-4

    1. Stevens, Wallace, 1879–1955 – Political and social views.
2. American poetry – 20th century – History and criticism.
3. Political poetry, American – History and criticism. 4. Modernism
(Literature) – United States. 5. Radicalism in literature.
I. Title. II. Series.
PS3537.T47537635   1994
811'.52 – dc20

                                        93-33404
                                          CIP

A catalog record for this book is available from the British Library.

ISBN 0-521-45384-4 hardback

This book is lovingly dedicated to
Samuel H. and Lois Gainsburg Filreis

Imagination has no source except in reality, and ceases to have any value when it departs from reality.

—Wallace Stevens

Ideas of Order was offered to the reading public of the thirties by a man not in the least ignorant of the issues or, for that matter, of the controversies and the codes.

—Stanley Burnshaw

A poem . . . is a kind of strategy for coping with a given scene or situation.

—T. C. Wilson, a radical poet, writing about Kenneth Burke

Contents

vii

Illustrations

Acknowledgments

Without the help of curators, special collections librarians, and archivists – in some cases help given over a period of years – it would simply not have been possible to write this book. I wish first, then, to thank John L. Beck of the Radical Literature Collection at the University of Maryland, Baltimore County; Ernst Bendix of the Staten Island Historical Society; Elizabeth Bishop and Carol Mackie of the Regenstein Library, University of Chicago; Eileen Cahill, formerly of the Rosenbach Museum and Library; Anne Caiger of Special Collections at UCLA; Bernard R. Crystal of the Butler Library, Columbia University; Kenneth R. Cobb at the New York City Department of Records & Information Services; Vicki Denby of Harvard's Houghton Library; Laura A. Endicott of Special Collections, Alderman Library, University of Virginia; Ken Ferraro, Bonnie Jean Woodworth, and Leslie Bernier, respectively, of the Archives, Corporate Library, and Records Department at the Hartford Insurance Group; Barbara Filipac of the John Hay Library, Brown University; Ann Flowers of the Special Collections Library, University of Michigan; Cathy Henderson and Ken Craven of the Harry Ransom Humanities Research Center, University of Texas; Bambi Landry of the Santa Fe Public Library; Mark Jones, Archivist at the State Library of Connecticut; Beverly Laughlin of the Hartford Public Library; Pruda Lood of the Hoover Institute Library, Stanford University; Kathleen Manwaring of the George Arent Library, Syracuse University; Robert A. McCown of the Special Collections and Manuscript Library at the University of Iowa; Kris McCusker of Rare Books & Manuscripts, University of Colorado; Timothy D. Murray of Special Collections, University of Delaware Library; Norma Ortiz of Special Collections, University of Arkansas Libraries; Sarah Polirer, formerly of the Harvard University Archives in Pusey Library; Jean F. Preston of the Department of Rare Books and Special Collections, Princeton University Library; Kevin Ray of Special Collections at Washington University; Virginia Renner and Sara Hodson of the Henry E. Huntington Library; Orlando Romero at the Museum of

New Mexico, Santa Fe; Linda Seidman of the University of Massachusetts; Raymond Teichman of the Franklin Delano Roosevelt Library, Hyde Park; Daniel Traister and Nancy Shawcross of Special Collections, Van Pelt Library, University of Pennsylvania; Cynthia Wall of Special Collections at the Newberry Library; John White of the Southern Historical Collection at the University of North Carolina, Chapel Hill; Patricia Willis and Patricia Middleton of the Beinecke Rare Book and Manuscript Library at Yale University; and Father Germain Williams of the Conventual Franciscan Friars, Albany.

I am also thankful to David Gross, Rachel Solar, Wendy Bach, Crystal VanHorn, and Eric Wertheimer for helping at various points with research. And for their extraordinarily energetic and capable three years' work as my research assistants at the University of Pennsylvania, I very gratefully acknowledge Matthew Larsen and Lynn Roland.

Alan Wald, Art Casciato, Harvey Teres, Jerre Mangione, and Stanley Burnshaw generously offered me their knowledge about the literary scene of the 1930s and varying (but invariably useful) advice about negotiating one's way through the period's arguments and counterarguments. My debt to Stanley Burnshaw is a deep one; he has been especially patient with me, always answering my questions at length and always instigating new ones. His sense of the 1930s is profound, as is his understanding of modern poetry: the combination has served me in ways that will be obvious, I trust, to readers of this book.

I'm grateful, too, to Allen Guttmann, Ellis W. Hawley, Peter Conn, Marjorie Perloff, Roy Harvey Pearce, James Longenbach, A. Walton Litz, Milton Bates, and Harvey Teres for having read portions of this book in draft. Peter Tarr and Daniel Traister each very carefully scrutinized and evaluated chapters at various stages; I owe both a great deal for those efforts, and for much more.

I am pleased also to acknowledge a number of generous people who took time to offer me information and/or guidance on certain issues: Kurt Albertine (Stevens's blood anemia); Wendy Flory (Pound-Tyler letters); William M. Ford (Latimer); John Fuller (Auden's "I have a handsome profile"); J. Hakes (T. C. Wilson), Madeleine Leippert Hall (Latimer); Ellis W. Hawley and Robert Himmelberg (business resistance to the New Deal); Herbert F. Janick, Jr. (Connecticut history); John Jeffries (Connecticut political history); Robert F. Kadlec (Latimer); William Koshland (Paul Hoffman, Knopf); Paul Corey and the late Ruth Lechlitner (Alcestis Press and Ruth Lechlitner); Marian Love (Latimer); Father Conan Lynch (Latimer); Stephen Maas (Willard Maas); the late Gerard Previn Meyer (Latimer); the late John J. O'Loughlin (Hartford insurance); Lyman Orton (Vrest Orton and Alcestis); Anna Moore Parks (depression-era Miami); Margaret Powers (James Powers); Peter Prescott

(Knopf); Charles A. Robertson (Latimer); Paul Rogers (Burnshaw's *New Masses* tour); Guy Rotella (Samuel French Morse); Margaret F. Sax (Eric P. Swenson); and Marc Simon (Latimer). Hunter S. Neal, Jr., Senior Staff Photographer at ITT/The Hartford, provided photographs from the *Hartford Agent*. A. Walton Litz, Milton Bates, Marjorie Perloff, John Richetti, David Wyatt, and the late Holly Stevens each gave me special encouragements at crucial moments.

My greatest debt is to Susan Albertine: keen reader and editor, dauntless literary scholar, intrepid partner, she continues to be, for me, "a planet's encouragement."

Grateful acknowledgment is made to the following: Alfred A. Knopf, Inc., for permission to reprint previously published material from *Letters of Wallace Stevens*, Copyright © 1966 by Holly Stevens; *Opus Posthumous: Poems, Plays, Prose*, by Wallace Stevens © 1957 by Holly Stevens and Elsie Stevens, renewed 1989 by Holly Stevens; *Collected Poems of Wallace Stevens*, © 1954 by Wallace Stevens. Lines from "Thoughts During an Air Raid" by Stephen Spender are reprinted with permission of Random House, Inc., from *Collected Poems 1928–1953* by Stephen Spender, © 1942 by Stephen Spender. Lines from "The Labors of Hercules" by Marianne Moore are reprinted with permission of Macmillan Co. from *Collected Poems of Marianne Moore*, © 1935 by Marianne Moore, renewed 1963 by Marianne Moore and T. S. Eliot; and also with permission of Faber and Faber Ltd. of London, England. The following poetry is reprinted by permission of New Directions Publishing Corporation: portions of poems in William Carlos Williams, *Collected Poems, 1909–1939*, Volume 1, © 1988 by New Directions Publishing Corporation; lines of "From the Paris Commune to the Kronstadt Rebellion" by Kenneth Rexroth in *Collected Shorter Poems*, © 1956 by New Directions Publishing Corporation; and lines from George Oppen's *Discrete Series*, which is contained in *Collected Poems of George Oppen*, © 1975 by New Directions Publishing Corporation.

I am also grateful to Marianne Craig Moore, Literary Executor for the Estate of Marianne Moore, for permission to quote Moore's letters to Ronald Lane Latimer, Wallace Stevens, and T. C. Wilson; to Ashley Brown for permission to quote Allen Tate's letter to him; to Madeleine Leippert Hall for letters and poems of Ronald Lane Latimer; to Steve Maas for letters and poems of Willard Maas; to Patrick Gregory for Horace Gregory's letters; to Stanley Burnshaw for his letters and poems; to Jane Morse for letters of Samuel French Morse; to Stephanie Craib for letters of Granville Hicks; to Bradford Morrow for a letter of Kenneth Rexroth; and to George E. Mathews, Executor and Successor Trustee of the Paul Corey Living Trust, for letters and poems of Ruth Lechlitner.

Excerpts from the unpublished letters of Elizabeth Bishop are used with the kind permission of her Estate, © 1993 by Alice Helen Methfessel.

The following archives and libraries have kindly extended me permission to use materials housed in their facilities (in most cases, though not all, such permission has entailed physical rights only): the Manuscripts Division, Department of Rare Books and Special Collections, Princeton University Libraries (Latimer's letter to John Peale Bishop and Allen Tate in the Tate Papers, and Stevens's to R. P. Blackmur in the Blackmur Papers); the Marjorie Allen Seiffert Collection, Special Collections Department, University of Colorado at Boulder Libraries (letters to Marjorie Seiffert); Special Collections and Archives, University Library, University of Massachusetts Amherst (Barrett Wendell's letter to Osward Garrison Villard); Yale Collection of American Literature, Beinecke Rare Book and Manuscript Library, Yale University (William Carlos Williams's letter to Latimer in the Williams Papers); the George Arents Research Library for Special Collections, Syracuse University (letters of Bryher, Isidor Schneider, F. W. Dupee, T. C. Wilson, and Stanley Burnshaw in the Granville Hicks and Horace Gregory Papers); the Rosenbach Museum & Library (letters between T. C. Wilson and Marianne Moore in the Moore Papers); Rare Books and Manuscripts Division, The New York Public Library, Astor, Lenox and Tilden Foundations (letters from Stevens and Mark Sullivan to Gilbert Montague in the Montague-Collier Family Papers); Special Collections Division, University of Arkansas Libraries, Fayetteville (letters of Lewis Mumford and Gerard Previn Meyer in the John Gould Fletcher Papers); the University of Iowa Libraries, Iowa City (letters to and from Ruth Lechlitner in the Lechlitner Papers); Washington University Libraries, St. Louis (letters from Maas and Morse to George Marion O'Donnell in the O'Donnell Papers; Elizabeth Bishop's letter to Anne Ford in the Bishop Papers); Henry E. Huntington Library, San Marino, CA (letters to and from Wallace Stevens in the Stevens Papers; Maas's letters to Sara Bard Field in the C.E.S. Wood Papers; and untranscribed portions of taped interviews in the Peter Brazeau Audiotape Collection); Brown University Library (letters of Willard Maas, Horace Gregory, and Porter Sargent in the John Wheelwright Papers [for both property and literary rights]; letters of Ruth Lechlitner, Harold Rosenberg, Ronald Lane Latimer and Willard Maas, and Alcestis Press materials in the Willard Maas Papers; letters of Maas and Latimer in the S. Foster Damon Papers); Harry Ransom Humanities Research Center, University of Texas at Austin (letters of Ben Belitt, Ruth Lechlitner, Ronald Lane Latimer, Kenneth Rexroth, Allen Tate, Wallace Stevens, John Wheelwright, Malcolm Cowley, Stanley Burnshaw, and Samuel French Morse in the Willard Maas Papers; Kenneth Fearing's letter to Carl Rakosi in the Rakosi Papers); The Poetry/Rare Books Collection, University Libraries, State University of New York

at Buffalo (letter of Ronald Lane Latimer and typescript of William Carlos Williams's "Guitar Blues" in the Williams Papers); the Houghton Library, Harvard University (letters of James G. Leippert, Witter Bynner, William Carlos Williams, and Stevens); Clifton Waller Barrett Library, Manuscripts Division, Special Collections Department at the University of Virginia (letters of Stanley Burnshaw in the Alfred Kreymborg Collection, #6561). Previously unpublished material found in several archives mentioned above by William Carlos Williams, © 1993, by William Eric Williams and Paul H. Williams, has been used by permission of New Directions Publishing Corporation, agents for the Williamses.

Small portions of this book were published, somewhat revised, as articles in *The Wallace Stevens Journal* 17, 2 (Fall 1993) and *Syracuse University Library Associates Courier* 27, 1 (Spring 1992).

Abbreviations

CP   *Collected Poems of Wallace Stevens* (New York: Alfred A. Knopf, 1954)

OP   *Opus Posthumous*, ed. Milton Bates (New York: Alfred A. Knopf, 1989)

WSR   Peter Brazeau, *Parts of a World: Wallace Stevens Remembered* (New York: Random House, 1983)

L   *Letters of Wallace Stevens*, ed. Holly Stevens (New York: Alfred A. Knopf, 1966)

Introduction

Do the drummers in black hoods
Rumble anything out of their drums?
—Wallace Stevens, "The Pleasures of Merely Circulating," 1934

Chroniclers and critics of the 1930s have argued among themselves so unremittingly about the cultural role of radicalism that the newest and most intellectually flexible among them are often hindered rather than liberated by the debate.[1] The bitterness of this fighting has made me somewhat reluctant to present *Modernism from Right to Left* as a call for similar contentiousness to commence among admirers of modern American poetry. It strikes me nonetheless that the almost total absence of such dispute in discussions of this poetry is one of the reasons why an auspicious direction in the study of modernism's relation to the "clever hopes" of that allegedly "low, dishonest decade"[2] remains largely untried. Another reason, not easily documented, is that those students rhetorically trained by American doctoral programs in literature during the past forty years to read poets like Wallace Stevens and Marianne Moore, and to a somewhat lesser extent William Carlos Williams, have not also been attracted to writing deemed "revolutionary" in the political sense. After the thirties – one decade when literary radicals *were* reading these modernists, as I will show – the exceptions have been only very recent.[3] As a corollary to this unwritten professional rule, it might be further supposed that insofar as critics of depression-era writing have, in Cary Nelson's words, "treat[ed] the political poetry of the period as a unitary phenomenon and reject[ed] it contemptuously"[4] (for "unitary" read "ideological" or even "Stalinist"), critics of Stevens's depression-era writing have congenially embraced his modernism, judging it elastic and accommodating (for these terms read "non-ideological" and "anti-Stalinist"). Obviously, the two groups haven't been talking to each other. Why not? Lively and productive, if often bitter, interaction between noncommunists and communists was a fortunate topic of study as soon as, in the 1960s, histo-

I

rians got out from under the proto-Cold War spell of Eugene Lyons's *The Red Decade* of 1941. Frank Warren's *Liberals and Communism* (1966) made its rejoinder to Lyons's thesis of "Stalinist penetration of America" not by claiming to the contrary that communism was "at most a very minor influence" on noncommunist thinking in the thirties, but by carefully describing points of intersection and crossing.[5] In one sense, then, my book presents a similar dialogue between those two positions on the matter of poetry – not for the purpose of finding some safe centrism (perhaps Warren's one flaw) but rather to point up a false distinction that separated modernism and radicalism in the first place.

In this book I, too, find Wallace Stevens's 1930s poetry accommodating and elastic. At the same time I attempt to realize these as having served as anti-ideological terms. In other words, such a reconstructive venture as this deliberately does not entail the usual assumption of intellectual inflexibility on the literary left. It is the main point of this effort to show how noncommunists' talent for what Kenneth Burke in 1937 astutely termed "casuistic stretching"[6] – in Stevens this skill manifested itself in two messily dialogical poems, "Owl's Clover" (1936) and "The Man with the Blue Guitar" (1937) – was partly intrinsic to the modernist penchant for many-sidedness, and partly learned from a bold new aesthetic left wing that was itself remarkably open and variable. This boldness I find in Burke's relentless emphasis on language, which created for him a critical disposition steeped in modernism and yet having the effect of reestablishing literature's value as social strategy and active power – this from, as Frank Lentricchia has correctly observed, "a charter member of the modernist avant-garde, . . . unswerving champion of Joyce, Williams, and Djuna Barnes."[7] Similarly bold was Edmund Wilson's *Axel's Castle* (1931). In the final words of that book, Wilson admitted that Joyce, Eliot, Proust, and Stein "tended to overemphasize the importance of the individual," were "preoccupied with introspection," and "have endeavored to discourage their readers, not only with politics, but with action of any kind." Yet when I read *Axel's Castle* as a whole, thinking of it as a work of the twenties catching up page by page to the thirties,[8] I am persuaded that Wilson was right to reserve the greatest measure of his ample critical power for modernism as having "revealed to the imagination a new flexibility and freedom." ("And though we are aware in [modernist writing] of things that are dying," Wilson concluded movingly and a touch desperately, " . . . they none the less break down the walls of the present and wake us to the hope and exaltation of the untried.")[9] Readers of Lucia Trent's and Ralph Cheney's spirited *More Power to Poets!* (1934) will be equally impressed, I think, by the authors' unswerving commitment as thirties radicals to several basic modernist breakthroughs. In "What Is This Modernism?" they assert their indebtedness:

> The breaking of "Do nots" is almost the only practice at which modernist poets work shoulder to shoulder. . . . The "Do not" which modern-

ists break in subject matter is that Pegasus must be kept in a paddock. *Any subject can be made poetic.* For poetry resides in the poet, not in the subject. Electric lights as well as stars, factory workers as well as birds. . . . In diction, modernists believe that no word can be too frank, too earthy, too strong. . . . Many modernists are intent on developing a new mythos. . . . To modernists poetry is not a sugared sedative.[10]

In the chapters to follow, I have brought to the foreground a great deal of new evidence that supports Burke, Wilson, Trent, Cheyney, and others' interactivist positions, especially in considering communist and radical noncommunist poets who made direct contact with famous modernists and their work. Proceeding in this way, I also hope to affirm the conclusions of two otherwise very different recent works, Alan Wald's *The Revolutionary Imagination* (1983) and Cary Nelson's *Repression and Recovery* (1989), where aesthetic left sectarianism is shown neither to have prevented experimental verse nor repudiated several basic elements of modernism.[11]

But even such recent revisions of the modernism-radicalism debate as Wald, Nelson, Harvey Teres,[12] Charlotte Nekola,[13] James D. Bloom,[14] Judy Kutulas,[15] and others[16] have recently managed has for professional and methodological reasons not been very easily achieved. Finding "the density, the generic ambiguity, and the understanding of . . . their own status as mediated and mediating" – in other words, qualities ascribed to modernist writing – in the work of Mike Gold and Joseph Freeman, Bloom has traced the "work[s] of recovery" that made his own possible. For every effort to clear the way made by scholars like Daniel Aaron (*Writers on the Left*) and Marcus Klein (*Foreigners*) during the busy twenty-year period bordered by these two books (1961 to 1981), "chronic obstacles" have been set up by the thirties' many retrospective antagonists. Scholars who get past the interpretations of ex- and anticommunists must still then confront those of "the 'Eliotic-Trotskyist' *Partisan Review* strain" that would reject out of hand Bloom's audacious notion that Gold and Freeman can be read for modernist features.[17] It is because interpretive infighting of this sort has continued among cultural historians of thirties radicalism that such documentary scholars as those named above have been forced not merely to be extrarigorous, sure- and even slow-footed, and at times very plainly descriptive in reorienting the literary history of the period; indeed, they have had to be "decidedly old-fashioned" (as Houston Baker suggested provocatively on the dust-jacket of Nelson's book) even while demonstrating faithfulness to the postmodern sense that "we resemanticize what we do recover."[18] Trying to put modernism and radicalism together again, these revisionists have been compelled to cast about for unusual (some would say digressive) historical approaches and literally to search for new resources that will enable such self-reflectively reconstructive acts to take place without merely contributing to a half-century-old argument another, however subtler and more luxuriously theorized position, predetermined by either the same old outright dismissals or outright acceptances of communism as a home-grown cultural force.

Wallace Stevens serves extraordinarily well, I contend, in the effort to work through and beyond that old familiar pattern. The choice of Stevens to play such a role, I realize, will strike some as incendiary if not just strange. He will be known to many readers as the author of the ubiquitously anthologized "Sunday Morning" (1915) and perhaps, too, for a series of quintessentially modernist poems-about-poetry in which a spectral second- or third-person pronoun behaves like a depersonalized, meditative *I*, quietly confessing to an eerily unimportant American life:

> There is a storm much like the crying of the wind,
> Words that come out of us like words within,
> That have rankled for many lives and made no sound.
>
> (*CP* 336)

Readers of such lines tend to ask: "Words that come out of *us*," really, or out of the speaker? And what rankling? And why – and how – so silent? Then, too,

> there is a man in black space
> Sits in nothing that we know,
> Brooding sounds of river noises. . . .
>
> (*CP* 444)

One cannot keep from wondering, Is it "we" – really all of us – who "know" this "nothing"? The metrical force and rhetorical straightforwardness of "there is a man" is qualified by this apparently unearned "we," which seems to draw an equation between, on one hand, some estimable singularity sitting remotely nowhere and, on the other, a powerful collectivity brooding on nothing. In *Wallace Stevens and the Actual World* (1991), largely a work of literary biography, I characterized Stevens as not so much typically remote as in fact involved, even at times preoccupied, with the world of political events and trends. I described, in short, the extent to which Stevens was capable of meaning more than "oneself" in his lofty-seeming "we." If my choice of the last period of Stevens's life and work, 1939 to 1955, from the beginning of World War II to the middle of the Cold War, was propitious, it was because my purpose could be served by showing Stevens's poetry engaging the issues of an era in which the dominant political culture increasingly featured and officially favored ideological disengagement (the postwar "end of ideology"). The story of American modernism's 1950s – really, its coming of political middle age long after it had come of *aesthetic* middle age – is also the story of the *making* of the aforementioned false distinction, invalidating ways in which radicalism and modernism had interacted in the 1930s in a 1950s-style narrative of the then-outmoded war waged between irreconcilable sides. (And, of course, once the sides were aligned in this way, the winner – "nonpolitical" modernism – could be declared.) There are many reasons why the thirties present a problem very different from the fifties. One of them is precisely that what happened to eminent modernists in the earlier period occurred *before* the fifties' invention of the myth of wholly separate radical and modernist spheres. I have already described how, in his last years, Stevens sensed the revision underway, and how, although his own sense of the thirties could not entirely resist being shaped by the fifties' version, the period was obviously alluring for him.[19] The reaction in the sixties *against* this fifties version of the thirties made it hard to trust deconstructions of the myth of separate spheres, such as Stephen Spender's obviously sincere claim that "my own Thirties' generation . . . never became so politicized as to disagree seriously with an older generation of writers who held views often described as 'reactionary.'"[20]

Any effort to get back to the thirties requires that one spend a good deal of one's resources describing the getting back. Participants have tended to return to the period again and again to present their own (revised) views. Their conflicting recollections make the archive fuller but discernment no easier. The old radical lumberman poet, Joe Kalar, predicted in 1970 that "[t]here will never be an end to books about the thirties," and I think he might be right.[21] Similarly, because the myth of separate modernist and communist spheres seems so important to its creators and adherents, there may be no end of speculation as to why "the modernist" Wallace Stevens reacted with such "strange disproportion"[22] to "the communist" Stanley Burnshaw's October 1, 1935, review of Stevens's *Ideas of Order* (1935) in the communist *New Masses*. Critical debate about the thirties seemed perpetual to Joe Kalar, by 1970 a veteran of many literary wars, because so many of the rhetorical provocations and counterattacks of the period – even the strong and not always fruitless rhetorical tradition of fierce self-criticism – were carrying over into cultural histories dealing with the period.[23] Little or none of this truculence has gotten into Stevens criticism, quite in spite of the fact that a great many full-length studies of Stevens's career, and a number of essays, raise the specter of Burnshaw.[24] Never, for instance, has anyone posed systematically the question of whether "Owl's Clover," the poem written largely in response to Burnshaw, discloses anything specific about Stevens's understanding of the issues that gave rhetorical force to the left. Nor, until very recently, have Stevens's critics felt prepared to begin with anything but the tired, Cold War-era assumption of "Burnshaw's misdirected Marxism."[25] Nor has it been asked whether the young Burnshaw, with his own special concerns about a moment Stevens's admirers readily assume was wholly his moment, was indeed representative of the cultural communism whose journal he used to evaluate *Ideas of Order*. In many ways he was not.[26]

In preparing to write this book, I read extensively in the private papers of communist and noncommunist poets who followed Stevens's efforts, poem by poem, in the thirties. This study disclosed, among other things, that the question of Burnshaw's representativeness – his having earned the privilege, as it were, to be the one to confront Stevens most forthrightly from the left – was an issue raised at the time. Willard Maas on the communist left, and Samuel French Morse on the center-right were among those poets who raised such a doubt. Maas once considered writing about Stevens, but soon moved away from modern poetry toward postmodern film and mixed media, and never did publish on Stevens. Yet, that Maas, then a *communist*, could privately assert, "[i]f I wrote one poem, just one, as good as any in Harmonium [1923] or Ideas of Order [1935], I would be willing to stop writing forever,"[27] speaks to the complexity of the situation. And Morse, who in the early fifties befriended Stevens and hatched plans to be his official biographer, told me that he had lost interest in the Burnshaw episode when poets' politics came to seem a less pressing issue than earlier.[28] Perhaps it is only just now possible – with archives, such as Maas's and Burnshaw's, swelling with incoming letters left and right, papers and materials both literary and "ephemeral" – to examine, in ample literary-political context, the noncommunist poet's declarations of interest in communism or the contemporaneous claim for "Owl's Clover" that it was intended as a "justification of leftism" (L 295), and to speculate in studies of this kind on the degree to which such claims are unreliable.

If we dismiss a nonradical poet's assertion of leftward movement as *thoroughly* unreliable, should we not then be prepared to explain why a poet as shrewd as Stevens could thus have had such a poor sense of how his poetry situated itself politically? In exposing a poet like Stevens to such a context, I realize that I risk (quite unintentionally) sustaining Irving Howe's chilly 1947 view that "Owl's Clover" was "rhetoric overrunning thought, a[n] assault upon a subject Stevens was not prepared to confront."[29] My ambition, on the contrary, is to suggest how similar is the risk of reducing *Burnshaw* to "myopic" and his approach to Stevens as "the coarsest kind of Marxian criticism."[30] Anyone who has read "Notes on Revolutionary Poetry," with its affirmative reference to I. A. Richards, its scolding of reductive communist assumptions about poetic form, its quotation of "revolutionary poems which are plainly precious," would not speak of Burnshaw's unreflective orthodoxy.[31] So, too, those who know of Mary McCarthy's brief grudging praise in 1936 for Burnshaw's grievance against the American Marxist obsession with content – "We have been so much concerned with *what* the author is saying," Burnshaw had written, "that we have neglected the concomitant question: *how* does he say it?" – would not assume radicals' dissociation from modernism.[32]

Taking both Stevens and Burnshaw a good deal more seriously, my portrait of the Burnshaw-Stevens episode in Chapters 5 and 6 is meant to be a portrait of American poetry at a crossroads. This stimulating brush with literary radicalism suggests that more eminent modernists than one might have guessed understood how their poems were going to be read by would-be detractors, and that they understood and even adopted a number of basic contemporaneous contentions about poets' standing in American society. In describing this "extraordinary" contact, to use Stevens's word for it (L 292), I aim, moreover, to locate poetic work generally representative of the noncommunist modernist. And I trust that the effort to see thirties poetics through the odd lens of Stevens provides a number of new suggestions about American cultural radicalism itself. One is that the thirties were *not* a period in which literary value necessarily went out of fashion, but rather, to quote Burke looking back from 1952, "a period of stress that forced upon all of us" – he meant the so-called "aesthetes" and communists both – "the need to decide exactly wherein the worth and efficacy of a literary work reside."[33]

Such application of Stevens will seem an annoyance to those who prefer to take their modernism "as if it were written from nowhere" (which is how Marjorie Perloff characterized the common view when commending Peter Brazeau for taking the trouble to interview Stevens's business colleagues). Consider that *Stevens*, not William Carlos Williams, or Kenneth Fearing, or George Oppen, or Charles Reznikoff, offered the following as a description of a poem he was writing:

> What I have been trying to do in the thing is to apply my own sort of poetry to such a project.+ [sic] Is poetry that is to have a contemporary significance merely to be a collection of contemporary images, or is it actually to deal with the commonplace of the day? I think the latter, but the result seems rather boring.
>
> + To What one reads in the papers. (L 308)

What specifically led me to write a book that describes the convergence of poetic isms is the postscript here: At the last moment, this American poet remembers that his correspondent might not know that "such a project" could have anything to do with the news. I am similarly compelled by the final misgiving in the quoted passage: that poetry collecting "the commonplace" risks tedium. Had Stevens here eschewed his usual rhetoric of qualified assertions, I dare say the comment could be deemed unremarkable and I would be the first to cast it on a large pile of other comparable statements made by poets in the period, in a bin marked "more easily said than done."

But the modernist whose 1930s Joseph Riddel rightly calls "the most revealing single period in his career"[34] was deadly serious when he spoke of poems responding "To What one reads in the papers." It cannot be denied that his comments in the months following the *New Masses* review suggest his wish to accommodate himself to certain assumptions of the literary left. These comments are too wide-ranging, and extend over too many letters, to be dismissed as whimsical. That he said he very much believed in "leftism," and hoped he was "headed left" (*L* 286-7), can perhaps be discounted as ironic or half-hearted, especially since he qualified the point by announcing that *his* left would not be "the ghastly left of MASSES." But he soon added that such contact as he had just had with the cultural radicals did allow a poet like himself to "circulate" – I use New Historicist pidgin here because Stevens did – and that it was in the last event "an extraordinarily stimulating thing" to find himself moving "in that *milieu*" (*L* 296). So, too, he deemed nonsense the notion some conservatives held that socialism and communism would "dirty the world" when carrying out their political transformations; although he admitted that the displeasure of dirtying would be the *immediate* effect, he significantly added that this would be true of any upheaval (*L* 292). At one point in this period he even permitted himself a bit of utopian thinking, speculating on what the world would look like if he were given the task of creating "an actuality" from scratch. He decided that it would look a good deal different from "the world about us" in many ways, though he declined to give the details of this vision; the prospect would merely be described in "personal terms," and he disliked people who spoke of such longing in personal terms (*L* 292). The "extraordinary experience" that contact with radicalism gave him led firmly to the conclusion that "one has to live and think in the actual world, and no other will do" (*L* 292), a signal shift, at least rhetorically, from his attitude of the *Harmonium* years. Internal order proceeded from external order, he said, as well as the other way around; he added that "the orderly relations of society as a whole have a poetic value" (*L* 305). He began to emphasize references to the "normal" in his poetry. He became obsessed with "how to write of the normal in a normal way" (*L* 287), a process he knew would create the main difficulty if he were to adapt his verse to any of the new poetic realisms.

Stevens also articulated the terms in which the advantages and disadvantages of "didactic poetry" and "pure poetry" could be argued (*L* 302–3). While he admitted to his publisher that he clung to a "distinct liking" for pure poetry, his manner of saying so revealed his awareness that this was a position one could put forth only defensively in an era when radicals like Max Eastman were reasonably attacking modernism as "The Tendency toward Pure Poetry" ("In place of a criticism ["of life," in Arnold's sense], these poets are offering us in each poem a moment of life, a rare, perfect or intense moment, and nothing more").[35] So Stevens, in saying now that he stood by pure poetry, insisted "at the same time" that "life is the essential part of literature" (*L* 288). Acknowledging "the common opinion" of his verse, that it was essentially decorative, he wished to counteract such a criticism by challenging the very terms *decorative* and *formal* (*L* 288). Asked to look back on his own "Comedian as the Letter C" (1922), he realized that, much as Malcolm Cowley had recently proposed in the last pages of

Exile's Return (1934), there was a distinct cultural construction of the recent aesthetic past, a twenties for the thirties. Stevens judged the obsession with the sound of poetry in "Comedian" explainable by the fact that "subject," by which he meant content, had not been as important in the teens and twenties as it was in the thirties (*L* 294). With hindsight granted by just six months, he glanced back at "Mozart, 1935," and decided that it took up the issue of "the status of the poet in a disturbed society" (*L* 292).

In each cultural period – high modern, radical, wartime, postwar – Stevens wielded a stock response in part to fend off further queries from correspondents. Before the thirties his response essentially was, *I write poems to become more myself.* But immediately after the Burnshaw encounter, at the height of the radical moment, this line became: *I write poems in order to formulate my ideas about and to discern my relation to the world.*[36] (When I asked Stanley Burnshaw if he would comment on my suggestion "that Stevens changed his attitude toward his own poetry because of [Burnshaw's] political response to it," he replied: "[Stevens] did want to prove that he was of the world and that he was responding to what I was referring to as reality. I don't think there can be any doubt about it."[37]) Most important – and I will return in the second half of this book to the precise points of impact – Stevens was speaking for the first time of the poet's link to Burnshaw's sense of reality as interactive. A poet saw poetry as helping to create what it sought in the world of events. This incessant change in language's relation to that world was, in itself, a reason why the lyric poet could persist poetically "now," in this historically minded moment, both marking history and being marked by history's traces: a dialogism between foreground and background, between the poem and its sometimes explicitly posited *now*, devised not in spite of but because of contemporary "complexity" (*L* 300).

My argument takes its first cue from Stevens's own contingent sense of "complexity"; just when it was in the noncommunist writer's special interest to turn toward radicalism, however tentatively and self-servingly, it happened that it was in the special interest of communist writers to involve him or her. Such coincidental shifting, it must first be realized, would have surprised few cultural figures then in the know, much as the convergence might seem astonishing today. One need only confer with any of the many surviving fellow travelers willing to talk about their radicalizations to be reminded, as I was when interviewing the noted ethnic memoirist Jerre Mangione, that "nearly everyone associated with writing and publishing whom one knew and respected was interested in some form of radicalism – and communism was always at least in the background."[38] The interaction, moreover, between noncommunists like Stevens and the literary-political forces of their time – forces set routinely into motion by journal editors, other poets, and especially reviewers – was remarkably dynamic. The new historicists' vaunted problem of seeing the tree *and* the forest (rather than one *for* the other), of circulating notions of background and foreground, could not be more acute than in such an instance.[39]

Though it is not a matter confessed in print by the many otherwise perspicacious readers of Stevens's 1930s volumes, *Ideas of Order* (1935), *Owl's Clover* (1936), and *The Man with the Blue Guitar & Other Poems* (1937), it has always seemed that for the purposes of studying the eminent modernist's defensive rhetoric, and to keep from losing one's own way in the tangle of the thirties' literary left, one had to steadily restrict oneself as a critic to *the modernist's* view of these extrapoetic forces. Such a procedure, while sensible if not unassailable, has given us just half the picture of the noncommunist's thirties. And it has reduced to simplicities the relation between, on one hand, the poet deemed utterly unique or uncommon and, on the other hand, what would seem to be the minor, ephemeral, even grubby, and finally inconsequential, aesthetic tactics used by mostly unremembered men and women. What does it matter, in assessments of figures like Williams, Moore, and Stevens still judged major a half-century later, if that common minority of poetic special interests behaves incorrigibly as a background? I have written *Modernism from Right to Left* believing that it matters a great deal. It is no less significant, I think, to come *at* singular poets like Stevens *from* that incorrigible, messy background, and (to mix and transpose the metaphor in this book's title) advance the analysis from back to front as well as right to left – in short, to find those sundry other poets', editors', and reviewers' arrogations of Stevens and modernism to have served their ends both perceived and unsuspected, even as (or perversely because) these ends seem forgettable in relation to Stevens's achievements or not nearly worth the tremendous effort and time required for documented retrieval. Yet in making literary-political use of him, after all, *they* constructed the setting in which he was read by still others, *and in which he read himself.* This is only most famously the case with the *New Masses* review provoking four-fifths of Stevens's longest poem. The same kind of effects, I will suggest along the way, result from the assaults by Orrick Johns on Moore, Willard Maas on E. E. Cummings, Mike Gold on Archibald MacLeish, Edwin Seaver on Horace Gregory, Eda Lou Walton on Robinson Jeffers, and Burnshaw, Johns, and H. H. Lewis on Harriet Monroe's *Poetry.*

There are many other such convergences of modernism and radicalism to be described, and this book is organized to do so. To imagine Stevens, the recently promoted, three-piece-besuited vice-president of The Hartford Accident & Indemnity Company, reading himself in the *Nation* in the early autumn of 1936 is, after all, an intriguing act of "recovery" best aided by particulars that tend to show that the editors of that fellow-traveling journal certainly knew what they were doing when they awarded their annual poetry prize to a work that Stevens later said expressed sympathy

with the antifascist Republicans in the Spanish Civil War. Still later, after
the falling out between the party-affiliated *New Masses* and a revived, freshly
anti-Stalinist *Partisan Review*, the editors of the latter disputatious project
knew exactly what cultural waves they were making when they solicited
and received five poems from Stevens. One last preliminary example of
cultural circulation contemporaneous with the Stevens-Burnshaw fracas
was the publication of three poems in the *New Republic*, whose literary
editor, namely Cowley, was suggesting that communism "can offer [the
writer] an audience, *not trained to appreciate the finer points of style or execution*
. . . but larger and immeasurably more eager than the capitalist audience."[40]
With Cowley's appointment to succeed Edmund Wilson at the *New Republic*, as was well known in both literary and political circles, the columns of
this "weekly became a playground of the proletarian artists and critics."[41]
As I will show in Chapter 5, Cowley's timely use of Stevens – Stevens's
appearance on just such a "playground" – was strategic in the ordinary but
not in the extraordinary sense; that is to say, the red-hot Cowley, busier
then than ever, would not have given a second thought to the ideological
significance of this otherwise odd-seeming meeting. And this is precisely
why such meetings are to be given a long second thought here. The relationship between Stevens and the *New Republic* resulted from just one of
innumerable forays of aesthetic left into right. It was a small but signal
provision in a fundamental unspoken agreement by which writers, literary
journalists, and cultural politicians traded freely on each other's rhetorics.
That process, called "historical" in every possible high and low sense, stipulated a good deal more ideological commingling than has been credited to
it. In an aesthetic era driven by a presumptuous feeling of "history" boldly
being made, basically pleasurable in ways often later denied, there was a lot
of "merely circulating" going on.

1

Which Side Are You On?

A man would have to be very thick-skinned not to be conscious of the pathos of Ethiopia or China, or one of these days, if we are not careful, of this country.

—Stevens

And so we sit in separate rooms, you
intimidated by the silence, vaguely
feeling all's not well, too tired to read,
too restless to lie still, too stirred
to trace this strangeness to its source.

—Edwin Rolfe, "To My Contemporaries" (1935)

Staring, at midnight, at the pillow that is black
In the catastrophic room . . . beyond despair. . . .

Speak and say the immaculate syllables
That he spoke only by doing what he did. . . .

The night wind blows upon the dreamer, bent
Over words that are life's voluble utterance.

—Stevens, "The Men That Are Falling" (1936)

I: STICKING TO THE FACTS

Wallace Stevens (1879–1955) did not save perhaps as many as ninety-five letters he received from his most regular correspondent in the 1930s, an odd man whom Stevens knew as "J. Ronald Lane Latimer." I am nearly certain that Stevens destroyed Latimer's letters; but the eccentricities of the relationship, a story in itself, await the third chapter to be described. Here it must suffice to say that as odd as this correspondent was – utterly anomalous among Stevens's exchanges – he was nonetheless crucial to that poet's developing awareness of the frenetic interplay between modernism and radicalism.

In 1935 Latimer formally sought and received permission from Stevens to pose specific inquiries about the poetry – questions which *were in fact ghostwritten by a well-connected communist poet who was at the same time a devo-tee of Stevens's work.* Since these letters do not survive, the precise question to which Stevens intended the following intriguing series of remarks as a reply must be deduced:

> I don't think that there is any secret to the merit of a poem. I mean by this that it is not a question of accuracy of conception or of expression. . . . There is no more secret about this sort of thing than there is, say, to the stock market. There are too many influences at work; there are too many people subject to influence. There is no secret to poetry, but undoubtedly you are right in saying that the influence of a work depends largely on this: that it must create what it seeks. There is no reason whatever why a poet . . . should not exist now, notwithstanding the complexity of contemporary life, and so on. Have you ever stopped to think of the extraordinary exist-ence of Milton, in his time and under the circumstances of the world as it was then? Milton would be just as proper, so to speak, today as he was in his actual day, and perhaps today, instead of going off on a myth, he would stick to the facts. (*L* 299–300)

Readers of these lines will reasonably feel an urge to read "Stevens" for "Milton," strange as the pairing might seem. The tone of the passage itself suggests that Stevens is pondering his own "extraordinary existence." If modernist writing in the thirties does not immediately seem to us today to "stick to the facts" – if Stevens's allusiveness does not call attention to itself quite as Ezra Pound's or Charles Reznikoff's or (in a different way) Marianne Moore's does – it is at least obvious that he constantly grapples with the problem of what such sticking would entail. Leaving aside for the moment the relevance of what modernists took to be Milton's politics, it is sensible to ask: Whence the homology of poetry and stock market?

One point revealed by the surprising relation is the letterwriter's appar-ent belief that what would seem a chance likening left the correspondent entirely unsurprised: It is my suspicion (the evidence, again, comes later) that Latimer's letter raised the issue specifically and with an ideological force Stevens was learning to meet in stride. The evidently uncharacteristic correlation of verse and economy permitted him a bit of griping about a dominant notion of the New Deal – the basic progressive tenet to which, under the tutelage of his ghostwriting comrade, Latimer was becoming a zealous convert: Rational planning brings forth intended results.[1] If cen-tralist theory irritated Stevens-the-business-conservative, what especially vexed Stevens-the-modernist-open-to-change was the theory's converse: Insofar as rational or "central" planning suggested results, from results one confidently reads backward to plan. The methodological point, in the letter significantly dated December 10, 1935, formed not merely a response to Latimer. It responded as well to prominent purveyors of a new and powerful national metaphor of "planning,"[2] such as the president of the United States.

On December 9 Franklin Roosevelt had defended his central economic scheme in a pivotal speech delivered in Chicago, reaffirming with characteristic assurance (and through ample newspaper coverage) that the relations between economic goal and economic fact, between New Deal imagination and depression reality, would yet be wholly rationalized. Here was Stevens, the next day, casually dictating a letter in his office at The Hartford Accident & Indemnity Company, arguing with skepticism and stealing a trope or two: No explanation of market forces, whether offered by far or moderate left, was plausible; no "secret" was to be discovered, no new deal to be struck, no trick played or comprehensive solution wrought, no fully confident reading tendered – *of stock prices or of poetry*. The forces at work on contemporary verse were largely beyond individual, let alone social, control. In the hands of poets like Stevens, during the New Deal, a talent for falling back on indeterminacy was one of the great, disarming prospects of the *conservative* argument, a contention that resisted both trendy radical totalization and liberal top-down rationalization. Those in business who denounced the "new relations between business and government" touted by liberal New Dealers and their allies on the left could do so by calling for a "Less Orderly Arrangement" of human affairs as a counterargument to liberal-left ideas of order. It was an interesting and temporary inversion of the usual conservative argument against disorder.[3] Whether Stevens's December 10 letter to Latimer responded specifically to the rhetoric of FDR's December 9 speech or more generally to the latest re-election rationale (there is no reason to dismiss a specific response out of hand, since the speech and its ramifications found prominent space in the December 10 issues of the newspapers Stevens read) his position as businessman-poet, his contention that there were "too many influences at work" to justify planning and regulation by those overconfident interpreters of the controlling forces, was not so much an irrational reply as unremarkably conservative.[4]

What *is* remarkable, I think, followed directly. Having reacted against what we must guess was Latimer's stated interpretive stance, namely that there *was* in the thirties a fundamental critical system or central grid or rational calculus by which to make whole order of poetry, Stevens then contradicted the skeptical position his own provocative poetry-stock market analogy had worked so hard to create. His letter continues by implying a rather sophisticated argument in favor of the poet's response to his social situation, "notwithstanding the complexity of contemporary life." The poet, he argued, could indeed "exist" in an era that threatened to remake him as a social figure, that pressed to disclaim his uniqueness. Such attitudes indicate that he had come a long way from the decade's first months and years, as I will show in Chapter 2. By 1935, Stevens was ready to suggest a flexible, mixed definition of the interaction between poetic, critical, and historical discourse. A poem could not be read by first reading the conditions that had given rise to it, conditions that could be rationalized later. Its hardest work was to create the very conditions that might allow it to be understood. Thus might a poet indeed "exist" in 1935 – of all pivotal years, for Stevens, modernism, and American literary culture at large – "notwithstanding the complexity of contemporary life, and so on." The winsome phrase "and so on" would signal to Latimer not merely the improvisational basis of Stevens's letter-writing (office dictation, here as almost always); it also bespoke his conception of poets' historical specificity as part of an original premise underlying the ideological assumptions of his correspondent's question. The habitual "and so on" here held out the possibility of agreement with the suppositions of his radicalized inquirer (Latimer) and meant, *Yes, and also those other things you mentioned in the question put to me.*

Yet if all this was supposed to sustain an argument against critical historicism – too many "influences" are at work, no full context for creation is recoverable, and so on – then the example of John Milton signifies at best an ambiguous endorsement of the argument. Stressing the unhistorical or "extraordinary" nature of Milton in his time, an idiosyncratic, transcendent Milton, Stevens simultaneously used the persuasive example of the seventeenth-century poet to support the opposite view. Milton did indeed exist "in his time and under the circumstances of the world as it was then" – that is, in a revolutionary moment. It was, tellingly, a point Stanley Burnshaw made in support of the idea that revolutionary crises incite "genuine poetry": "I do believe," Burnshaw wrote Harriet Monroe, the editor of *Poetry*, "that during the present decade something of the present turmoil will be distilled into genuine poetry, just as the 17th century English turmoil distilled itself into genuine poetry."[5] For his part, Stevens observed that Milton would be "just as proper, so to speak, today as he was in his actual day." No less than Burnshaw, he wanted to suggest that the poetic forms assumed by writing produced in the English revolutionary period were conditioned by a strong sticking to the facts. Here Stevens was following a depression-era trend in popular and some scholarly American perceptions of Milton. A popular use of *Paradise Regained* had Milton leading the intellectual charge against Mussolini in Abyssinia:[6]

> They err who count it glorious to submit
> By conquest far and wide, to over-run
> Large countries. . . .
> What do these worthies
> But rob, and spoil, burn, slaughter and enslave
> Peaceable nations . . . yet deserving freedom.
>
> (iii.76)

In the introduction to *Christ in the Breadline* (1933), a collection of three poets' work typified by Kenneth Porter's radical "To Henry Ford (Closer of Factories)," John Haynes Holmes confidently asserted that "poetry of this type is in the great tradition of English letters." At the top of Holmes's list one finds Milton, whose lines, constituting "art for humanity's sake," are "whips to lash the sins of greed, cruelty and pride."[7] It is but a short way from imagining Milton's genius thus pressed into the service of the realist subgenres ascendant in the American thirties, to beholding *Paradise Lost* as a text that, "instead of *going off on a myth*," would "stick to the facts." As the question Latimer hired from a communist compelled Stevens to consider a poet's contemporary position, so, according to Stevens's response, he and Milton, striving for universality yet beset by political insurgency, recognize the extent to which their forms are impressed and distorted by special demands of the day. The example of Milton finally works against Stevens's original conservative impulse to argue for indeterminacy in poetic as in market forces.

Stick to the facts was for Stevens a key, if perhaps philosophically sloppy, phrase, nonetheless useful in describing the noncommunist poet's response to pressures bearing down on his writing. These pressures persuaded Stevens to re-examine the power of poetic uses of "the object," of the work of referring itself, in ways that went well beyond post-Imagist rhetoric hailing "new" exactitude, and moved in the general direction of what radical poets were calling, inexactly, a poetic materialism – a poetry of "things" with an overt politics. Once a context can be described for the operation of those pressures, we will find that Stevens's poetic responses were often positive: he came to know his own acute historical imagination better by articulating several main tenets put forward by American literary leftists. To be sure, "stick to the facts," even when used humorously to *deride* radicals' writing, and here to re-imagine Milton in the 1930s, displacing Adam and Eve, as it were, onto the ground of the proletarian novel, refers back to a scenario as apparently improper as Stevens's argument overtly insisted it was "proper." As on other occasions, Stevens felt the need to mock the polemical mode of thirties realism: One only jokingly re-imagines Milton's first couple as Great Depression drifters, the original dispossessed farmers.

Stevens and other modernists sharing his shifting political ground spent more energy satirizing the new politically oriented realism than conceding its persuasiveness. But toward the mid-thirties the influence of cultural radicalism swelled, especially after the advent of a united front and then civil war in Spain.[8] This trend is obvious in the world of poetry, where, for instance, the assumptions of radical reviewers of Stevens's books began to be borrowed by his liberal and moderate reviewers. Thus over time the distinction between satirizing and acknowledging the rhetorical strength of the left became slim. When Stevens wrote a business colleague that such topics as collecting *objets d'art* "are not permissible subjects now-a-days. . . . Everything is overwhelmingly real now-a-days,"[9] he was resenting the pressure he felt to show concern for what he at one point dismissively called "the lower class, *with all its realities*" (L 291; emphasis added). Yet he also seemed able to measure the guilt he felt when speaking of his taste for fancy exhibit catalogues and books in a time of epidemic poverty. Even the terms "realism" and "real" now took on political meaning too automatically, for his taste. So ubiquitous and stylish a word as society was among the new terms-of-choice he abhorred. As early as November 1935 he seemed prepared to substitute for the word society a phrase evidently nonideological, one that would serve his purposes brilliantly a few years later in "The Man with the Blue Guitar" (1937) – "things as they are" (L 290). Yet even this apparent improvisation, as I will show in my final chapter, has its particular basis in the culture war then raging.

Some of the noncommunist poet's severest qualifications – unsympathetic readers tend to regard them as confusions – come only as the result of great rhetorical strain, one language trying very hard to oblige another. It is the strain of a person of Stevens's class and social position, who endures this pressure as itself one aspect of the new robust mode of the "real." Consider this manifestly confused testimony, for example:

> I then [in the twenties] believed in *pure poetry.* . . . But we live in a different time, and life means a good deal more to us now-a-days than literature does. . . . I am not so sure that I don't think exactly the same thing now [as before], but, unquestionably, I think at the same time that life is the essential part of literature. (L 288)

The statement evidently goes nowhere. Yet it shows the intensity of nonradicals' urge to honor themes and tones of engagement in thirties writing. They struggled with newly accepted terms, reformulating them by ideologically disarming them, re-situating them on an utterly uncontroversial literature-"life" axis. The strain having been disclosed by nonradicals' tortured language ("I am *not* so sure that I *don't* think exactly the same thing *now*, but, unquestionably, I think *at the same time*. . ."), only thus would they indulge the mode they had set out to resist. Only through such contortions, moreover, could Stevens claim to Latimer that noncommunist verse *does* take up the concerns of a "world" by retaining a rhetoric of the real and providing the poems with "actual backgrounds" (L 289).

In speaking of these "actual backgrounds," Stevens was answering yet another question Latimer had put to him. Asked to look back from the thirties to the Florida poems of his first book, *Harmonium* (1923), he reinvested the twenties with the backgrounds of the thirties, the meeting of the literary and the nonliterary. The result was a portrayal of his earlier poems not as generalizations but rather as detailed responses to a roughly recuperable "real." "I have been going to Florida for twenty years," he answered Latimer, "and all of the Florida poems have actual backgrounds. The real world seen by an imaginative man may very well seem like an imaginative construction." But the strong implication was that the "real world" so rendered was

not merely an imaginative construction. Clinging to the poetry-market
resemblance, nevertheless, Stevens acknowledged the obvious qualification
to the implied act of recovery. For if his correspondent were to take his
remarks and then "suggest any particular poem, I could *not* find an actual
background for you" (*L* 289; emphasis added).

Stevens had begun to re-imagine for the 1930s a 1920s largely controlled by programmatic conceptions of reality. Just when he was recognizing the reasons why many younger poets thought of themselves as "ham-
mering out beauty" (in Muriel Rukeyser's apt communist phrase),[10] he was
looking forward to the immediate future with renewed pleasure – not incidentally at a time when poems were coming very quickly to him. He began
to write that long poem in which he wrestled with "What one reads in the
papers" (*L* 308) – "Owl's Clover." As a follower of poetry and newspapers
both, he knew full well that exploring news narratives for poetic material
was itself a means by which the American literary left claimed to take sides
on the day's main issues, a constructivist mode summarized by a poet, Horace
Gregory, whose new communist-influenced verse Stevens was reading.[11]
("Have you heard the headlines, *death?*" was among these lines.)[12] In a
review of Aragon's *The Red Front*, Gregory observed that poetry was "[t]he
means by which [the revolutionary writer's] celebration of an event will
continue to be interesting and to carry revolutionary content long after the
immediate occasion is lost in the files of the daily newspaper."[13] *No Retreat*
(1933), the book Stevens read, was Gregory's attempt to inscribe the particular talent he praised in Aragon into his own work, and at the same time
to put modernist practice – and Stevens – in radical perspective. One of
the poems Stevens read in Gregory's new book, "Sunday Morning," subtitled "Rotogravure Section," was designed to show how far poets had
come from wistful lingering over coffee and oranges on a morning that was
now supposed to be reserved for anxious close reading of the Sunday supplements. This particular Sunday issue depicted one "inheritor of millions," a
scene that caused the speaker to contemplate "Intangibles of power / . . .
written in ticker tape / on private yachts" and other such "temporary"
setbacks.[14] To Alan Calmer, one of the editors of *Proletarian Literature of the
United States* (1935), communist elegies and odes "hail[ing] labor's triumphs
or lament[ing] its temporary defeats" often resembled "transcriptions of
newspaper items."[15] Gregory, brilliantly reversing accepted literary value,
modified his thirties-style twenties-bashing only insomuch as it meant laud-
ing a subgenre of high-modernist style that had been its most ridiculed
aspect: He hoped the new political poets would find "the possible *advantages* to be derived from *a decade of manifestos.*"[16] At the inaugural congress of
the League of American Writers, one young poet urged his colleagues to
turn out verse bulletins to be "posted on the walls of union meeting places."[17]
Kenneth Patchen's poem "This Man Was Your Brother" was meant to be

read as a "footnote for newsreel," and his "Leaflet (One)" was a leaflet partly consisting of journalistic snippets.[18] These were just the sort of media-centered aspects of literary writing – writing as bulletin, news brief, public notice, manifesto, pronouncement, dispatch, flyer, handbill, or leaflet[19] – that one supposes would have repelled Stevens unequivocally. But modernism and literary radicalism mixed. Note, for instance, that Patchen's poems "were eagerly sought after by publishing houses that exploited modernism"; so observed Joseph Warren Beach, looking back from the 1950s and gently mocking some radicals of the 1930s for showing such likeness to their modernist predecessors.[20]

To recover something of Stevens's attraction to these not-so-newfangled notions of the forms and purposes of poetry, one begins with the demonstrable fact that he read the newspapers regularly and scrupulously. What he found in the rhetoric and conventions of what we now simply call "the media" sometimes became the basis for his verse response to national and international crises and contentions,[21] despite the impulse, itself requiring examination, that prompted him and his Cold War-era supporters to conceal the fact of this debt. Even when his poetry's assimilation of contemporary public language is most difficult to see, even when Stevens's "clippings" more closely correspond to early-modern painterly shards than lyric of supposedly natural speech, some of his thirties poems can be said actually to support Marjorie Perloff's contention that cubist newspaper collage suggests not an evasion but a culturally responsive formal innovation.[22] *Radical poets by no means rejected this modernist form.* Kenneth Fearing's use of headline diction is perhaps most familiar, but the same is to be found frequently in the work of poets bearing out the credo that radical verse should engage "new forms and techniques . . . to express . . . the fast tempos and rhythms of the new world order" [sic].[23] One need look no further than Ben Maddow's headline-like use of bare syntax and deadpan juxtaposition in "The Communist Party of Germany," which begins: "Dead girl falls in Alexanderplatz. Coal / sells very dear."[24] "Another American poet described one radical Russian writer as having an admirable talent for "verbal contrasts" and, despite his revolutionary seriousness, an ability to enjoy the surprise caused by contrary "facts" offered merely for their contrariness – the poet was Louis Zukofsky (in a statement dated 1933), and the "writer" he was referring to was *Lenin*.[25] Such politicized juxtapositionism influenced Stevens's writing, if I may momentarily anticipate my reading of "The Man with the Blue Guitar," when his recognition of an otherwise overwhelming increase of information in the twentieth century was filtered by him to complement a *reactivation* (to use the term translated from Walter Benjamin) entailed in borrowing from public language. The fullest formal, tonal, and intellectual response to cultural radicalism, "a million people on one string" (*CP* 166) could be achieved through a multilateral approach to "the day's news" (*L* 311 n.8) –

significantly more flexible in Stevens's than in Ben Maddow's work, and argu-ably more than in Fearing's too. In "Blue Guitar," I will contend, there are as many responses to and compromises with modernism's literary-political de-tractors as there are cantos in the poem.

At the height of his interaction with the literary left, the end of 1936, Stevens put forward his concept of the political unconscious. The state-ment was public, in a lecture delivered at Harvard. "We are preoccupied by events," Stevens announced, "even when we do not observe them closely" (*OP* 225). He was asking a rather knowledgeable audience[26] to seek a rela-tion between his poems and contemporary crises. Once or twice, in his letters to Latimer, he had attempted to construct a new reading based on the application of this idea to his own work, but anyone who has read these letters knows it is an unfinished business. In one such letter, at the end of the paragraph quoted just below, he declared that his poem, "A Fading of the Sun," "is a variation of this theme"; he added, "possibly MOZART 1935 also is" (*L* 292). One wants to know more about what he calls "this theme," if only to have a commentary on the two poems, but searches in vain in the letter's preceding sentences for any helpful antecedent:

> So that there may be no doubt about it, let me say that I believe in what Mr. Filene calls "up-to-date capitalism." I don't believe in Communism; I do believe in up-to-date capitalism. It is an extraordinary experience for my-self to deal with a thing like Communism; it is like dealing with the Demo-cratic platform, or with the provisions of the Frazier-Lemke bill. Never-theless, one has to live and think in the actual world, and no other will do, and that is w[h]y MR. BURNSHAW, etc. has taken a good deal of time. (*L* 292)

Presumably "A Fading of the Sun" (1933) and "Mozart 1935" (1935) embody "a variation of *this* theme" because they deal with the question of why "one has to live and think in the actual world." The energy and precision with which Stevens places himself here, in relation to the declarations of now-unremem-bered congressional bills, party platforms, and economic tenets, make an un-derstatement of his definition at Harvard of political comprehension: he was indeed preoccupied with events and observed them rather closely. He seems to dare his correspondent to carry out the proposed project of reading eminent modernists politically. Here Stevens made it sufficiently obvious that he stood to the right of the communists, and, as we will see in Chapter 3, that is actually one thing Latimer wanted to know. He also claimed to stand to the right of the Democratic Party Platform and the Frazier-Lemke Act. Yet he simultaneously indicates that he had been liberalized enough to stand with Edward A. Filene, the international popularizer of business ethics, and sharp critic of capitalist business-as-usual.[27]

This nexus of contemporary political reference presents more than meets the eye. First is the ideologically eccentric suggestion of Edward Filene as a reformist alternative to communism. In speaking of "up-to-date capitalism," Stevens was doubtless alluding to a speech Filene had delivered just a few days before this letter was written. While Filene was well known for his progressive positions on a new "morals in business,"[28] and while he proposed an American economy responsive to "the masses of America"[29] and maddened red-baiters "with his rose-colored views of the Russia he visits,"[30] he was at the precise moment of Stevens's reference explicitly an anticommunist. A talk Filene gave after returning from a tour of the Soviet Union, the speech to which Stevens was probably referring a few days later, was reported in the *New York Times* under this headline: "E. A. Filene Warns Against Panaceas / Speech on Danger of Masses' Credulity."[31] Moreover, Stevens's politically knowledgeable remarks suggest that dealing with the Democratic Party Platform and the Frazier–Lemke bill was nearly as "extraordinary" as dealing with the communists.

Whereas Stevens saw Filene as a reasonable alternative to communism – instead of showing Stevens's proximity to Filene, the allusion confirms his distance – the reference to legislation sponsored by Lynn Frazier and William Lemke, a law designed to permit a farmer threatened with foreclosure to retain possession of property temporarily under court supervision (just thirteen days earlier ruled unconstitutional a second time)[32] was not the "extraordinary experience" Stevens's comments suggest. Ordinary, that is, unless one knew that it occasioned one of those ideological mixings of right and left that often sent him with renewed interest back to poetry. Although the bill capitalized on FDR's progressive rhetoric, New Dealers opposed it from the start.[33] So did the insurance business. Roosevelt's opposition, and two declarations of unconstitutionality, caused quite a "stir" in Hartford in fact, as "insurance executives den[ied] they will rush foreclosures on farms" now that they had been freed to do so with FDR's surprising help.[34] Stevens's daily life was bound up in a business that depended on the unimpaired "right" of lenders and insurers to supervise the repossession of property and equipment that had failed to perform as promised; in the early thirties, while all federal land banks held a farm mortgage debt of some $1.5 billion (of a total $8 billion), insurance companies alone were holding $1.75 billion.[35] The provisions of the law to which Stevens referred denied the insuring institution even the power to set sale dates for the defaulted properties. In Stevens's dense political analogue, then, the displacement of Filene on the political spectrum, superfluously leftward, was matched by the "extraordinary experience" of political convergence and crossing – FDR allied with insurance executives against populists calling for an extension of federal protection of farmers – caused by an otherwise standard piece of depression legislation meant to slow dispossession. I think Stevens's growing interest in the poetic possibilities of right-left crossing, similar to Kenneth Burke's, caused the Frazier-Lemke law to stand out

for him. Under the heading "Paradox," and nicely following a section on
"Confusion of Terms," Burke described his fascination with the fact that
"the political implications of *the aesthetic*" urged by radicals would to some
degree "involve a political alignment with the agrarians," and that this was
analogous to "the farmers, the only surviving American conservatives" being involved in a thoroughly "radical" rebellion and "whose interests make
[this movement] the equivalent of a radical group."[36] Stevens's sense of the
politics of modernism in his version of the analogue suggests that he meant
"*this* theme," an otherwise ambiguous phrase, to denote for his communist
interrogator the paradoxical politics of the poem "Mozart, 1935," where
the poet's unchallenged sense of aesthetic interiority is confused and contested
by an ideologically unfixable disruption outdoors threatening to come in:

> If they throw stones upon the roof
> While you practice arpeggios,
> It is because they carry down the stairs
> A body in rags.
> . . . the streets are full of cries.

(CP 131–2)

"Mozart, 1935," he noted here, "expresses something that I have very much
at heart, and that is: the status of the poet in a disturbed society" (L 292).
Stevens also mentioned to Latimer here his poetic rejoinder to Burnshaw and
the *New Masses*, the poem "Mr. Burnshaw and the Statue," part two of the five-
part "Owl's Clover"; he said he was just then "tak[ing] a good deal of time"
writing this rejoinder-in-verse. When that section was finally finished, "Owl's
Clover" retained a good deal of Stevens's nervousness about the New Deal and
private property barely hidden in the political dislocations of Lemke, Frazier,
and Filene. The world of "Mr. Burnshaw" in this satire is "a drastic community" in which the dispossessed violently become possessed, a dystopic "trash
can at the end of the world" where "the dead / Give up dead things and the
living turn away. / There buzzards pile their sticks among the bones / Of
buzzards and eat the bellies of the rich . . ." (OP 81).

2: AESTHETE (NEW STYLE)

For poets, as for novelists, playwrights, essayists, critics, and literary journalists, there were mainly two sides to every radical question. "Are you for
or against . . . ?" was nearly everywhere the interrogative prefix. "Are you
for, or against, Franco and Fascism?" demanded Nancy Cunard of her colleagues. "[I]t is no longer possible to take no side. . . . The equivocal attitude . . . the paradoxical, the ironic detachment, will no longer do."[37] To
the brightest among such unequivocal writers, André Malraux, for instance,
discerning and taking sides was but a prelude to tremendous efforts to
prevent one's own side from assuming qualities of its opposite. Other mod-

ernists – Arthur Davison Ficke, for example, despite leanings toward leftism – clung fast to the idea that their aesthetic had taught them the value of
eschewing side-choosing. In the following complaint that Ficke wrote to
his friend, the poet Marjorie Seiffert, note that he walks away from a confrontation with young radical companions, satisfied that *they* were the ones
confused, he the one clarified: "My little friends," he wrote, "who came to
see me keep shouting at me – 'Are you a communist or Fascist? You've got
to choose!' I say 'I'm neither, – and, furthermore, I don't got to choose!'
Which infuriates them beyond words."[38] Merely to ascertain sides *per se*
required a talent many noncommunist modernists possessed in spite of their
modernism – that is, notwithstanding an addiction to multi-sidedness, once
deemed the ultimate of constructions, now naturalized. That after perceiving sides a noncommunist poet sometimes sought to distort, confuse, or
qualify them – multiply them, explode them, as in cubist days gone by –
says less about a poet's positions than about the modernist idea of position,
the difficulties of choosing sides within modernist modes already conventional.

Despite popular belief, "Which side are you on?" could be a modest
inquiry. During and in the few years after 1935, it called for a relatively
uncomplicated renunciation of fascism rather than for a much more problematic support of communism. Nonetheless, the question was exacting
and searching. It provided Stevens a means of abjuring his conservative
peers' assumptions of his conservatism. "[W]hen Stevens took sides," Allen
Tate's version ran, "it was almost inevitably that of the practical and business world."[39] In literary circles generally, self-reflective poetic answers to
the oft-shouted – oft-*sung*[40] – question cross the political spectrum from
left through center and extend surprisingly far into the right, even the
Agrarian right.[41] From mid-1935 until the Nazi-Soviet pact of August 1939,
one needed to oppose fascism and not too loudly equate Stalin and Hitler
to be a member in good standing of the burgeoning alliance called by its
devotees "the sweetest bandwagon in all history"[42] – the Popular Front –
which perhaps more than any other political force prepared American intellectuals to endure (and, with a few exceptions, to support) the total war
against fascism of the next decade. Even when noncommunist modernists
seem to have resisted questions intended to ascertain partisan alignments,
their responses do not automatically reveal their poetry to have served no
ideological function or stood outside the arena of literary politics.

An assumption that this poetry does stand outside, however, underwrote
the depoliticization of Stevens in the late forties and fifties, critical acts on
which the great gestures of canonization in the sixties and seventies largely
depend. It was an easy job: in canonizing this particular noncommunist,
one had, it seemed, merely to ratify his own decision to omit the overtly
political "Owl's Clover" from the *Collected Poems* of 1954 and then to con-

strue "The Man with the Blue Guitar" (which was, of course, retained) as if that latter work bore no relation to its predecessor and was therefore not its partner. In order to liberate "Blue Guitar" from "Owl's Clover," Cold War critics needed, ironically, to accept the objections to Stevens's poetry of such prewar leftists as Burnshaw, Isidor Schneider, Dorothy Van Ghent, and Horace Gregory – to name only the four poets who, as communists or fellow travelers, published their reactions to Stevens in the Stalinist *New Masses*. All four basically agreed that, after some struggle, Stevens had failed to answer satisfactorily the main question of the day, had blundered in taking sides, had remained "confused" when other modernists' positions were "clarified." Later canonizing critics actually concurred with assumptions upon which Marxists based their opposition to Stevens, seeing him as a poet who happily, willfully, provocatively "stood alone" (as the communist Van Ghent put it earlier, borrowing from Stevens's poem "Anglais Mort à Florence"): a humanistic spirit committed to the inviolable individualist's lyric in a world of contingent but nonetheless hard facts threatening to crush just such a spirit. Van Ghent argued that the once anarchic avant-garde or "defeatist" lyricist soul put up insufficient fight against the world, setting itself feebly against those artists who were heroically choosing unified resistance, in Spain for example.

Van Ghent's brief reading of Stevens's "Anglais Mort à Florence," presented with her general case against Stevens, is hardly less acute for its materialist reductions. The question "Which side are you on?" was supposed to enable the interrogating antihumanist critic to disclose instantly the lyricized "confusions" of noncommunists who admitted they did not yet know enough about themselves to answer. These "confused" writers were potentially the Popular Front's most persuasive allies. Many modernists in the thirties were prompted to make some form of alliance with the Popular Front, even while taking aesthetic positions that seem inimical to the left. By leaving the most important political questions open while not denying that they are ideological constructions, Stevens came effectively to doubt his own, as well as others', overdetermined positions.

To underscore how poetic position-taking might produce unexpected effects, I have selected an off-putting example, well aware that any discussion of Stevens's *favorable* remarks about Benito Mussolini might better follow, rather than precede, the detailed descriptions of modernist-radical convergence below. Most readers with whom I have discussed Stevens's two surviving comments about Mussolini insist that the offense does not alter their views of his poems. Whether the poems can or should similarly offend presents a problem no different in kind, though very different in degree, from that which has at times impaired sympathetic historicist critics of Pound.[43] Contemporary public opinion polls do demonstrate, as Milton Bates intrepidly suggests, that Stevens was not "standing alone" among Americans in commending Mussolini. Yet the use of such polls begs the question of whether offense should automatically be taken anyway, without further contextualizing, so as not to imitate the subject's self-justification.[44] The polls Bates cites, moreover, were national. Insofar as local attitudes about Mussolini were reflected, or indeed shaped, by Hartford's widely read and venerable *Courant*, then Stevens's immediate social environment must have been a good deal more hostile to Italian fascism, and his opinion a good deal more unusual, than national surveys indicate. While Stevens was writing about fascist aggression, the Republican *Courant*[45] was rebuking Mussolini's policies – editorially, as on October 11 ("ITALY CONDEMNED"), and otherwise prominently (as in a page-one atrocity story that ran on October 18 announcing that Italian leaders had ordered chlorine bombs dropped on Ethiopian troops).[46] If the question is forthrightly "Which side is Stevens on?" then Bates's implied answer is: He seems, at least momentarily, to be on Mussolini's, but that was not so unusual.

The following statements were meant to defend remarks, made a few weeks earlier, that were less palatable still. Obviously Latimer's reply had challenged Stevens on the point; in this instance, it is particularly unfortunate that Latimer's letters to Stevens have not survived. I emphasize Stevens's qualifications:

> *While it is true that* I have spoken sympathetically of Mussolini, all of my sympathies are *the other way*: with the coons and the boa-constrictors. *However*, ought I, as a matter of reason, to have sympathized with the Indians as against the Colonists in this country? A man would have to be very thick-skinned not to be conscious of the pathos of Ethiopia or China, or one of these days, if we are not careful, of this country. *But* that Mussolini is right, practically, has certainly a great deal to be said for it. (L 295)

So the poet's extrapoetic sympathy with Mussolini – specifically in reference to the Italian invasion of Abyssinia; the "coons" are, horribly, the besieged Ethiopians – was founded on an otherwise shrewd recognition that he was confined to his ideological affinities by what was called "reason." Stevens seems well aware that his comments are marked by historical process. While such awareness, together with its potential for poetic openness, is overwhelmed (as well it should be) by the overt racism, the awareness nonetheless remains. His recognition of the impression made by the "day's news" – Japan brutalizing China; Italy invading Ethiopia; Falangist rebellion strangling Spain – allowed him to acknowledge at least the possibility that the corrupting power of fascism could cross racial, national, and ideological boundaries, and that potentially it affected all. He had rejected the it-can't-happen-here logic then typical of his nation and class: ". . . or one of these days, if we are not careful, of this country."

Here is where Dorothy Van Ghent's communist criticism went awry in handling the problem of lyric in Stevens's poem "Anglais Mort à Florence."

For the title of her *New Masses* essay, "When Poets Stood Alone,"[47] and as a refrain linking her general criticism of a dozen poets, Van Ghent used what she judged to be a reactionary assertion in "Anglais Mort": "But he remembered a time when he stood alone." "At the head of this essay," she wrote, "a couple of lines from Wallace Stevens stand as epigraph, announcing the bafflement and despair of a person who has lost orientation in a world where matter crowds out essence . . . and [for whom] mechanized institutions seem to exist solely for the purpose of overreaching themselves day after day in vulgarity and aimlessness."[48] This is the poem:

> A little less returned for him each spring.
> Music began to fail him. Brahms, although
> His dark familiar, often walked apart.
>
> His spirit grew uncertain of delight,
> Certain of its uncertainty, in which
> That dark companion left him unconsoled
>
> For a self returning mostly memory.
> Only last year he said that the naked moon
> Was not the moon he used to see, to feel
>
> (In the pale coherences of moon and mood
> When he was young), naked and alien,
> More leanly shining from a lankier sky.
>
> Its ruddy pallor had grown cadaverous.
> He used his reason, exercised his will,
> Turning in time to Brahms as alternate
>
> In speech. He was that music and himself.
> They were particles of order, a single majesty:
> But he remembered the time when he stood alone.
>
> He stood at last by God's help and the police;
> But he remembered the time when he stood alone.
> He yielded himself to that single majesty;
>
> But he remembered the time when he stood alone,
> When to be and delight to be seemed to be one,
> Before the colors deepened and grew small.
>
> (*CP* 148–9)

Van Ghent unsurprisingly assumed that the Englishman Stevens depicted formed a rough equivalence both to the speaker and to Stevens – that the three poetic identities shared a nostalgia for a lost social stability. Such a reading could only be sustained on the basis of another assumption, a common one. Since, secondly, the new order – against which the Englishman somewhat ambiguously depends on the police for protection – threatens to cut off his supply of aesthetic conventions, the old smooth flow of prosodic harmonies, it must thirdly be assumed that the new political order antagonizing the outmoded gentleman is the revolutionary one, especially as the old fellow's satisfying memories are of a time when one could stand *alone* – that is, when he was not compelled to define his needs only in relation to others'. At the risk of contributing another reduction to Van Ghent's, I have organized a three-part, left-to-right reading implied by communist criticism: (1) the new world order, presumed to be the making of the left, stands against (2) Stevens, who is presumed to side with (3) the outmoded Englishman (on the right). Reading leftward thus from cultural communism to what Burnshaw and others called the "middle ground," the Marxist critic suspects that the "new order," represented as invidious in the poem, coincides with the critical (not the poetic) subject on the left.

Such a reading is supported, to be sure, by several aspects of the poem. The dying Englishman depends upon music (the speaker specifies Brahms) to escort him back as his "dark familiar" to a time when the social formation was conceived as pleasantly individualistic, when the whole godly majesty of existence was revealed to each person in single truths: "He used his reason, exercised his will, / Turning in time to Brahms as alternate // In speech. He was that music and himself. / They were particles of order, a single majesty: / But he remembered the time when he stood alone." It is only one step from here, then, to the political criticism that the speaker was representing *himself* as the one remembering, that his salutary attitude toward the poem's lament endorses the act of recollecting bourgeois "particles of order" as a means of taking sides against the new whole of the discordant radical present, to which Van Ghent was in fact then zealously devoted.[49]

The poem in question was written during the first week of January, 1935. On January 8, Stevens was surely referring to it when he wrote Latimer, "The other night I took it into my head to describe a deathbed farewell *under the new regime.* And I am bound to say that I liked the result immensely for the moment (*L* 273)."[50] It might well be the case that Stevens wanted his own view to coincide with the Englishman's. His letter provides further evidence to support Van Ghent's implied conflation of speaker, Englishman, and Stevens. In it he reports also that he wrote the poem in the evening at home, "after a little music." He adds, after claiming that "writing poetry is a *conscious* activity" (emphasis added), that he can – perhaps *did* in the act of creating "Anglais Mort à Florence" – "stroll home from the office and fill the house with the most iridescent notes while I am ... changing to the slippers that are so appropriate to the proper enjoyment of Beethoven and Brahms on the gramophone" (*L* 273–4). It might be, then, that Stevens knew enough of the poem's potential detractors to play deliberately into the hands of radical analysis by appearing to underwrite the Englishman's nostalgia, and so, through the dying man himself, to mourn the loss of such music as a sustaining metaphor, particles of an old order.[51]

Yet one of the most willful acts of the poem – if, possibly, an act subverting every "conscious" attempt to make it what Stevens then claimed it was – lies in the situating work of the title, "Anglais Mort à Florence." This "deathbed farewell under the new regime" was, after all, set in Italy. On five of the eight days immediately preceding January 8, the day Stevens reported having written the poem, Mussolini's Italy was front-page news in Hartford as in New York. The French foreign minister had been spending that interval in Italy, where he was welcomed with what we now know was treacherous hospitality. On the seventh, an accord was reached between republican France and fascist Italy that precipitated, as some had guessed, heightened antagonism between Italy and England. Leaders of the latter anxious nation had urged the French on no account to deal with Mussolini. On the eighth, the *New York Times* and the *Hartford Times* each editorially expressed this typical American opinion: such pacts were to be praised because they helped make fascist ambitions "unrealizable"; the *Hartford Times* regarded negotiations with Mussolini as "something gained" in the hedge against Germany, while the *New York Times* ridiculed antifascist warnings of "[a]nother 'inevitable' war."[52] Such attitudes we might presume Stevens shared, judging from his comments on Mussolini later in the year.

But Stevens's poem responded to the convergence of lyric and historical imaginations as a formal as well as a strictly political answer to "the day's news" – in this case rather unavoidable news, especially to those, like the English, who, distrusting negotiation with fascism, will have found that week's news unavoidably bad news. Moreover, its French title places an Englishman knowledgeably in Italy, spiritually resisting representations of the contemporary Italian regime. The poet's later comments support this reading. He subsequently regarded the poem not so much as asserting one's dependence on religious philosophy for protecting oneself from the intrusions of the state upon the self as, rather, insisting that "a strong spirit (Anglais, etc.) stands by its own strength."[53] Thus, the political order against which the Englishman's old formal manner feebly contends was indeed the same order against which Van Ghent and other cultural radicals were contending – an odd but momentous ideological meeting. The nostalgia, from the speaker's view in proximity to the Englishman's nostalgia, makes each figure long for a time when such formal counterinsurgency was effective against those cultural fascists who were themselves, in Kenneth Burke's words, "against the harmonious." Stevens and Van Ghent thus set up "two kinds of against" (to use another helpful Burkean concept) that were nevertheless convergent.[54] Perhaps "Music began to fail *him*," to fail the Englishman, but it obviously was not failing the lyricist speaker. The poem itself offers sufficient evidence that a Stevensian spirit, *qua* modernist, continues a lyric resistance, just as the Englishman's premodern spirit withers under tremendous anti-lyric pressure in Florence, when "the colors deepened and grew small."

Stevens's modernism thus enabled him here to maintain some necessary separation from the Englishman in his contemporaneous account of his delight over the new poem. This achievement he described as having filled his house with "irridescent notes." The old Englishman, no longer able to distinguish elements of language, had become fuzzily nostalgic for the old sounds to such a degree as to be, in a sense, incapable of distinguishing "mood" from "moon": "Only last year he said that the naked moon / Was not the moon he used to see, to feel / (In the pale coherences of moon and mood / When he was young)."[55] Through the poem's endowing a deteriorating subject-position with great sensitivity to the intractable political predicament, a severe ideological press, it portrays an *ancien régime* aestheticist unable to construct a lyric ideology of the sort on which the poem that contains him is founded. This pre-elegy, with its slow tercets, might warn of spiritual collapse were its manifest lyricism not so positively a counterexample of such degeneration. The poem's political disposition might be revised accordingly: (1) Stevens endorses the subject of (2) the outmoded Englishman, who in turn resists (3) the "new regime." Thus a reading of the poem's commitment to the lyric might finally include rather than exclude terms of partisanship. Reading roughly from left to right, (1) Stevens endorses, presumably from the right, (2) an outmoded right, now insurgent, having turned to stand against, from *its* left, (3) the fascist or "new" right.

Charting the relations between critical detractor, speaker, and Englishman brings us only a little closer to discerning side-taking; we only know more specifically the form of the new right or "new regime" against which Stevens was prepared to have his poetic identities stand, no matter how bourgeois, enfeebled, or "alone." We can be more confident, at least, that Van Ghent was mistaken in her *New Masses* piece in assuming that this or any poem respectfully depicting a reactionary figure marks out a political "side" necessarily against her own. We also know better how effectively the noncommunist might depict the kind of side-taking itself then ascendant. It might be said that Stevens's speaker successfully extricated himself from his Englishman's predicament, but the Englishman's ideas about the lyric resemble those of Stevens's own earlier poetic self, the poet of *Harmonium*. One comes to see that the poem enacts contentions between the three tendencies that arose in Stevens during these critical years, and supplements the notion of a thirties construction of the twenties. The poem helped Stevens realize, as he later put it, that people must have something "external to them on which to rely" (*L* 348).

A first version of Stevens, embodied in the Englishman, is an endangered species, befitting the thirties view of the poet of *Harmonium*. This is the Stevens most closely resembling the Englishman himself. At certain moments in the poem, the thematized lyricism (the topic: an Englishman clings uselessly to forms) and the lyric mode itself (the reason this poem has come to be highly valued, by me and others)[56] become one and the same ideological element in lines close in sound and cadence to the Keatsian Stevens of the teens and early twenties:

> More leanly shining from a lankier sky . . .
> When to be and delight to be seemed to be one . . .
> His spirit grew uncertain of delight . . .
> He wás that músic and himsélf . . .
> That dárk compánion léft him únconsóled . . .

But in characterizing the Englishman, the poem acknowledges this style as itself a kind of *ancien régime*, debilitated because outmoded. Such explicit use of *Harmonium*-like lines could draw Stevens into the feeble resistance of an old politics-denying lyrical right against a new overtly politicized right utterly hostile to the lyric ("the new regime"). The self-revision confirms the distance between the noncommunist modernist whom Van Ghent rebuked as too much in love with sound (the poet "who stood alone" aesthetically in the "theme"-oriented thirties), and a newer, up-to-date Stevens whose poetry was disclosing modernism in the very act of becoming "preoccupied by events." A second Stevens, then, is the poetic figure the poem itself opposes, the poet who in several instances spoke "sympathetically of Mussolini" in his letters.

Yet a third Stevens here is the one I find most interesting – the modernist whose confusions make it possible to cast him as a representative "middle-ground" writer teaching himself to read the radical cultural position from right to left. This is the Stevens who could be "conscious of the pathos of Ethiopia," conscious enough to perceive the limits of his own position. This is the poet who, in the thirties, effectively recast, and to some degree recanted, his commitment to "pure poetry": an "esthete," perhaps, thought one reviewer of *Ideas of Order*, but "an esthete (*new style*)."[57] This keen witness, this ostensibly nonpartisan poet, observing the expiring lyricist (the Englishman) who in turn summons an inner strength to take sides against "the new regime," came to a position from which he could alter his own notion of the cultural place of poetry. Such a reading offers a rough analogue of the modernist, having come of age long before the radicalized period, now in the act of reassessing poetic growth: (3) Stevens as "esthete (new style)" in the process of learning to waive (2) the Stevens sympathetic to "the new regime" by rhetorically engaging (1) the outmoded Stevens of *Harmonium*.

3: SPAIN

Marianne Moore also assessed Wallace Stevens's politics in the thirties. Admiring the way Stevens's poems reveal that he "hates lust for power and ignorance of power," she drew a conclusion quite different from Van Ghent's. Moore was referring to a work that A. Walton Litz once called "one of Stevens's most moving poems,"[58] namely, "The Men That Are Falling" (*CP* 187–8). In the first half of the poem a man tries with yet-unexplained desperation to fall asleep in his bedroom. Soon it is midnight and he begins to comprehend an intense desire as the source of his restlessness, something lacking in him or perhaps in the day just passed. In the second half, there appears on the pillow of the sleepless man a severed head, bloody from riot and rebellion. The intrusion horrifies the man in his room. He contemplates the warring world for which this soldier died. The poem ends by returning to the possibilities of the poet's sequestered night, which is unchanged except for one thing, the poem itself – or, rather, the sleeper himself who is evidently constructing a privatized language about war: "The night wind blows upon the dreamer, *bent / Over words* that are life's voluble utterance" (emphasis added). These final lines identify the man in the bedroom as an anxious, hard-working poet, attempting to make of his own relatively insignificant, quiet suffering "voluble" words for the world's.

In Moore's suggestive reading of this poem, Stevens can "prove to us that the testament to emotion is not volubility" or, in other words, that some poets need not shout down dictators in order to express "hope for the world." Still considering "The Men That Are Falling," she added: "It is remarkable that a refusal to speak should result in such eloquence." By emphasizing Stevens's "refusal to speak" Moore meant refusal to speak *out*; the versified noisiness of many other poets she felt to be pretentious expressions of indiscriminate hope for betterment. Typical, surely, was the paradoxical wordiness with which the same theme of silence was used in other American poems about the Spanish Civil War, such as Genevieve Taggard's "Silence in Mallorca" – unremarkably derivative of romanticism ("O wild west wind"!), redundant ("Cry, we cry brothers, Comrades help us"), and cliché-ridden ("Mallorca, the first to fall, the last to die").[59] Who among Stevens's readers, knowing his hatred of the "lust for power," Moore wondered, would be surprised that he responded to the Spanish crisis in a manner that would deeply impress the editors of the *Nation*? "That 'The Men [That] Are Falling' should have received the *Nation*'s prize for 1936," Moore wrote, "is gratifying, however natural we feel the acknowledgment to be."[60] "Gratifying" while "natural," of course, because the expectation of Stevens's detachment was here refuted from inside insider politics.

Moore was not in error: Stevens had actually won the *Nation* prize for
1936.[61] It is hard to know if the *Nation* awarded Stevens its annual award
because its editors took his poem to express unambiguous political sympathy with the Spanish Loyalists, whose cause editorially preoccupied that
weekly from the moment war broke out.[62] Yet even as the *Nation's* feature
essays, and book reviews, and editorials demonstrated unbroken commitment to radical causes, the verse published in 1935 and 1936 did not particularly support or disavow its editorial policy.[63] Taking second prize to
Stevens's poem, and printed alongside it, John Peale Bishop's "Collapse of
Time" was downright counterrevolutionary.[64] That the literary editor was
Joseph Wood Krutch, a liberal whose cultural anticommunism we will later
find relevant to this story, only adds to the difficulty of measuring the
award's significance against the politics of the poem.

Ben Belitt, a regular *Nation* reviewer and assistant literary editor, had
persuaded Krutch to revive the annual poetry prize and was finally responsible for picking the winners that year.[65] Popular-front inclusiveness notwithstanding, communists assailed Belitt's promotion of Stevens at the *Nation*, even though Belitt, undergoing "apprenticeship to the politics of the
Nation," was quite willing to repeat "the pieties of the 1930s"[66] in, say, the
preface to his first book of poems. (He described his verse modestly as
"establish[ing] usable relationships between the personal and the contemporary world."[67]) In the *Nation* Belitt scathingly attacked earnings-minded
poetry anthologists as falsely democratic, and decried vanity presses ex-
ploiting poetasters for profit. This overt literary-political invective won him
praise from Eda Lou Walton and others.[68] But if there were breaks in Belitt's
"pieties," Stevens might have widened them. The poems Belitt published in
magazines and journals, preparing to collect them for *The Five-Fold Mesh*
(1938), suggested that Stevens's line underwrote them in a way that has
been observed by Belitt's critical admirers.[69] Even Belitt's most explicitly
political poem – "Charwoman: 20 Vesey Street" (the *Nation's* street address),
a work dedicated to Krutch – is sufficiently Stevensian to warrant attention
as such: "And keep that figure, while a watery arc / Trembles and wanes in
wetted tile, as if / It wrote all darkness down."[70] To pick Stevens for the
Nation prize, even the modernist whose work authorized the poem about a
"Charwoman," implied Belitt's sympathy for Stevens's particular "ordeal of
rediscovery" (that test "awaits the poet in the wilderness in which he has
newly set foot"). Such sympathy carried real risks.[71]

Of course, even among communists there were staunch defenders of
Belitt's prize-winning Stevens. Willard Maas, for one, supported not only
the choice for the *Nation* award but also Belitt's mostly positive review of
Ideas of Order and *Owl's Clover* a few months later. "I was interested to know
that I had a champion of my Stevens judgment," Belitt wrote Maas. "It was

arrived at with great care, but I should be interested to hear of what was said against it, though I suspect I know without being told." Belitt was certain to remind Maas and his radical friends of "the 'moral' judgment at the end"[72] of his December 12, 1936, review. That space was reserved for an important ideological qualifier: "It remains to be seen, however, whether such a doctrine" – as for instance "the violent mind" of the masses toward which Stevens was willingly, if anxiously, sailing (in the poem "Farewell to Florida") – "does not cut the Gordian knot with a sword of two edges: one to save and one to destroy."[73]

No matter, evidently, how complex were circumstances at the *Nation* as civil war in Spain broke out; nor that tensions between the *Nation* and the *New Masses* might even have made that year's prize strategically a rejoinder to literary leftists further left. The mere fact of this particular tribute, taken in combination with Stevens's much later suggestion that his poem was written in solidarity with the Spanish Republicans (*L* 798), has suggested to some that it might be best not to submit the poem to the sort of rigorous analysis and skepticism they have applied to his other poems of the period. A selective easiness comes about, I think, for the plain reason that, whereas "Owl's Clover" treats seriously an issue American critics find assailable (literary communism and its mimeticist reductions), "The Men That Are Falling" takes up a topic beyond usual antipolitical reproach, what many liberal academics continue to call, vaguely, "Spain." The simplest procedure is to repeat Stevens's explanation (he "did have . . . in mind" the Spanish Republicans) when rendering standard formalist judgment of the poet's desire,[74] or, if speaking about the witnessed heroism, one can be quick to note that the Spaniard who has "fallen" most importantly anticipates "the major man" of the 1940s, the hero whose activity exists beyond contingency and single cause.[75]

Another option is merely to repeat a version of Samuel French Morse's defensive praise. Morse quoted the most explicitly political lines of the poem ("Taste of the blood upon his martyred lips, / O pensioners, O demagogues and pay-men!"); was he thinking perhaps of the diction and tone of Harold Rosenberg's "Spanish Epitaph" ("O tall men of Hades / Have pity on this little one!")?[76] Then Morse announced that Stevens's "politics become more active with time, and more sound," while neglecting to explain how the poet, if figured alone in his room, might be deemed "active" or his politics now suddenly "sound."[77]

There have been two dissenters. Milton Bates mentions the poem briefly in his survey of Stevens's politics; he was the first to concede in print that the only evidence we have for the poem's sympathy with the Spanish Republic is Stevens's own Cold War-era gloss. This "elegy for the Spanish Loyalists," Bates observed, is "curiously ambivalent."[78] Meanwhile, Helen

Vendler rejected the usual unqualified praise of the poem on very different grounds; she has mistrusted the historical reading altogether. Vendler praised the first half of the poem, where the poet deals with "private loss" privately and not politically:

> He lies down and the night wind blows upon him here.
> The bells grow longer. This is not sleep. This is desire.
>
> Ah! Yes, desire . . . this leaning on his bed,
> This leaning on his elbows on his bed,
>
> Staring, at midnight, at the pillow that is black
> In the catastrophic room . . .
>
> (CP 187)

But when the soldier's head intrudes on "the psychic problem of private misery," Stevens mistakenly "turn[s] his attention to those moral 'words' of heroic action 'that are life's voluble utterance,' insisting that right action alone is the arena for the resolution of inner pain." The encroachment of the political into the private, foreign war into American home, suggests Stevens's failure to sustain the direction in which the meditation might have taken him: Politics becomes an excuse for opening the window to outer weather (to borrow Frost's terms) for defining what was just a moment before an inner storm. Vendler doubts Stevens's interest in the actual world at war. Poems resulting from such interest "turn the symbolic focus outward; as a result, they become forced."[79] Much as I dislike this reading, I take my cue from its wise mistrust of the critical clichés mustered by Stevens's predominantly formalist critics in unanimous support of a poem they nevertheless praise for taking ideological sides and for thus deriving special emotional power. No surprise, then, that such readings neglect to make a case for the pertinence of the historical moment inscribed into the poem.

The Spanish Civil War was a failed pronunciamento that became a protracted battle (1936–9) waged between, on one side, Carlists, Falangists, Requetés, royalists, business conservatives, the military, and the Catholic Church, soon collectively and imprecisely named "Nationalist," and, on the other side, dubbed "Loyalist," a loose popular-front coalition of anarchists, socialists, unionists, communists and other Spanish and then non-Spanish supporters of the republican government elected in the spring of 1936. It was a war about which, according to nearly every historical generalization made about it since, western intellectuals felt compelled to take sides. In this view, "an overwhelming majority of the American intelligentsia" regarded Spain as a testing ground for a war against fascism and for the antifascist rhetoric supporting a radical analysis in general.[80] Militarily and ideologically, Spain quickly became just such a fight. Given this perspective, the central question about the soldier in Stevens's poem, memorialized so sympathetically by the sleepless poet, would seem to be a simple one: On which military and rhetorical side had this soldier fought? Yet the poem itself offers slight internal evidence of the fallen man's affiliation, although his partisanship – a cause for dying, a motive for "speaking the speech / *Of absolutes*" – apparently does hold the key to the equally obscure desire of the poet:

> What is it he desires?
> But this he cannot know, the man that thinks,
>
> Yet life itself, the fulfilment of desire
> In the grinding ric-rac, staring steadily
>
> At a head upon the pillow in the dark,
> More than sudarium, speaking the speech
>
> Of absolutes, bodiless, a head
> Thick-lipped from riot and rebellious cries,
>
> The head of one of the men that are falling, placed
> Upon the pillow to repose and speak,
>
> Speak and say the immaculate syllables
> That he spoke only by doing what he did.
>
> God and all angels, this was his desire,
> Whose head lies blurring here, for this he died.
>
> Taste of the blood upon his martyred lips,
> O pensioners, O demagogues and pay-men!
>
> This death was his belief though death is a stone.
> This man loved earth, not heaven, enough to die.

If readers merely assume that this thirties poem is politically what Stevens said it was in the fifties, they do so because similar emotional memorializations have been given us in a flood of elegiac verse by Millay ("Say That We Saw Spain Die"), Rexroth ("Requiem for the Dead in Spain"), Rolfe Humphries ("A Gay People"), Maddow ("The Defenses"), Taggard ("Noncombatants"), Williams ("Wind of the Village"), Sol Funaroff ("To the Dead of the International Brigade"), James Rorty ("Elegy for the Spanish Dead"), Norman MacLeod ("After the Bombing of Barcelona"), Kenneth Fearing ("The Program"), James Neugass ("Give Us This Day"), Joy Davidman ("Snow in Madrid"), Archibald MacLeish (the verse-play *Air Raid*), Muriel Rukeyser ("Barcelona on the Barricades"), Edwin Rolfe ("City of Anguish"), William Rose Benét ("Catalonia"), John Berryman ("1938"), H. R. Hays ("Defenseless Spring"), and Theodore Roethke ("Facing the Guns"), to name only some of the many more or less active American partisans among poets. Williams, chairman of the Bergen County Medical Board to Aid Spanish Democracy[81] and contributor of his rendering of Miguel Hernández' poem to the collection *And Spain Sings: Fifty Loyalist Ballads Adapted by American Poets* (1937), held up "The Men That Are Falling" for special commendation in a review of *The Man with the Blue Guitar & Other Poems* that otherwise cast doubt on Stevens's alleged leftward movement. The poem about Spain, Williams wrote in the *New Republic*, "is the most passionate and altogether the best work in this selection." Indeed, "it is one of the best poems of the day . . . a lesson for us all."[82]

Even such contemporary accounts of Stevens's poem as Williams's, however, were written many months after American intellectuals' nearly unanimous enthusiasm for Loyalist Spain was assured and assumed; such sympathy peaked in 1937 and 1938.[83] Yet Stevens's poem about Spain, it must be remembered, was published in October 1936, and only after some time had been spent with it during the process in which submissions were judged at the *Nation's* offices. One account Belitt preserved confirms that the poem could not have been sent to the *Nation* later than September 17, and almost certainly its composition can be dated mid- or early September or even late August.[84] In short, Stevens's poem responds to a civil war only weeks old. It might well be among the very first poetic responses to the Spanish crisis by a non-Spaniard, James Neugass's "Headlines from Spain," published in the August 4 *New Masses*, being the *only* American poem on Spain I could find that was published earlier.[85] Unable to work from such impressions as were subsequently presented in Harry Pollitt's well-thumbed report "Building the People's Front" (not published until December 1936), or Auden's immediately famous moving description of Valencia (January 1937), or Van Wyck Brooks's lucid "Attack on Democracy" (April 1937), or MacLeish's popular "The War Is Ours" (June 1937), or Langston Hughes's verse-report from Barcelona (October 1937), or Stephen Spender's "Thoughts During an Air Raid" (May 1938), or Williams's tribute to Lorca (Spring 1939), or from any of the innumerable accounts of the Battle of Madrid by literary people – Spender, Lillian Hellman, Hemingway, Cyril Connolly, Edwin Rolfe, Gellhorn, Herbst, and Dos Passos (none before mid-October 1936, most much later) – Stevens's poem is an original work of political imagination. Not, like so much else, an "engaged" literary response responsive to other writing already designated "engaged,"[86] nor intended as a contribution to the thriving subgenre which pro-Franco poet Roy Campbell derided as "MacSpaunday"[87] and which Auden himself later dubbed "Daylewisaudenmacneicespender,"[88] it is an account of the alarm set off by another's bravery in a fearful, sedentary person piecing together a sense of the situation exclusively from nonliterary accounts.

Only in subsequent months would the choice between Loyalist defenders and Nationalist insurgents appear "clear-cut," and "the cause of Spain the cause of democracy and morality."[89] Only later would world opinion go solidly against the Nationalists when, during the Battle of Madrid, even conservative foreign papers accused the insurgent troops and their fascist allies of German-derived (and -assisted) *Schrecklichkeit*, the military tactic of shock that Picasso – yet another modernist facing left – would replicate in

Guernica six months later still.[90] Only later would public opinion in the United States be shaped by the arrival in Spain of famed writers like Hemingway; only later, 1937 and 1938, would literary sympathizers feel encouraged to hope that "public opinion would be aroused" by "Authors Tak[ing] Sides" in print, and that with the aid of unembarrassed political art "the farce of nonintervention might be brought to an end."[91] Only later could Rexroth suggest movingly in verse that "the unwritten books, the unrecorded experiments, / The unpainted pictures"[92] would have been written, recorded, and painted overwhelmingly by those on one side, not the other.

Before all this, however, when Stevens wrote what Bates has properly called a "curiously ambivalent" elegy, few Americans, including those on the left, thought the United States should make an effort to influence the war's outcome.[93] At the time, it was one radical writer's impression, indicative though exaggerated, that "the people on the left, liberal or communist, had not said a word or made a move."[94] Even the League Against War and Fascism waited to make its move in favor of the Loyalists. "For many liberals," a historian writes, "the war forced a hard choice between their desire for peace and neutrality and their hatred of fascism."[95] Given this indecisive if not momentarily neutralized atmosphere, we can consider the possibility that Stevens's fallen man was not to be read explicitly as a Loyalist soldier. By 1953, the poet might not have felt quite prepared to explain the poem's astonishing ideological ambivalence to a young postwar scholar, Bernard Heringman, who had written to ask, in essence, Which side were you on back then?

Early reports of the Spanish fighting in the American newspapers emphasized atrocities committed by the Loyalists in acts of revenge against insurgent soldiers taken prisoner and citizens who were found to support the rebellion. The terror of Málaga, for instance, was covered by the *New York Times* on July 26 and 27: 600 Nationalist hostages held on a prison ship were shot in groups in reprisal for an insurgent air raid.[96] At the end of August and in the first days of September, the *Hartford Times*, Stevens's afternoon paper, carried Robert G. De Pury's dramatic accounts of atrocities committed by retreating anarchist defenders; on September 4, under the shocking headline, "PRIESTS CRUCIFIED BY LEFTISTS," De Pury's lead was: "I saw this morning the bodies of two priests, crucified." Sorely pressed defenders had bound rebel prisoners – including priests and captured Moor soldiers – and placed them in various parts of the city under siege as targets for rebel attacks. The front-page story of the September 2 *Courant* told Hartford residents that in the streets of Irun one could hear the prayers of the "chained and shackled rebel hostages" mixed with the shrieks of shells fired at them by their own comrades. Among the Catholics shackled in the streets was one as eminent as the bishop of Valladolid.[97]

These horror stories reported from Irun, and frequent accounts of perpetrators of the notorious *paseos*, or gang assassinations, rapidly discredited the Republic abroad.[98] We may presume that in these first five weeks of the war Stevens could discount the biases of American newspapers whose emphasis on atrocities committed by the leftists is partly explained by the overwhelming isolationist sentiments of the American public which the newspapers sought not to contradict. He would surely have been made nervous by other less sensational reports disclosing how radical factions within the Loyalist alliance were taking advantage of the chaos to institute revolutionary programs in Republican-held cities. One can hardly imagine Stevens showing enthusiasm for the announcement of POUM leader Andrés Nins in the first days of September proclaiming that the dictatorship of the proletariat already existed in Barcelona; or for the anarchists of Seville, where it was reported that the rebel seizure of the city was being avenged by mass roundups and shootings of priests.[99] These incessant stories of atrocities committed by the left during the first phase of the fighting could hardly have foreshadowed, for Stevens or anyone else, a long war that finally would have to be narrated very differently: a conflict in which Franco's army, and his German and Italian allies, committed much more than their share of horrors. But Stevens's poetic response to the situation came exactly when, in Spender's words, "either side could strike the foreigner as heroic,"[100] and when pro-Republicans, particularly communists, were going to great lengths to distinguish between the depravity of the Church hierarchy and the decency of individual believers.[101]

The soldier of Stevens's poem is as likely to have represented for him one of the communist defenders as one of those rebel prisoners whose predicament he discovered under the horrifying banner headlines in Hartford on September 1 and 2: chained and shackled by the retreating Loyalists of Irun – or indeed crucified by them – and left to pray and be decimated by friendly fire. In the poem, the man who has fallen is, after all, a *rebel* – uttering the "*rebellious* cries" of his cause – and whose death requires Stevens to amend his appeal to "God and all angels" and to modify the religious notion of proper cause for death in such a way that the appalling demise of this man, who died for the world, can somehow be accounted for in an earthly language. (The very use of the term "rebel," then, itself a term used by the left to provoke the right, further complicates the subject's sympathy.)[102] The Loyalists' anticlerical fury would inform this lyric: While at first the sleepless poet directly entreats God and angels to "sing the world to sleep," soon, upon letting the actual world intrude upon the scene of his meditation, he discovers that the desire for belief, for a heaven, has been eradicated by the very same forces of disbelief that severed the soldier's head. If I am right that conservative coverage of the loathsome Battle of Irun impressed the poem, then it is because this event, as assimilated by a nation whose liberals were still largely isolationist, made clearer than other journalistic narratives that one side was fighting to preserve the traditional social role of the Church. Christianity's fictions, in Stevens's terms, had long sufficed for many as the fulfillment of desire for an aesthetic order, belief having brought the doubter through a dark night analogous to the poet's frightening intervals of silence. The Loyalists' belief in a terrestrial, not heavenly paradise was weakened by the tactical, not to say ethical error of making martyrs of the priests.[103] The phrase "for this he died" suggests that the poem's victim is a martyr in a modern post-Christian war; his bloody face on the poet's pillow forms an impression deeper than that created by the traditional Catholic relic, the *sudarium*, the imprint of Christ's face on the kerchief: "[A] head upon the pillow in the dark, / More than sudarium, speaking the speech / Of absolutes, bodiless, a head / Thick-lipped from riot and rebellious cries." Here, surely, is a victim of the great schemes of "demagogues and pay-men," of whom there were plenty on either side of Irun's embattled streets, or of the diplomatic aisles, where moral focus was as blurred as the nightmarish severed head of the dead.[104]

In revising rightward the poem Belitt prized on the *Nation*'s behalf, I am not, of course, talking about a poet who felt the least bit as Pound did, that "Spain is an emotional luxury to a gang of sap-head dilettantes."[105] And if Eliot's response to those who were collecting statements for the symposium, "Authors Take Sides," was to say he was "naturally sympathetic" but still felt "convinced that it is best that at least a few men of letters should remain isolated, and take no part in these collective activities,"[106] Stevens's poem, on the contrary, is designed to test in one poetic act the limits both of the poet's isolation and his isolationism.[107] Like "The Man with the Blue Guitar," and other poems in which Stevens consciously took up the structure of political argument, "The Men That Are Falling" distinguishes itself by confessing the narrowness of an American modernist's capacity for inscribing foreign action and by presenting a point of obvious moral contrast between the poet's confining American space and the hunger for foreign *Lebensraum*. Such confession, it must be noted, was hardly confined to modernists of Stevens's stripe. The radical H. R. Hays wrote "Defenseless Spring" with similar self-reproach in mind: "1200 killed in new raid on Barcelona – / And not a quiver in this lazy air!": "Defenseless spring, / Miraculous, dangerous season – / Caught like a sleepwalker / 40 stories up, / *Still* / *The wind feels good*."[108]

Stevens's poem formalizes an American aesthetic policy of isolation by doubting it – by finding in the course of such a meditation that isolation lacks moral legitimacy until private pain can be compared to that experienced by a world of sufferers existing bodily beyond the room, as it were, of the poem. Here again a talent for working with "[w]hat one reads in the papers" (*L* 308) is pertinent. To know that the Hearst papers were not the only dailies to use the well-worn justification of "human interest" for bold-facing every story about Spain that emphasized "any sort of violence, ca-tastrophe, or depravity,"[109] or were ready to repeat any partly confirmed story of "churches . . . desecrated, . . . [n]uns and priests shot down,"[110] is to know as satisfyingly much and as frighteningly little as the solitary speaker knows about the bloodied martyr. (I note how the same limitation of news-paper-knowledge as afflicts Stevens is implicit in the headline diction of Hays's first line: "1200 killed in new raid on Barcelona.") Stevens's *Hartford Times* equalled or surpassed the worst of what Allen Guttmann, in his na-tional search, found other American papers to have been printing. It must have been just as disheartening to read these stories in the war's first weeks, when "[n]inety percent of all the excesses" committed by the Republicans took place, as it was to sense the distortion. Quite aside from George Orwell's wonderment and disgust at the way in which, when POUM moved to the left of the Stalinist "far left," that faction was cursed as "Franco's Fifth Column" – indeed, even more dispiriting than that utterly cheerless theme in *Homage to Catalonia* – was the "dreariest" effect of all: Journalistic "screaming and lies" made pro-Republican press accounts "every bit as spurious and dishonest as that of the Right." "We all remember the *Daily Mail's* poster: 'REDS CRUCIFY NUNS,'" while on the left the *New Statesmen* treated one's noncombatant companions back home to Fascist barricades constructed of children's living bodies ("a most unhandy thing to make barricades with").[111] Confronted with mounds of atrocity stories, some verified, others "little more than fantasies," in his inquiry into "The Por-nography of Violence" of Spanish Civil War press distortions, Frederick Benson could cite only William James's observation that the same material provoking moral aversion to war's cruelty simultaneously provoked its share of perverse fascination.[112] Clearly Stevens means to have his speaker face down the temptation to let himself be visited by such rhetorical phantasms. But in the tempting comes an enlargement far beyond the poem to which Vendler would want Stevens to have restricted himself. The sleepless isola-tionist encounters the bodiless head with bloodied martyred lips on his pillow, speaking absolutes rhetorically derived from the right, and he grapples with aspects of political desire derived from the left, terrifying enough to rob him of sleep. Already Stevens was encountering, however re-motely from his bedroom and fleetingly in thirty lines, what Malraux described as the most troubling aspect of a Good Fight: the "recogni[tion] that each side takes on the characteristics of the enemy, consciously or unconsciously."[113]

4: IN THE CATASTROPHIC ROOM

Spain thus ideally located for Stevens the dimensions of his isolation. "Though a great public-political event," Spender wrote later, Spain "was

for many . . . a very personal involvement. Their reasons were moral before they were political."[114] If this is true, for instance, of Spender's own
"Thoughts During an Air Raid," a poem taught me in college as one of
the great political poems to come of the war, then Stevens's poem about
Spain keeps pace. Here are several sections from Spender's work:

> A hundred are killed
> In the outer suburbs. Well, well, one carries on.
> So long as this thing "I" is propped up on
> The girdered bed which seems so like a hearse,
> In the hotel bedroom with the wall-paper
> Blowing smoke-wreaths of roses, one can ignore
> The pressure of those names under the fingers
> Indented by lead type on newsprint. . . .
> Yet supposing that a bomb should dive
> Its nose right through this bed, with one upon it?
> The thought's obscene. Still, there are many
> For whom one's loss would illustrate
> The 'impersonal' use indeed.
>
>   . . . Then horror is postponed
> Piecemeal for each, until it settles on him
> That wreath of incommunicable grief
> Which is all mystery or nothing.[115]

The assumed claim of the poem, from its title on, is that it is set and was
composed in Spain itself. But it deliberately avoids deriving any of its power,
either as lyric or as argument, from its status as an eyewitness account or a
partisan's inscription. Spender deliberately cuts himself off from the actuality of the fighting, just as Stevens does by setting his meditation in his
bedroom. We find Spender and Stevens, two otherwise very different writers, on the same side of a dispute that raged throughout the literary left
during the thirties, notwithstanding the Popular Front. When Horace Gregory intrepidly confessed in the *New Masses* that, while "[o]thers can write,
do write in the heat of conflict[,] I can't" – "I must witness the conflict,"
he added, "then walk away and gain perspective"[116] – fellow communists
counterattacked. Edwin Seaver wrote: "Gregory is merely saying: All right,
. . . I'm for the Party; now let me write my poetry in peace."[117] At first the
dead came to Spender, as to Stevens, with a secondhandedness that Gregory honestly assumed was inevitable. For Spender, the dead were a list of
names literally impressed into newsprint; his poem admits his keen desire
to isolate himself, to gird himself in his bed – cooled after conflict in just
the way Gregory thought necessary. All three poets found it possible to
stand away with measures of success, while thematizing the illusion of presence, doubting the ideology of firsthand experience, and implicitly contradicting what Philip Rahv nastily called Spender's *"rejection* of introspection

and sensibility as ends in themselves."[118] The risk entailed in the strong radical preference for firsthand experience in Spain is that that experience can seem actually to recommend combat horror as a necessary condition of truth-seeking. In Edwin Rolfe's "City of Anguish," lines like "No man knows war / who never has crouched in a foxhole, hearing / the bullets an inch from his head, nor the zoom of / planes like a ferris wheel strafing the trenches" only qualify the conclusion that "War is your comrade struck dead beside you / his shared cigarette still alive in your lips." The poem seems to be more about good comraderie than about bad fascist aggression, and it only invites the right-wing scorn of Roy Campbell's "Wars Bring Good Times for Poets (Headline in a Daily Paper)."[119] Obviously introspection was significantly more complicated than the reductive state of inexperience Rolfe ridicules with his repeated construction "No man knows war / Who never. . . ." – who never charged a fascist battalion or who never ran from a strafing.[120] In a war zone, to which Spender was proximate and Stevens was not, such girding as Gregory described for radical modern poetry generally was required if one wanted momentarily to create and especially to preserve a poem qualitatively different from Campbell's utterly traditional form. That different sort of war poem, as Stevens saw it, accepted Rolfe's unmanly "never" as its preferred precondition for words; in such acceptance there is a recognition that the Spanish conflict, because of its particular ideological configuration, "began as a war of words and develops into a war about words."[121]

The point is that the Communist Party, in its way, understood this too: Claud Cockburn was among those hardliners who thought it silly that a writer, with an "exaggerated idea of physical action," felt "certainty . . . that *unless* he personally and physically fought he would cease to function fully as a writer." The sympathetic writer's job was to observe and write, not necessarily to fight.[122] After successful removal to a site of observation, the poem might itself then create an idea about position and cause a sudden end to isolation in both its political and bodily senses – a sense that Rolfe, in this respect following his mentor Hemingway, could not possibly inscribe in his poem, given its exclusivist standard of engagement.[123] Prepared otherwise to find the Communist Party "a hope for the future" and "necessary for living through these times of terror and destruction," Gregory knew enough, he said, to discern just when "it would be an impertinence for me to take sides" even while always generally endorsing radicalism,[124] and indeed Gregory's reputation among mainstream critics became that of "a poet giving expression to the inner intellectual and spiritual strains and dilemmas of the time" and "a sensitive instrument on which *the pulls in various directions* are recorded."[125] In Stevens's and Spender's poems alike, there is an incursion into the scene of private invention; the very act of "gain[ing] perspective," the politics of observation ridiculed by some

Marxist critics as counterprogressive, and celebrated by others as "sensitive" when Gregory described it ("I must remain in a position to observe," he said),[126] permitted the intensity of engagement so exalted in Spender's work of this period. The speakers of "Thoughts During an Air Raid" and "The Men That Are Falling" lose sleep over the fact that in poetry, to quote Spender, "the entire effort is to put oneself / Outside the ordinary range / Of what are called statistics" – to be able to imagine the single soldier dead and, in a poem about the world the dead man has given up, to say: The poem singing for a single life sings for all. "For *this* he died."

The Stevens of *Harmonium* would never have thought to make such a claim. Nor would he have had what we might call *the experience of inexperience* he described in December 1936, in his Harvard lecture. He recalled for his audience a recent visit to an art gallery, during which he had realized precisely why the exhibit held no interest for him; it was because "[t]he air was charged with anxieties and tensions." Few in his Harvard audience would have failed to realize what he meant: it was the time, after all, of Spain, the Battle of Madrid. "To look at pictures there was the same thing as to play the piano in Madrid this afternoon," Stevens told them (*OP* 226). A new sensitivity to "anxieties and tensions" in an American aesthetic context, capable of minimizing or trivializing an exhibit of art on a museum wall at a time of great anguish elsewhere, was going to change him. He had long pondered the relation of poets and their nourishing yet isolating rooms, but now the question of poetic separateness took its definitive political turn. He was prepared to pose the very questions communists and fellow travelers were then asking of each other; for instance, "Should Writers Keep to Their Art?" (as John Lehmann put it). Rolfe, in a poem quite different from "City of Anguish," offered in "To My Contemporaries" an answer to Lehmann's question and incidentally provided a contemporary gloss on "the catastrophic room" in "The Men That Are Falling": "And so we sit in separate rooms, you / intimidated by the silence, vaguely / feeling all's not well, too tired to read, / too restless to lie still, too stirred / to trace this strangeness to its source." Stevens also had recognized, as had Rolfe, that the very "scraping of your pen, furious on paper, / quickens the blood of the world" – blood that the pen helped the poet believe had slowed.[127] Rolfe's was an irony deeply inventive. For now, not only did Stevens feel that he "was as capable of making observations and jotting them down as anyone else," but he also wanted to adjust his individual "sensibility to something perfectly matter-of-fact" and admit that writing poetry was a matter of contributing "a bit of reality, actuality, the contemporaneous" to the latest concepts of *real*, *actual* and *contemporaneous*. In this evidently uncharacteristic way, Stevens proposed, he would most insightfully disclose himself (*OP* 226).

Such self-disclosure having been introduced as a possibility for Stevens during the thirties, we can return to his original remarks expressing *entente* with Mussolini, against which Latimer reacted strongly. His response forced Stevens to issue a clarification a few weeks later (the November 21, 1935, letter already quoted). The earlier remarks, Stevens explained, had been occasioned in part by his having come "across an amusing incident . . . in an English paper the other night." There he had found a political poem by James George Frazer ("the GOLDEN BOUGH man," Stevens reminded Latimer), written "for the purpose of calling Mussolini a dirty dog." Frazer's was, Stevens said, "a typical poem of ideas," and led him to consider why, even when poets want to express "the very general condemnation of Mussolini," they must not lose entirely the lyrical sense. This was shrewd depoliticizing through the renaming of a subgenre, for it clearly took Valéry's side against Eliot who had defended "Philosophical" poetry against the charge that a truly modern work would not be a "poem of ideas." Much time had passed, of course, since that argument had been offered in *The Sacred Wood* of 1920; now the "poem of ideas" had moved well to the left of Eliot's defense, to the point that Philip Rahv and William Phillips were employing it in their effort to integrate revolutionary systems of belief with the modern poetic structure.[128] Stevens's effort to separate himself not merely from Frazer's didacticism but also from the (alleged) radical renunciation of the modern lyric in general was complicated by the right-to-left movement of Eliot's notion of the great poet who deals with "philosophy, not as a theory . . . or his own comment, but as something *perceived*."[129] Having rejected this distinction, he then made his now-famous parenthetical remark, "I am pro-Mussolini personally." The parenthesis only underscores the difficulty of reading Stevens's response to issues concerning the literary radicals or of demonstrating how he became precisely aware of the well-marked boundaries drawn by ideological mapmakers around his otherwise tenable position.

Yet even here, at an extremely unyielding and insensitive moment, Stevens was searching for a new version of modernism that could contain a response to the events of the day – one that resisted the Rahv-Phillips assimilation of Eliot's great "Philosophical" poet. In other ways, too, Stevens was at this very moment deciding that the "typical poem of ideas" would simply not do. And it is just here, as he leans furthest rightward in attitudes expressed outside the poetry, that he distinguished himself most completely from Eliot and set the stage for his most significant intellectual and methodological development, anticipating certain poetic steps forward taken by many communist poets. Modernists preparing to face a threatened world, he began to understand, could not stand still ideologically any more than they could limit modern poetry willingly to a single generic formulation. "Unfortunately," Stevens wrote at the end of this letter, "I don't have ideas that are permanently fixed. My conception of what

I think a poet should be and do changes, and I hope, constantly grows"
(*L* 289). At almost exactly the same moment another noncommunist,
Stevens's old acquaintance Winifred Ellerman, or Bryher, stressed a similar sense of movement: "The complete left and complete right [are] meeting
to their intense surprise but with of course entirely different view points.
. . . [I]f Italy is not checked fascism may infect the whole of Europe . . .
[and yet] war will be made the excuse for fascist principles." In this letter
to Horace Gregory, Bryher posed the question implied but unspoken in
Stevens's new understanding of his own movement: "Where is one, in this
morass, going to stand?"[130]

A rhetoric of convergence, a common speech for opposed parties "meeting
to their surprise," would serve some modernists well from mid-1935 and
beyond – Bryher and Stevens, in addition to Moore and Williams. Their
journey from 1929 through 1934, however, had been especially arduous,
and I must now back up to it. During that earlier interval Stevens, like
Bryher, had ventured back into the world of political fact: First, he had to
come back to poetry itself. In the six or seven years preceding the market
crash, he had composed just a handful of poems, publishing fewer still.
That his return to writing coincided with the onset of profound change
surely recommends the usefulness of a look at the economic collapse as
Stevens saw it nearby, at the Hartford Accident & Indemnity Company and
in Hartford. He knew, at first hand, that his poetry-market analogy was a
key to taking sides in difficult times. "Everyone takes sides in social change,"
he wrote a few years later, "if it is profound enough" (*OP* 198).

Arrogations

2

The Poet and the Depression

Can our nation stand such a tax burden along with the other taxes necessary to liquidate the depression? . . .What will be the economic dangers of such a fund, and will it be too tempting to permit prudent disbursement?

—Earl C. Henderson, Connecticut General Insurance Company,
denouncing the Social Security Act as bad for business[1]

When [H. G. Wells] passes from the international to the interstellar, we hug the purely local. In the same way it helps us to see insurance in the midst of social change to imagine a world in which insurance had been made perfect.

—Stevens in "Insurance and Social Change," endorsing the Social Security
Act (*OP* 234)

People that live in the biggest houses
Often have the worst breaths.
Hey-di-ho.

—Stevens, "Hieroglyphica"

1: IDEAS OF NO GIVEN DATE

Not quite a year into the Great Depression, Stevens and his publisher, Alfred A. Knopf, agreed that there ought to be a new edition of *Harmonium*. Stevens decided to delete three poems and add fourteen. Most of the fourteen "new" poems had indeed been written after he brought the manuscript of his first book to Knopf in December 1922; yet none had been written after 1924. But poetry, or rather the status of poetry, had changed a great deal since Stevens ceased to consider himself a working poet. Imagining the shock Stevens felt when he realized that these transformations had occurred is not difficult. While evidence to support the point is slight, it is reinforced by the very reticence of poems with which he began again in the early thirties. Certain leftist uses of *Harmonium*, if he saw them, surely pushed him along. There were solemn radicalizations of "Sunday Morning," such as Horace Gregory's "Sunday Morning: Rotogravure Section," quoted in the previous chapter; Isidor Schneider's "Sunday Morning," with its feminine "late awakener," sitting among "Islands

49

in her bath," drying herself still later "like a midday fruit," and, like the woman in Stevens's "Sunday Morning," having a leisurely, unholy "Breakfast in noonbeam"[2]; and "Sunday Morning" by Ettore (or Hector) Rella. "[N]o pseudomartyr I," Rella's speaker announces, pondering ragged depression-struck charity collectors stationed on his city street, while he, meanwhile, sits aloft "on the edge of the endless space / where an unknown bird with enormous wings" descends in anapests and iambs unto "the dark place of Sunday."[3]

Even in the view of conservative poets, like the agrarian George Marion O'Donnell, an editor might now be justifiably condemned because "Too many of his poets are still back in the twenties, worrying about matters of technique."[4] (This editor, Julian Symons, admired and published Stevens.) Glancing back from 1936 – but recalling the recollection, in turn, in 1942 – the German antifascist exile Klaus Mann found the American thirties' sense of the twenties an odd but definitive phenomenon: "The same people who, ten years before, would have discussed the particularities of Picasso's style or the images of James Joyce, and Proust, now tossed about . . . the names of union leaders, intricate statistics and cryptic abbreviations – CIO, WPA, CCC, SEC, AAA." (Mann's was itself, of course, typically a forties view of the thirties, entailing a skepticism much easier to wield in wartime than earlier.)[5] A youthful but already well-established Malcolm Cowley, eyed by a still younger aspirant, Alfred Kazin, could seem editorially and personally to convey on one hand a sweet "love of good writing" and on the other a hard "faith in revolution." Cowley embodied the link between "the *brilliant* Twenties and the *militant* Thirties."[6] "Gone was the cynicism of the preceding decade," wrote William Phillips and Philip Rahv, "which had driven the artist to extremes of individualism." By allegedly "isolating art from society" the twenties modernist "had mystified the values of both."[7] At its most interesting, the radical poetry of the thirties inscribed its own sense of twenties formalism in *its* own form. An obvious instance is Solon Barber's poem spurning thirties nostalgia for the nightclub culture of roaring-twenties Havana; Barber rhetorically undoes a phrase Scott Fitzgerald might have at that moment meant affirmatively: "Let them return." Thus the thirties poet can knowingly use, and at once trivialize, typographical projects for reproducing intense moments of cultural freedom, and still with confidence address himself directly to a Cuban rebel:

> When you spouted revolution,
> when they sold you slaves in the market
> you were a germ in a seed. . . .
> Their voices fall, a whisper,
> on the waxed floors of your cabarets now.
> The ringing is lost in the rumble

of carts in your streets.
Things of the past or things of the past
forgotten. . . .

> Let them return to whisper
> in the madness of jazzbands
>
> P
> l
>
> a
>
> y
>
> i
>
> n
>
> g
> .

("Memory of Habana: a hot night")[8]

Rarely is the word "playing" given a value so negative, or modern typographical sport so ironized.

Although for Horace Gregory, with more extensive modernist connections than Solon Barber, it had once perennially seemed "difficult to perceive where mere experimentation ends and *actual writing* [sic] begins," there was no such difficulty in the thirties. "The period of wholesale experimentation, with its high mortality rate," Gregory concluded in 1937, "came to an end in 1929."[9] And, indeed, for poets like Gregory, Williams, Cowley, MacLeish, Millay, Taggard, Eda Lou Walton, Lola Ridge, Alfred Kreymborg, Gorham Munson, Maxwell Bodenheim, George Dillon, Walter Lowenfels, Edwin Seaver – even Stevens's old Harvard classmate Witter Bynner voted for William Z. Foster, the 1932 communist candidate for president[10] – to name only a very few who in the thirties became attracted to the left after having written a very different kind of poetry earlier, October 1929 was a window through which one saw one's earlier poetic self as narcissistic, too anxious about forms both traditional and broken, overcommitted to the "Cult of Unintelligibility and the Tendency toward Pure Poetry,"[11] inadequately prepared to "find an increased simplicity,"[12] and thus incompletely aware of the extrinsic pressures that had been shaping – and distorting – poetry all along. Stevens had good reason for similar retrospection. But the difference between him and these other poets made all the difference, for *they* had continued writing and publishing to the bitter end of the twenties. The same Genevieve Taggard who wrote "Blame Them" in 1929, with its lyric generalizations and unironic archaic quatrain –

> While she, so poison-ardent and so deft
> Traced in their love a fair picture of his pain;

Right hand the subtle assassin to her left:
Told all the mean geometry of her brain

– a few years later produced "American Farm, 1934," with its relentless, inordinate compilation of modified nouns:

One old shoe, feminine, rotted with damp, one worn tire,
Crop of tin cans, torn harness, nails, links of a chain, –
Edge of a dress, wrappings of contraceptives, trinkets,
Fans spread, sick pink, and a skillet full of mould. . . .
Jumble of items, lost from use, with rusty tools,
Calendars, apple-cores, white sick grasses, gear from the stables,
Skull of a cow in the mud, with the stem of dead cabbage.[13]

Many already mature poets' movements toward a new "engaged" position entailed just this stylistic nominalization. The noun-making was based somewhat upon a knowing effort to radicalize logical atomism's facticity – for instance, Wittgenstein's "The world is made of facts," such tenets having infected early forms of modernism with a fantasy of precise language constructed of perfectly named things. The dream was, to a great extent, shared by young political poets of the thirties, typified by Josephine Miles's wonderfully succinct appeal:

So scientifically score it
Chorus cannot ignore it.[14]

There were modernists whose movements toward engagement were much smoother than Taggard's, Alfred Kreymborg's, for example. But many who were "making the change" (as the communist poets' shorthand went[15]) made it in so clumsy a way as to be comical. Max Bodenheim's "Revolutionary Girl" seems hardly different from any of his earlier "girls":

you are a girl
A revolutionist, a worker
Sworn to give the last, undaunted jerk
Of your body and every atom
Of your mind and heart
To every other work.[16]

But however deftly making the great change was managed, all who made it would be judged by young doubters on the new poetic left – many, many writers who themselves had no twenties to look back on – as having given an "inevitable" shape to many modernist careers. "Inevitable" was a repeated word. Twenties-bashing, especially when executed by those poets who hadn't yet come of age in the twenties, made an inescapably radical thirties all the easier. Willard Maas's poem "Journey and Return" is about journeying back poetically in time to an imagined dissolute twenties ("We were in love with the movie queen / Kissing the celluloid dark"; "Pink animals of the sea / Touched by our hands"); here the twenties serves the young radical poet as a fantastically unified, prettified – and, please note, a metrically regularized – epoch from which one suddenly awakened into a new and clearer political moment *and* thus allegedly into an utterly new poetic. Correspondingly, the poem enacting such a "return" *itself* moves from lines like, "What toúch of hánd recálls the yéars" to new-era utterances conveying a fresher, tougher actuality that won't quite so easily scan: "With machínegúns moúnted on the wíndow sílls."

Poems like Maas's were meant almost as a warning to older modernists – designed to chart in themselves the passage from poetry apart to poetry *and* radicalism blended, as from dream to waking, from dulcet to harsh tones (to a disconcerting new-style dactyl like "machinegun").[17] Radical twenties-bashing was often more sophisticated than this, to be sure. The political radicalism of Hector Rella's "The Bone and the Baby" – Rella's very freedom as a modern poet to declare, in the middle of a lyric poem, "I WANT TO TELL YOU SOMETHING ABOUT RUSSIA" and "FIGHT DON'T STARVE" – is built into the verse itself. Rella wants us to know that he, because he is so young, is free to evolve politically as well as poetically, while eminent fifties-something modernists cannot do so without confession of past errors and some measure of self-contradiction. "I laugh at my brother who thinks there is room for revolution," Rella writes; but then again, "I'm not as old as T. S. Eliot / *I'll* make room."[18]

A brash, hopeful, evolutionist view of the sort Rella used to see himself and to exclude Eliot, if applied to Stevens, seemed then, as it does perhaps today, to misread the latter's career. So, too, with Maas's effort to make an instant myth of (alleged) twenties metric conventionality. From the perspective of 1931, Stevens could not say that he had come to the thirties either slowly or surely: the immediately preceding period had been one of almost total poetic silence.[19] Surveying the poems of *Harmonium* to decide which to remove and which possibly to revise, he was painfully aware of the distance between the acclaimed modernist past (from "Sunday Morning" of 1915 to the final *Harmonium* poems of 1921 and 1922) and the poetic dormancy of the present, 1931. What mixed impression would be conveyed by the addition to this new book of the "new" poems that were nearly as old as the old? Did the fourteen addenda truly "update" *Harmonium* for the crisis thirties?

The risk of a 1931 *Harmonium*, then, was the perception of abiding an anachronism that might have been fully realized before the project got underway. Written in early 1922,[20] published in *The Measure* in 1924[21] but left uncollected, "New England Verses" would have to endure comparison, if mistaken as "new," with William Carlos Williams's "mottled," low "facts" –

an american papermatch packet
closed . . .

> mottled crust of the stained blotter
> by an oystershell smudged
> with cigarette ash . . .
>
> words printed on the backs of
> two telephone directories . . .
>
> the printing out of line: portrait
> of all that which we have lost²²

– or one of his proletarian portraits: "A tramp thawing out / on a doorstep / against an east wall."²³ Compare these lines, from "Simplex Sigilum Veri: A Catalogue" and "The Sun Bathers," to the following stanza, outmoded from tone to foot – one of Stevens's "new" "New England Verses":

> Ballatta dozed in the cool on a straw divan
> At home, a bit like the slenderest courtesan.
>
> (*CP* 106)

"Dozed" conveyed comfortable indolence; "At home" an inwardness, and comfort again. "Slenderest" meant not famished here, but elegant, well-toned. Even "a bit like" is diffident of the merest force in simile. These contexts were, of course, controlled by Stevens, but nonetheless set off (six years belatedly) on their own politically incorrect course, a path of reception he could not guide.

Radicalized readers and poet-reviewers, Horace Gregory among them, might read these aphoristic two-liners – "New England Verses" is composed of sixteen titled couplets – as twenties verse taking deliberate potshots at the thirties. And whereas "New England Verses" would anticipate the epigrammatic style of "Like Decorations in a Nigger Cemetery" of 1934, it is important to understand what the earlier aphoristic condensations do *not* say. What they do not say largely depended on a literary-political context provided them by re-publication in 1931. Most readers of the new edition could not have known of the seven-year-old *Measure* version of "New England Verses," and would naturally assume a recent date of composition. One can read these couplets as having constructed a characteristic high-modern poem incidentally becoming a uncharacteristic depression poem; in so doing, one partially reconstructs how Stevens's "new" work struck readers who were themselves just then developing a keen collective sense of good and bad cultural timing.

The poem deliberately avoids the earnest tenor that Stevens at this date associated with social reference, and provides its alternative manner provocatively. If to any degree "New England Verses" manifests those conditions of its making about which, by 1931, it was obviously silent, the implication was that it carried somehow on Stevens's behalf some sign of *knowing* about conditions ignored. Take as an example couplet iv, the companion piece to another called "Soupe Aux Perles" (couplet iii):

SOUPE SANS PERLES

I crossed in '38 in the *Western Head*
It depends on which way you crossed, the tea-belle said.

The tea-belle is obviously scrutinizing the credentials of the elderly person who tells her of his journey across the Atlantic many years earlier. Her opening "It" is contingent on whether the speaker had crossed to or from the United States, a fact he or she – he, I'll assume – evidently neglects to state. The social standing of the elder will vary from one direction to the other, as the reasons for passage – for instance, immigration on one hand, an Englishman's New World sight-seeing on the other – might have differed.

To read this poem as, say, Horace Gregory or Eda Lou Walton would have read it in 1931, it helps to assume some vague caste-conscious critique of American life, a critique Stevens might have wanted to share: The culture was being commanded by a querulous new rich, a position embodied tonally in the sharp, upstart questioner. The title has helped place both the speaker and the tea-belle economically – both, it would seem, on the decline; the scene is set, after all, by soup without pearls. Judging only from two lines, one cannot know if the elder's remark is uttered as a matter of fact (to which the tea-belle would be responding pertly), or if the declaration conveys a fumbling attempt to impress her. In the latter case her retort exposes the crucial element of the elder's story that he might hope to hide: He crossed the *wrong* "way" on the *Western Head* if he wished now to qualify as impressive.

Looking backward through October 1929 to 1924 at the patrician companion to soup without pearls, with an eye to revising the twenties version of this poem, Stevens would also have re-read this:

SOUPE AUX PERLES

Health-o, when cheese and guava peels bewitch
The vile antithesis of poor and rich.

What Stevens did *not* do as he revised this poem for his new but belated edition is for me its only appealing aspect. The change he did make is one of just two slight (and evidently incidental) revisions for Knopf's 1931 *Harmonium*. Certainly the irony of "vile antithesis" raised the new, powerful version of contingent value. If we may judge from contemporaries, especially Gorham Munson and John Gould Fletcher, who had virtually marketed the thesis of Stevens's aestheticism, his verbal acuteness and emotional lassitude, a thesis that stuck,[24] it is clear that the 1923 readership did not fail to appreciate the irony. For them the aphorism might have been paraphrased as follows: At the sort of occasion on which the diners don pearls, delicacies serve (in a manner of speaking) to bridge that unfortunate gap between haves and have-nots; to that American crossing, one toasts and salutes, Good health!

The irony was so strong that a deliberate liberal illogic of cause and effect – when one culturally pleasant thing appears, another culturally unpleasant thing simply disappears – is overcome by the extraordinary imperviousness of the statement's maker. The thing made to disappear, moreover, is not a presence but a gap. As the speaker's snobbery deliberately puts off a reader with the couplet's excessive parading of devices – the French title; the archaism of "Health-o"; the comic tonal harmony of "bewitch" and "rich" – in order to understand what is *not* spoken about class difference the reader must ignore the obvious fact that the "poor" remain unaffected by the consumption of "guava peels" by the "rich." It perhaps needs saying at this point that it was possible in the thirties to be thunderously denounced for using French, regardless of context or the speaker's revolutionary credentials: "Why don't you speak in the language of the Mexican peasants and workers?" an editor of the *Daily Worker* screamed at Diego Rivera, who was trying to deliver a speech in French. "Why do you address us in the effete language of the effete European intellectuals?"[25] Given this tense atmosphere, I read Stevens's poem as a calculated counter-offense. Thus it carried certain risks. The irony could not function unless the reader could feel reasonably assured that most other contemporary readers – or, in other words, *both* "rich" and "poor" – could not possibly miss the rich irony of "vile." If by 1931 the poem's very deliberate act of estrangement, the evident lack of concern for distinctions between "rich" and "poor," would cause the reader fully appreciative of "rich" to be more than a little anxious about such a reflection of willful detachment from material conditions, the poem's irony simply would not function as it once had.

For one thing, the twenties-style irony derived its strength from the totalizing urge of the couplet form. But in the thirties, political poetry was often said to repudiate such a closed, aphoristic design. (Whether it did in practice is a question considered in Chapter 5.) Internal evidence surely suggests that as Stevens pondered *Harmonium* from this somewhat new perspective, he understood the formal outmoding of poetry like "New England Verses," as such repudiation laid the footing for one of the counterarguments included in "Blue Guitar" six years later. Not incidentally, the later poem is constructed of couplets so flexible and open, and so relentlessly enjambed, as to refute in itself claims of stanzaic limitation.

We do not know what immediate reasons Stevens had for revising the couplet called "Soupe aux Perles." Here is the revised version:

> Health-o, when ginger and fromage bewitch
> The vile antithesis of poor and rich.

The difference between "ginger and fromage" and "cheese and guava peels" is extraordinarily slight, so slight that one wonders why Stevens bothered at all. And the change is telling, for it would be absurd to conclude that Stevens was not aware of the extraordinary insignificance of his alteration when he inked this revision – nearly as absurd as arguing that he did not know what line he was not altering: the only other line in the poem. The revision is so overtly small that it seems to call even greater attention to the idea left unrevised, the vile antithesis sustained. It upholds the sentiment conveyed originally by the speaker once profoundly ironic, once slightly wealthier. This particular utterance, however outmoded, remains silent about the rhetorical conditions that once made it tenable (twenties excess, tonal as well as economic). Insofar as it expresses cultural urges to close the space between poor and rich – one supposes it can be argued that "guava peels" suggests a luncheon more sumptuous than does "ginger" – then the distinction is so slight as to reinforce the poem's willingness to leave the gap unbridged. In that case, it would have been better left alone. To the extent that all revisions of poems represent attempts to smooth over flaws, this particular adjustment thematizes the desire to fill in social and aesthetic breaches exactly as in the poem – for, brought over into a depression edition, the gap remains wide as ever, its continued health toasted.

Perhaps when Stevens put together his new *Harmonium* the change in the atmosphere remained imperceptible, although I am arguing that he was well aware of the shift even while proceeding this little way into the depression as if unaware. In either case, the critical response to the book could not have left doubts about the change. It was just then becoming feasible, in fact, to chart with accuracy such responses from left to right. Reviewers in the early depression period sought incessantly to make clear which side they were on, often at the expense of the book under consideration. Reviewing the emended *Harmonium* for *New York Herald Tribune Books*, under the ambiguous title "Highly Polished Poetry," Horace Gregory assumed that the added poems were written "during the intervening eight years," suggesting – how could he have known otherwise? – continuity and productivity. Yet he found that "The general impression *remains the same* and the polished surfaces *are still* unbroken" (emphasis added). This was a powerful implication, and handy. When radical poets subsequently wrote about Stevens – even when, as in the hands of H. R. Hays, the analysis eventually confirmed Stevens as "among the two or three best poets which the 1920s produced" – they almost invariably began with Gregory's assumption that one would always know where to find and place Stevens: "[T]he consistent polish and unchanging viewpoint manifested throughout [*Harmonium*] indicate that it may be considered a definitive example of his work. Any subsequent writing may add to his output, but it will probably not indicate a change in his personality."[26]

To arrive at his view of Stevens's sameness, Gregory first quoted a revision, the new, shorter version of "The Man Whose Pharynx Was Bad" (first published, 1924), in such a way as to suggest that work's point as follows: the poet of *Harmonium* might become "less diffident," but then again he might just as effortlessly choose diffidence again.[27] Gregory then suggested "that Wallace Stevens will not allow himself to grow beyond the limitations which he has imposed upon his talents. He remains static. His world, a civilized world in which all voices fall to a whisper and the expression of the face is indicated by a lifting of the eyebrow, is complete." His impression having been created by the inadequacies of the "civilized world" to which Stevens belonged, Gregory did not by the word "complete" mean to commend the poet. Only a few years earlier this word, applied to verse, might have been high praise indeed. For now a poetic "world" depicted as sufficient unto itself – or as "Highly Polished," per Gregory's title – could not possibly be responsive to the broken, depressed, and chaotic world beyond.

But Gregory's incipient political thesis – that Stevens betrayed his talent by reserving it for a "world" where, in Gregory's words, "melodies are sweet . . . and modulate to a dying fall and disappear in a rustle of silk" and where one feels "the immaculate top hat and stick are always" present – did not yet yield the fully radicalized criticism of Gregory's own *New Masses* essay of 1937. By this time, as poetry editor of that weekly,[28] Gregory seemed to one communist writer to hold "sole dominance in . . . the left-wing poetry movement" (an exaggeration, surely, but a telling one).[29] By then, six years after Stevens's reemergence, Gregory, restored to good graces at the *New Masses* despite a drumming received a few years earlier,[30] recognized that "political poetry as such cannot be divorced from other kinds of poetry" and quoted his own earlier judgment as having been largely mistaken. (Here is part of the 1931 judgment revised for 1937: "Wallace Stevens's sensibilities in writing verse had made it possible for him to view the world about him with singular acuteness.") To Gregory the *New Masses* editor, Stevens's vision was "dimmed by the effort to explain his 'position' in a medium ill-suited" to the crisis.[31] Indeed the 1931 piece ends with a hopeful view. Precisely because Stevens knows so well the civilized world of whispers and raised eyebrows, because his poems are "impeccable arrangements," Gregory's early-thirties Stevens was a candidate to "observe" capitalism in crisis. In his poetry one saw the effects of "the civilized artist thrust head first into modern society," the aptitude of a person with a sharp eye and ear and a compelling interest in small verities. *This* politically susceptible Stevens was indeed the poet who copied into his journal of quotations Desmond McCarthy's line on Arnold Bennett: "The mere habit of recording experience increases the chance of not having lived in vain."[32] It was a habit surely not unavailing in time of cultural emergency, now that, as Gregory put it, the "trained observer who gazes with an intelligent eye upon the decadence that follows the rapid acquisition of wealth and power" might catch up to the times.[33]

No insignificant issue, this politics of observation. Jack Wheelwright, a radical, pondering his alliance with the *Hound & Horn*, deemed it sufficient to reply to hard-line charges against that journal as a tool of the leisure class by noting how "cultural exploration had an inherent value even when detached from social activism."[34] Joe Freeman was pleased to defend *Ulysses* as "a marvelous mirror of the decay of capitalist civilization" and "a great book,"[35] while Granville Hicks saw that *Remembrance of Things Past*, a text usually assumed to have been loathed by the left, presented "a finer, clearer, more convincing picture of the decay of bourgois civilization" than *any* novel Hicks had found "written from the revolutionary point of view."[36] The same logic permitted no less an observationist than Henry James to undergo political transformation in the 1930s: "This 'new' relationship [with thirties writers], in which James became recognized as an innovator and as a profound critic of *the society through which he moved*, revived his power" (emphasis added). How exciting the aesthetic era in which Henry James was being recommended as having "something to say to those who wished to understand the intricate conventions and moralities of the ruling classes in America and England."[37] To notice "indolence" and "dissipation" was implicitly a political good.[38] But what of *representing* it in verse? A few radical critics, like Oakley Johnson, were asking this question explicitly of the novel, but it was not yet being systematically asked of lyric poetry.[39] C. Day Lewis in England was only making a start toward an argument against the sufficiency of observation when he urged poets to "Let your poem be a kiss or a blow: echo is no answer."[40] But, again, even if we leave poetry aside altogether, most critics of theatre and prose fiction assumed that left-ism in literature reflexively meant praising writers "standing waist-high in living as they write" and condemning those who "stay scrupulously on the sidelines, or press heatedly toward the center, or look aggrievedly or senti-mentally backward, or gaze prophetically ahead."[41] The ideology of first-hand experience, as I have suggested, had not been discerned as itself an aesthetic ideology. On this point modernists like Stevens gave particular assistance.

Other judgments of his 1931 edition bear similar marks of ideological confusion as Gregory's – a puzzlement created by the difference between general (though sometimes grudging) admiration for Stevens's virtuosity in the early twenties on the one hand, and, on the other, a still-vague, emer-gent sense of critical discrimination appropriate to the grimmer times. Eda Lou Walton, a poet motivated by an urban liberalism that soon turned toward radical activism (and possibly Communist Party membership),[42] was asked to review the new Stevens for the *Nation*. She could not keep from slipping into past tense ("here *was* a poet of the senses") even as she was appraising a poet known from a single book in two very similar versions. It was as if the revised edition signalled a position from which Stevens *must*, after all, have *moved* – along with so many others including the reviewer herself – despite his having produced just the one volume. Saying nothing that would imply a politically unconscious development, then, Walton instinctively projected onto Stevens in 1931 a poetic self that would be judged wholly anew. She noticed that he had "grown slightly more autumnal," even though in providing her readers such bibliographic information as she had at hand, she also remarked that the exclusions were largely incidental and the additions contributed more of the same old Stevens. Walton did notice that "The Silver Plough Boy" (1915) had been "repudiated" for the new edition, and speculated that this was because it typified the outmoded strain, "meaningless pretty imagistic verse": "A black figure . . . / seizes a sheet, from the ground, from a bush, as if spread there by some washwoman for the night. / It wraps the sheet around its body, until the black figure is silver" (*OP* 17). The "repudiat[ion]" had not been complete, some "pretty" poems having survived to the dirty thirties unbesmudged; Walton felt compelled to repeat the old saw about the poet's cold exteriors, his self-protections. Still, in updating the Munson-Fletcher thesis to the depression, Walton, like Gregory, vaguely anticipated a criticism she expected would soon be leveled against Stevens: he ought to inveigh less equivocally against misery. She quoted him (out of context) in anticipation of what would be, but was not quite yet, the liberal-left critique: Stevens "will not cry out in bitterness," she concluded. She was using Stevens to argue against those to *her* left who insisted that poets "play the 'flat historic scale' of memory" and "take momentary delight in 'doleful heroics.'" After defending Stevens against her own detractors who would have him externalize his bitterness, Walton then argued *against* calling Stevens "a 'Dandy'" on the grounds that indeed his poems portended "[h]is sincerity." He might, after all, play *some* "historic scale" – one that averted historical flatness.[43]

Raymond Larsson, once a well-known figure whom Kenneth Rexroth called "the best Catholic poet of his time,"[44] and by 1935 a Communist[45] trying his hand at political poetry,[46] was at this earlier point as confounded about Stevens as Gregory and Walton. Reviewing the 1931 edition for *The Commonweal* under the revealing title "The Beau as Poet," Larsson began with a definition of "objective" verse completely at odds with the growing use of the term for a new poetic -ism answering the altered world of much-depreciated things. If "Mr. Stevens's poems are objective" and "deal of objects [*sic*]," such "objects" do not quite convey the precise cultural currency of Kenneth Fearing's "pow, Sears Roebuck,"[47] Kenneth Patchen's "mile of Camel butts,"[48] Herman Spector's "tang of wrigley's gum: / THE FLAVOR LASTS. / . . . startling an idea of vengeance / THE FLAVOR LASTS,"[49] or Muriel Rukeyser's "billboard world of Chesterfields" (in a poem aptly called "Citation for Horace Gregory")[50] – typical poetic borrowings strongly suggesting the renewed desire to unify American poetry with the contemporary world of (as Stevens would soon somewhat misleadingly say of Williams) cheap bottles, newspapers, and soda ads (see *OP* 213-14). Stevens's "objects" were rather, to Larsson, a conservative's noncommercial acquisitions, assets "secure, certain, unchanging." Larsson's radicalized modernism still found "in the world of things something akin to security." His rock-solid Stevens, enviable insofar as he invested lyric energies in a world resistant to change, was nonetheless conflated with the altogether different Stevens Larsson clung to, a poet whose taste was no less "personal" in 1931 than before, and no less exotic – hardly "objective" even in Larsson's overbroad sense.[51]

Of several explicitly conservative reviews the new *Harmonium* received, Morton Zabel's is the one surely worth noting, for this commentary revealed already the defensive antipolitical politics forced upon *Poetry* in its last years under Harriet Monroe's famed, already mythologized editorship. Zabel's stance entailed a mainstream modernism delimited by the new mode that would itself seek to challenge the aesthetic experiments Monroe had long promoted. Through the end of the thirties Zabel would garrison modernism against materialist encroachments, such as Bernard Smith's liberal-left literary history *Forces in American Criticism* (1939), which Zabel deemed guilty of a "crudity of sympathy that keeps [Smith] in petty fear of admitting . . . sensibility as a critical instrument of infinitely greater importance . . . than popular or political passions" – a view that was not meant itself to seem a popular passion of an earlier day.[52] Zabel's evaluation of Stevens, published in *Poetry* in the December 1931 issue, made clear that from this moment no praise of Wallace Stevens could be printed without whole paragraphs devoted to anticipating and disarming a dissenter's voice – a voice, it is important to stress, that had not yet been clearly or widely heard. For Zabel, defending Stevens against an easily imagined detractor was central to his own uncertain situation at *Poetry*. If he was to maintain the stability Monroe had built for the journal – securing the publication of Stevens's "Like Decorations," for instance, shored up his position there, as did perhaps his dismissal of Stevens's *Nation* poem about Spain as "not . . . one of his notable performances"[53] – Zabel would have to imply in his editorial decisions and in his many reviews that the modernist revolution urged on American verse by *Poetry* was still a revolution and that its refuge remained Chicago.

To a far greater extent than Walton's, then, Morton Zabel's language implied a response to the expected radical attack. Unless he was protesting too much, why, in praising Stevens's "authority of instinctive symbolism and method," would the editor allow that the poems might seem to some critics "in these calmer days" to be, in hindsight, merely "the trickery of a topical vaudeville"? What unrest was *Poetry* disregarding with Zabel's *these calmer days*? Moreover, he insisted, this ill-mannered hindsight (whose hindsight? – the detractors are unnamed) deformed the Florida poems ten years old or older, "Fabliau of Florida," "Nomad Exquisite," "O Florida, Venereal Soil," "Floral Decorations for Bananas," by cutting them to fit today's (read *passing*) brawny historicist fashions. In fact, Zabel argued that Stevens's "style was not a conjuror's garment but an expression for ideas of no given date." Zabel's 1931 revision of Munson's 1925 dandyism thesis merely served to give the indicted aestheticist Stevens yet another hearing, but now in the context of a conservative argument that had history on its mind while necessarily denying it. While on one hand "realism" was the poetic -ism that could save Stevens's images from excess and "his morality from the illusory intellectual casuistry which betrayed most of his [early modernist] colleagues," at the same time it also must be true that "Mr. Stevens never urged the idea of obliterating danger by opposing it."[54]

Thus the Stevens who was partly reinvented for the thirties by a "High" Modernism held over from boom to bust is the poetic figure which the literary left would soon assail – to which, in turn, Stevens would react by, in his words, "heading left" himself. This was by no means a counterproductive circle of reputation and response. Stevens's radical readers reacted to his poetic claims as endorsed by conservative supporters – such as, aptly, Morton Zabel in Willard Maas's case and Harriet Monroe in Stanley Burnshaw's, and (erroneously) Marianne Moore in T. C. Wilson's – no less than they reacted to those poetic claims as we generally read them several poetic ages later, released now from certain literary-political tensions long since dissipated (although, of course, bound by others).

My point is that Stevens sought and stood on the ground of reception being cleared for him. Such a position defined the thinking and feeling aroused in and by poems he wrote *after* the anachronism of the "new" *Harmonium* was made critically evident *as* anachronism – poems that he then claimed, not surprisingly, were originally responsive to contemporary trends and forms. He would be able to claim this originality of "The Man with the Blue Guitar," even as that poem works as a counter-statement against its detractors by thieving, in Burke's words, "*their* vocabulary, *their* values, *their* symbols"[55] – because, as I will show, he had learned how a modern poem can draw into its own texture the "real" as alleged by his reviewers. But that would be later. When he began to take up writing again in the early thirties, after his seven-year hiatus, the "world" nonetheless seemed as never before an inextricable combination of, on one hand, compelling "actual" qualities of moral and economic bankruptcy, conditions discernible through newspapers and insurance work, and, on the other hand, an invention of its critics – a new intellectual left awaiting noncommunist response to that bankruptcy. The productive interaction between Stevens's poems and even his most reductive reviewers in the thirties was fuller and more complex than at any other period, principally because it served him and them as a precise homologue for the modernist collaboration with political fact.

2: THE NEW MORAL CLIMATE

Horace Gregory's 1931 review had leaned leftward casually and unofficially. In making his final point – that depression-era poetry ought at least to *observe* what had happened when a capitalist class pushed an entire society toward excess – Gregory had committed an error none of Stevens's radical critics in the thirties would entirely avoid. The rejoinder to modernist formalism issued on political grounds sometimes failed to admit admiration for enchanting sounds even as it might wholly rebuke the modernist's evident unwillingness to renounce "solitude and uniqueness" in favor of "get[ting] hold of . . . events . . . near at hand, and a solid framework on which to arrange them."[56] In Gregory's early assessment, but hardly less so in such later ones as Dorothy Van Ghent's and Isidor Schneider's (Burnshaw's is an important exception on this point), the implication was that the political critic could assail the modernist's bourgeois devices and issues, as well as his or her profession of neutrality toward them, and yet at the same time feel it to be "pleasanter," in Schneider's words, "to speak of Mr. Stevens's craftsmanship *which is an unending delight* and distinguishes him among his contemporaries."

So one potential link from right to left, particularly attractive to the communist Schneider, was the sound of poetry: either you had the ear for it or you did not. Schneider thought Stevens did. Stevens's poetry, wrote Schneider,

> comes as close to song, perhaps, as speech can. He has an extraordinary sense of the sound weights of words and his rhythm is an exquisite balancing of these weights; he plays deftly with assonances and internal rhymes and the subtlety of his alliteration makes a good workman in that line, like Swinburne, seem clumsy.

But praise like this did not soften the political attack. Guided by the rhetoric of "exquisite" and "subtlety," one could *still* manage a radical reading of Stevens's "Lions in Sweden" (*CP* 124–5) – the poem that served as Schneider's example of verse to be abhorred as culturally meaningless and yet to be valued as a system of "sound weights" stabilizing aural symmetries. Schneider inadvertently reinforced the great distance between savoring sound and accepting sense. "Enjoyment of such lines" – he was quoting the opening five lines of Stevens's poem – "requires that one be not scrupulous in regard to meanings." This assertion was only somewhat convincing as a way of putting a radical reduction to work in criticism. Because just this sort of reduction kept a few radical critics from approaching modern poetry at all – Mike Gold for instance – I should think it would come as no surprise that, as I will show in the final three chapters of this book, Wallace Stevens helped clear a winding path of approach, although he was – nay, *because* he was – an unlikely negotiator. What should make it still less surprising is our awareness now, these years later, aided especially by Cary Nelson's work, that many poets in the thirties themselves firmly believed (as the editors of *The Left* did) that "the capitalist system must be replaced by a collective state . . . with its foundation on the principle of economic liberation" while at the same time they unselfconsciously promoted an art "radical and experimental" for which "new forms and techniques must be hammered out."[57]

Despite this implicit promise of negotiation with high modernism, acute admissions by radicals that "great poetry" was being produced by modernist nonradicals were sometimes encumbered by dull tests for thematic agreement – this dullness being, of course, the trait for which the radical poetry of the thirties is almost solely remembered. For Isidor Schneider, long an accomplished lyricist, it was at times evidently quite painful to be applying such a standard.[58] Schneider felt that it was for critics of "*earlier* periods, when a limited audience for literature was assumed," to have viewed "the critic's function [as] primarily to discuss technical achievement." At the same time he fully realized that among American Marxist critics "the distinction between use and pleasure is too categoric": "Things made for use," he wrote in a personal letter to Granville Hicks, "like the flying buttresses of Gothic cathedrals[,] *give pleasure*," and "what is pleasure to one group may not be pleasure to another." Yet in the last event Schneider accepted "the responsibility of making an analysis of social function as well as of technique and judgment" and sought in any text what he called "the book's own meaning and its social character."[59] Upending such a careful balance between "meaning" and "social character" on one hand and "technique and [aesthetic] judgment" on the other was far less troubling for younger poets taking sharper aim at modernists – at the "older poets" – whom Edwin Rolfe felt left no more "than a fragmentary mark on their time or on ours." In naming names, Rolfe wrote: "To be important to a country's life, a poet must be more than a skilled versifier (Stevens)."[60] Implicated in this logic also, though far less plausibly than in Schneider's reading of Stevens's "Lions in Sweden" and Van Ghent's of Stevens's "Anglais Mort à Florence," one communist poet, Willard Maas, guest-editing a journal in which Stevens prominently published, knew that as a radical he must reject a poem submitted by e. e. cummings on the basis of "Cummings['] personal nastiness and Fascist tendencies." Maas added: "I . . . admit that Cumming[s]'s ballade was great poetry, but I'm agin' it just the same."[61]

Schneider's transition from the solemnization and canonization of Stevens's eloquence and "technic" to a denunciation on ideological grounds failed to integrate the two judgments; he was agin' Stevens just the same. Note Schneider's attempt to fashion the transition one might expect: Stevens's "sound is won at the cost of sense."[62] Schneider had simply not thought Stevens would want to stake an ethical position. The communist's argument about the noncommunist's split between sound and sense was that it fostered a poetry alleging immanent truths severed from contemporary moral considerations. These considerations might have brought into sharp focus the decayed material modernists put into poems in spite of basic affinities they themselves felt with the decaying class. In Horace Gregory's immature version of the sound-sense split in his 1931 review, sound was praised just to the degree that made sense theoretically acceptable. His vague parting hope, again, was that if Stevens knew the sounds of a regressive bourgeoisie intimately from the inside, could hear the rustle of silk, the dying whispers, and so on, his disposition toward sense would sustain an ethics potentially aligned with the radicals' condemnations. So Gregory's Stevens "gazes *with an intelligent eye* upon the decadence" of twenties-style success deemed excess in the thirties. Just such an approach to Marianne Moore, with her talent for obscure inventory, would have yielded similar results: What Gregory saw powerfully possible in Stevens he might have seen in Moore's thirties-style judgment of "The vast indestructible necropolis" acquired by "simple" Americans. From the inside of such accumulation she knew, as acutely as any poet at work during the depression, how when "we see the exterior" of such a "necropolis" we are discerning "the fundamental structure" ("People's Surroundings").[63] Thus, in an unpublished 1933 letter to Zabel at *Poetry*, Moore could actually say of Gregory that she was "in sympathy with the trend of his tastes" and prized his review of the 1931 *Harmonium*. There Gregory had not quite articulated what would become the liberal-left position on Stevens in the thirties, typified by Eda Walton's moderate reviews of 1936 and 1937: Insofar as Stevens's choice of "material" suggested incipient fascism to the left, his good lyrical ear countered with a cultural keenness that might imply, in turn, an acceptably negative judgment of a decomposing world. The aptitude for left-right compact among American poets here was actually never greater. When Moore was admiring Gregory for admiring Stevens's intelligent gaze upon decadence, she was able to affirm her own already well-developed ironic sense of, say, New Yorkers' "atmosphere of ingenuity" – "accreted where we need the space for commerce" ("New York") – and her profound commitment to the idea that Americans' materiality "answer[s] one's questions" ("People's Surroundings").[64]

Gregory's intuition about Stevens – and Moore's, if I am right as to why she liked Gregory's review – was directly on target, despite the fact that Gregory knew nothing about Stevens's deeply ambivalent reaction to his colleagues in the business community who took even the slightest advantage from the general economic collapse. There survives scant evidence – but it is strongly suggestive – of his attitudes toward colleagues' response to the crash; from this it might be inferred that Stevens knew well how to "get hold of . . . events . . . near at hand" and how poetry might indeed make "a solid framework on which to arrange them." He had not yet gotten into the habit of retaining carbon copies of outgoing personal letters, preserving only a small number of incoming ones. Correspondence pertaining to business, saved during his lifetime, was later discarded at The Hartford. From some of what remains, nonetheless, we can see that he was quite capable of criticizing, through the sort of "observation" Gregory coveted in Stevens's verse, a banking and business class to which many radical critics had no access whatever.

A glimpse of such a moral argument is offered by surviving letters Stevens mailed home during his February 1931 business trip to Florida. Far from being the pure escape from social realities often supposed,[65] these annual expeditions in the early and mid-thirties were cultural eye-openers. Since the early poems' tropes of fecundity and plenitude derived from his first regular southern visits, the fact that Florida was hit by depression harder than Connecticut – which is to say very hard – may have at first surprised him. After all, Connecticut had always been for him figuratively barren and in that sense "real." The "poverty" of *Harmonium* had been a New England matter. Now the binary tropes spread South as well as North. Reading through characteristic irony in his firsthand observations, one senses in the extant materials dated 1931 a special awareness of the totality of the economic and social disintegration. "The old Royal Palm Park," he wrote his wife Elsie, "is now merely a parking space for the world's greatest collection of second-hand automobiles. This has not been a good year for the town [Miami]. Even the weather has been depressed."[66]

On this trip he met up with his friend James Powers, who had worked with The Hartford and had literally capitalized on others' bankruptcies. By 1931 Powers was striking out further on his own. In the midst of the local collapse, the ambitious young man was actually flourishing. He "was setting up a [J. C.] Penn[e]y business down there" – in Miami, where he and his wife Margaret were residing.[67] On all other occasions Stevens enjoyed his friend's company immensely – and Margaret Powers's as well (one knows this, if only from the poem he wrote about a riotous evening spent with them).[68] Here, though, the poet seems to have been disturbed by an untimely display of new-found comfort: "[W]e ran into Jim Powers who went down to Miami with us on the same train. He was looking very smart and pleased with himself. He told me that he had 'a car that runs,' a mural, etc. *Well, if I had not met him here some years ago and taken him away he would have none of those things*" (L 261; emphasis added). Stevens's attitude toward the young businessman's good fortune is stern, an uncharacteristic moral tone doubtless conditioned by the fact that the letter to Elsie was written just before he went off to settle a "bank case" in a once-wild town, West Palm Beach, that had taken a severe and particularly unexpected plunge.[69] Powers might have decided to remain in association with the recently ruined Richardson Saunders, an engineer, developer, bank officer, and investor in one, with whom Stevens had had business relations in Florida since the mid-twenties. Saunders was an intimate whom Stevens sought out when passing through Miami. If the young Powers had stayed with Saunders, he would hardly have been in a position to gloat about the acquisitions of autos and murals. Poems subsequently engaging the florid Florida scene would be altered accordingly to this new contingent sense of the place: "The pillars are prostrate, the arches are haggard, / The hotel is boarded and bare," even though "despair," thus quite safely rhymed, would seem wrong for the local "ecstatic air" ("Botanist on Alp [No. 1]," *CP* 135). (Similarly, one wonders if the line "Marx has ruined Nature, / For the moment," given this special context, points not to Marxism as the cause of ruin but as ruin's momentarily accurate predictor.) Business appraisals of Key West used a negative rhetoric rich with suggestion, dwelling on local fecundities in a way that might be said to borrow from the pre-depression Stevensian lexicon of "O Florida, Venereal Soil," "Floral Decorations for Bananas," and "Nomad Exquisite": "The jasmine, the almond, the bananas, the cork-tree, the coco-palm, and the oleander flourish on Key West's coral island, but the City of Key West, in sore straits after appeals to State and Federal Governments, is . . . in what amounts to a receivership"[70] – but I am arguing, of course, that the influence moved powerfully in the other direction. With such bank cases as he could skillfully bring to settlement – and a few, surely, that he could not, for example perhaps his friend Richardson Saunders's – Stevens came to know better than most of his business colleagues, and doubtless better than any of his poetic contemporaries, that the difference between praiseworthy prosperity and blame-worthy bankruptcy was a very slender one.

That thin line separating black from red was nowhere more apparent than in southern Florida, long blooming in the businessman's poems and letters[71] but now "boarded-up and bare," car-lots where its grand hotels had stood. Personal good fortune was no reason for confidence any more than insolvency was for blame. The concept and rhetoric of depression-era "blame" is important here. Year-round Key Westers, bitter about being "Bottled in Bonds" and watching helplessly "the glory and [then] decay" of their town,[72] began angrily turning against the "suitcase industrialists and the real-estate sharks" and their "partners the writers and floaters of bonds," impressions Richardson Saunders the banker-developer and James Powers the bond-writer might have left. While Stevens was there to help manage "[t]he escape from bond slavery" by working out surety payments for construction and banking failures, he must have felt the sting of a local feeling that "Florida towns have had too many such business men."[73] In Stevens they would have been blaming the wrong man. He wrote of Powers:

> He would, I suppose, have sta[ye]d here [in Miami] in association with Richardson Saunders, he would have prospered as Saunders prospered, he would have had a finger in [J. C.] Penn[e]y's affairs here and have been in the banks with Saunders and then when the banks closed he would have been in the same position that Saunders is in today: out of a job. Actually, however, while Saunders is out of a job and although not to blame is blamed. Powers is here in possession of everything that Saunders has lost.[74]

Let us return to the lines from "Lions in Sweden" that Isidor Schneider quoted as his example of Stevens's sound won at the cost of sense:

> No more phrases, Swenson: I was once
> A hunter of those sovereigns of the soul
> And savings banks, Fides, the sculptor's prize,
> All eyes and size, and galled Justitia. . . .

The best Schneider could do with this poem was cite, and then overstate, its "virtuoso's mastery." But technical mastery is far from the poem's most striking feature. Nevertheless, once its "beauty" had been exaggerated, Schneider could broadly appeal to the experience shared by many of Stevens's readers, left and right: *Stevens resisted reference to the scenes, issues, and events known commonly to others.* In "Lions in Sweden," Schneider insisted, one could not read the "falsification of the conventional sculptural treatment of the allegorical figures."

Schneider was alluding to "Fides" and "Justitia" in the opening lines he quoted, and to "Patientia" and "Fortitudo" in the next few. Even in the aestheticist terms the communist critic momentarily adopted for the purpose finally of excoriating these terms as divorcing sound from sense, he dramatized his complaint. The poem's point about the "problem of old and new forms, of refreshing the past," as Litz has put it, is reinforced by the deliberately "outworn turns of poetic diction." This diction is as willfully obsolete as "those dead classical images," the sculptured lions "which decorate our public buildings."[75]

Offered on behalf of recuperating a motive for referentiality in Stevens, Litz's reading in effect belatedly answers Schneider's main charge. For Litz the rhetoric and diction of the poem suit themselves to the point about that which is "outworn." What Schneider unnecessarily mystified by dubbing a "falsification," an adaptation of allegorical figures as social defigurations, was not difficult to locate in the poem after all: his assumptions of Stevens's unwillingness to construct political reference directed critical attention toward what the communist conceded in the first place were flexible, versatile allusions. The poem provides allegorical figures tightly

stretched to cover a world of indemnified banks and depression-era dishonesty, for instance, Fidelity (from "Fides" as invested faith or "Trust") –
old symbols of value gone south. To make the point that "ideas suffer"
when Stevens's poems become most lyrical – which is to say, when they
merely achieve the status for which many twenties-style formalists valued
them – Schneider was thinking less of Stevens's talent for configuring historical forces than of the modernist critical tradition, which the critic,
troubled by his own ungainly materialism, wanted programmatically to
oppose. Given Schneider's complaint about allegory stretched too far for
the sake of recognizability and good sense, I note with interest the poem
"New York, Cassandra" in Gregory's *No Retreat*,[76] the 1933 collection Stevens
read – a book praised by the left.[77] "New York, Cassandra" "stretched" Apollo,
Cassandra, and Cerberus – "Give Cerberus a non-employment wage, the
dog is hungry" is one line – almost beyond recognition, so that these figures might cover, in Gregory's subsequent lines, "insurance [that] went to
the banks" and the figurative "lions caged in Wall Street," their "claws . . .
merciless."[78]

Reading Stevens as he did, Schneider could only ignore how even the
lines he quoted from "Lions in Sweden" as evidence of mere gorgeous
nonsense did engage in the very hard work of representing depression –
and not so unlike Gregory. Schneider then fell prey to his own criticism,
lulled by sensory "enjoyment of such lines," and surmising, rather than
confirming, by close reading, that Stevens's habit of not being "scrupulous in regard to meaning" was sustained in this poem. The critic thus
missed an alternative reading, the sense of which he only then would have
begun to appreciate: It might have stressed the relation between the outmoded lions and the "savings banks" they decorate and protect.

The following attempt, keeping to Litz' spirit of revising the implications of an "old" historicist critic for a later time when details of Stevens's
daily business are accessible, situates itself in the debate about modernism
precisely where Isidor Schneider's *might* have. The "Sovereigns" of "Lions
in Sweden," are, after all, coins as well as generally signs of regal power.
And excessive fault-finding, itself a "fault" the speaker of the poem intends
to redress, is simply a matter of discovering what related political and moral
irresponsibilities were betokened by a currency that had become merely
souvenir. Identified as distinct from someone named "Swenson" in the first
line, the speaker tries to analyze Swenson's situation in as many ways as he
can create figures for the sovereigns that are apparently his great concern.
They are in the "soul" of things. Second and equally, they are reduced to
"souvenirs." And third, they are protected (inadequately, it turns out) by
once-kingly (sovereign) allegorical figures: the lions that were supposed to
have been guarding the banks. Thus the poem is quite logically organized.
Each new part of the argument begins with an if-clause: "If the fault is

with the soul. . .”; second, “If the fault is with the souvenirs. . .”; third, “If
the fault is with the lions. . . .”

> But these shall not adorn my souvenirs,
> These lions, these majestic images.
> *If the fault is with the soul*, the sovereigns
> Of the soul must likewise be at fault, and first.
> *If the fault is with the souvenirs*, yet these
> Are the soul itself. And the whole of the soul, Swenson,
> As every man in Sweden will concede,
> Still hankers after lions, or, to shift,
> Still hankers after sovereign images.
> *If the fault is with the lions*, send them back
> To Monsieur Dufy’s Hamburg whence they came.

Obviously, when reading “Lions in Sweden” Schneider could not have
checked his conjectures about its rhetoric against the tone of Stevens’s letters disavowing slack depression-era business strategies. Probably Elsie
Stevens alone knew, for instance, of her husband’s feelings about the suc-
cesses his friend Powers and others were enjoying at the moment of
Richardson Saunders’s and other friends’ bankruptcies. Nor, anyway, did
the *New Masses* editor see even generally in Swenson’s relation to the speaker,
in the very lines he quoted, how pressing is the speaker’s desire to understand the assignment of culpability in crisis. The speaker wants to know
how and why crisis-time fault-finding might seem to have originated in
the language used in times of boom to refigure conditions (soul, souvenirs
and lions in the poem amount finally to the same false but necessary sense
of security) – or, in Stevens’s language for Saunders’s depression collapse,
how and why some people were “blamed” while others were not.

One of the people who was in fact blamed, who was “at fault,” in the
poem’s repeated phrase, was the well-known banker, Eric P. Swenson, director and chairman of the National City Bank of New York, son of the
famous Swedish investor, Svante Magnus Swenson. New evidence gathered for the portrait of the Alcestis Press in Chapter 3 makes it possible to
date “Lions in Sweden” more confidently than before – and earlier, the
spring of 1934,[79] a time when Swenson and other powerful figures at National City were being sued by small account-holders for having set up a $2
million loan fund in November 1929 as a way of aiding high-ranking bank
officers distressed by the market collapse. This was a major catastrophe in
its own right. But it was also deemed by radicals, consumerist liberals,
moralizing ministers, and business conservatives alike as symbolic of the
failure of Hoover-era non-regulation:[80] the costly bail-out of banks that
had made ill-advised loans, taking the form of reorganization, liquidation
or resuscitation,[81] fueled radical attacks on investment capitalism as a whole.[82]
The situation caused one of those intriguing American moments when the
interests of the ambitious but frustrated middle class and those of radical

critics converged. *Collier's* told its middlebrow, newly white-collared audience that "'BANKSTERS' MUST GO," while its writers were covering the National City scandal.[83] Even among insurance executives, holding their own, there must have been some bitterness about the fact that whereas in 1931 banks and insurance companies had been at the same low level of new industrial capital ($14.3 million for insurance, $11 million for the banks), by 1934 there was a gigantic disparity in recovery (the banks by then had reached $193.3 million while the insurance companies were floundering at $3 million).[84] The "LETTERS FROM THE PEOPLE" section of the *Hartford Times* gave the phrase "THE PEOPLE" nearly its most radical sense, in spite of the paper's cautious editorial views, printing letter after letter from enraged Hartford residents like the one excoriating the "money mad men" of the local Savings & Loans "who have more than they can ever use, but are imbued with an insane desire for still more."[85] Raising the issue of what in the newest cultural shorthand was called "the banks" – a broader term than our own concise "S&L" – and emphasizing especially the problem of securing small depositors' "savings," moderate Hartford residents could sound rhetorically very much like the nascent communist Sid in *Waiting for Lefty*, groping monosyllabically for answers to "what is wrong with us in the money sense"[86] and speaking in Sid's guileless insurrectionist diction.

The National City trial was momentarily the rage. Swenson had been asked to act as a trustee of the insiders' reserve – ridiculed in Vincent Pecora's *Wall Street Under Oath* as "the so-called morale loan fund"[87] – out of which unsecured loans were plentifully made "to help retrieve the personal fortunes of certain officers and employes."[88] Taking the stand in the spring of 1934, Swenson defended the plan by citing the good hard work done by officers of the bank during the 1929 crisis. He refused to assent to the suggestion made earlier by a prosecution witness, an economist, that a "fair" salary for a director of the bank in 1928 would certainly have been closer to $400,000 than to the $1 million Swenson's bank been paying. Swenson told the court he personally approved no-interest loans to other officers "solely from the standpoint of the stockholder."[89]

"No more phrases, Swenson," Stevens's poem begins, sternly. "*I* was once / A hunter of those sovereigns of the soul / And savings banks." The speaker clearly distinguishes himself from Swenson, while at the same time establishing himself as an insider. Each had sought old forms of value. Each had been "Trained to poise the tables of the law, / Patientia, forever soothing wounds." But there the similarity must stop. Something happened (in an event at which the poem only hints). "But," the speaker chastises, "these shall not adorn *my* souvenirs." Then, as the speaker examines the several ways in which the key phrase "at fault" is ethically relevant in such a situation, he disarms Swenson's key point of defense by acknowledging that every person "hankers after sovereign images"; that is to say, the desire for the old valued forms does not abate during crisis. Yet conditions have changed, something that Stevens's Swenson refuses to admit and the shrewdly opinionated speaker has belatedly recognized as improper – after, that is, having conducted some business of his own (*I too* was once. . .).

For refusing to allow the refiguration so deftly analyzed by his demystifying critic, Swenson must accept this poem as a stern lecture from a fellow insider. If the banker's defense was in fact that he did not know the market would fail to recover promptly – "All, from the President of the United States down," Swenson argued in court, "said the country was sound and that the upturn of business was near" – the speaker's critical response in the poem lies in the trust that *insiders*, normally allies, place in sovereigns, the images we erected and should have known would wear out as protectors.[90] If the meaning of this imagery disintegrates, send them back to Sweden whence they came, where they were first configured.[91] Whereas Swenson's flimsy defense was that what would seem to be a great deal of money in 1934 had simply not been a lot in 1928,[92] the speaker's critical response is: If the fault lies with the souvenirs, it should never be forgotten that the souvenirs are consequential only insofar as they derive value from "the soul itself."

What made the poem so refreshing a response to the economic crisis is the first argument the poem offers to chastise Swenson. "If the fault is with the soul," the ex-capitalist speaker argues, "the sovereigns / Of the soul must likewise be at fault, and first." We can fairly guess Stevens's response to one contention frequently made by defendants in the well-publicized National City trial: The special funds and loans had been organized most of all for the beleaguered bank officers at the vice-presidential level. Accordingly, corporate vice presidents were caught with hands redder even than Swenson and other presidents and directors. (In two cases brought before the Senate Banking Committee, vice-presidents were found to have borrowed $300,000 each at no interest: One had paid back just 3 percent of the principal; another had not put up a penny in collateral.)[93] The bank's former chairman argued that loans made during the period of crisis kept vice-presidents' ambitions from "becom[ing] dulled."[94]

All this presented, from the businessman's position, an economic argument obviously posing as a moral argument, a version of Eric Swenson's sincere view that vice-presidents working hard during good times deserved to recover losses without risk during bad. "Unless the man of energy" can be part of "his own organization," his hankering will fade. Capitalism requires incentive: "[t]he ultimate goal of every one of our employees was entrance into the vice presidential ranks. *The office of vice president was always open to those who proved their fitness for the position.*"[95] The poem, and the punning rhetoric of trust and mistrust, fidelity and infidelity, on which it is founded, came at a moment of particular sensitivity, for Stevens had himself just then risen to corporate vice-presidency at The Hartford, having been a key participant in "the famous coup" that seems to have made him, not normally a player of corporate hardball, wary of general claims about what the National City bankers were publicly calling "fitness" for such a station. The "upheaval," conveying Stevens to a level that the newspapers were reporting as pivotal and precarious, resulted from a countermove made against an attempt to force out Stevens's ally, James Kearney. The countermove worked; Kearney became The Hartford's president, and Stevens was rewarded for loyalty.[96] When Kearney's feat was disclosed in the February 1934 issue of the *Hartford Agent*, Stevens was featured prominently: "Four New Officers of the Htfd. Accident and Indem. Co.: Wallace Stevens Elected Vice-President."[97]

My point is that the flaws in National City's defense were not just obvious to a political left that vociferously condemned Swenson and his greedy colleagues. (Oswald Garrison Villard, to whom the young Stevens had once been introduced as a fellow of "marked literary aptitude" in pursuit of a job as journalist at Villard's *Evening Post*,[98] interpreted the Swenson case as having proved that "Wall Street has not got much time left to set its house in order."[99]) The popular moral reaction against the bank's position, summarized by Rexford Tugwell's "Banking for the People," and Proctor Hansl's "Years of Plunder,"[100] coincided with new systemic arguments against capitalism that were reaching into government, religion, and business. The result of the convergence induced by this and similar cases, a temporary alliance New Dealers like Tugwell maximized while pushing through new federal banking regulation, was a depression-era moral rhetoric that politicized writers and speakers, those who would never have been expected to join the public invective against the capitalist hankering after sovereigns. The rector of the Grace Protestant Church in New York, for instance, wrote his sermon one Sunday that spring in reaction to the bankers' argument in the National City trial that "the man of energy" must be rewarded else his "ambition becomes dulled." The rector called for radical realignment of *currency* and *soul* in new relation to one another, similar to the way in which Stevens's poem tonally and symbolically organizes its warning. "American business," this response ran, "had better undergo a conversion." While the bankers' defense insisted that "greed for huge money gain is the only stimulus in American business which will keep a man's ambition alive,"[101] Stevens's insider speaker, much like Villard from the outside, was suggesting loftier, less self-interested contentments as the alternative. The case against Swenson tested usual neat analyses of what had gone awry in the American theory of value.

Notwithstanding his recent ascent to the vice-presidency, Stevens considered himself one of the exceptions to the category of the American businessman who in his father's day had been called the *man of energy*; so, indeed, Garrett Barcalow Stevens repeatedly reminded his son Wallace when the young man was wavering in the decision to join the nine-to-five life.[102] The reasons for this cultural resistance, I suggest, were not confined to a psychological parent-child struggle setting father's characteristically American expectations of an ambitious business-minded son against the son's feminized, Europeanized hopes for a career as writer, however important that contest might have been to the development of a gendered nine-to-five figure in Stevens's verse (in such works as "The Common Life" and in the final cantos of "Blue Guitar").[103] The adult Stevens simply did not "hanker" after sovereigns, even as the response to all the incentives which Swenson and other prominent businessmen assumed worked innately. Despite his participation in the 1934 coup, his attitude toward corporate advancement at The Hartford was so much an anomaly that few of his insurance colleagues ever got over it.[104]

In the year 1932, a difficult financial year to be sure, Stevens did purchase his suburban home, and two years later did establish his office along The Hartford's "executive row." His comments to Jim Powers about what it took to meet expenses suggest that spending money on so substantial and secure a possession as a house merely prevented him from frivolities (*L* 266). While doubtless Stevens did not believe "the soul" in any strict sense to be the ultimate solution, a pure alternative to sovereigns – while he was not the ex-capitalist his speaker was – his poetry deftly borrows from the language of moral positioning to point up a reflection on the importance of correlating economic and ethical-egalitarian arguments in times of crisis. For the moment, then, not unlike the Manhattan rector calling for the radical reform of American business, Stevens was sustaining the newest popular argument against business abuse. Stevens and the rector, and many others who denounced superfluous profit-taking in a period of general privation but had not taken the time to denounce it before, were participating in an exciting ideological commingling of moral and political forces against the system as it was.

Here Stevens's placement of Edward A. Filene's reasoning should seem even more distinctive than earlier. His approving citation of Filene was meant as a signal to the left-moving Latimer, a clear message sent through the example of a business ethicist and New Deal booster. The signal was sent knowingly: The position against Swenson could move the poet rhetorically leftward insofar as it meant endorsing A. A. Berle's reformist "New Moral Climate" in the life of American business.[105] "*So that there may be no doubt about it*" – "it" being his sympathy with reform – "let me say that I believe in what Mr. Filene calls 'up-to-date capitalism.'" The statement put Stevens even more deeply in the political mix. And the importance of such involvement cannot be underestimated, given the ideological convergence making feasible many New Deal reforms, changes deeply affecting the insurance business. If the "profit system . . . is destroyed in America," Filene wrote, "I am sure, it will *not* be destroyed by Communists. . . . It will be destroyed by those very business men who believe most profoundly in the profit system."[106]

3: A DIRTY HOUSE IN A GUTTED WORLD

The ideological irony Edward A. Filene observed was not confined to the notice of New Dealers. Stevens had ample access to it, and I understand this to warrant a foray into the rhetoric of the insurance business, with anticipatory glances at its effect on Stevens's thinking and writing, in order to discover just how ample that access was. My reading of such areas evidently inimical to poetry as the impact of regulatory reforms on insurance, for instance – as well as government-provided insurance, the rhetoric of advertisement, cultural "threats" felt from within The Hartford, and Stevens's interaction with friends having New Deal assignments – suggests to me that the particular mixing of 1933 and 1934 excited this modernist's resourcefulness in ways that are not to be seen in his poetry until 1935 and after. One historian has argued that businesspeople at first "suspended" their ideology in welcoming and entreating certain New Deal reforms.[107] Although I do not think business ideology at The Hartford fundamentally shifted in this period (rather, it absorbed liberal rhetoric of change), I am intrigued by the fact that for Stevens ideological "suspension" might be just the right term. What is interesting is that insofar as Stevens felt doubled, the business self took its positions somewhat in advance of the modernist self, even as the two drew stimulation from the same sources. Stevens's entry into this zone of convergence, a special space where right and left were momentarily meeting, and indeed exchanging places in reacting to such reforms as the National Industrial Recovery Act (creating the NRA), was wider than might be expected by those who take the view that, unlike Williams in medical practice, or Archibald MacLeish in legal practice, Stevens minded his own business in business.[108] That he most certainly did not can be suggested merely by his short essay "Insurance and Social Change," a piece downright progressive when put next to conventional insurance rhetoric of the time. This meant more than showing his relative open-mindedness; he was demonstrating to his business colleagues that the Social Security Act was not going to supplant, but actually would re-establish the role of private insurance in American society, raising what advocates of the new system called "The Specter of Insecurity," but in modest, persuasive terms.[109] He seems also to have implied that the criticism of nationalized insurance as bad for business, a denunciation common among his cohorts, was disingenuous, part of the propaganda battle waged against state regulation on ideological grounds even when the practical effects were positive. Earl Henderson of Connecticut General, publishing in the local business magazine *Metropolitan Hartford* – "Providing for one's loved ones and one's own old age has been the insurance companies' purpose in society"[110] – was hardly alone in his recalcitrance. Hartford companies complained that their own retirement plans made social security "redundant."[111] In the *Hartford Courant*, the paper whose editor habitually put the very word "depression" in quotation marks (as one would an outlandish claim),[112] a group of employers made page one when they condemned required federal withholding by favoring "security" through economic expansion (or "trickle down").[113] Hartford business leaders were not shy about their view that the main task of the Connecticut Unemployment Commission was to sort out the "professional whiner[s]" and "protect the . . . community from . . . dangerous legislation" that might result from local sympathies with the unemployed.[114] Against all this Stevens responded by calmly suggesting that the supposed slippery slope toward socialism was actually a level playing field being looked at from the wrong business angle.[115]

Stevens's senses were aroused particularly in this early period of depression, I think, because the question of intellectual partisanship that so interested him – "Which side are you on?" – was itself being called into question by the most powerful of partisans, by those New Dealers whose early strategy for wide acceptance of ideas like social insurance, "long repressed as radical or un-American,"[116] actually depended on *masking* political difference. In "Choose Your Ism Now," James Warburg implied that political choice was merely going to entail the "choice" of crossing over, with everyone else, to the side of business reform: "Millions of people who would deny indignantly that they were Socialists, or Fascists, or Communists, would vote in favor of any number of alterations in our economic system."[117] Indeed New Deal legislation put many business conservatives in the awkward position of *defending* restrictions on competition and *seeking* government-financed bail-outs. Meantime, many liberals found themselves calling for the *relaxation* of the very antitrust laws their ideological progenitors had put in place to keep big business in check. Arthur Schlesinger, Jr., an admirer of political crossovers much in the tradition of Filene, later saw this as "a continuing struggle . . . replete with irony":

> For it was the businessmen who wished to turn their backs on the free market and set up a system of price and production control; and it was the New Dealers who opposed them at every turn and tried to move toward a functioning price system and a free market. If the business image of NRA had prevailed, the result would very likely have been in time to put the private economic collectivism thus created under detailed public regulation and thereby bring into existence the very bureaucratic regimentation which business accused the New Deal of seeking for itself.[118]

It meant a good deal of place-changing as well as role-trading. Even the embattled new chairman of Swenson's National City Bank "openly advocated strict government regulation and control of investment,"[119] hastily abandoning, as many did under similar strain, a free-market libertarianism for what in the 1950s came to be called a "new" conservatism, allowing certain state intervention. And a former president of the same besieged institution began to organize a Committee for the Nation to Rebuild Prices and Purchasing Power, a group accepting the very concept of price support business had denounced a few years earlier as bolshevist encroachment.[120] Critics of the NRA hardly knew what American political rhetoric to use in attacking it. Hartford's august *Courant* featured this confusion. When NRA's constitutionality was in doubt, one headline read, "PRESIDENT'S INCLINATION TOWARD RIGHT OR LEFT SUBJECT TO SPECULATION."[121] Who could have thought, just a few years earlier, that Stevens's fellow executives would be *distressed* when the worth of the casualty-surety companies was (once again) to be appraised on the basis of market value? This inverted resistance was no surprise to anyone who knew how to read the rhetoric with which the retreat from freely floating value had first been brought off: "the group felt that the market value of securities had declined so much [back in 1931] that the market *no longer represented the true values.*"[122]

No surprise, either, that business conservatives of the insurance world hailed the Reconstruction Finance Corporation (RFC) in its aggressive FDR-era incarnation. Temporary nationalizations (low-interest takeovers dubbed "rescues" by insiders) of "weak and rickety and unsound insurance companies," a process "gradually putting the Federal government into the insurance business,"[123] were *applauded* in insurance centers like Hartford, by people who had recently been staunch better-business-with-less-government types, and *denounced* by others who had long supported state regulation and intervention. To fill a special zone of convergence, created by ideological disorientation as much as crossing, NRA planners summoned an unusual breed – the antitrust conservative. Among the most eminent of those called upon, Gilbert H. Montague came to Washington to plan not only how to encourage trade associations while regulating them, all while *easing* antitrust laws – but also how to justify for conservatives who were happily adjusting to the free market a liberalism *sanctioning* combinations.[124]

Gilbert Holland Montague, as it happens, was one of Stevens's oldest and dearest friends. The two had moved through Harvard College in the same class, had a great deal professionally in common, and maintained regular contact for fifty-five years after leaving Cambridge. The many letters between them have been overlooked[125] because Stevens doubtless kept Montague's replies and carbons of his own outgoing notes filed as business papers (destroyed at The Hartford after Stevens's death when records distinguishable as "personal" were being removed for preservation). They are also neglected, I suspect, because Stevens's extant letters to Montague, those the latter saved, are filled with easily passed-over comments: "Your address on PATENTS AND CARTELS does me good"; "I was really interested in your remarks on Lawrence Lewis"; "[T]he Antitrust Division of the Department of Justice doesn't go about things in a way to make people care much whether those who attack it are right or wrong."[126]

But Montague was no drone. Among his other friends and correspondents were a host of principal Roosevelt liberals: A. A. Berle, Hugo Black, William O. Douglas, Felix Frankfurter, Jerome Frank, Sidney Hillman (co-founder of the CIO, planner of the NRA, and FDR's confidante), and Claude Pepper.[127] And then there was Franklin Delano Roosevelt himself, not merely a correspondent but Montague's former economics student at Harvard.[128] The same Montague hobnobbing with New Dealers – and whose reformist views, aired in a Harvard classroom, might have shaped the ascendant economic philosophy in undiscernible ways – could also receive appreciative letters from John D. Rockefeller, Jr.[129] and from conservative columnist Mark Sullivan, who claimed to know Montague's *Rise and Growth of the Standard Oil Company* (1903) "line by line."[130]

To be sure, Montague's support of the NRA soon soured (he had always preferred to see "the regulation of business" remain in "the hands of the courts" and not "vested in some commission or bureau");[131] and a few years after helping create the NRA out of the regulatory void he was decrying it as a monster, overcodified and capricious.[132] But however much Montague came to mistrust the power of executive-branch agencies after 1932, he loathed nothing more than the way in which his colleagues in business law had helped Herbert Hoover as Secretary of Commerce vindicate the decision "to view with great alarm" (and then to undermine) Justice Department proceedings against corporate monopolies.[133] As the New Deal came in, he was "flirting with corporate statism."[134] It was natural, therefore, that Stevens's friend would willingly support the NRA, at least initially. From his position as chairman of the NRA Committee of the New York State Bar Association, Montague urged attorneys to set up the Blue Eagle in their office windows even though they had been exempted from its restrictions, and got good press in doing so.[135]

That Gilbert Montague's dogged reformism did not play well in the insurance centers only makes his influence on Stevens's attitudes toward fair practice even more remarkable than otherwise. Hoover's anti-antitrust "alarm" had set off bells in Hartford, too, as Stevens's friend made enemies by intrepidly questioning why abundant written evidence of price-fixing agreements had not elicited outright confessions of guilt from insurance executives, and why tough penalties had not been imposed during an investigation of insurance collusion.[136] Montague's byword, well known among businesspeople, was "reasonable profit"; beyond it, he felt, lay the sort of corporate greed that had very nearly ruined the American economic house in 1907, and again in 1929. It must be noted that when progressive conservatives like Montague spoke publicly of "reasonable profit," never allowing "profit" to stand economically unregulated as grammatically unmodified, it was widely understood that "reasonable" was the basis of everything. The concept was borrowed from elsewhere and attached to New Deal restraint-for-recovery rhetoric on limited profit-taking that, nonetheless, at the time went radically against traditional business assumptions.[137] The effect on Stevens's "Insurance and Social Change" is direct: "[W]e have advanced remarkably [toward universal indemnification]; and future advances seem to be not fantastic but certain. It is all a question of remaining solvent, a question of making a reasonable profit. Agents have as much at stake as any group in the making of a reasonable profit" (OP 236).

If, as I have already argued, Stevens's new ideas about contingency came from an eclectic mix of poetic and nonpoetic sources, certainly his friend Montague was prominent among the latter. A main question of concern in the poetry was how one should respond to "changes incident to unrest," as the poet scrupulously put it in "Insurance and Social Change." Montague was among the few conservatives to urge insistently for conditional, constantly changing senses of American freedom. In a stirring speech, "The Coronation of the Democratic Principle," delivered before the Colonial Dames of America on the occasion of the 150th anniversary of the American Constitutional Convention,[138] Gilbert Montague "preferred flexibility to certainty," and advocated, in quoting Oliver Wendell Holmes, "play . . . in the joints of the machine" of legal interpretation. "'A word,' Justice Holmes has remarked, 'is not a crystal, transparent and unchanged; it is a skin of living thought.'"[139] These relativist ideas about language, alien to rhetorical traditions of conservatism but already rich in legal liberalism – especially Holmes's with its suggestive homology of literature and law – appealed in specific ways to Stevens, who admired any approach to the fluid, adaptable "word" that could nonetheless get away with quoting Gibbon approvingly and speak of certain legal writing as absolutely "sacred text," all while, again, providing a strong sense of contingency and posing "vital questions affecting the whole people"[140] – undaunted, in short, by the democratic mess a "number of men in a mass" can make (in Stevens's phrase [CP 206]). "'The time is past,'" Montague quoted Justice Brewer, "'. . . when any living man or body of men can be set on a pedestal and decorated with a halo.' . . . Changing social conditions require new remedies."[141] Montague's openness to "remedies" shaped "Insurance and Social Change," the latter appearing in the Hartford Agent of October 1937,[142] a few months after Stevens's friend's speech was delivered and published. He was drawing confidence from the close association of Montague's two main principles, liberal conceptual adaptation to "changing times" and conservative-corporatist "reasonable profit." That combination added up to Stevens's open-minded affirmation of increased socialization in his industry:

> [T]he activities of the insurance business are likely . . . to make one reflect on the possibilities of nationalization, particularly in a period . . . so easily to be regarded as a period of transition. Yet the greater these activities are: that is to say, the more they are adapted to the changing needs of changing times (provided they are conducted at a profit) the more certain they are to endure. (OP 236–7)

Not quite as discernible perhaps, but nonetheless compelling, is the importance of Montague's Colonial Dames of America speech to the poem Stevens published in (of all public forums) the *New York Times* a month after his essay. The poem was "United Dames of America," in which a captivating "orator spoke" of how best to abide the farthest-flung state of fluidity – a Dantesque state indeed, where faces floated like gusted leaves. The speaker in the *Times* poem, distinguished from the "orator" but evidently in basic agreement, extends the orator's discussion to describe a scene in which all the notions of contingency of all the jurists one might quote come together in an extreme state of individual right – "the orator spoke: 'The mass is nothing . . . / The mass is no greater than // The singular man of the mass'" – so that the "Coronation" in Montague's elevated title figure, used with a democratic irony (given the admiring quotation of Justice Brewer), could not, in Stevens's hands, ever quite take place: "There are not leaves enough to crown, / To cover, to crown, to cover – let it go. . . ." (CP 206).

"Contingency" was and is, of course, a basic insurance term[143] – more powerful in insurance than elsewhere because its very use, especially in images for public consumption, could change as conditions changed. To change the scope of contingency, in effect, meant changing how change was defined. In the coming years this was precisely the quality of American business (and university) culture Russell Kirk in *The Conservative Mind* claimed confirmed both the ubiquity and the utter failure of liberalism. But Kirk's and other conservatives' somewhat later view that everywhere in American life "change was preferred to continuity"[144] mistook for something classically liberal what, at firms like The Hartford, can only be called a hegemonic approach to change. Too grand a point can hardly be made of a factor so basic: If the concept of contingency, the changing sense of what might change, had long served The Hartford well (a huge pledge summarized disarmingly in "We cover every contingency," that soothing advertising axiom; and a testimony to the flexibility with which types of policies were being modified and repackaged for the times), then it wasn't an affirmation of a liberal assumption so much as it was a deliberate (and profitable) confusion of conservative and liberal ones. Good as its favorite word, The Hartford facing the depression years was ever prepared to write new

kinds of insurance as frightful contingencies arose. And yet the company's
deeply seated conservative rhetoric – its historic presentation of stability,
permanence, rock-solid assurance – militated against the new accommo-
dations to change. The result was a torrent of little confusions in the rhetoric with which the company represented itself to its own people. This representation, which was always about representation, caused a clash of lan-
guages about American life that quickened Stevens's effort to distinguish
himself from the rhetorical demands of his work in certain conceptual categories, while submitting to the trend in others. Where social insurance –
the Social Security Act of 1935 – was concerned, he sought most obviously
to distinguish himself; where the threat of Labor unrest was concerned,
poems of 1933 and 1934 show how he mostly went along.

One lucrative "New Field of Insurance" at The Hartford was "in providing protection for directors of companies against possible suits for dam-
ages" under new strict provisions of the Securities Act.[145] The fidelity and
surety departments enlarged the so-called "blanket bond" to cover distressed
banks and growing government agencies, both prominent depression features. It was "the only certain way" to indemnify against insider acts of
bad character.[146] The boom in dishonesty that made the insider's sover-
eign-bashing invective against Swenson in "Lions in Sweden" possible,
made central one of Stevens's specialties. He was up to his hips in dishonesty:

> It may seem morbid of an embezzler to keep a memorandum, yet many
> of them do. It may be mere neatness. Public officials seem to be a little
> less fastidious. They collect taxes without making records. In such a case
> we look for people with receipts. Tellers in savings banks take money
> from their cash and make charges against inactive accounts. In such a
> case the bank tries to persuade depositors to bring in their books. ("In-
> surance and Fidelity Claims," *OP* 238)

Easy as the tone is – Stevens's two surviving insurance essays are far more
stylistically familiar than any other piece in the *Hartford Agent* and *Eastern
Underwriter* of that period – all the managing of dishonesty that fell to Stevens
was complicated enormously by the depression as many problems converged, often bringing estate cases into the realms of dishonesty insurance
and depository bonds on failed banks. "You are on the bond of the admin-
istrator of the [deceased] husband's estate," Stevens wrote. "The $50,000
consisted of cash on deposit in a bank which failed several years after you
gave your bond. A, B, and C will settle for $10,000 , but X, Y and Z want
$50,000 . What had you better do?" (*OP* 238–9) Stevens knew the solution,
of course. He brilliantly solved such dilemmas throughout the depression,
some say as brilliantly as anyone then or since. Manning Heard, Stevens's
assistant beginning in 1933, recalled in 1976 that the "terrifically big bank
failures" kept Stevens "always, always busy" during the thirties:

> [A]ll the banks were closed. And we'd written – in those days it was com-
> mon to write – depository bonds, which . . . meant that we, the company,
> guaranteed as surety the repayment of a deposit primarily to public institu-
> tions. And the banks were failing right and left, and we were having quite
> some difficult times because . . . if the company would have had to pay the
> liability on all the depository bonds that [were] outstanding in banks that
> were closed, the Hartford would have gone broke.[147]

There were some near disasters. When Henry Ford risked a \$7.1 million
deposit with Detroit's failing Union Guardian Trust Company, attention
immediately turned toward Hartford, where it was known that blanket policies had been issued by The Hartford to guarantee Ford's personal funds in
various banks – a policy perhaps written under Stevens's supervision, though
no evidence of it survives. Fortunately for The Hartford, it was discovered
that the policy had lapsed in 1931 and the company was safe from Ford's
stubborn refusal to put up collateral to help the RFC save the bank.[148]

Of course there was a mint to be made from depression-era dishonesty, and The Hartford took full advantage, sure to decry patriotically the
"alarming rapidity" with which "dishonesty losses are increasing," and yet
hardly able to contain glee at the new wide business vista: "Blanket Dishonesty Insurance should enable alert agents to capitalize on a golden opportunity," wrote a ranking member of The Hartford's Fidelity Department.[149] Here was not only a chance to write big new policies, but to
demonstrate to its clients the firm's great talent for contingency. One resourceful form of dishonesty coverage, euphemized as "Loss Prevention
Service," was described as covering "the *Moral* side of the risk" by providing for the investigation of the suspected employee.[150] A new "Protection against Collusion" indemnified losses sustained by employers at the
hands of "unscrupulous" employees and extended coverage to workers "acting in collusion with others who are not employees," a gainful reform
demonstrating that The Hartford responded to the "elastic and varied requirements of modern business methods and . . . follow[ed] the kaleido-
scopic changes which are being made so rapidly in the business world today"[151] – those "changes" being, in this instance, inventive ways of corporate deceit in a time of managerial chaos.

The Great Depression, in short, made it possible for such "changes" to
be covered by greatly enlarged senses of "contingency" – a series of larger
and larger blank checks written against social stability. And by all accounts
Stevens was among the most "imaginative" in the country (*WSR* 67) at
accommodating rapidly changing conditions in his cases: The process of
adapting, not to mention the insurance trope itself, was compelling. The
very same "imaginative" claims man later wrote of a "spirit . . . imprisoned
in constant change" (*CP* 472). The poet who confronted Burnshaw's sense
of imminent change somewhat on Burnshaw's terms did know conceptu-

ally what it was "To live incessantly in change" (*OP* 82). Despite Manning Heard's doubt as to "how [Stevens] could separate his mind between poetry and all that's involved in poetry and this mundane, realistic surety-claims world" (*WSR* 67), Heard's and other colleagues' description of a businessman who took unusual pleasure in cases' contingent twists, helped mature the modernist willing, first, "To confront with plainest eye the changes" attending his ideas (*CP* 289); second, to make an intellectual program of "It Must Change" even given "the fluctuations of certainty" celebrated under that very heading (*CP* 395); and third, in the thirties, to see a productive irony in materialists' conceptions of the ideal. This last benefit of contingency was just a few long poems away: Their sense of "final" conditions, no less than his own, was "beyond the compass" of the change materialists themselves hoped to bring about (*CP* 168).

What is extraordinary about the opposition to the New Deal at The Hartford – which in my reading impressed Stevens sufficiently with its conservative fears as to delay slightly his response to the related theoretical possibilities of change – was that it coincided with a perception of new benefits to be gained from the increased fear of failure in other businesses (with insurable risk somewhat diminished by government intervention) and a deep involvement in the activities of the abundantly financed work of new federal agencies. It is clear that The Hartford directly benefited from Roosevelt's timely declaration of the bank holiday.[152] It is similarly evident that long-term advantages would be won from the regulatory wisdom of people who shuttled between Hartford and high "inside" New Deal positions, for instance, at the RFC.[153] Insurance companies held more U.S. Government securities and public utility securities than ever.[154] The Department of Agriculture worked with The Hartford in developing the new field of crop insurance, then untried.[155] Federal housing programs, WPA construction projects, all made more lucrative work for Stevens's department, as construction sureties were hardly less necessary in government-financed than privately sponsored building.

And yet the same corporate breath that aspired to funds coming from New Deal agencies lamented in the old conservative ways. "It's refreshing, in these paternalistic days," wrote one member of The Hartford's Surety department, "to find people doing things for themselves."[156] Another officer complained of "One Way Liberality" in the courts, inveighing against regulations – "unprincipled provisions" – that hindered The Hartford's ability to add new categories to the "misfortunes we insure against."[157] And the very same Securities Act that was hailed as providing a new sort of protection for bank directors expecting depositor suits was criticized on another day as big government run amok, "impos[ing] restrictions and burdens which go far beyond the necessities of the occasion." The insurance executives who collaborated on this public statement declared at the same time that

they had "no desire to criticize the course of necessary reform nor to indulge in any spirit of partisanship."[158] If New Deal-bashing went with claims
of cooperation and nonpartisanship, what similar cynicism caused one
member of Stevens's department to contribute the lead article to the December 1933 *Hartford Agent*, "CHECK UP ON GOVERNMENT'S PUBLIC WORKS
PROGRAM IN YOUR VICINITY"? This man frankly admitted that public works
meant "countless opportunities" for new profits: "With this great recovery
program getting under way your opportunity to secure additional revenue
in insurance commissions should not be lost sight of." As if the amplitude
of the "opportunity" were not plain enough, alongside this article the *Agent*
ran a photograph of the Grand Coulee Dam.[159]

The Hartford's Advertising Committee worked overtime to guarantee
the contradictory tropes of stability and contingency. This *particular* depression was *just one of many* The Hartford had already endured: "1837, 1848,
1873, 1893, 1907, these are dates that recall the more desperate periods
successfully survived." How unusual for Americans outside the insurance
world to speak of the 1929–39 economic catastrophe in such a way! De-
pressions were natural, periodic, even familiar, not catastrophic. And yet if
the company's ads could rhetorically reproduce current events with fright-
ening-enough suggestiveness, they knew, The Hartford's policies will be
that much easier to sell. "The Advertising Committee recognizes the fact
that there is enough in the news of each day to attune the ear of the substantial citizen who has accumulated insurable property to any agent's so-
licitation." In other words, to speak in the language of depression made
insurance an easy sell among a newly insecure class of people.[160]

Thus the corporate self-description Stevens lived with daily throughout
the thirties politicized natural disasters by attaching them to ostensibly
depoliticized images and slogans. Phrases punning on political foreboding
saturated both in-house and public rhetoric the poet heard and, to some
extent, engaged. The great flood of 1936 – causing a prolonged regional
loss of power, a crisis Stevens mentioned in one of his letters[161] – ruined
the downtown offices of some Hartford businesses. An ad aimed at making
the uninsured not a little nervous, especially those whose ears were "attuned" to the political threat from beyond. A photo of a flooded office, its
records awash, ran above this boldface warning, "IT CAN'T HAPPEN HERE,"
satirizing not those who insufficiently feared fascism (a contingency no
insurance would indemnify), but those who, with more pertinent foolish-
ness, disregarded *uncontrollable* disasters (see Figure 1).[162]

In contrast to the small businesses and homes needing The Hartford's
insurance depicted in the *Agent* as already destroyed, The Hartford itself was
figuratively – and as literally as possible – indestructible. "The office here,"
Stevens wrote Latimer, "is a solemn affair of granite, with a portico resting

on five of the grimmest possible columns." This was the poet's way of
metaphorizing such solemnity and grimness as would successfully keep out
poetry-loving bohemians who would want to visit him: that his publisher's
printer and spouse, both wearing shorts, might call on him at the office
before "stop[ping] at some nearby rest-house and change to something more
bourgeois" was "one of the hilarious possibilities of being in the insurance
business" (L 283). The Hartford took its semblance to granite more seriously (see Figure 2), though no less tellingly, in its effort to distinguish its
space from the public's, stressing throughout the thirties the security of the
home office:

> For the great pillars on the portico of the Hartford's Home Office, the
> architects chose granite. . . . No stone but granite was acceptable for the
> Hartford's own building, for its strength – and as a material expression of
> the unshakable stability of the Hartford itself. Just as an architect speci-
> fies granite of tested strength, so the buyer of insurance can safeguard his
> values with test insurance.[163]

Fortress imagery was part of a rhetorical strategy to suggest The Hartford as a safe and thriving human area impenetrable to devastating natu-

"IT CAN'T HAPPEN HERE" .... Oh! No??

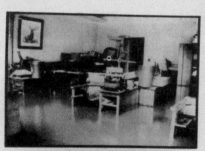

Waiting for the water to go out in the Hartford's Lewis Street office.

Claim service under difficulties.

Aside from the temporary interruption of light and power, the "great flood" of 1936 did not affect the Home Office of the Two Hartfords. As previously noted in *The Hartford Agent*, printing presses were silenced several days and tabulating machines and automatic dictating machines were stopped. Certain Hartford offices were less fortunate. The Hartford, Connecticut, local claim office of the Hartford Accident and Indem- the office was operated from the home of Manager Bradenbaugh where the staff reported each morning. The regular mail was over to the Hartford. As soon as the flood receded several members argued their way through police and militia lines and tramped up

Figure 1.   "'It Can't Happen Here' . . . Oh!, No??" *Hartford Agent* 27, 11
(May 1936), 243. (Courtesy of The Hartford Group.)

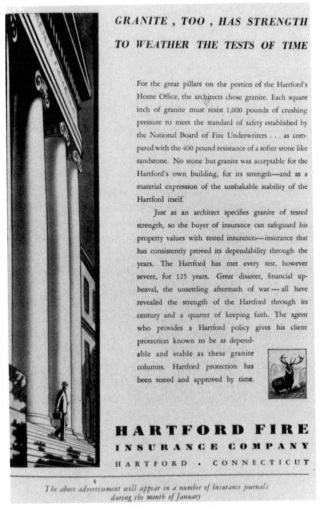

Figure 2. "Granite, Too, Has Strength to Weather the Tests of Time," *Hartford Agent* 27, 6 (Dec. 1935), opp. p. 168. (Courtesy of The Hartford Group.)

ral and social elements outside, all while private homes were constantly depicted as never-quite-safe from hungry masses. One of the ways The Hartford urged its middle- and upper-class customers to add its Residence Burglary Policy was to associate the risk with the potential invasion by the homeless – the very image of invasion leftist poets were taking up with obvious delight (for Kenneth Fearing, the word "Dividends" meant no "defense against grey, hungry, envious millions").[164] A full-page drawing in the *Agent* showing an ill-clad, unshaven man rifling through the clothing drawers of a homeowning man slumbering soundly in the background bore this provocative caption: "Many a man has 'lost his shirt' through failing to carry a Hartford Residence Burglary Policy."[165] The scene was not meant to appear to pray upon middle-class fears of emerging proletarianism, of course, but merely to be clever. The same, I think, must be said of Stevens's remark to his successful young friend Jim Powers: "I think that buying a house is the best thing that I have ever done," and yet "because of the depression, there are so many burglars about that . . . [p]eople actually go to bed leaving lights burning all over the house in order to fool the bums. . . . Holly and Mrs. Stevens have been trained, in the event of a break, to offer to make breakfast and show any visitors round."[166]

Yet the sense of risk was hardly less real to Stevens, who wanted silence and time for poetry to be main merits of his house, than when it was strategically implied by The Hartford, which wanted to benefit from the social crisis in more conventional ways. The poet might make a joke worthy of the *Agent*'s most aggressive anxiety-inducing advertising committee. Upon receiving a review by the poet Ruth Lechlitner, who suggested that Stevens's new poems made him "obviously open to attack" from the literary radicals,[167] intellectualizing sentiments more sharply expressed by Genevieve Taggard's poem "Interior" ("A middle class fortress in which to hide! / Draw down the curtain as if saying, *No*"),[168] he wrote Latimer that "We are all much disturbed about a possible attack from the Left." For all its lightheartedness, the witticism vividly imagined "the best thing that I have ever done" wrested from him: "I expect the house to be burned down almost any moment" (*L* 313). When in 1932 he bought the colonial on West Hartford's Westerly Terrace, it was precisely when the house as the officially optimistic figure for American society was being subverted by fifty-two radicalized American writers, painters, and critics who signed an "open letter" to other intellectuals, urging noncommunists to join them in supporting the Communist Party ticket for president: "The United States under capitalism" was "like a house rotting away; the roof leaks, the sills and rafters are crumbling."[169] The fearful image was conjured by contenders on either side of the question, by *Agent* ad men in images of homes ravaged that might have been insured; as by poets like Leonie Adams, Langston Hughes, Orrick Johns, Matthew Josephson, Alfred Kreymborg, Countee Cullen, Cowley, Gregory, and Schneider, who collectively deemed the American house unsalvageable, indemnified or not – and in poems such as James Neugass's "The Hour of Lateness" where

> There are . . . rats running in the roof-beams, ants
> Chewing at the foundations.
> Death-beetles tick under the wall-paper, punctuate the evening quiet
> Of families gathered at home . . . [170]

and one of Alfred Hayes's lively communist villanelles:

> These nights one hears a creaking in the hall,
> The sort of thing that gives one pause
> The crack is moving down the wall.
> We must remain until the roof falls in. . . .
> The crack is moving down the wall.
> Defective plaster isn't all the cause.[171]

Ruth Lechlitner, chiding depression "Statisticians" as "Seekers of meaning under change," knew, too, that the great causes of decline were best evidenced in "Abandoned houses, grey-swaying on granite, / . . . flowers like ghosts / . . . the broken gate."[172] What, then, of the generation to come after the American homeowner had, as it were, "lost his shirt"? They, wrote Stevens, will see

> The spring clouds blow
> Above the shuttered mansion-house,
> Beyond our gate

and thus

> Will say of the mansion that it seems
> As if he that lived there left behind . . .
>
> A dirty house in a gutted world. . . .

The thrilling fear of disappearance, of leaving nothing possessed of oneself behind – and, what's more, a "blank" in which once had been invested so much feeling, "what we felt / At what we saw" – was strong enough in Stevens to send up from him, as from the radical poet Lechlitner, an utterly "*literate* despair," "A Postcard from the Volcano" (*CP* 158–9) as a small but meaningful check against unmodified despair.

4: LABOR DAY, 1934

Much as Stevens disagreed with business colleagues about the impact of social insurance – the logic and disarming tone with which he revealed his relatively progressive position give hints of strategies of convergence he would adopt in 1935, 1936, and 1937 – he was still quite susceptible, in 1933 and 1934, to the rhetorical instigations against upheaval that he heard all around him. The threat of May Day agitation in 1932 and 1933, after the tumultuous Hartford observances of 1931 during which a placard reading "JOIN THE COMMUNIST PARTY" was permitted a place just beneath the speaker's podium (see Figure 3), caused The Hartford to issue and then energetically sell "Riot and Civil Commotion Protection." In the *Agent* labor unrest was "just another example of what happens when the lawless element runs amok. Where will the next trouble break out? . . . [I]ndustry is passing through a period of readjustment involving constantly increasing difficulties between capital and labor. *The time is psychologically ripe.*"[173] Conservatives and New Dealers alike had qualms about the least predictable element of their plans, specifically that pertaining to "the masses" – sentiments reflected in the deeply ambivalent feelings of Donald Richberg, one of FDR's most powerful recovery advisors and, along with Montague, an NRA planner. "There is no taskmaster," Richberg wrote privately, "like a multitude on the march."[174]

Stevens's conservative poem, "The Drum-Majors in the Labor Day Parade," addresses the marching multitudes, voicing doubts about the capacity of American radicalism, and radicals' poetry, to maintain a sense of playfulness sufficient to the innovation demanded by their cause. That the poem expressed new doubts at a particular, disconcerting moment – the unforgettable instant, in Alfred Kazin's recollection, "when the first wild wave of hope under the New Deal had receded"[175] – makes it all the more interesting as an anticipation of the special inventiveness of "The Man with the Blue Guitar." For Kazin that moment was Labor Day 1934. He felt it to be an especially bad time for such a let-down, since that day found the young man again waiting on the infamous assignments bench at the of-

Figure 3. Communist Party rally, May Day 1931, *Hartford Courant*, May 2, 1931, p. 1. (Courtesy of the *Hartford Courant*.)

fices of the *New Republic*, hoping for a few dollars' worth of reviewing to be doled out by editor Cowley. For Stevens, of course, firmly employed in Hartford and in no need of the quick reviewer's cash many of his contemporaries absolutely required, the sort of worker's holiday he presumed would give the laboring classes greatest pleasure was deliberately *not* the celebration his poem's speaker observes as he eyes the drum majors who lead the local Labor Day parade. Much as Kenneth Burke's ideas for "Revolutionary Symbolism" urged radical writers to "rethink your representations of workers" and generally to "attend to the machinery of representation" was an attempt at complicating communist "dialogue with the uncommitted,"[176] the fourth stanza of "The Drum-Majors in the Labor Day Parade" complicates what is otherwise Stevens's dull criticism of labor's celebratory rationale – with this question: "Are they really mechanical bears, / Toys of the millionaires, / Morbid and bleak? (*OP* 70) For the question is not merely designed to discredit the Labor Day participants (any more than Burke wanted his rhetorical position to be thought deviant by hardliners in the League of American Writers, to whom he presented it). These lines go much further than the dismissive manner of the poem's opening stanzas, asking, in sum: Do not the workers on holiday risk seeming to be exactly what their severest critics say they are: automatons, unfree, dependent on capital?; limited by reliance on their antagonists, and rendered predictably uninteresting?

The poem doubts if by Labor Day 1934 unionists knew imaginatively how to use the ceremonial day off to the best advantage of their cause. In fact, a nationwide strike had been called by the United Textile Workers of America (UTWA) to commence on Tuesday, September 4, the day after that year's holiday. It would seem that unionists' timing was indeed perfect for winning the hearts and minds of fence-sitters, those previously indifferent to labor's newest symbols. After all, dozens of New Deal officials had long been scheduled to deliver enthusiastic Labor Day addresses, to hail unprecedented friendly relations between the federal government and the organized American worker (what wonder, when one considers that the number of federal unions had grown astonishingly from 307 in 1932 to 1,788 in 1934).[177] Labor Day was greeted by a full page of stories in the *New York Times* stressing the importance of unionism to economic reconstruction, under a rare eight-column headline: "THE NATION PONDERS A PIVOTAL LABOR DAY."[178] The shrewd timing of the textile strikes made it difficult for Harry Hopkins to do anything but ignore the furious letter he received from businessmen who complained that "That Man in the White House" was actually encouraging Labor Day strikes by announcing in advance that he would offer relief to the strikers under the auspices of the Federal Emergency Relief Administration. While

recognizing the need to help those suffering from "involuntary unemployment," business condemned aid to UTWA strikers as "fraught with grave
dangers to our economic and social stability."[179] *Time* marked that September as the moment when "Private fulminations and public carpings
against the New Deal . . . bec[a]me almost a routine of the business
day."[180]

In response, popular reformers were inspired by unionists' celebration
of their new-found power to give wildly optimistic Labor Day orations.
Fiorella LaGuardia's enraged conservatives.[181] While the call for a national
strike found nearly unanimous support among southeastern workers, in
Stevens's New England the textile locals were not entirely convinced.
They planned to open the mills as usual after Labor Day. Hartford, however, an industrial city where unionism was now especially strong, became the regional exception. From there it was reported that the locals
would dramatically exceed UTWA's national strike plan by calling for
walk-outs in every affiliated branch of their industry.[182] Workers left the
mills, set up "flying" squadrons in trucks and cars to move through strike
areas while picketing, clashing with factory guards, re-entering the mills,
and unbelting machinery. The National Guard went on duty throughout
Connecticut. Thirty miles beyond Hartford's city limits, 1,500 pickets
fiercely battled Connecticut state troopers.[183] If the Labor Day parade was
to become, from 1934 forward, a grand annual affair in Hartford, this one
was especially important, marking a resurgence of local labor muscle and an
increased gap between middle- and lower-class public opinion.[184]

Stevens's poem imagines a doubtful middle-class response to a Labor
Day claimed to be "pivotal" by a popular anti-business position satirized
here as too inflexible to make its own argument:

THE DRUM-MAJORS IN THE LABOR DAY PARADE

If each of them wasn't a prig
And didn't care a fig,
They would show it.

They would throw their batons far up
To return in a glittering wheel
And make the Dagoes squeal.

But they are empty as balloons
The trombones are like baboons,
The parade's no good.

Are they really mechanical bears,
Toys of the millionaires,
Morbid and bleak?

> They ought to be muscular men,
> Naked and stamping the earth,
> Whipping the air.
>
> The banners should brighten the sun.
> The women should sing as they march.
> Let's go home.

If only the paraders did not take themselves so seriously – were they not such prigs; were their "banners" not so dull – the poet's dazzling inventions could be deemed the result of their effort, not his. A baton tossed, for instance, could return transfigured, "a glittering wheel." But the Labor Day paraders *are* prigs (stanza 3): They are flat, over-earnest, unremarkable. The poem's speaker, and not these Labor Day drum majors, can claim provocatively to know what will "make the Dagoes squeal." The poem politicizes a strategy Stevens had already mastered: in his terms, he disarms his imagined antagonists by outperforming them.[185] Its logic advances directly to his own characteristically priggish "ought."

The "if" of the first stanza gives way to the second and third, where the speaker could suggest a few "good" qualities the paraders lack. The third stanza simply repeats the negatives, extending the mockery. But after the fourth stanza asks its co-opting question (are they really "mechanical bears"?), the fifth, using its knowing "ought," proposes a mediated solution, implying what the workers on holiday ought to do to make their parade truly representative and poetic representing truly inescapable. If the goal of the parade was indeed to demonstrate labor unity and to awe local detractors with its essential power, then the celebrants "*ought* to be muscular men," miraculous (not ordinary) laborers, *Stakhanovets*, in the term then trendy among Russophiles: "*Naked* and *stamping* the earth." In this he obviously discerned the basic aesthetic appeal to the poetic left of marching masses and strikers, idealized by young radicals like Muriel Rukeyser. ("[P]oetry," no less than the "picket-line," Rukeyser wrote in a poem, was designed "to master pride and muscle fluid with sun.")[186] The banners carried on Stevens's Labor Day "should" be so bright as to improve upon the daily sun; and the women "should" sing.

But a purpose fundamental to Stevens's willful syntactical choices of tense and mood makes this idealized scene distinctly *not* the Labor Day of then and there. Nor, obviously, were these choices going to affirm the evident aesthetic confidence disclosed in many, many meters not nearly as "Naked and stamping" as Rukeyser's, such as

> It was a new thing for a poet to make his stanzas
> out of a picket line;
> and *hear music* in the plain speech of plain people,[187]

for "It" – *this* poetry – was hardly "a new thing." Its claim of innovation and resourcefulness needed some healthy doubting, as did Genevieve Taggard's implicit suggestion that her political poems achieve a comparably robust gait:

> . . . they hobbled with anxious steps
> To keep with the stride of the marchers, erect, bearing wide banners.
>
> Body sings best when feet beat out the time.
> Translated song, order of bold rhyme, –
> Swing the great stanza on the pavement. . . .[188]

There were on the poetic left, of course, doubters about whether such gait indeed marked a "Metric advance" – Josephine Miles, for instance, who observed in a sequence published in *Poetry* just as Stevens was writing about Labor Day, that

> All our footsteps, set to make
> Metric advance,
> Lapse into arcs in deference
> To circumstance.[189]

Kenneth Patchen was similarly skeptical:

> I'm tired of all they say: "How do you say 'worker'?
> Make it ring?" Near the run-down factory
> The hills still climb to cloud and silence. . . .
> We bring no boxed solution; our flags
> Stream out for use, not trumpet-masses.[190]

In Stevens's sense of "Labor Day," although far more critical than Miles's, such "deference / To circumstance" made a whole irony of metrical advance sufficient to match social imagination. Patchen's poem, "A Letter to the Liberals," is a reproach aimed to his right from further left, yet its criticism interestingly permits Stevens's poem to manage a right-left convergence against what for him was a similarly facile poetic center.

Stripped to its predicated constructions, Stevens's poem reads as follows:

> If each of them wasn't . . .
> And didn't care . . .
> They would . . .
> They would . . .
> But they are . . .
> Are they really . . . ?
> They ought to be . . .
> . . . should brighten . . .
> . . . should sing . . .

The grammar of if-then surmise gives way incrementally to "rhetorical" interrogative (that is, predictably answerable with the word "really" stressed), which, in turn, gives way to modal forms ("should brighten," "should sign") used, in turn, for ironic obligation, condition, assumption, expectation, and advice-giving. Having thus out-organized the laborers in a ditty apparently half-hearted (but, I would argue, in fact cannily constructed so as to *seem* easy and dismissive), the speaker finally turns away, with an imperative addressed to a figure, until then unmentioned, a bystanding intimate: "Let's go home," presumably "home" to more important matters. In quitting the scene he has described, he is not merely turning away from the corresponding commotion; obviously, he is reacting as well to Rukeyser's sort of sure-footed idealization.

It hardly needs saying that Stevens was making much more than was necessary of the "eagerness on the part of *some* [radical poets]," as Cowley later put it, "to renounce the art of making patterns out of words."[191] The radical poets he read – among them Gregory, Maas, Lechlitner, and Norman Macleod – revealed no such eagerness. Macleod's "Communist Day Song," published in *Left Front* (official organ of the Midwest Region of the John Reed Club[192]) even characterized "the steel song that factories sing" as "cauteriz[ing]," not liberating, "the brain of multitudes"; Macleod's lyric would have to suggest in itself an *alternative* for those "forcibly attuned to the swing of machinery" and "disciplined with clash and clangor." To be sure, Macleod's verse, with very little clangor, expressed confidence that the "steelsong" would be changed into the "singing of multitudes," but this case is not made in terms compelled by the machinery that enslaved, as anyone could discern just by looking at Macleod's utterly regular lyric on the page. "Steel song," a phrase appearing at the beginning of the poem, must in the end be tempered into "steelsong" – with that small but evidently crucial difference suggesting a forging of political hardness and thoughtful prosody.[193] Notwithstanding the resistance to reduction in the radical poetry he read, then, certain exaggeration of such antiformalist positions as those Cowley disparaged would do things to Stevens's stanza that in the long run won him admirers from the left, including the four poets just mentioned. The following comparison between a stanza from a poem by Cecil Day Lewis and part of one from Stevens's "Blue Guitar" might begin to show where the fear of poetic priggishness in the Labor Day poem would soon take the nonradical. To a lover who would have him lower his revolutionary guard, Day Lewis writes:

> Hands off! The dykes are down.
> This is no time for play.
> Hammer is poised and sickle
> Sharpened. I cannot say.[194]

Answering a poetic detractor much like the earnest speaker of Day Lewis's poem, Stevens writes:

But then things never really are.
How does it matter how I play

Or what I color what I say?
It all depends on inter-play . . .

. . . these I play on my guitar

And leave the final atmosphere
To the imagination of the engineer.
                    (*OP* 103)

Of course each stanza represents an extreme style of the poet. Stevens finally rejected the canto just quoted for the long poem, but very little might have been done to make it of a piece with the stanzas he did publish. The oxymoron driving the whole work is present here as a nice irony (the poetic engineers, serving as the guitarist's detractors, lack the imagination for creating "the final atmosphere" they crave). The pretense of diffidence about one's lines is obviously checked here too by attempts at lyric control ("it" *does* very much "matter"). When the "Blue Guitar" stanza fails, and this one does, many or most of its four-footed lines are end-stopped; in the lines quoted one finds only one of the enjambments so familiar to readers of the final version. In the worst instances, the effect can be ridiculous, undermining the conceptual flexibility or "inter-play" that I read as the poem's most significant contribution to the argument about the role of poetic form in the social-poetry movement. (Later in the rejected canto the same failure leads to versification resembling that of Dr. Seuss:

I could not find it if I would.
I would not find it if I could.

I cannot say what things I play, . . .

And since they are not as they are,
I play them on the blue guitar
                    (*OP* 103)

Nothing C. Day Lewis could do, on the other hand, would rectify the impression of imitative fallacy. That is, the form of the stanza cannot possibly help us to believe in the force of the sentiment conveyed by "This is no time for play." Yet just this belief is required to overcome various strong pressures courted by the love lyric itself, a subgenre this poem tries to politicize by thematic rather than stanzaic inversion. The quatrain has all of the metrical and generic cues readers of poetry traditionally look for in "playful" verse. The effect of "play," though it has been introduced negatively (announcing: *this refuses to be a poem about play*), is to suggest in the end, rhymed so plainly, that a bit of play is precisely what the poet needs if "poised" is to be recognized as among his qualities. Three-stressed rhymed lines, three-fourths end-stopped, cannot help but give the impression, as it did in 1943 to one *politically sympathetic* critic, "of sentimentality all compact . . . strik[ing] a false note." The "resourceful, sincere, and integrated poet will steer clear of this danger."[195]

What J. Hillis Miller wrote in 1965 about Stevens's "witty" "nonsense" poems, which "by destroying the ordinary . . . meaning of poetry in a mad improvisation [put Stevens] suddenly . . . in tune with something else," is true as far as it goes.[196] Miller's sought-for "something else" becomes much clearer, I suggest, when one learns that the "singsong rhythm" was not rare but all around, that it had *not* been spurned by Stevens's most self-consciously political contemporaries. Nor, then, did his shrewd use of poetry's "hoo-hoo-hoo, / Its shoo-shoo-shoo, its ric-a-nic, / Its envious cachinnation" (*CP* 131) stop at "efface[ment] before reality." The strategy of confronting the new public rhetoric in light satire was one he would attempt a number of times. "Hieroglyphica," like "Labor Day" written in 1934, did its slight work with a similarly strong sense of resistance; it, too, is one of the poems Miller would describe as making a "linguistic paste":[197]

> People that live in the biggest houses
> Often have the worst breaths.
> Hey-di-ho.

This is a silly, disarming refrain. The two-liner I take to be a "found" quotation (as a postmodern poet would say, generally following the modernist practice of Gertrude Stein) derived from a radical slogan or axiom, and overdetermined by its assimilation into the ditty form Miller has admired. With literally no rhyme or reason, and a purely dismissive *self*-mocking polemic, it proclaims *Down with dwellers in big houses! They stink!* In doing so it specifically mocks the poet who would express confidence that buying the spacious colonial for his family of three was the "best thing" he had ever done. The other stanzas are of a piece:

> The humming-bird is the national bird
> Of the humming-bird.
> Hey-di-ho.

> X understands Aristotle
> Instinctively, not otherwise.
> Hey-di-ho.

> Let wise men piece the world together with wisdom
> Or poets with holy magic.
> Hey-di-ho.
>
> (*OP* 69)

By ironizing the trendy word "national," rendering it a false category, Stevens makes that which is deemed *national*, after all, a concept imaginable from the radical perspective of a creature unmoved by artificial boundaries and concocted designations. It finds especially ridiculous such trifling designations as "the national bird." The world "[o]f" *this* bird will not be reconstructed by reason, but rather by "instinct," by "wise men" and "poets" whom we should trust to "piece . . . together" things as they ought to be.

"Polo Ponies Practicing," something of a companion piece to "Drum-Majors," observes the opposite social spectacle: the privileged class at sport. The disarmament of ideological claims works identically, doubtless encouraged by Gregory's tentative political approval of Stevens's power of social observation. Once one's work was automatically associated with the communists, as Gregory's soon was, it was more difficult to make this claim for oneself. Gregory's 1935 description of his own poetry as art made by an "outsider" failed to convince anyone: "This may sound strange and 'nonpartisan,'" he wrote. "I believe my value as a writer depends upon a gift of observation."[198] Making full use of the ideological freedom "observation" can be granted the "outsider," "Polo Ponies" absorbs counterclaims likely to be made against the scene it whimsically idealizes. It depoliticizes the phrase "old order" by noting that claims made against the "old order," against the splendid decorum or orderliness embodied in polo, are themselves "old" claims:

> The constant cry against an old order,
> An order constantly old,
> Is itself old and stale.

When the poem continues, then, it moves toward the situation the speaker has intended to describe – polo ponies practicing – as definitively of the present; this entails turning away from detractors' counterargument, for these critics' complaints seem not "Here." The maneuver forces declarations against polo to become arguments against a "world" that is positively "the world of a moment." "[M]oment" is a slippery term indeed, neither quite securely in the lexicon of the historical imagination nor merely a sign of temporality (suggesting physical fast pace, suitable for lyric praise). The ditty was composed strictly in the rhetoric of observation:

> Here is the world of a moment,
> Fitted by men and horses
> For hymns.

The world of polo, which its detractors contend is a "world" ignorant of worldly conditions, is nonetheless "the world of a moment." The speaker smoothes over a major thematic problem with an epistemological nicety. The world of polo is "of a moment" only in the sense that the poet, in verbally apprehending it, makes it motionless in a "*brilliant* air," "In a *freshness* of poetry," even though its challengers, repudiating the social specificity of this mannerist, high-caste pastime would mean "the world of a moment" in a very different way. An observed yet constructed world, resisting complaints that it is not of the world, is to Stevens not only "the world of the moment," but also well "Fitted . . . / For *hymns*," suited to verse well defined and even muscular. Poetry like that described in the poem – but not the poem itself – puts the greater part of its energy into situating itself spuriously but usefully above the politics of observation, "Beyond" radical repudiation, past hearing the deadly "constant cry against an old order":

> Beyond any order,
> Beyond any rebellion,
> A brilliant air
>
> On the flanks of horses,
> On the clear grass,
> On the shapes of the mind.
>   (*OP* 70)

Mailed to T. C. Wilson of *Westminster Magazine* on July 19, 1934, "Polo Ponies Practicing" matches the Labor Day poem to come six weeks later. The earlier work offers a poetry forbearing the inducements of working-class scenes and themes as the best sources of new, fresh, clearly defined "hymns" chanting the here and now. And it provocatively depicts a *non-*proletarian scene in offering its hymn as example. Neither poem crosses the line from mockery to respect when reproducing the rhetoric of New Deal-era reform. The strong man playfully idealized for the poetic Labor Day parade that would outdo the parade of September 3, 1934, it is true, is roughly borrowed from the popular and ubiquitous local idealizations of liberal and radical Labor. If Stevens even for a moment deemed his strong men idealized, such a thought is not believably manifested in the poem. The mock speedily succeeds any possibility of such an ideal; the poem engages a positive image passingly; and the satire is broad. The same is true of "Hieroglyphica."

The "national bird" in effect was the ubiquitous (and, to some, hatefully rapacious) American eagle painted an eye-catching New Deal blue. "The bird," it was familiarly called – a symbol the Roosevelt administration had shrewdly reinvested with political symbolism in order to gain popular recognition of its NRA,[199] including, successfully, at The Hartford[200] – is embedded in Stevens's satire. No surprise, of course, that a poet would be responding even vaguely to the massive effort to psychologize the symbol in public discourse: "When every American Housewife understands that the Blue Eagle on everything that she permits to come into her home is a symbol of its restoration to security," proclaimed NRA chief Hugh Johnson, "may God have mercy on the man or group of men who attempt to trifle with this bird."[201] Foes of the New Deal joined adversaries of this sort of centralized symbolic management, just "so much incantation, advertising, and radio sound,"[202] and proceeded to deconstruct the Blue Eagle like no other Roosevelt image. "The American Eagle, that noble bird before it was painted blue and turned into a Soviet Duck," wrote the anonymous author of *Frankie in Wonderland*, should be mentioned only with sincere "apologies to Lewis Carroll, the originator and prehistorian of the New Deal."[203] "Hieroglyphica" was no scurrilous *Frankie in Wonderland*, of course, its mock of national planners' media incantation deftly encoded: As satisfyingly distinct from the brazen but carefully packaged "national bird," the negligible hummingbird is the *national* bird only in the world of the hummingbird. It is what it is and ought to be, and the poem that suggests as much is, in a sense, a counter-incantation: "The humming-bird is the national bird / Of the humming-bird. / Hey-di-ho."

Stevens's failure at this turning point to engage seriously the object of his political satire may be contrasted with the relative success of "Lions in Sweden." If there the speaker chides Swenson, one of the bankrupters, it is also clear that he understands Swenson's difficulties from inside – was himself once a hunter of sovereigns. Herein lies the main lesson Stevens would begin to learn from the political debate. "The Man with the Blue Guitar," the most successful of the poems responding to the challenge of the literary thirties, would encounter its antagonists through disarming forms of inclusion.

Stevens's "Like Decorations in a Nigger Cemetery" (*CP* 150–8) is as antagonistic to the new public rhetoric of the thirties as "Polo Ponies Practicing," "Hieroglyphica," and "The Drum-Majors in the Labor Day Parade." But its persuasiveness on this point is attributable to another factor. Had Stevens published "Drum-Majors," for example, with its reaction against Labor Day, in the *Nation* or the *New Republic* or the *Partisan Review* – in just a few years he would publish poems in all four – he would have been criticized, possibly attacked; poems much less antagonistic to workers were attacked. It might not have been timidity so much as a shrewd sense of his poem's politics that kept "Polo Ponies" for T. C. Wilson's obscure *Westminster Magazine* and "Drum-Majors" for *Smoke* of Brown University; it is possible, too, that Stevens considered himself unprepared to reenter prominent circulation. In either case, his decision to take "Like Decorations" to Monroe's and Zabel's *Poetry*, where the new generation of politicized poets would at least read him if not respond to him, was a relatively bold move. For while, as we will see, "Like Decorations" is replete with formal arrogations and provocations, its epigrams are not nearly as assailable as the preceding 1934 poems. And to the extent that even these other poems were to be considered politically harmless, their context in publication certainly reinforced this view. Publishing in *Poetry*, on the other hand, was in itself now something of a retrogressive statement, especially a poem taking as much space as "Like Decorations" (which Zabel, thrilled to have Stevens back,[204] placed first in the issue). Williams was one of those provoked by the poem: he later referred to it as "that haphazard congeries of snippets which I find not what one should expect today" from an important poet.[205]

5: THE TEDIUM OF BEING RARE

Stanley Burnshaw pointed out many years later that the provocation of "Like Decorations in a Nigger Cemetery" begins with its title. He speculated that if it had been called "Like Decorations in a *Sheeney* Cemetery," there would have been greater contemporary outcry.[206] When Stevens acknowledged that the title had been suggested by Judge Arthur Powell of Atlanta, one of his companions during southern business trips – the poem is dedicated to Powell – and that it really did analogize a cemetery set rudely aside for impoverished blacks, he was making the point in order to explain a formal similarity: "The title refers to the litter that one usually finds in a nigger cemetery and is a phrase used by Judge Powell last winter in Key West" (*L* 272). Among the Hi Simons papers at the University of Chicago is a letter from Powell recalling the incident:

> We were walking in Key West when I stopped to look through a fence. I explained that I thought it enclosed a graveyard, as some of the rubbish looked "like decorations in a nigger cemetery." He was interested when I explained the custom of negroes to decorate graves with broken pieces of glass, old pots, broken pieces of furniture, dolls heads, and what not.[207]

The fifty epigrams, together a rough irregular assortment, are themselves structurally "like" – similar structurally to – the "what not" in Powell's modern and outwardly enlightened comparison of a "curious" low-cultural fact and an alluring arty abstraction.

It would be wrong, I think, to trust entirely Powell's later attempt to convince the suggestible Hi Simons that "the title is fitting" wholly because the poem is "itself an olio" – wrong to assume that the title's suggestive likeness is indeed solely a formal matter; that no value moves from structure to sentiment; that the verses hang together formally but not substantively in the manner suggested by the image of the decorations in the segregated graveyard. For the likeness does certainly extend to a number of vital matters then at hand, to the audacious social position assumed, for instance, in epigram ix:

> In a world of universal poverty
> The philosophers alone will be fat
> Against the autumn winds
> In an autumn that will be perpetual.

Surely the "poverty" meant here was not wholly philosophical (as in "The Snow Man," thirteen years earlier, where it most certainly was). "Judge" Powell's bit of folk wisdom, reaffirming his own status as Stevens's elite "pine-spokesman" dispensing "memorable if somewhat malicious"[208] phrases serviceable as modernist poem titles, contributes more, obviously, than merely a sense of structure to the relation between "universal poverty" and seasonal perpetuity. By reading a structural trope of *found art* in the title phrase, Stevens registers first-hand knowledge of the particular way in which impoverished victims of Deep South segregation honored their dead with such fragments of domesticity – broken furniture and dolls' heads – as could whimsically be found at hand, all while he leaves himself wide open to the objection that he naturalizes and makes quaint a certain philosophical facility and lethargy: in *that* "world," one of actual ritual whimsy, the "philosophers *alone* will be fat." But since the poem is anything but facile or lethargic – for one thing, it challengingly consists of stanzas-as-found-objects – I take it that a certain distance from custom, naturalized to be as inevitable as autumn's approach, will have been achieved in fifty attempts to get at the inadequacy of Powell's beguiling cultural analogue.

In epigram ix and elsewhere, "Like Decorations" uses its resemblance to imagism to naturalize the Great Depression, much as at The Hartford depression-era catastrophic homelessness was depoliticized to be rendered a threat analogous to the "perpetual" cycle of periodic flooding or storming. It will be surprising to some that many radical poets of the period, referring to "this bitter season," similarly played it both ways; Stevens, in "Like Decorations," using the same rhetorical strategy, makes it explicit. Thus the particular use of imagist and Romantic natural tropes in "Like Decorations" (seasonal cycle, inevitable decline, sharply perceived change, downturning) contrasts favorably with the same tendency in the work of dozens of self-described political poets I have read, who implicitly claim to have made pointed political reference while nonetheless using a fully natural imagery. Isidor Schneider's poem "Now" (with its repeated ugly term "Nowness," ambiguously both meteorological and social) describes a seasonal condition that "quiets an old homesickness" even while it also suggests disappointment with the way things politically are.[209] Geoffrey Grigson's "About Now" (1936) is another instance:

> In this bitter season, I discern the reality
> In the bigness of the black leaves. . . .
> I discern the reality in the bromide
> Of the lighted window from the
> Empty street,
> In this bitter season.

For "*this* bitter season" we are obviously supposed to read *the depression* as well as *winter*, an era of emptiness, dislocation, homelessness. Grigson's title, "About Now," and the refrain "In this bitter season," work hard at simulating referentiality. But finally this effort does not accomplish even as much as Stevens's "In a world of universal poverty." Franklin Folsom's six-part poem "These Days" handles the seasonal trope similarly: the homeless speaker of part 1 is cold, but *why* he does not say. My point is that Folsom, known as a prominent figure in the communist-allied League of American Writers, presumed he would not have to dissociate seasonal from political.

So his lines – "I am left no warmer / in my winter than before – / by having fitness to be" – equate cold with a condition that is permanent unless we do something politically about it, and the phrase "These Days" (like Schneider's and Grigson's slippery "Now" and Grigson's "this bitter season") is supposed to mean the thirties. But Folsom's poem appeared (in *Poetry*) with many other by-then traditional *vers libre* nature lyrics where cold is merely transitory and "These Days" merely winter.[210] Working rhetorically against the referential facility and lethargy in Folsom and Grigson, Stevens's ninth epigram in "Like Decorations," typical of others in the series, postpones reference to conditions that would justify the separation of fat philosophers from general privation. Only in the third line of four ("Against the autumn winds") do we get the naturalized circumstances, after the connection between "universal" and "philosophers" has knowingly disfigured "poverty." When considered in the light of the evident liberal economic truism that down-turn was intrinsic to the long prior rise, certainly the first spurious fact (that thinkers thrive when others starve) is presented as a depression-era value seemingly neutral. It seems to me, here and elsewhere, that Stevens's poem contains many signs that it is keenly aware of its arrogation – whereas, surely, Grigson's and Folsom's lyrics, utterly unprovocative, never account for such an effect.

Epigram xviii also bears signs of this awareness:

> Shall I grapple with my destroyers
> In the muscular poses of the museums?
> But my destroyers avoid the museums.

This shrewd tercet uses something of the strategy that enabled "Drum-Majors" to disarm the parading workers by out-conceiving their own proletarian ideal. Presuming they could not themselves imagine it, Stevens imagines for them their own strong men marching. Here he supposes his antagonists' position, assuming their wish to do battle with him. But he brings in by analogy the site of combat; that it takes place in a museum is by no means a necessary condition of the antagonism. Here as ever he wisely selected the place of rhetorical war, for *the museum* was already a figure in the arsenal of the communist left aimed at twenties-style decadents, for instance in Michael Gold's widely debated, savage attack on Thornton Wilder. Gold based his criticism on the opinion that Wilder's subject matter presented "a museum . . . not a world. In this devitalized air move the wan ghosts he has called up, each in 'romantic' costume. It is an historic junkshop over which our author presides."[211] Isidor Schneider's "To the Museums," its refrain urging four times "Come to the museums, workers," beseeches them to transform into labor's muscular poses every pointless form of art:

> under each gleaming nude
> paste this label: "This is the working woman, this is her

worker's body,
undeformed."[212]

Even Paul Rosenfeld, a noncommunist to be sure, whose work Stevens closely followed, complained in an essay called "Bread Lines and a Museum" that museum art should be less what one finds in the galleries and "more generally useful . . . direct untheoretical contact with things . . . a shock of reality."[213] When configuring his antagonists' ideal – the same muscular men his speaker imagined for the Labor Day parade – Stevens came upon the likeness to the classical sculptural pose. But once these figures are displaced onto his ground, sequestered in museums and mockingly aestheticized as art objects, although he has agreed to grapple with them on their terms, he might be said to win the bout: These lowly antagonists are not the sort of people who frequent museums, despite Schneider's repeated entreaties ("Claim what [art] is stored here. It is yours. / Labor of artists"). And insofar as the antagonists *do* "avoid the museums," they might not even be aware of the muscular poses they "ought" to strike.

The typical epigrammatic strategy of "Like Decorations" is to offer two or three benign, unassailable propositions, and then to suggest a difficult relation between these and a final, usually more densely aphoristic one. Here is canto xxiii:

> The fish are in the fishman's window,
> The grain is in the baker's shop,
> The hunter shouts as the pheasant falls.
> Consider the odd morphology of regret.

The plain realism of the first three observations – three given facts of abundant common life, like Pound's "Study in Aesthetics" from his book *Lustra* – understates the mild, ironizing imperative "Consider," which is used to initiate the expressiveness of the final line. "[R]egret" implies placidly that such pre-industrial marketplace facts are no longer easily found in the real, much as Pound's speaker is "mildly abashed" when he cannot quite see why young Dante in the market at Brescia takes special "satisfaction" in stroking "The fish in the boxes."[214] Though they go forward from the same modern tradition, Pound's and Stevens's final lines are crucially different:

> *Pound*: And at this I was mildly abashed.
> *Stevens*: Consider the odd morphology of regret.

For Stevens the vividness of the scene conjured by facts of premodern abundance demonstrates that the grateful contemplation of these old forms is very much alive, and that the poet, taking the village scene apparently to heart (although without Pound's speaker's sense of "I"), takes a step "barefoot into reality," as Stevens put it in a later poem (*CP* 423).

But "Like Decorations" takes many backward steps as well. In effacing the nostalgia for the-realism-of-imagism in xxiii, epigram xxiv sheds some light on the bitterness of xxii with its "comedy of hollow sounds":

> A bridge above the bright and blue of water
> And the same bridge when the river is frozen.
> Rich Tweedle-dum, poor Tweedle-dee.

The first lines of xxiv mislead us into thinking that the tone of xxiii will be sustained in its successor. But the last line radically changes that tone. It is obvious that Stevens is not really interested in the substance of the simple observation – a bridge over a river – but in formal analogues that might spin off conventionally associated signs. The "same" bridge in changed circumstances is not really the same (spanning over something that has changed), and yet it is the same (still *over* in the same way; the relation does not yield.)

Between the first observation and the final aphoristic fragment of xxiv, Stevens offers no grammatical coupler to help his readers read the relation: no easy subordinator (such as "which," used in epigrams xi and xxi); no position-fixing preposition ("against," in ix, the "universal poverty" epigram); no conspicuous logical turn ("Yet" in xvi, xxxii, xxxiv and xliv; "if" in xl; "Granted" in xxvii; "But" in the "muscular poses" epigram, xviii); no ironically flat transitional phrase (for instance "On terms / Like these . . ." in xxviii). Are "Rich Tweedle-dum, poor Tweedle-dee" meant to comment on the relation described above, or on another kind of difference analogous only by relation? Yet Tweedle-dum and Tweedle-dee are commonly known as two forms of the same figure. The burden of difference obviously falls on "Rich" and "poor," precisely as it did when Stevens left unrevised "Soupe Aux Perles" in "New England Verses," instead working ultrafine distinctions between "cheese and guava peels" and "ginger and fromage." It would be as if, here, he tinkered with "Tweedle-dum" and "Tweedle-dee," finding some other version of sameness. An utterly uncontroversial if not tautological assertion – a bridge over a river in summer remains a bridge over a river – leads quickly to the arguable suggestion that differences between "rich" and "poor" might naturally be deemed coincidental. The tone of "Tweedle-dum" and "Tweedle-dee," like that of "fromage" succeeding "cheese," suggests: What's all the fuss over such conceptual differences? When many of Stevens's modernist friends joined radicals in the "Open Letter" for the candidacies of Ford and Foster two years earlier, they saw no difference between poor Hoover championing the rich and rich Roosevelt championing the poor (under the heading "Are There Two Parties Or Only One?" they wrote: ". . . just as Tweedledum is the logical *alternative* of Tweedledee").[215] For Stevens, unlike his radicalized friends, insofar as difference *is* largely subject to similarity, so the barely hidden aphorism in xxiv runs: These issues are just more water under the bridge. Kreymborg and the other radicalized poets voting Communist in 1932 were of course not nearly so casual about the "logical alternative" being no real alternative at all. "Like" in the poem's title phrase, "Like

Decorations," suggests, too, that the cultural site of formal relation is expendable, even though that contradicts Stevens's own explanation of the title, in which the poems are structurally like "rubbish," where "Nigger Cemetery" is *necessary* to the point (no cemetery for the "rich," after all, suffers decorations so identically modest as to warrant description as "what not").

Epigram xxv then finally discharges the realism that had been achieved in all seriousness in xxiii.

> From oriole to crow, note the decline
> In music. Crow is realist. But, then,
> Oriole, also, may be realist.

Establishing the hierarchy, the first two propositions identify realism as low on the poetic scale. "But, then" again, it is not enough; Stevens wishes also to claim "realism" for the higher end. This epigram takes up one of Stevens's intermittent arguments against the new realism: There is a "reality" other than that pointing to conditions in "decline." There is a "realist" for every condition, not only that of lowly "crow," who by being called "realist" has been unnaturally elevated, but of oriole as well.

Epigram xxxiii returns to the claim that orioles are realists too. It picks up another of Stevens's doubts about the new social realism: do people need and want the same things? The poet of "Like Decorations" fears the resulting monotony, dreading what will happen to the modern lyric when, in the figure of "The Man with the Blue Guitar," "a million" people choose to play "on one string" (*CP* 166)? I was not surprised to find, when reading the poem in Stanley Burnshaw's personal copy of *Ideas of Order*, that this was one of just two epigrams the young Marxist had marked fifty years earlier:

> For all his purple, the purple bird must have
> Notes for his comfort that he may repeat
> Through the gross tedium of being rare.

Should the elite bird *choose* to make monotonous sounds, it is because he has become bored with his rarity. Stevens makes it quite clear that even when the purple bird assumes that "crow is realist," he nonetheless gives a royal performance. Grigson, the poet-editor who heard in Stevens's poems "the little staccato notes of a stuffed goldfinch in a gilded cage" – "[w]ind the key, the wings begin to lift and shiver, the little dead beak opens and shuts, and the invisible clockwork sets the invisible little drum of notes revolving"[216] – did not take into account the shrewd inclusiveness, the range (as it were) of the particular bird of xxxiii here.

"Like Decorations" concedes that aesthetic rarity craves realism even while judging the latter to be hardly less a manner to be put on, and only somewhat less manifestly an artificial style. What would the fish in the fishman's window be without the line "Consider the odd morphology of

regret" to put a point on the observation; and what is the Brescia market
without the otherwise recalcitrant "I" of *Lustra* abashed by its modernist
version of density? These were ideas one would think had long since been
resolved in modern poetry, which partly accounts for the "tedium" that
Grigson and Burnshaw evidently assumed was wholly unintended. But
obviously Stevens felt a need to replicate the risks for a new era, clear as
they were: for poetic "realists" there can be little but "the *decline* in music,"
the same "flat historical scale" Eda Lou Walton knew others would expect
Stevens to play. The realist views his or her poetic -ism as designed to
privilege what is low and unprivileged.

   Now that realism has been declared just another style, the way has been
paved for even greater provocations. Epigram xli first suggests that nature
has thus far been able to return "Each year" to provide its vast "disguis[ing]"
of the human clutter; but that clutter is given in such a way as to doubt the
worth of mechanist ideas, for instance that the quality of life is advanced in
an art informed by technology:

> The chrysanthemums' astringent fragrance comes
> Each year to disguise the clanking mechanism
> Of machine within machine within machine.

In order to understand this epigram as satire, one must know something of
the poetry it was conspicuously misrepresenting – the emergent "Dynamo"
school that drew its power as a program from incessant, unapologetic exal-
tations of machine over nature. Even Willard Maas, a committed lyricist
and at one time an opponent of the Dynamo style, urged poets to

>   Build poems of girders
> skyscrapers of salvation
> dynamos of rhyme
>   metallic songs. . . .
>   Bridges of deliverance.[217]

Such poets were taking Williams's willfully unnatural "metal rose" (implicit
in the early-modern tenet "Make It New")[218] to industrial extremes. Poets
were "riders of steel stallions" making "electric songs of speeding lights!":
"we lay the base / . . . of marxist machinery . . . / and arms like hammers
strike stars."[219] The redemptive sign in Stevens's invective against poetry-
become-"clanking mechanism" is the word "astringent," then, as it quali-
fies what is otherwise an obvious denunciation of the Dynamo poets'
"American Worker" with his or her "Arms, hands, fists, bred by machine
into the precise / swift strength of pistons, hit[ting] like the 20th Century."[220] Nature has its own way of expressing an ironic attitude, antagonistic to what is erroneously deemed a distinctly twentieth-century trait. In
making his case for that particular irony, Stevens's poetry is never more
categorizably "modern" than here, much more than merely a belated lyric
Luddism or an "antimodernism" of the sort that has described for early-

modern conservatives.[221] The modern machinelike lyric, from Williams's metal rose onward – more to the point, from the vorticists and futurists, the latter group unmentionable on the American left – had had its own effective cleansing bitterness. Spender's idea that "Machinery, . . . instead of being against us, [is] on our side" was at least as old as modernism itself, not by any means a dictum invented in the thirties.[222] Stevens wants merely to reaffirm an already old poetic truth. Epigram lxi is not, then, merely a refutation of the "verse of the 'Oh, Grandmother Dynamo, what great big wheels you have!' school," such as that made passingly by Stephen Vincent Benét in his antipolitical foreword to Rukeyser's first book. Benét wrote: "I do not intend to add . . . to the dreary and unreal discussion about . . . proletarians. . . . [W]hen Miss Rukeyser speaks her politics . . . *she does so like a poet . . . and she does so in poetic terms.*" In speaking so confidently of "poetic terms," Benét obviously hoped for something far above the fray of poetic movements – hardly a sufficient way of describing Rukeyser and surely an ineffective way of responding to Maas's and others' new "metallic songs." But when Stevens refers to the "clanking mechanism / Of machine within machine within machine" he is thinking not only of that object which, for example, Rukeyser's "The Gyroscope" presents, but of a modern poem generally as, at bottom, a brilliant machine in itself: he does acknowledge the basis of the modern in "Power electric-clean, gravitating outward at all points" insofar as that power refers to the poem itself – so that indeed poets might do what Rukeyser urges them to do: "find what traffic / you may have with your silences."[223]

Epigram xlii satirically projects a god that, while particularized, is yet the creator of strings of monotonous forms lacking distinction. This is the "God of the sausage-makers." Epigram xliii extends the irony of quantity:

> It is curious that the density of life
> On a given plane is ascertainable
> By dividing the number of legs one sees by two.
> At least the number of people may thus be fixed.

The implications here move at once leftward and rightward: The natures of people are not determined merely by totaling the number in the mass, while a mass is finally more powerful than the number of its constituents. Stevens's invective against quantity is surprisingly restrained. He takes some evident pleasure in others' fantasies of ultimate ascertainment. "*It is curious*," he notes, that there are those who believe in the value of quantitative measures; something, at least, will come of it. An enviable tone of certitude, for one thing, as conveyed in Gregory's enumerated "million men and a million boys" who "*know what they mean*" when they "Knock down the big boss,"[224] and in Burnshaw's soon-to-be-mobilized "scattered millions / In mill and farm and sweatshop."[225] In this sense the epigram mildly proposes to poetic social realists that sometimes they are merely taking a census when they claim to be empowering the millions counted, foot by regular foot, in their verse.

Epigram xlvii begins to recommend a way out of present conditions by slowly reversing the related Great Depression metaphors of lowness and dullness. We have seen this in Stevens's letters to Elsie about James Powers and the disasters of southern Florida: grand hotels becoming parking lots, even the weather itself "depressed." Economic and spiritual reconstruction would take place when things were "made bright and shining once again," a phrase for the poetic project he took quite seriously when later using it to describe figurative preconditions for the recovery of war-torn France in the late forties (*L* 527). His language about the depression perfectly matched his anxieties about the new long poem: Its tone as a whole, he feared, "might be a bit low and colorless." The "gaiety and brightness" (*L* 273) lacking in southern Florida he soon found similarly lacking in "Like Decorations." Here is xlvii, a halting attempt to seek out an object for, as it were, light verse:

> The sun is seeking something bright to shine on.
> The trees are wooden, the grass is yellow and thin.
> The ponds are not the surfaces it seeks.
> It must create its colors out of itself.

The first two lines state, respectively, the solution underway and the condition requiring attention.

Finally, however, such a solution must get going of its own accord. Conditions to be shined upon have nothing evidently to do with the agent of reconstruction: "The ponds are not the surfaces it seeks." Rather, in order to lift us out of our depression, the sun cannot perform its basic generative function by focusing on abundant life below. The pattern repeats itself elsewhere. If epigram xxxi had been one of those portions of the poem conceding the power of realism to predict and then describe a "teeming millpond" where "The actual is a deft beneficence," by xlvii the epigrammist finds himself in a position to recognize that for all the "beneficence" actuality has in store, a world "teeming" with "men and the affairs of men" (epigram xxxv), here, too, the "actual" cannot renew brightness to itself.

It had not been four days after sending the poem to Morton Zabel at *Poetry* before Stevens seemed already prepared to retract the ahistoricism of the forty-seventh epigram ("the sun is seeking something bright to shine on"). He wrote Latimer about his new poem, his longest since "The Comedian as the Letter C": perhaps the poet's mind was not the main source of the lamenting tone in these epigrams. If one has grown unused to writing so pithily, the "inhuman" environment inscribed in that art might seem somehow to fabricate despite him. Poetry, in this tension between stanzaic control and authorial autonomy, seemed "to receive its impulse from circumstances which more often than not would be cheerless to anyone except the poet" (*L* 272–3). Much of the poem would seem to follow from this shrewd generalization, but the fiftieth epigram surely does not.

Going against the rest of the poem by restating the otherwise naturalized political argument explicitly in the contemporary political language of its antagonists, the fiftieth epigram was undoubtedly added last, and indeed, I would venture to guess, at the very last moment. It began with a straightforwardness uncharacteristic of the other epigrams: "Union of the weakest develops strength / Not wisdom." This shift in rhetoric can be explained, I think, if one sees in the final epigram, first, a response to events taking place precisely as Stevens believed his poem was complete and, second, a certain retreat from the very choice of the epigrammatic form. The response and the retreat were closely related. The conservative adage in the final epigram's first line, virtually lifted from the political commentary in the papers that week, seemed to be driving Stevens to a statement not containable by the structural pithiness that had earlier seemed satisfactory. Nor was it controllable by the old Poundian tenor of posed abashment, serving otherwise as the poem's foundation.

He finished the work he now judged to be "cheerless" in the days preceding December 6, 1934; that was the day he mailed it to *Poetry*. The argument made in the final epigram had just then resurfaced with intensity: Business conservatives organized and published their legal response to what they considered the greatest sin of planned reconstruction: collective bargaining.[226] The poem does assail the "Union of the weakest," but not by refusing to acknowledge potential strength of the weak, rather by noting in too succinct a way that the majority would never be the sort necessary to become an "all" capable of redressing natural decline. It clearly mattered to Stevens, just when he sought a resting ground for his poem, that opposition to collective bargaining, established in the NRA's seemingly undemocratic section 7a, countered the central New Deal notion that a majority of the workers in a given company had the legislated right to grapple with management on behalf of all workers.[227] The ensuing debate led to a court test of the collective bargaining provision; expected to result in a judicial counterattack, and timed with the election of the pro-labor 74th Congress in November 1934, the case commenced with fanfare during the first days of December.[228] Despite liberal majorities in the new Congress, this challenge marked the beginning of the end of local union strength under the NRA that only a year earlier, in Hartford's "NRA Night," had drawn 20,000 marchers, along with a hundred floats, thirty bands, and the singing of "Marching Along Together" and "Happy Days Are Here Again,"[229] and only three months earlier enabled the show of strength that in turn incited Stevens's Labor Day poem.[230] Again, to skeptics the particular shock of the moment was what one liberal historian of the New Deal has called an "irksome obligation on employers," namely that when an employees' election was held, subsequent to a strike, the strongest element within a company was qualified to act for all.[231] When Stevens's last epigram was composed, employers and employees were said to "have made terrifying fists at each other."[232] Note the epigrammist's final view:

> Union of the weakest develops strength
> Not wisdom. Can *all* men, together, avenge
> *One* of the leaves that have fallen in autumn?
> But the wise man avenges by building his city in snow.
> (emphasis added)

The question in lines 2 and 3, following the political counterassertion of lines 1 and 2, is a highly charged, thirties version of a similar assertion made in "Six Significant Landscapes" eighteen years earlier:

> Not *all* the knives of the lamp-posts,
> Nor the chisels of the long streets,
> Nor the mallets of the domes
> And high towers,
> Can carve
> What *one* star can carve,
> Shining through the grape-leaves. (emphasis added)

In this "Significant" landscape, its imagism typical of the earliest poems collected in *Harmonium*, the precision strike caused by the natural image (by *one* brilliant star shining), opposes human conditions (carved by the world's knives, chisels, mallets) even as it merely expounds an ironic ratio. Stevens knew quite well, I think, how the first week of December 1934 augured a very different time for such poetry. Not only was it possible to question the "wisdom" of collective human activity, but the stakes could be raised in other ways as well: The unionized "weak"-become-"strong" sought to "avenge," not merely "carve," well-wrought individualist work, no matter how carefully that work was inscribed by an awareness of the knives, chisels, mallets it had chosen not to use. The last line of the poem offers a solution that was finally not the compromise prepared for in preceding epigrams, but instead an attempt to assimilate the claim of "aestheticism" made against unpolitical poems written in a political age – a gesture akin, in other words, to Archibald MacLeish's attempt to express ideological compatibility by identifying a common enemy in the question "Who recalls the address now of the Imagists?" But in the long-lined "Invocation to the Social Muse," where that question was posed, MacLeish was not being so smart as to frame the very question in verse that reminded his detractors of the outmoded form. Thus Yvor Winters's reply, "A Postcard to the Social Muse," could expose MacLeish's liberalism so ruinously. Winters's usual spareness was rarely so politically pointed:

> Than to engage with those
> Of small verse and less prose
>   'Twas better far to play
>   At bouts-rimés.[233]

After forty-nine apt reminders of "small verse," Stevens lastly (I think mistakenly) had meant this: The wise person might offer alone – as opposed to the strong person in concert with others – not oriole meeting realist crow halfway, but purple bird singing monotony whenever he damned well pleased. Yet the rare bird avenged decline by creating, provocatively, something the union of the weakest deemed in all ways inessential – a *pure* product of the imagination, "his city in snow."

If Stevens took steps back after advancing, however, it seems logical that some force was calling him forward. For Eda Lou Walton and Isidor Schneider, for example, both of whom would object to Stevens's new poetry on the grounds that he was not moving swiftly enough into the thirties, similar scrutiny of their work would have been cause for tempering that complaint, even as the poetic side Stevens took at the end of his late-1934 poem seemed anathema. The ratio of diction I suggested above – imagist "carve" to politicized "avenge"; dream-city and its brilliant pleasure domes in the early poem to "all men" working "together" unwisely in the later – might well have sent Walton and Schneider back to their own earlier work abashed. For the movement revealed there is different only in degree. Their poetic transitions, stanza by stanza, were swifter than Stevens's, yes, but no less uneven. Here is Walton's depression-era "Portrait of an Old Man":

> In this high noon of loss, that had grown hot
> With all that in the morning mattered not,
> No leaf would drift, nothing would happen less
> Than instant death.[234]

And here her Millayesque "Enigma" of 1925:

> In you I wander like a little child
> Seeking ripe berries in a thicket wild,
> Stooping and turning in my way to see
> Where dogwood or white violets may be.[235]

As an example of the poetry for which Schneider is remembered (when he is remembered at all), here is an extract from his address to a "False Revolutionist" (1934):

> But most beware
> when he calls you rare
> better than the others;
> that is his knife
> to stab your brothers.[236]

Schneider, who was writing political verse at least as early as 1920,[237] more successfully than most poets resisted a thirties-style second-guessing of the twenties. Nevertheless, one finds in poems like his "Dawn" something surprising – not quite the manner of Stevens's precious "New England Verses," perhaps, but a slight observation so precisely derivative of imagist-*chinoiserie* meter that, knowing the date of the work to be *1930*, one would be remiss *not* to read it as I have read Stevens's "New England Verses." This is the whole of Schneider's "Dawn":

> O auroral obfuscation! –
> lace sleeves over the hárd grásp of dáy.[238]

I take it that in 1930 the radical poet still wanted to lure his detractors to condemn him for the niceties of "lace sleeves" and for the pale romantic archaism of "O auroral obfuscation," just in time, that is, for the two final feet to do their hard stomping. If that is even this slight poem's proletarianized strategy, surely in the latter-day imagism of the fiftieth epigram Stevens had learned something of the aesthetic moment to which it did not belong.

3

What Superb Mechanics

I love the idea of bringing out a proletarian . . . poet in a deluxe edition! These lovely incongruities!

—James G. Leippert, a.k.a. Ronald Lane Latimer[1]

I think there ought to be a new deal / free from authors over 40 // Suggest you look up J. G. Leippert.

—Ezra Pound to Parker Tyler[2]

Latimer is an extraordinary person who lives in an extraordinary world.

—Stevens (L 391)

1: MR. HYPHENATE LATIMER

However tempting it may be to dismiss J. Ronald Lane Latimer, the fact is that he might have provided the most important literary friendship Stevens ever had; certainly his importance during the thirties is unmatched. He formally posed questions about very recent poems, in a manner that elicited the most revealing replies Stevens had yet offered anyone about his work. Latimer, moreover, was not just inquiring about Stevens's new poems, but was *publishing* them as well. The Alcestis Press materials scattered in odd archival corners verify Latimer's cajoling, sometimes infuriatingly blunt encouragements as having persuaded Stevens to write and publish regularly again, and to think about how new poems worked as a unit. "Owl's Clover" might owe as much to the Stevens-Latimer exchanges of 1935 and 1936 as indeed to Burnshaw's *New Masses* review.

Remarkable in itself was that Latimer could have sustained his enterprise in the middle of the depression, an extremely difficult time for all publishers, let alone publishers of verse. It was a time when Little Brown's new third colophon, *Non refert quam multos sed quam bonos habeas* [Fewer and Better Books], was hailed by Little Brown's Alfred McIntyre unbecomingly in *Publisher's Weekly* as "Birth Control for Books,"[3] and when, as Stevens said, Alfred A. Knopf, Inc. "cannot possibly be interested in publishing poetry." "Better" in "Fewer and Better" did not, whatever McIntrye's and Knopf's pretensions, mean volumes of poetry. Of course Knopf was in fact publishing some contemporary poets,[4] but the business was truly imperiled; books of verse were indeed among the first type to suffer cutbacks, and Stevens's remark was not much of an exaggeration. Alfred Knopf himself, hard hit but genial as ever, would not have disagreed with Stevens's observation that "selling poetry now-a-days must be very much like selling lemonade to a crowd of drunks" (L 284).[5] John Crowe Ransom, paying tribute much later – and noting that through Knopf he was "proud of having a sort of family connection with Wallace Stevens" – nonetheless was going somewhat out of his way to mention that "*Poets too* are to be found in Alfred Knopf's clean, well-regulated stable"; this was really praise, for Ransom, ever the admirer of profit, knew that "poetry is always the speculative item on the publisher's book list."[6] That amidst the depression, when "speculative" was itself a dirty word, Knopf readily granted Latimer, a brash nobody, permission to publish new work by Wallace Stevens in strictly *limited editions* – Little Brown's "fewer and better" taken to extreme, as the Alcestis contract specified Latimer's exclusive right to do Stevens "deluxe" – implicitly acknowledged Knopf's sense of how badly trade editions of Stevens's sort of poetry would fare in the mid-thirties. Knopf did certainly want, in the long run, to remain Stevens's publisher, hoping for better times. A market that had netted American publishers $42 million in 1929 was cut in half by 1933 (214 million new books sold in 1929, just 111 million four years later).[7] In a single depression year, the number of poetry books issued in the United States dropped by more than 20 percent.[8] Alan Strook, the business manager of the *Hound & Horn*, described the dismal scene for Ezra Pound in Italy: "It is palpably no longer true that books are worth even the paper they are printed on. . . .The book business is so pell mell that it is impossible to tell from day to day what will happen. . . . [T]his is no time to put out books." And Strook, hardly otherwise a radical, insisted that the only way good work would see print was for writers to wait until "such idiots as Doubleday, Doran's, Scribner's . . . [are] wiped out."[9] What Strook evidently did not realize – but Pound shrewdly did – was that a tide was turning toward small, semi-collective presses,[10] run by people precisely like Latimer, prepared to endure "unimaginable austerities," as he once put it, in order to float a few books of contemporary poetry "on very little but nerve."[11]

If Latimer was the most important literary friend Stevens had, he was also, without a doubt, the oddest. Latimer's activities make it hard to imagine that he and Stevens related personally on any level. That they did relate, and with relative ease notwithstanding the correctness and formality of Stevens's other friendships, is further new proof that the mid-thirties were for him a period of surprising openness to strange new ideas and manners. And "J. Ronald

Lane Latimer," by all evidence, struck a figure as disconcerting as alluring. His closest allies were haunted by him. Ruth Lechlitner, one of the Alcestis Press poets, once dreamed that Latimer broke into Willard Maas's apartment to steal the manuscript of a play they had been writing. She wrote Maas that her association with "Jay" was the "first experience, in all dealings with people, that has completely upset me."[12] And Maas, for a time Latimer's closest friend, defended him as long as he could to the other Alcestis authors, but finally confessed his feeling that his own publisher and colleague was a "psychopathic worm."[13] Allen Tate later remembered Latimer as "a fly-by-night opportunist." He couldn't fathom why "Stevens took him seriously and wrote him long letters about his poetics."[14]

Latimer's eclectic interests kept him busy. During the time he was regularly publishing and corresponding with Stevens, he began planning a narrative biography of Ernest Dowson,[15] was enrolled in business school,[16] became an initiate into the order of St. Francis, in Albany, for which he took a short-lived vow of chastity and wore a monk's robe and cowl in private,[17] was engaged to a young woman from an established Rensselaer family while living with a succession of three men in Greenwich Village,[18] and was giving away a small sum of money he inherited at his mother's death as if he himself were "passing out of the picture."[19]

His obsession with pseudonymity has certainly contributed to the difficulty historians and critics of modern poetry have had in locating basic information about his important publishing project.[20] Maas was instructed to address him "*exactly* this way: J. L. – only initials."[21] His own printer, the person who set the type of *Ideas of Order*, knew him only as "Mark Jason"[22] and "Mark Zorn."[23] Maas's modernist mentor, S. Foster Damon, tired of keeping up with all the pseudonyms, began referring to the young publisher as "Mr. Hyphenate Latimer."[24] At a time when Maas was in *daily* contact with Latimer, even *he* expressed doubts that he could keep the names straight.[25] Robert Fitzgerald decided that there really was no such person as Mark Jason, that Maas had all along been running *Alcestis* by himself.[26] Latimer wrote to Sherwood Anderson as Martin Jay,[27] Witter Bynner as James Leippert (his given name),[28] Ezra Pound as Leippert in 1932 and as J. Ronald Lane Latimer in 1936 (Pound evidently thought he was dealing with two people),[29] and was introduced to Milton Abernethy, the radical editor of *Contempo*, as Jay Martin.[30] "Imagine the applause when Latimer arrives in N.Y.," he signalled Maas in advance of one trip from Albany. "Leippert is dead, you must forget you ever knew him – & Mark Jason has resumed his right name, Latimer. But Latimer must remain an unknown quantity – who he is, where he is, what he is – is a mystery. I love pseudonymity for its own sake."[31]

Needless to say, this made business dealings with the Alcestis Press sometimes impossible, and difficult at best. During his periods in Albany, where he stayed with his moneyed uncle, Frederick Lane, and seems to have led a

secretly *conventional* life, Maas was left behind in New York to respond to
letters from authors whose business with various Latimer pseudonyms could
only be wildly guessed at. Maas complained, that he was sending back evasive, invented responses to precise editorial questions, answers to which only
Latimer could know.[32] Shortly after Alcestis published John Peale Bishop's
Minute Particulars, the proud author dropped by the Alcestis office at 335 Fifth
Avenue, merely to arrange for a copy of his book to be sent to Louise Bogan,
who might give it and the press prominent notice in the *New Yorker*; but
Bishop, already uncomfortable with promoting his own book, found no one
there, and had to resort to sending telegrams all around town, one of which
later discovered Latimer in Albany.[33] No less influential a critic of modernist work than William Rose Benét seemed agreeable to reviewing Stevens's
first Alcestis book, *Ideas of Order*, in the *Saturday Review of Literature*, but
mistakenly addressed his inquiry to "Miss Lane"; Benét became so incensed
at being unable to get a fix on the press, let alone the editorial gender, that
Stevens finally himself had to intercede on Latimer's behalf.[34] Allen Tate,
whose book *The Mediterranean & Other Poems* was finally published by Alcestis
after thirteen months of miscues and postponements, a lag that rankled him
no end,[35] told George Marion O'Donnell (who knew of "Leippert"), that
"Leippert disappeared." "[W]e heard nothing," Tate lamented. "Now there
is *Latimer*. . . . However, the discovery of James Leippert in a new role shakes
somewhat my confidence in Latimer."[36]

For Stevens, whose dealing with literary and nonliterary acquaintances
had been almost exclusively by mail, and who kept an efficient system of
records and updated addresses at the office, Latimer presented relatively little
problem. Indeed Stevens seems to have enjoyed the relationship more than
he might have otherwise *because* of the peculiar indefiniteness of his new
publisher. Like no other Alcestis poet, Stevens assiduously tracked Latimer's
every off-beat movement, with special doggedness during the last months of
the press, when he had to send letters to his publisher in care of "The Green
Shutters" (a gay bar along Charles Street), "The Grab Bag" (the grocery store
owned by one of Latimer's male lovers), or through one Vivian Stock at an
Albany address bearing no evident relation to Latimer (but where, as it
happens, I found Latimer's sister fifty years later).[37]

Stevens remained mostly unentangled, to be sure; as in his later ten-year
friendship with José Rodríguez Feo, he watched, followed, and enjoyed
Latimer, but balked at a certain point of closeness.[38] Only once did Stevens
really get caught up in his editor's unorthodox life. He met Lew Ney of the
Parnassus Press, Latimer's printer through mid-1936. Latimer and Maas had
been playing a game with Ney, politically a radical, a penniless man whose
"chief possession" was "a font of exquisite type" (*L* 283). Coming to the
Alcestis office to bring installments of proof sheets of *Ideas of Order*, Ney met
Maas but never saw Latimer himself, whose eccentricity it was the main rule

of the game to glorify. For Ney Maas referred to Latimer only as Mark Jason, letting on that Ney's Alcestis jobs constituted merely one of many projects this Jason had undertaken, that Jason was spending $10,000 on fine editions.[39] In reality Latimer and Maas, nearly destitute themselves, were well behind in making payments to Ney for his work (later, Latimer's poverty would force him to sell off his furniture and then, as a last resort, his rare books).[40] As Ney began to discern the real reasons for the secrecy, he sought a means of blackmailing Alcestis. Soon Stevens arrived in person, bearing the corrected proofs of Ideas of Order. Finding no one present at the Alcestis office, he telephoned Ney at home in Brooklyn; Ney came to town, allowing Stevens to deliver the "precious" (L 282) proofs by hand. Having made the printer come a long way, Stevens thought it proper to ask him to lunch, "which I really very much enjoyed" (L 283), during which Ney "had a great deal to say about Latimer, most of which I was sorry to hear."[41]

Stevens wrote Maas to clear the record. The letter shows Stevens's great receptiveness to Latimer's strangeness: "Perhaps [Latimer] could not have done as much as he has done without doing some of the things that Ney likes to talk about. . . . If Latimer had been a millionaire, both in money and in sympathy, he could not have done more for me than he has done."[42] This is not to say that Lew Ney's attempt to blackmail "Mark Jason" through Wallace Stevens had no effect whatever on Stevens, who was careful to protect his own reputation, especially among his colleagues at The Hartford. He did, after all, destroy Latimer's letters. (In 1934 Stevens was still storing in his office files at least some of the letters Latimer was sending;[43] it could only have been at some later point, then, that he decided to discard them, retaining only the carbons of his replies.[44])

When Latimer mentioned his desire to leave publishing altogether and to go into business, Stevens, who by then was one of a very few who knew of Latimer's enrollment in business school, assumed the young man's interest in insurance to be genuine and tried to help.[45] And as the usual problems of the small depression-era publisher began to mount, presumably made worse by rumors Ney was already spreading, Stevens continued to send his new poems. "At least Stevens sticks by us," Latimer wrote Maas at one especially desperate moment, "Bless the man."[46] Stevens did stick by Latimer, and not just the once when the risk of collaboration was wholly personal. He showed enormous patience and consideration when discussing with Latimer the possibility of doing a collection that would bring together all the recent work.[47] Stevens believed firmly, he told Maas, that Latimer was doing "as much for poetry in this country during the last several years than anyone else than I can think of."[48]

And Latimer stuck by Stevens. It was energetic and unqualified encouragement, and it made a great difference. Latimer rated Stevens highest among Eliot, Williams, Moore, and Pound,[49] and tirelessly promoted Stevens's verse just at a time when his poetic self-esteem was lowest. He told John Peale Bishop of his desire to make Stevens better known: "Wallace Stevens hasn't had the recognition he deserves. . . . I have as great an admiration for the poet as I have for the poetry."[50] Latimer knew everything about the latest little magazines, the more peripheral the better; before making his first approach, he had carefully followed Stevens's every halting step back into poetry, memorizing lines printed in the short-lived *New Act* and speaking knowledgeably of the Stevens poem in Chapel Hill's *Contempo*.[51] He felt that Stevens was "generous" in contributing to the *Alcestis Quarterly*, and spoke of his letters as "a real delight."[52] In many ways, it was an ideal poet-publisher association, especially at a time when advances were shrinking, production delayed by strikes, corners justifiably cut, and many otherwise good relations strained. Stevens's courtesy, in return, only amplified Latimer's support of the poetry; the greatest surprise awaiting the scholar who might pursue the Alcestis archive, aside from Latimer's communism, is the magnitude of the editor's campaign for Stevens's reemergence. Only Latimer's exertions made it possible for the number of poets discussing Stevens's two Alcestis books to exceed by many times the number of copies actually printed – a compelling twist in publishing supply and demand only possible with limited editions.

While attending Columbia College (see Figure 4), James G. Leippert and a few college friends had set up the *New Broom and Morningside*, and soon the *Lion & Crown*. To say the young man had a prescient eye for modern poetry is an understatement: As an undergraduate he published Charles Reznikoff, Carl Rakosi, Basil Bunting, Norman MacLeod, Conrad Aiken, and Gertrude Stein, and was one of the earliest advocates of George Oppen.[53] He could demonstrate a remarkable poem-by-poem familiarity with *An "Objectivists" Anthology* soon after its appearance.[54] Thus Williams could hardly scoff at so ambitious an editor, who now proposed an all-Williams issue at a time when such offers were unimaginable. He took the idea of the number to heart, and negotiations concluded eventually in the decision to have Latimer become William Carlos Williams's principal publisher – and that he might have remained, had not James Laughlin come along precisely when he did.[55] At various points Latimer and Williams discussed publishing the *Embodiment of Knowledge* manuscript,[56] the novel *White Mule*,[57] and the very beginnings of *Paterson*.[58]

As early as February 1933, Stevens had agreed to contribute to the Lion & Crown series of paper-bound selections of American poets. Leippert approached Tate by informing him that Stevens had already agreed to have "Peter Quince," "Le Monocle de Mon Oncle," and "Sunday Morning" reprinted along with, in Leippert's words, "some unpublished poems" otherwise unidentified.[59] By the end of April his list had already expanded to include Pound, Moore, Williams, Stevens, Tate, Bishop, H.D., MacLeish, Robinson Jeffers, and

Leonie Adams.[60] Sometime in June, Stevens sent his work (in care of "Martin Jay"; for some reason, the other poets had been approached by "James Leippert").[61] In midsummer the *Lion & Crown* gave way to the journal that would become *Alcestis*, though it was first to be called *Flambeau* and then *Tendency*.[62] Five of the eight new Stevens poems Latimer would publish in the first number of *Alcestis* were actually solicited for *Flambeau* and were in the editor's hands a full *fourteen* months before publication. (It is likely, thus, that "The Idea of Order at Key West" and "Evening without Angels" were written as early as mid-1933.)[63] By November 21, 1933, Latimer was soliciting contributions, writing on flashy *Tendency* letterhead (now pretentiously subtitled "A Magazine of Integral Form") and mentioning the illustrious names of his contributors, among them Erskine Caldwell, Aiken, Moore, John Gould Fletcher, Robert Frost, Mark Schorer, the radical Meridel LeSueur (fresh from wide circulation in one of Edward J. O'Brien's anthologies) – and Stevens.[64]

Figure 4. James G. Leippert at Columbia University, 1932. (Courtesy of Madeleine Hall.)

Putting *Tendency* aside, in early 1934 Martin Jay began to search around for a new idea. He wrote an acquaintance – it was Willard Maas, whom Latimer as Leippert had known from the Columbia English department – describing his notion of "a poetry quarterly which will aim to be the ultra-quarterly," and immediately mentioned that he already had in his possession new unpublished Wallace Stevens material.[65] Maas deferred his main objection to the nature of Latimer's program: the ideological implications of Fewer and Better. Many radical poets' poverty was so extreme (Maas was no exception);[66] their craving for sympathetic publishers so strong; their challenge to fancy limited editions still so relatively disorganized – that it was not unusual for Maas to feel he must hold his political nose when reading about Latimer's ideas for *Alcestis*. "Knowing your taste in rare editions, etc. I'm looking forward to a pretty ritzy spread, but wouldn't care if it were pink toilet paper if you could get out a new first-rate quarterly."[67]

Fortunately for the collaboration, Maas probably did not know about Leippert's own attempts at poetry. If he had, the scent of pure poetry on pink paper would have been too strong to ignore. "Monstreth," a poem "J. G. Leippert" submitted to the leftish *Contempo* – where Stevens published "The Woman Who Blamed Life on a Spaniard" just at this point – homo-eroticizes an Eliotic line:

> Over these roofs the chill
> light of the shadowed moon
> held in the sooty snow,
> twists & is gone again.

> Feeling ironical hands
> reach and reveal the cold,
> press and withdraw again
> into the gutter's folds.[68]

As "Martin Jay" he was also attempting imitations of Hart Crane, about whose gay life he was an earnest collector of anecdotes.[69] (One dense effort, "Poem for A.T.P.," includes phrases such as "Orondure of reversal," "sardonic revocation of desire," "Green tumult in this universe of flesh," "chromatic conclaves on this heart.")[70] Perhaps Latimer's development of a keen eye for modern poetry is all the more remarkable because his sense of himself as a poet was obviously so poor; if so, of course, it would not be the first time an uninventive poet became an inventive editor. Maas was impressed by his friend's ambition and knack for signing big names. By the time Latimer asked Maas to be his associate, the young editor could boast of having in his editorial drawer two long poems in the Stevens group, "as fine as he's ever done" (among them "The Idea of Order") and two short poems (probably "Nudity at the Capital" and "Nudity in the Colonies") as well as "four more Stevens" submissions, which Latimer had the luxury to "save . . . for a later issue." He was already speaking of doing a book – six months before he actually proposed this to Stevens! – called *Ten Poems of Wallace Stevens*, in an edition that would be strictly limited to one hundred signed copies.[71]

In just two and a half years with Latimer, Willard Maas would put himself in touch with some of the most influential figures in American poetry. Four issues of *Alcestis* brought out twelve poems by Stevens, three by Williams, nine by Cummings, four by Bishop, three by Fletcher, as well as the work of Blackmur, Damon, Robert Fitzgerald, Merrill Moore, Parker Tyler, and younger poets, all political radicals: Jack Wheelwright, Harold Rosenberg, Schneider, Rukeyser, Lechlitner, and Maas himself. Of the volumes of poetry Latimer published under the Alcestis imprint, only two first books, Maas's and Lechlitner's, were by little-known writers. The rest of the list is astonishing: Stevens's *Ideas of Order* and *Owl's Clover*, Williams's *An Early Martyr* and *Adam & Eve & the City*, Tate's *The Mediterranean*, Bishop's *Minute Particulars* and Robert Penn Warren's first book of poetry, *Thirty-Six Poems*. Latimer and H. D. nearly closed a deal on a book, after publishers had begun to ignore her.[72] The book he sought to do of Elizabeth Bishop's work would have been her first. As early as 1932 Latimer was urging Pound to let him publish new *Cantos*[73] and four years later approached Pound about doing a *Collected Poems*.[74] He was also prepared in 1932 to put out an entire issue of Louis Zukofsky.[75]

2: HEADED LEFT

Immediately after the publication of *Ideas*, Latimer asked and was given permission to pose questions to Stevens about the poetry. In the decisive period between *Ideas* and *The Man with the Blue Guitar*, Latimer's queries, many of them addressing the connection between poetry and social change, left distinct impressions on Stevens's changing idea of order. Although in response to Latimer's request to be permitted to ask questions Stevens warned "It would depend on the questions. It goes without saying that I should try to answer them, but whether I could remains to be seen," he did answer them, and rather systematically.[76] Even as he dodged a few ("I am going to skip your question about fascism") he could hardly resist some response ("Fascism is a form of disillusionment with about everything else") (*L* 295). It is obvious that these questions appealed to Stevens in some very fundamental way. Yet it is a fact that they were written by a communist – it was Willard Maas – whom Latimer hired to write them:

> *Confidential* (I don't want my literary sins to ever find me out . . .): I am in
> need of a "ghost" of sorts. . . . I want 50 pertinent *intelligent* questions on
> Marianne's *Selected Poems* and 50 on Stevens's *Harmonium* and *Ideas of Order*
> (or 50 each on the two Stevens if it cd/ be done). . . . I want to pop the
> questions at S. & M. now, while I have contacts . . . & I am so excruciat-
> ingly busy. . . . The remuneration isn't high ($10 – $15 total), I'm aware. . . .
> But the questions *must* be intelligent & really get at the meat of the works.[77]

So *this* is how Stevens came to ponder, as he began "Owl's Clover," not merely fascism as a "form of disillusionment," but also "whether I feel that there is an essential conflict between Marxism and the sentiment of the marvellous [*sic*]." Stevens's reply of December 19, 1935 (*L* 302) alone suggests that some rendition of the following questions had been posed:

> Q. Do you think art is or should be "to a greater or lesser extent didactic"?

> Q. If you were not working in business, could you devote your lifetime purely to poetry, . . . "leading the special life" of the intellectual?

> Q. [D]oes a poem about some natural object emanate from the object or from the poet?

> Q. Are there any specific reasons why in your poetry you favor Latin over Teutonic or "German" vocabulary?

Although Stevens's responses were "simply . . . off-hand" and he did not "want anything that I say in these letters to be regarded as anything more than a bit of letter writing," some answers were conscientiously evasive, for instance his reply to the perhaps leading question about German influence. Others were quite casual. One wants to know exactly what questions Maas and Latimer asked that provoked the long letter of October 31, containing Stevens's initial comments about Mussolini. (Had the interviewee perhaps smelled a rat?) Latimer and Maas began to put the same or similar questions to Marianne Moore at just this time. Because one of Moore's responses quotes part of the question, we can confidently guess that the diction of the questions posed to Stevens was also straight out of Emile Burns's just-then popular *Handbook of Marxism* or Engels' freshly translated *Socialism, Utopian and Scientific*.[78] Note Moore's reply: "I am not sure that I understand the second question – with regard to '*the mastery of facts as associated with the possibility of more effective action in the historical sphere*.'"[79]

Stevens and Moore each evidently understood the political position from which Latimer was now coming. We have already seen some of Stevens's responses – for instance, "I hope I am headed left, but there are lefts and lefts" (*L* 286). Moore, earnestly answering the awkward question she claimed she did not quite understand – surely she meant that it had been so dully put – wrote to assure Latimer that, as far as "the possibility of more effective action in the historical sphere" was concerned, poetry was largely immune to ideological pressure: "I would say that aesthetic expression is, with me at any rate, a kind of transposed and protected doctrine of existence."[80] Four days later she wrote again, having had time to ponder Latimer's purposes in asking such questions. In the meantime, a complimentary copy of the Alcestis edition of Williams's *An Early Martyr* had arrived, and she took the occasion of overturning Latimer's communist rhetoric to mention her disapproval of Williams's new radicalized manner: "I wish in [Williams's] desperation against the unchangeable and the abominable he need not come so near ruining his thrust. There is nothing like it when it comes straight. One is maddened sometimes into taking the wrong revenge. Perhaps we are all maddened, and not steadied enough to say what is wrong or what right."[81]

It is hard to know how completely Stevens sensed Latimer's leftward move. He seemed less certain in his resistance to others' political writing than did Moore. She was firm about Williams's ruinous radical "desperation against the unchangeable," whereas Stevens merely said, "I don't like any labels, because I am not doing one thing all the time" (L 288). Latimer's (or rather Maas's) question was apparently here, "Which means more to you, poetry or life?" and Stevens admitted after a few paragraphs that he was then at work on "Mr. Burnshaw and the Statue" of "Owl's Clover," trying to "reverse the process" of the communist responding to the poet by having the poet respond to the communist (L 289). He was now doing "one thing" at one time, after all; it might be interesting to say in letters how that felt *while* he was writing the poem. "Even in its present condition I should be able to trace a process of thought: analyse for you what I have written, and by that means illustrate by a poem which might seem largely gaseous the sort of contact that I make with normal ideas" (L 289).

Because Latimer as he corresponded with Stevens was increasingly obsessed with the notion of normalcy as a political (or rather anti-political – anti-gay and anti-communist) construction, Stevens's sense of his "contact . . . with normal ideas" cannot but be taken in the context supplied by Latimer's radicalization. Whatever interest in radicalism Latimer developed at Columbia – our only hint is that he roomed with someone whom his sister later described as an "evangelical" communist[82] – remained dormant until Maas became associate editor. But by the time Stevens had gathered the last poems into the typescript of *Ideas of Order*, Latimer's radicalization was well underway. He made a five-hour drive to hear a speech by Earl Browder.[83] He arranged to dine with Corliss Lamont, specifically with the intention of educating himself about the intellectual left wing.[84] He took to referring to himself as "the Albany Bourbon playing *Defender of the Faith*," supported Horace Gregory's poetry against conservatives' complaints, and described an angry letter from George Marion O'Donnell as written "in reply to my exalted defense of Marxism in literature."[85] By July 1935, he was expressing to Maas his real interest in "the publication of Communist literature"; Maas was thrilled by the prospect, and arranged to discuss the matter seriously.[86] A little later he officially joined the Communist Party of the United States and his "party assignment" was to work with the Workers Alliance. He did "some studying" of Marxist theory at the communist-run Workers' School.[87] Eventually he wrote a letter to the editor of the *Partisan Review* as "one member of the Communist Party" prepared to tolerate the work of that breakaway journal.[88] He even tried his hand at revolutionary poetry, though these were no more

publishable than the earlier imitations of Eliot and Crane. The new lines nonetheless document the changed thinking of Stevens's publisher, even if they utterly impugn its originality. It is quite enough to know how his "Battle Hymn"
begins: "Now we have come here to this last duty, called by revolution, the necessary / work of destruction that eventually brings / order from chaos & a final
peace." Other poems among the papers Latimer sold to the University of Chicago are similar.[89]

To be sure, the man who founded Alcestis Press in 1934 and published
Stevens in the first issue, was not yet *then* the revolutionist of "Battle Hymn."
On the contrary, as Stevens would have clearly seen, *Alcestis Quarterly* was provocatively conservative. The editorial statement introducing the first number plainly criticized "art for propaganda's sake." If the poet chose "to attack
social evils (as Messrs. Spender and Auden do)" he made "his art merely the
instrument of an economic theory." "[O]r should he (like Mr. Stevens and
Miss Sitwell) rather try to capture and intensify the beauty of things as he
sees them?" Though Latimer had agreed here that every poet "must make a
definite choice" between the two sides, *Alcestis* had at that point chosen
"purely artistic (as opposed to social) ends."[90] His swift radicalization coincides with the growth and then official party approval of the Popular Front
in 1935, and it is not atypical. But the effect of this change on Stevens cannot be underestimated, since here was someone who had, after all, named
him – along with Edith Sitwell – in the very act of marking out the reactionary argument.

Although Maas's new influence at Alcestis cannot properly be described
as communist "boring from within" (for one thing, Maas was only briefly
secretive about his communism), and while proselytizing Latimer was a
friendly and open matter and hardly the cloak-and-dagger sectarian strategy
of post-thirties mythology, the transformation of Latimer's attitude toward
poetry and publishing was spectacular. When he and his friends had prepared and compared ranked lists of American modernists back in 1934,
before the Alcestis project got underway, Latimer couldn't for the life of him
understand why the communist Maas had left Eliot entirely off his list.
Maas decided that that was the perfect moment to come out of the ideological closet.[91] "I personally might wish to see some revolutionary poetry
published," he wrote, and Latimer soon knew exactly what he was getting
in his associate editor. He strongly promoted Latimer's publication of Williams, knowing Williams was generally "on our side."[92] *An Early Martyr*,
Maas argued, was the most important of all Williams's works.[93] A year into
the venture he knew why "Maas can find nothing to admire but the format" in Allen Tate's book.[94] Maas tried to discourage Latimer from publishing Warren and Tate.[95] He asked Wheelwright's advice and received this:
"Perhaps your friend Jason could be persuaded that radical poets are the
modern argonauts. Work that way & see if you can nail him down more

securely, or he will turn." (He added: "I did not turn radical in order to get something to say but rather found that what I said turned me radical.")[96] Then Maas recruited Ruth Lechlitner to help him draw Latimer's attention to the communist argument against the Fugitives and their conservative protégés.[97] And when the attempt to block the publication of the Agrarians failed, and Lechlitner was angry with Latimer to the point of refusing to have anything more to do with Alcestis (and withdrawing her own book manuscript), Maas usefully calmed her: *Tomorrow's Phoenix*, Lechlitner's book of radical verse, emerged under the Alcestis imprint as planned.[98] Maas worked with closely with Lechlitner, who in spite of her Stalinism at this point was a regular reviewer for the *New York Herald Tribune Books*. He involved her in several important Alcestis decisions that tended to radicalize the venture. And he tried to arrange things with *Books* editors Irita Van Doren and Belle Rosenbaum so that the Alcestis books would go to Lechlitner for review rather than to the more traditional Babette Deutsch, even when, in Tate's and Warren's cases, and possibly also Stevens's, the result of such a maneuver might be a politically unsympathetic review.[99] There is no specific evidence to confirm my suspicion that the uncommon delay in the production of Tate's book was politically motivated (if it was, Latimer knowingly approved), but it is clear that energy and resources reserved for *The Mediterranean* were diverted to Stevens, and that Tate was "alarmed" about the evident bias.[100]

While Maas was never quite certain of the depth of Latimer's ideological commitment, its effect was satisfying enough. He acknowledged his friend and editor in the last poem in his own Alcestis volume, *Fire Testament*. "Accolade for the Sun," dedicated "To J. Ronald Lane Latimer," metaphorizes Latimer as the poetic left's great emerging patron, "flame for our thoughts, fire for our singing," equal in fervor to the sun itself.[101]

So the radicalization of Alcestis began the moment Maas wrote a rejoinder to Latimer's "inane" editorial in the first *Alcestis Quarterly*, to which the communist had taken "violent exception."[102] Damon had warned Maas not to worry too much over political differences, adding that, after all, in the inaugural issue Maas could be found in print alongside the best Stevens Damon had seen in years – quite a compliment to both Stevens and Maas from a powerful literary arbiter of the day.[103] But Maas, ignoring this moderate advice, and hoping for sustained comparisons to Stevens *and* a reliable communist aesthetic in the journal, fired off a letter to the editor (never printed) expressing disappointment that he had been an invited contributor and yet had not been given advance warning of the magazine's reactionary stance. He dismissed as naive Latimer's division of art into two schools (one for propaganda's and the other for art's sake), and urged the founder of *Alcestis* to read "Marx and Lenin and learn any number of things about poetry and art and their function."[104] In a separate letter not for print Maas urged Latimer to allow the two of them to "experiment" with the "issue regarding our differences," that issue being whether "there is good revolutionary poetry." Latimer then agreed that the fourth number of *Alcestis*, already scheduled for the summer of 1935, would be explicitly designated a "Revolutionary Number."[105] From that moment until July 1935 Maas surveyed the radical poetic field widely in Latimer's name, recruiting communists for the special issue and playing up the firm commitment to revolutionary verse. He was especially pleased that the revolutionary number would come out just as Stevens's book did – "imagine coming out simultaneously with STEVENS!!!!"[106] – convinced that the effect of such seemingly deliberate timing would be to assure his doubtful comrades of the high seriousness of Latimer's association with the eminent modernists. For reasons that will be made clearer in Chapter 5, *Maas never wavered in his judgment that Stevens's poetry made him an exception among incipient fascists, and never complained about its politics even while reproving so many others'.*[107] Maas assumed from the fact that Stevens admired his poetry – Stevens said so more than once,[108] then agreed to write a letter of recommendation in support of Maas's application to the Guggenheim Foundation[109] – that Stevens might feel similarly about his radicalism. (Stevens wrote Maas that his book "is filled with delicacy and delight and makes me feel that a number of things may be happening in the world I know nothing about."[110] He said as well that he hoped Maas would use Lechlitner's radical poetry as the basis for "telling the story of the Alcestis Press as it deserves to be told."[111]) And one of the special thrills of radicalizing *Alcestis Quarterly* and Alcestis Press, and of bringing Stevens along by association, was to be able to refute the claim of his closest political friends, for instance Lechlitner, that Latimer had fallen into the hands of the Eliotic Agrarians. He could hardly wait, he wrote Latimer, to hear what O'Donnell, a southern conservative, would think about the revolutionary number,[112] and he was elated at the alliance implied by the Alcestis brochure he helped design, namely that Maas's own poems, "whether . . . of love or revolution," were "*suggestive of Wallace Stevens' serenity*" (emphasis added).[113]

Maas kept Latimer informed about his work on the special issue. As press time neared he assured Latimer that the poets they would print in *Alcestis* 4 were indeed "*very close* to the group you represent in your last issue, *only they are Marxists*."[114] He felt that the aspects of that "last issue" (*Alcestis* 3) most persuasive of the journal's appeal to both sides were offered by Stevens: "Sailing after Lunch," "Meditation Celestial & Terrestrial," "Mozart, 1935," "The American Sublime," and "Waving Adieu, Adieu, Adieu." How exactly the revolutionary poets of number 4 were "very close" to Stevens in number 3, excepting their definitive "social" emphasis, must have made Latimer wonder – as it must have made Stevens wonder, in the very likely event that Latimer passed along Maas's intriguing evaluation. But it is clear that when Maas wrote that he wanted to make the revolutionary number "*strictly revo-*

lutionary on the *broadest* possible basis *despite* the fact that my sympathies are *all* with the Communists," he was not saying anything that would strike most radical poets as contradictory or illogical.[115]

Stevens in any case received the fourth issue of *Alcestis* and realized surely that no poetry journal was going to remain free from the influence of the left, even one that only three issues earlier had proclaimed a position inimical to this development. If it is at all significant that Stevens saw Alcestis moving rapidly left and considered himself, for better or worse, implicated in its reputation, it is especially important that as Alcestis made this move radical readers, poets, and editors would be gaining access to Stevens in their own context. When Harold Rosenberg applauded Maas's work with Latimer, saying "[I]t's a good idea to take over a bourgeois instrument and make the most of it," he meant that the special issue would slant the others.[116] Aside from the revolutionary poets of number 4 – among them, Rosenberg, Schneider, Wheelwright, James Neugass, and Rukeyser (Maas chose her emphatic "Child and Mother," which begins "Revolution shall be toy of peace to you, / Children")[117] – there was Lechlitner, already well known as a mainstream reviewer, announcing that Burnshaw was the best poet of the *New Masses* group.[118] And for Stevens there was, once again, Williams with whom to contend: Williams's "Fine Work with Pitch and Copper," published in number 4, was tonally and methodologically of a piece with the other leftist contributions. Stevens knew that Williams was writing to Latimer about the day *when* the revolution comes (not *if*); doubtless he saw that Latimer greatly admired "The Yachts," radicalizing *terza rima*; probably, too, that Williams was urging Latimer to be the one dauntless publisher to bring out Zukofsky's anthology of worker's poetry.[119]

Having brilliantly managed official relations between Latimer and the communist poets, Maas considered it only a matter of course that he would send all Alcestis books – certainly his own book *Fire Testament* and Williams's *An Early Martyr*, but also Stevens's *Ideas of Order* – to the communist *New Masses* for review. We must not now make the mistake of interpreting such a decision as anomalous or accidental. Latimer routinely approved, comprehending the politics of reviewing.[120] On Monday, July 7, 1935, Maas wrote Latimer in a business-as-usual tone that should inhibit any temptation to assume belatedly that the forces bringing Burnshaw and Stevens together were extraordinary rather than ordinary. "I am so glad you felt you could give New Masses review copies," Maas wrote. "I merely sent Stevens's prospectus to [Isidor] Schneider with a note." He wrote again the next day: "I think it will be no end of fun reading their reviews, especially if some good critic like Schneider gets them, and I imagine he'll do them himself since the books are worth keeping to say the least."[121] With this new information one cannot conclude that when Isidor Schneider handed over Wallace Stevens's *Ideas* to Stanley Burnshaw at the offices of the *New Masses*, two poetic spheres converged eccentrically. For it was in the routine course of publication and reception that Stevens would be read, and criticized, by the thirties left. Burnshaw, seeing *Ideas* placed on his desk, never assumed once that writing on Stevens would be anything *but* "no end of fun." Asked recently if he remembered receiving and reading the book, Burnshaw laughed and said, "Rather, yes. I was fascinated. . . . I greatly admired what he had done in *Harmonium*."[122]

3: THE POLITICS OF LIMITED EDITIONS

Stevens seems to have known all along that putting out his new poems in expensive limited editions could only hurt his case with the left. Indeed, because of his informed sense of the American economy he was more keenly aware than most poets that "the status of the book de luxe is disintegrating about as rapidly as other things de luxe."[123] Occasionally he would tell Latimer directly that he was "appalled" at his editor's taste for fancy editions.[124] Latimer made no apologies for the high quality of his projects: "We shall use an Italian hand-made paper," he once blithely wrote Maas, "and a highly unusual but lovely french type known as Incunabula. It's an exotic type and hasn't been used in this country more than two or three times."[125] The all-rag Alcestis *Ideas of Order* held fifty-four pages of text and no fewer than seventeen blanks. It cost $7.50. (Kenneth Burke's 351-page *Permanence and Change*, nearly seven times the length of Latimer's production of *Ideas*, was one-seventh the price. A complete, unabridged *Ulysses* was published by Random House at about the same time, at $3.50. H. H. Lewis's radical *Salvation* cost twenty-five cents. Knopf's 2000 copies of *Ideas* itself would be priced at $2.)

If Stevens's giving hints of discomfort – being "appalled" when Latimer seemed inclined to overdo it – did not serve to warn Latimer of a new politics of Fewer and Better, then a number of others, Maas, Lechlitner, Wheelwright, Williams and, later, James Laughlin, warned him explicitly. When Maas wrote that he was delighted by Latimer's interest in educating himself about "Communist dialectics" and in publishing "Communist literature,"[126] a discussion about the basic materiality of books began. It ended with Latimer coming all the way around from the right, where a certain sophisticated but unarticulated bibliophilic materialism, utterly unassociated with Marxism, had always intrepidly put the work of typesetter, designer, and editor on an equal footing with authorial labors.

Even assuming that such a theoretical move could be smooth – it never is – there remained other basic problems. Lechlitner wrote Maas: "My objection to the Alcestis books (one objection, at least) is that they cost too much per copy for the people to be able to afford."[127] As she was about to sign her contract with Alcestis for the publication of *Tomorrow's Phoenix*, she warned, "I don't approve of limited editions in general."[128] Wheelwright felt similarly: "As for submitting a MS to Alcestis: I would be glad to do so, but

I hope the price comes down as it seems very high to me and certain to deprive authors of their public."[129] Even Laughlin, the young well-to-do founder of New Directions – "crawling with enthusiasm," said Stevens[130] – did not purchase Alcestis books because of "scruples about the price."[131] Laughlin admired Latimer's taste and hoped that Alcestis could align its ideas about publishing more with contemporary circumstances and "be able to bring the same good poetry *to the general reader*"[132] – as he sincerely hoped New Directions books would do. One way in which the socially conscientious publisher could respond to the depression was to produce books cheaply; another, often but not necessarily related to the first, was to make them available to "the people," as Lechlitner was recommending. Maas described the greatest success of recent American revolutionary poets as a breaking down of the boundary that had kept older modernists from modern readers; only the irresponsible publisher stood potentially between them.[133] Certainly this was Williams's most vehement position on the matter, as paraphrased by Paul Mariani:

> [W]ho knew better than Williams himself the futility of getting out deluxe editions for the few who could afford them, as Latimer was doing for him[?] . . . Cheap paperbacks were probably the closest approximation modern society had to getting the poem out by word of mouth, "next to Homeric singing [as Williams put it] and a universal stage." After all, it was publication that had become the weak link in getting the word out: fine paper, fine type, managerial costs, distribution costs. . . . What was needed now, then, was for the hundreds of Woolworth's five-and-dime stores across the country to serve as the medium in Depression America to get books . . . out to the people. Later someone might do the deluxe editions for art's sake. But for now: cheap and wide distribution and availability.[134]

As Latimer and Laughlin both painfully realized, this was much easier said than done. Williams's strong political position – to my mind he would hold no stronger – needed qualification of the sort he was not then inclined to make. Others' bitterness about Fewer and Better seemed equally impractical. Stevens at least recognized and accepted that this was no time for Knopf to be publishing poetry like his – that even in a trade edition he might get favorably reviewed but would not sell in large numbers when publishing was as precarious an enterprise as any other. Perhaps here again Stevens's own sharp moral discernment of the climate for business offered him insights which radicals might have consistently shared but which many did not – Williams among them, despite his robust practical streak.

While Williams would seem to toe a party line at least on the politics of Fewer and Better – publication had become the "weak link," and economics largely determined design and styling – Williams's position was not so ideologically unambiguous after all. What he appreciated most about writing was having power over the end result, and that, with Latimer, he had. "I'd rather have what work I've done come out in fine small books," he readily admitted to Latimer, "than in any other way – but I feel hedged round – would rather not appear at all than to become precious – it affects everything, gets under the skin, into the bone at last."[135] On one hand, then, Williams "felt funny being published in an expensive format which no one ever saw," while on the other, he freely "admired the craftsmanship and design that the small fine press could give a poet's work."[136]

If getting out his proletarian verse-portraits in a run of 165 copies seemed an "incongruity," surely a much greater incongruity would have been leaving them altogether unpublished.[137] Maas's arguments for cheap editions and wide distribution contained the same impossibly doubled expectation. As he discussed with Latimer plans to bring out communist literature, Maas thought Alcestis "might publish Spender and Lewis *deluxe.*"The books must be "printed as cheaply as possible" yet, somehow, "still printed *distinctively.*"[138] The complaint about price was a necessary sign of the radical position. While in the cases of Williams, Maas, Lechlitner, and Wheelwright it certainly was just that, the same could not be said for Zabel, who wrote Maas to ask if he might obtain special, cheaper copies (perhaps bound sets of proofs that were otherwise to be discarded).[139]

Nor should it be supposed, conversely, that communists opposed limited editions as a matter of course. When in 1935 Burnshaw and James Daly discussed founding a limited-editions press, there was no hand-wringing about the political correctness of such a venture.[140] What counted against a deluxe edition, if anything did, was the use to which it was put, the claims implied by the context of publication. John Reed's *Tamburlaine, and other verses* (1917), a prized possession on radicals' shelves, got its value from rarity and fine paper: Just 450 had been made. (A jacketless, well-thumbed, unsigned copy in 1991 was worth $350.) This was Henry Hart's favorite point about presswork throughout his generation's radical period. The Equinox Cooperative Press issued handsome, fancy limited editions of the Hickses' biography of John Reed (1935) and Reuben Osborn's *Freud and Marx* (1937). Isidor Schneider's *Comrade, Mister* (1934), "an 88-page book," Hart later recalled with pure pleasure, has fine "paper that forty years haven't brittled, an attractive layout of the type (Bodoni Book), and a binding of pristine originality." Granted these are *much* later words, chosen long past Hart's red days as editor of *The Writer in a Changing World* (1937). Still "attractive layout" and "pristine originality," or even "deluxe," were not nearly the epithets among book-loving radicals that might be assumed.[141] In January 1935 the *New Masses* carried a prominent advertisement for the book *Hunger and Revolt: A Revolutionary History of the World Crisis*, promoting it as: "LIMITED! AUTOGRAPHED! / DELUXE EDITION / ONLY 100 COPIES!" – a book that could be obtained through the *Daily Worker* at the exorbitant price of $5.[142]

Just as this ad appeared, the Party was beginning to take a new line on limited editions. The "Call for an American Writers Congress," which would provide the basis for forming the League of American Writers, the most prominent of the cultural popular-front organizations, proposed a number of subtle changes anticipating the official Comintern policy shift six months later. One of these preliminary changes was the call for "wider distribution of revolutionary books and the improvement of the revolutionary press, as well as the relations between revolutionary writers and bourgeois publishers and editors."[143] If radical writers began to work with potentially sympathetic editors and publishers, the result would be better exposure of revolutionary writing, even if that meant in limited editions. Certainly Willard Maas's instincts as a radical poet, in having agreed to come on as Latimer's associate editor six months earlier, would be roused by this new call. It came at the time Latimer was persuaded to give over editorial control of the "revolutionary" issue. It is hardly an accident that two days after the League's "Call" was published, Lechlitner was writing Maas that if she could think of any more "left-wingers for the secret" she would tell him without delay.[144] The "secret" was hardly a subversive conspiracy – again, Maas never once, in the several hundred letters I have seen, felt himself to be infiltrating Alcestis.[145] That Latimer should now publish communists was openly advocated, and Maas found the situation thrilling. As Lincoln Steffens put it when engaging the liberal E. A. Filene in Modern Age Books: "I love to let a capitalist say things to a Red that Reds prefer to tell capitalists."[146]

The whole point of the new Alcestis policy, as a matter of fact, was that it was itself less a strategy of concealment – Reds speaking to Reds through capitalists – than an open invitation to associate freely and candidly with "bourgeois publishers and editors" previously anathema under left-sectarian policy. Now that the communists were urging radical writers to make radicals' writing available in any way possible, there could be no single, self-evident "line" on limited editions. This is not to say that the *New Masses* would cease its vigorous campaign against the reactionary idea that poetry was written for a special, small class of readers. Orrick Johns's review of Moore's *Selected Poems* (1935), to take one of many examples, expended a good deal of its energy attacking T. S. Eliot's promotion of Moore; when Eliot claimed that "the genuineness of poetry is something which we have warrant for believing that a small number, but only a small number, of contemporary readers can recognize,"[147] Johns replied that on the contrary "good art . . . should be of a nature to be desired by the largest number of the people." "No critic of a great age that I know of," Johns wrote, "has felt his praise of poetry grow as its number of admirers diminished. [But] Mr. Eliot says just this."[148]

To no one's surprise, Allen Tate was coming at the issue from Eliot's direction. Unlike Eliot, though, Tate deemed Fewer and Better just a matter of smart, self-respecting business, and he made this case directly to Latimer:

Withstand all accusations of elitism and political retrogression; concentrate simply on making a profit. Contrary to liberal belief, Tate argued, the ordinary trade edition of a book of poetry did not reach even the small public that existed for it, selling perhaps 200 copies. The limited edition of 200 copies responsibly filled the need created for it; the people who will own the book will be the people who truly wanted to become its readers.[149]

Tate was surely right on the quantitative matter of copies sold, though his argument fails a simpler test. The price of the limited editions he wanted Latimer to continue publishing, on his own principle of good literary business unencumbered by an ideology of mass printing, was as a matter of fact exorbitant *even for the poets themselves* – the best representatives of Eliot's very special class of readers, Tate's stable market. Samuel French Morse, already Stevens's great admirer – eventually aspirant to the role of official biographer – would seem surely to be one of those special readers; yet Morse could not afford to buy Stevens's *Owl's Clover*.[150] Even the president of the Poetry Society of America did not have the cash handy to buy an Alcestis book at $7.50.[151]

Stevens's respectful interaction with Alcestis demonstrates that he saw good poetry and reliable publishing as integrally creative activities – that he knew Latimer deemed "these editions [to] represent my attempt to be creative"[152] and admired the editor-publisher as "one of those writers who never write."[153] Especially when "the status" of books was "rapidly . . . disintegrating," Stevens sensed that "[a]ll that remains intact is the printing of it, because, of course, the printing involves the artist."[154] The same modest expectations he held about making money from his poems[155] he assumed Latimer to hold about publishing them. In suggesting this point he came closer to Latimer's view than any of the Alcestis poets, communist or reactionary, Maas or Tate. If Latimer felt pressure from his other poets to sell books and secure reviews in prominent places, Stevens obsessed no more about selling large numbers of the books he wrote than Latimer obsessed about selling large numbers of those he published (*L* 296). And if the other Alcestis poets, not having taken the time to see the actual circumstances in which Latimer was forced to operate – the loans assumed, the debts evaded – could not abide inevitable errors and delays,[156] then Stevens was unusual in being extremely generous in this regard.[157] He was keenly interested in publishing as a physical aspect of producing poetry. "It is easy enough to accept a wellmade book without realizing how much has gone into it," he wrote to compliment Latimer on the production of *Owl's Clover*. He added, "I hope that the reviewers do *you* justice," meaning that the book should be read as a thing in itself alongside notions it conveys textually (*L* 312; emphasis added). It is remarkable enough to imagine Stevens spending an evening reading the Alcestis limited edition of Lechlitner's *Tomorrow's Phoenix*, a book of unapologetically radical lyrics, but still more extraordinary that he would come away with a clear sense that the effect of Lechlitner's political poetry was bound up intellectually as well as literally in the work that went into making the book – an effect Lechlitner's unpublished correspondence shows was wholly devised.[158] When she wrote of poetry's "superb mechanics," she meant poetry as a labor of great change: In the poem she felt to be the book's best,[159] "Of What Superb Mechanics," she began by addressing the poem itself, the very marks pressed onto the page:

> Of what superb mechanics are
> The wheels of change, the cycle driven;
> And what equation for a star
>
> Set us in motion? You and I . . .
> Behold us as we multiply.[160]

"As I sat reading TOMORROW'S PHOENIX last evening," Stevens wrote Latimer,

> I thought how necessary it would be to an evaluation of the book to know what had really gone into it. I mean not only Miss Lechlitner's struggle with the world and the people in it, but your own struggle with the world and the people in it, and even the devotion of the man who set the type. What a love (it is nothing else) for the things they love this shows on the part of each one of the three![161]

Publication was a bargain struck between poet and publisher (and "the man who set the type") in which the poet was only holding up one end if reviews were favorable; he enjoyed confronting his own – and occasionally, as with Lechlitner, others' – poetic discourse as "a particular deed of language," in Jerome McGann's phrase; publishing poems with Alcestis made them more than ever for Stevens, and excitingly, "an institutionalized event in communication which takes place according to certain rules and possibilities, and which has particular ends in view." This sort of bibliographic historicism, a revitalized critical discourse, has been speaking of the way in which poems that are read through "their documentary codes" provide readings no less concrete than other kinds of readings.[162] In the case of *Ideas of Order*, a year earlier, the integration of book-as-thing and text-as-idea seemed to Stevens just the right mix of creations. The mix also satisfied Maas no end, which shouldn't be a surprise, for it was just the sort of awareness the literary left was trying so energetically to inspire in American poets – works of art informed and literally impressed by superb mechanics that send them on their course beyond a mind. Stevens beheld a sample of the type Latimer had chosen for the book and said, "the size of it seems even to influence the effect of the poem."[163]

Of course the particular "effect" Stevens had in mind – "just a bit precious"[164] – was not specifically what the left hoped for when they called for materialism to embrace books. Yet the very same intense interest in synthesized intellectual and physical process, attention to the work and workers involved in the operation, led Stevens, in perfect harmony with Maas, to take a position about the printer's role that the young communist greatly admired. Latimer, in his outrage at the rumor-mongering Lew Ney, had decided to leave the printer's name off the colophon of *Ideas*, even though, as Maas argued, Ney was largely responsible for the labor that made the book what it was; for Maas it was a significant crisis of political conscience, even though he shared Latimer's personal dislike of their printer. When Ney read Latimer's letter informing him that his name would be deleted from the colophon, he was "very sad," as Maas reported it back to Latimer. "I really believe you might get more out of him by conceding his name as designer of printing as he has it on the colophon," he wrote. "As he said, 'Here I sit up nights working on yours [Maas's] and Stevens['s] book, trying to make it perfect in design and I won't even get credit for it. . . .' [I]t's just his name as a printer."[165] Latimer had tried to convince Maas that Stevens "seemingly doesn't care" if the printer's name is left off even a hand-made book, but there is no evidence of such an attitude in Stevens's letters to Latimer. On the contrary, second- and third-party correspondence suggests that he did care greatly about Ney's role, and when Maas convinced Latimer to raise the issue with Stevens, the poet approved the colophon with Ney's name, took care when handling page proofs to correct an infelicity in the wording,[166] and "complimented [Ney] on make-up and again talked of beauty of type, etc."[167] The now-rare Alcestis *Ideas of Order* properly bears the identity of the printer who set the book by hand and distributed the type afterward.

Maas could only applaud this sensitivity – on the left it would be routinely called a "political sensitivity" – as exceeding that in many of his comrades'. But it did not come in the usual way, for Stevens's interest in publishing as a taxing, physical yet in itself creative procedure doubtless arose from his attitude toward managing his own elaborate insurance work. Those who recall Stevens at The Hartford have generally remembered that when he was preoccupied by the work it was because of his fascination with the process.[168] His "business" advice, then, was very unlike Tate's: he reminded Latimer that publishing is like "the practice of law, or . . . running an insurance office," where the idea that "everything depends on sales," rather than being an end in itself, is an occasion for great intellectual investment. This was "in the long run the most fascinating part of the work."[169]

When Williams finally saw *An Early Martyr* he seems to have shifted his posture on limited editions, at least in order to pay Latimer due compliment. First he said, "I have always taken the attitude that it didn't make the least difference how a thing was printed so long as the quality of the writing was good" – a statement that contradicted the political position he was taking all along when expressing his discomfort with publishing at Alcestis. Nevertheless, he added, "This is the first time I have been inclined to change that opinion. Really, the appearance of the page as you have chosen it is superb."[170]

Latimer was not unaware that in Williams's case – if not in the case of Maas, who was far more ideologically orthodox – he would have to appeal to the poet's desire to see his work distributed widely. He proposed to do Williams's *Collected Poems*, an offer Williams took very seriously; the plan involved a "masterpiece" limited edition on "fine paper" at $15, and then a month or two later a trade edition produced from the same type beds on "ordinary paper" at $2.50 or $3.[171] When Williams asked about the legal arrangements, Latimer made the tactical error of explaining how he and Stevens had come to an agreement: Stevens had retained copyrights while Latimer had reserved the right to publish "deluxe firsts," so that Stevens would be unencumbered in his decisions with Knopf to publish "later, *cheaper* editions" (emphasis added).[172] But Williams did not want to make Stevens's sort of arrangements, enlightened or not. His horror of publishing books that were "precious" again intensified. It may be that the not-always friendly rivalry with Stevens was bringing out the worst in him. In large part this must be explained by the weakness in Williams's political position on limited editions relative to Stevens's surprisingly strong one.

With Williams, nonetheless, Stevens could not win; it revealed an attitude about Stevens in the thirties assumed by some contemporaries and passed down semiconsciously through decades of assumptions about the book-form Stevens's elitism took: If Stevens stood firmly by Alcestis and continued to publish in editions that the poets themselves could not afford to buy, let alone the masses, then Stevens's work was politically incorrect; yet if Stevens returned permanently to Knopf he would be selling out to big interests, gaining access to print for which he didn't have to work poetically hard, making poetry for profit. In a mood stirred by these thoughts, Williams sat down to write his review of *The Man with the Blue Guitar & Other Poems* for the *New Republic*. He drafted a spiteful first paragraph later deleted. In several manuscript versions he takes the particular ideological double standard further. Not only does he upbraid Stevens for returning finally to Alfred Knopf, a bourgeois publisher; he also makes Knopf's commercial book seem at the same time *like a precious limited edition*! Here is one version of the excised false start:

> Stevens has got himself published by a reputable commercial house. He is one of the few modern American poets to experience capital investment. More power to him. They've given him an attractive volume in bright yellow boards, costing them, I don't know, four or five hundred dollars. It's a good buy.[173]

An earlier opening ran this way:

> Without capital investment the market for poetry, like every other market, regardless of values, will slump. Poetry here is in a chronic slump. But Stevens has got himself published by a good firm.

A still-earlier draft began with: "Money is power, a power." Here Stevens was

"one of the few modern American poets to experience capital investment. . . . Maybe there is money in it. Who knows."[174]

If Stevens was hard to place politically, and seems to have brought out confusion in everyone, even in Williams, who among poets knew him best, the
confusion certainly extended to the very means by which Stevens's poems
were produced. After complaining enviously of Stevens's reversion to Knopf
– Williams himself, after all, craved a financially stable publisher – he wrote
what in the *New Republic* became the published opening of the review:
"The story is that Stevens has turned of late definitely to the left. I should
say not. . . . No use looking for Stevens there – without qualifications."[175]

Convergences

4

The Rage for Order

compilations of notes
Things   mosaic
　—pencilings made by Stevens in his copy of Marianne Moore's *Selected Poems* (1935)

Williams had that rather silly language theory. . . . Wallace Stevens was more of an influence, I think. At college I knew "Harmonium" almost by heart. . . . But I got tired of him and now find him romantic and thin – but very cheering, because, in spite of his theories (very romantic), he did have such a wonderful time with all those odd words, and found a superior way of amusing himself . . . . [B]ut HARMONIUM certainly made a big impression on me in 1932 or 33. . . . He shouldn't have tried to theorize, perhaps.

　　　　　　　　　　　　　　　　　　　　　　—Elizabeth Bishop in 1964[1]

It should be said of poetry that it is essentially romantic as if one were recognizing the truth about poetry for the first time. . . . [T]he romantic is referred to, most often, in the pejorative sense, and this sense attaches . . . to some phase of the romantic that has become stale.

　　　　　　　　　　　　　　　　　　　　　　　　　—Stevens (*OP* 183)

[W]hen a culture begins to take the descending curve . . . the speed of the fall is great. . . . No longer are the old questions of technique alive.
　　　　　—Orrick Johns, reviewing Marianne Moore in the *New Masses*[2]

The contemporary romantic is a revolutionist.

　　　　　　　　　　　　　　　　　—Stevens, in a notebook jotting[3]

I: OBJECTIVISM AND SENTIMENTALISM

Williams was understandably surprised when Stevens called him a romantic. Surprised, yes – but the feeling soon gave way to anger, and Williams held for years a grudge that has been described many times since William Van O'Connor decided back in 1950 that Stevens was "refus[ing] to accept the connotations . . . the terms *romantic* and *realist* usually hold in our time," or, in other words, that Stevens was confused.[4] Williams had not realized, when the epithet "romantic" was first attached to him, that Stevens was himself searching for what through much of 1934 and 1935 he repeatedly called "the new romantic."

Nor could Williams have known then that Stevens was projecting onto others what he wanted for himself.[5] If Williams and his objectivist allies had perceived Stevens's projection as such, it might have helped to explain why Stevens put such odd and contradictory readings into that irksome preface to Williams's *Collected Poems, 1921-1931* (1934), a piece that had been written for the Objectivist Press of Louis Zukofsky, Carl Rakosi, and George Oppen. For here, in an essay planned as early as September 1933 and which Williams received and read in December, and undoubtedly passed around among the objectivists,[6] Stevens made claims about Williams's romanticism seemingly abhorrent to the members of that group. It seemed to indicate that Stevens wanted to take Williams in a direction in which they would never consciously go. Yet, as I hope to show in telling the story of Stevens's strange neoromantic moment, by the end of 1935 his sense of poetic "things" was broadly in line with their own.

Much less flattering than the word "romantic," perhaps, was its clumsy cousin "sentimental." Actually, Stevens did not really mean sentiment so much as, in his words, "the *reaction from* sentiment." Williams's poem "'The Cod Head,'" he wrote, "is a bit of pure sentimentalization; so is 'The Bull' .... What Williams gives, on the whole, is not sentiment but the reaction from sentiment, or, rather, a little sentiment, very little, together with acute reaction" (*OP* 213). This ironization of sentiment was actually a radical standard of the day. In Kenneth Patchen's line, "We can't get there by taxi-cab or sentiment,"[7] where "there" means nothing less than political martyr-dom, "sentiment" is wonderfully diminished by juxtaposition with the everydayness of "taxi-cab." Stevens, I think, was observing the same of Williams, a perception that was quite similar to William Phillips and Philip Rahv's criticism of Williams's political trendiness: "W. C. Williams," they wrote in "Literature in a Political Decade," "merely added the proletariat to his store of American objects."[8] And even Joseph Freeman's otherwise uninsightful preface to the poetry section in *Proletarian Literature in the United States* was keen to this modernist sleight-of-hand: when "relatively established poets . . . came to the important decision" to write poems expressing political opinions, they saw that "the art for art's sake doctrine" had in early modernism been "made a little more respectable by transformation into the new scientific-sounding term, 'objectivity.'"[9] But the difference between Rahv and Phillips and Joe Freeman on one hand and Stevens on the other was that the latter had obviously gotten significant pleasure from Williams's poem "Brilliant Sad Sun," with its distinctly post-romantic imagism-*cum*-proletarianism, its relentless nominalizations, its unremitting clarities, its "hard facts" – that combination of features suggesting to some poets then, including the Patchen of *Before the Brave* (1936), a tenable relation between one strain of modernist poetics and political radicalism. Harry Roskolenko, a socialist and later member of a radical anti-Stalinist splinter group, fashioned in his verse an "Aesthetics in Our Time" mindful of the way in which it at times merely reimagined imagism put to revolutionary uses, "the phrase, the image / shattered by shock of falling glass and rock" – the main effort being "*to hollow, not hallow* / in briefer intensity of leaner language, / not fattened in the mind's ornate theatre."[10] The radical poet H. R. Hays similarly saw that "facts are the preoccupation" of the objectivists while "the socio-economic bias of much of contemporary thinking puts a premium on facts as a basis for argument,"[11] and Louis Zukofsky welcomed the fact that "in Marx's economy, of all economies, alone there is substance for doing the new canzone."[12] Onto Williams's "Brilliant Sad Sun" – notwithstanding its dependence on "facts," a "bias" Hays would approve and an "economy" Zukofsky's Marx would allow – Stevens knowingly affixed the term "sentimentalized"![13]

Something was happening here other than an attempt to name, or willfully misname, Williams's newest aesthetic ideology. According to the reading presented in this chapter, the designation "new romantic" was already for Stevens far more strategically significant than conceptually coherent. Note that he hardly differed in this respect from Stanley Burnshaw. In his own complaint against Zukofsky's lauded objectivist number of *Poetry* (1931), Burnshaw described the objectivists' version of Williams as traditional and even "charming," both terms intended as profanities.[14] In this climate, Stevens's criticism of Williams actually gained currency among radical poets expressing reservations about objectivism. At least one such radical, Hays, understood that Stevens's use of "sentimentalized" was meant somehow to justify the discrepant use of the word "antipoetic."[15] Another, the poet Charles Henry Newman, in an essay titled "How Objective Is Objectivism?," disputed Williams's claim that he "discards sentimentality (because it is 'unreal') for objectivity" and concluded that "Wallace Stevens . . . aptly" sees sentimentality coming in again through the back door.[16]

Stevens felt a powerful urge to classify in literary-historical terms Williams's obsession with low-cultural verities, the distinct American objects advertised by (in Stevens's words) "signs [for] Snider's Catsup, Ivory Soap and Chevrolet Cars" and gleaned from the "rotten newspaper" (*OP* 214) to which democratic modernists like him deliberately subscribed. And yet the same poet whom Stevens saw willingly finding *materia poetica* in that local rag, and whose poems picked sociably through the city dump, at the same time "dwells *alone* with the sun and the moon" and "dwells in an *ivory tower*" in order to grant from on high such a view of the cultural low (emphasis added). "Something of the unreal," Stevens wrote in the preface, "is necessary to fecundate the real; something of the sentimental is necessary to fecundate the anti-poetic" (*OP* 214).

Only in these astonishingly qualified ways was Stevens able to concede, for the moment, that Williams and poets doing similar work were credible poetic objectivists. But he fully understood that Williams and Zukofsky and their colleagues had made what Michael Davidson calls a "fatal pact between modernist objectivism and materiality."[17] Antipoetic material that did not eschew referentiality, a belief in the very "possibility of matter to think" (in Zukofsky's phrase),[18] a preoccupation with phrasal reproductions of the American everyday, displayed in, say, Rakosi's "666 for colds and fevers";[19] or Oppen's mere use of the word "Frigidaire" (of a piece with Patchen's "taxi-cab" but more forceful) and a ringing depression-era phrase in headline diction, "man sells postcards," in a poem pointedly called "Bad times";[20] or, in Williams's own objectivist interval, his feeling for

> *surfaces* of all sorts
> bearing printed characters, bottles
> *words* printed on the backs of
>
> two telephone directories (emphasis added)[21]

or the soda sign in "The Attic Which Is Desire," a view boldly replicated on the page,

```
★ ★ ★ ★ ★ ★ ★ ★ ★ ★ ★

★                     ★

★         S           ★

★         O           ★

★         D           ★

★         A           ★

★                     ★

★ ★ ★ ★ ★ ★ ★ ★ ★ ★ ★[22]
```

– all these inscribed "surfaces," these lucid presences, these "historic and contemporary particulars,"[23] Stevens was working hard to fathom as deeply sentimental! It was a shrewd move. Roskolenko's rule of thumb – "hollow, not hallow" – might be understood as just a new sort of the traditional hallowing. Indeed the next point in Stevens's piece on Williams was that the sentimental and the antipoetic finally shared common ground. This, Stevens felt, was going to define a new romantic in such a way as to create, potentially, an alliance that would include radicals like Trent and Cheyney, who based their political poetry on the modernist tenet "Any subject can be made poetic," and modernists like Stevens himself, who saw "That the whole world is material for poetry" and "That there is not a specifically poetic material" (*OP* 189).

Williams was mistaken if he thought Stevens was not fundamentally enamored of those early thirties portraits of the everyday, attracted now to the measuring mind quite as much as to the interpreting mind, to objectivist presenting as much symbolist meditating[24] – and perhaps thus to Zukofsky's brand of objectivism generally. (The extant evidence is such that it might never be clear how attentively Stevens read Zukofsky, Oppen, Rakosi, and Charles Reznikoff beyond the "Objectivist Number" of *Poetry*,[25] notwithstanding Marianne Moore's recollection that "he had been reading Zukofsky and liked the work"[26] and at least one strongly suggestive letter Stevens wrote Rakosi.)[27] Nor did Williams see how the term "romantic," if fastened just so, could make facticity palatable to a modernist who had nurtured himself on symbolist forebears but was nonetheless trying to prepare himself to look beyond "the solitary realm of his own mind" for and at "things." "Romantic" was becoming a literary-political term for Stevens, signifying his strong craving for a contemporary poetic. Such a strategic use of the term would take him several conceptual steps forward, even as its application to Williams could do nothing but serve as a shorthand for an indictment against modernist backtracking – from objectivism's advance beyond imagism, backward, say, to teens- and twenties-style Amygism or naive orientalism.[28]

As muddled as his 1934 preface must have seemed, I am contending, Stevens knew what trouble he was causing. In hinting at a romantic aspect of objectivism, he was going well beyond any then-known connotation or criticism of the objectivists' much-touted reaction against settled modernist rhetoric; in turning around the charge of poetic rhetoric as a form of self-delusion[29] and associating it with romantic sentimentalism, he was also effectively doubting their sometimes reductive adherence to "the real," their alleged unwillingness to see a whole forest for a particularized tree.[30]

The objectivists keenly sensed this criticism, we can be certain; after all, they saw themselves as providing the link between the imagist revolution, in which Stevens and Williams had both had a hand,[31] and the social revolutionist's immediate "object," presented rather than meditated. And Stevens's contentious description was offered with similar contentiousness from the literary left. Having been brought into American view by Burnshaw in his book *André Spire and His Poetry* (1933), Spire's poem "Peasant Women," quite similar to Williams's so-called proletarian portraits,[32] was met with this comment by a socialist reviewer: "Here is obviously a sentimentality born of mere empirical observation of external details with no ability to ascertain the basic relations that determine them."[33] For

Stevens no such Marxist rhetoric – not even a bad imitation of it – was ready for trying on quite yet; for him it was not that Williams's objectivism neglected to spell out "basic relations" that "determine" rendered externalities. He did wisely see "[t]he ambiguity produced by bareness" (*OP* 214) that might be remedied in a frank admission of metaphysical fullness, however unfashionable such an admission might be.

Despite his own doubts about how objectivism could manage sentimentality, then, and notwithstanding whatever tentative alliances new modernist -isms were making with the left, Stevens told Latimer in 1935, in answer to one of Maas's hired queries, that he was thinking again about a modernist past, as it were, when he had "liked the idea of images and images alone" (*L* 288). He knew, in other words, the value of an imagism updated by new-fashioned poetic materialists. He understood how some radical poets might approve, as Ruth Lechlitner did, of "the strong social implications beneath" Williams's surfaces, and how the same radicals could look back on the modernist revolution and see the basis of just that: "[W]e can now see," wrote Lechlitner, "that there *was* import" in the imagist "cumulative meaning back of the object as symbol" – in imagism as a "renascence of realism."[34] "Now" it was possible, too, that Stevens's attention could be caught by Williams's unironic sense of fortunate "fine weather" suffusing depression figures in poems such as "The Sun Bathers": the thawing tramp, the "begrimed" war vet, the "fat negress."[35] So, too, in a poem showing Oppen at his most avidly proletarian, a steam-shovel operator, satisfyingly steadfast in "*firm* overalls," offers the contentment of locating his machine's almost bodily response in deftly managed muscularity, to boldly idealized physical proficiency. The "falling" at the end of that quintessentially objectivist poem in Oppen's book *Discrete Series* thus was not to be lamented or deprecated in the least, nor meant as a value in decline, but a kind of modernist unionism.[36]

Efforts to understand the state of the association between Williams and Stevens at this confusing moment have been made even more difficult by Stevens's projection of his search for a new romantic onto Marianne Moore as well. In early 1935 Stevens was asked by the young radical poet T. C. Wilson to write a review of Moore's *Selected Poems*. A little later in the year, as it happens, Moore was writing a review of Stevens's *Ideas of Order*. Putting together unpublished materials in the Wilson, Moore, and Stevens archives, one can see how deeply Moore's review of Stevens was influenced by Stevens's review of Moore, even while the former was still being drafted, for T. C. Wilson had enthusiastically made himself an intermediary between Stevens and Moore. Stevens and Moore did exchange a few letters directly in this period. But Wilson received letters from Stevens describing his new romantic, and *Moore's* new romantic; Wilson then quoted to Moore excerpts from Stevens's comments about Moore. In Moore's responses she was reacting to Stevens as conveyed to her by Wilson; and, as we will see, Wilson was selective in his extractions of Stevens's letters. While Stevens wrote to Wilson and Moore about neoromanticism, he was also describing it to Latimer as an approach to his new ideas of order, just as he was organizing the manuscript of poems for the Alcestis Press limited edition that would soon take that title. While Williams saw that Stevens's introduction had clarified the basic differences between them, now that the thirties had elicited from both poets general prose statements about what Williams was regularly calling "things," Moore decided that Stevens's introduction to Williams's book demonstrated a basic *similarity* between the two men. In her own review of Williams's Objectivist Press *Collected Poems*, she saw Williams as a bee attracted to the flower of representation, yet "drugged with romance." "[A]nd," she added, "Wallace Stevens is another resister, whose way of saying what he says is as important as what is said. . . . [P]oetry in America has not died, so long as these two 'young sycamores' are able to stand the winters that we have, and the inhabitants."[37]

Complicating the situation still further was Stevens's sense of the pejorative connotation of the literary-historical term "romantic" as it was used in this period. Even the most theoretically sophisticated faction on the left denounced its use. What we might for the moment describe as a thoroughly strategic and mostly untheorized literary radicalism, as exemplified by Granville Hicks's "Our Revolutionary Heritage," had taken to using "revolutionary" as a synonym for what Kenneth Burke called, in registering complaint, "that humanist word 'romanticism.'" Burke saw that Hicks, in his effort to "claim nearly every outstanding American of the past for the cause of revolution," had merely substituted "revolutionary" for "romantic." Thus, said Burke, Hicks "was able simply to reverse the humanist attitude toward romanticism, taking as a *good* what had formerly been a *bad*. But romanticism is not *per se* revolutionary."[38] The much commoner form assumed by radical disapprovals of "romanticism becom[ing] decadent," the version far more accessible in the intellectual weeklies, repudiated "over-emphasized . . . feeling" as "an escape from reality" (in Eda Lou Walton's nasty appraisal of Robinson Jeffers).[39] Since Stevens would take to heart the project of circumventing the pejorative reading of romanticism, whether elaborately negative like Burke's or plainly negative like Walton's, it must be recognized that the romantic was not in Stevens's view merely misconstrued by those who used the term in the popular sense to re-name (and denigrate) intuition and to wield doctrinal axes against poetic "sensibility," but also by a sophisticated aesthetic left that deemed the term pejorative because, unlike "revolutionary," it merely "noted the attitude of rejection that ran through all nineteenth-century romanticism."[40] This was to be precisely T. C. Wilson's complaint about Stevens as expressed privately to Moore – that Stevens sustained a prepolitical "attitude of rejection."

Stevens seems to have been aware of this particular pejorative romanticism. Looking back from 1940, he narrated for Hi Simons the 1933–35 episode, stressing that the search for a new romantic was disappointingly similar to the quest conducted by many other poets for a utopia to be induced by the revolutionary left. He recalled "the time when I, personally, began to feel round for a new romanticism." He remembered that by the phrase "new romanticism" he meant a renovation of aesthetically satisfying faith: apparently, following his already well-established convention, an epistemologically enabled "fiction" that would "suffice" after orthodoxies of transcendental belief had been once and for all repudiated. During this search, one special form of neoromanticism – namely communism – "almost stole the show," Stevens recalled, understating the thirties comically (L 351). "*Communism is just a new romanticism*," he obligingly explained to Simons (emphasis added). While "I believe in any number of things that so-called social revolutionists believe in . . . I don't believe in calling myself a revolutionist." I think he meant that insofar as communism was a new romantic form, and insofar as he saw the neoromantic compulsion to be methodologically modernist while sentimentally old-fashioned, he would have entertained communism as a poetically valid possibility. But this merge of romanticism and radicalism – especially in 1940, with much turmoil behind him – could not have indicated his readiness to do "everything practically possible to improve the condition of the workers" (L 351).

Although most new uses of the term "romantic" had by 1934 or 1935 been defamed by politicization, Stevens deliberately used the phrase "new romantic" during a period in which he was gathering together recently published poems, composing new ones, and organizing all of them for his first book in a dozen years. On March 25, 1935, the day before he informed Latimer that he had turned over his book manuscript to his secretary at The Hartford to be typewritten, he wrote T. C. Wilson that he had decided "Williams represents a somewhat exhausted phase of the romantic" and that it was time, finally, to turn to "Miss Moore." It was she, he said, who was "endeavoring to create a new romantic" (L 279).

Meantime, Wilson was energetically engaged in his correspondence with Moore, sending and receiving letters that took up the engrossing problem of Stevens's reputation in the thirties. Wilson was finishing his career as a doctoral student at the University of Michigan, had already published poems and reviews in *Poetry*,[41] and was an associate editor of *Westminster Magazine* when Stevens published three poems there.[42] *Westminster* was rapidly gaining its high standing, for which Wilson was largely responsible.[43] The issue containing new Stevens work also included poems by Williams, Oppen, and Maas, and Williams's essay on H. R. Hays.

The controversial subject of Stevens's new work arose when Wilson wrote Moore excitedly that he and Ezra Pound were co-editing a "special poetry number" of *Westminster*, planned for 1935, and soon called by all parties "The Westminster Anthology."[44] Pound wanted to recruit mostly young writers for this selection, Wilson told Moore, but would be willing to include poems culled from the big names, including Moore herself, Williams, Eliot, "etc."[45] Moore responded by suggesting five unheralded poets to her own liking: William Justema, associated with the once-prestigious *Hound & Horn*; Winifred Ellerman, or Bryher, then editor of *Life & Letters*; a recent Vassar graduate, Elizabeth Bishop; Melville Webber, whose film *Lot in Sodom* Moore had reviewed in *Close Up*;[46] and one W. W. E. Ross, of Toronto, whose "Irrealistic Verses," a sequence of extraordinarily traditional poems, were appearing just then in *Poetry* and in whom Moore saw great "ability" (she herself had published Ross's work in the *Dial*).[47] Evidently ignoring the suggestion of Bishop ("I do not think she is quite ready for print"[48]), Wilson did agree to seek W. W. E. Ross, but Pound later vetoed the idea of including any such "Irrealistic Verses" in an anthology in which he had a hand.[49]

By the beginning of 1935, Moore was wondering why Pound had excluded Stevens. She could not have known it, but Pound had long tried to ignore Stevens's work[50] and, when hearing of Zukofsky's plan to have Stevens write the preface to the Objectivist Press Williams, wrote: "yaas yaas Mr Wallace Stevens IS back in Bill's epotch, the retiring daisy esthete."[51] Nor, moreover, could Moore know that the latest version of Pound's dismissal of Stevens came on broadly political grounds:

> Stevens' ?????? the amateur approach, the gentle decline to take responsibility of being a writer ??? . . . or am I wrong ? . . . It is not Stevens['s] ISO-LATION, but his damnd laisser aller attitude RE/ *his* writing that gives me the ache. . . . "Boundt, haff you gno bolidtical basshuntz?" said Slovinsky in 1910.[52]

Wilson, undoubtedly also a recipient of Pound's acid opinions on Stevens, was losing, though not as rapidly, his own "bolidtical basshuntz" for the businessman-poet from Hartford. He explained (and translated) for Moore Pound's rationale for the selection:

> [Pound] does not feel that "neat and orderly expression" is of value unless accompanied by [an] awareness . . . of the "crude, yes crude ambience." . . . [I]n all cases, he has shown preference for verse dealing with strikes, murders, decadence, the decline of capitalism. . . . I suppose this accounts for his omission of Miss Bishop, Mr. Ross, Mr. Webber, Mr. Justema, Wallace Stevens, and several others.[53]

The company Stevens was keeping here presented a confusing lot; no less confusing to Moore, probably, was Wilson's ill-founded assumption that

Pound was moving leftward. Further, she could understand why Pound's "preference for verse dealing with strikes, murders, decadence and the decline of capitalism" would provide him reason to include Williams and other objectivists such as Oppen – as he did – even though Pound had already expressed dislike of Williams's "Proletarian Portrait" on the grounds that it was unremarkably didactic (the woman in the poem "might have done as well in Russia as in Passaic," was Pound's crack):[54] "Her shoe in her hand she is looking / intently into it – // pulls out the paper insole to find the nail // that was hurting her."[55] Yet Pound did decide also to include Moore's "Frigate Pelican," a poem embodying the "neat and orderly expression" that Pound, per Wilson, was thunderously denouncing.[56] Moore might have fretted a little about appearing with "this *most romantic* bird" (line 41; emphasis added) in such a politicized context, however successfully Pound contaminated and contradicted Wilson's editorial leftism.[57]

Just then Stevens emerged from his silence in a big way: "Like Decorations in a Nigger Cemetery" appeared prominently in *Poetry*, filling ten pages of the issue. Reading that epigrammatic series in special relation to Pound's political program for *Westminster*, Moore wrote *Poetry* editor Zabel:

> I am glad to see Wallace Stevens placed first. He is perhaps not at his maximum but valuable things occur all through the series. . . . *Ezra Pound's dissent from Wallace Stevens in favor of economic verse** does not hinder one from knowing that Wallace Stevens is unusually "talented"; and I am convinced that Mr. Ross and Elizabeth Bishop are talented.
>
> * for the anthology Mr. Wilson has been assembling.[58]

Moore's reiteration of her interest in the verse of W. W. E. Ross is barely explicable, despite Harriet Monroe's support.[59] That she was constantly endorsing Elizabeth Bishop before Bishop had published a single line outside Vassar is one of the celebrated gestures in modern American literary history. Hardly less effective was Moore's willingness to stand by Stevens during this trying time, as her fearless defense of him in a review of *Ideas of Order* would soon reveal. But, again, what she saw in Ross is hard to fathom. So hard to fathom, indeed, that Stevens, exhorted by Moore to read a collection of Ross's sonnets, *Sonnets of ER* (1933), reacted so strongly against the outmoded rosiness there that he wrote a poem embodying his critical response. Moreover, the poetic retort to Ross – and, by implication, to Moore's sense of the romantic – incited notions about poetry's relevance to the depression, ideas largely uncharacteristic of other poems Stevens wrote this period. Presenting to Stevens a gift copy[60] of Ross's sonnets, Moore's first provocation was her suggestion that in Ross's poetry one might see a version of Stevens's: "In reading this book I thought of you a number of times."[61]

In the last section of *Sonnets of ER*, a sequence of sonnets declaring qualified relation to romanticism by going under the title, "Somewhat 'Wordsworthian,'" appears a strikingly undistinguished poem, "On Solitude":

> There is a sadness lies in solitude.
> Go to some hill when sunset gilds the sky,
> And gazing west to watch the bright sun die
> Below the clouds with gaudy colors imbued,
> See the tall lonely pines as still they brood
> Moving their branches as if solemnly,
> Urged by the evening breezes fitfully,
> And standing as for decades they have stood.
> All, all is silence and the setting sun,
> Fading from sight but not from mind has left
> And world to solitude given over. Now done
> The day, and all is now bereft
> Of earthly joy, the sun's companionship,
> As lonely as the sea-borne empty ship.[62]

It is difficult to imagine how Moore was seeing the faintest reflection of Stevens here, although she might have been thinking of his "Autumn Refrain," a sonnet published in the *Hound & Horn* in its Humanist moment – a work expressing its own reluctant relation to romanticism by indicating how for Stevens the grackles' hard skreak and skritter had muscled off preferable soft "words about the nightingale." And there, after all, Stevens did use the "sorrows of the sun" to set the scene. The sun of "Autumn Refrain" was a foregone thing, rendering untenable a romantic renewal for modern verse. But Ross's "gazing west to watch the bright sun die" stipulated genuine sadness only intellectually. In poetry like Ross's the setting sun makes merely for gorgeous sunsets; there are forced syntactic inversions ("the clouds with gaudy colours imbued"), uninventive meter ("Fáding from síght but nót from mínd has léft"), and imperatives lacking any force ("Go to some hill"). In Stevens's "A Fading of the Sun," on the contrary, he began by reacting against this point:

> Who can think of the sun costuming clouds
> When all people are shaken
> Or of night endazzled, proud,
> When people awaken
> And cry and cry for help?

Insofar as it counters Ross's "setting sun" ("*Fading* from sight but not from mind"), "A Fading of the Sun" also responded, generally, to pejorative romantic tropes (the clichés of solitude, sadness, the fitful wind, the dazzling natural scene, and so on). It represented an educated poetic guess as to the tendency in his work that had led Moore to read *his* neoromanticism into Ross's. The result was that Stevens pushed himself away from poems like "The Brave Man" – the brave man there is the sun facing a new day – and toward a revised romantic he deemed appropriate to the thirties. In this context the opening lines might be paraphrased as follows: Can any poet today continue to speak of "the sun costuming clouds" in the hackneyed sense (Ross's "sunset gilds the sky . . . / Below the clouds with gaudy colors"), when so many desperate people "are shaken," crying out for the poet's special form of "help"? What is the "responsibility of being a writer" – to borrow from Pound's "bolidtical" objection – in answering or at least reproducing that cry? The "fading" of the sun marked the degeneration of such romantic tropes. If Ross could say, in "Irrealistic" verses for the realistic thirties, that the disappearance of "earthly *joy*" is a function wholly natural, Stevens would have to express uncharacteristic doubts. My point is that he very knowingly did:

> If joy shall be without a book
> It lies, themselves within themselves,
> If they will look
> Within themselves
> And cry and cry for help?
>
> (*CP* 139)

"A Fading of the Sun" was published in November 1933, its composition precisely contemporaneous with the introduction Stevens was then submitting to the objectivists for Williams's *Collected Poems*. To prepare for this, Stevens re-read Williams's work and found a number of poems of special interest: "Ah, Madam," Williams wrote in "Brilliant Sad Sun," "what good are your thoughts / *romantic but true* / beside this gaiety of the sun / and that huge appetite?"[63] Questions raised by Moore's promotion of Ross, and the presentation of the sun in "A Fading of the Sun," were now finding answers in a vague but coalescing program. "It will be observed," Stevens wrote, "that . . . the person addressed in 'Brilliant Sad Sun' [has] been slightly sentimentalized. In order to understand Williams at all, it is necessary to say at once that he has a sentimental side. Except for that, this book would not exist." The reading of Williams's *gay* sun in relation to the woman's *abject* poverty thus justified Stevens's rather shockingly plain opening remark that Williams "is a romantic poet." ("This will horrify him," Stevens confessed. "Yet the proof is everywhere" [*OP* 213].) Horrifying to Williams as it might have been, Stevens's reading of "Brilliant Sad Sun" was perfectly consistent with the undertaking then forming. Williams's poem is another proletarian portrait and, at that, an expression of and for the very people who "are shaken" – the condition that Stevens had recently suggested in "A Fading of the Sun" put tropes like Ross's "sun costuming clouds" at the utter dead end of romanticism. If Ross was indeed *somewhat* Wordsworthian, the woman Williams addresses in "Lee's

Lunch" was able to locate the "gaiety of the sun" in the midst of impoverished scantiness, in sadness and sorrow, the sort of sorrow that caused Stevens finally to offer the depression-shaken people in "A Fading of the Sun" good bread and meat in the closing lines:

> The tea,
> The wine is good. The bread,
> The meat is sweet.
> And they will not die.

Williams's new romanticism – based on the ostensibly antiromantic idea that a poet was to be less interested in the word as symbol and more in its concrete reality[64] – taught Stevens that economic depression would arouse (and its poems would visually contain) not old images of the sun, but new inventive ones, replicated from the bold, typographically brawny menu lying on the counter at Lee's Lunch:

> Spaghetti   Oysters
> a Specialty   Clams
>
> and raw Winter's done

The subsequent question gets directly at the surprising psychoaesthetic abundance of poverty, and yet conveys the emphatically spare look of the poet's page:

> What are your memories
> beside *that* purity? . . .
>
> What beauty
> besides your sadness – and
> what sorrow
>   (emphasis added)

2: A MORE SUBTLE WAY OF REFERRING

The dilemma posed, at opposite lyric extremes, by Ross's old-romantic "On Solitude" and Williams's new-romantic "Brilliant Sad Sun," had already been articulated by Stevens in a series of poems written in 1932 and 1933. These roughly form a group in which the tone is reticent and the implied background is the cultural failure of belief: "The Sun This March," "Autumn Refrain," "Snow and Stars" and "A Fading of the Sun." They seem collectively to say: A depression-era poet cannot submit to a degenerate romanticism, a misplaced optimism (where, after the monumental failure of structured belief, one turns merely, for instance, to a gorgeous sunset); and yet, one cannot merely articulate despondency. The latter disillusioned or "defeatist" position, in a period increasingly dominated by radical utopianism ("bitter . . . despair" entailing "a [hopeful] challenge to revolt"[65]), risked being read as part of a political as well as an aesthetic reaction founded on "pathological introspection."[66] Moore might have un-intentionally implied this criticism when she likened Stevens to Ross, whose irrealistic verse was so much less devoted to thirties-style realism than Stevens ever wanted to seem; evidently, it helped push him toward the new modes. And T. C. Wilson, arguing his own leftist poetic ethics for Moore while Moore was preparing her Stevens review, took just this view, making it the basis of an ideological criticism that Stevens would soon hear directly from Burnshaw.

Poems comprising the next distinct group – works of 1934, chief among them "Winter Bells," "Gray Stones and Gray Pigeons," "Evening without Angels," and "The Idea of Order at Key West" – suggest that Stevens made a clear decision in the process of trying on a neoromanticism for 1935. Halfway from the disinterested ironist Stevens of the late teens and early twenties to a neoromantic Stevens of the thirties that never quite came into being, he would test the possibilities of a Humanism then current. That Stevens could use such -isms more or less interchangeably is merely an-other sign that he was willing to allow himself to be placed within several seething controversies. Once he could find himself so positioned, in other words, he might then discover how the opinions defining these disputes were themselves often confused, even at times mutually inclusive. By the fall of 1933, when he wrote his piece for the objectivists, he managed to bring opposite terms together in that odd but unreductive version of the romanticist-classicist argument that had raged in the late twenties, a feud that in the early thirties still commanded the attention of modernists left and right.[67] This was certainly the case with the so-called "Humanist con-troversy," in which the *Hound & Horn* figured famously.

Stevens was in contact with editors and critics at the *Hound & Horn* from 1929, when he began corresponding with Richard Blackmur, through 1932, when the magazine published the sonnet "Autumn Refrain." If dur-ing the period in which Stevens was loosely associated with the *Hound & Horn* he was looking toward it and to its editors to help him settle on a definition of modern poetry that would account for its post-Christian as-pect, it would have been propitious for him to learn that in the fight be-tween the orthodox Humanism of Irving Babbitt and the Humanism of the so-called "revisionists," the *Hound & Horn* was coming squarely down on the side of the revisionists; the latter group, in the words of one of the editors, called on *all* Humanists "to cease decapitating the Hydra heads of romanticism."[68] That is, while romanticism was still a "pariah" in the of-fices of the *Hound & Horn*, it was not generally thought that Babbitt's mis-take was in thinking the romantic could never be renovated into an ac-ceptably modern form. The unwavering group, led by Babbitt and Paul Elmer More, responded to the revisionist challenge with a collection of essays under the title, *Humanism and America*. The revisionists countered with *The Critique of Humanism*. Even if Stevens did not wish to take sides here – though my point is that he would have sided with the revisionists because Babbitt's followers precluded the possibility of a new romantic – a side was chosen for him. One of the essays in *Humanism and America*, Stanley Chase's "Dionysus in Dismay," reproved Stevens by name for belonging to a faction of modernists who disabled the "romantic devotion to what is picturesque in the storied past" and who displayed "the consciousness of intellectual defeat and spiritual dismay."[69] Whether or not it was designed as such, "Autumn Refrain" must have seemed to some at the *Hound & Horn* a confirmation of Chase's decision to place Stevens with the revisionists. Merely by its stress on the word "gone" – "The skreak and skritter of evening gone / And grackles gone and sorrows of the sun, / The sorrows of sun, too, gone" – the poem emphasizes what is checked, perplexed, inert or, in short, *stilled* (". . . and being still, / Being and sitting still, something resides . . . / the stillness is in the key") rather than stressing what humans are capable of imagining. The titular word "Refrain" points in the prosodist's sense to a repeated theme, and as well to the tone or attitude of the poem itself, double work that causes signs and sounds of reticence to proliferate:

> gone . . . the *moon* and *moon*,
> The yellow *moon* of words

> I *have never – shall never* hear . . .
> Though I *have never – shall never* hear that bird . . .

> the *stillness is* in the key, all of *it is*,
> The *stillness is* all in the key. . . .

>   (CP 160)

If one were to follow closely a development along these lines in Stevens's new poems, as Blackmur did after "Autumn Refrain" had come his way,[70] one could have seen a movement from high modernism to some other critical creed that might have provided a model of Humanism realized in modern poetry. But the Humanist line, whether orthodox or revisionist, mapped another dead end for Stevens in this period of searching.

The migration from "Autumn Refrain" to "Winter Bells" and "Gray Stones" to "The Idea of Order at Key West" can be characterized as a move from disillusionment over the ineffectiveness of certain modernist attachments to romanticism (grackles, alas, replacing the nightingale), to an obsession with the failure of the church, to a new confidence in the human capacity to realize the satisfying law of inhuman proportion. In "Gray Stones and Gray Pigeons" the archbishop's holiday departure is an obvious symbol for a church emptied of belief; what remains is the material church (CP 140). In "Winter Bells," something of a companion piece, the physical site of belief (specifically, here, a synagogue), its vestments, chimes, and so forth, leads naturally to the idea that the believer would follow "the custom / For his rage against chaos" and "go to Florida one of these days," where, with a Stevens poetically vacationing, he would find a new form of sufficient fiction in "the little arrondissements / Of the sea there" (*CP* 141). Of course this "rage against chaos" would lead Stevens directly to the next, momentous step: "The Idea of Order" of 1934 is almost certainly contemporaneous with "Gray Stones" and "Winter Bells."[71] The rage against chaos in "Winter Bells" suggested Stevens's endeavor to try on for size some raiment of Humanism, to follow the tenet of Babbitt to which even the revisionists still solemnly subscribed, notwithstanding their feeling that their mentor had overdone the otherwise justified attack on romanticism. This was the Humanist principle of "proportionateness" – that one ought to live by "Nothing too much," ought, in the view of the more moderate Humanists, to borrow whatever one could from the configurations of classicism before submitting to the modern appeal of romanticism (thus a *rage* for *order* in Stevens's terms was not contradictory). Too, as Babbitt himself concluded, "the world would have been a better place if more persons had made sure they were human before setting out to be superhuman."[72] In shrewdly breaking down the fallacious Humanist distinction between classicism and romanticism, the French critic Ramon Fernandez explained how "romanticism" had come to earn and deserve its pejorative sense. "The idea of the inhumanity of the work of art," Fernandez wrote, "is one of the most uselessly false ones ever produced by *debased romanticism* in its reaction against *genuine romanticism*."[73] Looking back on the thirties from the forties, Stevens explained his brief venture in Humanism specifically in relation to "Winter Bells," yet in terms that generally support a correlation between the "natural substitute" offered in "The Idea of Order at Key West" and Williams's "romantic" passion for cultural objects:

> [T]he strength of the church grows less and less until the church stands for little more than propriety, and . . . after all, in a world without religion, propriety and a capon and Florida were all one. . . . [T]he Jew [of "Winter Bells"] is a good example of the man who drifts from fasting to feasting. I ought to say that it is a habit of mind with me to be thinking of some substitute for religion. . . . My trouble, and the trouble of a great many people, is the loss of belief in the sort of God in Whom we were all brought up to believe. Humanism would be the natural substitute, but the more I see of humanism the less I like it. . . . In its most acceptable form it is probably a baseball game with all the beer signs and coca cola signs, etc. If so, we ought to be able to get along without it. (*L* 348)

"The Idea of Order at Key West" concedes a main Humanist idea – Babbitt's notions of proportion and poise – while yet moving away from the centrality of the human:

> and yet its mimic motion
> Made constant cry, caused constantly a cry,
> That was *not ours* although we understood,
> *Inhuman*, of the veritable ocean.
>
> (*CP* 128; emphasis added)

The qualification of Humanism here is overt, but becomes even clearer when the poem challenges the critic whom the *Hound & Horn* editors coveted for their journal – namely Ramon Fernandez. The tone is one of admiring but confident refutation:

> Ramon Fernandez, *tell me, if you know*,
> Why, when the singing ended . . .
> . . . why the glass lights, . . .
> Mastered the night and portioned out the sea.
>
> (*CP* 130)

After establishing that the poem itself provides a voice singing a song beyond us and yet ourselves, the argument turns to the critic with – coincidentally (and misleadingly) – the floridian name, suggesting that he might clarify the situation: We beseech you to describe, though it might be reasonably doubted that you can, not the effects of the rage for order but why the vital need resides in us (a neoromanticism), and is yet an even measure outside or "beyond" us (a neoclassicism).

> Oh! Blessed rage for order, pale Ramon,
> The maker's rage to order words of the sea,
> Words of the fragrant portals, dimly-starred,
> And of ourselves and of our origins,
> In ghostlier demarcations, keener sounds.

In an essay translated by one of the *Hound & Horn* editors and publicized as one of the fruits of the merger of that magazine with the *Symposium*, Ramon Fernandez, writing "On Classicism" in recognition of "the centenary of romanticism," and undertaking to invalidate the distinction between the two, observed the following about the rage for order: "The desire to judge, and to order one's life by judgment, concerns more than mere abstract activity; it is no intellectual game, but a vital need." The human compulsion to order the stimuli and things around oneself implied for Fernandez, as for the neoclassicist, a "renunciation of the wealth of feeling." Such disavowal of "feeling," however, means "only that man, after having proved his powers, wants to complete and harmonize them by adapting them more exactly to the world and to himself, and that he accepts all the consequences of this exactitude." We must once again take romanticism seriously, Fernandez argued, if only because "the great weakness of the neo-classicists is that they set out to *feel* only what they have already *comprehended*."[74]

There is no way to be certain Stevens saw the Fernandez essay, but it seems to me very likely. Letters from Blackmur to Stevens confirm that he subscribed to the *Hound & Horn,* and generally indicate that he followed it issue by issue.[75] When the editors announced that the magazine would merge with the *Symposium,* they publicized the names of writers and critics who would contribute to the inaugural issue, both in the pages of *Hound & Horn* and elsewhere, such as the *New York Times,* where Ramon Fernandez' piece on classicism was prominently listed.[76]

Through his correspondence with Blackmur, Stevens was to realize that there was much more ideologically to the *Hound & Horn* group than Humanism. Allen Tate's "The Fallacy of Humanism" would have appealed to Stevens less as a form of reaction than of revisionism.[77] But it was Blackmur who first fully explained to Stevens how the new critical school, led by I. A. Richards and his student William Empson, could somehow be contained theoretically by a single literary magazine that also more or less successfully contained Humanists and Agrarians. Tate, for instance, had reviewed Richards's *Practical Criticism*[78] in such a way, Blackmur felt, as to "point [out] the beginnings of clarity in my confusion"; he envied Tate's certitude, worried about his own lack of it, and told Tate that "the *way* in which I have examined Cummings and Stevens" (the latter in his essay "Examples of Wallace Stevens") was one of two basic ways "of examining poetry" – the other being, presumably, Tate's. Blackmur implied that Tate, being more ideologically assured, saw one side of Humanism and not two at once, and might have handled Stevens more coherently.[79] By 1933 the agrarians, no longer heavily invested in the *Hound & Horn* project, could refer to Blackmur among themselves as "a prize old lady," evidently for his lack of theoretical mettle;[80] and by 1934 Blackmur and Tate had broken on political grounds.[81] Blackmur was looking ideologically elsewhere. He earnestly approached Cowley to express an interest in the "consequences involved in a writer's becoming a radical"[82] and he dined with *New Masses* editors, Horace Gregory included, an event creating the feeling that "Blackmur is a much more forthright person than you would imagine from his writings."[83]

⸎ But at the end of 1931 and in early 1932, when Stevens and Blackmur were corresponding about the long essay on Stevens's poetry, the concept of "ambiguity" had not yet received so angry a cultural reading as it later would. Blackmur sent Stevens a draft of the essay, apologizing for failing to treat the author as if he were "dead a century." He wanted to know if Stevens would "give proximate glosses to certain individual poems," in particular "The Emperor of Ice-Cream," so that the critic would know if he had "distorted your meaning beyond all justice."[84] Stevens's reply, dated November 16, 1931, explicated "The Emperor of Ice-Cream" (1922) by updating "ambiguity" to the social-realist thirties and by distinguishing his use of the term from obscurity, equivocality, or evasion. First he wrote, "If

I am right in identifying a certain ambiguity as essential to poetry, then I am wrong in explaining, because, if I destroy the ambiguity I destroy the poem." He also knew that if he endorsed ambiguity as "essential to poetry," he must be certain to stress for Blackmur that "Ambiguity does not mean obfuscation," and that the poem does not avert reality but, on the contrary, takes a "respite from the imagination" by working with commonplace realities ("dresses of every day, work clothes; cast off newspapers").[85]

> Let the wenches dawdle *in such dress*
> *As they are used to wear*, and let the boys
> Bring flowers *in last month's newspapers.* . . .
>
> Take from the dresser of deal,
> *Lacking* the three *glass* knobs. . . .
>   (CP 64; emphasis added)

Even when reread forcefully as a thirties poem, this could never quite corroborate Oppen's "object[s] sharply defined" (in Williams's phrase);[86] nor Williams's "undistorted," "solid," "stable" things "standing squarely against abstraction" (in Rakosi's phrase);[87] nor "brilliant sensual appearance" integrated with "grim but real underlying significance," to use Williams's semipolitical trope of descriptiveness thirties-style.[88] Yet Stevens's new sense that "[a]mbiguity does not mean obfuscation," a view attained when he was asked by Blackmur to look back at his own early work, was a significant advance toward the special social acuities of "Owl's Clover" and "The Man with the Blue Guitar."

The November 16 letter to Blackmur is important not only, then, because it provides a fine thirties reading of a twenties poem. It also suggests that Stevens was, at least generally, familiar with Richards before Blackmur, in his immediate reply, associated Stevens's explication with the notion of ambiguity put forth by Richards's protégé Empson. Blackmur was delighted by Stevens's willingness to go further than even he himself would have in the effort to establish "ambiguity as the *explicit* value of poetry." Citing Empson and Richards both, he noted that Stevens would "see how much I have made use of the word [ambiguity] in the paper on you" – this "paper" being the comprehensive "Examples of Wallace Stevens." He urged Stevens to read *Seven Types of Ambiguity* and identified Empson's (and to some extent his own) relation to the master: "Empson was a student of I. A. Richards at Cambridge, and when I asked Richards if the dedication, which said *I A Richards told me what to put in the book*, was true, Richards said yes; only I couldn't have done the putting myself."[89]

Had Stevens read *Principles of Literary Criticism* as studiously as Blackmur seemed to urge him to do, he would have had sufficient forewarning that Richards's influence could be seen all over "Examples of Wallace Stevens," the first sustained analysis of Stevens's rhetoric, the essay that would do more to distinguish, and to some degree canonize, Stevens criticism *as criticism* than any other evaluative response of this period (or, arguably, any afterward). If for I. A. Richards one had to move through a poem in "experimental submission" – the illiberal concept so disparaged by F. R. Leavis[90] – for Blackmur, similarly, regarding *Harmonium*, "Reading Mr. Stevens you have only to know the meanings of the words [prior to reading] and to *submit to the conditions of the poem.*"[91] Blackmur's essay on Stevens accepted Richards's effort to raise the "standard of response" to art by his organicist insistence on close reading. The result was a critical style that strikingly matched the substantive goal: to find poetry's "poise, stable through its power of inclusion," in Richards's words, "not through the force of its exclusions."[92] In the passage quoted below, though it is but a mild example of Blackmur's unusual prose style, one easily sees how the instrumental idea of critical analysis could accommodate the early Stevens "by a style not merely instrumental," in Denis Donoghue's apt phrase. Donoghue has keenly understood that Blackmur's insights are gained "from among the accruing possibilities of the words," Stevens's words as quoted no less than Blackmur's own – "not messages to be delivered but possibilities waiting to be discovered just under the surface or aslant from it."[93] Blackmur wrote of "On the Manner of Addressing Clouds" in the following Richardian way: "The whole thing *increases in ambiguity* the more it is analyzed, but if the poem is read over *after analysis*, it will be seen that *in the poem* the language is *perfectly precise*. In its own words it is clear, and becomes vague in analysis only *because the analysis is not the poem.*"[94]

Blackmur seems rather deliberately to have borrowed from Richards a science of words' behavior, though, again, in a style more akin to Stevens's in that it bears out the inclusivity Richards stipulated for poetry but could not quite commit to his own prose. That programmatic affinity seemed to be clinched by the way Stevens's "Autumn Refrain" was editorially designed to accompany Blackmur's "Examples": It strongly suggested that the *Hound & Horn* had recruited the new Stevens poem to authorize Blackmur's approach (see Figure 5), with Stevens's "skreaking and skrittering" in the poem endorsing Blackmur's opening-paragraph riff about this poet's "striking . . . collection of words."[95] But an unmentioned English cousin was connecting these kin. For Blackmur's Stevens, "words, like *sensations*, are *blind facts* which put together *produce a feeling* no part of which was *in the data*" (the Richardian emphases are added).[96] Again deriving confidence from Richards's attachment to utility, Blackmur believed that a practical criticism could refute both the critics who "dislike" Stevens because he seems "finicky," and those "who value the ornamental sounds of words but who see no purpose in developing sound from sense."[97] On the contrary, Blackmur's essay began, sound and sense in Stevens are perfect interanimations, to use Richards's term, and through the Richardian method Stevens could become a poet whose every choice of meaning

AUTUMN REFRAIN

EXAMPLES OF WALLACE STEVENS

THE skreak and skritter of evening gone
And grackles gone and sorrows of the sun,
The sorrows of sun, too, gone . . . the moon and moon,
The yellow moon of words about the nightingale
In measureless measures, not a bird for me
But the name of a bird and the name of a nameless air
I have never — shall never hear. And yet beneath
The stillness that comes to me out of this, beneath
The stillness of everything gone, and being still,
Being and sitting still, something resides,
Some skreaking and skrittering residuum,
And grates these evasions of the nightingale
Though I have never — shall never hear that bird.
And the stillness is in the key, all of it is,
The stillness is all in the key of that desolate sound.

WALLACE STEVENS

THE most striking if not the most important thing about Mr.
Stevens' verse is its vocabulary — the collection of words,
many of them uncommon in English poetry, which on a
superficial reading seems characteristic of the poems. An air
of preciousness bathes the mind of the casual reader when he
finds such words as fubbed, girandoles, curlicues, catarrhs,
gobbet, diaphanes, clopping, minuscule, pipping, pannicles,
carked, ructive, rapey, cantilene, buffo, fiscs, phylactery,
princox, and funest. And such phrases as "thrum with a
proud douceur," or "A pool of pink, clippered with lilies
scudding the bright chromes," hastily read, merely increase
the feeling of preciousness. Hence Mr. Stevens has a bad
reputation among those who dislike the finicky, and a high
one, unfortunately, among those who value the ornamental
sounds of words but who see no purpose in developing sound
from sense.
    Both classes of reader are wrong. Not a word listed above
is used preciously; not one was chosen as an elegant substitute for a plain term; each, in its context, was a word

Figure 5. Facing pages from the *Hound & Horn* 5, 2 (January–March 1932), 222–3. (Courtesy of the Henry E. Huntington Library.)

would be deemed controlled. "Not a word listed above is used preciously," Blackmur boldly asserted after quoting a list including "curlicues," "ca-tarrhs," "gobbert," "clopping," "pipping," "pannicles," "buffo," "fubbed" and "fiscs"; "not one was chosen as an elegant substitute for a plain term; each, in its context, was a word definitely meant."[98]

There is no external evidence that Stevens read *Principles of Literary Criticism*, even after Blackmur had strongly praised the book in correspondence. But we do know that after "Examples of Wallace Stevens," with its deep debt to Richards's method and specialist's tone, Stevens purchased Richards's *Coleridge on Imagination* (1934); his copy survives in the Huntington Library. It was one of the few books in which he marked passages, made marginal notes, and indexed his responses to the argument on the pastedown and flyleaf.[99] It could not have come into Stevens's library at a more appropriate moment, for Richards's effort to offer a materialist rewriting of Coleridge's distinction between imagination and fancy would provide a very new romantic indeed, at least one against which Stevens would measure his own haphazard program. His many prose explanations of neoromanticism during 1935 bear the influence of Richards's psychologically modernized Coleridge, as do two poems, "Table Talk" and "Sailing after Lunch" (both also of 1935).

Richards was of course already well known for his psychoaesthetic experiments at Cambridge, during which he asked his audiences for descriptions of their responses to poetic word choices. *Coleridge on Imagination* makes plentiful use of his earlier conclusion that an ideal of interpretive fitness or rightness could be reformulated in rational terms denoting an adequacy of stimulus and response.[100] That there finally exists a normative response to color-words, for instance, was an assumption carried over from earlier forms of practical criticism into the 1934 analysis of Coleridge's reaction to Gray's sonnet "In Vain for Me the Smiling Mornings Shine." Richards agreed with Coleridge that Gray's selection of color-words ("reddening," "golden") "obfuscates the whole emotional response" to the poem,[101] which makes it thus an instance not of imagination but of fancy. The moment of imaginative creation should be characterized by a special acute awareness or "vigilance"[102] toward the whole range of responses to the conditions the poem puts into words and by the choice of some words and not others to give order to these responses. The point to which Stevens would first react – it had always troubled him – was that all our "past choices" worked together to coax or wheedle us into making fit, precise decisions in the moment of producing a poem. This was just Blackmur's strongest claim for *Harmonium* in "Examples," and Richards repeats the idea generally in *Coleridge on Imagination*:

> What should guide us is our experience of life and literature – not as represented haphazardly and schematically in formulable opinion, but as it is available in a power of choice, "the representative and reward," as Coleridge calls it, "of our past conscious reasonings, insights and conclusions." It will be the modes and capacities of distinguishing that have been developed in these past reflections, *rather than the conclusions we came to*, that become the source and sanction of the choice.[103]

In "Table Talk" Stevens satirically administered a psychoaesthetic test on himself, providing a glance at a science of words' behavior that has failed, even while it nicely reinforces Richards's inclination to stress the difference between poetry and ordinary discourse (mere "Table Talk"). The point of the poem is that the choice of color-signs made in it produces little sense. The act of making and then scrutinizing choices wrests what little else controls the poem's considerable energy. The poem argues that "Life . . . is largely a thing / Of happens to like, not should," or, in other words, that poetic choices are not matters of "happens *to like*" – not Richards's complex though measurable system of interests – but merely "the way things happen *to fall*."

> . . . why
> Do I happen to like red bush,
> Gray grass and green-gray sky?
>
> What else remains? But red,
> Gray, green, why those of all?
> That is not what I said:

Not those of all. But those.
One likes what one happens to like.
One likes the way red grows.

It cannot matter at all.

(*OP* 73)

By denying the self-explicating critic-speaker any access to a creative men-
tality, by moving with playful quickness past a close analysis that might
have distinguished between one's choice of "green-gray" as mentally separable from plain "gray" or plain "green," Stevens anticipates not only his
critics' desire to systematize *Harmonium* into color schemes – in which
green would mean the "tough, diverse, untamed," point-blank real (in,
say, the Yucatan section of "The Comedian as the Letter C" [*CP* 31]),[104]
blue would signify the imagination (in, say, "Anecdote of the Prince of
Peacocks" [*CP* 58]), and so on. He also learned to lie in wait for readers
like Hi Simons and Bernard Heringman who dared ask reductive questions about the critical value of such systems. After locating in Mallarmé's
sonnet "L'Azur" the strictly symbolic blue that "runs all through Mallarmé's
poetry," Simons suggested to Stevens that "with you, blue usually stands
for . . . the life of the imagination."[105] The 1935 poem anticipated a reply
to such totalizing: "It cannot matter at all." One's words are organized
because they "happen" to "fall" together in one way merely as opposed
to another. The response to Richards was thus characteristic: Stevens was
refusing to allow the text to be turned into the meaningful inkblot; if
pushed toward symbolic self-actualization and other such therapies, he
would deliberately produce, as he did in "Table Talk," a text that resisted
its function as a normative structure while not designed to elicit "normative" responses.[106]

"Table Talk" is, to be sure, a rather disingenuous form of the counterargument just described, since of course its construction is hardly as casual
as its title and idea suggest; its random choices are precisely rhythmic and
rhymed. Yet if I am not wrong to suggest that its literary-political strategy
was to show a psychoaesthetic test failing miserably in his own case – if
Stevens was resisting Blackmur by lightly suggesting that "My readers will
get no mere normative structure from me" – then Stevens had indeed learned
from Richards's Coleridge the distinction between fancy and imagination.
"Table Talk" served him overtly, in other words, as an egregious example of
fancy – expressly in Coleridge's terms as quoted by Richards in *Coleridge
on Imagination* from Coleridge's conversation, *Table Talk*: ". . . That the images [stimulated by fancy] have no connexion natural or moral, but are
yoked together by the poet by means of some accidental coincidence" (*Table
Talk*, June 23, 1834).[107] Thus Stevens challenged the Richardian rendering
of the romanticist distinction by making a poem, itself apparently offhand –

the title sets the easygoing pace, suggesting idle conversation – consciously beguiling the theoretical expectation of stock response while qualifying the immediate reflex so entirely that it implicitly argued for a working out of experiences much newer and fuller, much more plastic and less impulsive (more postmodern, really, and less modern) than Richards's scientific assurance would allow.

Enfeebled, then, by its own strategy of satirizing a conception deemed a basic or "primary" poetic function, "Table Talk" has not impressed Stevens's critics.[108] (Even he, it seems, had little time for it once it was written, and left it unpublished.[109]) "Sailing after Lunch," however, taking up Richards's reading of Coleridge's idea of imagination, succeeded finally in catching the wind of the critical concept it began by satirizing, making the result something Stevens liked well enough to place first in the book manuscript he was preparing for Alcestis.

The poem begins by making yet another call for a new romantic. The initial problem to be faced in the neoromantic project in the thirties was that romanticism had by then fully earned its pejorative connotation. The poem implied that Stevens's goal was to gain a fresh view of romanticism through the formal resemblance between the functioning of poetry and sailing a boat. That there might then have been something wrong with the craft, as it were, of his poetry suggests that the poem would at least criticize the failure that had led to this condition, or would find a way out:

> It is the word *pejorative* that hurts.
> My old boat goes round on a crutch
> And doesn't get under way.
> It's the time of the year
> And the time of the day.

Stevens next satirizes the notion of normative psychological and physiological responses to poetry, introducing the poet-boatsman-speaker as an exception to this faulty principle:

> Perhaps it's the lunch that we had
> Or the lunch that we should have had.
> But I am, in any case,
> A most inappropriate man
> In a most unpropitious place.

To further the satire he grafts onto a famous Coleridgean refrain a rather willful conception of poetic history:

> Mon Dieu, hear the poet's prayer.
> The romantic should be here.
> The romantic should be there.
> It ought to be everywhere.

After a bold turn away from such literary self-consciousness, he returns to the boat-poetry analogy by modifying it: What prevented the modern poet from finding his own motion freely was the crustiness of conceptions of romanticism; this, then, was the cause of the problem originally introduced:

> But the romantic must never remain,
>
> Mon Dieu, and must never again return.
> This heavy historical sail
> Through the mustiest blue of the lake
> In a really vertiginous boat
> Is wholly the vapidest fake. . . .

He then begins afresh, now taking somewhat more seriously the distinction between referential and emotive functions of poetry:

> It is least what one ever sees.
> It is only the way one feels, to say
> Where my spirit is I am,
> To say the light wind worries the sail,
> To say the water is swift today. . . .

The result of saying and doing only and exactly what one feels leads finally to the imagination momentarily triumphant. The poem itself succeeds in lightening the musty old Romantic sail. A transcendental quality of poetry is restored, and the poet, catching wind of the imagination, finds a direction of his own:

> To expunge all people and be a pupil
> Of the gorgeous wheel and so to give
> That slight transcendence to the dirty sail,
> By light, the way one feels, sharp white,
> And then rush brightly through the summer air.
>
> (CP 120–1)

On March 12, 1935, Stevens sent this new composition to Latimer and wrote:

> This particular poem is one that I have had in mind for the first poem in the book. . . . While it should make its own point, and while I am against explanations, the thing is an abridgment of at least a temporary theory of poetry. When people speak of the romantic, they do so in what the French commonly call a *pejorative* sense. But poetry is essentially romantic, only the romantic of poetry must be something constantly new and, therefore, just the opposite of what is spoken of as the romantic. Without this new romantic one gets nowhere; with it, the most casual things take on transcendence, and the poet rushes brightly, and so on. What one is always doing is keeping the romantic pure: eliminating from it what people speak of as the romantic.
>
> I realize that a poem, like anything else, must make its own way.
>
> (L 277)

Notwithstanding the astute use of "pejorative" in the stanza advancing the poetry-boat analogy, the most enlightening aspect of Stevens's self-imita-

tive explication is that it directly addresses the relation of theory and ex-
planatory power. The encumbrances created not by romantic theories but
by theories of the romantic, presumably including this one, prevent poetry from going in its own direction. The poem must itself "make its own
way" as a critical theory of romantic inheritance, fully despite the idea of
"explanation" redacted in prose for Latimer. To speak in such a way of
romanticism is to keep a new romantic from freeing poetry to catch
imagination's drift, to find its heading, its literary-historical way. The poem
is itself an "abridgment" of a poetic theory and is, at least partly, the result of Stevens's reading of Richards's peculiar rendition of romanticism
(not Coleridge's verse but "what people speak of as" Coleridgean). *Coleridge
on Imagination* might have suggested the analogy that gets the poem going. In a final chapter on the evident difficulty of contemporary poetry,
Richards argued that a poem is not always a thing said but ever a way of
saying it (precisely Moore's assessment of Stevens in her review of Williams's
Collected Poems). In the last chapter, one that damned him in the eyes of
many committed modernists, Richards offered a series of analogies to help
us understand the essential directionlessness of the "way" of saying. Only
when we separate the said thing from the way it is said do we find the
meaning of the poem to be an effect of mental impulse. One of the analogies from instinctive motion Richards drew on here was already a favorite of Stevens – "the pigeon's flight," the use of which, matchlessly at the
end of "Sunday Morning" (*CP* 70), enabled Stevens to suggest precisely
this: Poetry extends its own wings merely to do so, not to make a point
of the particular descending but on behalf of the aesthetic effort of clo-
sure and definitive descent. Another of the analogies Richards offered to
explain what he meant by directionlessness was "the tacking of a boat."[110]
Once it can be established, however, that the poetry-boat analogy failed
because the theory of poetry that suggested the analogy was itself impaired
("My old boat goes round on a crutch . . ."), the poem could only begin
by claiming that it cannot quite yet begin (". . . And doesn't get under
way.").

The second stanza, trying to find the etiology of the trouble ("Perhaps
it's" due to this condition or that), extends the satire begun at the end of
the first: the time of year must be wrong for the imagination or, to be
needlessly specific, perhaps the time of day. If, as Richards argued, sensations provoked by poetry are conditioned in part by physiological states –
even by hunger, he suggested in *Principles of Literary Criticism*,[111] or the
position of one's head, or even the condition of one's blood[112] – then surely
Stevens has no trouble moving from the romantic poem that cannot find its
direction to the satire of a new antiromantic reading of romanticism that
merely encrusts it by speaking of poetry reductively as a system of bodily
interests. Does the science of interpretation really expect to extend this far?

If, as Richards suggested, the "Western ethic tends to find its sanction in biology" (a passage in the Coleridge book Stevens marked),[113] and if to read a poem aright one must pass through the "jungles of neurology,"[114] so, too, would dyspepsia deform our response! "Perhaps," Stevens satirically discovers, "it's the lunch that we had." Richards's idea that the literary critic was occupied with the health of the creative self as a doctor the health of the body[115] might be operating as well in Stevens's satire at this humorous point. For Richards's analogue of poem, critic, body, and doctor came to Stevens at a moment of acute sensitivity. Just weeks before the poem was finished, Stevens's own physician, disclosing the poet's high blood pressure (200/115 four minutes after mild exercise), in combination with a hypertrophy of the left heart and worsening obesity – he was now 235 pounds – had put him on a ruthless diet with dreadful warnings that if he did not get exercise and restrain himself at table he would suffer a heart attack or stroke.[116] During his annual February visit to Florida Stevens did not nearly hold to his regimen.[117] Here, then, I dare say Stevens was testing Richards's audacious physiological claims against his own bloated body; representing his personal poetic crisis-state as an extreme "system of interests"[118] seeking to satisfy "appetencies,"[119] he smoothly satirizes the thought that one's lunch could actually condition one's response to a poetic thought or, even more self-mockingly, the lack of one's lunch ("the lunch that *we should have had*"). And by extension he casts doubts on Richards's notion that poetic theory ministers to one's health. In this reckoning, the point about the failure of romantic imagination cut both ways. He could resist, as he did in "Table Talk" for different reasons, theory as coercive therapy, or what Geoffrey Hartman has called Richards's "*benevolent* normativeness"[120] – could refute, that is to say, the boldest claim of Richards's reading of the modern reaction to romanticism, namely that there exists an altogether "appropriate" reader, that all people are ideally the same when they experience sensations, including sensations excited by words arranged as verse.[121] The satire of Stevens's second stanza concludes accordingly: Whether or not the purely physiological fact of one's lunch, as it were, could prevent the romantic poem from getting under way – "*in any case*" – Stevens must offer himself as the exception to the democratic aspect of normative response: "A most *inappropriate* man / In a most *unpropitious* place."

By making a refrain from "The Rime of the Ancient Mariner" sound like a critical polemic, by deliberately telling and not showing, Stevens then allows his satire to respond to the modern theorist's sense of the romantic (*Richards's* Coleridge), not to the poet himself – not to Coleridge's essential *frisson* (produced by the Mariner's terrible isolation) but to a literary history that has risen up all around it. If Stevens was seeing reviews of *Coleridge on Imagination* that spring, he might well have been familiar with that common complaint: Richards was imposing his methods on

Coleridge in such a way as to be able to find the fancy/imagination distinction everywhere and S. T. Coleridge nowhere.[122] Certainly the "poet's prayer," conjuring the presence everywhere of the Coleridge of one's theory, is ironic. The boat of the modern poet has been crippled by "This heavy historical sail." So, despite the claims Richards was making for a "new science"[123] as a new reading of romanticism, the romantic "must never again return," for the heavy historical sail, the unwieldy aesthetic theory, was itself "the vapidest fake."

Yet it is at this very point, when the satire is sharpest, and when, apparently, the project of romantic renewal was sinking by the weight of its own cumbersome equipment, that Stevens approaches the problem in a fresh way, introducing a distinction he borrowed from Richards's Coleridge. In a passage Stevens marked in pencil and indexed in his own copy of *Coleridge on Imagination*, Richards credits the kind of inspiration that irked F. R. Leavis and others: "a *projective* outlook, . . . the doctrine that we project values into nature," which Richards, coming back to the issue later, summarized as follows: "The mind of the poet creates a Nature into which his own feelings, his aspirations and apprehensions are projected."[124] (For the word "poet" in Richards, we are right to read "critic" also, as I think Stevens did.) In another passage to which Stevens's extemporized flyleaf index refers him (and us), Richards discusses the emotive function of poetry and theory. Here Stevens's penciled note to himself reads: "[page] 14 – affinities of the feelings with words or ideas." Richards had always made a point of bringing "feeling" into the realm of readable common signs, impulses theretofore considered beyond the reckoning of interpretation. The referential function of language is merely "capable of directing thought to a comparatively few features of the more common situations" of life. "But *feeling* is sometimes a more subtle way of *referring*."[125] In *Coleridge on Imagination* Richards went even further to restore feeling to the realm of interpretable signs. Whereas "feeling . . . [is] a word which, especially in the plural, has often to-day a derogatory tinge and is associated with vagueness and sentimentality," romanticism could get well beyond this pejorative sense by urging the poet to rely on feelings as the ground of ideas. Here Richards quotes Coleridge writing Southey in 1803, using a figure that extends Richards's likening of poetry to a motion impelled by wind: "Ideas *never* recall Ideas," Coleridge wrote, "The Breeze it is that runs thro' them, / it is the soul, the state of feeling – ."[126] And in order to ready oneself critically to read feeling as a "more subtle way of referring" than seeing, it is sometimes necessary, even when analyzing the *visual* arts, "to avoid the word 'see.'"[127] Here is Stevens's version of the distinction: "It is least what one ever *sees*. / It is only the way one *feels*, to say / Where my spirit is I am, / To say the light wind worries the sail." Once one moves away from the referential function of language toward an emotive function as altogether another form of referring – once one realizes that poetic language expressing feeling need not be vague or sentimental, as pejorative romanticisms would have it – one can *say*, in Coleridge's words (a 1796 letter to Thelwall, quoted by Richards and marked by Stevens): "I am a mere *apparition*, a naked spirit, and that life is, I myself I," or, in Stevens's words, "Where my spirit is I am."[128] This is truly to "expunge" referentiality in poetry and to become, without apology, "a pupil / Of the gorgeous wheel." (In the same letter to Thelwall that struck Stevens, Coleridge confessed his pure love of language, of Plato's "dear *gorgeous* nonsense" [Coleridge's emphasis].) It is indeed the effort of exchanging "people" for "pupil," submitting to the gorgeous sounds of words even (evidently) at the expense of sense, finding the "Awareness of words as *words*," as Richards insists was Coleridge's idea,[129] that immediately precedes the sudden rising light wind of imagination, that will fill the newly romanticized sail of the boat of modern poetry.

3: MISERY IS NOT TO BE BORNE

Two weeks after mailing "Sailing after Lunch" to *Alcestis Quarterly*, Stevens finished arranging the poems for *Ideas of Order* and told Latimer that it was an arrangement "based on contrasts" (*L* 279). The book typescript was finished on March 26. A day earlier Stevens had responded to T. C. Wilson's invitation to review Moore's *Selected Poems* for the *Westminster Review*. He would probably have to decline to write such a review, he warned, though it was possible if Wilson could wait until autumn. But he took the opportunity to describe Moore's poetry as a form of the new romantic, and here revised his assessment of Williams. His point serves to explain "Sailing after Lunch," though Wilson had not of course seen the poem:

> *I do not think that I can undertake Miss Moore's volume. . . .* Miss Moore is not only a complete disintegrator; she is an equally complete reintegrator. From that point of view, it would suit me very well to go over her poems, *because I think that what she does is really a good deal more important than what Williams does. I cannot help feeling that Williams represents a somewhat exhausted phase of the romantic, and that his great attractiveness is due to the purity of his form.*
>
> *On the other hand,* it seems to me that Miss Moore is endeavoring to create a new romantic; that the way she breaks up older forms is merely an attempt to free herself for the pursuit of the thing in which she is interested; and that the thing in which she is interested in all the strange collocations of her work is that which is essential in poetry, always: the romantic. But a fresh romantic. Anyhow, whether or not that is what she intends (even though unconsciously) it would be interesting too, if on a careful review of her work the work supported it, to apply her work to that theory. (*L* 278–9)

When T. C. Wilson quoted Stevens's comments on Moore's neoromanticism in a letter to Moore written a few days later, he omitted the portions I have italicized.[130] Perhaps he edited Stevens's letter in such a way because, as he told Moore, he had not asked Stevens if he could do so (although he was "sure that he would not object"). Nevertheless, Moore's perception of Stevens's comments on her own romantic aspect did not have the benefit of two basic points: She could not have known that Stevens had said he would probably *not* undertake the review; nor could she have been aware of Stevens's view that her own success as a new romantic would have to come after Williams's comparative failure. Moore's pairing of Williams and Stevens, in her review of the Williams book Stevens had introduced, had obviously not reconciled the two; it would have meant a great deal to her to have the match confirmed by Stevens's own words.

Soon Stevens did agree to write the review of Moore, and Wilson arranged to get him a copy of her book. By May 27, Wilson had in hand the typescript of Stevens's notice (a version not extant). He quoted portions of it in a letter to Moore. One part quoted is slightly different from the review later published, suggesting a last layer of revision by Stevens and perhaps another lost typescript: Wilson characterized this version by telling Moore that Stevens's "prose has ardor even in its coolness."[131] Those who, with Celeste Goodridge, hold to Moore as not only a "brilliant reader of her contemporaries,"[132] but also (in Kenneth Burke's phrase) "a study in stylistic scruples,"[133] can imagine how deeply Wilson's appraisal of Stevens's chilly prose would have struck Moore as she waited for the Stevens review. Readers of that piece ("A Poet That Matters," in *OP* 217-22) less inclined to accept Goodridge's thesis that Moore's "essays and reviews" – more, in other words, than her poems – "allow us to reconstruct the public dialogues she had with the writers she valued most,"[134] can judge variously as to whether Stevens's endorsement of Moore's 1935 selection was qualified; at times he appreciated her "real toads" in "imaginary gardens," and at other times he seemed to think she spent too much time "sticking to the facts."

But Wilson's private comment to Moore about Stevens's ardent coolness was hardly straightforward, and sheds light on his attitude toward T. S. Eliot's introduction, which was bitterly attacked by the communists. Not the least of Eliot's radical detractors was Burnshaw; in Burnshaw's poem "Mr. Tubbe's Morning Service" Eliot was "This wizard of the cult, Despair," "find[ing] / . . . Blinders for all his tender boys."[135] Even Burke, no hard-liner against high-modern pessimism, was left unreassured by Eliot's theologized movement "from negation to the 'negation of a negation.'"[136] Moore herself expressed a bit of reticence about having gotten Eliot of all poets to create the context in which her new book would be judged. "[I]n consenting to let Faber + Faber publish my collection," she wrote Stevens,

"I had no thought of involving any one person in a defense of me."[137] Suspecting the value of Eliot's preface during a period when T. C. Wilson's political allies were sometimes brutally rejecting "the negative features of Eliot's precisian criticism,"[138] Wilson himself certainly chose an odd line to cite for Moore as his favorite: "I especially like [Eliot] saying, '. . . to feel things in one's own way, however intensely, is likely to look like frigidity to those who can only feel in accepted ways.'"[139] In relation to Wilson's tactful characterization of Stevens's review of Moore as cool, the repetition of Eliot's anticipation of a misogynist left that would insinuate Moore's frigidity suggests that Wilson found Moore and Stevens similarly lacking in feeling (a momentary figurative feminization of Stevens that must have made it psychologically easier to attack him as well). Many years later, in a 1964 memoir of Stevens, Moore attached to Stevens Eliot's line on her: Stevens's poetry, she remembered, was "a consummate refutation of the impression that life must be frantic."[140] Moore often wrote this way about herself, and, at least in 1935, when literary-political lines were drawn, deemed Stevens and herself an aesthetic pair in reaction against a newly dominant mode. Not surprising, then, that Moore responded to Wilson's quotations from Stevens's typescript by expressing "happiness to have a connection with an article by Wallace Stevens about poetry, of the sort you refer to having got from him." "[B]ut," she added, perhaps not fully prepared for the straightforward way in which Stevens said she too was a new romantic, "I am astonished by what you quote from it."[141]

Moore's astonishment only encouraged Wilson to decide to come clean and to make explicit his ideological problems with Stevens. Complicating things further, Eliot was by now asking Moore to review Stevens for the *Criterion*,[142] and so Wilson's political criticism of Stevens had an unintended timely effect. Her response to Wilson's criticism was to defend Stevens (and herself) without making a single compromise with the radicals. Her *Criterion* review was really, in all respects, a counterargument stipulating no enemy, as the position against which it defended Stevens was specific but unnamed.

Moore now lent Wilson some of her copies of Stevens's poems in various periodicals, including numbers 2 and 3 of *Alcestis Quarterly*, the latter number containing "Sailing after Lunch," and this set the stage for Wilson's first direct critique:

> I find Stevens' direction, as expressed in these and other recent poems, somewhat disturbing. I mean, these poems are evening poems, spoken with a "dying fall," very beautiful and even perfect of their kind, but pervaded by a willingness to accept defeat or the next thing to it. All of them seem to me the words of a man who is "bidding farewell, bidding farewell" in lovely cadences, . . . My objection, I suppose, is not so much an aesthetic one as a moral one. . . . when he says:

> What is there here but weather, what spirit
> Have I except it comes [from] the sun?
>
> ["Waving Adieu, Adieu, Adieu," *CP* 128]

the attitude is one which is distasteful to me, which is, in my opinion, basically anti-intellectual, amounting to a denial of the poet's real and greatest function.[143]

Even if Moore did not already know Wilson was then a Stalinist – she might have ascertained this from his contribution to the March–April 1935 symposium in *Trend*[144] – Wilson hinted at his position here, briefly quoting the point in Gregory's review of *Harmonium* that would be taken up by the left in forming its response to Stevens. While Moore had repeated praise for Gregory's 1931 review as recently as 1934 – later she stuck by her view that it was "the perfect description of Wallace Stevens"[145] – there was no avoiding the fact that the 1931 review had anticipated the left in reproving Stevens's world-unto-itself where the "the immaculate top hat and stick are always" present and the "melodies . . . modulate to a dying fall."[146] Moore knew that Ann Winslow's *Trial Balances* was in press (to be published that October); in this volume, established poets were paired with younger ones. As Stevens was matched with onetime objectivist Martha Champion (*OP* 215-16),[147] Moore was paired with Elizabeth Bishop, and Cowley with the radical Alfred Hayes. Moore knew already that Gregory was sponsoring T. C. Wilson. One of the three poems Wilson was publishing there was "Let Us Go No More to Museums," which conscientiously follows Gregory's point about the airless world in verse like Stevens's: "Let us go no more to museums and stand / Exalting memorials of some dynasty we have no part in."[148]

Gregory's preface to Wilson's *Trial Balances* poems made it clear that the young poet addressed great social problems while permitting "no facile solution." Here Gregory went so far as to connect his approval of Wilson's radicalism ("He is not merely angry at a world of darkness and disorder; he is here to warn us") to Stevens's assessment of Williams's objectivism. Thus Stevens could be seen standing with Wilson, "the 'antipoetic,'" and a new verse "fully conscious of the world" on one side, while "*so-called* 'poetic' values" of the modernist mainstream stood conservatively on the other: "To accept [Wilson's poetry] one must grant the right of the poet to be fully conscious of the world in which he is living, a world in which Wallace Stevens' definition of the 'anti-poetic' remains in juxtaposition with the so-called 'poetic' values."[149] In *Trend* Wilson observed among young poets "the almost unanimous adoption of an attitude toward the existing order that is left in its sympathies," an inclination "as desirable as inevitable."[150] Wilson sustained his Stalinism at least until the end of 1937, when he was dismissing *Partisan Review* Trotskyites as "nitwits" and commending Williams's rejection of *Partisan* in favor of the *New Masses*.[151] Gregory planned to have Wilson succeed him as a member of the *New Masses* literary board.[152] Wilson and Gregory regularly exchanged thoughts on the left; Gregory's private about-face on Stevens, notwithstanding the assumption of Stevens's sympathy in the *Trial Balances* preface, deeply marked the line Wilson was now drawing for Moore.[153]

Wilson's ideas about Stevens – that his poems accepted defeat and eschewed hope, that he denied the writer's ethical responsibility – held to what was perceived (wrongly) as a basic party line, but it was the first such criticism Marianne Moore heard directly. This was the affirmative strategy for warding off the "defeatist" modernist mode that continued to follow *The Waste Land* and was still producing poems no less "hopeless" than that great original – derivatively dreary works in which "fascism yawns" because "phosphorescent worms emerge . . . / the eliots, the ezra pounds / play[ing] jazztunes of *profound regrets.*" (So one of the radical Dynamo poets complained,[154] while on the right it was said that Eliot's "penetrating analysis of modern spiritual ills" was being *mistaken* "for cynicism and despair."[155] Note that some left-leaning liberals were capable of seeing in Stevens, as Eda Lou Walton once did, "the very extreme of the Wasteland theory."[156]) In an essay, "Hopefulness and Left-Wing Literature," Wilson wrote blandly that "Marxism . . . is an instrument of analysis which enables the writer to discern the dialectical interaction of forces and events."[157] Eleven years later the communist word-stock had mostly fallen away from his critical prose, but Wilson retained the critique of Stevens he had developed as a radical, and in the following revealing comparison of Moore and Stevens lamented Stevens's indifference to poetic ethics: "[W]hereas for Stevens 'poetry is the imagination of life' and the poet's morality is 'the morality of the right sensation,' for Miss Moore 'art . . . is feeling, modified by the writer's moral and technical insights'. . . . Moore believes that creative activity entails ethical and moral as well as esthetic responsibilities."[158]

Moore's reply to Wilson's communist charge of defeatism, aside from suggesting that she was learning to classify current political rhetoric, took a first step toward a lasting judgment on Stevens (declared in 1940): Stevens "seems to live in an unspoiled cosmos of his own," but at the same time "he is so constitutionally incapable of self-treachery that his poetry becomes for us *a symbol of hope.*"[159] The very intensity of his inward turn caused him to be so flawlessly himself, so utterly not what was expected of him by others, that it produced the utopian "hope" which in turn prevented poets like Wilson from seeing a plausible ally to an ethics of reading. This was a tricky argument. In order to advance it Moore had to concede that Stevens's interiorizing caused, on the contrary, "mental strife," inner pain somehow evident in the poetry and thus recognizable to "society" as a whole if its members would just try to read Stevens's modernism sympathetically. Stevens's "great accuracy and refracted images and averted manner," Moore wrote Wilson, "indicate to me a certain interior reconcentration of being. One who has borne heat and burden as well as he has, and as long as he has, is very deeplaid. I feel sure that the support he needs would not come from general society but from men – men . . . who are aware of his mental strife and . . . his interior debts and insufficiencies."[160]

Before T. C. Wilson could print Stevens's review of Moore in *Westminster Review*, the magazine folded. Fortunately, Wilson was serving as an American representative of Bryher's *Life & Letters*, having been introduced to the journal by Moore,[161] and was able, with Stevens's permission, to place the piece there, where it did not appear until December.[162] He allowed Wilson to show the typescript to Moore, and on July 12 explained its connection to "Sailing after Lunch," a point Wilson evidently did not pass on to Moore. "Both the poem SAILING AFTER LUNCH," Stevens wrote Wilson, "and the note on [Moore's] SELECTED POEMS are expressions of the same thing. . . . People think in batches. The predominating batch today seems to think that the romantic as we know it is the slightest possible aspect of the thing." Since the British "feel . . . badly about the romantic," it was fine with Stevens to have the piece appear in England (*L* 282).

Stevens's review of Moore presented the new romantic in a final, if not definitive, form: "the romantic in the pejorative sense merely connotes obsolescence, but that the word has, or should have, another sense." Thus it provides yet another gloss on the rescue of Coleridge in "Sailing after Lunch." It permitted him also to determine that Babbitt's attack on romanticism could be accommodated to the idea of Moore's neoromanticism, since in criticizing romanticism – according, at least, to Stevens's quotation of him – Babbitt had at least used the romantic in a high literary-historical (not in the low or pejorative) sense. "[W]hen Professor Babbitt speaks of the romantic, he means the romantic," Stevens wrote shortly after defining the romantic in a nonpejorative form ("strange, unexpected, intense, superlative, extreme, unique, etc.") by quoting Babbitt in the course of excoriating that form (*OP* 220–1). The Moore review also allowed Stevens to acknowledge Williams's abhorrence of the 1934 preface. Stevens did not name Williams outright. Yet the poet he had in mind was nonetheless clear to those who knew the story – the objectivists, Wilson, Moore and Gregory (from letters sent by Wilson to each), and Williams himself: "It is absurd to wince at being called a romantic poet" (*OP* 220).

There was much more at stake here than Williams's soreness. Stevens's review of Moore also deliberately defined a neoromantic that would be irritating to the left, in an effort, I think, to counter the cultural practice that pointed out to poets like Moore the contradiction between bourgeois lyric form and "genuine" feeling. When Stevens alluded to this antiformalist rhetoric – speaking of "a time like our own *of violent feelings*" – he was obviously trying to imagine radical detractors. Making his case negatively, Stevens left himself no logical choice but to describe Moore as a counterexample. She was the poet refuting thirties-style "violent feelings" with her own violent feelings that nonetheless preserved "scrupulous,"[163] even "rigid" (*OP* 217) form. Being a romantic poet, Stevens wrote, "means, now-a-days . . . in a time like our own of violent feelings, equally violent feelings and the most skilful expression of the genuine" (*OP* 220). The "genuine" response to one's vehemence, poetic and social, in other words, was not necessarily violence released flood-like into free form, justifiable as that might seem "in a time like our own." Stevens was coming to admire Moore, then, because "If the verse is not to be free, its alternative is to be *rigid*," and in sustaining formal rigidity against all ideological odds the new romantic still replied, with apt contemporaneity, to "violent feelings."

This unstylish logic certainly helped Stevens explain why the preference for feeling over seeing in "Sailing after Lunch" led finally, but almost imperceptibly, to a "slight" and paradoxically controlled "transcendence." What Stevens would mean a year later by "the pressures of the contemporaneous" and six years later by "the pressures of reality"[164] was anticipated painstakingly here in the belief that a formal feeling comes in a counterviolence answering incursions of unfair aesthetic expectations. To underscore his rejection of the prevailing idea that the proper retort to outer violence was exclusively a poetry of reality – real toads in *real* gardens – Stevens came close to identifying by name poetic radicalism as the offending -ism. This parting shot missed its mark, but it nonetheless recalls the letter in which he asked Latimer to imagine what sort of poetry Milton would be obliged to write were he writing in the thirties; he too "would stick to the facts" (*L* 300). "The school of poetry that believes in sticking to the facts," Stevens now wrote in the review, "would be stoned if it was not sticking to the facts in a world in which there are no facts" (*OP* 222).

In late October, as Moore was preparing her review of *Ideas of Order*, T. C. Wilson pressed his case further. He granted Moore's earlier point that Stevens's struggle might be seen in his very composure (it is also Stevens's notion about Moore in his review). But Wilson disliked the facile solution evidently offered by Stevens's suggestion that "When all people are shaken" they can merely look inwardly for a cure. By the end of his presentation of this point Wilson had worked himself up into a full communist heat, complaining of the defeatism and – in Kenneth Burke's not entirely negative term – the "acceptance" of the nonradical poet, a defeatism similarly repudiated by other young radicals like Kenneth Fearing, who might call images of "Darkness" and "bitter[ness]" in another's poetry "the chief offenders" as signs of a "weakening of [a poet's] grip upon the external world,"[165] and by Muriel

Rukeyser, in *Theory of Flight*: even darkest "night in this country," in the hands of the revolutionary artist, could become "deep promise of day, / . . . busy with preparations and awake for fighting."[166] For Wilson as for Rukeyser, not only is "misery . . . *not* to be borne," even though it seemed to be "borne" in Stevens's poetry. But there was a still harder edge to the accusation: "[T]hose who have made thousands of souls crippled . . . *will have to answer for it*." Here is Wilson's rejoinder to Moore:

> WS' humility is surely not the least of his qualities, and his composure, which must have been obtained not without struggle, shows itself in his ability to look a thing full in the face, no matter how disrupting it may be and have his own spirit strengthened thereby rather than, as happens in so many cases, be overcome by what he has seen. A poem like "A Fading of the Sun" indicates that WS is alert to what I cannot but think it must give him pain to look upon. I myself . . . should not be capable of the reserve and certitude which Mr. Stevens displays. . . . [I]t is *ultimately* true to say that "If they will look / Within themselves" "They will not die." Yet I think that it is first necessary to make it possible for these people to look within *themselves*, and I at any rate could not in looking upon their misery and incomprehension speak as Wallace Stevens does. Such misery is not to be borne, and will not be much longer, and those who have made thousands of souls crippled in spirit, body and vision will have to answer for it.[167]

Moore wanted to go no further with the debate. By now she had written out her defense of Stevens, and it was shortly to be made public. She did reply to Wilson's strongest letter, but only to close the subject deftly by saying, "Purblindness regarding Wallace Stevens ought not to be one of our current misfortunes in letters," and by selecting as her response only the initial positive point Wilson had made: She wished, she said, that she herself had succeeded in saying in her review just what Wilson had said in his letter – "about Wallace Stevens's composure as the result of struggle." She also noted that Latimer had written her to request advance copies of the *Criterion* containing the review.[168] She sent Latimer one of these, and this was the very copy that reached Stevens,[169] who then said of Moore: "She is one of the angels: her style is an angelic style" – as unique, he added, as Gertrude Stein's.

4: FORTIFY THE AUTHOR

Stevens was right about the singularity of Marianne Moore's reviewing style. He would not have been alone in approaching her poems from the general direction of her prose. Always her prose is a pastiche of phrases quoted from the book under review, spliced with her own aphorisms, fables and epigrams – an act, as Burke deemed it, of stouthearted yet amicable collaboration, a "carving [of] a text out of a text."[170] Moore's defense of Stevens was so mindfully compressed into this pithy intertext that it has been easy to underestimate just how precisely her thesis was attuned to emergent leftist criticisms of Stevens – just how strong a defense it is, and how important to the whole crucial story of the cultural reception of *Ideas of Order*.[171]

Typical is her sympathetic reading of the antirealist purple bird of "Like Decorations," epigram xxxiii. It must be discovered in a single phrase: "while maintaining one's native rareness in peace." "Peace" is the key interpretive word in this passage, as conditions of turmoil would not very easily justify the state of being rare or precious. Her will toward "imitative appreciation," in Goodridge's phrase, having the effect of "collaps[ing] the distinction between commentary and text," was never stronger than here.[172] Another phrase compresses a reading of "Anglais Mort à Florence" and "Lions in Sweden" into one critical assertion, braving the mixed metaphor and yet rhetorically splendid in its own right: "guarded definitions but also the unembarrassing *souvenirs* of a man and '. . . the time when he stood alone.'" Her reading of epigram xxiii in "Like Decorations" – "The fish are in the fishman's window" – took Stevens to be criticizing the depression-era "fatalist" who ponders the fish, baked goods, hunted pheasants no longer plentiful, "surrender[s] to 'the morphology of regret,'" and desists by "drowning in one's welter or woes, dangers, risks, obstacles to inclination." Moore's review, in short, brilliantly depoliticized Stevens. In her hands the purple bird, as patient as a photographer taking a time exposure, "classifying," "botanizing," rejecting the grossness of realism, put forth "a series of guarded definitions" and, standing alone, suggested itself as a fully natural thing. "[L]ike the language of the animals," and not at all the artificiality of the aesthetic human, Stevens's poems were slyly but intuitively persuasive, "a system of communication whereby a fox with a turkey too heavy for it to carry, reappears shortly with another fox to share the booty." Having accomplished this naturalization, she concluded with a jab at literary politicians, pushing even further the idea that Stevens's status as purple bird is an instinctive one and thus not subject to charges of wrong or right, left or right:

> Serenity in sophistication is a triumph, *like the behaviour of birds.* The poet in fact is the migration mechanism of sensibility, and a medicine for the soul. That exact portrayal is intoxicating, *that realism need not restrict itself to grossness*, that music is "an accord of repetitions" is evident to one who examines *Ideas of Order*; and the altitude of performances makes the wild boars of philistinism who rush about interfering with experts, negligible. In America where the dearth of rareness is conspicuous, those who recognize it feel compelled to acknowledgement.[173]

Moore's 1935 review was as clear a message to Stevens as to his political critics: Among your high-modernist colleagues, it promised, there will be those who are prepared to defend you against the "fanatics."

But if Stevens missed such a message, there was soon another even clearer one. As was so often the case in this era of literary wars, reviewers picked up cues from each other: the next leftist attack on Stevens to materialize (Burnshaw's commentary had already been published a few months earlier) was a reaction against Moore's defense of Stevens's rare purple bird in her *Criterion* piece. This was Geoffrey Grigson's "A Stuffed Goldfinch," which appeared in Grigson's upstart *New Verse*,[174] where Stevens's claim (and Moore's defense) of rarity was answered by the charge of artificiality. Stevens was the stuffed finch of the title. Now Moore defended Stevens privately, and strongly. She wrote him on March 10, 1936, assuring him that Paul Rosenfeld (whose essay "Authors and Politics" established him firmly among literary anticommunists),[175] W. W. E. Ross (against whose old romanticism Stevens had already reacted), and Eliot (whose introduction to *Selected Poems* had occasioned the opening shot in the left's assault on Moore) – all these "good minds" – deserved protection against "a cohort of fanaticals." The fanaticals were waging a war on the few talented and free writers who had reached "the pinnacle of deserved triumph which a fortified author enjoys." And, she added, shrewdly reversing the usual accusation, the fanaticals regarded this pinnacle "as imperialists do the regalia of the Tower." She urged Stevens not to respond to Grigson and the others, but to continue shining light on his own work, keeping off his own page "the critical shadows that darken lines and pages they cannot produce." She assured him, in what amounted to a second review of *Ideas* for his own eyes, that "Ideas of Order is an enviable unity," "a kind of volume-progression on certain individual poems of previous years."[176] A year later, when *Owl's Clover* exploded like a bomb in some quarters, Moore repeated the terms of her defense: he modeled "an unkilled and tough-lived fortitude"; worse still (given the direction in which Stevens felt he was heading), she wished just what "the tenantry" wished for "persisting members of an aristocracy" – namely "'long life to it'"![177]

What is astonishing about Moore's offer of reassurance to Stevens at a time when he was stirred by leftist approaches was that she herself had been much more brutally rebuked. Compared to Orrick Johns's left-sectarian review of her *Selected Poems*, Burnshaw's and Grigson's of Stevens were mild indeed. If there was to be any defense, it should have involved Stevens coming to the ideological defense of Moore; but he obviously did not think for a moment of using his review of Moore, where he was chiefly concerned with carving out his own "new romantic" position, as Moore used hers of him, as a bold riposte to their political critics. Orrick Johns, conceding Moore's "scrupulous" choice of words and forms, countered that "a pearl is found in a sick oyster." Johns argued in his notice that Moore's poetry in the last twelve years had declined along with her culture: "[W]hen a culture begins to take the descending curve . . . the speed of the fall is great. . . . No longer are the old questions of technique alive." Eliot's introduction gave not the least comfort, as Eliot-bashing had become a favorite leftwing sport, the rules of which are only now being rewritten.[178] To Max Eastman *Ash Wednesday* was an "oily puddle of emotional noises";[179] to Grigson, Eliot had "recognized his falling price and tried to jack it up with grass stems";[180] to Fearing, he was "an Englishman in theory, a deacon in vaudeville, a cipher in politics" (a line Burke quoted with relish);[181] and in T. C. Wilson's reckoning, it was the duty of poets "to go on from where Marx left off," with "New perceptions requir[ing] new forms" so that "the rhythms of 'The Waste Land' are hardly appropriate to a worker's song."[182] For Orrick Johns the mere fact that it was Eliot who introduced Moore, claiming to "speak for a small and thinning class," spoke volumes about Moore's milieu. The comment prefatory to *Selected Poems* "not only reveal[s] the minds to which he speaks," wrote Johns, "but the street, the door number, the spindly old sofa on which he sits and the faces in the drawing-room corner by the window." In this view, Moore's poems were "washed and stiff-dried," their meanings "bled-white," and she resided in "moral isolation" within the "fiercely self-protective and competitive tradition" Eliot's introduction prescribed for her.[183] The tenor of Johns's piece suggests that when she (and Eliot) needed to be found and ferreted out, the literary left, having positioned her so unequivocally on the continuum of ideas about order – so precisely in that stuffy old parlor, primly posed with Eliot – would know just where to look. Such ridicule produced an approach very different from Burnshaw's to Stevens, as we will see in the next two chapters. In fact, Burnshaw's point was precisely the opposite: one does *not* know where to place Stevens politically – that being both the problem and the possibility.

Long after the new romantic moment had passed, and when only Williams still stewed in bitterness about the epithet, Moore continued with what she had begun in her review of *Ideas* during the politically charged months of 1935 – to speak of Stevens in terms resistant to the left, terms which in large measure Stevens's critics have adopted. "Unanimity and Fortitude," Moore's February 1937 review, written for *Poetry* and covering both *Owl's Clover* and (for a second time) *Ideas of Order*, defended Stevens again provocatively. Red flags were sent up everywhere. At one point she spoke provocatively of the "awareness of if not the influence of T. S. Eliot"; at another she made sure to cite "egress" and "negress," of all possible choices, as the example of Stevens rhyming "just right," to laud at every cost Stevens's "playfulness" in pulling such a stunt.[184] Still more intrepid was this: "[w]e see [in Stevens's new work] the salutary effect of insisting that a piece of writing please the writer himself before it pleases anyone else." Moore's willingness to measure herself unambiguously against the literary-political standard helped both Stevens's supporters and detractors in the difficult project of measuring him. Seeing "Unanimity and Fortitude," Samuel French

Morse, already then a strong Stevens adherent, knew immediately that Moore's notice would serve him as a counter to the left. "Marianne Moore's review of Stevens was just of my taste," he wrote Zabel. "*I wonder if Stanley Burnshaw will see it?*" Assuming that by this point Stevens was "tired of trying to explain himself" in political terms, Morse saw Moore as supplying just such a rationale.[185] Moore's review was what suggested to Morse that a then-recently published poem, "A Thought Revolved" (*CP* 184-7), would cause a renewed radical attack. "I should like to know what the boys are going to say about" *that* poem, he added.[186] Moore knew that Stevens was just the right poet for refuting utopian claims because he had an ear sharp enough to quote the left's basic *lack* of hope back to itself. In other words, to say of "bourgeois poets" (as Edwin Rolfe did) that "Certainty and hope are beyond them" itself risked a form of hopelessness.[187] In her own inscribed copy of *The Man with the Blue Guitar & Other Poems*, containing the abridged "Owl's Clover," she copied out on one of the blank leaves at the end of the book lines from Stevens's "Mr. Burnshaw and the Statue" that accomplish just such a satirical feat:

> The thing is dead . . . Everything is dead
> Except the future. Always everything
> That is is dead except what ought to be.[188]

The new romantic episode elapsed so rapidly, and was followed so promptly by the Burnshaw episode, that we have little choice but to take seriously Stevens's later idea that the poet's attraction to communism had been a form of his attraction to the romanticism deeply embedded (but denied) in objectivism. This "romanticism" served fleetingly to express utopian or post-Christian longings for a new sense of order, an aspiration he felt temporarily, but nonetheless strongly. The encounter with literary communism would serve him similarly.

Yet if the radicalism of the *New Masses* was to be accommodated to a search for the supreme fiction that had characterized his interest in the new romantic, it would require a good deal of formal and thematic elaboration. It would take, it seemed, an unimaginable broadening of Burnshaw's literary radicalism. Still it is a matter of fact that at the very point at which the communist left turned toward Stevens – and thus, of course, Stevens was turned toward them – aesthetic policy had itself shifted to the Popular Front, under the auspices of which the very "casuistic stretching" that Stevens needed to adapt communism to the new romantic was itself employed by the communist left in the effort to "claim nearly every outstanding American . . . for the cause of revolution"[189] – including Stevens. When it was in Stevens's interest to reach out, the new romantic having finally failed to embody what he had badly wanted, it was also in the interest of the left to reach out to him. The convergence would seem simple, just as, in some hands, "Owl's Clover" would seem the rather simple result. But we must recognize that Stevens's "interest" in the left was created by his unconscious habituation to a literary world that had already been shaped by the left. He realized the contingent relation between what he deemed the special romanticism of American communists and the polemical poetic movement toward things as they are. In the early thirties this crossing produced objectivists and their latter-day-imagist allies moving left, and disclosed Moore in relative motion moving right. Thus Stevens had come to see the importance of a "keenness for actual things" in his own new poetry. And as he emerged from the neoromantic moment, Burnshaw appeared to hurry him along in a direction he was already going. Perhaps when he corresponded a few years later with Carl Rakosi, one of the first objectivists, he was recalling, as much for himself as for Rakosi, the excitement the new mode had stirred in him:

> [W]hat excites you most of all is real things, and that your allusions to other things are merely to accentuate actual objects and people. In short, you view the imagination as a foil, something for contrast. If I am right about this, you have exactly the kind of mind that appears to be required in contemporary poetry. I don't say this with reference to the use of the imagination, but with reference to keenness for actual things.[190]

5

Turmoil in the Middle Ground:
Politicizing the Lyric

The words Right and Left perhaps mean more today than at any time in the history of American criticism.

—Horace Gregory[1]

I hope I am headed left, but there are lefts and lefts, and certainly I am not headed for the ghastly left of MASSES.

—Stevens to Latimer (*L* 286)

But the test of a revolutionary position is not in *what one rejects* . . . [n]ot in the "push away from," but in the particular "pull toward" one selects to match it.

—Kenneth Burke in 1936[2]

1: FORCES IN THE KNOW

Earnest readers of the *New Republic* in 1935 must have been just a little startled to see this poem printed in the June 5 issue:

DANCE OF THE MACABRE MICE

In the land of turkeys in turkey weather
At the base of the statue, we go round and round.
What a beautiful history, beautiful surprise!
Monsieur is on horseback. The horse is covered with mice.

This dance has no name. It is a hungry dance.
We dance it out to the tip of Monsieur's sword,
Reading the lordly language of the inscription,
Which is like zithers and tambourines combined:

The Founder of the State. Whoever founded
A state that was free, in the dead of winter, from mice?

What a beautiful tableau tinted and towering,
The arm of bronze outstretched against all evil!

(CP 123)

Certainly Morton Zabel would have been surprised at the convergence of Stevens and this journal of "social emphasis." Just a few months earlier, Zabel's column on "Recent Magazines" in *Poetry* concluded with lines quoted from Stevens as counterexample to the "social emphasis" of "journals like the *Nation* and the *New Republic*." Of "two groups" of poets, "the formalists and the social critics," Zabel suggested, "the latter [were] naturally more prominent and well-chosen by the [*New*] *Republic* editors." Zabel and others in the mainstream modernist movement always admired poetry in the *New Republic* gathered by long-time literary editor, Ridgely Torrence, whose "place in New York journalism," since his retirement from the post, "has not been filled." But "[t]he present poetic policy of the *New Republic*," by which Zabel was referring to Edmund Wilson and his successor Malcolm Cowley, "will do well if it revives the standards Mr. Torrence maintained."[3] Indeed, the desire on the part of the *New Republic* to publish Stevens in 1935 would not seem at first to support Cowley's radical conclusion to *Exile's Return* – the conversion of lost-generation writers to communism, he wrote, was indispensable to their maturation as writers – nor endorse the friendly editorial advice Cowley, quite unlike Torrence, doled out to radical contributors and reviewers (such as: "Watch out for poems that readers can't understand and be very good to regional and descriptive poets"[4]). Nor indeed would Cowley's pursuit of Stevens seem to accord with the fact that, in Kazin's reckoning, "Cowley redirect[ed] the literary side of the *New Republic* in the direction of a sophisticated literary Stalinism."[5] Yet "'The New Republic line was, for the most part, a polite echo of the [communist] party line,' and, despite occasional wavering, 'more consistently Stalinist' than even *The Nation*."[6] Not even very polite: In 1935, as Frank Warren pointed out in *Liberals and Communism*, the editors agreed together to "deabsolutize liberty," a bold theoretical renunciation of liberalism's concept of human rights as pure and unconditional.[7] Cowley acknowledged that he and his fellow editors sought a more or less "synthesized" policy governing political and literary departments alike – "to blend skillfully the economic, social and cultural in their presentation of America." And when this synthesis later came under criticism from liberal English literary journalists, especially at *Scrutiny*, who were less theoretically enamored of editorial centralism; when it was said "that political opinions, and especially Marxist opinions, play too great a part" in review assignments and acceptances for publication, and that if there had to be editorial unity, it would be better to base it on "values derived from literature instead of politics" ("[p]oetry in particular" was pointed out) – then Cowley, in reply, was prepared to defend the *New Republic* just the way it was.[8] Even after the Popular Front officially closed out the "Third Period" on August 2, 1935, Cowley was still turning back poems because they were "decorative and perfumed" and in his rejection letters might simply quote back to the poet politically offensive phrases.[9]

While it is accurate to say of Cowley's editorship, as Daniel Aaron has, that his goal was to "*mediate between* the 'art as a weapon' school of literary judgment and ivory-tower subjectivism,"[10] this does not lead necessarily to the conclusion that Cowley believed anything but that communism created a climate in which the artist functioned *most effectively*. Imagine, in such an editorial setting, the reaction caused by Stevens's submission of "Re-statement of Romance" (published in the March 6 issue), "Sad Strains of a Gay Waltz" (May 22), and "Dance of the Macabre Mice" (June 5) – verses neither "regional" nor "descriptive," nor easily divisible from the large, apparently unsuitable category of "poems that readers can't understand," poems in which "decorative" if not "perfumed" lines could be found. In "Dance," for instance, frolicking mice decipher "the lordly language of the inscription" on a hero's statue, "Which is like zithers and tambourines combined" – precisely, it would seem, the sort of all-sound-no-sense dandyism Cowley had consciously left behind when he disavowed his status among "the 'exiles' and *transition* group"[11] and quitted an editorship at the exuberant high-modernist *Broom* (where Stevens had published).[12]

And yet Cowley could not but print these new Stevens poems. The general motive is ascertainable even as any specifically articulated rationale was lost when editorial correspondence at the *New Republic* was scattered into private collections.[13] Nonetheless it was Cowley who initiated the contact in early 1935. He had learned, from Zabel at *Poetry* who was just then learning it from Maas at *Alcestis*, that Stevens was assiduously back in the poetry-writing business. Cowley replied to Zabel, thanking him for the "tip" on Stevens, and implied that he would be writing The Hartford immediately. He must have done so.[14] By February, Cowley was appealing to the conservative modernist Zabel, in a strategy that would characterize the poetic plan at the *New Republic* from this point on, seeking Zabel's approval of what verse they were printing (and ostensibly on grounds much nearer "aesthetic" than "ideological"). "Do you think our poetry's looking up?" Cowley asked hopefully in a typical letter.[15]

Such interaction between the *New Republic* and *Poetry* at this particular point is instructive, because it came after months of a very different association. Cowley had spent the previous year trying to foist onto a horrified Monroe and a bemused Zabel a series of disorderly, tumultuous poems by various proletarians, one enthusiastically described as a seventeen-year-old "Kentucky hillbilly . . . now back on the farm," another an inmate in the New Mexico State Penitentiary who composed sonnets about "his sexual inversion" and misadventures "with some boys in a C.C.C. camp" – not exactly *Poetry*'s sort of poets.[16] (On the back of one of these letters, Monroe scribbled a note for editorial eyes only: "Probably Cowley's discards – I see nothing for us."[17])

If, to say the least, 1935 brought a shift in relations between the *New Republic* and *Poetry*, the general cultural purpose driving the *New Republic*'s ambition to publish Stevens can be fairly approximated, revealing a sense of the political instability entailed in reading the poem. "Dance of the Macabre Mice" is, in nearly anyone's account, a satirical poke at "The Founder of the State." "Whoever founded / A state that was free, in the dead of winter, from mice?" But from what position – from what side – is "the State" mocked? The line just quoted might be said, in a conservative's (let us imagine Zabel's) contemporary reading, to satirize utterly the politicized language it engages: Right mocking the way left ubiquitously mocks (or glorifies) "the State." Yet that reading seems unsatisfactory because it is willfully severed from the interests and inducements of the remarkably animating context created in that *New Republic* issue by pieces on Jane Addams, the NRA, and a National Folk Festival, a communist roundup of labor news, Louis Hacker's hatchet job on Frederick Jackson Turner's posthumous magnum opus, and Cowley's ingenious communist assessment of Margaret Mead's work with the Arapesh[18] – a reading, in other words, suggested only by the poem's later, permanent setting in *Ideas of Order*, the arrangement mostly managed by Stevens. The historical setting that could not be managed was in some ways the one that made possible the very point his mice were making about the word "free." Stevens had no notion, of course, that his poem would follow immediately from Hamilton Basso's brilliant brief study of the demagogic Americanism of Father Coughlin,[19] but having been approached by Cowley for poems, and having long been a reader of the *New Republic*, he could and should easily have imagined something of the way in which a piece of "lordly language" and an "arm of bronze outstretched against all evil" might resonate in this as opposed to another intellectual congregation. (We must not forget that this was the era in which Harvard's aging Charles J. Bullock routinely opened his first lecture each semester by grimly declaring: "If anyone came to my house with the *New Republic* I would pulverize his skull with my cane."[20]) The politics of a poem, in this period particularly, did not nearly stop at creation, for creation itself in some manner anticipated a friendly or hostile readerly condition. Basso's sense of Coughlin's heroic, but hateful, inflations once helped a certain reading of Stevens's satire. So would any reader's sense that the editors just then favored a "deabsolutized" theory of rights. While speaking ironically of freedom, and trotting out that common theme, the state, the poem, after all, puts that pervasive phrase *in the mouths of mice*, authorizing beings of such hilariously small stature to issue forth the ardent exhortation that dwelling on such an issue as the historical struggle against evil was getting them (and people) nowhere. "At the base of the statue, we go *round and round*," say the mice. "What a beautiful history . . . !" And: "What a beautiful tableau tinted and towering, / The arm of bronze outstretched against all evil!" These final lines might be said indeed to have ironized not only the founder's, but all such rhetorical escalations ("outstretched against *all evil!*") – even, that is, the revolutionary bombast of those whose unambiguous business it was to oppose founders of the state. From the thoroughly disarming point of view of the mice, then, *any* such struggle against trends often indiscriminately called "evil," not to mention "*all* evil," can be reduced by a kind of natural history to static, frozen images such as the defenseless bronze statue in winter, notwithstanding its representation of valorous deed. Something of similar significance, I think, took place when Stevens was perceived in relation to other verse Cowley chose to run that month. Here it is easier still to see how Stevens's satire might cut one way only, against one kind of politics and for another: against a once heroic, once well-founded (American?) state issuing forth claims for individual rights and freedom that might in turn be deemed fallacious by a later, less reverent though diminished perspective. Such a liberal-left rendering of Stevens before "Owl's Clover" worked well when read with Philip Cornwall's "Twilight at the House of Morgan" (in the *New Republic* of June 19), where the refrain,

> Hell on wheels past the House of Morgan,
> Hell on wheels past the House of Morgan,

criticizes the power of the great by allowing the diminutive (poor children in this instance) to play.[21] Josephine Miles's "For Futures," published in the same issue as "Dance of the Macabre Mice," while a good deal less frolicsome than Stevens's and Cornwall's poems, deals similarly in political irony:

> When the lights come on at five o'clock on street corners
> That is Evolution by the bureau of power.[22]

If "[t]o Cowley everything came down to the trend, to the forces that seemed to be in the know, and in control of the time-spirit"[23] – this, another of Kazin's characterizations, would nicely explain the editor's own sense of what would entail a "*sophisticated* literary Stalinism" – then Stevens should be included as a small but nonetheless crucial part of Cowley's plan.

It is just here that we may see how the new liberal-left context created by and for Stevens's poetry set up a dialogue between Stevens and the increasingly influential aesthetic ideology of the thirties – interaction that finally prepared him for contact with Burnshaw, further left, a few months later. The circle of readings inciting readings draws tighter. Take Howard Baker's reading of "Dance of the Macabre Mice": Preparing his Autumn 1935 essay to run in the inaugural issue of the new *Southern Review*, Baker was obviously influenced by the assumed political context afforded the poem in the *New Republic*, even as Cleanth Brooks's and Robert Penn Warren's more purely aesthetic *Southern Review* was designed as something of a rebuttal to Wilson's and Cowley's going belle-lettristic concern. "Dance," to Baker, signaled Stevens's new interest in the "government and its *inability to change* as the necessities of *the people* change." He also noted that in general Stevens's new poems "deal openly with specific references of the last few years, going so far as to mention names like Ramon Fernandez and Karl Marx [the latter, again, in 'Botanist on Alp (No. 1)']."[24] And if Cowley's need to run "Dance," whether strategically or accidentally organized to shore up a besieged left editorial position (regularly challenged by those further left at the *New Masses*), in turn shaped Baker's reading of Stevens's poem as amenable to cultural liberalism, it must also be recalled that Stevens read and liked Baker's essay at a time when *he*, in turn, was writing new poetry and was alert to criticism from communists. Such circuits of reception can and should be followed. The reasons for the new presumption of Stevens's developing sympathies – a few months before Burnshaw's review was deemed by some to have set back that emerging reputation – are thus deeply involved in the attachment of poet to publication, a relation that as a matter of course remained unspoken and largely unrecorded.

It is possible to conclude of this relation – keen as Stevens was to the vicissitudes of bringing his new work to market – that he remained wholly attentive to the special circumstances that would develop for his poems when at this moment he was choosing to send them to the *Nation*, the *New Republic*, and (on the other end of the spectrum) to *Poetry*. Extant evidence supports his complete cognizance in several special revealing instances; the case of "Mr. Burnshaw and the Statue" is an important one. After all, Stevens sent the poem he described as "simply a general and rather vaguely poetic justification of leftism" (*L* 295) to be published in the fifth *American Caravan* by his old acquaintance Kreymborg, a poet of his own generation and once a member of the loosely organized New York group of the teens, publisher of Stevens's early *Others* poems – someone, it was widely known, who had "gradually neared a clear revolutionary position," in Burnshaw's words.[25] As the Popular Front took hold, the literary left dropped names of "name" poets like Kreymborg, Bynner, Bodenheim, Gorham Munson, Edna Millay (at times),[26] and Williams (often) – older poets and once "high" modernists deemed more or less of Stevens's stripe, who had seen the light and were now committing themselves to radical poetry – a move that soon had the ironic effect of creating "a new literary snobbism of the left."[27] Why, when he was not particularly a fan of Kreymborg's *Caravan*,[28] did Stevens want his poem to appear there? The answer lies in his recognition of two facts: that he was sending a poem bearing in its very title the name of a *New Masses* editor to a friend known as a communist, whose *Caravan* work had always aimed at "accomodat[ing] a progressively broader" writing and denouncing "passive and recessive attitudes,"[29] and, that he – Stevens – was likely to appear with a contingent of such reds as Kreymborg could get past anticommunist co-editor Paul Rosenfeld. One reads "Mr. Burnshaw and the Statue" alongside work by Richard Wright, Bob Brown, Evan Shipman (a.k.a. Manuel Gomez), Don Gordon, Paul Corey, Meridel LeSueur, Lechlitner, Rukeyser, Burnshaw, and Kreymborg.[30] What Stevens surely did not suspect was *Kreymborg's enormous personal loyalty to Burnshaw*, which was due in no small part to Burnshaw's constant private and public praise of the older man, commendation that "will do much toward establishing you from the Marxist point of view as our leading and most important poet."[31] Not long after "Mr. Burnshaw and the Statue" arrived at the *Caravan*, the telephone rang at the office of the *New Masses*; it was Kreymborg on the line for Burnshaw, warning his comrade well in advance that a verse-reply was to be published, and providing Burnshaw an opportunity to write a brief prose statement to appear with Stevens's poem – and perhaps something further:[32] the unpublished correspondence proves that Burnshaw was actually given the chance to write a reply-in-verse.[33]

> BURNSHAW: Kreymborg telephoned, "You've just been immortalized." . . .
> I said to [him], "Gee, that's terrific. But is it a good poem?" He replied,
> "It's wonderful." I asked, "What does it say?" He laughed, "Search me!"
>
> *What did Kreymborg tell you about Stevens?*
>
> BURNSHAW: . . . [I]n the thirties he admired him very much.
>
> *Even though Kreymborg was then politicized –*
>
> BURNSHAW: – a red-hot Communist! He was one of the hottest.
>
> *And he had nothing negative to say about Stevens's recent poetry?*
>
> BURNSHAW: No. He just thought, as I did, that one should publish poems
> that might have some influence in bettering the world as it was at the
> time.
>
> *And yet as a Communist he put into print a rejoinder to you, his political ally
> and friend.*
>
> BURNSHAW: He thought ["Mr. Burnshaw and the Statue"] was wonderful – the whole idea that *The Caravan* received a long poem by Stevens
> that had to do with the . . . *New Masses*. . . ![34]

2: REFORMING MODERNISM FROM WITHIN

Poetry presented noncommunist modernists with a political development quite distinct from the left incrementalism of Cowley's *New Republic* and

Kreymborg's *American Caravan*. The *New Republic* that had published "To the One of Fictive Music" in 1922 under Torrence was one thing, then, and the one publishing "Dance of the Macabre Mice" in 1935 under Cowley indisputably another; yet no one who read "Dance" in the June 5 issue and decided, as Baker did, that it augured a new Stevens thought twice about drawing a clear line between an old and new *New Republic*. The Stevens published in *Poetry*, however, quite a different story, betold a magazine's troublingly arrested center-stage history. The thirties provided many if not most of its worst moments. What possible new direction could be taken by Zabel, Zukofsky, Gregory, George Dillon, and other up-to-date friends of the journal in a period when Monroe was continuing to run the magazine, despite now describing herself as having "earned a place by the fire" and "reached a less stressful stage of life's transit"?[35] (Stevens was one of the few poets to whom she wrote forthrightly in this vein: "I shall be quite willing to retire and write my memoirs. . . . I think I have done my share."[36] She hoped she could "personally conduct you to certain places in Peking," as she wrote nearer to the end, an unavailing wish since she knew better than anyone at the time the imaginary construction of Stevens's orientalism.[37]) In this mood Monroe's main editorial vice, an "open-door policy" toward poets whom she herself at times deemed dull,[38] was less in check than ever; it let in a flood of uninventive poems by Howard McKinley Corning, Flora J. Arnstein, Hertha D. Luckhardt, Marion Louise Bliss, Carla Lanyon Lanyon, W. W. E. Ross, and this by Albert Edmund Trombly:

> .Enough to be:
> To feel that little though she take heed of me
> Nature had need of me or I should not have been –
> Nature who proffers no explanation
> And needs no justification. . . . [39]

Publicly, Monroe remained aloof from the "sub-literary," considering politics in any strict sense to be beyond her ken and literary politics to be wholly a function of personal differences. Dealing with such quirky, not to say explosive figures as Pound and John Gould Fletcher had taught her plentifully the central role of temperament in poetic disputes. Yet to say this habit enabled her to depoliticize all political discourse is an understatement. A ferocious argument between Pound and Gregory, taking up the important issue of one poet's "fog-horn voice for Mussolini" on the right, and another's "bolshevickly ignoran[ce]" on the left, could cause Monroe to say, in all seriousness, "I don't see why two amiable poets would be upset about an economic issue."[40] To be certain, Monroe did the right thing by many proletarian writers, so long as they maintained an agreeable tone. But her good-natured handling of impoverished poets was only a result of personal sympathy. In the early thirties she treated the left-wingers, especially indigent ones, with "almost killing kindness."[41] Yet as for the content of poems sent her by these same impoverished poets, she was generally quite oblivious. When Japan began flexing imperial muscles in Manchuria, and exactly as the United States was sending the Marines to Shanghai to keep open its own economic open door, Maas asked Monroe: "Can't you say something against all this war talk? – poems, editorials, anything but something! Not that all our shouting will do any good, but what right have we to call ourselves humans, let alone poets, if we don't cry out against this ghastly sickening thing?"[42] Monroe did not merely reject the antifascist "War-Talk," the poem Maas sent to right the cultural wrong he had described for her in such urgent tones. She did so on the grounds that its expression of fears of another impending war was unfounded and irrational, criteria for acceptance that fittingly struck Maas and Van Ghent as political indeed. "The Orient seems to flare up easily," Monroe wrote to justify her view of the poem's insignificance: "I don't think Europe and the U.S.A. can afford another war." Maas's political verse, she warned him, was "mostly sound and fury, signifying nothing, don't you think?"[43]

Monroe's mistrust of all forms of didacticism is understandable to anyone who knows how and why Pound's early counsel became at times a form of psychological abuse, "'didactic'. . . to the point of violence," inflicting a pain Monroe still felt when she used that phrase near the very end.[44] Privately, however, she was less inclined to restrain her closely related aesthetic and political conservatism, never seeing it as working against the modernist "revolution" over which she had presided. When Gregory, a personal friend and perhaps her most regular correspondent in the final years, suggested "a proletarian number of *Poetry*" as late in the radical era as May 1935, Monroe hesitated, offering the excuse that *Poetry* had run special issues featuring the "regional" and the "racial" ("like the recent Chinese" number), and others "involving a school or method" (such as the objectivist number). But, she maintained, "we have never had a number based on some *subject* or *point of view*" – assuming modernism, of course, not to be a "point of view." Would the all-prole issue "be a communist number," she asked, " – propaganda either direct or implied? Of course I am not a communist – the system seems to me wholly contrary to human nature. And if I did believe in it I doubt if I should think *Poetry* the place to set it forth."[45] The false distinction between region, race, school, method on one hand – an odd-enough grouping – and, on the other, "subject or point of view," sheds some doubt on Monroe's understanding of the literary-political possibilities of the objectivism she was among the first to promote; even *it* she classed with the essential (that is, the apolitical) group. She refused to move poetic -isms from the personal and psychotheological to the political. ("Poor Zukofsky! –" she wrote Gregory, "too bad he can't stand on his own feet, such as they are! Young communist just because he must follow someone, something."[46]) When she heard that Isidor Schneider – once a faithful submitter of lyrics to *Poetry* ("My glances buzz like puzzled bees / about the reticence of buds"[47]), now a *New Masses* editor and as steadfast a communist as there would ever be among American poets – had been asked to serve on a poetry awards committee, Monroe was utterly aghast.[48] Pound's estimation in 1930 that "Miss Monroe has *occasionally* mutilated a work by excisions"[49] was perhaps a few years premature, but by 1934 mutilation by excision and revision was commonplace, as were unfathomable choices from among submissions-in-series. Many poets continued to accept such decisions silently, but what spread the reputation of *Poetry*'s politics, already low enough, was that poets on the left, increasingly bold and feeling empowered, began shouting back. It hardly matters that there was no particular antiradical pattern in Monroe's rejections and blue-pencilings, only that it was discerned by radicalized as well as liberalized poets who had long been publishing in *Poetry* – not just by such radicals as Schneider, Burnshaw, Maas, Gregory, Lechlitner, Fearing, Rosenberg, Orrick Johns, Rolfe Humphries, and T. C. Wilson, but also by liberals such as Belitt and future editor Dillon. Orrick Johns had submitted a fierce poem – "Nothing has scathed me, / Nothing ever; nor ever will. / I have touched pitch" – only to find that Monroe's hand and blue pencil turned the metrically forceful line "I have loved pitch and lust and hell" into "I have loved pitch and lust and *vain deviltries*" and that "the mistress" in the same poem had been transformed by Monroe into "the bride," not nearly Johns's sentiment.[50] This sort of thing doubtless had struck poets in the teens and twenties as but a prudish strain in an otherwise innovative editor. Not so now. From the editor's perspective this "turn" from proto-political deference to partisan defiance must have been bewildering. After all, Johns had long been sending Monroe notes in praise of *Poetry* as "a real anchor in a turbulent world," with "a strength . . . due to its *high position above querulousness and cliques.*"[51] Less than a year after that letter, he mailed her the following wild rebuke:

> I think the poetry published in POETRY including my own lately is tripe. I think POETRY ought to end its career. Why? Because it cannot see the turn. The turn has come. In what direction is this turn? In the direction of positive social necessity. . . . My poetry, all my life, has at least been incitation to action. The men of fame of my time have always been Professors of Triviality, masters of false gods, seekers of cold, passionless finesse, Yeats, Eliot, whoever. They are dead. And well dead. And dead with Pound on top of them. . . . You have tried to destroy me. You have sabotaged me with cheap, low faint praise. I will outlive you all. Why? . . . Because I am still young and can sing the working class!!![52]

Stanley Burnshaw, a hundred times more tactful than his friend and comrade Johns, refrained from any sort of vituperation until (in his view) provoked. Monroe rejected and returned five samples of Burnshaw's "industrial poetry," from a manuscript then called "Pennsylvania Mill Town" –

poems that had been written during his stint working in a Pittsburgh steel mill and only later collected in *The Iron Land* (1936); but he politely kept trying. "You will find," he wrote Monroe, "that I have *no axe to grind* as far as these poems are concerned."[53] When he did push in those months, he courteously pushed: "I have always felt," he wrote her in 1932, "that the only aspect in which *Poetry* did not reflect *all* of the American poetic activity was in its small proportion of poems dealing with the main currents of the time, i.e., industrialism, social adjustments, etc. While realizing this I was quite sensible to the poverty of genuine poetic production in these times. *I am not one to lay down a program for poetry.*"[54] Privately, however, Burnshaw felt very much as did Johns; he wrote Kreymborg about his speaking tour for the *New Masses*, which took him through Chicago, adding that he did

> see Harriet Monroe, and I was again amazed at the sheer decay and stagnation of the *Poetry* office. I don't know why I am so polite to her still, she is such an incurable reactionary and ass. She still thinks that *Poetry* is revolutionary. Etc. What an idiot, making fun of communism as just another ism. She seemed rather politely distressed when I told her what you were doing.[55]

For Monroe, the poetic "rank and file" continued to be a category reserved for people like the club-woman Mrs. Carl I. Henrikson, president of the genteel "Friends of Literature," who, upon hearing of *Poetry*'s possible financial failure, was (in Monroe's words) "brave enough to say, 'It shall not stop!'"[56] All the evidence suggests that Monroe in her last editorial years had little inkling that such a precious use of "rank and file" would be loathsome to anyone; or that her statement, "Big business men, I found, were not afraid of experiments"[57] in publishing poetry – a line she penned when celebrating her magazine's fortieth volume in 1932 – would set actual "Big business men" like Wallace Stevens to wonder what was becoming of *Poetry*.

And Stevens would have known the particular politics of *Poetry* – or, at least, how a literary politics was going to be impressed upon Monroe, Zabel, and Dillon each in turn. It was not merely that Stevens was an attentive reader from the magazine's genesis in 1912 and that he gave special encouragement to its editors even when he was not publishing there regularly.[58] Could he be blamed if this was in part because his own reputation was so closely linked to that of *Poetry*? The importance of the connection cannot be overestimated: When critics on the left and admirers in the modernist mainstream alike contemplated the achievements of *Poetry*, they almost invariably included Stevens as a central player in Monroe's "New Poetry" movement. It did not help that Monroe's memoir was making its timely appearance, and that her story of "discovering" Stevens figured prominently;[59] after her death, even *The Baltimore Sun*, extraordinarily ignorant of modern verse, displayed the requisite level of cultural literacy to drop the name "Wallace Stevens" when doubting if certain "poetry in America in the twentieth century could ever [have been] written" without Monroe.[60] Every time *Poetry* was attacked on political grounds, Stevens must have felt at least vaguely compromised. For the *Sun*'s unknowing judgment was widely shared. He was obviously part of "the still-born 1912 renaissance" ridiculed by Burnshaw in a 1935 statement.[61] From "the abortive poetry revival of 1910–1920," Edwin Rolfe wrote in a 1935 issue of the *Partisan Review*, "Wallace Stevens is remembered by *Harmonium*; he is no longer a living poet."[62]

Examined at a distance of a half century, the ideological shocks and buffetings felt at *Poetry* would seem typical of a noncommunist journal still priding itself on tolerating aesthetic innovation and change. Monroe's studied apoliticism was giving way to Zabel's defensive and at times cantankerous reaction. Zabel's position, in turn, lasted a few years anachronistically into the popular-front period, when many if not most other literary journals began accepting the invitation to politicize – to publish leftish if not credentialed radical poets regularly, and to take up, as *Poetry* finally did under Dillon's direction, a few of the causes advocated by the literary left, such as the federal subsidization of writers.

Zabel tried to meet the left head on. He made no bones about discussing in print the "crudity of sympathy that keeps [the Marxist critic] in petty fear of admitting beauty."[63] As the reviewer of Gregory's *Chorus for Survival* (1935) he worked hard to deny the relevance of his friend's radicalism to his great poetic success: "Gregory is grouped among writers of social revolution. . . . But this distinction is incidental to his fundamental qualities. The sincerity and art that have gone into his books should be major assets to any cause, but they are too substantial to need or allow partisan coercion."[64] Zabel's attitude had not budged in the four years since 1931, when in his re-evaluation of *Harmonium* he wrote, as we have seen, that Stevens's greatness derived from "an expression for ideas of no given date" – that is, from its wonderful resistance to historicist approaches – and because "Mr. Stevens never urged the idea of obliterating danger by opposing it."[65] Now "sincerity" was to be judged "fundamental" while a poet's "authorization. . . . of official orthodoxy" was just "incidental." As Zabel and Monroe discussed the future direction of the magazine, in a series of honest memoranda, he hoped they would both "be resolute, and vigorously anti-second rate," remaining true to singular, unalterable poetic value, firm as aesthetic absolutists: "The *One*, dear H.M., remains; the *many* change and pass."[66] What he meant by the changing, passing "many," of course, was the literary left. "No," he wrote Monroe again, "P cannot be downed by cliques. . . . A muscle-bound magazine. . . . has certain uses, but it can seldom gain the rank to which POETRY aspires." Thus he urged not wholesale changes but "reform from within" (his phrase). And here precisely, in

Zabel's plan, is where Stevens's new work would be especially effective. Zabel's program meant that Stevens would be drawn to the reform-mod-ernism-from-within camp against those – including, at different points, Zukofsky, Maas, and Gregory – who were campaigning to make *Poetry* "muscle-bound." In December 1934, as Stevens prepared "Like Decora-tions" for what was in essence his return to *Poetry* after thirteen years away,[67] Zabel seized editorial space to assail the *New Masses* as a place "where the proletarian argument allows room for no other" and to imply that Stevens's appearance in *Alcestis Quarterly* offered the necessary literary-political alter-native. He found Latimer's aestheticist editorial leading off *Alcestis* 1 fantas-tically reactionary, and supported it in part by implying Stevens's support:

> To those who take literature as seriously as life [Latimer's statement] may be a damaging heresy, *but in an age of opinionated violence we are inclined to accept such intentions gratefully*, and to renew with Mr. Stevens the ameni-ties of a "Delightful Evening" [*CP* 162; one of Stevens's poems in *Alcestis* 1] in his familiar manner:
>
> > A very felicitous eye,
> > Herr Doktor, and that's enough,
> > Though the brow in your palm may grieve
> >
> > At the vernacular of light
> > (Omitting reefs of cloud):
> > Empurpled garden grass. . . .[68]

Only in an era in which aesthetic value was itself besieged, Zabel was saying, would a magazine as important to poetry as *Poetry* endorse a posi-tion as backward-looking as Latimer's was just then. That an organ operat-ing (for the moment) in accordance with such nineties-like precepts was becoming a hospitable place for Wallace Stevens's "felicitous eye" eyeing "Empurpled garden grass" was for purists like Zabel a further sign of bad times. And there were plenty of moderate, anticommunist poets on hand, Morse for one, to reinforce the editorial traits Zabel once urged on T. C. Wilson's editor-in-chief at *Westminster Magazine* – namely "sense, prudence, and somewhat more respect for names and ideas tha[n] you seem to be using."[69] "[T]o have new work by Williams, Stevens, Marianne Moore," Morse wrote Zabel about *Poetry*'s good prospects, "is more than good. *This one path* for good writers must be kept open."[70] But as Morse was posting such encouragement to Chicago, Zabel was already doubting the cautious strategy of domestic reform. His fears that *Poetry* would go "unread by people who count"[71] had not been the least bit allayed. He resigned from *Poetry* still believing, however, that the best way to restore to power the magazine that "once was the regular organ for Wallace Stevens"[72] was to publish Stevens again.

Some observers believed that Zabel had been "forced out" in favor of

George Dillon by those who felt *Poetry* risked its central position by failing to align rapidly enough with the new political modes.[73] This is not
entirely accurate. For one thing, Zabel had badly wanted out, and he too,
after a time, urged Dillon to come along to Chicago. For another, Dillon
was hardly going to turn away *Poetry*'s regulars, including Marjorie Allen
Seiffert, a particular favorite of Monroe ("How refreshing," Dillon assured
Seiffert soon after his takeover, "to read some good lyric poetry in this
age of versified dialectics").[74] But that a bloody coup could so rapidly become the theory of choice among Zabel loyalists who mourned *Poetry*'s
slipping standards no sooner than they mourned the death of Monroe is
especially telling. And it is true that Zabel's selections had been called into
ideological question. Thus for *Poetry*'s leftist readers – the archives I have
consulted confirm that many left-wing poets read the successive issues of
Poetry as leaves of tea telling political fortunes – the thirteen cantos of
"The Man with the Blue Guitar," Zabel's last important acquisition for
Poetry, were put in a politically awkward and ambiguous position. When
the arrival of Stevens's new poem was greeted triumphantly at the offices
of *Poetry*, Dillon had begun to work closely on editorial decisions and
policy, and was already making his mark by volubly supporting Auden and
Spender and suggesting that *Poetry* strive for a commoner touch by com-
peting for popular-cultural attention on "the newsstands of the country,
along with the *New Republic* and *Theatre Arts Monthly*."[75] It was becoming
rapidly clear that Dillon was trying to take *Poetry* leftward, promoting writers little known to *Poetry* readers, such as Franklin Folsom, executive secretary of the communist-allied League of American Writers;[76] seeing that
Maas and H. H. Lewis were awarded each an annual Guarantors' Prize;[77]
permitting an avowed communist to guest-edit a "Federal Poets Number";[78]
and editorially endorsing the Coffee–Pepper bill.[79] The all-WPA issue
brought in a flurry of letters from radical poets hailing the return of
contemporaneity to *Poetry*: "All cheers to *Poetry* for that!" hailed Ruth
Lechlitner,[80] who had already written Dillon to say that from her radical
perspective "the journal is much improved."[81] Whereas Monroe and Zabel
had been fairly cool to H. H. Lewis while he was publishing his collections *Red Renaissance* (1930), *Thinking of Russia* (1932) and *Salvation* (1934),
Dillon immediately showed great interest, accepting Lewis's "Farmhand's
Refrain" –

> Our neighbors in Russia "belong" at least,
> No landlord impugning their worth;
> Have much consolation of goods increased,
> If not the sole havings of earth.[82]

Dillon, not stopping there, was pleased to award "Farmhand's Refrain" the
Harriet Monroe Lyric Prize.[83]

When Maas began telling his communist friends of his new association with Dillon, they "were unable to cover up their surprise that POETRY would feature a group as left-wing as this";[84] he wrote that since Dillon supplanted Zabel "the magazine has improved 100%," "has become definitely left-wing in tone," and he lauded the willingness to publish poems "more left-wing than any I've been able to place anywhere – and that includes NEW MASSES."[85] So efficiently was the *Poetry* that published "Blue Guitar" making up lost ideological ground that during a New York City radio show, A. M. Sullivan's popular *Poetry Hour*, the magazine was attacked for "publishing 'propaganda' poetry," an irony that delighted communist writers at the height of the Popular Front.[86]

Dillon could not have had a free hand to accomplish at *Poetry* what he did in 1937 and 1938 if Monroe and Zabel had not been so recalcitrant back in 1934 and 1935. What first infuriated the *New Masses* poets was the forceful combination of Zabel's strategy of picking and choosing occasions for counteracting the leftist trend and Monroe's habit of blithely ignoring literary politics altogether. If Stevens was reading *Poetry* closely when this antagonism burst into open conflict, as is almost certain,[87] he would have seen a strong hint of his own immediate future. Apparently encouraged by Zabel, Monroe emerged this once from her public silence on literary politics and lashed out against the left in an editorial, "Art and Propaganda." The principal target of her attack was Stanley Burnshaw.

3: POETRY CANNOT BE QUIET ANYMORE

What seems to have started the battle between Burnshaw and *Poetry* was Maas's deviation in reviewing for *Poetry* the anthology of *New Masses* poets called *We Gather Strength*, featuring Rolfe, Herman Spector, Sol Funaroff, and the talented "lumberman-poet" Joe Kalar. While "American revolutionary poetry as a whole [had] never risen much above the doggerel level" – a wrongheaded assumption in itself, even considering Maas's own verse alone – these young poets, in a conscious effort to incorporate modernism, to "imitat[e] Eliot, Cummings, and Williams," had only made matters worse, in Maas's view; "small [that is, lower-case] letters and phonetic rhetoric make a poet neither modern nor revolutionary." Maas found Kalar in particular "more interested in *impressing us with his poetic modernity* than with the deplorable conditions and hopes of his fellow lumberjacks,"[88] and noted in passing that A. B. Magil had "degenerated into an official writer for the Communist Party."[89] Maas soon learned that he had gone too far (and, my point is, he had). The next moment the same brash Maas was writing to Monroe, admitting a "most regrettable error" and pleading that his comment about Magil's intellectual depravity be stricken in page proofs ("to write officially for the C.P. [as Magil did] I personally do not consider degeneration").[90] But this deletion was for Burnshaw insufficient. Soon after the review appeared in *Poetry*, the *New Masses* responded; Burnshaw wrote angrily to *Poetry*:

> Willard Maas, who reviewed 'We Gather Strength' for Poetry, feels that his remark about the *New Masses* [quoted above] is quite misleading because of his review. Accordingly, as his review stands his beliefs are falsely represented. He has written a letter calling for an explanation. We published this and I think you ought to do this. . . . I note with considerable regret your characterization of *New Masses* poetry. . . . But I do not want to agitate. . . . [91]

Poetry did not strike back until the first reports arrived from Monroe's supporters describing Burnshaw's lecture tour of eastern and midwestern cities. He gave lectures on "Revolutionary Literature in American Poetry" and "Culture and Fascism."[92] On the road the young radical discovered, as he wrote Kreymborg from Wisconsin, that "the Communist Party of the United States has forged a kind of chainwork binding together the intellectuals of the cities in a common purpose with the workingclass."[93] No doubt the heady feeling conveyed to Kreymborg in Milwaukee stayed with the traveler as far as Missouri, where a particularly rousing speech upset at least one *Poetry* subscriber, who fired off to Monroe a fearful letter. The editorial Monroe then wrote, while beginning with an expression of her willingness to "pause and listen" to "the earnest Russ-minded communists," concludes that it would not be the "duty" of *Poetry* magazine "to accept and spread before our readers such half-baked efforts at class-conscious poetry" as were being accepted and published by the likes of young Burnshaw at the *New Masses*. She suggested that that journal "and other enthusiastic organs of the left group" should create a separate sphere in which political poets might choose to reside. She pointed out that Burnshaw must be a recent communist convert, alluding to his "Eartha" sequence, published in *Poetry* only a few years earlier, as lyric poetry now abandoned for "poetry with a 'message'"[94] – assuming that the communists' demand for "message" had unequivocally repudiated the lyric. It had not, and the Stevens of "Mozart, 1935" shrewdly knew this, as I will argue. It had not been the leftists, *so much as the noncommunist modernists*, who were moving the lyric beyond Gilbert Murray's strict metricist's sense and John Drinkwater's conservative stipulation of the form as "the product of the pure poetic energy unassociated with other energies"[95] toward something that might tap those "other" cultural energies. Looking for obvious, even ostentatious examples of an association between traditional lyric and "other energies" among poets of the left, one might search no further than Lola Ridge's 1935 sonnet sequence on the Sacco and Vanzetti executions, *Dance of Fire*, celebrated as such in its time,[96] or Rolfe Humphries's angry rejoinder to "a tendency [among some on the left] to minimize the importance of lyric poetry: I think such an attitude is a betrayal, not a defense, of culture. The ardor that goes into pure song, like the ardor that goes into revolution, is a vital and important manifestation of the human spirit; and no one devoted to either should ever disparage the other."[97]

To be citing Burnshaw's party-sponsored tour, then, gave Harriet Monroe leave for imprecise blame-shifting about the alleged sad fate of the lyric, and she quoted her frightened Missouri informant, whose lamentation that "[p]oetry cannot be quiet any more, and talk about fields and streams and meadows, or gallant gentlemen and ladies, or the spots on a butterfly's wings" served cleverly to set off Monroe's own evidently more tolerant position: "It is *not impossible* that *some* communist poet *may* write an immortal poem" and publish it in *Poetry* (emphases mine). That not every poet's aim was to produce poems for the ages, rather than for the age, did not occur to Monroe as any sort of option as she sought to fend off the right wing of her own constituency. Constant grading against permanence had sustained *Poetry's* choices through several distinct aesthetic eras – and was only now finally articulated as policy defensively political. This trend would have been evident even to readers of *Poetry* who took Monroe's side against Burnshaw. The distinction was clear in so uninformed a counterargument to the literary left, and in so prominent a place, that I suggest it clarified both modernists' and radicals' subsequent ideas on the subject a year prior to the Stevens-Burnshaw rendezvous. Assuming resourcefully that all poetry was propaganda of a sort, Monroe went on to draw the distinction as follows:

> If an artist's chief interest is the turn of a phrase, a new color-scheme or rhythmic pattern, some delicate half-tone of beauty perceived by a sensitive ear or eye, his propaganda will float so high in the upper esthetic air that ordinary denizens of the common earth will be blind and deaf to its meaning, to the self-important message it would write upon the sky. On the other hand, if an artist's chief interest is a communistic or social "revolution," he will be utterly unable to keep that interest suppressed in his art. . . . If all art is propaganda, a heroic effort to convert the world, its force comes from the artist's spirit and not from his will – that is, it is a force elusive, intangible and free, not to be directed or confined.[98]

Ostensibly creating a middle position, she was deliberately expecting the impossible; a revolutionary poem that *Poetry* would want to publish would have to be lyrical in her narrow antiideological sense of the genre.

Notwithstanding its tide of anticommunist clichés, Monroe's counterattack did distinguish itself signally from other reactions against communist poetics. For one thing, she at least conceded the propagandistic function even of extreme literariness, choosing rather to focus the rebuttal on how and why the lyric form was irreclaimable in the "Russ-minded" poetry

Burnshaw called for. In using this tactic, Monroe's criticism was quite different from that of the anti-Stalinist liberal Joseph Wood Krutch, whose essay "Literature and Utopia" primarily lamented poetry's default as our purest cultural form and the related forfeiture of "proper" poetic perspective. ("What [America] needs is cultivation not indoctrination" was Krutch's slogan.)[99] Monroe's rejoinder to Burnshaw was also basically different from Paul Rosenfeld's "The Authors and Politics," where the great sin was the radicals' abuse of "the historic." Unlike Monroe, who had no problem with such baseness as came from unadorned poetic observation – and had promoted her share of it during *Poetry*'s imagist days – Rosenfeld mistook objectivism for communism and then misread both as unwittingly acquisitive: The radicals were abusing philosophical materialism, he felt; by being so obsessed with "production" and so addicted to the materiality of *materia poetica*, they tended only to reinforce American rapacity. "Instead of fighting the country's already overdeveloped [greed]," he wrote, " . . . they have to all purposes been trying to identify the cause of literature and art with *materialistic* desires."[100] Monroe was not really concerned with Rosenfeld's bitter quasi-philosophical ironies of political left assuming "object"-oriented qualities of right. Her main concern was to draw a line between what she saw as exclusive cultural realms, and to name the sides: on one hand Burnshaw at the *New Masses*, Cowley at the *New Republic*, and so on; on the other, Yeats, MacLeish [*sic*], Tate, and *Poetry*, "holding their ground more quietly."

From the moment Monroe's editorial appeared, Burnshaw waged war on *Poetry*'s tactic of exclusivity. The confrontational tone of these retorts perhaps concealed a much more interesting and progressive turn of logic, the very turn that turned Stevens from observer to contestant. The *idea* of convergence, in short, was ahead of the *rhetoric* of confrontation. Monroe's notion that poetic art and poetic politics were exclusive and separable gave Burnshaw no choice but to speak of inclusivity. It is telling, then, that Burnshaw mistook stylistics for thematics when summarizing "the Monroe letter" in a personal letter to Kreymborg: It was to be read, he insisted, as part of his own general ambition "to '*humanize*' the whole business of poetry criticism. . . . [at] the New Masses."[101] He was being generous to both sides, for the signs of confrontation were there from the start. He suspected that Zabel was somehow originally behind Monroe's uncharacteristic jeremiad, and I think he was right.[102] Burnshaw was incensed at Zabel's demand that the rejoinder be abbreviated, and so arranged to run it in the *New Masses* as well as in *Poetry*. The uncut *New Masses* version was given a title typical of the cultural practice then still dominant, but it badly obscured the latent theme of inclusivity: "The Poetry Camps Divide." To be sure, the titular trope picked up from where Monroe left off – when *she* named the divided sides and unwittingly played into the hands of the left's sectarian talent for nasty periphrasis. It was a naming of unnameables that Burnshaw could not but welcome gladly since his sectarianist impulse was, at first, to advance the confrontation as energetically as possible in order to expose Monroe's real literary politics. So he told her: "You have drawn the line with admirable clarity." Allen Tate she had placed accurately, he pointed out, adding that "Tate, as you know, has been about as shameless a reactionary as the South has been able to compound so far." Note that Burnshaw also conceded Monroe's placement of the noncommunist liberal MacLeish on the right (he had earned a "first place among the incipient Fascists of American poetry"). By this point the pitch was getting higher, as Burnshaw was quite willing to see the differences between *Poetry* and the *New Masses* clearly stated even while disallowing Monroe's general distinction between poetry and politics. While the latter magazine fought "with and for a class that is rising into power," the former put up its "solid front of reaction." He saved his harshest ridicule for Monroe's hope that someday *Poetry* would publish a revolutionary poem that would earn the status of "immortal," suggesting that "revolutionary poets are hardly going to elect for their masterpieces an organ surviving on a capitalist subsidy."[103]

In response to her claim that he was merely a cheeky new convert to communism, he ascribed such assumptions to the way in which the obdurate modernist mainstream journal, far from inspiring poetic development, retarded it. It was true that his own "Eartha" poems, a lyric sequence Monroe had admired "only four years ago,"[104] had been accepted for publication in *Poetry*; yes, but only after she had prohibited other poems he had submitted — and *they* had been revolutionary poems.[105] Here was the rub: The poetic spheres Monroe deemed separate intersected a great deal more than she realized.

> Frankly, Miss Monroe, [Burnshaw wrote,] I find it almost unbelievable that an intellect as unusual as yours finds it difficult to understand and condone the point of view expressed by those of us who feel the desirability and historical necessity of a proletarian revolution. . . . *Don't you grant that the political awareness of revolutionary writers is nothing less than a logical necessity of intellectual awareness, since politics and culture are now proved inseparable?* (emphasis added)[106]

4: POPULAR-FRONT POETICS

The Burnshaw-Monroe debate was important not only because it provided modernists a close-up view — in a journal modernists like Stevens knew well and whose editors they generally still respected — of a self-consciously modern literary institution responding very defensively to incursion from the left, and not only because it was probably Stevens's first sighting of the young Burnshaw, a view likely to have shaped his own response a year later in "Owl's Clover." In that poem Stevens discloses a detailed understanding

of the exchanges between the two positions epitomized by Burnshaw and
Monroe. Their dispute is important, too, because it gave modernists a basis
for accounting the differences between contentious and remediative ex-
pressive modes – modes that I would argue paralleled the favored "presen-
tational" and the scorned "meditative" forms of modernism at issue within
objectivist reforms-from-within-modernism.

In the year that passed between the Burnshaw-Monroe and Burnshaw-
Stevens incidents, much will have changed in the rhetorical association of
poetic left and right. So much indeed that even noncommunist poets who
were not closely following leftist tendencies would still have known enough
to distinguish Burnshaw's criticism of *Ideas of Order* from his criticism of
Monroe's thesis of separability. To perceive the two approaches as ideological equals would be to misread basic development from the sectarian mannerism of the Third Period (1928–33), in which the communist critic saw
noncommunist poetry emerging out of a "fascist unconscious," to a revisionist or latitudinarian aesthetic (1935–39) that Burnshaw turned toward
Stevens, entailing an interpretive practice in which what was dormant in
noncommunist poetry was not its fascism but conversely its potential for
contributing to social change.

Literary-left sectarianism, distinguished by intense "adventurism" and
"ultra-leftism" and actually a good deal of frankness, was typified, and in
some ways invented, by the confrontational reviewing style of Mike Gold,
whose "Out of the Fascist Unconscious," a brutal attack on MacLeish's
"Frescoes for Mr. Rockefeller's City," articulated a notion of the political
unconscious. This interpretive practice enabled the communist literary critic
to read antagonism to revolutionary change as latent even when the writer
under question was consciously a near or imminent ally.[107] "One became so
adept at handling these concepts," Alan Calmer readily admitted just a few
years later, "that it was easy to prove how political reaction lurked behind
the purest love sonnet."[108] Even after breaking with both the party and the
New Masses in the summer of 1936, Burnshaw, behaving very unlike Calmer,
did "my duty by my Party and my Self" and never once spoke against left-
sectarianism publicly.[109] If he had repudiated his former position, he might
have described a few of his own essays and reviews of 1933 and 1934 that
were modeled on Gold's contentious manner and held pretty closely to the
theory of the fascist unconscious. "A New Untermeyer Product," not nearly
Burnshaw's staunchest piece of the period, took on *Poetry: Its Appreciation
and Enjoyment* principally because Louis Untermeyer was not "able to re-
solve the critical 'controversies' of, let's say, an Archibald MacLeish vs. Mike
Gold" and because, even in chapters dedicated to a category of great currency, such as "The Poem as Weapon," Untermeyer "contain[ed] not the
merest mention of the recent infuriated debate about art and propaganda."
(True enough: In 1934 political satire was being described in this book as

largely caused by "personal grudges" and as meanness arising from physical deformity, Byron's club-foot and Pope's hunchback.)[110] Untermeyer was merely "the perfect liberal." "Unfortunately," Burnshaw wrote, "people will be sold this book."[111]

American poets were affected by the sectarian cultural tactic in a number of ways. The most important consequence was that it forced both insiders and outsiders to develop a good sense of timing. For poets deeply committed to communism, the effect is easily described: It kept them policing themselves. Maas's anxiety about the dedicatory poem to S. Foster Damon introducing his first book – Damon was not in the least a political ally – serves well as an example: "[I]t's such an *exalted* piece," Maas confessed, "Jesus, spare me from the Marxians when they read it!"[112] A little more difficult to describe is the way in which the sectarian line pushed away other, less officially faithful poets by inducing the very same trepidations that kept Maas close. The example of MacLeish, whom Burnshaw called "McBosh," is well known.[113] Horace Gregory's case is perhaps more suggestive of how such estrangement conditioned radical standing. When he deviated in "One Writer's Position" – avowing that "the Communist Party has proved to me again and again that it is the only group retaining a hope for the future," he nonetheless confessed that he stood "somewhere outside the circle of all groups"[114] – one of several replies, Meridel LeSueur's "The Fetish of Being Outside," wondered: "[W]hy want to be an outsider when you see and admit sight of the Promised Land as Gregory does?"[115]

Somewhere between Maas's submission and Gregory's (temporary) resistance was the most common means of dealing with the narrow Third Period line – to outlast the inevitable slight deviations, disaffections and returns. There were probably dozens of small, mostly unadvertised rehabilitations and reversals for each one remembered today, and this was the aspect of literary communism most visible to Stevens (while least visible to his interpreters in later decades), as poets moved quietly in and conspicuously out of the journals he read, giving him a good look at literary-political "circulation" in advance of the Popular Front. For Cold War-era historians of American communism, who not surprisingly underestimate the value of circulation, this also happens to be the most ridiculed aspect of ultra-leftism – described for instance by Howe and Coser in 1957 as "a tendency fundamentally terrifying, even if sometimes comic in its manifestations";[116] and it was the special brand of literary self-destruction advertised prominently a few years later by *Partisan Review* modernists, who would dramatize the shift from Third Period to Popular Front, and at the same time, focus on a degradation ritual as the ultimate weakness of the communists' cultural routine. (Of all those radical writers who had once contributed more than two items to the *New Masses*, Herbert Solow tabulated in

Partisan, one in every four had subsequently been designated "enemies of mankind.")[117]

But there was much more to ideological circulation than self-criticism, degradation, hypocrisy, and betrayal. Timing was everything; and in this Burnshaw and Stevens were unusually well met, both masters of good timing. Yet even among writers on the left, the talent for measuring passing aesthetic opportunities is an extremely hard one to characterize. Nevertheless, I am sure it is the key to distinguishing acuteness from dullness in "social poetry" of the period.[118] De facto poetry policy at the *New Masses* meant that a poem submitted there tended to be deemed "good" if it *anticipated* shifting lines of alliance in some way, and one way was itself wholly aesthetic. (My point is that this was no less true after the advent of the Popular Front than before.) When one submission to the *New Masses* from a communist poet was rejected, that aspirant, himself an editor at another journal with its own line, could then reject the work of another poet using the rationale by which he had himself first been spurned. There might not have been, as Burnshaw has persuasively explained to me, forthrightly stated political standards governing rejections at the *New Masses*, but the ripple effect outward, from communist through fellow-traveler poets, from toe-the-line to fellow-traveling journals, and then to formerly recalcitrant journals like *Poetry* under the liberal Dillon, can be clearly discerned. In June 1934 Burnshaw returned one set of poems sent the *New Masses* with the mild admonition that they "seem to us too chock full of startling imagery and so we can't use them."[119] Six months later (as the Popular Front was dawning) the poet whose work Burnshaw had rejected himself rejected another's, submitted elsewhere, as "counter-revolutionary in tone,"[120] to which the third poet (Jack Wheelwright, an active radical) responded: "Alas, the radicals do not understand poetry and the poets do not understand the revolution."[121] Even during the period in which left sectarianism was official practice guiding party-affiliated projects, such policy, especially when it came time to justify acceptance or rejection of poems on ideological grounds, was hardly monolithic. A poem, having deviated once, might itself be changed because of its slightly shifted relation to social conceptions. Describing an ode that had been rejected, a poet wrote with a tone of self-accusation that might seem surreal now, but was rhetorically commonplace then. It "is *no longer* counter-revolutionary," the poet wrote his editor, "and I am sorry you do not feel able to run it"; one notes with some astonishment that the words of the poem had not themselves been altered.[122] In the special language leftist poets used to describe their work to each other and to editorial allies, a poem lived an ideologically athletic life of its own. The talent for good timing – for reading the way in which a text's reception, though not the text itself, was the changing thing, not year to year but month to month – meant a great deal to one's hopes of having poems appraised as dynamic. When mailing a cycle of nine lyrics, "The Great Dark Love," to Granville Hicks, himself then deemed orthodox (in the fifties Howe and Coser dubbed Hicks "the chief Keeper of the Norm"[123]), Burnshaw felt he must confess that "these lyrics are not immediately related to Marxism," and he meant the word "immediately" as a matter of time, not of ideological space. The hypothetical critic mounting that charge, Burnshaw insisted, "could not say that they did not exhibit a nostalgia for something other than the present, even though the future they seem to ask for is far far ahead. I personally believe that they are 'timed' in a period after the world will have been communized."[124] Burnshaw knew foot for foot, stave by stave, how his own poetry was evolving. But he was enough of a cultural materialist, a practiced if not a theorized one, to realize what was important to his poetic career: his extraordinarily sharp sense of the relative rate of change in the literary-political environment that produced that poetry and of the rhetorical measure with which the two often differing rates might be advantageously compared. Maas, whose evolution Stevens was watching at close hand, provides a case in contrast. With not nearly Burnshaw's sense of timing, Maas realized what a difference six months could make. His retraction of the assault on *We Gather Strength*, appearing under the bland headline "An Improvement," told readers much more about the reviewer than the reviewed, with its confession that the original negative notice had been written a half-year prior to publication: By then "the entire editorial staff of the New Masses ha[d] been changed." "I *now* feel," Maas lied, "that . . . at last we may hope for a real revolutionary poetry movement in America."[125]

   Because third-period practice created such complications, for some bewildering but inspiring, for others disorienting and ruinous, it is too frequently assumed that the shift to the Popular Front in August 1935 gave only great relief and vastly simplified matters – that noncommunist circulating could suddenly commence and give pleasure; that for all liberals, "American Communists suddenly became all sweetness and light, clean-cut disciples of American virtue" (as one historian mockingly put it).[126] In this view, helpful though at times dismissive and even in Stevens's case reductive, it would seem that the new disposition, urging communist critics to open up the ranks of the literary left to as many potential allies as possible and by speaking of the "left" in broad and inviting antifascist terms, alleviated the necessity of keeping a scorecard to know the players – as it would obviate both the incessant choosing up sides and the tough appraisal of reactionaries' naming of partisans. In this reading, offered either for unconditional praise or more often as anticommunist ridicule, the literary Popular Front is mostly or solely remembered as the happy bandwagon Joseph Freeman later described for Daniel Aaron, and every bit as "elastic and benevolent" as Kazin later recalled,[127] for under its auspices "the dichotomy between poetry and politics disappeared, art and life were fused"[128] and "everyone was invited inside."[129] Given the "sudden infatuation with bourgeois culture,"[130] the rise of "an unembarrassed, radical middle class"[131] – indeed an all-out rejection of "Social Democratic drivel to the effect that fascism was 'a revolt of the middle classes'"[132] – the very worst diagnosis that could be made for a moderate or apolitical writer described a temporary illness: *confusion.*[133] In fact, however – and this is especially important when considering Stevens's attraction to what he plainly called "leftism" in the autumn of 1935 – the shift to the Popular Front that was large enough in theory to include himself, Williams, Millay, and MacLeish with room to spare, while perhaps simplifying the communists' dealings with governmental policies (in the fight against the rise of Hitler, and soon in urging Western intervention in Spain), did not simplify the dealings with artists, lyric poets in particular. What it did for modern American poetry, actually, was fashion out the old policy, the policy of interpreting in noncommunist texts a fascist unconscious, a concept that might be conversely called a revolutionary unconscious. The act of interpretation now obliged was no less complex than before: The people's front critic was licensed to investigate what the poem under consideration did not know about its own latent *endorsement* of social change. Allies could be found in almost any poetic -ism, just as before incipient fascists could be found almost anywhere.[134] Hardly a simplified situation. Nor was there anything simple about the temporary "reassembly of forces" Raymond Williams recalled in "The Politics of the Avant-Garde": "Surrealists [mixed] with social realists, Constructivists with folk artists, popular internationalism with popular nationalism."[135] Since the "all art is bunk" line was out – it was now deemed "incongruous to find it in a poem," as Isidor Schneider warned Ruth Lechlitner – radical editors and poets were left to seek formal congruities and to judge "bunk" work by work, which is what most of them thought they should have been doing all along.[136]

The fact, moreover, that among American literary leftists expressions of popular-front ideas and attitudes preceded the official Comintern announcement by some months[137] only makes Burnshaw's approach to Stevens and Stevens's response to Burnshaw still more difficult to decipher. In May, at the first American Writers Congress, Joe Freeman suggested that it "is not necessary for a writer to subscribe completely to the political program of the proletarian party in order to aid the workers; it is unnecessary for him to abandon poetry for organizational activity."[138] The statement merely recapitulated what many radicals had been saying privately and publicly for months. Matthew Josephson, for instance, another writer of Stevens's generation who had gone left, had been speaking of putting on potentially sympathetic writers only "minimal demands, broad enough to embrace people of various persuasions."[139] A *New Masses* article had argued still earlier that any "writer . . . honestly looking for something better, can cast his lot with the working class. In time he may become . . . acclimated and naturalized."[140] An essay on literary interpretation that preceded the official announcement of the Popular Front by five months fell into certain old traps (MacLeish's notorious "Frescoes," yet again, was said to be "of 'considerable beauty' but . . . *nevertheless fascist in content*"); yet the same piece managed also to articulate a significant theoretical step toward popular-front poetics. It was "dangerous" to argue merely that a "poem expresses what [its] author meant to express," for that would exclude nonradical poets who were unconsciously revolutionary, whose writings were more insurgent than they themselves had yet become, and whose lack of knowledge about provoking social change it was now the job of the revolutionary critic to disclose. Thus the royalist Balzac and the mystic Dostoyevsky were deemed "significant largely because they expressed *what they did not mean to express*."[141] Moreover, as we have seen, the "Call" for the American Writers Congress, in the first weeks of 1935, urged communist writers to begin working with bourgeois editors and publishers. Even if Willard Maas had not joined Alcestis Press primarily for this reason (to help radicalize poets like Williams and, indeed, Stevens), Maas's notion that "the revolutionary number" of *Alcestis Quarterly* would greatly benefit by being precisely timed with the appearance of Stevens's *Ideas* from the same press might have seemed, from the perspective of the following autumn, to have been a splendidly coordinated example of popular-front publishing.

For the book-reviewing routine at the *New Masses*, and for Burnshaw in particular – and thus, for Stevens – the rise of communist latitudinarianism did cause some important changes. Burnshaw's essay, "Middle-Ground Writers," widely admired, served as a kind of popular-front primer for communist and fellow-traveling reviewers. When a writer learned that simply to *be* a writer entailed opposition to fascism, his or her work would be politically clarified. The "confused" or middle-ground writer was "striving toward ideological clarification," and it was the job of the reviewer to meet him or her part way. He or she must cease wielding a "bludgeoning criticism" and put aside "the skull-cracking method"[142] made famous by Gold's "bumpy, erratic, disjointed" reviews that blasted Gertrude Stein as a "literary idiot," Sherwood Anderson as a "cockroach aristocrat," Edmund Wilson as a "high-bosomed Beacon Hill matron entering a common street car"[143] – a procedure flawed because it utterly ignored the indivisibility of form and value and drove potential allies away. Leaving Gold's bumpiness behind with some relief, the critic now smoothly showed how the writing under review expressed a "condition of creative crisis."[144] Thus by theorizing about the new reviewing policy well in advance of taking on the Stevens assignment, Burnshaw eased the critical difficulty of explaining the rationale for his Stevens review, although when he wrote his commentary on

Ideas of Order in September, the role of the radical as guide and ideological clarifier had just then become an orthodox one whereas it had been unofficial when he wrote the theoretical piece. But, again, the Popular Front did not simply indicate that the reviewer who once scored incipient fascists and now encouraged unconscious revolutionaries was also suddenly free to sanction noncommunists as he pleased. In fact, the new approach merely set up a freer-*seeming* set of guidelines that, for reviewers in particular, could be as inhibiting and as strictly constructed as the old confrontational line. At least in earlier days if you were too sympathetic to an incipient fascist, you were yourself subject to being called one; now, with the new openness, there was a certain amount of insisting on openness. It was no simple matter psychologically.[145] We have already seen how Burnshaw, responding to Maas's review of the *We Gather Strength* poets in *Poetry*, cracked some skulls – writing to *Poetry* to insist Maas had actually changed his mind, urging Maas to write a letter of retraction[146] – all fully in spite of the fact that Burnshaw, in his own much later judgment, "thought [at the time] that on the whole the poetry the *New Masses* was publishing was pretty lousy."[147]

Another remarkably different example of Burnshaw's reviewing strategy survives. This time Maas himself wanted to savage a book of nonpolitical lyrics for its lack of revolutionary themes – *Poems*, by the activist progressive Californian Marie de L. Welch.[148] But Burnshaw, taking a latitudinarian line, suggested strongly that Maas "make a few revisions" in his notice. "I know that no one could get the impression from [Welch's] book that she is very sympathetic to the revolutionary movement or that she has actually done revolutionary verse," but her publisher had stifled her good ideological proclivities by "enforc[ing] certain restrictions"; certain lyric poems not admitted into the collection, Burnshaw promised, did after all show "definite *indications of a left tendency*." He added: "In view of these facts don't you think the tone could be *somewhat more tentative*? . . . I am all for giving people a chance unless they have proved themselves outright bastards."[149] Maas did revise his brief review of Welch for his editor,[150] and the final version printed in the *New Masses* reveals two closely related tendencies that have much to do with Stevens's reception. First, aesthetic latitudinarianism would not necessarily involve greater adeptness at dealing with the lyric. Second, the new reviewing policy, however open to middle-ground writers, could itself involve a version of the old skull-cracking procedure, structurally if not tonally. In the instance just mentioned a communist was brought around to sympathize with a noncommunist just as surely as the communist had been brought around when he prematurely criticized Dynamo poets as uninventive. The revised version of Maas's review included this sentence: "Here is a mind that contains a healthy outlook on phenomena of nature and one that *unconsciously* revolts against pseudo-popular philosophies of annihilation." Burnshaw's editorial impression is clear: "[O]ne misses certain pieces that have appeared under her name in current reviews – poems that have shown more of a *left tendency* than any included in this collection."[151] Despite the turnaround on Marie Welch, obviously no established way was being developed for reading a "left tendency" in lyrics like hers.

5: MUSIC OF A TOUGHENED SORT

The lyric – not only Welch's, of course, but also Stevens's – fit into that small but growing crack in communist poetic theory. This is not to say that the deeper the crack, the weaker the edifice. Popular-front poetics was a brilliantly effective hegemony in its own right, designed to absorb flaws, and having the effect of encouraging beliefs such as (among the modernists) Williams's that "you can't sacrifice technical perfections to *any* cause,"[152] and (among the radicals) Humphries's, that "the same man [*sic*] may be a good lyric poet and a good Communist."[153] It was by virtue of an openness to the noncommunist's lyric that communist verse could get beyond conservative rhetorics like Drinkwater's and Murray's and broaden the form's musical trope so that intellectual no less than specifically aesthetic work could become intrinsic to the traditional compositional element in lyric – which is, indeed, the enlarged definition of the lyric now accepted as standard. Lechlitner's poem, "This Body Politic," boldly urged "Be lyric, poet" because radicalism heaped upon radical poets so many unwieldy symbols ("The State supplies / Stag-heads for the flaccid bowels, / Hawks for the meekest eyes").[154] Harold Rosenberg wrestled metrically with what doubtless seemed to him the required use of the slow-footed word "organization." It played havoc, obviously, with a two- and three-stressed unrhymed "modern" line, but there the poem in which this metric struggle takes place itself bears signs of Rosenberg's doubts:

> And the organization
> Is it an organization?
> How many volunteers?
> Whom does it inspire?
> What man that planted a
> Vineyard and not drunk
> The first wine?

This brief poem – "The Bureaucrats" – slips into a pastiche of catchphrases, somewhat in the manner of Fearing, only to be brought up short with the heavy metrical requirements again of "the organization" (both the word and the system to which it refers):

> Do us honor   Generals
> And foreign visitors
> Are pleased with us   Yes

Women too already
And automobiles
Up there

But the organization
All the washed-out stuff is seeping steadily back? . . . [155]

David Wolff, before going off to fight in Spain, made his pact with modernism in "Remembering Hart Crane": If "the riveters of the real / bridges
[are] invisible to you forever," it is because Crane has died and not because
he never understood the real. And although Wolff evidently felt his elegy
would not be complete without telling Crane directly of a "new bridge we
project," a "Party of one weld" and "living steel," the middle of the poem
credits Crane for having understood how

> the first-class of U.S.A.,
> whose coin, like gilt, is lethal on the skin, encouraged
> into their smooth imperial Caribbean

Crane himself, "in pajamas last seen madly smiling." The unabashed
radicalization of Crane and his bridge here − conspiracy theories to explain how imperialists drove him mad and to a watery death, how capitalists underwrote a bridge "whose first pier destroys the tenements" − is
supported, not contradicted, by the direct and admitted influence of Crane's
lyric line on Wolff's, especially obvious in passages most politically bitter
(for example, phrases like "their smooth imperial Caribbean").[156] And Harvey
Breit, then a member (with Harry Roskolenko) of a an ultraleft anti-Stalinist
splinter group and still lamenting the absence of a truly revolutionary party,
was in virtually the same breath praising Crane and favorably comparing
him with Stevens and Williams. Crane's singing was "in a big tradition," Breit
wrote with the same fervor he reserved for his own and others' "Revolutionary
inadequacies."[157]

Such talk as Breit's is typical of the letters I've found in the archives. And
such problems as Lechlitner, Rosenberg, and Wolff faced as poets are quite
common among the radicals whose work I have read. Indeed, in my view
the American mid-thirties marks a significant moment in the lyric's long
thematic evolution. In "Mozart, 1935," Stevens deliberately engaged the
lyric's foundational musical principle to make unmistakably manifest the
contribution of modernism to revisionist poetics. As early as Maas's review
of Welch − and it is just one of many similar instances, save that there the
evidence fully survives − it was clear that in order to read a noncommunist
lyricist as unwittingly sympathetic to social change, the radical critic had
to find a way to make the movement of the lyric, from bad to good on the
sliding scale of politically ascribed values, the poet's very theme. The critic
would make "sensibility" metaphorically thematic as "substance" ("sensibility" was allegedly bad if pure, "substance" allegedly good if pure),[158] or,

in Edmund Wilson's terms, would thematize structural "coherence" as intellectual "significance." The critic would have to make central the very shift of communist poets toward the lyric as means by which radical poets, *always insufficiently radical*, expressed credibly the "confused," "anxious," "desperate" condition that led the noncommunist poet under moral scrutiny to "seiz[e] handfuls of things he feels sure of" – that classic lyric gambit.[159] Once the sound of poetry had been itself made the material of the poem – a material the radical critic could claim he or she helped produce in the act of searching for signs of unconscious alliance – the disengaged poet, now theoretically split into two, into an unconsciously political and a consciously nonpolitical self, became an "organized" or ideologically "clarified" artist who could begin to "play the present," in the crucial metaphor of lyricism in Stevens's "Mozart, 1935." The noncommunist poet began to seek the apt subgeneric frame for the "confused" poet-self, the decadent, "disorganized" identity enamored of sounds severed from sense – the poetic identity revealed in Stevens's verse that made Richard Blackmur only a little nervous and caused Marianne Moore to issue uncalled-for praise, she being utterly undaunted by the left. ("Wallace Stevens," Moore would write, "is as susceptible to sound as objects were to Midas' golden touch" – and in saying so she set up one of the great mixed ratios in modern poetics.)[160]

Trying to find their own ways through this dense critical atmosphere, in which it was fashionable to observe confusion in others *while admitting it for oneself*, Stevens's liberal and leftist reviewers, following Burnshaw's topography plotting the middle ground, began remarking that the author of *Ideas of Order*, and in turn *Owl's Clover* and *The Man with the Blue Guitar & Other Poems*, could now be discovered in the process of motioning toward "themes of commanding contemporary stature" while standing steadfastly by the lyric. They saw that he was making a "movement toward a poetry of statement" safely within what was earlier deemed a thoroughly nonthematic concern for old rhythms and (mere) "poetic effects."[161] Whether a communist poem could ever be founded on a "love" of "fragments saved" from a broken-up world, to quote Burnshaw again; whether a formalism for 1935 was tenable: These became main themes of the artist struggling against ideological disorientation. And it must be pointed out that Burnshaw was saying throughout 1935 that communist poets were no less "confused" on the point, having been forced into the position of reinventing the importance of prosody as if no pre- or noncommunist poet had ever reached that point. "*[D]o not forget what I have discovered*: rhythm," wrote Kenneth Fearing to Carl Rakosi, using "discovered" in all seriousness; "Nothing without it is poetry; and, of course, I do not mean iambic pentameter."[162] Rakosi the objectivist must have felt that his good friend Fearing the communist was trying to manage a certain trading of poetic places. Stevens, I am suggesting, felt similarly about the comments of his radical correspondents and reviewers. Ben Belitt's judgment that Stevens's new "music is . . . of a *more toughened sort*, pruned of bravura and *merging the logical with the lyrical*"[163] conformed to the ideas Burnshaw expressed in "Notes on Revolutionary Poetry" and "Middle-Ground Writers": What revolutionary poetry and criticism had been lacking, Burnshaw argued in one essay and strongly implied in the other, was a sense of the entanglement of political meaning in poetic form. During the era of the Popular Front communist critics were making up lost formal ground while liberal critics were seeking to redress their own earlier blindness to political "content." When liberal reviewers were praising Albert Halper's novel *The Chute* for its political content, knowingly disregarding its very clumsy writing, a prominent communist critic insisted on panning the book solely because it failed to meet "literary standards"; thus the aesthetic was deemed another of the left critic's "responsibilities." ("I as a critic," Granville Hicks wrote, "and the New Masses as an organ of the left wing have certain responsibilities – to writers, to readers, and to the maintenance of literary standards." This reviewer's judgment stood in spite of the strong sense among editors at *New Masses* that in the era of the Popular Front they should at all costs avoid "dealing harshly with a friendly and important writer.")[164] The very fact, moreover, that in making his own points about the politics of form Stanley Burnshaw felt he could cite and endorse I. A. Richards's quasi-scientific efforts in declaring the indivisibility of form and "content"[165] suggested that curious theoretical alliances would be forged in the process of trying to reinvigorate the radical movement through a deliberate return to the aesthetic in poetry. Thus a *New Masses* editor openly broke with Anglo-American Marxist conventions for rebuking Richardian materialism. This, it should be noted, was a time when William Phillips, in his essay "Form and Content," was lambasting Richards in *Partisan Review* for advancing an "indecisive, evasive approach to content" because his "milieu . . . contains no groundwork of affirmative belief."[166]

Viewed from the point at which Burnshaw turned his eye toward the revolutionary unconscious in poems like "Mozart, 1935" and "Sad Strains of a Gay Waltz," Maas's and T. C. Wilson's "aesthetic-deviationist" tactics, which had both poets calling for the greater assimilation of communist verse by the lyric, were now actually paradigmatic for reading Stevens as political. Leftist poetry now needed a strong dose of what was clumsily but significantly called the "modern subjective lyric," the poem of individual feeling. In a purely strategic sense this line contributed to the idea (much ridiculed in the late forties and fifties) that the communist cultural movement should recruit modernist eminences, like Burnshaw's compatriot Kreymborg. When in "Notes on Revolutionary Poetry" Burnshaw proclaimed that "[t]he mode of expression indigenous to the cultural group *will determine the forms*," he was opening the way for big names moving left. The assumption here, interestingly, is that the lyric was native to the individualist class, and since the left was now courting bourgeois allies, it was in effect courting the lyric as well. To prove that he was committed to the notion, he bravely quoted as bold counterexamples "passages from revolutionary poems which are plainly *precious*,"[167] written by radical poets who remained unnamed in the essay for reasons Burnshaw recently told me were "tactical."[168] To be sure, certain poetic forms were still then to be decried as "fragments saved from the splintering wreckage" of a civilization that had provoked the great modernist revolt in the first decades. But the impulse to save such fragments, by the thirties, threatened to revive charming euphonies in rear-guard efforts to divert younger poets' attentions from American modernism's moral flaws (Eliot and Pound were said to be chief malefactors in this regard; Stevens, Moore, Millay, and Cummings less so; Williams rarely). To show that modernism's radical inheritors could discover the unmarked route between Freeman's uninventive sonnets (per Burnshaw) and Funaroff's slavish Eliotisms (per Maas) was precisely the rationale that guided Maas's boldly heterodox selection of the revolutionary poetry for *Alcestis 4*, and led him to explain to Latimer that the "lyrical radicals" (including Burnshaw's *New Masses* colleague, Isidor Schneider) were writing poetry *similar* to that of the poets of *Alcestis 3*, which featured Stevens's "Sailing after Lunch," "The American Sublime," and "Mozart, 1935." So, at least in Maas's view, Stevens was to be found along that unmarked way between traditional lyric and modernism. Lechlitner encouraged Maas: "I like the lyric stride. I've always felt that revolutionary poets have been afraid of lyricism and adopted prosy and ponderous style with deplorable results."[169] Maas's strictly confidential version of the radicals' new approach to the lyric made Stevens's usefulness clearer still: "You are right about Stevens in one way," he confessed to the west-coast radical Sara Bard Field who had raised the touchy subject:

> I couldn't ever be that detached but I must respect him for his magnificent rhetoric, his sense of form, his cerrebration [*sic*], his celebration of the ecstasy and the world of colored peacocks and unreality made real with delicate fire-tongues and insistent cymbals and tambourines. He is, in his best work, a joyous dancer, a trifler touched with visions, dancing to a Bach fugue. . . . Stevens finds his particular celebration out of tune today, [but] he is trying also desp[e]rately to find, to make, "order out of ideas."[170]

That a communist poet could say such things to his mentor cogently refutes the usual view of the thirties that "[t]he times conspired *against the lyricist* unless like Stevens he chose to sing largely unheard."[171] Obviously Stevens was not going unheard. Nor, more important, was the lyric by 1935 a victim of conspiracy. Rather, I contend, it was a unique beneficiary.

6: PLAYING THE PRESENT

Calling a lyricist to a piano Stevens knows is out of tune with the times, "Mozart, 1935" begins by directing this poet-figure to continue nevertheless playing sound over sense ("hoo-hoo-hoo," "shoo-shoo-shoo," "ric-a-nic") and to "practice arpeggios" for the purpose, apparently, of diverting the speaker's attention from the battle being waged nearby. But the threat is near: People have been throwing stones on the roof from the streets outside the room in which the pianist has been instructed to take his seat. The poem has begun, then, by suggesting itself as contributing to a diversionary tactic, a fine looking away from trouble:

> Poet, be seated at the piano.
> Play the present. . . .
>   (CP 131)

And yet, in its own time, this poem emerged as the one work William Rose Benét could say "most clearly" expressed "[t]he poet's attitude toward the epoch in which he finds himself."[172] How was such a double politics possible? "Mozart, 1935" immediately discloses a will to counter complaints of pure poetry, to refute that charge heard regularly from Stevens's critics, to find "his particular celebration *out of tune* today" on his own if necessary; and, in short, to meet the communist Maas's "*respect* for his magnificent rhetoric" at least halfway across from right to left. That Stevens's poetry was all music and no ideas became the repeated refrain of some of his leftist critics. Even so eager a devotee of the communist lyric as T. C. Wilson, we recall, expressed the point privately to Moore by insisting that Stevens's work was too much "of the senses."[173] Perhaps more important, the notion that the old tyranny of form held sway over Stevens was becoming the obligatory lament of many nonradical critics who were unaware of the extent to which the left had already touched them. Benét, in his review of *Ideas*, inadvertently quoted Stevens against himself; tellingly, it was also a passage Burnshaw marked in the copy of *Ideas* he used for preparing his review:[174]

> Is the function of the poet here mere sound,
> Subtler than the ornatest prophecy,
> To stuff the ear?[175]

Rakosi, in "Domination of Wallace Stevens (1925)," could begin by calling out in much-felt debt, "Clear me with this master music," and yet finally express doubts about all those "happy unities" issuing from "the grave interior."[176] Then there was Untermeyer, the liberal whose entrepreneurial anthologizing had come in for much blunt left criticism, passing on a bit of the same. "Often enough a [Stevens] poem refuses to yield a meaning," Untermeyer wrote, "but 'Academic Discourse at Havana' and 'The Idea of Order at Key West' surrender themselves in an almost pure music."[177] "[A] pity," lamented twenty-eight-year-old Theodore Roethke in the *New Republic*, "that such a rich and special sensibility should be content with the order of words and music and not project itself more vigorously upon the present-day world."[178] Even Roethke, whose "vegetal radicalism,"[179] according to Burke, would soon create in him a much stronger sense of Stevens's stylistic influence, was prepared to insinuate the logically false antagonisms: "Sensibility" (that fighting word)[180] inhibits vigor, as "the order of words and music" obstructs the use of contemporary themes. Yet *play the present* was Stevens's instruction to his modern Mozart.

"Mozart, 1935" indeed answers these particular grievances, openly at first, and then more discriminatingly in the last lines. In the end Stevens will have employed one tenet of the literary left to counter another, the main allegation of pure poetry. Finally he will have thematized the lyric "confusion" conveyed by the disorganized artist, for it was this lyricist, not the self-aware "clarified" one, who must be invited to use his "Singing Strength" (in Kreymborg's prepolitical Whitmanian phrase freely adopted by the left)[181] to give voice to the cries of the people in the streets. In this special liberating sense, the noncommunist lyric was designed to preach primarily to the converted as a means of converting itself. Not merely the "toughened" music that Belitt soon heard Stevens performing, then, but a great deal more: "music . . . merging the logical with the lyrical."[182] If Stevens was using "Mozart" to answer the indictment directly at first, the answer begins with the very title, which indicates that among the levels of poetic subject-position – Stevens's, the speaker's, and the pianist's – the speaker is conscious of the inappropriateness of what he calls upon the pure poet to play, even as he risks presenting an image of the masses familiar from The Hartford's mob-psychology explanations of dissident activity. The title allows Stevens to say for the speaker, in other words, *Surely you can find a Mozart for my time of crisis.*

The provocation first entailed the mere use of Mozart. By far the most famous and perhaps the most ferocious third-period communist attack on a bourgeois writer, Mike Gold's homophobic abuse of Thornton Wilder, had been incited by Wilder's "rootless cosmopolitanism" and his engagement of "the most erudite and esoteric themes one could ever imagine." Wilder's writing was reprehensible because it was "all about Angels, and Mozart, and King Louis, and Fairies."[183] Through the very title, then – "Mozart" and "1935" separated by the mere comma, suggesting one element in, or in relation to, the other – the speaker distinguishes himself from the addressed pure poet, implying that if one should be criticized for fingering a *divertimento* in 1935, the attack cannot be aimed at this modern ingénue, who is, after all, tutored by the more conscious poet-figure, by far the worthier antagonist of the two: he, in short, is the Stevensian figure of capable imagination, sheltering a beset *poète maudit* while half-wittingly exposing him to public dangers – imagining a certain outmoded art form as downright instigation.

In beseeching such a political innocent to be seated at the piano, the speaker admits his audacious sense of cause and effect:

> *If* they throw stones upon the roof
> While you practice arpeggios,
> *It is because* they carry down the stairs
> A body in rags.

And *so* "Be seated." Ignore whatever disturbances 1935 may heap upon you; *you* play strains stirred not the slightest bit by what has been happening around you. Yet what is happening – if only because it is at this point so much an intrusion and so scarcely explained – has impressed the music's audience (and thus, of course, the poem's). The implicit pun on "strain" was much in poetic currency, synonymous with "confusion" and always used self-referentially. Similarly current was the exposure of aesthetic havens as prisons. Kenneth Patchen's "Loyalty Is the Life You Are" notes hauntingly how "our eyes are the eyes at your windows gentlemen / our hands are the hands at the latches of your doors" – but then: "I think the strain is good gentlemen."[184] Stevens likewise acknowledges extra-aesthetic forces at work on the lyric. One's arpeggios are perhaps disfigured but not in the way the poet-player plays but by the present concentrated hearing the lyric will receive. One can hardly imagine ignoring the stone throwers. Here the auditors are themselves making sound in return; no passive listeners they. Those plunks on the roof provide a new metronome for 1935 art. This, then, is strong internal evidence that Stevens knew what constituted the provocation of the poetic revolutionists' willfully arhythmic beat – Rukeyser's irregular meter burst by industrial-strength spondees, for instance:

> now that the factory is sealed-up brick
> the kids throw stones, smashing the window,
> membranes of uselessness in desolation.[185]

After having worked hard to establish himself as something of an expert on free-verse prosody, and eschewing as naive the "Cause, Not Craft" mode of Gold and a few other exaggerators,[186] Burnshaw, ever a purist on the point, observed sourly to Kreymborg: "Rukeyser seems to be the one to praise these days." He meant, in part, that the less one seemed to care for the metric tradition, the greater the chance of left-wing fame.[187] Obviously, though, Rukeyser, following her elder Lola Ridge in this respect, was thinking about relations between radicalism, prosody, and gender in the subversive sense meant by Ridge when she addressed "Russian Women" collectively: "You swing of necessity into male rhythms / that at once become female rhythms. . . . / in you there is no peace, / but infinite collisions."[188]

Still more disturbing to the speaker of Stevens's "Mozart" than such arpeggios-turned-stones is the fact that "they" – the street masses, the stone throwers, the unwitting inventors of the subversive new music – have now suddenly appeared *inside* the house. They are to be seen, after all, carrying *out* that unidentified "body in rags." The poet-figure in Stevens is nowhere more profoundly shaken than when his conception of art in "1935" is challenged on its own indoors terms, as "they" threaten that conception inside and out. The poem's increasingly deliberate lack of internally consistent logic intensifies this sense of confusion, for the battle enacted here between the intrinsic and the extrinsic *must* get at the inmost construction of what Stevens had deemed poetic language, quite as much as it upsets the plain antagonistic sense it carries. Cause and effect are completely disturbed. Does the pure poet's act of practicing arpeggios have anything really to do with the stone throwing? Is this so *because* "they" carry down a corpse? Had the ragged body held the life of friend or foe? Does its raggedness suggest a metricist ally who had become demoralized? Was his death, as it were, an inside job? Stevens sensed, I think, that left-against-left malevolence was the literary left's weakest point: The difference between, on one hand, Schneider's stern "Portrait of a False Revolutionist" and Stevens's "Mozart, 1935" is the latter's playfulness; Stevens's Mozart deliberately produces what Schneider calls "the indoors art:"

> He'll chant red song
> like a cricket all day long,
> if you let him hum
> *safe and warm*
> *out of the storm.*[189]

Ideological falsity having been turned around, Mozart endeavors no such "chant": Stevens's shrewd version of Schneider's poem – it had appeared in *Alcestis Quarterly* – discloses a trope latent in Schneider's False/True antinomy for revolutionists, namely Indoor/Outdoor. He poses a great danger when "you let him hum." The poem necessarily cannot explore the implications of preventing him from such "safe" "indoors" humming, and that is a point "Mozart" takes up. The speaker now urges the pianist to be "the *voice*, / Not *you*" – to speak indeed for others as well as himself. The pronominally reflexive is really deftly transitive, and depression-era selfhood becomes seen by self as object – not "be thou" but "be thou / *The voice*" of the people:

> Be thou, be thou
> *The voice* of angry fear,
> *The voice* of this besieging pain.

Literalized outsiders are hurling stones at the house, and "the streets are full of cries" – perhaps, or perhaps not, because the pure poet is making all sound and not singing a song of social significance. In the middle of the poem the speaker's strategy is evidently to implore the pure poet to practice well the very reverberations of his opponents. If in being merely oneself (in "be thou" reflexivity) the artist in 1935 must adapt the voice that shouts down one's art (be thou *this voice*), then one must oneself bespeak one's besieger. Soon the speaker becomes shrewder still:

> Be thou that wintry sound
> As of the great wind howling,
> By which sorrow is *released*,
> *Dismissed, absolved*
> In a starry *placating*.

"The voice" that had seemed to oppose a Mozart for 1935 is now fully naturalized. To the poet of pure sound, the artist who knows the sound itself and not the reasons why the sound is heard, the streets of cries augur the confused howling of the winter wind, a howl to be quelled by the precision and utter clarity of the stars. Through this disembodiment of sound the speaker will finally recognize that in such expression of anger sorrow might be diminished. So the piano playing does, after all, smooth over the contradictions of "1935" currency on one hand and outmoded "Mozart" on the other, absolving and placating the voices raised up by one against the other.

Kenneth Burke, too, was considering the vexing question of why at certain historical moments "the lyric tends to fall into th[e] bin" (along with, more specifically, the ode, he noticed). It was because such a form "invites us to snatch whatever mild pleasures may be at hand, and call it a day," because, in other words, the lyric is generally but not inherently conservative. He – like Stevens in my reading – found that while the lyric consorted theoretically with intellectual "acceptance," tending to take up an issue and quickly "call it a day," in certain special instances it bore close "relation to the broader frames of adjustment."[190] "Mozart, 1935" is one of the special instances Burke was hoping for. Conceding the general view that by 1935 many of the old lyric forms had "ended" in the minds of most – or otherwise had been popularized as

> Dress our economics
> In the best harmonics.
>
> We'll sing a song
> With Social Significance
> There's nothing else that will do[191]

– Stevens's speaker insisted intrepidly that "*We may return to Mozart.*" The feat was to be accomplished not by shutting out of one's lyric the streets full of cries, fear, and anger and the throwing of stones, but rather by giving voice to these elements within a lyric that had made a theme of its own potential loss – retuning itself within a "frame of adjustment," in Burke's

sense, and playing to conditions that formally allow it. The contrast between Stevens and Moore on this point – and at this very moment – is
instructive. For Moore the diversion itself would ultimately "persuade" one's
leftist detractors, as indeed it finally did[192] – the act of playing the past in
order to conjure a lost time when one had leisure for "'charming . . .
notes'" and access to an art that improvised without constraint. For Stevens
the poet must face and play (and thus in turn *adjust*) the present, no matter
what the antagonism induced by contingent notions of responsibility. He
was obviously thinking of his own poem when, sometime in the spring of
1935, he marked in pencil the following passage in his copy of Moore's
Selected Poems:

> the piano is a free field for etching; that his "charming
>   tadpole notes"
> belong to the past when one had time to play them
> to persuade . . . [certain ignorant people]
> . . . .
> that one detects creative power by its capacity to conquer
>   one's detachment. . . .[193]

Stevens knew such "a free field" for the modernist avant garde no longer
really existed – that the freedom of free art, of *Poetry's* sort of Americanized
vers libre, for instance, had bred a kind of tyranny which the new generation
of emancipated poets were repudiating; this was an acute post-liberal assessment he would not elaborate until much later,[194] but it was here in the
making. Then again, Moore, working hard at reading the new Stevens as a
stay against literary-political chaos, prepared to see in "Owl's Clover" a
continuation, not a disruption, of the *Harmonium*-like past. She jotted the
following note while preparing to write her review of that new poem:
"*Owl's C. int[eresting]* especially as it fits into the other work."[195]

7: DON'T MOURN, FORMALIZE

"Sad Strains of a Gay Waltz" picked up where "Mozart, 1935" left off. An
old significant form has become obsolete, but is there a next step to be
taken? The speaker here makes evident his attitude toward the necessity of
the question. The question has upset him. If he answers affirmatively, a
"mode of desire" may have been squandered. "*Too many* waltzes have ended"
already, and now what? In "Mozart, 1935" the ideological basis of this ca-
lamity never quite came clear – aptly I think. The detractors were typically
ill-used outside agitators, unseen rebels with unnamed cause. In "Sad Strains,"
however, Stevens's initial conservative impulse finds no check, and blame
for the loss of the civilized modes is placed squarely on the masses, "these
sudden mobs of men, // These sudden clouds of faces and arms." This
counterargument is one Stevens would use later to explain what was wrong
intellectually with unionism: He never quite got beyond the sense of the

fiftieth "Like Decorations" epigram, as unions would always merely express the natural desire of all people, in this case the working class, to be happier than they are; they want more money; they remain greedily untheorized.[196] Because in "Sad Strains" this simple argument is expressed in terms set out by "Mozart, 1935," the point is suggestively critical: Here the masses are incapable of understanding how the very forms they have supposedly helped their intellectual leaders to break can still contain the most effective articulation of their desires. While the people at large are, he grants, "An immense suppression, freed," at the same time they are artless

> voices crying without knowing for what,

> Except to be happy, without knowing how,
> Imposing forms they cannot describe,
> Requiring order beyond their speech.
>   (*CP* 122)

After this the lament can be repeated with a touch more reformist zeal: "Too many waltzes have ended." Reading this, the radical poet and reviewer Ruth Lechlitner referred to the "sudden mobs of men" – and to Stevens's use of phrases like "sudden mobs," "masses of men," and "millions" – as metonymy for what one critic has called "that decade when the crowd was made the sum total in American expression."[197] "Only the momentum of the motion of masses," wrote the young radical Whittaker Chambers in a poem called "October 21, 1936" (1931), "has any meaning."[198] For Chambers as for Stevens, the strength of masses derived from their likeness to "the moving masses of clouds" (to quote Chambers's poem again), yet Stevens's, not Chambers's, use of the image provoked Lechlitner's unsurprising conclusion that Stevens "refus[ed] to admit the desirability of the union of the mass in an 'orderly' life." On these grounds, "Stevens is obviously open to attack from the left," and he will be remembered not for "his ideas" but for his "superb mastery of form."[199]

Yet despite the disappointment the poem conveyed about the left to the left, the premise of "Sad Strains" is nevertheless a major admission that poetic forms are no more or less historically contingent than poetic objects. Too, the tone can be read as conciliatory and resigned:

> *The truth is that there comes a time*
> *When we can mourn no more over music*
> That is so much motionless sound. (emphasis added)

Here the very tenor of self-criticism, that productive but much-maligned communist subgenre, begins to enact Stevens's accommodation to the new political turn in criticisms of *Harmonium*, namely, again, that he was a poet of mere music. "Sad Strains" is clearly founded upon self-revision, truly the "plangent eleg[y] for Stevens's own poetic self" that Harold Bloom sees. But it is not so much "Hoon's Last Stand," as Bloom would also have it,[200] as a recognition of Hoon as another "most inappropriate man / In a most unpropitious place" ("Sailing after Lunch"). "[P]lace" is both space and marked time, an era. With "Sad Strains," then, Stevens came to know perfectly well where – that is, to what moment in time – his poems must go from *Harmonium*. That realization is certainly the sense of his intertextual nod to a poem of 1921, "Tea at the Palaz of Hoon": in "Sad Strains" we read, "And *then* / *There's that* mountain-minded Hoon." The echo of the old poem entails the diction of casual letting go, a relinquishing of the recent high-modernist past of art's "free field," the field on which Moore in her own brilliant way remained (and, in less generous view, to which she was unfortunately confined).

Stevens now knew why and how Hoon must be revised for the mid-thirties: "Now, for him, his forms have vanished." Thus, in the October 1935 *New Masses* review, Burnshaw did not particularly radicalize criticisms of *Harmonium* already commonplace; rather, he repeated points about the flaws of the early poetry in order, finally, to express hopes for the new work. As Burnshaw himself later noted when he reprinted the review with a commentary, his harshest criticism came in speaking about what Stevens had been. Burnshaw assumed Stevens's reputation as "an incomparable verbal musician," and reminded his readers that the poet's second book was coming long *after* "it was tacitly assumed that one read him for pure poetic sensation; if he had a 'message' it was carefully buried."[201] Insofar as Burnshaw's review counseled Stevens to revise *Harmonium* in new work, not to mourn but to formalize the poetic past in the poetic present, this was merely, after all, an idea Burnshaw would have gotten from Stevens himself – from "Sad Strains," I would contend, where to see only the criticism of the artless masses or "mobs of men" was to miss the beginning and end points of ideological adjustment and relocation. Burnshaw clearly felt that "Sad Strains" addressed itself to the left. (I was not surprised to find it the most energetically marked in Burnshaw's personal copy of *Ideas*.) In the famous review he cited "confusion" in Stevens's presentation of the "'sudden mobs of men' [who] *may* have the answer," even though, he added, Stevens was quick to qualify with irony and escapist rhetoric.[202] Thus, Burnshaw's new sense of ideological perimeters could immediately extend to Stevens, even if Stevens's inclusion merely followed logically because his own confusions so conveniently articulated the confusions of others also "in the throes of struggle for philosophical adjustment."[203] My point is that the Burkean adjustment to which Burnshaw referred can nevertheless be read in the poems to which his commentary was a response – not only in "Owl's Clover" but also in *Ideas*. The rhetorical turn in "Sad Strains" came as Stevens understood the structural principle that would make "Owl's Clover" feasible. The cries of the masses might themselves assume effective form in revealing desire more fully than the antiquated waltz: "Yet the

shapes / For which the voices cry, these, too, may be / Modes of desire."
Stevens and Burnshaw were matching "may" for "may," possibility for possibility. This poem of self-revision, self-criticism, and reconciliation – not
of attack or counterattack – came precisely at the moment Stevens's very
idiom conceded as transitional ("there comes a time / When . . . "). It
concluded by proposing, though not yet in itself providing, a very new
version of the old self-involvement. A Stevens rhetorically prepared for the
immediate future "may" be "Some harmonious skeptic" who would retain
his fundamental music, restore the "intrinsic" power of poetic construction
(language "Will glisten again with motion"), and yet help "unite" poet and
detractor under a single literary banner.

6

Toward a Rhyming of
Opposites: "Owl's Clover"

APHORISMS ON SOCIETY is somewhat pretentious. . . . [L]et's stick to OWL'S CLOVER. I
enclose a new title page with that title. The point of this group in any case is to try to
make poetry out of commonplaces: the day's news; and that surely is owl's clover.
—Stevens to Latimer, May 1936 (*L* 311, 311n.8)

I'd love to write some poems about love. Don't laugh. . . . [R]egimentation and the
movement aren't cause and effect.
—Stanley Burnshaw, in a letter to Alfred Kreymborg[1]

1: WHAT FATE ASSIGNS TO THE MOMENT

Thus Burnshaw, moving tentatively one way, met Stevens moving tentatively the other, on a ground much wider than commentators on "Owl's
Clover" have appreciated. Joseph Riddel, writing about "Poets' Politics,"
decided that "Stevens is arguing on nonpolitical grounds, or on prepolitical
grounds, that he has misunderstood Burnshaw just as Burnshaw had confused poetry with politics."[2] In this view "Owl's Clover" is a "defense of
poetry which managed, almost *miraculously*, to *survive the time* in a way
Burnshaw's poetics did not,"[3] as if a poem self-consciously of the left could
ultimately control its canonical destiny as it made the perilous journey
from "red decade" through cultural cold war. When first considering the
situation in 1958, Riddel exaggerated the staying power of "Owl's Clover" exactly as he underestimated the influence of popular-front poetics,
of which Burnshaw's "Turmoil in the Middle Ground" is a classic instance.
For such a poetics, and an ample understanding of its interactive strategy,
is thoroughly imbedded in Stevens's poem. So, too, in arguing that "Owl's
Clover" "achieves nothing whatever in the way of a satisfactory answer to

Mr. Burnshaw's complaints," critics who agree with Lucy Beckett[4] seem to assume that Burnshaw's and Stevens's positions were both essentialist and irreconcilable. On the contrary, the main point of Burnshaw's criticism, and of Stevens's long poem-response, was to propose continual inter-ideological struggle as a model for negotiating opposing positions *that were themselves shifting*. Only recently, with literary histories such as Wald's and Nelson's, which have been, in turn, influenced by the controversial New Left assumption of a home-grown American radicalism – the very axiom that irks historians holding to Theodore Draper's view[5] – has it been possible to look deeply into the connection between the historical Burnshaw and "Owl's Clover" to see how *both* sides demonstrated, as Nelson generally puts it, that modern "poetry is too diverse to fit any simple model of party influence."[6]

Of course as Burnshaw himself endured the passage from the thirties to the fifties, to what he called "our anti-Marxist midcentury,"[7] he reached certain conclusions about how Stevens critics were then treating his role in Stevens's development – conclusions that in many ways anticipate Nelson's political brand of postmodern flexibility. By 1959, working as an editor at Henry Holt, his radical past seemingly well behind him, Burnshaw knew enough of intellectual anticommunism, and of McCarthyism's deepest cultural implications, to have realized how, and why, critics of Stevens's poetry had not read the 1935 review perceptively, when they had bothered to read it at all.[8] Burnshaw was well aware that he had written and published this easily stereotyped sentence: "It is the kind of verse that people concerned with the murderous world collapse can hardly swallow today except in tiny doses." Yet *it*, it must be remembered, had not been *Ideas of Order* but *Harmonium*. The reviewer's next remark had deployed the popular-front strategy, urging Stevens to move from the earlier aesthetic position: "And *it* is verse that Stevens *can* no longer write," with "can" – not "must," or "should" – very much in the syntax of the new heterodoxy.

In fact, Burnshaw in 1935 had not been so far from Stevens's own rhetorical position: "There comes a time / When" Hoon's bourgeois self-preoccupations – modernism's neoromantic *nothing-but-I* conceit, as in "I was the world in which I walked, and what I saw / Or heard or felt *came not but from myself*" (*CP* 65) – might be changed and enriched by the effort to replicate a mass voice while not denying the powers of subjectivity. It is true that Burnshaw felt in the autumn of 1935 that the time for such change was *now*; true, too, that "Mr. Burnshaw and the Statue," and the three other poems in the sequence Stevens wrote after the Burnshaw review appeared, may not provide quite the "satisfactory answer" to Burnshaw's "complaints" that critics seem to expect when reading the poem. Yet the last four poems in the series do respond intellectually to the interplay between modernist poet and communist expectations: the dialectic of "speculations, questionings, contradictions," the methodological self-scrutiny the Popular Front called for, even while, as Cowley later misleadingly joked, the policy only seemed to be a relaxation of policy ("Let sleeping dialectics lie").[9] An example of such exchange:

Stevens in *Harmonium*:	What is one man among so many men? What are so many men in such a world? Can one man think one thing and think it long? . . . . For realist, what is is what should be.
	(CP 41)
Burnshaw's response in "Turmoil in the Middle Ground":	Realists have been bitter at the inanity of Pope's "Whatever is is right," but Stevens plunges ahead to the final insolence: "For realists, what is is what should be." And yet it is hard to know if such a line is not Stevens posing in self-mockery. One can rarely speak surely of Stevens's ideas.[10]
Stevens's counterargument in "Mr. Burnshaw and the Statue":	Everything is dead Except the future. Always everything That is is dead except what ought to be.
	(OP 78)

Burnshaw, for his purposes, was not wrong to comprehend Stevens's variation of Pope's Augustan aphorism as a contradiction of realism in the contemporary radical and post-imagist modes. But he admitted that he could not read Stevens's ideas well, since Stevens might be putting into Crispin's mouth here the detested idea that what is real is what ought fancily to be, not what plainly is. Yet Stevens's counterargument-in-verse shows that he sensed irony in Burnshaw's unwillingness to find any creditable form of realism driving the desire to put in language what ought to be. Bent on useful criticism, Burnshaw might have missed a chance, in this view, to use Stevens's early work for finding an incipient utopian strain. In "Mr. Burnshaw and the Statue" Stevens was satirizing not only Burnshaw's dystopian mode, the kind of skull-cracking historicism that had allegedly destroyed every literary thing it had touched in the years preceding the Popular Front. At the same time Stevens did just what Burnshaw himself supposed it was Stevens's acknowledged talent to do: to pose in self-mockery, to make his own ideas hard to discern. Yet in this instance the voice that gets heard is Burnshaw's.

The issue of *New Masses* containing Burnshaw's review appeared on the first day of October, and by the last of the month Stevens had already finished writing "Mr. Burnshaw and the Statue," the second poem in the "Owl's Clover" sequence (*L* 289). In late January 1936, he was "getting along with" "The Greenest Continent" (*L* 306), a third. At that point he knew "Owl's Clover" would not be complete until after the fourth and fifth poems were added. These would be "A Duck for Dinner," complete in mid-April,[11] and "Sombre Figuration," finished by May 16 (*L* 311).

The scene of "The Old Woman and the Statue" is localized – a park. It is nonetheless a representative scene: "*Another* evening in *another* park." We see a "group of marble horses," a sculpture that is unique and central (the animals have been centered in a circle of trees) and yet which reflects the natural setting (the trees' gusted leaves seem to race along with the horses). After section i has fixed the park locale, section ii describes what the sculptor had known about the context the park would offer his monumental statue. Section iii then discloses what he had not known about this context. Once it has been established that the statue does indigenously befit the park, section ii can state its conclusion unsurprisingly, beginning with "So much the sculpture had foreseen:" The colon suggests that the stanza to follow will describe what the artist was capable of anticipating in the context produced for his art on location. Here the equestrian statue is a thing in itself, intrinsically describable: "marble leaping," "white forelegs taut," "heads held high," and so on. And to the extent that the statue can be described in terms extrinsic to it, the comparative context is altogether climatic:

> *clouds of* bronze imposed
> On *clouds of* gold, and green engulfing bronze,
> The marble leaping *in the storms of light.*
> (*OP* 75; emphasis added)

Thus the sculptor's art has arisen, we are to believe, from his talent for imagining – in other words, anticipating – the way sunlight *would* play on folds and edges. He had foreseen, apparently, how the rotten leaves from the trees would swirl around the horses, "in immense autumnal sounds." Even in the midst of change – seasonal change – he knew in advance the meanings his art would make as he held firmly to his conventional sense of aesthetic context.

So it is the particularly difficult task of section iii, as a counterargument for disputing the sculptor's standard theory of design, to point out in a voice other than the sculptor's what he had not in fact known about the conditions the park would furnish at this historical moment. Poetic meiosis, a negative suggested so strongly that it sticks in the mind like a positive, is rarely as forceful as this:

> But her he had *not* foreseen: the bitter mind
> In a flapping cloak. She walked along the paths
> Of the park with chalky brow scratched over black. . . .
> (*OP* 76; emphasis added)

As Stevens explained, "she" is a woman of the depression, "So destitute that nothing but herself / Remained": a street person, a "vagabond" in the old sense, a "bag lady" in the new. Now we know that the sculptor has been guilty of creating a piece of art that does nothing for her. Or, if he *had* been thinking of her, in artistic practice the thought had "repressed itself / Without any pity." Those "golden clouds that turned to bronze," the terrestrial context, yielding a thing-in-itself without reference to the fractious social world, "did not touch her eye and left / Her ear unmoved" (*OP* 76).

Section iii makes a case *for* the indigent *against* the statue. Insofar as the artist does not foresee how the significance of his art will gather when it is placed amid the society for which it is designed, there is a danger. So section iv would seem at first to attempt a reconciliation of the two positions and a somewhat more inclusive definition of context:

> The mass of stone collapses to marble hulk,
> Stood stiffly, as if the black of what she thought
> Conflicting with the moving colors there
> Changed them, at last, to its triumphant hue.
>
> (*OP* 76)

This was precisely the counterargument presented by Kenneth Patchen in his verse-preface to *Before the Brave*, also of 1936. Patchen's speaker calls for a literal deconstruction of heroic national art, a reversal of the heroicizing process that returns art to raw blocks and starts anew:

> Turn out the lights around the statues.
> Unlock the vaults of unhewn stone; put down
> An order for new men. . . .
> Their time is up. . . . We take power.
> We're sorry they left so little.[12]

And for some lines in section iii of Stevens's "The Old Woman" it does seem that the park-dwelling poor have similarly won the day, that the sense of Patchen's revolutionary speaker has crept inside the Stevensian "as if" – that a representative of sudden great change, the Old Woman herself, has persuaded the park's designers that the heroic statue, with its grand, natural imagery, is inappropriate to local place and time. The old art "built a world we could not use," as Patchen put it. By the end of the section, however, we rediscover the Old Woman "Thinking of heaven and earth," traipsing through the fallen leaves around the statue – striding alongside only what the sculptor *had* foreseen. We are to believe, evidently, that she has adjusted herself somewhat to the natural setting theorized in the sculptor's original design; the section ends with what she, in her turn, does not know.

Section v continues to qualify the Old Woman's claims against the unreality of the statue. Stevens has asked his reader, in effect, to imagine how the Old Woman's presence prevents a nearby budding yew from blossoming into brilliance in the evening, the time of day dominated by her dull, homeless meanderings. Now it is not so much the sculptor who has neglected the poor woman, but (somehow) the indigenous site itself! Now what has remained "Untroubled by suffering" is not the imagination but the very "brilliant" possibility of nature (OP 77–8). In this sense, too, the poem can further endorse the notion that the sculptor had indeed envisioned his art's pretty context, given inarguable "brilliance," extrinsic and real. Note that the most assured language in this first poem comes just here in v, but after the case for the Old Woman has been made in section ii: In the poem's final lines we are asked to imagine the park once again "Without her" – that is to say, before and after her presence. "Without her," indeed, the budding yew, incapable of disclosing its effulgence in her presence, is to be seen

> Branching through heavens heavy with the sheen
> And shadowy hanging of it, thick with stars
> Of a lunar light, dark-belted sorcerers
> Dazzling by simplest beams and soothly still,
> The space beneath it still, a smooth domain,
> Untroubled by suffering, which fate assigns
> To the moment. *There* the horses would rise again. . . .
>   (OP 77–8; emphasis added)

The final point raised against the Old Woman's argument is based on a bold, basic rhetorical confusion: It is both post-revolutionary and conservative, "Untroubled" at turns because trouble has passed and because the speaker is impervious to "suffering." The confusion of lefts and rights seems especially provocative when one considers the way in which the poem engages a long-forgotten but once-ubiquitous leftist lyric subgenre, used exclusively by leftist poets: depression park poems. The subject of such poems was typically a radicalized artist figure observing or addressing (and sometimes proselytizing) a pre-political indigent. Burnshaw's "New Youngfellow (Draft of a Park-Bench Incident)," published in the first issue of *Dynamo* (1934) and collected in *The Iron Land* (1936), has "A shabby man on a bench" ask "a young man [who] slunk nearby": "Well, son, has the New Deal dealt you a job?" "No, of course," is the answer, and the "Park-Bench Incident" ensues. In the end, the wizened speaker, prepared "to ship off to Russia," imagines the son he never had "ready to go to war / in our third, last revolution." The narrative frame, once set, does allow Burnshaw in the thick of the poem to present lines more characteristic of his non-narrative lyrics, such as in the italicized thoughts of the shabby man:

> (. . . *today your tour of the world begins; tomorrow*
> *let's hope you'll know its sting*
> *of fierce sweet mutiny driving your heart and bones*)
> Who am I to be grinning too queerly?[13]

The subgenre produced tropes a good deal less remarkable. In Kreymborg's *The Economic Muse*, a poem called "The Depression" begins:

> It's pretty hard to sing of moonlight now,
> Of benches in the park. . . .
> I'd like to if I could, but here somehow
> Are shadows, beggars, shadows, and the rain's
> A dripping, soppy, clammy winding-sheet
> Indifferent to the tragedies of men,
> Indifferent as the many passing feet
> That makes the beggars rise and drop again.[14]

In Isidor Schneider's "Jobhunt," the dispirited figure is urged by the speaker to conceive of himself as statuary in a way similar to Stevens's management of the Old Woman and Mr. Burnshaw –

> rear yourself like architecture;
> make trim cornices of hair

– although finally in Schneider's poem, his sense of the depression is hardened by the realization that he cannot seem to anyone as monumental as the park itself, cannot summon the uniqueness or singularity to warrant being observed by others, and returns to the glumness of merely observing ("Within the tattered park / you watch the fountain quench / alternate moments of the sun").[15]

T. C. Wilson made his own contribution to this radical subgenre:

> To sing a song and sing it
> Over and over . . .
> Though the words don't fit
> And the tune's dead wrong –
> Is all there's left for most men.
>
> They make an ominous music where
> They sit, and they sit everywhere.
> Have you not heard them in the park
> Humming the time away,
> The heavy empty time?[16]

By imagining the scene a destitute park-dweller has prevented, then, and by reserving the poem's most deliberately "poetic" language for it – "the sheen / And shadowy hanging of it," "dark-belted sorcerers / Dazzling by simplest beams and soothly still" – Stevens's park-bench poet believes he can conceive of conditions the destitute want, even as depression park songs such as Wilson's incited humility in radicals knowing they should prefer the "dead wrong" song overheard there to their own. By describing natural events in the park that preceded the Old Woman's accusations against the statue's disengagement from context, the speaker of "Owl's Clover" can, on the contrary, transfigure everything he had not "foreseen" into an appealing final condition, "a *smooth* domain," allegedly putting the lie to left-right difference. Despite all other signs of ignorance, in this mediated view human suffering is recognized as a remediable state, a condition "which fate assigns / To the moment." In that special not-knowing, that domain where contradictions are smoothed over even as they are clearly identified by the park's homeless – at that exact moment and place, "*There*" – the statue (and in the larger sense, all depression-era art) can be reinstated, stronger than ever in making claims on the imagination, much stronger than before the Old Woman's argument momentarily carried the day. At this point the speaker can hardly contain his new-found rhetoric of realism: "How clearly that would be defined!" (*OP* 78).

2: THE DRASTIC COMMUNITY

By the time Stevens looked back on "Owl's Clover" from the perspective of 1940 in order to explicate the poem in detail for Hi Simons, he was claiming that in preparing "The Old Woman and the Statue" he had learned how the "confrontation" between "reality (the depression) and the imagination (art)" was best managed dialogically. He had come to know, he recalled, "the energizing that comes from mere interplay, interaction" between opposed positions conversing. In his own post-depression interpretation, the first poem of the sequence succeeded finally in changing the minds of both the sculptor and the Old Woman. For the sculptor it meant a shift from a kind of happy, narrow formalism (a sculpted form praised for its severance from social context); for the Old Woman, a shift from a grim, moralized mimesis (art unself-reflectively bespeaking the day's crises). This convergence had been managed, he told Simons, by "[c]ross-reflections, modifications, counter-balances, complements, giving and taking" (*L* 368).

While it is true of "Owl's Clover" as a whole that it carried on such a negotiation between one political and one apparently nonpolitical position – but really two political positions: one distinctly radical and the other indistinctly in the "middle ground," "confused" – it was simply not true of this first poem. Whatever was motivating him in 1940 to remember "Owl's Clover" as if it had led him almost from the start to that conclusion about the value of "counter-balances . . . giving and taking," its origin lay in the momentous change coming over the literary-radical disposition between the time the first poem was written and that of the four following. That is to say, Burnshaw's October 1 review not only set Stevens going again some two or three months after the first section was published in the *Southern Review* (it had been a good deal longer, doubtless, since it had been composed); too, his "doing a great deal of writing" after Burnshaw's review, between October 1 and November 15 (*L* 294), focused what he later selectively recalled had been the guiding formal principle all along. This principle held that verse susceptible to depression actualities structurally replicated the encounter between modernism and politics designated by modernism's (now former) arch-antagonists. This meeting depended utterly on voice given to a position certified by the opposition as acceptably persuasive. It was a risky procedure that would then move the whole – the poem subsequently involving and increasingly containing detractors' positions – in the general direction of an intrepid antagonist-turned-ally who was to be half-invented. The related acts of, first, providing equal time, and, second, involving by containing and semi-reinscribing one's adversaries enabled the poet to claim that he had learned the still-greater rhetorical principle of incessant change.

Only with "Mr. Burnshaw and the Statue," the poem Stevens wrote with a specific detractor in mind, and even more successfully in "A Duck for Dinner," the fourth poem, did Stevens learn the lesson about the relation between the specific radical conception of the middle-ground writer and the general principle conducting the incessantly changing conditions that were making his poetry problematic. It was just the lesson promoters of popular-front poetics were then beseeching modernist eminences to learn. In his energetic effort to re-educate himself and realign his work with the most current ideas, and in trying to sharpen his already acute sense of good literary-political timing, Stevens implicated his verse in a political irony that was intrinsic to the latitudinarian move, and this is, to me, the poem's most impressive strategy. By arguing in "Sombre Figuration," the last "Owl's Clover" poem (*OP* 96-101), for a form of modernism that would somehow maintain a *fixed* principle of order, positing an inviolable political unconscious as a means of characterizing incessant change, Stevens finally offered a significant contribution to the methodological position Burnshaw was advocating, a last powerful tug on the line moving American modernism from fascist to antifascist unconscious – methodologically from Gold to Gregory. In this sense, Stevens did have something substantive to add to Louis Lozowick's communist notion that an artist's inextricable relation to society must be that of an "activist who depicts changing reality in a manner which makes his own work a factor toward further change."[17]

The chief problem with the argument of "The Old Woman," then, was its failure to name the opposition fairly and squarely. There can be little question as to what and whom the sculptor represented there: His advocacy of "the imagination" over "reality" is relentlessly Stevensian. Yet the Old Woman's position was never once characterized specifically enough for any reader to know whom or what she represented, to ascertain if she spoke greedily for herself, wretched and hobo-like, or selflessly on behalf of a whole destitute class, conscious and radicalized.

Among the flaws of "Mr. Burnshaw and the Statue," on the other hand, is not its failure to name the left. The Old Woman's position had not the great advantage of responding to a review in the *New Masses*. Beginning with "Mr. Burnshaw and the Statue," the rhetoric of the verse in "Owl's Clover" is sharpened by that "extraordinary" contact (*L* 292). In view of

Stevens's sense of popular-front logic, and of the logic guiding the argument between Burnshaw and Monroe, the poem is what critics say it is –
"the one major betrayal of his poetic genius,"[18] "an almost total failure,"[19]
"incontrovertibly Stevens's poorest performance" and "his largest failure"[20]
– *only* when he fails to name or characterize the opposition as belonging to
the world of political rhetoric. When he comes closest to abstracting from
the Old Woman's argument – in the course of describing the brilliant yew
that would bud before and after, but not during, her intrusion – he arrives
at his grammatical object: He has put himself syntactically into the position
of having to say exactly who or what has kept the yew from brilliance. Yet
he cannot quite or will not finally name her argument in words whose
coherence derives from positions external to the poem. He wants to say,
*The park would be brilliant without the Old Woman's sort of argument, and had
been brilliant before.* But before *what*? What happened to diminish brilliance?
The answer, I think, is willfully "gaudy bosh":

> Without her, evening like a budding yew
> Would soon be brilliant, as it was before
> *The harridan self and ever-maladive fate*
> *Went crying their desolate syllables. . . .*

In arriving at its syntactical object thus – in reaching the characterization
in a summary phrase or two of the Old Woman's whole complaint against
the heroic statue – even the most hopeful readers arrive, not coincidentally,
at the language for which "Owl's Clover" is notorious. But this is just the
opposite of what critics have habitually cited as the bad "rhetoric which
resulted when he tried to argue rather than create,"[21] for, in my view, Stevens
was trying to "create" here when he *should* have been arguing. "Owl's Clover" is "bad" at exactly the moments when Stevens lost, not gained, his
political nerve, when his well-developed rhetorical habit of *polyptoton* (like
that of John Ashbery, Stevens's successor in this respect)[22] – of leaving dense
layers of pronouns unsorted and unnumbered – was least restrained by the
world of sects, partisans, encoded communicants, a myriad nameable -isms.
(It is one of the reasons, I think, why Ashbery's style flourished in the
ideological 1960s of all decades; close readings of Ashbery's verse, rather
than the usual general admiration for his shrewd resistance to reference,
lead us rhetorically back to Stevens's management of the densities and severe dislocations of public political discourse in the 1930s.) Note, in the
passage from "The Old Woman" quoted above, for instance, how after the
words "she" and "her," the phrase "*their* desolate syllables" comes some lines
in advance of the other "voices," which remain even then unidentified.

Reaching his chief rhetorical defense *against* ideologically informed argument within the poem itself, Stevens thus lapsed back into the premature
political strategy of "Sad Strains of a Gay Waltz" and "Mozart, 1935," a
plaintive conservative diction that had worked, anyway, in the short poem

but not necessarily here in the extended mannerist satire. By moving from
the brief flexible lyric of early 1935 to the sometimes intractable blank-
verse satire of late 1935 and early 1936 he was *not* in that one very important sense changing his aesthetic position relative to Stanley Burnshaw's: It
had been Burnshaw, in the essay "Notes on Revolutionary Poetry," who
designated "satire" as one of just "two types of revolutionary verse
remain[ing] largely unexplored."[23] Insofar as Stevens had failed to name
exactly "their [but *whose?*] desolate syllables," the vague voices of early 1935
were consumed by the nonhuman, unassailable song of the wind. The people
and their voices remained indistinct in a lyric skillfully disarming them by
merging them with a ceaselessly shifting but natural current. This presented
not a variable, political doctrine metaphorized as wind, but an inarguable
force against which one pushed bodily back:

> Their voice and the voice of the tortured wind were one,
> Each voice within the other, seeming one,
> Crying against a need that pressed like cold,
> Deadly and deep.
>
> (*OP* 77)

With an invitation from the literary left in hand – and also, I would suggest,
Burnshaw's call for the radical re-exploration of satire as genre – Stevens responded swiftly and directly to the *New Masses* editor, making quite certain
this time to locate from the start the origin of claims against the statue:

> MR. BURNSHAW AND THE STATUE
>
> The thing is dead . . . Everything is dead
> Except the future. Always everything
> That is is dead except what ought to be.
> All things destroy themselves or are destroyed.
>
> These are not even Russian animals.
> They are horses as they were in the sculptor's mind.
> They might be sugar or paste or citron-skin. . . .

Complaints against the statue articulated in the first section of "Mr.
Burnshaw" are extensions of the Old Woman's position. The horses are so
entirely constructed "in the sculptor's mind," it might be wondered if they
have been made of mud, sugar, cream, paste, fruit skins. They might have
been "Left here by moonlit muckers" – might just as well have been those
puffed-up items one buys at Schwarz's as made of marble, solid, substantial.
They are not real. Insofar as they constitute Stevens's symbol for art in the
depression – here the argument picks up a hint from the very timbre of
Burnshaw's changing *New Masses* voice – they are "images / Made to remember a life they never lived" (*OP* 78).

One basic difference, however, between the Old Woman's grievance
against the sculpture in the first poem and Burnshaw's objection in the
second is the satirization of the argument in the second. The satire was

possible, of course, only to the extent that Stevens could give voice to the objection, its bitter criticism of the present. "Always everything / That is is dead except what ought to be" is a proposition viable only if the position is presumed to be extreme: "Always" and "everything," especially in tandem, tonally corrupt a reasonable-sounding "ought." The assertion is, after all, carefully timed to coincide with the new communist position conveyed by the radical reviewer. The voice of section i, belonging undoubtedly to the "Mr. Burnshaw" of the title, gripes that "These are not even Russian animals." So whereas the Old Woman's position only briefly had its say in the second section of the first poem, after the case for art had already been presented, in the second poem there is a discernible shift in strategy: The counterargument speaks first. Section ii contains the artist's response, addressed to the muses. In section iii the communist argument briefly offers a counter-counterresponse. Section iv continues the artist's apostrophe to the muses and forms yet another response to Burnshaw.

When Simons asked Stevens if "Mr. Burnshaw and the Statue" did not indeed contain, first, "ironical" representations of Stanley Burnshaw's position and, then, "your rejoinder," he had the right idea but misnumbered the sections; he believed sections i, ii and iii had voiced Burnshaw's position and iv and v the poet's rejoinder.[24] Asked to identify the sections as discrete positions or points of view, Stevens chose to describe the poem as a narrative interrupted by two apostrophes, which were in reality "short hymns of reconciliation." Burnshaw was much closer than Simons to Stevens's sense of the poem's interactive strategy, although he never got the opportunity to tell Stevens so. Yet the record, unpublished until now, is clear: When Burnshaw was given a chance by his comrade Kreymborg to include a reply in the very same *American Caravan* that would first print Stevens's "Mr. Burnshaw," he contemplated *poetry* as a reply-in-kind, and discussed submitting a series of eight linked personal poems "even though they might make me seem to be a fascist – what right has a red to mourn the death of his mother? – I'll take the risk." In other words, according to Burnshaw's sagacious sense of the negotiation between communist left and modernist middle-ground, the apt counter-counterargument to Stevens's counterargument was not yet another restatement of the original objection, but a demonstration by daring example of communist poetry willing to lean a little generically to its right.[25]

If it is assumed that section i is a distorted restatement of "Turmoil in the Middle Ground" put into Stevens's blank verse, and that section ii, the poet's response, an apostrophe to muses, is a "hymn of reconciliation," then it is possible to imagine ways in which the poem as a whole enacts the rhetorical strategy and power of popular-front poetics. One thus imagined the very "casuistic stretching" Burke saw after 1935 as the cultural radicals' new formal asset. Does not Stevens instruct the muses to reconcile themselves to conditions posited by the literary radicals in section i, and in a stanza full of entreaties that read as grammatical imperatives, tell them to "Come," "Entwine," "Chant," "Bring down," and, finally, to "Agree"? Are they not *urged* to chant appropriately "sibilant" requiems for the figure destroyed by contemporaneous pressures which were created out of social context? By section iii, indeed, the destroyed statue has been removed, replaced and renamed, and it is only then evident that the muses, who sang for the lost likeness, were not the ones responsible for the inscription that hilariously moved Marxist rhetoric from reductive empiricism to aesthetic self-reflexivity: "*The Mass / Appoints / These Marbles Of Itself To Be / Itself*" (OP 80).

By section iv, it is clear that by responding to Burnshaw in a seemingly inappropriate and archaic mode, an invocation to muses, and by engaging "short" hymns of reconciliation to interrupt the "narrative" exposition of Burnshaw's complaints, the provoked nonradical imagination was threatening to silence the opposition altogether. The advantage that had been gained by allowing Burnshaw to speak first might be lost if in section iv the speaker would absorb, and render illogical, the contention that poetry retains the special critical strength to reveal the distinctions between present and utopian conditions by ceding the power and function of language to the muses instead of the masses. He knows the danger of this procedure, and he rather half-heartedly asks the muses to go ahead and "Disclose the rude and ruddy at their jobs" – to cause him to sing a proletarian song. What then follows is a brief but fascinating attempt, which is not the least bit attractive for its proletarianism, but rather for its knowing use of the helpful radical-romantic example of Shelley – whose genuinely "revolutionary ideas" William Phillips defended bitterly against Eliot's rendering them "adolescent";[26] and for whose "mystic hash" Mike Gold infamously confessed admiration. ("Let me confess it now," Gold wrote, "I took Shelley literally. One half of me was proletarian. . . .The other half was full of the most extraordinary mystic hash."[27]) As Stevens later explained to Simons, the reference to Shelley in "Mr. Burnshaw and the Statue" was meant to help elaborate his suggestion that "Communism is *just* a new romanticism" (L 351): The Shelleyan lights of "Owl's Clover" "are not going to alter the structure of nature" yet "will have transformed the world" (L 367). Conceiving precisely of the paradox Mike Gold's radicalized neoromanticism admitted, Stevens's speaker was suddenly freer suddenly than ever to temper revolution by slinging some "mystic hash" of his own. He imagines "A time in which the poets' politics / Will rule in a poets' world" (OP 80). But then, cleverly, he engages one of the mainstream modernist arguments *Poetry* under Monroe and Zabel had gathered up against Burnshaw, namely that *all* poets, not only radicals, "Complain and prophesy." So, too, *all* "good" poetry – to Monroe in particular, we recall – had to be counted as propaganda, if any had.

In the logic of the response of section iv, then, a world ruled by poets would paradoxically "be / A world impossible for poets," who, in order to be poets must make claims against the world as it is – although not, according to the left's own new aesthetic strategy, necessarily for a new world. In that sense poets "are never *of* the world *in* which they live," and we are back to Gregory's rhetoric of "observation." Replying to one argument insisting that the modernist was too much committed to the rightness of whatever is, he assumes that the noncommunist poet had always been stating objections in response to a different argument, and that so long as he remained a poet "of" a world *not* ruled by poets, he would continue to put forward similar criticisms.

It is surely a sign of confusion, in the contemporaneous communist sense of the word, that in reply to this, his own argument (in iv), the modernist could conceive of no direct rejoinder from the radical. So, too, it is doubtless a demonstration of Stevens's awareness of the terrible indistinctness between the two positions presented in the progression of sections that section v, which ought to have been given over to the antagonist position, begins: "A solemn voice, not Mr. Burnshaw's says . . ." Section v then presents the political apocalypse. Buzzards "eat the bellies of the rich," while "the sun / Shines without fire" and the sculptor is discovered, dead on this apocalyptic ground, decapitated. A lizard obliviously squats where once belonged the artist's bright eye. If the unorganized tramp's lament of the Old Woman became an ideology proper in the first sections of "Mr. Burnshaw and the Statue," by section v it has gone horribly awry. The sculptor, not merely the sculpture, is dead. "Everything" is dead. The solemn voice, describing the scene, *not* Burnshaw's, tells with irony too bitter for Burnshaw of "a hopeful waste to come" (*OP* 80–1).

Moving on from this catastrophe, the considerable energy of section vi is expended by the poet's promises to ascribe to his muses a devotion to the concept of radical change. "It is only enough," he says earnestly, "To live incessantly in change." Just below the section in which the Popular Front should have been given space to respond, then, the noncommunist speaker's strategy entails allowing a voice not of the communist left to forecast the failure of the revolution in v by revising the concept of "change" sufficiently so that in vi, it will be recognizable even to the muses, whom he has addressed decorously as "Mesdames" throughout the poem but never more loftily than here. The example of change that follows the seemingly radical generalization – that we must adapt both to the idea and to the condition of constant change – is the sudden but hardly shocking premonition of autumn in the midst of summer. It is hardly "so great a change" as that exhorted by the tone and underscored by the political context. Finally, in the final proposition of section vi, this has become "*archaic* change." Notice, however, how the naturalization of leftist importunities about poetry's commitment to change has a final effect. As a result of the "hymn of reconciliation" mediating communist and modernist, the two positions have met on "the middle ground" first marked out by the communist. If in order to reach such a ground Stevens's sectarian Burnshaw has given up the hard apocalyptic edge on his conception of change, then Stevens's latitudinarian Burnshaw is willing to instruct the muses to fear no longer the communist jeremiad against individualist inspiration. "Shall you, / Then," he asks the muses finally,

> fear a drastic community evolved
> From the whirling, slowly and by trial; or fear
> Men gathering for a mighty flight of men,
> An abysmal migration into a possible blue?
> (OP 82)

The answer to the question is obviously, *No – fear no longer*. Except for the phrase "into a possible blue," which is unmistakably Stevensian, these lines, notwithstanding the tone of "abysmal," might just as well have been Rukeyser's in *Theory of Flight*. The muses have learned well that they have nothing whatever to fear from revolutionary tropes. Once the attack from the left can be renamed a united front against stasis, section vii of "Mr. Burnshaw" is feasible with its celebratory dancing and its structural assimilation of the new communist credo. That assimilation need not bear out merely Alan Calmer's only somewhat exaggerated definition of popular-front poetics as calling for an end to first strikes against potentially antifascist writing, "regardless of . . . even its hostility to communism."[28] For "Owl's Clover" also at this moment harmonized with Kenneth Burke's more sympathetic revisionist efforts to describe the "Communist job" as "mak[ing] clear why the *imperium in imperio* method cannot work" and showing how and why "one may spend too much effort in attacking what need not be attacked, and what should not be attacked."[29] By the end of "Mr. Burnshaw and the Statue," the speaker has asked the muses to sing for themselves, "In the glassy sound of your voices," and to repeat in "long recitation" at least the *harmless* portion of the reflexive revolutionary inscription: "*To Be It-self*" (OP 83).

3: HARMONIES BEYOND KNOWN HARMONY

"A Duck for Dinner," the fourth poem in the sequence, reasserts the dialogical structure of the first two. Like them, it begins by alternating arguments between poet and left. After the unspecified Old Woman, and the specified Mr. Burnshaw, the fourth poem names a "Bulgar" to be the radicals' spokesperson. Stevens thus identified him for Simons (L 371). The pattern of political exchange in "Owl's Clover" is by this point explicit: "A Duck for Dinner" opens with the phrase, "The Bulgar said . . ." and the contentions that follow are clearly framed by quotation marks. Whatever twistings of the argument the poet or poet-sculptor cannot resist will be obvious. In section ii, the first rejoinder to the Bulgar, the speaker ad-

dresses a mythic American pioneer, who comments on the Bulgar's positions. The Bulgar then explicitly responds in section iii ("Again the Bulgar
said . . ."); another rejoinder, in section iv, follows. In section v, it is no
longer possible to identify the speaker ideologically, though he cannot logically be any of the figures to whom he refers in the third person. The last
section, structurally as well as thematically a "hymn of reconciliation," concludes by bespeaking a "We." Here is a fortunate pronominal shift that sets
the stage for "Sombre Figuration," the fifth and last poem, where "Owl's
Clover" culminates in a latitudinarian, Burkean "we," absorbing, restating
and reenlisting opposing positions and offering thereby a stirring portent
of destruction discernibly fascist, a prospect "we" can all agree to deter.

In his opening speech, the Bulgar addresses Stevens directly, as "you," a
park-bench poet, an observer of the working poor passing a summer Sunday in the park – in what Stevens conceives as "his" park. The Bulgar
claims that the poet must use the power culturally allocated to him by his
leisure, by his observer's sense of the park, to help the immigrant poor to
rise as far as they can. They will be empowered despite him if they must,
the poet is notified. They want his voice even if it remains uncommitted,
but they will in any event articulate their own position. "If you caricature
the way they rise, yet they rise," the Bulgar warns in a basically friendly
way. He pleads with the poet to let them speak, for if he lets them speak
distinctly, they will persuade the poet to let them play things as they are.
They will enjoy the park as casually and neutrally as he does. As a mini-
mum of sympathy, the Bulgar exhorts, revise *this* poem's park poetics sufficiently to re-imagine the Old Woman as an immigrant – she who has been
without apparent ethnicity or cultural associations. "*At least*," says the Bulgar,

> ". . . conceive what these hands from Sweden mean,
> Massed for a head they mean to make for themselves,
> From which their grizzled voice will speak and be heard . . ."

Obviously the task for the poem assumed by both positions is to rebuild in
it the head that had been removed by Mr. Burnshaw's revolutionary imagination. And the implication of the Bulgar's otherwise cordial argument is
that Stevens, without the masses, knows inadequately what he had thought
was his park, if indeed his purpose was to reform the statue, the symbol of
his own poem.

To have allowed this argument the poet was being, from his view, chari-
table indeed. Left to speak unencumbered from his own position, he would
have claimed ample unqualified knowledge of the park. Here, as earlier in
the poem, his sense of the scene was founded on virtually daily experiences
in Hartford's largest park, where, as his daughter recalled, "ideas could come
and breed and grow."[30] In early years, he had spent summers and holidays
tramping across southeastern Pennsylvania hills;[31] later, when working as
an attorney in Manhattan, he spent long off-season Sundays following the

edge of the Jersey palisades.[32] From 1916, however, his feeling for natural
landscape was for the most part confined to frequent walks in Elizabeth
Park. Yet "confined" is hardly the right word for this near-urban space
where this suburban modernist could "always find something *new*" and
which served as "a perennial vacation at hand."[33] While "It doesn't sound
worth while," as he later wrote, "merely to see Nature in the picnic sense"
(*L* 507), on the other hand Elizabeth Park was so spacious and so varied –
its woods, rock gardens, lawns, greenhouses, a lakelet with ducks, and rose
gardens and a rustic rose-house (the first such open to the public in the
United States) so continually alluring – one could learn to forget one was
close to the growing industrial city that he knew he had chosen as his
permanent home.[34] Stevens's park was undergoing a change during the
thirties, like so many other public places. The very idea of metropolitan
parks, rekindled by city officials' desire to create a (largely false) sense of
mobility in the urban masses,[35] inspired what even a sympathetic historian
of thirties public landscape has called "the New Deal's brash meddling with
nature," it being a conceptual as well as a material meddling.[36]

So strong a desire for "Nature in the picnic sense" now as never before
ran headlong against typical though mostly unexpressed anxieties about
the mixing of classes and ethnicities that would be largely unavoidable. The
deep relation between the day-to-day politics of urban turmoil and the
rampant new "recreation movement," whose promoters were Jesse Steiner,
Robert Moses, and the powerful National Recreation Association, was going
to be left unexamined in Steiner's "Challenge of the New Leisure" (an
article calling for increased federal funding of recreation, and featured prominently in the *New York Times Magazine*). Nevertheless, the goal of calming
and containing a population working harder than ever and getting nowhere, or not working at all and thus with plenty of "leisure," was quite
evident.[37] Connecticut was a special target of the leisure theorists. From
January 1934 to July 1935, the state soared from fifteenth to second in
average relief benefits paid out; by mid-1935 some 6,500 families in Hartford received direct relief.[38] As the New Deal called attention to the possibility of public work as a form of relief, the public, with a new awareness
among the working classes of government services and basic entitlements,
began visiting such places in unprecedented numbers.[39] A public works
program conceived by the Park, Aviation and Street Departments won national commendation for its inventiveness.[40]

Hartford's public spaces were improved by various underemployed arms
of the WPA, beginning in June 1935.[41] And Hartford's many federal project
laborers would feel freer than before to return in their leisure to parks
they had themselves helped to improve. These were Italian-Americans from
Hartford's East Side, many of whom were hod-carriers,[42] and doubtless
some African-Americans as well, whose total segregation from suburban

West Hartford – one black citizen in 1934 called Hartford "the Alabama of New England" – may have been somewhat eased by WPA workers, many of them quite skilled,[43] moving from project to project in parts of the city and its suburbs to which they were unused.[44] A plan to build three million dollars' worth of federal low-cost housing in Hartford was hysterically attacked at a public meeting just a little while before Stevens wrote his poem – attacked not merely because the plan brought government into competition with local landlords, and because leisure-theory zealots like Steiner who associated with such projects sounded dangerously like socialists,[45] but also – perhaps primarily – because it all augured further changes in Hartford's racial demography.[46]

For many reasons, then, Stevens was likelier in 1935 and 1936 than before, on his daily and especially Sunday strolls, to see those "sprawlers on the grass" who became the chief protagonists in "A Duck for Dinner," and for whom the Bulgar speaks. Stevens's curiosity about the utilization of his park by the working class presents a strain throughout his career left largely unscrutinized.[47] The contrary theses, for instance, of "Contrary Theses (II)" (1942) are the abstract, "grand mechanics" of nature on the one hand, and observed social particularities, "The negroes playing football in the park," on the other (CP 270). There the natural outstrips the human, no matter how interesting, observable or intrusive the witnessed social phenomena. The "contrary" was negotiable insofar as "The flies / And the bees still sought the chrysanthemums' odor" (CP 270), no matter how dire the economic or how tense the political circumstance. If he had gone ahead with "On the Presence of Italians in Parks," the title of a poem he left unwritten,[48] one imagines a similarly naturalized resolution of difference. Though the confusions and intrusions of the social would routinely terminate in the natural, even in the "picnic sense" of the metropolitan park, such sociological observations fascinated him. John Rogers, who later described himself as having served as "executive manservant" along "executive row" at The Hartford, got the distinct impression from Stevens that he could trace the individually psychological if not the cultural roots of superior behavior in the servant-master (and black-white) relationship – no small irony, this alleged awareness, since the point Stevens was making was specifically for the benefit of his "manservant." "Once . . . he ventured this opinion," Rogers remembered:

> He said that he noted that when he was a boy in Pennsylvania and they had the servants, used to hire – his mother used to hire servant girls. And he said, "You know," he said, "I never saw any difference between the servant girls and the lady, you know . . . but," he said, "it's an interesting thing looking at human beings." I remember he said this, he said, "They always seem so more secure when they felt somebody else is under them socially." You know, and he said he thought this was a human trait.[49]

Almost exactly thirty years before "A Duck for Dinner," Stevens, then very much the urbanite, wrote in his journal:

> It would be curious to establish, in a slum, two parks, the first with flowers and rambles but without seats; the second without flowers or especial rambles but with seats. The curiousness would be in seeing who used each, and how. – Parks . . . are generally filled with the lower classes. Our park here, today, a Sunday, was thick with Italians and negroes. So, too, often for the aesthete, museums etc. are visited by the lower classes, to the exclusion of the upper. Undoubtedly these things are important in modifying the natures of those who frequent them + [sic] are, thus, a phase of that police system under which order, very largely, rests.[50]

Stevens made this observation in New York on April 29, 1906 – a Sunday. But here, thirty years later, was a very different Sunday, in an era in which the park could no longer serve covertly in the stead of police imposing order, no longer "curious[ly]" modifying the natures of the working class. I had not realized, until reading about what Galen Cranz aptly calls "the politics of park design," that "park use on Sundays" has presented a wholly separate category for analysis;[51] for Stevens, who made his park visits on all seven days, but extended stays on Sundays, the differences of tone between weekday and Sunday park users must have been quite distinct. The depression-era Sunday in question reversed his early analysis of parks as social control: Now "they," with special confidence, modified the park rather than the other way around. They could "rise a bit / On summer Sundays." The inevitability of the change comes from the Bulgar's powerful claim that change occurs slowly and surely: "True," he admits, gradualizing the revolutionary argument,

> only an inch, but an inch at a time, and inch
> By inch, Sunday by Sunday, many men.

If the Bulgar's park people had not changed in their attitude toward leisure, it was leisure with a difference. Having hardly progressed from 1906 in one sense, "they" were still only half-consciously "there," in the park, "Forgetting work, not caring for angels, hunting a lift," seeking "The triumph of the arcs of heaven's blue / For themselves, a space and time and ease" (OP 91). But now, additionally, they were permitting the park-bench poet to allow their "grizzled" voices to "be heard": With this the observer, in Horace Gregory's sense, has become a subject, and the poem has returned to the subgenre typified by Burnshaw's "New Youngfellow (Draft of a Park-Bench Incident)" and another radical park poem, Hector Rella's "The Bone and the Baby," a little more sympathetically. The final section of Rella's poem is precisely the invasion of the proletariat Stevens imagined from his perspective: a communist organizer, bearing a picture of "LENIN TRIUMPHANT," enlivens a disorganized lot of homeless and

leads them FIGHT DON'T STARVE in a swarm
toward the private park in the best part of town

the noise of their approach
BARBARIANS FROM THE NORTH
quivers along the scented flesh
of the bourgeois fresh from his sunday bath

the men and the women
exiled by the man in the park to his subconscious mind.[52]

The poet-speaker of Stevens's poem can only *admire* the way in which this "swarm" of people allowed the park to modify their natures. There is ample evidence to suggest that Stevens himself saw the local park as a place where he, similarly, could pass time "forgetting work," where even he could "feel" sentimentally as if he had become the observed Other. (At times, of course, such sentimental liberalism, associating park with freedom, only reaffirmed the racist typing it intended to supplant: "When on a soft summer evening I walk in a place where there are sweet peas," Stevens once wrote, "or, better still, a place where there is woodbine [Elizabeth Park is known for its woodbine], I feel that I have laid off my Aryan habits and that I am a big fat colored person" [L 604].) What was disturbing was not the desire on the part of the Bulgar to come to the poet's liberating park to rest; there was also, far more transgressive, the claim that the workers "rise" and concomitantly speak. Stevens's understanding of the scene coincides with a powerful tenet of the leisure theorists — that recreation is itself a "form of expression."[53] Thus Stevens's claim for the Bulgar (that ascending means declaring), like Rella's claim for his homeless, sets up a contrast, not a correspondence, between the literal uprising of the park poor and the ascent of Venus into the unchanging sky (lines 2-3 of section i). The Bulgar's people are meant to mature on their own social and political terms and rise qualitatively as themselves, unassimilated American newcomers with sharp Italian eyes, low-English noses, Swedish hands "massed" to reconstruct the statue in their own image — "for a head *they mean to make for themselves*" (OP 91).

In section ii, the poet's first rejoinder, he tries to reverse the Bulgar's argument by addressing a culturally *undifferentiated* American pioneer (OP 91–2) — in some sense a cultural forerunner (but not racial progenitor) of these modern immigrants, nobler than they, distinct for his heroism, selflessness, and willingness to move beyond the cities. In suggesting this connotation, Stevens, wittingly or not, tested popular-front enlargements of Bulgar from Burnshaw, from élite party critic to representative worker, with shrewd, counterproductive reminders of left-sectarian rhetoric and a certain once-respectable tradition of progressive American historiography. First, he was making cunning use of Mike Gold's invocation of the rugged American type in the wicked attack on MacLeish's "sneer" at the immi-

grant left: "Who is there in America today," Gold challenged the poets, "to
carry on the revolutionary democracy of the pioneers?"[54] Stevens was also
engaging a basic character of Frederick Jackson Turner-style "sectionalist"
theory that had deeply influenced the subsequent radicalization of American historiography in the thirties; Turner's "common man," still then la-
beled a "progressive" concept but already completely outflanked on its left,
was, after all, "an undifferentiated American" largely denying difference.[55]
The pioneer's era, in Stevens's "progressive" but similarly outflanked historical sense, was a time when "men were to be ends in themselves," in the
poem's phrase. Trying hard to distinguish this "buckskin," this heroic "crosser
of snowy divides," from the Bulgar and his people, the speaker provocatively advises the pioneer to make the nativist-reactionary "America Is for
Americans" argument, not the least bit Turnerian, but familiar to Stevens from
the intense race- and class-conscious Boston of his Harvard years:[56]

> Are the cities to breed as mountains bred, the streets
> To trundle children like the sea?
>
> (OP 91)

The answer: Obviously not.

The speaker of section ii then attributes to this pioneer a studied nationalist principle for denoting his muscular deeds, proletarianizing him in
effect, and compares this principle negatively to "these" cultureless park-
dwellers, themselves would-be proletarians. Yet had not the pioneer of old,
for all his admirable roughness and baseness, taken time to study "the print
/ Of London, the paper of Paris," and to know "the Italian lives"? And had
he not learned, in Mike Gold's vexing sense, just what it was that made
him so radically different? These fine, Europeanized cultural source-texts,
the intellectual foundation even of the American roughneck, were merely
"gaudy bosh to *these*," condemned as effete by today's anti-intellectual cultural newcomers. "*Their* destiny is just as much machine / As death itself."
Once this divide-and-conquer strategy has done its work to distinguish
foundational pioneer from transgressive immigrant, the speaker urges the
reinvented pioneer to see how "These lives are not your lives" and, in nationalist diction – "O free, / O bold" – to mount the heroic statue *just as it
was* and ride "your horses straight away" (*OP* 92).

The Bulgar's response to this historically preposterous argument is so utterly devastating – as we will see, it is armed with another negative review in
addition to Burnshaw's – that, realizing perhaps how it disgraces the invocation to the pioneer in ii, Stevens later attempted to load the opening phrase by
changing it from "Again the Bulgar said" to "Again the *acrid* Bulgar said" when
he revised the poem. The Bulgar's counterattack cuts nonetheless to the heart
of Stevens's lingering pre-political aestheticism. His poetry here was still said to
be "Infected by unreality," still too enamored of its sounds to be intelligible as
a presentation of observed "things." "There are more things / Than poodles in

Pomerania." And in a reference doubtless to the poem itself in progress, the very poem that contains him, the Bulgar notes that the poet is "rapt round / By dense unreason, irreproachable force." He attacks the speaker's position for its vagueness: The speaker alleges to have adopted the masses' terms, and yet he continues to speak abstractly of clouds of turmoil and change, in his usual unassailably natural figures: "These bands, these *swarms*, these motions, what of them?" Particularly demoralizing is the Bulgar's use of a special critical figure in attacking Stevens's new art as yet "Infected by unreality":

> This man
> Is all the birds he ever heard and . . .
> . . . .
> Is cast in pandemonium, flittered, howled
> By harmonies beyond known harmony.
>
> (*OP* 92)

If Stevens was to give the "grizzled voice" of the Bulgar's masses their due say, poetically, he could not yet claim to know "crow" realism and at the same time hold to the position of the rare "purple bird" (as he had only several years earlier in "Like Decorations").

The ornithological conceit to which Stevens has the Bulgar refer was Geoffrey Grigson's. Shortly before Stevens began writing "A Duck for Dinner," Grigson's nasty brief review appeared in the English *New Verse*, a journal to which Stevens subscribed and knew well enough to characterize as the production of a "group."[57] Stevens was to Grigson "The Stuffed Goldfinch" that Marianne Moore had immediately felt needed defending – the rare bird as poet, unreconstructed since *Harmonium* despite all cultural changes. While acknowledging that *Ideas of Order* contained "fewer . . . peacocks" than *Harmonium*, Grigson still saw in Stevens's verse "the finicking privateer . . . *observing nothing*." Note the direct contradiction of Gregory's hopeful thesis, which had expressed political possibility, William Phillips's revisionist "sensibility of choice."[58] Parodying "The Idea of Order at Key West," moreover, Grigson deemed him the "single artificer of his own world of mannerism." ("She was the single artificer of the world" was the offending line [*CP* 129].) Actually, when Grigson made the passing suggestion that *Ideas* presented the "thin-fingered *undemocratic* American" of *Harmonium* who survived into the thirties, it was the only point where the *New Verse* charge against the stuffed bird was figuratively and rhetorically associated with literary radicalism.

By inscribing a reply to Geoffrey Grigson in "A Duck for Dinner," at around the time he was elsewhere calling Grigson and his "group" political propagandists and nothing more (*L* 309), Stevens was showing that Burnshaw's review was still much on his mind. But Stevens also knew from *New Verse* that Grigson and Burnshaw were radical upstarts of very different orders. As a matter of fact, Grigson, regarded by American poets as "bellig-

erent" but also "eclectic,"[59] made his magazine notorious for its "vitriolic style
of reviewing," and from that, as well as Grigson's early support of W. H. Auden,
was imputed a radical editorial disposition.[60] Yet Grigson pugnaciously inter-
rogated the Auden-Spender-Day Lewis claims for communist poetry; suggested
(of Day Lewis's *A Hope for Poetry*) that "propaganda . . . is always achieved at
the expense of the poetic";[61] and hoped that readers would not "damn NEW
VERSE politically where damnation is invalid"[62] – all while saluting Auden not
for his politics but for "his love, his versatility, his plain cleverness,"[63] "the first
English poet for many years who is *a poet all the way round.*"[64] The Grigson
refigured in "Owl's Clover" was indeed the one known principally for publishing Spender and Auden in *New Verse*, yet the editor was deliberately promoting
primarily the Spender who felt "that the communist poets do *not* understand
. . . working-class conditions" and primarily the Auden who was capable of
"*indifferent* verses about communism," such as:

> It's no use turning nasty
> It's no use turning good
> You're what you are and nothing you do
> Will get you out of the wood.[65]

They might be read as "defeatist" lines, to be sure,[66] and are in several ways
reminiscent of the Stevens of "Table Talk," in tone and diction, as well as in
expressing the conservative side of the modernist attraction to operations
of chance:

> Granted, we die for good.
> Life, then, is largely a thing
> Of happens to like, not should.
> (*OP* 73)

Grigson was hardly the stick figure casually cited in critical assessments of
Stevens's reaction to the review in *New Verse*.[67] Crucially, Stevens was realizing at this moment precisely how *he* had come to be known to Grigson's
"group" as the embodied summoning of "all the birds he ever heard" (in the
Bulgar's Grigsonite words). It seems to me quite likely that Stevens was coming
finally to regret the bluntness with which he had assumed a political position
for the symposium conducted by Grigson in *New Verse* back in October 1934,
an erring zeal not at all necessary for gaining Grigson's admiration – stri-
dency which "A Duck for Dinner," with its echo of *New Verse*, was thus intended to redress. Samuel French Morse, who just a few years later was already worrying about radical misapplications of Stevens, perpetuated the mistake by telling his friends that the *New Verse* symposium had been strategically "very silly and pompous" so as to extract from big-name poets "some
secrets that can [later] be used as clubs by Grigson and his pals."[68] The situation must have seemed really quite desperate. What would seem obviously to
be an attack from left to right actually presented so flexible and unpredictable a cultural view that Moore could be defending Stevens against Grigson

from the left[69] almost exactly as Grigson himself was praising Auden as an "Elizabethan *Fool*-cum-artist" and MacNeice as an "X-ray-eyed *Elegant*"![70] Zabel, thrilled to be pointing like-minded anti-radical readers of *Poetry* toward major poets' responses to Grigson's symposium, was especially delighted by the poets' collective demonstration of "the fact that social and political *non-partisanship* still prevails *against* the demands and challenges that crowd the air."[71] To Grigson's symposium question, soliciting comments on the importance of "the people" to poets, Stevens had contributed this uncharacteristic reply, which served perfectly, in Grigson's review of *Ideas*, as a club for flattening any subsequent elegance in Stevens, just as Morse later feared: "Inability to see much point to the life of an ordinary man," Stevens had fired back, goaded by the questionnaire into uncommon syntactic terseness. "The chances are an ordinary man himself sees very little point to it."[72]

It is as if Stevens allowed the Bulgar, that ordinary man, to have studied closely a slightly earlier Stevens – the Stevens who had been in previous pre-popular front months an unwitting ideological controversialist. Here the detractor questions the poet's timely commitment to the role of the American commoner, the Bulgar himself, in "Owl's Clover." Only after reproducing Grigson's critical figure, the rare bird refuting the American Marxist cliché of a monotonous, middle-class republic "where no birds sing," as Edmund Wilson put it;[73] only after allowing that *Ideas* could be criticized for leaving unmodified the conscious aestheticism of *Harmonium* (Stevens's alleged *rage* for order was actually "flittered, howled / By harmonies beyond known harmony") – only then could "A Duck for Dinner" restate and update Grigson's symposium question:

> Is each man thinking his separate thoughts or, for once
> Are all men thinking together as one, thinking
> Each other's thoughts, thinking a single thought,
> Disclosed in everything . . . ?
>
> (*OP* 93)

This inquiry is logically calamitous for the speaker who had been claiming that the chief problem with rendering the masses' voice in verse was that voice's multiplicity. Yet the Bulgar was arguing that masses could think and speak as one. To that Stevens would not find an appropriate response until "The Man with the Blue Guitar," in a work answering "a million people on one string" with complex, inimitable chords in stanzas constructed seemingly as operations of chance. For now, he produced replies in section iv of "Duck" by backtracking to the parody of the left inscribed in "Mr. Burnshaw," satirizing the sort of music the Bulgar's masses love, a

> "Concerto for Airplane and Pianoforte,"
> The newest Soviet réclame,

and thus by re-imagining the aesthetic dereliction of the revolutionary utopia on his terms.

Here again "Owl's Clover" slips into the language for which it is notorious: aphoristic but programmatic, giving the feel of "snippets" – Williams's
term for "Like Decorations" – yet long in metrical feet, its rhetoric half-
quoting and garbling slogans against which Stevens's speaker-artist is supposed to have been cautioning us, for instance "As the man the state, not as
the state the man" (OP 93). The revolutionary conception of mankind
might mean "this mob" – in other words, the reductive left of "Sad Strains,"
the sort that appears one night at the house of a modern Mozart for a
session of stone-throwing, a left incapable of conceiving the forms that
would lend their complaints a stirring, lyric voice. The only way to modify
such a counterattack is to turn sharply, in the sudden realization that merely
to be able to conceive of such a failed future is at least some evidence of the
imagination. Where the imagination is concerned *some* is tantamount to
all, this being an early version of the august minimalist of Stevens's last
poems: "Yet the absence of the imagination had / Itself to be imagined"
(CP 503). "Yet to *think* of the future *is* a genius" entails no less strenuous a
turn, its syntax a great deal more disconcerting. If the depression-era artist
can be guided by such a sharp turn toward renewing imagination's talent at
handling reality, then *some* statue, *some* form of art as symbolically central
to life lived commonly, might be restored to its full place "on *enormous*
pedestals." The canonizing gesture this time is agreeable to all parties.

Sections v and vi proceed from this last movement away from counterattack, acknowledging, as in vi, that "These people have / A meaning within
the meaning they convey" (OP 95). In the end, Stevens converged on a
"we" to exceed politically controversialist arguments. "We" must altogether
face the crisis of the time. "We" have no choice but to come to the park for
our own reasons. The strong ending of "A Duck for Dinner" is achieved in
an insistently pronominal united front of poet and people:

> How shall *we* face the edge of time? *We* walk
> In the park. *We* regret *we* have no nightingale.
> *We* must have the throstle on the gramophone.
> Where shall *we* find more than derisive words?
> When shall lush chorals spiral through *our* fire
> And daunt that old assassin, heart's desire?
>
> (OP 96; emphasis added)

This "we" is familiar from other poems. There is an implied relation between radicalism and neoromantic nostalgia in the line about the nightingale. In 1934, just fifteen months earlier, "we" would have extended only
so far as neoromantics; as I have suggested, even then those so named might
reject the label. The particular "we" of early 1936 marks an advance from
poems produced during the "new romantic" moment, for in the otherwise
steady course of Stevensian rhetoric from the mid-teens to the mid-thirties, "we" has meant "one" or "I" until this very point in "Owl's Clover." In

preceding sections the structural grammar was founded, almost xenophobically – paradoxically for a poem set in a public park – upon *them* standing against that sacred, once-inviolable *I*.

4: DELETE THE SPRAWLING PORTENT

In the winter of 1936–7 Stevens began composing "The Man with the Blue Guitar," and a year had already passed by the time Knopf published a trade edition of *Owl's Clover* by pairing it with the newer poem. The job of extracting Stevens from a political context, largely a post-thirties phenomenon, was already under way by this point – the *we*, so hard-earned in the last movements of "Owl's Clover," overwhelmed by the restored context of *I*. It was at least in part a witting strategy at Knopf, where there was always a certain, not unreasonable view of Stevens's special cerebral strengths as well as social weaknesses; some evidence in the firm's files of the earlier strategy survives from the forties.[74] Of course, submerging "Owl's Clover" in a book called *The Man with the Blue Guitar & Other Poems*, in which the reader would come across Stevens's longest poem merely among "other poems," was no conscious antipolitical conspiracy on the part of Knopf's editors or Alfred Knopf himself, then a supporter of liberal causes and a self-described New Dealer.[75] For one thing, the eclipse of the lesser by the greater poem actually supported the point Stevens himself made by demolishing "Owl's Clover" – a second thought that could reasonably be deemed authorial, indicative of Stevens's thinking all along. The Knopf dust jacket seemed only to confirm, in other words, Stevens's own belated but seemingly definitive retractions from political reference. Here, too, timing was all. "In one group, *Owl's Clover*," that dust jacket reads, "while the poems reflect what was *then* going on in the world, that reflection is *merely* for the purpose of seizing and stating what makes life intelligible and desirable *in the midst of great change* and great confusion" (emphasis added). The blurb continues to speak of "Blue Guitar" as part of a poetry "we" will need as "we *are entering*" a new phase of aesthetic individualism – a "we" very different indeed from the sense of the plural in "Where shall we find more than derisive words?"

Samuel French Morse, overcoming his own decades-old anxieties about Stevens's political reputation, and somewhat resisting "aesthetic value" by favoring the unspecific over the referential in Stevens, chose the first version of "Owl's Clover" as copy-text for *Opus Posthumous* in 1957. It was an act of editorial recovery more subtly predictive of later refutations of his scholarly profession's "irrational commitment to poets' final wishes" than he knew then or could explain as a matter of literary history.[76] The "Owl's Clover" Stevens cut by 198½ lines[77] was stripped of the definiteness that had briefly made it a contribution to cultural politics. The Bulgar's people, for instance, in losing their identities, were cut off from the definite ethnicity and national character that had made them attractive as poetic subjects. Bared of their Balkan shoes, Moldauan bonnets, Viennese watch-chains, Russian beards – their "being part," their "feeling the strength" (*OP* 92–3) – the Bulgar's immigrant people, in the condensation and revision of section iii of "A Duck for Dinner," were even more susceptible than before to the charge that they were "stock figures" straight out of "what is now called *Victorian ideology*," a criticism Stevens had genuinely feared when he was first writing "Mr. Burnshaw" (*L* 289; Stevens's emphasis).

The clearest indication of Stevens's deferred anxieties about political reference is, of course, the total purging of Stanley Burnshaw. All signs of "Mr. Burnshaw" were eradicated in the cut version, even though the poem still logically and rhetorically contained its response to the *New Masses* review for those who knew to look for it. "Mr. Burnshaw and the Statue" became "The Statue at the World's End." No longer was the voice that speaks part v – now part iv, the original part iv having been deleted entirely – introduced by "A solemn voice, not Mr. Burnshaw's says . . ." The Bulgar, now the "acrid" Bulgar, as we have seen, is granted a mere six lines in which to deliver what had been his disconcerting opening monologue on the will of the park's new masses to rise. His warning to the poet – "If you caricature the way they rise, yet they rise" – had been excised. And in "Sombre Figuration," the last poem, most of the meditation on the awful portent of fascism was removed (*OP* 98–9; III: 15–38, 41–8). Drawing rhetorically upon the democratic poetic tradition of Walt Whitman's "The Sleepers" in order to add democratic strength to the antifascism of popular-front poetics, "Owl's Clover" had once provided some of Stevens's strongest lines:

> High up in heaven a sprawling portent moves,
> As if it bears all darkness in its bulk.
> But this we cannot see. The shaggy top
> Broods in tense meditation, constantly,
> On the city, on which it leans, the people there,
> Its shadow on their houses, on their walls,
> Their beds, their faces drawn in distant sleep.
> This is invisible. The supporting arms
> Reach from the horizons, rim to rim,
> While the shaggy top collects itself to do
> And the shoulders turn, breathing immense intent.
> All this is hidden from sight.
> It is the form
> Of a generation that does not know itself,
> Still questioning if to crush the soaring stacks,
> The churches, like dalmatics stooped in prayer,
> And the people suddenly evil, waked, accused,
> Destroyed by a vengeful movement of the arms,
> A mass overtaken by the blackest sky,

Each one as part of the total wrath, obscure
In slaughter; or if to match its furious wit
Against the sleepers to re-create for them,
Out of their wilderness, a special fane,
Midmost in its design, the arms grown swift,
The body bent. . . .

(OP 98)

Gone in a year's time was this powerful suggestion that the prospect of evil, a political catastrophe that "Can Happen Here," would exploit "the form / Of a generation that does not know itself."

When critical interest in "Owl's Clover" extends to this cut version, it is usually because it reveals Stevens's discovery in "The Man with the Blue Guitar" that "present-day verse technique" had by the thirties been threatened because its "language and rhythms bear no relation to modern life," as Edmund Wilson put it when describing the poetry scene at large.[78] Or, in other words, because the evisceration of "Owl's Clover" just prior to the composition of "Blue Guitar" discloses how at that moment Stevens was keenly aware of what the poet Robert Fitzgerald, himself fleetingly a literary fellow traveler,[79] called in his review of *Blue Guitar* the "insistent . . . rhyming [of] these opposites."[80] "[T]hese" become ideological "opposites" when one reads the poem politically. Yet despite the exhortation of the Knopf dust jacket, what was "*then* going on in the world" to which in "Owl's Clover" Stevens reacted, was still "going on" in early 1937, when Stevens braved the contentious world again in "Blue Guitar": The ascendancy of fascism; the new hegemony of the American liberal-left under the New Deal; the increasingly resonant demands of the American working class. (And all three issues are addressed in the new poem.) Only the Spanish Civil War would have become material for poetry when Stevens commenced to write new poems in the latter half of 1936. As we have seen, it too became part of new work. The main difference was that in "Owl's Clover" he had learned how to evade certain "pressures of the contemporaneous" in order to present things as they are with a fuller and formally more elaborated sense of realism – as "Blue Guitar" would claim – than many of the poetic "realists" of the day. Curiously, as 1936 became 1937, Stevens and T. C. Wilson were finally agreed as to what the very next poetic step would be. "[W]hat we want today," Wilson wrote, "is not abandonment of realism but an extension of it to include another dimension – which is that the object is also a symbol, inherent in the material."[81] "I cannot bring a world quite round," Stevens wrote, "Although I patch it as I can" (CP 165).

7

A Million People on One String

It was never quite clear whether we were supposed to express our political views or influence people to have other political views.

—The composer Arthur Berger, reflecting on Stevens's lecture at Harvard, December 1936 (*WSR* 163–4)

Stevens . . . comes a little more than half-way round, to the "rose" of the "red."

—Samuel French Morse, reviewing *The Man with the Blue Guitar & Other Poems*[1]

But then things never really are.
How does it matter how I play

Or what I color what I say?
It all depends on inter-play. . . .

—Stevens, in a deleted canto of "The Man with the Blue Guitar" (*OP* 103)

[Art's] purpose . . . is to make existence tolerable to those who are compelled to accept Things As They Are.

—Joseph Wood Krutch

1: THE RATIONAL ELEMENT

Nineteen thirty-six: trouble at Stevens's beloved Harvard. The confrontation that began when a high Nazi official embarrassed President Conant by responding generously to an alumni fundraising appeal only raised the pitch of hissing and whistling at newsreels in Cambridge theaters, and further fueled those who drove to Washington one night to raise the Soviet flag over the Supreme Court building.[2] George Charney (Harvard class of '28) returned to the Yard as organizational secretary of the Party's New England district, having been invited to debate the Italian Consul. A thousand students jammed the hall.[3] Roger Baldwin ('05) and Corliss Lamont ('24) teamed up to remind their cohorts that the Massachusetts anti-red flag law had been written so broadly as to make Harvard crimson illegal in public display. They took the occasion to serve notice that no college had produced "heretics and rebels . . . as continuously" as had Harvard.[4] In June of that year, alumni and students witnessed a protest against the teacher's loyalty oath that had been enacted by the Massachusetts state legislature. Grateful for any faculty support, student radicals heard exhilarating official pleas for a renewal of academic freedom.[5] The state representative who had written the bill and pushed it through while shouting "Reds are getting control of Massachusetts schools!"[6] was brazenly parodied by the Ivy orator: "I see loose morals, fast living and – horrors! – free thinking. . . . Perhaps Harvard is a mine of communism. Perhaps Red propaganda is being circulated among the undergraduates . . . [Y]ou parasites, you bolshevists. . . . But . . . soon the good old capitalistic system of [Alf] Landon . . . will be with us again."[7]

The air of the 300th commencement was charged with these and similar bitter strains, causing an institutional nervousness among loyalists of an old order[8] only intensified by the keynote address given by Franklin Delano Roosevelt ('04) at the formal tercentenary ceremonies in September. The president (and candidate) elaborated freedom of thought pointedly so as to include "understand[ing] philosophies we do not accept and hopes we find it difficult to share" (and so it was said he was being "soft on communism").[9] Porter Sargent, long a rebellious Harvard observer, saw a celebration "electric with surprises, both of suppression and inspiration," though generally "the radical element was kept under"[10] and "[s]ons of Harvard who had most to contribute were forgotten, while doddering old dodos were given place."[11] On the very day of the Roosevelt visit – surely it was thus timed – a group of alumni including Cowley, Hicks, and Dos Passos circulated a pamphlet criticizing Harvard's institutional stand on the Sacco and Vanzetti case (a few weeks later it was correctly charged that Harvard officials had intercepted and suppressed the pamphlets).[12] The Tercentenary Ode, delivered by the poet Hermann Hagedorn ('07) on September 17, no less didactic than such odes before or since, turned out additionally to be, of all things, a converted radical's windy plea:

> What of the night, Harvard? What of the lamentation
> Under your window, the moaning of multitudes? . . .
> What of the dearth, Harvard?
> What of the hunger?
> The trampling feet, the drums rolling? Youth, in vacuity,
> Gasping for daybreak!
> What of the night, Harvard?[13]

We can be confident that talk of these and other odes and episodes reached
Stevens, if not from such university mailings and magazines as always found
him in Hartford then through rampant alumni rumoring. His closest Harvard
contacts were colleagues from his own Harvard years (1898-1901). By the time
he accepted the invitation to come to Harvard to deliver the Morris Gray
lecture, he was sure to have known of the latest troubles incited by his famous
radical friend Porter Sargent,[14] who had remained in Cambridge, specialized
in institutional reform, and was by 1936 known as "the saltiest commentator
on U.S. education."[15] (In 1935 he had written of Cambridge's Old John the
Orangeman, who asked a silk-hatted Harvard clubman what VERITAS signified
on the Harvard shield, to which the clubman replied: "Oi doan exactly know
the Latin, sor, but it manes 'To Hell wid Yale'" – to which Sargent added, "So
truth means to any group what they want it to."[16]) Sargent was then loosely but
productively associating with a group of leftist alumni (including the socialist
poet Jack Wheelwright) in order to stage a protest during tercentenary events
to decry the new limits on academic freedom. While contracts of two economics instructors were not being renewed – the Harvard left would charge that
the dismissal had come because of the instructors' "liberalism" and "sympathies
with organized labor" (one dared write a book on the C.I.O.)[17] – the effect on
remaining untenured radicals and moderates alike, as Sargent put it to Wheelwright, would be to keep "teachers timid at Harvard as elsewhere."[18]

    A "new diversity," thus termed, quite favorably described by College
sophomore Arthur M. Schlesinger, Jr. as created by Middle Westerners,
public-schooled Easterners, and the few admitted Jews, was reinforced by
journalistic denunciations of the club system as "exclusive little organisms"
breeding "[a]nti-pacifism, anti-radicalism, anti-Semitism" and "excellent
material for a mob." The perceived threat of "diversity" – ever the
buzzword – made the physical counterattacks of 1936 possible, and even
socially rewarding in some circles, such as "shav[ing] a Communist's head"
(as at MIT) and "the furious destruction of the rooms of conspicuous radicals."[19] The radical *Harvard Critic*, and local units of the National Students'
League and the Student's League for Industrial Democracy (forerunner of
SDS), all operated under the Harvard Student Union, which liberals leaning left praised as having "interest[ed] the ordinary undergraduate in . . .
the problems of the world,"[20] and liberals leaning right denounced as colo-
nized by Stalin's youngest dupes.[21] Harvard's chapter of the Oxford Group,
its members pledging not to support the government in any future war,
actively participated in the big 1936 Student Anti-War Strike (involving
perhaps 750,000 students nationally); it was movingly supported by
radicalized alumni like poet Hermann Hagedorn. "There could be no
doubt," Howe and Coser later observed, "that the work . . . of the cam-
pus Communists was yielding handsome results."[22]

    This, then, was the contested Harvard to which Wallace Stevens publicly posed the following provocative question:"Does anyone suppose that the vast mass of people in this country was moved at the last election *by rational considerations?*" Using crisis rhetoric similar to that in Hagedorn's praise for the no-war pledge, the distinguished Morris Gray lecturer also observed:"We have a sense of *upheaval.* We feel *threatened*" (*OP* 229–30; emphasis added). Surely the lecture reads as a good deal more ideologically robust than otherwise, when many people like Hagedorn can be placed rhetorically – indeed poetically – in the noisy background. Hagedorn's essay on the Oxford Group, running in the *Advocate* concurrently with Stevens's visit, warned of "anything possible in the way of upheaval," characterized American lives "as confused as the world around" them, and spoke of "impending disaster" and a "mania for destruction."[23] Typifying many such calls at Harvard, versified and not, Hagedorn's solution was persistently thematic and unambiguous:"[R]esistance" meant specific resistance to war. But what of Stevens's sense of resistance? What, for him, was threatening? His references to besieged Madrid, discussed at the beginning of this book, were no less sympathetic for brevity (*OP* 226). What could this poet have meant, then, by implying at the same time that if Americans had voted rationally on November 3, 1936, just a few weeks earlier, things would be different? That FDR would not have defeated Alf Landon? Returning to a Harvard much changed since his turn-of-the-century days there, Stevens also called for "resistance" by name, resistance against "the pressure of the contemporaneous" (*OP* 229–30), and any clue to a political reading of his return to Harvard – we know that members of his audience were trying to construct one – lies in that phrase. So does a similar reading of the long poem he wrote immediately afterward.

Stevens was suggesting to his Harvard audience that while a poet might or might not get swept up in the social and political "upheaval," he or she should attempt to "collect oneself against all this in poetry as well as in politics." A poet might resist "all this" by converting an "ominous and destructive circumstance . . . into a different, an explicable, an amenable circumstance," and might continue to transfigure the world's plight until it was no longer disturbing. "Resistance is the opposite of escape. . . . There can be no thought of escape" (*OP* 229–30).

This is not what Stevens would mean a few years later, in April 1941, when he spoke at Princeton of "resisting or evading . . . the pressure of reality,"[24] for in December 1936 "resistance" meant courting hard prewar dissensus, whereas three and a half years later it could mean escaping into easy wartime consensus.[25] The difference between the two suggests reliably at least one basic difference between the forties and the thirties. In early 1941 it was assumed that Americans were prepared to acknowledge the reality of the crisis (a campaign against fascism that the United States was ideologically readying itself to enter), even as many, like Stevens, were not similarly prepared for American intervention.[26] But in 1936 there was still plenty of doubt. Measuring their shifting positions against positions deemed indisputable by others, many writers knew, as Stevens surely did, that being for or against "things *as they are*" meant standing "for" or "against" art attentive to a settlement of the crisis. This made the "pressure" that interested him.

In using the phrase "pressure of the contemporaneous," in short, Stevens was referring less to "reality" than to realism. By then he knew full well how poets calling themselves political made realism itself a main matter of art. While reality continued to issue shocks and surprises, requiring constant inventiveness, realism, a conception vying among contending conceptions for the power to oversee poets' attention to crises, was beginning to produce predictable results as the liberal-left coalition widened and brought in forms once deemed inimical to political art. Poetic "realists" could not but concur with Stevens: "The only possible resistance to the pressure of the contemporaneous is . . . the contemporaneous itself." Yet for those willing to submit to pressures for engaging a definitive "real," it was particularly easy to forget that realism was no less a manner or style than any other.

Stevens's Morris Gray lecture, "The Irrational Element in Poetry," advanced its sense of the political unconscious accordingly. He understood how poetic ideologies succeeded one another, how and why the writer "who has been brought up in an *artificial* school becomes *intemperately real*" (emphasis added). Freedom operated at the risk of becoming just another settled aesthetic convention. The simple example he offered was Picasso's "obsession of freedom" (*OP* 230). If freedom in the arts were a truer freedom, then "fastidiousness" would not be "repudiated as an abomination" so involuntarily; nor would "Social Fact" be so hard to reconcile aesthetically with "Cosmic Vision" (he was citing an essay on Picasso by Christian Zervos). There was a point beyond which committing oneself to what one called "the real" entailed not knowing how unfree had become one's formalized preferences for that reality. Nor did the up-to-date modernist – in a way, he was himself speaking as an early postmodernist – quite see, as he did see, that "'destroy[ing] the barriers which art . . . impressed on the imagination'" (*OP* 230) only erected new barriers. "You can do as you please, everything matters," Stevens said. "You are free, but your freedom must be consonant with the freedom of others."

Horace Gregory might have come to mind as a perfect example of such an up-to-date modernist, but in making his point at Harvard Stevens named no contemporary American names. He did name names of the dead, and his analogy to the poetry of Edgar Allen Poe was apt and persuasive. Why had Poe's tintinnabulations once appealed to American ears, but did so no longer? "You are free to tintinnabulate if you like," Stevens deftly wise-cracked for his audience, "but I am equally free to hold my ears"! What else could explain why a poet's own earlier work "becomes as obsolete for himself as for anyone else"? At certain historical junctures poets submerged themselves in the aesthetic moment that tended to judge an earlier poetic self-consciousness to be more or less unreal.

The argument was itself rather freely borrowed from the Marxist critique of aesthetic ideology, even as it seemed to be aimed at disparaging certain naive American versions of the same. In a precisely contemporaneous statement, Gregory, now *New Masses* poetry editor, asserted in *Story* that "newer poetry is less affected by an early acquaintance with Joyce, Eliot and Pound and . . . is *no longer concerned with mere verbal experiment.*" The most effective style "has a hard, clear surface."[27] This position permitted much twenties-bashing: In the thirties "writing itself should be more decisive, clear and outspoken than most of the work written in the preceding decade."[28] "There is no 'style,'" Mike Gold had said (deliberately without style), " – there is only clarity."[29] Helen Davis contributed an extreme version of Gold's invective against style, in a poem for the magazine *Cambridge Left*, "Come Words Our Tools": Words, "Work[ing] ten times harder now" that "Hitler and hunger laugh at what you've done," will "Plot out their needed course in lovely steel / Plain demonstration, evident and clear."[30] Never mind that steel, no matter how "lovely," is not "clear." Unless one decides that Davis for some reason meant "Come Words Our Tools" to exempt itself from its own demand for direct steel-hard demonstration, or wanted to court a basic formal irony that would at any rate undermine the call for "clarity," her error in thinking will be apparent to anyone who glances at the work on the page: Davis's poem, after all, is a perfectly regular sonnet. There were radical sonnets, to be sure, that formally augmented an anti-rhetoric rhetoric advocating "Plain demonstration." Marvin Klein's striking "Sonnet to Disintegration" is an example, with its octave consisting of widely-spaced disconnected phrases, clinging to the integrations of sonnet but just barely.[31] Kreymborg's "American Jeremiad" makes a similar clinging its main topic, so that his sonnet is about a traditional sonnet that for reasons of political conscience never gets started:

> It's pretty hard to sing of moonlight now,
> Of benches in the park and lovers' lanes.
> I'd like to if I could, but . . . [32]

But in Helen Davis's wholly conventional Petrarchan form little, if anything, is plainly demonstrated; nor should it necessarily be, of course. Yet consciously "radical" writers of lines like "No seasons ever dawdle for the plough" cannot at the same time pretend that such phrases aren't what they metrically and syntactically are. These writers are constrained by old unrevised formal rules, textual practices accepted as given. "Radical" poems like Davis's do not for themselves make the necessary case for radical artifice – the sort of knowing engagement of the rhetorical feints and syn-

tactical maneuverings of lyric poetry's formalities that can imply acceptance of what postmodern poets, some of them political radicals, would
call "the word as such." Stevens (and Kenneth Burke) felt the requirements
of a "frame of acceptance," not to temper the words-as-tools idea, but actually to sharpen it. When Mike Gold once set the language of proletarian
letter-writers in blank-verse stanzas, surely the result, the forceful poem
"Examples of Worker Correspondence," cannot be said to stand unmedi-
ated by the poetic process. To read the poem is to know that it was Gold
who chose to lineate the workers' prose, of course, and then to realize that
he chose with skill:

> But our heárts were dárk with ánger
> We márched in thóusands to her gráve[33]

Even if these were actually the words in the workers' letters Gold or the
New Masses had been sent, and even if three stresses in the first line quoted
also actually were internal rhymes ("hearts," "dark," "marched") in the original document, nonetheless Gold was making, as well as finding, poetry.[34]

Putting the lie to Gregory's, Gold's, and Davis's seemingly indisputable
understanding of "style," then, Stevens at Harvard intrepidly maintained
that while a style might be "hard" it could never quite be "clear." The
signified could never be utterly visible through the texture of signs set in
verse, in spite of some radical axioms about the coming glorious cessation
of style and the emergence of an uncorrupted textual surface. To the degree
that twenties poetry could *aid* poets of the thirties – and in a larger sense
modernist artifice could thus *sustain* radical attitude – all parties to the
agreement would first have to admit that "style," even the one designated
"clear," was always laid in the traces of another style.

Offering this analysis, Stevens's sense of the left's impression on him was
never more apparent, and yet in ideological terms he was turning it around
– a strategy perfected immediately afterward in "Blue Guitar." He knew
precisely why "[t]he Mallarmiste becomes the proletarian novelist," and he
depended on a form of historicism as the basic conceptual tool for beholding the changing role of the artist even as the false consciousness of the
proletarian novelist was his target.[35] He saw that the noncommunist poet
undergoing partial conversion to left-sanctioned "clarity," to words as "lovely
steel," might endure the change without ever making himself or herself
conscious of the pressures shaping the contemporary notion of
contemporaneity. To be able to make that very point, of course, indicated
acute awareness. His provocative example of the Mallarmiste metamor-
phosing into a proletarianist did not in fact exaggerate the transformation
undergone by some of his own generation (a few old friends among them).
His own sense of a twenties for the thirties might even discern a *1936* for
1937: Looking back on his own very recent development, he acknowledged
in his Harvard lecture that he had attempted to write "Owl's Clover" by

allowing "a confronting of the world as it had been imagined in art and *as it was then in fact*." He then described for his audience the Old Woman of the first poem: she was simply "a symbol of those who suffered during the depression."

What, then, of Stevens's declaration about Roosevelt's landslide? The statement was much more complicated, after all, than it must have seemed to his audience – many, if not most, of whom would not have been followers of Alf Landon.[36] Stevens meant only to remind his audience that aesthetic ideology, even that which was founded on resistance and dissent, has a discernible way of marking the work of artists, especially when those artists are not conscious of how such pressure tends to exclude other cultural forms. And what is a cultural form but a vehicle bearing a contending concept of reality? It was assumed that being a noncommunist in the Soviet Union only meant that it was bewildering to interact aesthetically with reality as it existed there; too, that being a non-Nazi in Germany entailed a severe limitation that was similar not morally, perhaps, but structurally (OP 229). Why, then, was it not also true that American mimeticists, implicitly validated by New Deal engagement of artists as cultural journalists and liberal-left conceptions of artists as documenters, held non-mimeticists to a version of reality in the same basic way?

It was in this particular controversial yet insightful context that Stevens used a phrase just then resurgent among liberal and leftist anti-isolationists: *It can't happen here*. A year earlier it had been the title phrase of Sinclair Lewis's novel, and Granville Hicks was correct on October 29, 1935, in predicting that it would "raise the issue of fascism more sharply than it has been raised in America before."[37] By October and November of 1936 the title-phrase itself had already become culturally axiomatic, as the Federal Theatre Project re-ignited Lewis's "red flame" by opening a stage version simultaneously put on by eighteen FTP units nationwide, prominently including Connecticut's.[38] The new currency of "It Can't Happen Here" was carefully timed by the organized intellectual left to coincide with the presidential election: "Wherever the Democrats and Republicans were not campaigning last evening," a sympathetic reviewer wrote, "Mr. Lewis and his conspirators were . . . warning against political dictatorship."[39] We must have no illusions, Stevens announced at Harvard just a few weeks later, about being able in the long run to resist any ascendant way of comprehending the real. "We no sooner say that it never can happen here," he said, "than we recognize that we say it without any illusions" (OP 229).

The words "It Can't Happen Here," of course, carried with them the implication that "It" – fascism powerfully despecified in an already characteristically Stevensian way – *can* "happen" in the United States. Stevens's use of the phrase was not meant to seem the least bit remarkable. He assumed, I think, that it would be appreciated as a matter of routine political reference.

When turned around, however, and used against the unified liberals and radicals who put forward the massive federalized arts effort in twenty-one theatres just at election time, the same axiom could be managed by conservatives in attacks on the New Deal more pointed than the WPA's vague, unmentionable fear of Roosevelt's demagoguery (unmentionable because the Theatre Project owed its life, after all, to New Deal centralism). The most complete turning-around was managed by Hooverite doubters like Mark Sullivan, whose regular column ran in the *Hartford Courant*. Sullivan explained to his readers that "It" in "It Can't Happen Here" actually meant "the arising of the *American* dictator" who inspired in the public a "worship of the state," which was, to Sullivan, both a fascist practice *and New Deal hallmark*.[40] A certain element of the right, then, typified by Sullivan's fears of New Deal absolutism, felt itself enabled by this particular radical "It" to speak most forthrightly of "protests and resistances" in turning liberal rhetorical strategy against a dominant form of liberalism. Shrewdly using the phrase, Stevens could express anxiety about an epoch of political culture in which "your freedom must be consonant with the freedom of others," while playing upon deep partisan ambiguities (*OP* 230).

Although it is hard to come by, there is evidence that this keen political decontextualizing came across to a few doubters in Stevens's audience. Among the three or four hundred people who attended[41] his lecture at Harvard in December 1936 was the student Arthur Berger. Berger clearly understood Stevens's play on modernism from right to left: He and his roommate Delmore Schwartz knew that Stevens did not mean to eschew "reality" and sensed Stevens's special insightful way of warning his audience that *it* — political repression become aesthetic — can happen here. For at Harvard in 1936 Berger, Schwartz and their friends, aspiring artists and musicians, were feeling the same pressures as noncommunists. They took Stevens's talk as wise counsel on making the most of one's awkward position. "[T]hose of us wanting to be artists [were] being pressed that we had to have a message to the people in our art, influence the people," he later recalled. "It was never quite clear whether we were supposed to express our political views or influence people to have other political views." Stevens's visit to Cambridge was exactly what Berger needed, he later said, to "contemplate the good in the midst of confusion" and yet not fall into the trap of living "apart in happy oblivion" (*OP* 225, 224). "What Stevens had to say touched some very sympathetic chord in us," Berger has said, "because we were grappling with these problems."[42]

The sentiments of the Harvard lecture — which Peter Brazeau properly described as a concentration of many ideas Stevens had already developed in response to Latimer's questions (*WSR* 162) — led Stevens in the winter of 1936–7 to an important realization. If he was to continue with the problems of "Owl's Clover" in new work, it would have to incorporate his new ideas about the closely related ironies of aesthetic freedom and politicized realism and the way in which contemporary crises – fascist rebellion in Spain; radical unionism; court-packing – impress themselves on a poem "even when we do not observe them closely" (OP 229). The notion of contingency in the Harvard talk and the structure of interaction between a poet and his detractors in the next major poem are indeed a close match.

2: THINGS AS THEY ARE

In preparing the audience to hear portions of "Owl's Clover" that December day, Stevens had given a tangled description of his recent work. Actually, what he described resembled not so much the poem he had just published as the astonishing improvisations of the poem he was about to compose. Of course his hearers could not have known either that he was ready to write again at length or that there was anything significant in his overwrought sense of timing. Certainly not from this: The poem "is what I wanted it to be without knowing before it was written what I wanted it to be, even though I knew before it was written what I wanted to do" (OP 226). Through the winter he wrote a poem nearly as variable as the one that had to be imagined from that convolution. A few productive months later he announced that he had already completed twenty or thirty sections of "The Man with the Blue Guitar," adding, with a confidence uncharacteristic of other periods of composition, that he might have ten more in his head.

Such confidence holds but the slightest clue to the poem's structural power. Its variability actually obtains from an exhilarating insecurity. The guitarist of "The Man with the Blue Guitar" frets over his position to such an extent that these frettings are taken by detractors within the poem itself as clear signs of weakness. The main difficulty arises when one tries to identify the detractors with any consistency. Are the arguments "they" use to rebut the guitarist wholly the poet's creations and original to the poem? The sheer inventiveness entailed in the work's every other aspect makes the detractors – a "they" whom readers evidently should already know (perhaps from the Old Woman, Mr. Burnshaw, and the Bulgar) – central to the guitarist's eventual emergence as expertly improvisational.

In the dialogical narrative of the poem, the talent for invention derives directly from the vigor the guitarist gains by improvising a reply to the detractors. Both the reply and the vigor are based on an adaptation of their terms. In this sense the poem demonstrates, as Frank Lentricchia has put it (summarizing Raymond Williams), "that hegemony . . . is best understood dramatically . . . [and] agonistically."[43] "Blue Guitar" is a drama in which both sides believe, with Burke, that "[t]he victory of one 'principle' in history is usually not the vanquishing, but the partial incorporation, of another."[44] Thus *positioning*, the poem's key political-aesthetic trope and pun, is so important. Stevens's "they" and their positions have given shape to the guitarist's very posture; in canto i, posturing is literally at issue. Only by means of his constantly shifting relation to his guitar can the guitarist acquit himself ably in presenting the idea of position (what might be called positionality) as itself his position – by admitting, intermittently, that he attempts to disguise the very fact that he *has* a position.

And he seems to have so many positions. His guitar is at different points agent, means, method, envoy, device, vehicle, contrivance, gizmo. It is an instrument to be tried on, adjusted, and maneuvered (canto i), an adhesive and accessory in one (ii), a buzzing means to an end that must be coped with or managed just right (iv). It is a sharp tool, knife, nail and hammer (iii). Then again it is abstract, an apparatus constructed of place and space and resisting change (vi), a form of the self clawed by an irrational form of the self (xvii), a noisy swarming of thoughts (xxvi), a means of defiguring the figurative mask (xxix), a shape in an overcast sky (ix). It is also a vehicle conveying the object back to poetry (xviii), a mode of involuntary, painful posturing somehow affording nuance and even at times inspiring rhapsody (xxxi). By then it has already served well as a device for playing off two positions at once (xxiii) and as an object to which may be assigned the sudden strength to be both the reason and resolution of a thunderstorm (viii). It is the thing to which is transferred the power of invention (ix). It is also, at points, improvisation itself (xx). So mutable a central figure would seem to make the narrative of the poem equally directionless. To be sure, the arguments put forward by the poet, his detractors (always "they," never dramatized or named as in "Owl's Clover") and by a third, authorial voice, do range widely – from the hurtful, moralizing contentiousness of v to the strumming supplications of xx. There is also the jeering polemic of iii, the brooding compromise of vi, the rollicking antagonism of x, the defensive insistence of xxviii, the confident entreaty of xxxii, the mocking counterattack of iv, the willing deliberation of ii.

The very forms argument can take would seem to heed the incessant inventions and variations of the guitar and its strings – would seem, that is, to assume no pattern or organization *despite having the status of argument.* In this view the poem is, as one admirer has put it, "[l]ess argument than improvisation."[45] Yet Stevens's feat depends on the poem's preventing the two categories of argument and invention from becoming exclusive; this mode results from a convergence of modernist noncommunists and their would-be detractors. That *forms* of argumentation constantly shift is itself the consistent argument the poet is trying to make for – on behalf of, not in spite of – his detractors. The figure of guitar and its strings served brilliantly to display what Burke was just then calling "Attitudes toward the Incessant Intermingling of Conservatism and Progress";[46] fine tuning and constant re-tuning displace the heavy uncalibrated hand pounding at art produced otherwise from this "intermingling." The guitarist's strings are not only metal jangling (iii), buzzing fibers picked that come easily untuned or go cold to the strummer's touch (vii); they are also strains of contemporary life, practiced and played, in effect, from the complex modern score of "attitudes toward history," in Burke's sense – figuratively arrows of argumentative direction (ix), wranglings between ideas (xxxiii), chattering lines of debate (v), even skins on which to thumb (xxv) or drum (x) the measure of the lyric line. This is the clearest way of explaining how and why in the end the poem's cantos play upon the agonistic rhetorics of American politics – why they develop into cables slung through an industrial suburb in crisis (xxx) and mark lines of tension between bosses and workers (xxxi).

To follow the major variations of the central phrase in this work, "things as they are," is to learn that, despite the immense pressures to innovate and modulate that would seem to bear on any poet who is to use a single phrase twenty times in the poem's thirty-three cantos (and five more times in six cantos later deleted), the variable meaning of the phrase does have rhyme and reason. At the outset "things as they are" points to an incontrovertible world of manifest conditions. This is the pseudo-objectivist definition given it by them, the detractors. Even the guitarist, when responding in the first canto of dialogue, engages "things as they are" in their reified sense. In canto ii the guitarist responds further to the detractors' argument by accepting and extending their definition of "things as they are" as verities just far enough so that the concept can seem to him unattainable; thus the set of objective conditions that they hope he will find and retain for his poem become, in his new and improved view, impossible to render in words.

But soon the phrase "things as they are" develops an intertextual twist: Canto vii, for instance, re-imagines the dystopia of "Mr. Burnshaw and the Statue." That Stevens seems to have added this canto later[47] reinforces my sense that it considers as a whole the poem's place in his thirties work. It marks a significant rhetorical advance over the "clanking mechanism" derided in "Like Decorations," which had perhaps left Stevens's criticism of the Dynamo school indistinct from Stephen Benét's (ignorantly denouncing "the 'Oh, Grandmother Dynamo, what great big wheels you have!' school"). Here, however, "creeping men" have become "mechanical beetles never quite warm," while things as they are have been cut off from everything under the warming, humanizing sun. Their reactions are founded on an original pride for early-modernist uses of the machine shared by left-detractor and poet-guitarist alike. The mechanists' failure lies ironically in a god-like naming – a poetic genesis the guitarist continues to believe is his and his alone, especially now that his detractors are reduced to making sunless insects: "And shall I then stand in the sun / . . . *and call it good*" (emphasis added):

> The immaculate, the merciful good,
>
> Detached from us, from things as they are?
>
> Not to be part of the sun?

That this particular strategy will imminently miscarry is evident in the intellectual flatness of the phrase immediately following: "To stand / Remote and call it merciful." The guitarist can already sense – but, again, given the order in which the cantos were composed, it might have been a looking back – that his inventive form depends utterly on a rhetorical dialogism learned from detractors *whom he nonetheless calls mechanists*, reductive, crude, unfeeling, and "cold." But the old outmoded self-involvement has begun again to intrude, itself a reduction (like Munson's and Fletcher's early views of the dandy). Sadly but momentarily, then, "The strings are cold on the blue guitar" (*CP* 168).

Later the slogan, "things as they are," is repeated to reassure detractors who doubt the validity of realism's extended geography. The dialogue between imagined and real, thought to be temperamentally right and left – of "serene" voices in the clouds (aesthetic right) and the "grunted breath" of the detractors (aesthetic left) – play "year by year" a meta-poetry in a style answerable to both, poetry *about* the contingent concept of things as they are (xxiii). And now this poem has itself become that sort of poem. Thus the detractors' idea of things as they are is again refuted, even as it is borrowed from liberally. Still, a main point against them has been clinched, for even *their* version of the poem is finally a poem about poetry.

In later cantos, the speaker romps with the hard-won concept, playing freely upon the variations that had first given the detractors so much trouble. The world itself – the sense of "things" secured by evidently fixable objective conditions, asserted earlier – is now dismissed by a mere capricious gesture, in a thumbing of the nose:

> He held the world upon his nose
> And this-a-way he gave a fling.

All variations of reality remain to be impulsive, beat out by a petulant thumb on the skin of the blue guitar-*cum*-drum. Ordinary worldly things on which others would have the guitarist-poet percuss, common things like cats and trees, are indeterminate, aqueous and unfixed – in other words "irrational" specifically in the surrealist sense ("liquid cats // . . . did not know the grass went round").[48] Here in canto xxv things as they are – the concept – is itself stretched out like a skin, or (to mix the metaphor at Stevens's urging) is itself fluid. Stevens knew from "Mr. Burnshaw" – and, as I have argued, from lyric deviationists like Maas, Lechlitner, Rolfe Humphries, Wheelwright, and Burnshaw himself – how political realism could now be broadened to include "things as they were, things as they are, / Things as they will be by and by . . . " (*CP* 178). The phrase "by and by,"

easygoing, yet forward-looking, certifies the point rhetorically. Reality becomes paradoxically most definitive when a writer dallies over it a little,
even if he or she somewhat passively awaits it – a direct descendant of
"Table Talk" belatedly seen as having been a concession to Practical Criticism via Burnshaw's special use of Richards.

The morning song of canto xxxi discharges the restrictive definition
of "things as they are" originally proposed by the detractors. Finally, using a rhetoric that anticipates the grandly programmatic "Notes toward a
Supreme Fiction" (1942), the guitarist imposes a restriction of his own
making: "*It must be* this rhapsody or none, / The rhapsody of things as
they are." The song of reality is actually ecstatic, multi-toned, and impulsive – not fastidious, monotonous, or constant. "Things as they are" is
wholly a matter of performance. The form of argumentation finally involves not the artist's critics' demand but his own. It must be exactly what
he says it is; therefore, it will be mannered and inexact! (*CP* 182-83). By
xxxii, then, only the phrase "things as they are" itself remains to be altered
for the purposes of attracting the subject: "things as they are" is now, finally,
"You as you are." The point is posed as a question, with the stress on seeming ("as") as it delimits being ("are"): "You *as* you *are?*"

The answer to this question lies in the confidence required to be able to
abdicate the object and yet remain liable to reality: "You are yourself. The
blue guitar surprises you" (*CP* 183). What "surprises" the man with the
blue guitar is the power granted his assigned agent for transforming not so
much unfortunate reality as realism – not only things as they are but a
literary politics putting into play a certain forceful revisionist rhetoric of
the real. Indeed, "The Man with the Blue Guitar" reproduces a basic literary-political controversy in its very structural choices, no less assiduously
than does "Owl's Clover," that much slower-footed target for the deadly
aim of political readings. But what controversy?

3: A LITTLE PATIENT EXPLAINING

The argument carried on between the poet-guitarist and the detractors is
no more original to the poem than that between the poet–figure and his
various named and unnamed antagonists in "Owl's Clover." In this fundamental way the two poems are very closely related. Each position is inextricably connected to the radicalized critical rhetoric of the thirties, as even
a general sense of the detractors' argument reveals. What is original to
"Blue Guitar," of course, is the "simple enthusiasm and imaginative energy"[49] with which the antagonists comport themselves canto to canto.
This is obviously what distinguishes the poem of 1936–7 from the poem of
1935–6. Yet in moving with Stevens to "Blue Guitar" from "Owl's Clover,"
we ought not to conclude, without looking closely into the situation, that

he was putting distance between himself and the contentious literary world that had deeply marked and (in the view of some) had ruined "Owl's Clover."

On the contrary, the poet-guitarist finally endorses a sense of reality constantly changing. And so he is himself changed further by the very conceptualization of change – a dialogical idea of order already worked out in Stevens's historical imagination. If the detractors' insistence on a reality entails actualities, an epistemology no longer to be denied its place among modernist precisions, then the era's literary-political skirmishes, including several described in the previous chapters, become helpful in locating "The Man with the Blue Guitar" as the modernist's contribution to both positions. The way in which Stevens learned to allow his poet-figure to experiment with – to "patch" (canto i) – a concept of reality, will be recognizable as the strategy of the poems in the "Owl's Clover" sequence, a familiarity supporting a similar approach to the new poem's involvement in the bitterest arguments of the time.

One such argument particularly supports the point. This is the exchange between Joseph Wood Krutch on one hand (and his defenders, for instance the liberal critic Charles Glicksberg, writing for the antiradical *Sewanee Review*), and, on the other hand, Philip Rahv, Harold Rosenberg and the not-yet-anti-Stalinist *Partisan Review*. Krutch's "Literature and Utopia," published in the *Nation*,[50] was fiercely attacked by Rahv in "How the Waste Land Became a Flower Garden," published in *Partisan* in late 1934.[51] Rosenberg joined the fracas in his negative review of Krutch's *Was Europe a Success?* in the April-May 1935 issue of *Partisan*.[52] Glicksberg's defense of Krutch appeared in 1936.[53] The strongest detractor, Rahv, in analyzing Krutch's insistence on creating a "special counter-revolutionary category: artist," challenged Krutch's characterization of the radical writer and his use of "things as they are" to support an argument that Rahv claimed had nothing to do with realism.

To Krutch, Rahv contended, partly quoting his adversary, "The revolutionist is busy proving that 'Things As They Are' can no longer be borne, while the artist 'is busily proving with his songs and his tales that it can.'" According to Krutch's narrative of recent literary history, when the writer-as-Bohemian of the teens and twenties had "grown grim" in the thirties he merely gave up his windsor tie for the "flannel shirt of the worker" and swapped one mode of reproducing "Things As They Are" for another. Where this artist went wrong, the argument continued, was in claiming that the newer mode dealt with reality more faithfully and responsibly. This position, in Krutch's hands and played upon by Stevens's guitarist, concedes the contradiction and proceeds nevertheless to defend it quite explicitly as such – as "a paradox which may be stated thus: The chief function of fiction and drama and poetry is not to make anything or anybody better. It is not to improve society any more than it

is to improve morals. Its purpose, rather, is to make existence tolerable to those
who are compelled to accept Things As They Are."[54]

In Glicksberg's counterattack he pointed out the basis of Krutch's argument in "the *as if* philosophy of vital illusions" – the "*as if* construction" of
Hans Vaihinger, as he noted. The point situated Krutch's position on positioning in a way that would have attracted Stevens, whose interest in how
poetic constructions made "existence tolerable" by offering a concept momentarily sufficient, reached back to *Harmonium*.[55] Krutch's distinction –
his opponents contended that it was a false one – between the reformer
whose concern is "with what he can do to the world" and the poet whose
interest is "in what the world is doing to him" was, in Rahv's words, merely

> a crude attempt to counter the Marxist exposure of [art's function in society]
> *by wiping out the particular historical context in which it operates.* . . . By applying
> his chloroforming technique, Krutch manages to obscure this fatal meaning.
> The artist makes existence "tolerable to those who are compelled to accept
> Things as They Are." But the plain fact is – as a glance at any newspaper will
> show – that economic conditions compel the masses to revolt against, not to
> accept, things as they are. (emphasis added)

By 1936–7, when Stevens assimilated this argument, the situation had
changed to the point where the party line, having first excoriated Krutch,
had then to account for his sense of things as they are; it was Dimitrov, in
announcing the Popular Front, who insisted, after all, that the "masses must
be taken as they are, and not as we should like to have them."[56] Stevens was
prepared to assume basic elements of Krutch's view as conditioned by this
broadened sense: First, that among those most strongly "compelled to accept Things As They Are" is preeminently the artist; second, that insofar as
"things as they are" constitutes realism as an aesthetic form-among-forms,
"things" yield the pressure on artists to accommodate the contemporaneous.

Krutch had irritated the sectarian left not because he challenged realism
but because he suggested a connotation of the phrase "things as they are"
that offended political realists who had unwittingly raised one form of
realism to the level of an absolute value. The slogan as Krutch provocatively
used it referred primarily to the artist's project (to the conventional deno-
tative gesture). Only secondarily, if at all, did it suggest the people's existence deemed aesthetically describable. In this view, what changed was not
the real but the way in which modes of realism were adopted and then
superseded. Rahv's Marxist counterattack, then, involved the strategy of
reformulating *the phrase Krutch had himself stolen from the revolutionary moment* when he conferred upon "things as they are" the status of ideal presentation. The implication of his rhetorical theft doubled the power of the
stolen phrase and belatedly – after 1935 – set into motion shrewd noncommunist realizations such as Stevens's: A truth often suffers more by the stress
of its defenders than from the arguments of its opposers. Nevertheless, if an

artist refused to play or only grudgingly played things as assailed truths, it would be said he invariably ignored actuality.

From the very beginning, of course, "The Man with the Blue Guitar" operated within a discourse making the charge of invariability. Is not canto i a dialogue between two versions of positionality, each hoping to retain "things as they are" for its own polemical purpose?

> The man bent over his guitar,
> A shearsman of sorts. The day was green.
>
> They said, "You have a blue guitar,
> You do not play things as they are."
>
> The man replied, "Things as they are
> Are changed upon the blue guitar."
>
> And they said then, "But play, you must,
> A tune beyond us, yet ourselves,
>
> A tune upon the blue guitar
> Of things exactly as they are."

Only insofar as canto ii then allowed the guitarist to elaborate his position (in the first person) could iii permit the detractors to respond. And only as canto iv contained the guitarist's rebuttal could v be so liberally given over again to the detractors.

The dialogue between two positions would seem to be clear enough without the help of Stevens's gloss. But when Hi Simons questioned the arrangement[57] a few years later, Stevens insisted that the poem was a sequence: "[O]ne [canto] really leads into another, even when the relationship is only one of contrast" (*L* 359). Seeing no formal continuities between "Owl's Clover" and "The Man with the Blue Guitar," some readers of the latter poem have followed Morse's conclusion that for "Blue Guitar" Stevens had *not* chosen "discourse" as his mode[58] or Riddel's that the poem is more improvisation than argument. Sam Morse found that "the seesawing back and forth between what the man with the blue guitar said and what 'they' said" became "monotonous," but this is perhaps because these opposing "figures" seemed to him, as to others who have severed one poem from the other, concocted for the occasion rather than as representatives of fierce political contentions.[59] Far from abandoning the dialogue between Krutch's and Rahv's positions after the first group of cantos, the poem developed from them an authorized voice that threw open the possibility of reformulating a sense of the phrase inextricably associated with the radical argument – "things as they are."

Canto ii allowed the guitarist to elaborate on his argument from i. Despite the detractors' insistence on a static depiction of things as they are,

> "Things as they are
> Are *changed* upon the blue guitar."

He began with a rather disarming admission: An artist's ideas about the imperfection of his presentation of reality could themselves serenade the real. "I cannot bring a world quite round." But he claimed a talent for patching. If he sang of the ideal human figure, it was of course not a person but the figure of a person, and through this invention he could "reach through him almost to man." This was the purest form of argumentation, for the rhetoric was largely set by the guitarist's ambition to persuade. The "if"-proposition tempted the detractors to imagine the guitarist's best effort at singing "almost to man," and to credit him for very nearly missing things as they really are. Finally, it asked the opposition to take a word from his poetic lexicon – "serenade" – for denoting his sincere lyric efforts: "*Say that it is the serenade / Of a man that plays a blue guitar.*" As the literary left was provoked by Krutch's preference for sweetness over light – "[L]iterature," he said, "is really concerned with finding a way of looking at things. . . . [T]hanks to the fact that his most important life is led inside his mind, he can make even his thoughts about imperfection delightful"[60] – so the guitarist's detractors were provoked by his claim that he was making a close approach to people as they live every day.

Their rejoinder, in canto iii, began with a knowing nod to the previous argument. "Ah, but to play man number one" acknowledged the sincerity of the guitarist's point (*ah, yes but* . . .). Yet, it then offered a strange picture of "things" as they would be if the guitarist had his own way with human figuration; he dissected that figure, extracted from it only what he wished, and finally destroyed it as subject-become-object. Thus the detractors in iii extended the guitarist's notion of patching to the point where it was exposed as an invasive procedure. The detractors took the guitarist's "play" as a euphemism for destroy and deny. "To play," in this list of parallel infinitives, became "To drive," "To lay," "To nail," "To strike," "To tick," "[to] tock" and finally "To bang." The tone of the rebuttal, having begun with an easy, nodding "Ah," now modulated to satiric irony: If *this* was going to be the guitarist's way of turning a subject "true," of "Jangling the metal of the strings," then the detractors wanted nothing to do with it. Canto iii revealed Stevens's shrewd understanding of how the literary left would criticize what Krutch had called the radical writer's obsession with what "he can do to the world."[61]

So in iii the detractors subject the guitarist's polemical language to a sort of historicist analysis; in iv the guitarist, replying in kind, borrows a central radical image to make his strongest counterargument. This, of course, was a basic form of the radical claim, in the phrase of Kenneth Fearing, which Burke enjoyed quoting, that under the aegis of political realism "millions of voices become one voice" as "millions of hands . . . move as one"[62] – a strong claim on Stevens's noncommunist mind from the time of "Sad Strains of a Gay Waltz" with its unconscious "sudden mobs of men."

The radical poet in Fearing's, Burke's, Kenneth Rexroth's and others' poly-
phonic conception sang not for himself or herself alone but *as* a million
people. Rexroth wrote:

> They shall rise up heroes, there will be many,
> None will prevail against them at last.
> They go saying each: "I am one of many."[63]

Stevens's guitarist began to challenge this particular notion by branding it a
reduction in precisely a way Burke appreciated, with his aversion to any
strategically unnecessary reduction. For the moment, the guitarist uses the
phrase "things as they are" as something commended by his antagonists and
rejected by him. He asks, Is this impossibility truly the world of art "they"
want to bring about?

> A million people on one string?
> And all their manner in the thing,
>
> And all their manner, right and wrong,
> And all their manner, weak and strong?

The guitarist's answer, it is to be assumed, is *No*. The poet's disposition is
not, he insists, conditioned by unanimity, nor by predictability or popularity. His strings are too thin, too finely tuned, to be fingered by all those
rude hands. His variations are programmatically unprogrammatic, lively
but subtle, causing sounds as natural as those of seasonal cycle:

> The feelings crazily, craftily call,
> Like a buzzing of flies in autumn air. . . .

Having reasserted aesthetic individualism, the guitarist returns to "things as
they are" as a slogan once verging on hurled epithet. It is now modified to
suit his position and yet retains its basic force:

> And *that's* life, then: things as they are,
> This buzzing of the blue guitar.
> (*CP* 166–7)

In forming the guitarist's answer here the speaker shows yet again a
familiarity with the literary-political rhetoric of the moment – with the
image of the diligently unanimous millions in, say, Lola Ridge's "Fire Boy,"
where "Comrades" (a word "containing both thee and me, but not stopping at me or thee") are addressed as "each knowing in you the millions'
strength";[64] or Taggard's "And Mighty Poets in Their Misery Dead": "Welders
and diggers, puddlers of steel, millions / Strong, simple, disciplined, – the
essential men: / . . . Mechanics, steady and daring, heroes without praise"[65]
– or MacLeish's notorious "Invocation to the Social Muse": "How to take
to one's chamber a million souls?"[66] Stevens's central trope, the guitar, led
him to enliven a critical cliché: among American idioms for monotony are,
plays on one string, plays the same song again and again, and *knows only one*

tune well. The guitarist's counterattack, by its mere choice of figure, sustains his criticism of the realists. No matter what the instrument, the playing is the same: "all their manner" the same, always; no matter if they are "right" or "wrong," "weak" or "strong."

Stevens's free use of his detractors' self-criticism depends, I think, on reproaches made against American literary radicalism by its own most intrepid supporters, who sought greater idiomatic and figurative diversity. Somewhat tired of efforts like Sol Funaroff's ingenuous celebration of the power plant at Denieprostroi – "And new loves burn with tigris eyes / Billions of kilowatt hours,"[67] lines Burnshaw still loves to mock for their naive Russophilia[68] – some radicals, even before the Popular Front, called for "variation" in radical writing; they wanted to hear revolution's great claims crazily craftily calling. "What I do not like about the *New Masses*," one otherwise devout reader wrote, "is the affectation of idealized proletarianism, *the monotonous strumming on the hardboiled string*, the hostility to ideas on other levels than one, the contempt for modulated writing and criticism, the evasion of discussion."[69] James Neugass, in his poem "A Landscape of Negatives," went a good deal further, characterizing present circumstance by its lack of variation ("No ships rear among the distant fixed waves / . . . No smoke comes from the tall marine smoke-stacks"). He was implying that a new order, political no less than aesthetic, would transform objects that "give *no* hint of internal concentration" into ones that gather variability from within. Thus, for Neugass, the radical poet sets up a world of heterogeneity to counter one

> Where there is no interplay of movement, no melody,
> No rhyme, where the blank texture of surface
> Is not relieved by the play of recurring action.[70]

"Blue Guitar," in Neugass' sense, thinks deeply about "internal concentration" and "interplay" – and a return to rhyme as itself "the play of recurring action" – in ways that take precise advantage of a modulation that radicalized (and supposedly antimodernist) adherents of the real themselves sensed would be required if they were to persuade the vast noncommunist modernist realm, through the very sort of "dialogue" they found in Stevens's poem. There were, of course, a diversity of reasons motivating such calls on the literary left, but they fall into three general categories. Some expressed cravings for aesthetic variation. Some, like Neugass', assumed that if the present sign system itself engendered "no interplay" then poets should advocate a new system based on that structural principle. Others wanted to contract a purely strategic "middleman . . . [to] do a little patient explaining" on behalf of "people [who] have had glimpses of the true picture."[71]

The guitarist becomes just such a patient explainer, even as he energetically and unpredictably offers up his variations, and even as he knows, as a modernist, the problematic nature of "the true picture." Thus Stevens took up a main point of dialogic revisionism in contemporary radical literary theory – a point he would see being made in the *Partisan Review*, which we can be certain he read regularly.[72] Of course frequent attacks continued to impugn the aesthetic individualist "who wishes to replace the whole world with himself," as Leon Trotsky put it. But it was now being noted (though not by Stalinists, to be sure) that Trotsky, while holding contempt for those willful modernist obscurantists like Andrei Bely, those blue guitarists among social commentators, had never meant to deny altogether the importance of such writing as contributing "*internally convincing* . . . moments of lucid psychology" to the "greatness" of poetry. This expansive view of radical art might catch even Walt Whitman in the widening net of sanctioned "pre-revolutionary" writers. After all, had not Whitman's "radical" "I am one of many" logic held that "An individual is as superb as a nation when he has the qualities which make a superb nation"? Among the revolutionaries, then, poetry's claims could indeed call "craftily," and even "crazily."[73]

Stevens could also shrewdly deny both the validity and usefulness of the rigid, separable poetic spheres, categories identified by his hopeful yet fault-finding critics, such as Eda Lou Walton with her leftist "Two Worlds" thesis purporting to explain the modernist split personality,[74] and young Charles Seymour in an essay called "Wallace Stevens: A Study in Contemporary Minor Poetry." For Seymour, writing in the Yale literary magazine, the *Harkness Hoot*, which had gone left under the editorship of Eugene V. Rostow,[75] the division between the poet "as the socialistic maker of a system, . . . a credo for his fellow-men" and the poet as "the individualistic maker of a beautiful thing worthy of existence for its beauty's sake" ante-dated the form of thirties side-taking that how affected wholly the structure of Stevens's work. Of course, Seymour was thinking of *Harmonium*. But now it was the notion of the left itself to blur the distinction between sufficiently engaged and somewhat disengaged. So Stevens could pick up a guitar overtly imaginary – a *blue* one! – for the purposes of marking new ground under the left's own slogan for realism. Seymour's essay was surely on Stevens's mind when he pondered the choice of tropes for responding to the new literary left in "The Man with the Blue Guitar" during the winter of 1936–7. For when Seymour's piece had appeared in Gene Rostow's radicalized *Hoot*, it had been accompanied by a large drawing depicting a besuited businessman strumming a guitar, and bore this disconcerting caption: "Although his guitar has but one string, Mr. Wallace Stevens makes merry music" (see Figure 6).[76]

4: PERHAPS IT GIVES

Not surprisingly, the guitarist's detractors are offended by doubts about "things as they are" as an instrument played by a million hands. Whereas canto iv

Although his guitar has but one string,
Mr. Wallace Stevens makes merry music.

Figure 6. Sketch of Wallace Stevens, *Harkness Hoot* 4 (November 1933), 27. (Courtesy of the Beinecke Rare Book and Manuscript Library, Yale University).

contains the guitarist's sharpest invective, v follows with the detractors'. It begins:

> Do not speak to us of the greatness of poetry,
> Of the torches wisping in the underground,
>
> Of the structure of vaults upon a point of light.
> There are no shadows in our sun,
>
> Day is desire and night is sleep.
> There are no shadows anywhere.
>
> The earth, for us, is flat and bare.
> There are no shadows.

Perhaps when this fifth argument is disconnected from the political dialogue in the opening movement of the poem – just as it was detached when it first appeared in print along with just one other canto, in *Twentieth Century Verse*[77] – the praise it generally receives will seem deserved. But its participation in the discourse about poetic realism, so very much a part of its deliberate arrangement, is at this point needlessly simple. It presents a position too easily contested despite its ultimately misquotable opening line.

"Do not speak to us of the greatness of poetry"! With a grammar of imperative and an idiom of admonition, as if to say "we will have no more of that business," the line is addressed to the guitarist who has been arguing for the supreme subtlety and transcendent place of poetry. Again, one must discern antagonism only from the dialogic giving and taking well under way, else the caveat resembles entreaty. But in refuting "the greatness of poetry," the third canto was much more proficient than this fifth. In iii the detractors focused on the analytical potential of the artist who had unthinkingly placed himself in a category separate from other people. Here, in vi, the leftist detractors put forward a positive argument to counter the guitarist's unearned confidence in the "greatness" of poets. But they create alternative categories so obviously rigid (literally night and day), and take sides in a dispute that reminds us of another contention so categorically old (the earth is flat), one must appreciate Stevens's deliberately reductive parody of the detractors' invective in order to recognize how and why he is disfiguring the radical argument. The canto puts into the mouths of the detractors the claim that everything under the sun is perfectly distinct and clear – that there are no grey areas. The claim had become conventional in the work of some radicals who wanted poetry to repudiate the visionary's objects in favor of perfect clarity. Insofar as clarity casts a shadow, it is because the revolutionary subject stands boldly with the sun – in these lines by Cecil Day Lewis, for example:

> Here it is. There fall
> From him shadows of what he is building: bold and tall –
> For his sun has already mastered the misted horizon – they seem.
> Indeed he casts a shadow. . . .[78]

By doubting this aesthetic ideology of clarity, Stevens was quoting from doubts already expressed by leftists, for instance by Josephine Miles:

> When the mind is dark with the multiple shadows of facts,
> There is no heat of the sun can warm the mind.
> The facts lie streaked like the trunks of trees at evening,
> Without the evening hope that they may find
> Absorbent night and blind.[79]

Fortunately, in the dispute about the greatness of poetry, between on the one hand the guitarist, with his sense of "multiple shadows [even] of facts," and on the other some version of Day Lewis's hard line, canto v concludes with an expression of the sort of utopianism that successfully attracts both the guitarist as we know him thus far in the poem and the poetic mind of Stevens as we know it from the verse-apologies for *Harmonium* in *Ideas* (such as "Sad Strains" and "Mozart, 1935"):

> Poetry
>
> Exceeding music must take the place
> Of empty heaven and its hymns,
>
> Ourselves in poetry must take their place,
> *Even* in the chattering of your guitar.
>   (emphasis added)

Surely a point of confluence runs here between three positions – the two already made explicit (guitarist's and detractors'), and a third, a narrative and evidently authorial presence, the poem's central subject whose art entails assigning pronouns to the other two ("he" and "they"). Each of the three can consent at least to the idea that religion has squandered its value and that in art one finds a means of putting something human in its place.

But as aesthetic left and right converge by each avowing the loss of God, so the key term "place" in the key post-Christian idiom of substitution ("must take the place") connotes one thing to the guitarist and quite another to the pronoun-defying detractors. In their bitter attack on the guitarist's initially earnest claims for a modernism reaching "beyond" (yet containing) the world as it is, they are obviously not calling for just another version of transcendence – neither a new theological form stipulating heaven, nor a "new romantic" form palatable to realists such as was presented in the last lyric tacking in "Sailing after Lunch" (in spite of I. A. Richards's materialist assistance).

Nor, then, in borrowing the Stevensian phrase "Poetry / Exceeding music," do the guitarist's detractors intend a new temporarily satisfying fiction, no matter how supreme, to replace the outmoded. These particular realists are just what Krutch's aesthetic radicals deny they are (but *are*), notwithstanding the caricaturing they suffer at that anticommunist's hands. Do they not want poetry to seek the ground of a flat, bare world? Do they not hunger for an epistemology somehow eschewing epistemological self-consciousness, a mimeticism somehow avoiding all word-world reduction – things to be known only and exactly as they are? They will admit the flatness and bareness of an earth they shall inherit from earlier "excesses" typified by flashy modernist *opsis*. At that revolutionary moment, triumphant yet somehow untranscendent, a collective poetic identity ("Ourselves") becomes the subject of the poem. Ingeniously, it is no less flashy than modernist self-reference, yet one can only characterize it as earthy.

To reach that final point of flatness-in-depth, "they" willingly serve the end of mediation, by tolerating, for strategic purposes, the guitarist's improvisational modernism. That mediation is based on the guitarist's politically impudent idea that "*Poetry*" should indeed be the sole subject of the poem. Of course, "they" discover in keeping pace with the guitarist's strummings through thirty-three variations that to accept the guitarist's modernist mode is to accept inevitably all his ideas about the supposedly inhering structures of modern art. It is a major formal concession, devastating to the rhetoric of flatness. At canto vi the detractors have reached the decisive moment in their own reactive aesthetic course, where a new human verse will tolerably be heard "*Even* in the chattering of your guitar" (*CP* 167).

If in canto v both parties, modernist and modernism's left detractor, could call for "Poetry // Exceeding music" in the contentious inflection of the *detractors*, in vi this opening argument is explored as possible grounds for fuller aesthetic reconciliation. The radically new human poetry, allowing the common person to adjust to the catastrophe (as it were) of heaven's hymns, is "A tune beyond us as we are." Readers cannot help but note how the idea is borrowed without apology from the detractors' initial paradox. The thirties guitarist will learn to play "A tune beyond us, *yet ourselves*." But the paradox runs deeply, as canto vi calls for "A tune beyond us as we are, / Yet *nothing changed* by the blue guitar." This goes more directly to the heart of the matter than did the detractors' opening shot. It contests the guitarist's first claim that "Things as they are / *Are changed* upon the blue guitar."

The sixth canto then scrutinizes the ambiguity of the detractors' word "place" in v. Poetry, it was argued there, must take the place of heaven's hymns. Of course, the *place* of poetry – its chosen tonal and generic value or standing (earthy or transcendent; common or "great") – is at the very heart of the controversy. "Place" inheres in the revolutionary idiom of the detractors' case and cause: We will tolerate "even" the chattering of your blue guitar, they said, if we ourselves can finally *take the place of* the former fiction-providing powers we detest. Canto vi, responding to this contest of sufficient fictions, depoliticizes the latest connotation of "place" by altering the central phrase of the poem to include it: "[T]hings as they are" becomes "the place / Of things as they are."

This rhetorical strategy – to borrow a phrase from the other side and patch it, tick it, tock it, bring it 'round to support one's own position – remains unremarkable until in canto vi the speaker, by depoliticizing the detractors' revolutionary rhetoric, sets up an argument favoring the guitarist that seems otherwise to be voiced by *them*. The speaker refers to himself and to ostensibly like-minded people as *us* and *we* (as in the detractors' cantos previously). Moreover, the canto is addressed to a *you* associated with the guitar – obviously the guitarist. But in the end of this pivotal sixth argument, the collective or social voice, the *we* presumably congruent with *they*, endorses a position *only the guitarist* could have endorsed previously: "A composing of senses of the blue guitar."

Whose position, then, has been articulated by the speaker of vi? A voice there, new at that point, mediating detractors and guitarist, whose interest was not one side or the other but the act of side-taking itself, assumed an authorized positionality not "beyond" contested ideological positions but containing them. In Stevens's view, I think, this shifting, postideological subject could demonstrate that an ostensibly disinterested examination of poetic side-taking was no less deliberate a taking of sides. Indeed, such a move supposed the sort of comic detachment, typical of Stevensian modernism, against which one side always did battle. The poem is never again as polemical as iv (favoring the guitarist's position), or v (favoring the detractors) – except in the brash tenth canto where ideological convergence fuels a blaze of subversion.

With the important exception of canto x, then, to which we will return, the remaining cantos in the work tend to adopt the guitarist's tone and usage while spending their greatest energies adjusting to the detractor's issues and ideas. Certainly xv is an example of this.

> Is this picture of Picasso's, this "hoard
> Of destructions," a picture of ourselves,
>
> Now, an image of our society?

The authorial subject seems formally to accept Picasso's multiperspectival fragments. Accordingly he replicates his world and himself as belatedly politicized cubists might disintegrate "image[s]" of "society" no less than of themselves. What connection, then, has been made between this inscription straining at unrecognizability and a "society" evidently bent on destroying itself in like manner? One possible model was indeed Pablo Picasso, whose modernism, the left in 1937 was contending, made way at last for political expression popularly understood.[80] Are "destructions" part of an art deemed social? Is "social poetry" a genre of modernism providing formal replications of society's disintegrative crises or, alternatively, a form that can be precisely comprehended by the disintegrating elements of society?

Less obviously inscribed here is the radicalized poetry of Alfred Kreymborg, whose prepolitical "Parallels" was a valiant attempt to convey the same modernist self-doubting – the sort made infamous by Williams's "Portrait of a Lady" – in "open," often enjambed, repetitive couplets-in-series strikingly similar to "Blue Guitar," and implying the same basic poetic confidence. But the crucial difference is that Stevens's four-stress line moves quite a bit faster and more freely than Kreymborg's pentameter:

> I digress? Where was I? What did I say?
> You really don't mind having me this way?

> It soothes you? Does it truly? I'd have meant
> To play our commonplace an instrument
>
> As subtle as a clavichord or spinet,
> With many spider-grained illusions in it.[81]

The detractors are not present in canto xv (except perhaps by proxy in the lone reference to Picasso) any more than they are realized in Kreymborg's "Parallels," but their original argument has shaped Stevens's severe self-doubt, finally confessed. If things as they are are being destroyed, for instance by war (in canto xvi), language conveying consciousness, presenting an "image of . . . society," is much in doubt: "Am I a man that is dead?" asks the poet, and "Is my thought a memory, not alive?" (xv; CP 173).

The detractors also hover silently over canto xxii. Moving furthest from the detractors' spell, the poem frankly stipulates poetry as having been the matter of the poem all the while. This overdue admission recalls the way the poem began and anticipates the way it will conclude: "From this the poem issues and / To this returns." Because of the context provided this moment by the poem's inscribed radical detractors, its actual radical detractors could safely *commend* a poem about poetry as "*justified* in his hands," meaning Stevens's. And that is exactly what T. C. Wilson suggested to Gregory and Marya Zaturenska after reading "Blue Guitar" a first time. Canto xxii, Wilson noted, "is a beautiful *Ars Poetica*, . . . [e]specially the last two lines, which are pure Stevens and exact and luminous":[82]

> From these it takes. Perhaps it gives,
> In the universal intercourse.

It should be no surprise, actually, to find a radical poet – even the very same communist who, as we have seen, had criticized Stevens's work in 1935 as "amounting to a denial of the poet's real and great function"[83] – praising "Blue Guitar" in 1937 for expressing the idea that when "the imagination comes to nothing . . . [w]hat is really propitious . . . antagonizes it." After all, Stevens himself could competently make just such a reading of his poem (L 362). He also described how "discord exaggerates the separation between its elements" and how "we look forward to an era when there will exist the supreme balance between these two, with which we are all concerned." It made no difference, of course, that immediately after Stevens suggested that "[t]he idea can be extended socially," he warned: "this is not what is intended" (L 363). T. C. Wilson and other radicals nonetheless saw in "Blue Guitar" how the noncommunist modernist was capable, in Rukeyser's terms, of dancing "our" dialogical "mechanic dance" by allowing "all opposites affirm your contradictions / . . . of merging conquered blast and counterblast"[84] or, in Burke's terms, of engaging "uses of diversity" and "carrying out a 'perspective by incongruity' for 'heads I win, tails you lose' purposes."[85] The dialogic of "Blue Guitar" was precisely such a success among its potential detractors, as I hope to demonstrate shortly in

a right-to-left arrangement of the critical responses; for the moment it
suffices to observe the important concurrence of Burke. Burke's eclectic
Attitudes Toward History (1937), precisely contemporaneous with "Blue Guitar" and its similar structure of give and take, was demonstrating to noncommunist skeptics that a radical rhetorician, steeped in the modernist
turn against flaccid late-Victorian idealism, could actually admire the way
in which Marx "stole" bourgeois rhetoric "for the proletariat," describing
for this theft terms that helped radical readers understand the "Blue Guitar" strategy of reproducing mutual borrowings between left and right.

    Borrowing is the key term for this emergent aesthetic. Stevens's arroga-
tion of "things as they are" should have delighted communist poets like
Edwin Rolfe, despite Rolfe's bold judgment a few years earlier that Stevens
was "no longer a living poet": Found or appropriated slogans, Rolfe believed, have "a chanting musical, poetic qua[l]ity which could very easily
be adapted to poetry." Yet Rolfe spoke of the idea of poems as patchworks
of "widely known, meaningful" phrases found in public discourse as if
that idea were not itself a borrowing from the very poets – Eliot, Pound,
Moore, Crane, even Sandburg – whose constructivist modes he unfortunately dismissed.[86] Stevens's and Burke's similar understanding of borrowing did go to that next level. "The stealing back and forth of symbols,"
Burke wrote, "is the approved method whereby the Outs avoid 'being driven
into a corner.'" In Burke's sense, Stevens, who would easily operate among
the "Ins" when he so chose for the sake of gaining rhetorical power, was
proceeding methodologically and symbolically as if an "Out," thieving
phrase-symbols from his detractors, including T. C. Wilson, themselves
imagined in the act of a like thievery – all parties avoiding the poetic corner.[87] Here, for Stevens as for Burke, a keen, virtually postmodern conception of political words as words, an understanding of the way in which
these words interact with forces outside their spheres of origin, was what
would earn very high praise from Bernard Smith in his progressive *Forces
in American Criticism* at the end of the decade:

> [Marxist critics] have not effectively dealt with the problem of communi-
> cation. The Marxist uses innumerable words differently from the way they
> have traditionally been used. These words mean things to him that are quite
> different from what they have heretofore meant. That is a natural conse-
> quence of a revolution in social, moral, and psychological values. But he is
> communicating with people who have carried over the habits of speech
> acquired in the traditional environment, and he is constantly trying to per-
> suade people outside his movement that his methods and ideals are cor-
> rect. Hence communication is always difficult, often confused, sometimes
> frustrated. It is a problem of immense significance, yet there is only one
> Marxist critic in America, Kenneth Burke, who is energetically and seri-
> ously concerned with it.[88]

Since Smith also made a point of noting that Burke had been a "pure esthete" in the twenties, the implication was that only such a critic could so strongly focus on representation.

From a Burkean "perspective by incongruity," then, which emerges in the thirteen-canto interval Stevens put in between the opening conflict (i through x) and the final evolution (from xxiii) of a representative person – indeed, a working-class man – in the last cantos (xxx through xxxiii), comes a poetic justification that reformulates what was originally the social realist's ideological motive as a persuader-by-words. Things exactly as they are are dire and miserable enough in themselves to support calls for great change and no modernism seemed required to obtain a view of this particular version of the New. Yet once things as they are have become elements of the guitarist's version of realism – exact yet subject to variability – the poem may return to the issue with which it began. Thus in its final three cantos, "Blue Guitar" shrewdly reverts to the detractors' argument by choosing to "evolve a man" who would seem to qualify for service as the representative in poetry "they" demanded.

This "man" is a variation of Stevens's earlier representative figure, an "old fantoche" like Crispin of "The Comedian as the Letter C." But he is Crispin distinctly proletarianized. Although still hankering for "A Nice Shady Home" "And Daughters with Curls" (CP 40, 43), he has become a lineman for the electric company. The guitarist has reserved a characteristic antipoetic stance for him: He labors "at the cross-piece" on a utility pole, "Supporting heavy cables" that are "slung through" an oxide-stained industrial named Oxidia (a form of "oxide" set in paradoxical relation to elements of the utopian "Olympia").

> From this I shall evolve a man.
> This is his essence: the old fantoche
>
> Hanging his shawl upon the wind,
> Like something on the stage, puffed out,
>
> His strutting studied through centuries.
> At last, in spite of his manner, his eye
>
> A-cock at the cross-piece on a pole
> Supporting heavy cables, slung
>
> Through Oxidia, banal suburb,
> One-half of all its installments paid. . . .
>
> Oxidia is the soot of fire,
> Oxidia is Olympia.
>   (xxx; CP 181–2)

One need only vaguely remember how the earlier tropes of lyric strings can be stretched this far to know what tune can be played on these thick cables by these rude hands – a song that will return to the effort to lyricize leftists seeking reconciliation with the sound of poetry. Rukeyser's figure,

doubtless borrowed from Crane's "Proem" to *The Bridge*, is similar to
Stevens's:

> Speak to me
> world hissing over cables, shining among steel strands,
> plucking speech out on a wire, linking voices
> reach me now in my fierceness, or I am drowned.[89]

Stevens's various descriptions of his own "banal suburb" help identify the
utility man's Oxidia. It must have seemed to him a good deal like his Hartford, in short, which he once described as the "typical industrial suburb, stained
and grim" (*L* 790), residential ("One half of all its installments paid") yet
unclean (fouled "From crusty stacks above machines"). This worker lives and
labors in a revolutionary utopia slowly becoming a middle-class hell. In Oxidia,
the electrical workers' transvaluation of Olympia, the person Stevens's poem
evolves is empowered to contend against his employer, despite the fact that
in xxxi the guitarist sets up the strongest possible naturalization to offset this
organized human power, as if to assert, despite the employee's new-found confidence, that the strong morning sun stands firmly on the side of the employers. Here "The employer and employee contend, / Combat, compose their
droll affair."

The beginning of the work-day is thus no cause for celebration or
aubade. To Stevens generally, morning light announces rather the urgency
of readying oneself for a practical attack upon the poetic sensibilities:
"Morning is not sun. / It is this posture of the nerves." The "sinister sun"
can be poetically debilitating. It can "obliterate the memory of a poetic
promise"[90] because it called forth poet and worker from their houses just
the same, auguring a day that each would admit consisted of thoughtless
energy expended in the actual world of American work. Writing of canto
xxv, the world-thumbing canto, Stevens later said, "People go about their
accustomed jobs, unconscious of what is occurring." Often psychologically a casualty of the same depthlessness, he was by no means unqualified to be addressing the problem of "stupid people [witnessing] the spectacle of life, which they enjoy but do not understand" (*L* 361). Stevens's
poem "The Common Life" (1939), with its grimy, geometric "down-town
frieze" consisting of "church steeple" and "stack of the electric plant" side
by side, and matching shadowless men and one-sided women (*CP* 221),
is not an expression of contempt for this commonality so much as knowing commiseration. The last canto of "Blue Guitar" speaks knowingly of
"the only dream they knew" (xxxiii). The argument leaves us as the future is slowly reached through negotiation between employer and employee
in the poem's last movement as between guitarist and detractors in the
first. The blue guitar, as it were, advocates an instrumentalism. Ideological difference is finally being handled through a reconciliation of political
and aesthetic antinomies. It was the same disconcerting lesson that George

Oppen had learned about the daily sun just before he left behind the following sort of lyric for Communist Party organizing:

> It brightens up into the branches
> And against the same buildings
>
> A morning:
> His job is as regular.[91]

The process of daily assault, which Stevens sensed as discerningly, I think, as the hard-working Oppen, signals the movement toward a genuine giving and taking between the modern and the political, "a wrangling of two dreams."

Stevens's shrewdest move in "Blue Guitar" might be in predicting such a cultural shift in the final cantos: "*Here*," then, "is the bread of time to come," the last canto notes in elaborating "That generation's dream." "[I]n Monday's dirty light," back at work, "The employer and employee will hear" nature's most attractive sparkling and shrieking, but this natural poetry cannot keep them from "continu[ing] their affair." The guitarist can only take up his guitar and assume, as it were, "this posture of the nerves," the contention between finally reconcilable positions, "As if a *blunted* player" tries to play what remains of the American imagination so sorely tested. Yet when in xxxiii the poem restates the distinction between night and day from the detractor's argument for clearly delineated positions in iv – finally, he says, "we shall sleep by night. / We shall forget by day" – one sees how the qualification that follows makes a workable exception of the imagination. These night-and-day delineations do obtain in a daily world,

> *except*
>
> The moments when we choose to play
> The imagined pine, the imagined jay. (emphasis added)

Stevens had learned to play the guitar of the imagination in the service of a negotiated settlement between positions that continued to draw power from claims of irreconcilability. Such claims were made in political retrospect even before the thirties expired – as early as 1938, when Babette Deutsch lamented the loss of MacLeish's twenties poetry of "intrinsic value," forfeited when the poet "was diverted" in the thirties "by the noises of a panic-stricken crowd *below* him" (emphasis added). When Deutsch spoke of "he," she meant the modernist generally as much as MacLeish specifically: "But times change, and we with time. . . . He began to hear, louder than the silence in which he watched a moving shadow, . . . louder than the jays in the apple-trees, the clamorous voice of the city."[92] But Stevens's "imagined jay," hardly signifying the regression to the poetry of "intrinsic value" Deutsch mourned, made complexity of two reductions, creating "moments" when "the clamorous voice" of Oxidia would actually augment the choice of playing the imagination. It is a mistake, I think, to read "the imagined jay" as the poetic element either left behind or neglected in the new era that Stevens characterized in his Harvard lecture.

Similarly, it is a mistake to read the "dream" of the final canto as a utopian dream. Nor did Stevens simply conclude his poem "on a softer note,"[93] as if the lessening in tensions between "employer and employee" was due to a backing off by either side of the dispute. He felt, rather, that it was no longer necessary to exaggerate the utopianism of his detractors. The thrust of the concluding canto is to allow the guitarist a long-prepared-for moment of discovery ("*That's it,*" he says), yet the discovery is the sophisticated Burkean non-solution for offering "a few final solutions." In that key phrase there is a subtle further relaxation of absolutist diction, a spirit of rhetorical mediation. Such a spirit emerges from the heated interaction of opposites – from the "rhyming of opposites" (as Robert Fitzgerald saw it),[94] always a lyricist's finest ploy. There is only a strategic solution to be found "in Monday's dirty light." To sing of this political reality is not to sing necessarily of the perfect future "time // To come," an extraordinary Sunday morning of new fictive belief, but of things as they contemporaneously are on any ordinary American Monday: "It must be *this* rhapsody or none, / The rhapsody of things as they are."

Note the special, inclusive sense of "rhapsody." Among Stevens's "few final solutions" is a willingness to borrow terms from the ongoing "droll affair" of employers and employees for his most ecstatic utterances, musical yet free and irregular. The end of the poem makes thematically clear what the interactive structure of the whole implies all along – that modern poetry overtly and incessantly lyric is no different from other forms of political language in inscribing opposing voices; that each discourse entails a response to other discourses.

5: TWO KINDS OF AGAINST

With Burke's sense of offering "a few final solutions" in hand, we return to the modernist who entered the realm of political commentary by suggesting to a progressive audience that Roosevelt's 1936 landslide was a sign of pressures nearing the point of crisis. Looking back from "Blue Guitar," we realize that the long poem set in motion by the Harvard visit of late 1936 was received by the liberalized literary world of 1937 with open arms. Once again modernist provocation led directly to convergence. *The Man with the Blue Guitar*, book as well as title poem, played remarkably upon the times as the times had played on it, recreating externally the interactions it had used for itself internally. We have seen that its counterarguments contain readings suited to a wide range of politically charged elements. In reproducing an ideologically contentious environment in its very structure, the poem itself organized the disarray of literary-political conditions that would come to judge it. It succeeded in no small part, then, because it anticipated the way in which it would embolden Stevens's critics to support him explicitly on the grounds some of the same critics had used to exclude him earlier.

The new poem fared well, in other words, because it expended its considerable energies imagining the sympathetic consensus for its detractors in the manner of the guitarist appropriating their positions in the poem. That was its interideological project, creating a sense of context close to that Fredric Jameson has found (and admired) in Burke's version of "ideological analysis." In a Burkean sense, then, "Blue Guitar"

> brings into being that situation to which it is also, at one and the same time, a reaction. It articulates its own situation and textualizes it. . . . [T]his simultaneous production and articulation of "reality" by a text is reduplicated by an active, well-nigh instrumental, stance of the text toward the new reality, the new situation, thus produced; and the latter is accompanied immediately by gestures of praxis . . . to overemphasize the way in which the text organizes its subtext.[95]

The critical situation "Blue Guitar" thus produced is nothing short of remarkable in its congeniality. T. C. Wilson, having a few years earlier found Stevens's new work "disturbing," could now be "amazed at what Stevens can do with a simple image." Wilson even praised poetic self-referentiality, while Morse, approaching the poem from the opposite political direction, could see some "red" in Stevens's "rose" at a time when Morse himself was working hard to prove to his young rebellious peers that in the United States "older poets are the better rebels and the truer ones" (oddly the reverse of the English situation, he noticed).[96] Taking Stevens's new work on what a reviewer understandably believed to be his or her own stable terms, *but which are indeed the rapidly shifting terms of the poem*, reviewers of *The Man with the Blue Guitar & Other Poems* tended to reiterate the guitarist's argument by ascribing to it a new and satisfying ideological harmony between themselves and the modernist moving from right to left.

No such harmony, of course, had been created by "Owl's Clover." The chief failure of the earlier poem was in not carving out a large enough space for its own acceptance. Such a default, however, should not necessarily have contributed to the general view that "Owl's Clover" was "an almost fruitless detour that Stevens momentarily mistook for the right path," as Lucy Beckett has put it – that "right path" being the straight and easy road to "Blue Guitar" where the old "spare exactness" could be happily reinstated.[97] The later poem did engage what I have called the "revolutionary unconscious" of its predecessor, in useful combination with what Fitzgerald noted was the poem's lyric rhyming of opposites, thus forging a consensus for itself. In this respect mainly it structurally attains what "Owl's Clover" could not – hardly what Beckett had in mind when she described it as "an aberration."[98] "Owl's Clover" did create for Stevens critical conditions that would allow him at once to come *and* be brought up to date.

Tracking Stevens's reception, one begins productively with Morse. Aside from seeing in early-modern "rose" an acceptable form of thirties "red," Morse understood how "Stevens has made concessions which are all to the good"; and to say just that was a significant concession in itself. "The Man with the Blue Guitar""goes progressively forward to a conclusion."[99] Morse's private thoughts on Stevens are in the same vein but more revealing, since their recipient surely shaped the revelation: Morse was writing, after all, to Willard Maas. "[Y]our 'social consciousness' is thoroughly grounded in your experience," Morse wrote, referring to Maas's struggles as a gay communist, "and the dogmas take a terrible beating from you. It is a good thing." Irritated that "Literature is becoming politics, nowadays," Morse urged Maas to look in Stevens's verse for an answer to the radical parties:

> It is awful and wonderful to me to see Gregory rejecting Wallace Stevens [in the *New Masses*] because the best of the recent Stevens knocks the rather spineless verbless verse of Gregory into a cocked hat. To put it another way: Gregory is interested in propaganda (in a good, perhaps, rather than a bad sense) whereas Stevens is interested in poetry.

In one way, of course, Morse's use of "Blue Guitar" as an approach to Maas merely reverted to Harriet Monroe's separate spheres. But at the same time, his sense of interaction between modernism's rebellious detractors and modernist eminences – those "older poets" whom Morse took to be "true[r] rebels" – is the closest any contemporary observer came to describing the extraordinary way in which "Blue Guitar" moves freely into an ideological space from outside. "Gregory," Morse wrote Maas,

> refuses to admit that part of his experience which is not already compatible with a given ideology, whereas Stevens is able to admit, and does admit, *experience which is more or less incompatible with his ideology, an ideology constantly changing, becom[ing] more inclusive.* Hence, Stevens, to me, is the real poet, doing a poet's work, making incompatibles compatible.[100]

Morse assumed that the modernist elders could finally be looked to for ways out of radicalism's antipoetic jams. That assumption itself began to travel a little left, a first stop being Dillon's now-liberalized *Poetry*. For a review, Dillon shrewdly turned to Fitzgerald, a poet and translator admired from both sides of the aisle. Fitzgerald obliged by finding that Stevens's new cadences produced "public significance." Finally "Stevens has given himself room to be explicit" even in the most variable of lyric modes. He has avoided the "exertions of sterility" of poets like Yvor Winters whose "grim classicism" is "like the classicism of the Fa[s]cists" and "an index to our historical disorder." With the help of his detractors Stevens was achieving the "easy ring of dialogue" and so raised the "issue of behavior or justice." Fitzgerald added that Williams had been wrong to suggest in his *New Republic* piece that "Blue Guitar" overemphasized Stevens's argument. (Stevens "argues with an objector who complains that he . . . does not speak of things as they are," Williams had written. Thus Stevens revealed himself as "a troubled man who sings well, somewhat covertly, somewhat overfussily at times, a little stiffly, but well. . . . [T]his book is in a way one long argument.")[101] Pointedly dissenting from Williams, Fitzgerald concluded that Stevens's "subject" was engaged by an open mind; it was nothing less important than "the decline of the West."[102]

Here and elsewhere Stevens was being accepted as a thirties poet who had "forsaken any desire to devote himself to building beauty apart from life." From "Lions in Sweden" forward, Stevens would not abide such a false distinction between "beauty" and "life." But he did, I am certain, appreciate the way in which reviewers who could describe such leftward inclination could unwittingly reproduce the guitarist's counterargument-by-distortion. And in, of all places, the New York Times: Eda Lou Walton, hopeful of Stevens's ideological transformation for her own reasons (as Morse and Fitzgerald were optimistic for theirs), announced in the Times that Stevens's new series moved "toward a leaner poetic analysis of the real world" and when the blue guitar is "strummed it changes the recitative concerning actual life."[103]

Meantime Gregory was gathering up his own special motives for revising his earlier assessments of Stevens. Mostly restored to his former good standing at the New Masses,[104] Gregory finally engaged in a bit of communist self-criticism: He quoted his own 1931 review ("the decadence that follows the rapid acquisition of power") as a means of restating his position on positionality in the review Morse criticized for Maas. Morse obviously had little trouble accepting Gregory's agreement with poets and critics far to his right, "that Wallace Stevens's sensibilities in writing verse . . . made it possible for him to review the world about him with singular acuteness." To be sure, in "Blue Guitar" Stevens's brightness was somewhat "dimmed by the effort to explain his 'position' in a medium ill-suited to the demands of exposition." Nor would Gregory concede "that the poet himself was 'left' in sympathy or that his primary intention was to write political poetry." And yet, again, Gregory felt that Stevens's evident political gesture compelled the New Masses editor to apply the popular-front credo: "If [a poet's] . . . work is mature and centered in our culture, we, as critics, should be able to interpret from it the character of the society in which the poet lives." Finally, then, the revisionist act was the object of criticism and not its subject: "Mr. Stevens's desire to restate his relationship to a 'blue guitar' throws light upon matters of concern to writers in existing society." Gregory found the depiction of "Oxidia, banal suburb, / One-half of all its installments paid" sufficiently "convincing."[105]

Of all the responses to The Man with the Blue Guitar, the most interesting is the one from the critic whose positions most closely resembled those of the guitarist's detractors. This came from Ruth Lechlitner, a talented (though now neglected) radical poet in her own right. Her notice appeared in the *New York Herald Tribune* and played a great part in shaping her own ideas for a political verse play, *We Are the Rising Wing*. It seems particularly apt to turn to Ruth Lechlitner in the end, for she had never been reticent about expressing her admiration for noncommunist modernists, and yet held intractably radical views – voted for Earl Browder; took on the hard work of "build[ing] up a sale-contacting list of names" for the League of American Writers;[106] befriended (and literally, at times, sheltered, at her and Paul Corey's farm) such "movement" artists as Schneider, Maas, Richard Wright, Willie Seabrook, Si Kaplan, and Jerre Mangione.[107] Not only did Lechlitner admire Stevens's modernism, Corey remembers, but she also felt that in her reviews "she was giving him a chance to mingle with the thinking of the poets of the 30s."[108] Stevens had read her book carefully.[109]

To say what she really wanted to say about *The Man with the Blue Guitar* was a complicated, even torturous, matter for the otherwise unemployed Lechlitner, for she hid the extent of her radicalism from Irita Van Doren and Belle Rosenbaum, her *Herald Tribune* editors whose proffering of regular assignments formed a financial lifeline in hard times. While Van Doren and Rosenbaum might indeed have known something of their reviewer's political associations – many radical writers were out of the closet by this time, and worked throughout the publishing world – they cut and rewrote Lechlitner's reviews in such a way as to suggest political toning down.[110] Thus the encoded way in which Lechlitner's *Herald Tribune* piece urged the guitarist's politics leftward: The reviewer seemed to be holding her distance, a rhetorical necessity that fascinatingly reproduces in the poet-reviewer relation the relation between guitarist and detractors – and generally, as I have been arguing, that between eminent modernist and aspiring communist. Whether because Lechlitner really found in Stevens's new work a "left tendency," as Burnshaw had in Marie Welch's, or because at the height of the Popular Front she could somewhat more frankly emphasize this tendency in her *Herald Tribune* reviews, Lechlitner approvingly cited the wrangling between workers and boss. She concluded that Stevens's satire was "never heavy." She quoted his poem "A Thought Revolved," declaring that "in this our troubled time" he too supported the people's search for

> an earthly leader who could stand
> Without panache, without cockade,
> Son only of man and sun of men,
> The outer captain, the inner saint
>
> (CP 185)

– knowing full well that these were the sort of terms often enough used on the left to describe Lenin or, quite often still, Stalin.

When Lechlitner turned her attention to the tenth canto of "Blue Guitar," she was keeping to the spirit of her assessment of Stevens's politics – the temper of the assessments I have cited, and others even more willing to beckon Stevens from his left.[111] Lechlitner read canto x as proving the poet's willingness to oppose fascism. She undertook to endorse the guitar as tool or device for disarmament, its tendency to assuage dependent entirely on its handler. Here, she herself was moving from didacticism to instrumentalism, and met Stevens halfway, precisely as and why Burnshaw had met him. "The guitar in the hands of the poet," Lechlitner wrote, "becomes a torch against dictators."

To make any sense of this reading, one must first assume that by seeing in canto x of "Blue Guitar" an endorsement of the opposition "against dictators" Lechlitner had not meant to refer to a dictatorial *left* – had not meant Stalin, that is. Rather, of course, she meant that here Stevens was intellectually joining the resistance against the European dictators. She read the phrase "pagan in a varnished car" as referring to a figure who courts popular adulation from a motorcade, as often pictured in the newspapers, and assumed him to represent a fascist stumper. It is worth supposing what caused this reading, given that there is little in canto x to help one specify the ideology of the mocked demagogue. Lechlitner was surely influenced by the fact that the *Nation* had awarded its annual poetry prize to "The Men That Are Falling" (the penultimate entry in *The Man with the Blue Guitar & Other Poems*), in part, as I suggested in Chapter 1, for what the *Nation* took to be Stevens's expression of sympathy for the Spanish Loyalists.

Surely, also, Lechlitner was reading specific political sentiment into the rebellious rhetoric of canto x, assuming that the poet-guitarist who would speak so enthusiastically about political overthrow ("the touch that topples men and rock") would be looking leftward from the right to cause some trouble. The string of confident imperatives – "*Raise* . . . columns," "*Toll* a bell," "*clap* the hollows," "*Throw* papers," "*Behold* the approach of him," "*Roll* a drum," "*Cry* aloud" – itself emulates the syntactical "tendency to give orders" frequently lauded by radical poets and critics.[112] "I offer as armor against sharp derision / Deliberate decision," Josephine Miles wrote in her poem "Imperative": "Get up now and go."[113] Indeed, in Harold Rosenberg's praise of Burnshaw's line "Build a world fit for the bloodborn free!" (from the final poem in *The Iron Land*, 1936)[114] one may be seeing a specific basis for Stevens's counter-syntax. Here is Stevens's canto as it appeared in the Knopf arrangement:

> Raise reddest columns. Toll a bell
> And clap the hollows full of tin.
>
> Throw papers in the streets, the wills
> Of the dead, majestic in their seals.

And the beautiful trombones – behold
The approach of him whom none believes,

Whom all believe that all believe,
A pagan in a varnished car.

Roll a drum upon the blue guitar.
Lean from the steeple. Cry aloud,

"Here am I, my adversary, that
Confront you, hoo-ing the slick trombones,

Yet with a petty misery
At heart, a petty misery,

Ever the prelude to your end,
The touch that topples men and rock."

These many years later I was able to discover a good deal about the canto that Lechlitner did not know when she understood it to signal Stevens's arrival as an antifascist. Nonetheless a disappointing political misreading that befell *her*, in the verse play *We Are the Rising Wing*, which borrowed forms and figures from "Blue Guitar," might have warned her of the risks entailed in interpretations founded on such basic ideological assumptions. Knowing that Stevens did not necessarily mean to scold a dictator on the right only underscores the value of Lechlitner's and the other reviewers' new premise of modernists' politics. Lechlitner could not have known, obviously, of Stevens's much later gloss. During the Cold War, he called the demagogue in the poem "Harry Truman as god" – a telling anachronism, I think, since one does not think of Hitler or Mussolini as political progenitors of Truman (*L* 789). Obviously Stevens had another sort of demagogue in mind.

Nor could Lechlitner have known that Stevens had submitted an early version of the canto to *Poetry* for publication in the May 1937 issue, six months before Knopf published the whole. No correspondence survives[115] to help explain why Zabel or Dillon eventually excluded this canto from the selection of twelve Stevens sent, but the typescript of the rejected version of what became the tenth canto in the complete series here bears the number "III." It would have been placed third, that is, in the *Poetry* group of fourteen; and it was intended, when Stevens made his selection in late March, to follow cantos ii and ix (as numbered in the Knopf book), and to precede cantos xv, xvii, xviii, and six of the final seven cantos of the poem (xxvii through xxxiii, less xxxii).

The magazine selection began with the guitarist's *response* to the detractors' side of the dialogue in i, but readers of *Poetry* did not have the benefit of i. Lines such as "Although I patch him as I can" thus made little sense when they could not be read as the defense of a position against mere tinkering with a system that required overhaul. Nor can the entreaty "Say that it is a serenade / Of a man" be understood to address anyone in particular; here the guitarist is urging the detractors to speak about things in his manner, as only readers of the whole would know. Following this, in the *Poetry* selection, ix advanced the argument rather harmlessly, continuing the effort of the first-person speaker to retain the blue guitar for the production of "a form, described but difficult." The patching of ii signified merely the earnest attempt of a writer sensing the limitations of poetry in the most general way.

For whatever reasons, Stevens chose not to admit the detractors' voice into the *Poetry* selection. It is an instructive exercise, then, to read the canto Lechlitner praised – thinking of it as following from ii – as part of the guitarist's argument. After all, the only sensible alternative is to read it as a form of Burke's "Two Kinds of Against," a mock resisting not only the political power of the second-rate powermonger, but also the poet who claims that words overthrow regimes. The early version of the canto is briefer and concludes differently:

> Raise reddest columns. Toll a bell
> And clap the hollows full of tin.
>
> Throw papers in the streets, the wills
> Of the dead, majestic in their seals.
>
> And the beautiful trombones – behold
> The approach of him whom none believes,
>
> Whom all believe that all believe,
> A pagan in a varnished car.
>
> Subversive poet, this is most rare.
> Forward into tomorrow's past![116]

By 1940 Hi Simons of Chicago, a frequent visitor to the *Poetry* office, had somehow learned of the existence of this early unpublished version of canto x; he quoted the deleted lines back to Stevens when asking for a gloss. Stevens's response, other than to say he had "forgotten that this [canto] was submitted to POETRY," is, I think, telling: "I thought that subversive poets a la mode were getting nowhere fast" (*L* 360). The generalization seems to confirm his special design for the for-*Poetry*-only arrangement, where political subject and object are somewhat turned around: the "Subversive poet" is addressed by an invisible authorial voice (the one commanding the poet to orchestrate and then disrupt the demagogue's parade). This subject audaciously satirizes the entire proceeding – that is, mocks dictator *and* poet together. The poet sees the emperor's newest rhetorical clothing, a threadbare metabelief. The only thing each citizen believes about this leader is that all other citizens believe him. The slogan with which this early version of the poem concludes is put in play by the instructing, authorial figure, but it is the politicized sound-bite characteristic of *both* demagogue and subversive: "Forward into tomorrow's past!"

Nor, of course, could Ruth Lechlitner have dated the composition of the poem as precisely as we can these decades later, and in doing so speculate on specific rather than general political circumstances that might have made the subversive canto possible. Again, it was in March 1937 that Stevens first told Latimer of the series, which was then nearing completion, most of the cantos having been written earlier in the winter.[117] One demagogue of the moment – just then more than ever, in the view of many Americans – was here at home: Franklin Roosevelt had won a second term by the overwhelming margin Stevens had provocatively minimized at Harvard. Then Roosevelt began his effort to pack the courts, a move decried as vastly exceeding presidential powers and defended, by Roosevelt himself, as entirely consistent with democracy. The forces of reaction in the high court, he said, would otherwise prevent the people from benefiting from his programs. At this, the president's critics now regularly called him a dictator – the lucid Dorothy Thompson, for instance; and Gilbert Montague's voluble friend Mark Sullivan, syndicated in the *Hartford Courant*;[118] and also Felix Morley, later president of Haverford College, who heard the Fireside Chat of March 9, 1937, and felt then "for the first time" that Roosevelt had all along been traveling down "the highway to dictatorship."[119]

Now let us back up a few weeks. FDR had been inaugurated a second time on January 20, and the *Courant* in Hartford had carried a large photograph of the landslide victor riding in an open car ("a pagan in a varnished car"!), delighted by the cheers of two hundred thousand who had come to see the parade despite a cold rain.[120] The inaugural address avoided the specifics of new policy altogether; to his critics it was now becoming obvious that this leader, "[w]hom all believe that all believe," did not intend merely to "patch it as I can," in Stevens's phrase – "not merely to do a patchwork job with second-hand materials," as FDR himself put it – but would undertake to build "on the old foundations" a "better . . . future," to remake the American system from the bottom up. His acceptance of the obligation of "leading the American people forward along the road over which they have chosen to advance" used language right out of his widely quoted campaign book, *Looking Forward*.[121]

Now, again, the poem: *Forward into tomorrow's past!* If this axiomatic borrowing was indeed designed to turn political invective inward – to reach the American leader – then the version of the canto Stevens produced after its withdrawal from early publication in *Poetry* told not of a common but of an uncommon gesture of poetic subversion. The authorial voice, having called upon the guitarist to organize the demagogue's parade, then urges him to shout out his resistance: "Here am *I*, my adversary, that / Confront *you*."

Many years later, trying to remember this particular canto for Renato Poggioli, who sought the poet's views for the purposes of an Italian translation, Stevens neglected to maintain the distinction between the invisible authorial subject and the guitarist's song of political opposition. In this

revealing recollection – not incidentally, a retrospective characteristic both
of Stevens's and America's 1950s – the poet figure had himself become the
"subversive poet" ("most rare"!), somewhat contradicting the 1940 statement for Simons, in which the "subversive poet" seemed tonally more Kenneth Fearing than Wallace Stevens. "*I* address him but with hostility," he
told Poggioli, collapsing self-doubting poet into fiery subject-position: "*I
deride & challenge him*" (emphasis added). Lechlitner and other leftists
were not mistaken, then, to understand Stevens's apparently deep urge to
speak in decipherable American political code, although if Lechlitner knew
that Stevens's range of reference in this instance left room for Roosevelt,
she might not have written so friendly a review. Nonetheless, Stevens was
only pointing out what Lechlitner knew from the misreadings caused by a
remarkably similar figure in her *We Are the Rising Wing*: a demagogue on
parade, named "The Great I," proffering fascist grandiloquence, while his
detractors "whistle / Him back," shouting him down in four-stressed lines.
Then a figure named "The Miracle-Maker" ponderously tells an assembled
throng of believers:

> American millions, I, your miracle-maker,
> I, your leader and law, holding your separate
> Lives in my hands . . .
> I weep as a father weeps
> When his children disobey, strike back at him
> Who loves them best![122]

Lechlitner had wanted "The Miracle-Maker" in her poem to present an
American fascist demagogue that would remind audiences of Father
Coughlin, and she was dejected, but not shocked, when even her most
politically sympathetic audience misunderstood the verse to be expressing
a criticism of Roosevelt that might be either radical or reactionary.[123] She
knew precisely what Stevens had put into his canto, I think, and her position, momentarily, became his. Rexroth's and others' radical polyphony –
"I am one of many" – could be turned ideologically around while losing
little in the way of subversive lyric force.

The fieriness of the canto causing such contemporary and subsequent
puzzlement, and the unsure place of "Blue Guitar" in the canon after modernism – in the conformist interval, we might say, between modernism
and postmodernism – indicates how surprisingly comfortable a poet like
Wallace Stevens could have become working in a mode in which
adversarial relations were to be casually played out with intense thirties-
style dialogic. This, I have argued, is one of the structural blessings – it is
no less than that – bestowed upon American forms of modernism by the
radical moment. For all the bombast and recklessness in Max Eastman's
communist account of modernism's decline in *The Literary Mind* (especially

when he scolds "The Cult of Unintelligibility" as inherently apolitical),
he was surely right about the politics of modernism on three counts: First,
that modernist poetry had become, by the thirties, "the most sincere and
natural thing in the world to write, that any poetry will be [deemed] modernist which ignores the reader or looks upon him as a mere excuse for
speech;" second, that "modernists . . ., who talk about words as though
they were a material as simple in its values as dyed chalk or porcelain,
have followed the opposite course"; third, and most salient, that modernists have "ignored the strategy of communication."[124] So much for the stereotyped communist critique of modernism as a critical and theoretical
dead end, for these are precisely complaints made later, by poets and critics who would not think of themselves as having much in common with
communists of Eastman's stripe. "Blue Guitar" shows, too, that modernists themselves need not have been toeing the communist literary-critical
line to recognize these three failures. Here Stevens was perceiving similar
predicaments for modernism: first, in this poem's willful acceptance of formal constraint (both as a matter of stanzaic form as well as the requirements of the "improvisation," which is thus not the least bit "natural");
second, in its willingness to engage words-as-such; and, third, in its conception of meaning as incessant strategic positioning. When in later, chillier
times – 1953 – Stevens was recollecting for Poggioli the red-hot atmosphere that produced "Blue Guitar" in 1937, he concluded with a telling
thought on modernists' failure to speak out volubly for or against the rebellion already nearing the end of a major phase – their inability to see
their own rhetoric as strategy. Had it been fear that modern poetic language was still too elevated to be of use as ethical significance or historical referent? Yet as we have seen, his anxieties were not merely those of
the modernist feeling old and out of place but often those shared by radical
poets as well: Poets, of whatever political ilk, might simply not be heard.
"I may have cried out Here am I," he wrote Poggioli, "and yet have stood
by, unheard, hooing the slick trombones, without worrying about my English" (L 789).

The regret of 1953, two years before Stevens's death, and coming at a time
when his and modernism's official relation to American cold-war culture was
being affirmed (in spite of his conscious efforts), was too little and late if he had
meant to redirect the course of criticism. It did lend belated but needed support to Marianne Moore's keen assessment of modernism's cultural role: While
unpretentiously (yet in so many other ways ostentatiously), Stevens "hates lust
for power *and ignorance of power.*" Moore had reached this conclusion after
reading *The Man with the Blue Guitar & Other Poems.* She asserted, too, that
Stevens's poems showed no less than that "there is hope for the world":"They
embody hope, which in being frustrated becomes fortitude; and they prove to
us that the testament to emotion is not volubility."[125]

Stevens never said such a thing forthrightly. Moore had a knack for saying on behalf of modernists in the 1930s things they no longer wanted or dared to say for themselves. Struggling for restatement in the "red decade" – wrestling with how "[m]y conception of what I think a poet should be and do changes," in Stevens's words (*L* 289) – these challenged figures looked to others to discover a new language for self-definition. Stevens also searched for confirmation in his wide reading, finding the following in 1937, in a volume by (of all writers) Jacques Maritain:

> It is less difficult for the philosopher than for the artist to be in disagreement with his period. . . . [B]y depending on the intellect of his time and pressing it to the limit, in the concentration of all his languor and all his fire, . . . the artist has a chance of reshaping the whole mass.

Stevens carefully wrote out the passage in his notebook,[126] confident, I think, that he had been thoroughly renewed by those two closely related poetic exertions: "depending" on the era and at the same time "pressing" back. His sense of lyric "concentration" and footloose "languor" modestly predicted much poetry to come after modernism's evident antipoliticism had failed several more severe tests in the forties and fifties. It predicted, that is to say, the work of poets consciously deriving both radical opinions and poetic processes from sources now more easily nameable and acceptable as such. But occasionally (and I think increasingly) this basic debt to Stevens's thirties does surface in the very new – in the postmodern, which in American poetry has had a way, quite recently, of returning back, for instance, to the lyric form of cultural slogans-as-contrivances. Using the figure "Strumming Language" in 1977, for instance, Edward Dorn was surely acknowledging an obligation to the related tropes of counterargumentation and incessant variation in "Blue Guitar." "Any language," Dorn said, "takes a risk by leaving itself open to new constructions and to uncontrolled usage." More important is Dorn's sense – not only, thus, a postmodern feature, but residually and selectively, I contend, a modernist one as well – that the poet should "spend a lot of the day monitoring the flow of news and so forth, watching how the language is being used." How else might lines such as "Poetry is *not* mostly government product" sustain, not invert, a latter-day radicalism?[127] Do let us remember that the poet who wanted "To live in the world but outside of existing conceptions of it" (*OP* 190) was a modernist poet borrowing from radicalism, not a radical poet borrowing from modernism. But let us also remember that it might have been the other way around.

Notes

Iowa	Special Collections, University of Iowa
JHB	John Hay Library, Brown University
KB	Kenneth Burke
Massachusetts	Special Collections, University of Massachusetts
Michigan	Hopwood Room Collection, University of Michigan
MM	Marianne Moore
MZ	Morton D. Zabel
N	*The Nation*
Newberry	Newberry Library, Chicago
New York Public	New York Public Library, New York
NM	*New Masses*
NR	*The New Republic*
NYHTB	*New York Herald Tribune "Books"*
NYT	*The New York Times*
P	*Poetry*
PLUS	*Proletarian Literature in the United States: An Anthology,* eds. Granville Hicks, Joseph North, Michael Gold, Paul Peters, Isidor Schneider, Alan Calmer (New York: International Publishers, 1935)
PMP12-35	*Poetry* Magazine Papers, 1912-1935 Series, Regenstein Library, University of Chicago
PMP36-53	*Poetry* Magazine Papers, 1936-1953 Series, Regenstein Library, University of Chicago
PR	*Partisan Review*
Princeton	Special Collections, Firestone Library, Princeton University
RLC	Special Collections, Regenstein Library, University of Chicago
RLL	J. Ronald Lane Latimer, a.k.a. James G. Leippert, Martin Jay, J.R.L.L., "Jay," Mark Jason, and Mark Zorn
RML	Rosenbach Museum & Library, Philadelphia
SB	Stanley Burnshaw
SRL	*Saturday Review of Literature*
Stanford	Special Collections, Stanford University
TCW	T. C. Wilson
Virginia	Special Collections, Alderman Library, University of Virginia
WCW	William Carlos Williams
WM	Willard Maas
WS	Wallace Stevens
WSJ	*Wallace Stevens Journal*
WUL	Special Collections, Washington University, St. Louis

Introduction

1. Indeed, "The Long War" is the title Judy Kutulas has given her new book about the entire literary left of the 1930s (forthcoming, Duke Univ. Press); she describes "a paralyzed historiography." This "Long War" has been fought mainly between generations – imprecisely designated "old" and "new" left. "In order for there to be a new history," writes Theodore Draper with bitter irony in his attack on New Left historians, "there must be an old history to be fought and vanquished" ("American Communism Revisited," *A Present of Things Past* [New York: Hill & Wang, 1990], p. 120). But the battlelines are crossed. Compiling a cultural history of the League of American Writers, Arthur D. Casciato, like Kutulas, found himself burdened not only by the insistence of older partisans, whom he otherwise admired, "that the participants' perspective should always be privileged," but also by the fact that when Old Left detractors of New Left scholarship discredit the communist left of the thirties, they also sometimes needlessly demoralize young nonparticipant scholars "who would recover [the left's cultural] achievements *as well as its embarrassments.*" Here, the young scholar can feel somewhat coerced into dealing primarily with "those disillusioned radicals who have reconciled with the dominant culture"; the results can be counterproductive (Arthur D. Casciato, "Fighting Words: The Third American Writers' Congress and Rereading the History of the 1930s." Paper presented at the American Studies Association, 1988). An accessible discussion of the generational significance among historians of what in *Towards a Democratic History* (1966) Jesse Lemisch called "history from the bottom up" is provided by Jonathan M. Wiener's mostly descriptive yet nonetheless sharply criticized essay, "Radical Historians and the Crisis in American History, 1959–1980" (*Journal of American History* 76, 2 [September 1989], 399–434). One of Wiener's antagonists, although describing himself as generally an ally, is Herbert Aptheker of the unrepentant "old" left; his "Welcoming Jonathan Wiener's Paper, with a Few Brief Dissents" (*Journal of American History* 76, 2 [September 1989], 443–5) submits that "Wiener's essay suffers from an ignorance of . . . the period preceding McCarthyism" – to wit, the thirties (443).
2. W. H. Auden, "September: 1939" (later "September 1, 1939"), *NR*, October 18, 1939, 297; Auden finally referred to this work as "the most dishonest poem I have ever written" (quoted in Edward Mendelson, *The Early Auden* [New York: Viking, 1981], p. 330).
3. Among WS's critics, cogent, knowledgeable observations about the modernist engagement of radicalism are emerging from James Longenbach (*Wallace Stevens: The Plain Sense of Things* [New York: Oxford Univ. Press, 1991]); Harvey Teres ("Notes Toward the Supreme Soviet: Stevens and Doctrinaire Marxism," *WSJ*, 13, 2 [Fall 1989], 150–67); and Andrew Lakritz ("Stevens's Statue and the Rancor of History." Unpublished chapter in a book manuscript on WS, MM and Robert Frost). See also Robert Emmett Monroe's "Figuration and Society in 'Owl's Clover,'" *WSJ* 13, 2 (Fall 1989), 127–49; for Monroe, "Stevens is a lucid political thinker" (147) and no less than "the

most promising major poet of his generation for a cultural analysis" (127). The reassessment of WS's thirties may be said to have been initiated by Milton A. Bates's *Wallace Stevens: A Mythology of Self* (Berkeley: Univ. of California Press, 1985); see especially pp. 155–94. SB has reentered the fray, adding his "Reflections on Wallace Stevens," *WSJ* 13, 2 (Fall 1989), 122–6, and a published interview conducted by AF and Teres ("An Interview with Stanley Burnshaw," *WSJ* 13, 2 [Fall 1989], 109–21).

4. Cary Nelson, *Repression and Recovery: Modern American Poetry and the Politics of Cultural Memory, 1910–1945* (Madison: Univ. of Wisconsin Press, 1989), p. 171. Such contempt has a long critical tradition, beginning immediately as the decade closed: even Halford Luccock, whose *American Mirror: Social, Ethical and Religious Aspects of American Literature 1930–1940* (New York: Macmillan & Co., 1940) boldly praised the work of Kenneth Patchen, Muriel Rukeyser, Kenneth Fearing, and HG, was sure to warn his readers that the "Depression found constant expression in . . . verse which need not be dignified by the august term of poetry" (p. 140), staying clear of the likes of H. H. Lewis, and apologizing constantly ("It might seem fantastic to claim for Fearing's metrical extravaganzas the qualities of serious ethical criticism" [p. 227]).

5. Frank A. Warren, *Liberals and Communism: The "Red Decade" Revisited* (Bloomington: Indiana Univ. Press, 1966), p. 3.

6. KB, *Attitudes Toward History* (1937; reprinted Berkeley: Univ. of California Press, 1984), pp. 229–32.

7. Frank Lentricchia, *Criticism and Social Change* (Chicago: Univ. of Chicago Press, 1983), p. 85.

8. See Bernard Smith, *Forces in American Criticism: A Study in the History of American Literary Thought* (New York: Harcourt, Brace and Co., 1939), pp. 376–7 n. 1.

9. Edmund Wilson, *Axel's Castle: A Study in the Imaginative Literature of 1870–1930* (New York: Charles Scribner's Sons, 1931), pp. 297–8. Lest there be doubt about Wilson's radicalism in 1931: see "An Appeal to Progressivism," *NR* (January 14, 1931), 234–8, a bitter attack on liberals for "betting on capitalism" (237). Later Wilson recalled that, for him, "these years were not depressing but stimulating. One couldn't help being exhilarated at the sudden unexpected collapse of that stupid gigantic fraud [Big Business]" (*The Shores of Light* [New York: Farrar, Straus, and Young, 1952], p. 498).

10. Lucia Trent and Ralph Cheyney, *More Power to Poets!* (New York: Henry Harrison, 1934), pp. 107, 108.

11. Wald, in turn, has credited Paul Buhle for "tell[ing] the story 'whole'" – for "putting Marxism and Communism in a larger setting, and . . . showing the diversity and interconnections of the Left experience" (*Labour/Le Travail* 24 [Fall 1989], 294–5). Nelson's aim has been to reject "[t]he myth" that political poetry "was always formally conservative, thematically monochromatic, and rhetorically wooden. . . . [On] the contrary, this diverse and highly interactive period of political poetry is one of the real treasures of our literary heritage" (*Repression and Recovery*, p. 102).

12. Harvey Teres, *Banners and Wings: Politics, Imagination, and the New York Intellectuals, 1930–1970* (New York: Oxford Univ. Press, forthcoming.)

13. See Charlotte Nekola, "Words Moving: Women, Poetry, and the Literary

Politics of the 1930s," in *Writing Red: An Anthology of Women Writers, 1930–40* (New York: Feminist Press, 1987), pp. 127–34.

14. James D. Bloom, *Left Letters: The Culture Wars of Mike Gold and Joseph Freeman* (New York: Columbia Univ. Press, 1992).

15. A portion of Kutulus' *The Long War: The Literary People's Front and Anti-Stalinism, 1930–1940* has been published as "Becoming 'More Liberal': The League of American Writers, the Communist Party, and the Literary People's Front," *Journal of American Culture* 13, 1 (Spring 1990), 71–80.

16. To some extent Terry A. Cooney, *The Rise of the New York Intellectuals* (Madison: Univ. of Wisconsin Press, 1986), can be counted among these. "[M]odernism had appealed to . . . many writers of the twenties . . . in part for its aura of radicalism in culture, and nothing was more characteristic of the intellectual life of the decade than the attack on business culture by literary intellectuals. For some the move toward Marxism in the thirties would clearly be little more than a continuation of this pattern" (p. 32). The problem with Cooney, and to a lesser degree Teres, is that they ascribe such a synthesis mostly to the *PR* group, led by Rahv and Phillips; my purpose, like Nelson's in particular, is to include many kinds of political radicals, not restricted to the anti-Stalinists who became leading anticommunists.

17. Bloom, *Left Letters*, pp. 3, 7–8.

18. Nelson, *Repression and Recovery*, p. 52.

19. See AF, *Wallace Stevens and the Actual World* (Princeton: Princeton Univ. Press, 1991), pp. 242–77.

20. Stephen Spender, *The Thirties and After: Poetry, Politics, People (1933–1975)* (London: Macmillan & Co., 1978), p. 9.

21. Joe Kalar to Warren Huddlestone, July 24, 1970 (quoted in *Poet of Protest, Joseph A. Kalar: An Anthology,* ed. Richard G. Kalar [Blaine, MN: RGK Publications, 1985], p. 318).

22. James Baird, *The Dome and the Rock: Structure in the Poetry of Wallace Stevens* (Baltimore: Johns Hopkins Univ. Press, 1968), p. 254.

23. See, for example, the furious exchange provoked by Draper's "American Communism Revisited" when that essay was first published in the *New York Review of Books.* Responses appeared as "Revisiting American Communism: An Exchange" (*New York Review of Books* 32, 13 [August 15, 1985], 40–4). See also Michael Goldfield, "Recent Historiography of the Communist Party U.S.A.," *The Year Left* 1 (1985), 315–56; Paul Buhle, "Historians and American Communism: An Agenda," *International Labor and Working Class History* 20 (Fall 1981), 38–45; Kenneth Waltzer, "The New History of American Communism," *RAH* 11 (June 1983), 259–67. Self-criticism is nearly as important a factor among historians of American communism as attacks from detractors: Even a leftist scholar of the American left as established as Buhle can apologize with surprising readiness for his *Encyclopedia of the American Left* (New York: Garland Publishing, 1990) when challenged from his allied left (see "An Encyclopedist's Lot," *N* 250, 14 [April 9, 1990], 498–501). For a classic instance of self-criticism in the thirties, see Louis Aragon's "From Dada to Red Front," a confession of the earlier "error" of having been attracted to dadaism (*NM* 15, 7 [May 14, 1935], 23–4).

24. Most recently: John Timberman Newcomb, *Wallace Stevens and Literary Canons* (Jackson: Univ. of Mississippi Press, 1992), pp. 100–14; and Longenbach, *The Plain Sense of Things*, pp. 131–2, 137–8, 141–7. Among the others are Bates, *Mythology of Self*, pp. 172–6, 183–6, 193; Lucy Beckett, *Wallace Stevens* (Cambridge: Cambridge Univ. Press, 1974), p. 113; Frank Doggett, *Wallace Stevens: The Making of the Poem* (Baltimore: Johns Hopkins Univ. Press, 1980), p. 121; Frank Kermode, *Wallace Stevens* (Edinburgh: Oliver and Boyd, 1960), pp. 63–6; George Lensing, *Wallace Stevens: A Poet's Growth* (Baton Rouge: Louisiana State Univ. Press, 1986), pp. 126–7, 148; Frank Lentricchia, *Ariel and the Police: Michel Foucault, William James, Wallace Stevens* (Madison: Univ. of Wisconsin Press, 1988), pp. 214–15; A. Walton Litz, *Introspective Voyager: The Poetic Development of Wallace Stevens* (New York: Oxford Univ. Press, 1972), pp. 204–6; Louis Martz, "Wallace Stevens: The World as Meditation," *The Yale Review*, n.s., 47 (Summer 1958), 517–36; Monroe, "Figuration and Society in 'Owl's Clover'"; Samuel French Morse, *Wallace Stevens: Poetry as Life* (New York: Pegasus, 1970), pp. 148–51; Joan Richardson, *Wallace Stevens, A Biography: The Later Years, 1923–1955* (New York: William Morrow, 1988), pp. 109, 129, 202; Joseph N. Riddel, *The Clairvoyant Eye: The Poetry and Poetics of Wallace Stevens* (Baton Rouge: Louisiana State Univ. Press, 1965), pp. 114, 120–34, 289–90; Riddel, "The Contours of Stevens Criticism," in *The Act of the Mind: Essays on the Poetry of Wallace Stevens*, ed. Roy Harvey Pearce and J. Hillis Miller (Baltimore: Johns Hopkins Univ. Press, 1965), pp. 252–4; Riddel, "'Poets' Politics' – Wallace Stevens's *Owl's Clover*," *Modern Philology* 56, 2 (November 1958), 118–32; Herbert J. Stern, *Wallace Stevens: Art of Uncertainty* (Ann Arbor: Univ. of Michigan Press, 1966), pp. 13–15, 165–6; and Donald Sheehan, "Wallace Stevens in the 30s: Gaudy Bosh and the Gesture's Whim" in *The Thirties: Fiction, Poetry, Drama*, ed. Warren French (Deland, FL: Everett Edwards, 1967), pp. 149–57.

25. Abbie F. Willard, *Wallace Stevens: The Poet and His Critics* (Chicago: American Library Association, 1978), p. 23. It has been more than a decade since Willard wrote that "The impact of this review on budding Stevens criticism cannot be overemphasized, not because of any cogency or acuity in the critic's comments, but because of the profound effect these comments had on the poet himself and on those who then and now study Stevens" (p. 35). Lisa M. Steinman (*Made in America: Science, Technology, and American Modernist Poets* [New Haven: Yale Univ. Press, 1987]) has concluded that "Burnshaw, a poet in his own right, was far more sympathetic to Stevens than Stevens admits" (p. 209 n. 52).

26. Typical of SB's private descriptions of intellectual and editorial life at *NM* is a letter to AK confessing as early as 1934 that "I shall not be able to continue at the New Masses," where literature was becoming "an excrescent act rather than a compulsion" – sentiments "strictly entre nous" at the time (SB to AK, July 9, 1934 [Virginia, AK Papers, #6561, b1]).

27. WM to Sara Bard Field, August 14, 1937 (HL, C.E.S. Wood Papers, WD166[20]).

28. WM had just read for RLL's Alcestis Press the manuscript of *Owl's Clover* – or, alternatively, *Aphorisms on Society*, which WM thought "a lousy title" –

when he informed RLL of his view that "it is unfortunate" that "Granville
Hicks, Burnshaw, et al . . . have been the mouthpieces for Communism in
the literary field" (WM to George Marion O'Donnell, May 26, 1936 [WUL,
O'Donnell Papers]). Samuel French Morse followed the "Owl's Clover" controversy, and by 1937 expressed to Morton D. Zabel at *P* his hope that WS's
poetic course would not be too much perturbed by SB; Morse hoped SB
would see, and be sufficiently refuted by, MM's latest review as by WS's
then-recent poems (Morse to MZ, February 11, 1937 [RLC, MZ Papers]).
In Morse's review of *Owl's Clover* and *The Man with the Blue Guitar & Other
Poems* in *Twentieth Century Verse* (8 [January–February 1938]), he concluded
that WS had "picked the wrong man to represent the Marxist imagination"
(167).

Despite his important decision as editor of WS's uncollected writings in
1957 (*OP*) to reprint the first and longer version of "Owl's Clover," giving a
fuller sense of the initial reaction to SB, Morse later predicted, after speaking with WS about the issue, that WS's critics would overestimate the importance of the episode (interview with AF, Milton, Massachusetts, January 7,
1983). The only thing that saved "Owl's Clover" "from the worst excesses of
the social and political poetry of the period" was WS's "refusal to take the
attitude of an artist on 'bad terms with society,'" wrote Morse in 1970 (*Poetry
as Life*, p. 155). Morse had evidently pondered, or drafted, an essay on WS in
1939 (Morse to George Marion O'Donnell, June 23, 1939 [WUL]). As a
student of Theodore Morrison six months earlier, Morse had written an
essay that attempted a Freudian reading of "Owl's Clover" (Morse to
O'Donnell, December 30, 1938 [WUL]).

29. Irving Howe, "Another Way of Looking at a Blackbird," *NR* 137 (November
4, 1947), 16–17.
30. Riddel, "Poet's Politics," p. 118.
31. SB, "Notes on Revolutionary Poetry," *NM* 10, 8 (February 20, 1934), 20–2.
32. Mary McCarthy and Margaret Marshall, "Our Critics, Right or Wrong, [Part]
IV: The Proletarians," *N* 141, 3674 (December 4, 1935), 654. They wrote of
"the pent-up traditional aestheticism within the Marxist critic" (654).
33. KB, "Preface to the Second Edition," *Counter-Statement* (1931; reprint Berkeley: Univ. of California Press, 1968), p. xvi.
34. Riddel, *Clairvoyant Eye*, p. 105.
35. Max Eastman, *The Literary Mind: Its Place in an Age of Science* (New York:
Charles Scribner's Sons, 1935), p. 84.
36. See, e.g., *L* 306.
37. AF and Teres, "An Interview with Stanley Burnshaw," 110.
38. Interview with AF, February 23, 1990 (Philadelphia). "[A]lmost all writers,"
Kenneth Rexroth remembered in 1971, "to a greater or lesser degree moved
to the Left" (*American Poetry in the Twentieth Century* [New York: Herder and
Herder, 1971], p. 107. The perception, strongly felt more than a half-century
later, was even more strongly felt then. In January 1938, Dorothy Van Ghent
wrote: "[M]ost contemporary poets are Marxists" ("When Poets Stood Alone,"
NM 26 [January 11, 1938], sec. 2, p. 44).
39. For accessible descriptions of the problem of background and foreground in

New Historicist writing, see Jean E. Howard, "The New Historicism in Renaissance Studies," *English Literary Renaissance* 16, 1 (Winter 1986), 13–43; Jerome J. McGann, "The Scandal of Referentiality" in *Social Values and Poetic Acts: The Historical Judgment of Literary Work* (Cambridge: Harvard Univ. Press, 1988), pp. 115–31; and H. Aram Veeser's introduction to *The New Historicism*, ed. Veeser (New York: Routledge, 1989), pp. ix–xvi.

40. This was part of the original epilogue to Cowley's *Exile's Return* (New York: W. W. Norton, 1934), and published in *NR* 79, 1016 (May 23, 1934), 34–6; emphasis added. It was omitted by a somewhat embarrassed Cowley from later editions, and finally reprinted in *Think Back on Us: A Contemporary Chronicle of the 1930's*, ed. Henry Dan Piper (Cardondale: Southern Illinois Univ. Press, 1967), pp. 56–62. For Cowley's explanation, see *The Dream of the Golden Mountains: Remembering the 1930s* (New York: Viking, 1980), pp. 222–3.

41. Lillian Symes, "Our Liberal Weeklies," *Modern Monthly* 10 (October 1936), 8.

Chapter 1: Which Side Are You On?

1. On central planning as an idea attractive to radicals and liberals alike, see Warren, *Liberals and Communism*, pp. 50–61.

2. In pro-New Deal, and specifically anti-Hoover rhetoric, the word "planning" in itself had great force; see, e.g. Richard Hofstadter, *The American Political Tradition and the Men Who Made It* (New York: Alfred Knopf, 1967; originally published 1948), pp. 308–9. "Central planning" was the emphasis of the so-called first New Deal.

3. The counterargument, favoring a "more orderly arrangement," emerged from the likes of Edward A. Filene, whose work, as we will see, WS followed; see "The New Relations between Business and Government," an address Filene delivered before The American Academy of Political and Social Science, Philadelphia, January 5, 1934 (reprinted in *Speaking of Change: A Selection of Speeches and Articles by Edward A. Filene* [New York: Former Associates of Edward A. Filene, 1939], especially p. 88).

4. Defending his economic policies in anticipation of the 1936 reelection campaign, Roosevelt reminded his Chicago audience that while "the economic life of the United States is a seamless web," the country had been enabled to endure the "emergency of 1933" because of government planning. Though the market was "many-sided," it was, in the new dominant view, wholly predictable. The text of this speech was quoted in *NYT* (December 10, 1935, p. 12). If WS was, as I suggest, responding to Roosevelt's latest great claims for the New Deal, then he also probably saw, in the same day's financial section, a report noting that a high portion of Americans polled thought there was too much federal regulation of business; another report concluded that the president's speech "failed yesterday to invest the stock market with much spirit" (37). Roosevelt's speech was still more prominently covered in *HC* (December 10, 1935, pp. 1, 2, 10). An editorial characterized the speech as signifying a new push toward "*centralizing control* of production" (p. 10;

emphasis added). Roosevelt had indeed argued that a centralized economy was inevitable since the forty-eight states separately "never were able and never will be able to legislate or administer individual laws adequately" (quoted in *HC*, p. 1).

5. SB to Harriet Monroe, October 22, 1932 (RLC, PMP12–35).
6. A letter to the editor of *NYT*, "Milton on War," October 9, 1935, p. 22. See also A. M. Witherspoon, "Milton Is Still Timely" *SRL* 11, 646 (April 27, 1935), 2–3; J. M. French, "Milton as a Historian," *PMLA*, 50 (June 1935), 469–79; and A.S.P. Woodhouse, "Milton and His Age," *Univ. of Toronto Quarterly* 5 (1935), 130–9, a survey of "the new literary history" in Milton studies (133).
7. John Haynes Holmes, "Introduction," *Christ in the Breadline . . . by Kenneth W. Porter, Seymour Gordden Link, Harry Elmore Hurd* (North Montpelier, VT: The Driftwind Press, 1933), p. 4.
8. Spain provided, Malcolm Cowley wrote, "the one issue on which they agreed" – "they" being "literary rebels" otherwise unwilling "to march with others in disciplined ranks" (*Exile's Return: A Literary Odyssey of the 1920s* [New York: Viking, 1956; reprint of the revised 1951 edition], p. 295).
9. Unpublished, untranscribed portion of Peter Brazeau's interview with Wilson Taylor, July 1976 (HL, HM 53898).
10. "Citation for Horace Gregory," in *Theory of Flight* (New Haven: Yale Univ. Press, 1935), p. 77.
11. WS to HG, February 2, 1933 (ALS, HG Papers, b12).
12. HG, *No Retreat* (New York: Harcourt, Brace and Company, 1933), p. 43.
13. HG, "Le Front Rouge," *P* 42, 5 (August 1933), 284.
14. HG, *No Retreat*, pp. 7–8.
15. Alan Calmer, "Portrait of the Artist as a Proletarian," *SRL* 16, 14 (July 31, 1937), 4. The description is subject to some irony, for by 1937 Calmer was repudiating some of the radical modes he was describing.
16. HG, "Introduction," *New Letters in America* 1 (New York: Norton, 1937), 10.
17. For a skeptical report of this and similar versions of communist poetics, see Matthew Josephson, *Infidel in the Temple: A Memoir of the Nineteen-Thirties* (New York: Alfred A. Knopf, 1967), p. 366.
18. Kenneth Patchen, *Before the Brave*, pp. 59, 89.
19. At the first American Writers' Congress, Jack Conroy said: "To me a strike bulletin or an impassioned leaflet are of more moment than . . . the technical manner of Marcel Proust and James Joyce" (quoted by Cowley, *Golden Mountains*, p. 275).
20. Joseph Warren Beach, *Obsessive Images: Symbolism if Poetry of the 1930s and 1940s* (Minneapolis: Univ. of Minnesota Press, 1960), published posthumously, ed. William Van O'Connor, p. 250.
21. See AF, *Stevens and the Actual World*, pp. xvii–viii, 12, 26–8.
22. In *The Futurist Moment* (Chicago: Univ. of Chicago Press, 1986) Perloff argues that "the formalist critique of collage on the part of the New Critical Right is matched on the Left by a *distrust of collage's semantic heterogeneity*" (pp. 73–4; emphasis added). Supported in this instance by her reading of Walter Benjamin, Perloff has always been concerned with the way in which

mechanical process moves from "the 'detach[ment of] the object'" through "its 'reactivat[ion]' elsewhere" (p. 73). *The Futurist Moment* recovers collage as a *political* "way of reintroducing the public discourse into the poetic field" (p. 74), a point I take to be crucial in any attempt to manage WS's use of such discourse, though it be a discourse of liberal-left and not of right. This argument is obviously supported by Picasso's daily dependence on news articles, cartoons, and photographs from the French communist newspaper *L'Humanité* for *Guernica* (see Phyllis Tuchman, "Guernica & 'Guernica,'" *Artforum* 21, 8 [April 1983], 45–6).

23. Editors' preamble titled "Left!," *The Left: A Quarterly Review of Radical & Experimental Art* 1, 1 (Spring 1931), 3.

24. Ben Maddow, "The Communist Party of Germany," *Dynamo* 1, 3 (Summer 1934), p. [1].

25. Zukofsky was replying to complaints lodged by leftists against *An "Objectivists" Anthology* denouncing it for neglecting to affiliate itself with the proletariat. I paraphrase a typescript dated March 3, 1933 (RLC, PMP12–35, b41, f4).

26. See *WSR*, pp. 162–5.

27. "Filene Sees Press Unfair to New Deal / . . . Assails 'Banker-Minded,'" *NYT*, December 22, 1935, p. 7.

28. See the 1934 lecture of this name, published in *Morals in Business* (Berkeley: Univ. of California Press, 1935).

29. Granville Hicks labelled Filene "a Boston merchant with a reputation for liberalism" (*Part of the Truth* [New York: Harcourt, Brace and World, 1965], p. 76).

30. V. P. Krull, "A Letter to the Board of Trustees [of Vassar College]," January 26, 1937 (Hoover Institute Library, Stanford University, *National Republic Papers*, b306, f "Vassar").

31. "E. A. Filene Warns Against Panaceas," *NYT*, October 18, 1935, p. 25; an excerpt was printed on October 20 ("An Improved Constitution," sec. 4, p. 8); see also "Eliminating Loan Sharks," October 29, 1935, p. 20; and *HC*, October 18, 1935, p. 10. The speech, called "The Contribution of Our Secondary Schools to Better Business and Industrial Conditions," is reprinted in *Speaking of Change*, pp. 15–31. In a speech of July 1935, Filene's idea that "Economic democracy is now at least thinkable to an ever growing number of business minds" was qualified by his basic suspicion of New Deal planning and expansiveness: "I do not wish to state this too optimistically, for we can't always bank on trends" ("New Deal Growing, Filene Tells London," *NYT*, July 11, 1935, p. 10). Before the Moscow trials, few liberals suggested, as Filene did, that fascism, communism, and chaos proposed roughly equivalent economic alternatives.

32. As with the Filene story, WS's remarks were doubtless prompted by the very recent news that this farm debt relief law had, for a second time, been declared unconstitutional ("Frazier-Lemke Act Held Still Invalid, Although Amended," *NYT*, October 22, 1935, p. 1).

33. See "Roosevelt Disapproves Frazier-Lemke Bill," *NYT*, April 11, 1934, p. 4. On left opposition to the bill, see J. T. Flynn, *NR*, "Other People's Money,"

November 6, 1935, 361; and "Why the Frazier-Lemke Bill is Bad," *N*, May 20, 1936, 633–4.

34. "Insurance Executives Deny They Will Rush Foreclosures on Farms," *NYT*, May 29, 1935, p. 11; "Report Stirs Insurance Men," *NYT*, December 5, 1935, p. 1; "Reports on Farm Properties Acquired through Foreclosure by Banks and Insurance Companies," *NYT*, December 2, 1935, p. 2.

35. Marriner S. Eccles, *Beckoning Frontiers: Public & Personal Recollections* (New York: Knopf, 1951), p. 110: "It was clear from these figures that any step taken to check the further foreclosure of farm-mortgage indebtedness would indirectly benefit and help maintain the solvency of the farmers' creditors – the banks, insurance companies."

36. KB, *Counter-Statement*, p. 118.

37. Nancy Cunard, "To the Writers and Poets of England, Scotland, Ireland and Wales," June 1937, sent in the names of Aragon, Auden, Pablo Neruda, Tristan Tzara, Cunard and others (quoted in Valentine Cunningham, "Neutral?: 1930s Writers and Taking Sides," in *Class, Culture and Social Change: A New View of the 1930s*, ed. Frank Gloversmith [Sussex: The Harvester Press, 1980], p. 45).

38. *This* in a postscript to a letter Ficke wrote Seiffert to lament the "insane, wicked confusion which historians call 'History'" (Arthur Davison Ficke to Marjorie Seiffert, September 17, 1936 [Colorado, Seiffert Papers]).

39. Tate to Donald E. Stanford, June 15, 1975 (Stanford, Donald E. Stanford Papers).

40. Florence Reece wrote the poem (mostly sung) that began "Which side are you on? / Which side are you on?" after armed police plundered her shack in an effort to find her strike-organizing husband; the interrogative took hold as a battle cry.

41. The archives of communist and fellow-traveling poets are full of letters that speak of "coming over" from right to left in a language engaging the rhetoric of side-taking. When George Marion O'Donnell, a poet closely allied with Tate and John Crowe Ransom, began showing his friends a new poem, "Death's Photography," the communist WM responded by writing, "I think you are coming over, which does not imply a conversion, but does imply . . . that there seems *only two sides these days and you naturally were destined to oppose Fascism*" (WM to O'Donnell, August 14, 1937 [WUL, O'Donnell Papers]; emphasis added).

42. Joseph Freeman to Daniel Aaron, 1958 (quoted in Aaron, *Writers on the Left: Episodes in American Literary Communism* [New York: Harcourt, Brace & World, 1961], p. 270).

43. For a lively summary of the most recent round of charges and counter-charges, see Nelson, *Repression and Recovery*, pp. 242–3 and especially 320–2 n. 267.

44. Bates, *Mythology of Self*, p. 183 n. 34.

45. For more on *HC*'s rearguard Republicanism, see John W. Jeffries, *Testing the Roosevelt Coalition* (Knoxville: The Univ. of Tennessee Press, 1979), p. 35.

46. *HC*, October 11, 1935, p. 14; October 18, 1935, p. 1. Incidentally, the charge of chemical warfare was later proved false.

47. Van Ghent, "Where Poets Stood Alone," pp. 41–6.

48. Ibid., p. 46.

49. After citing WS's theme as "the imagination as an ordering function in a disorderly world," Van Ghent speaks of "[t]he man who remembers the time 'when he stood alone,' when the police did not have to prop him up." She notes that WS's poetry has "gradually lost much of . . . [its] imaginative fervor" as "its theme of decaying imagination becomes more overt" ("When Poets Stood Alone," p. 46). As Dorothe Bendon in the early thirties, Van Ghent had planned an extended stay in Moscow with WM (see letters from Bendon in the WM Papers, HRC, many undated, one dated June 15, 1932; and WM to Harriet Monroe, December 27, 1932 [RLC, PMP12–35, b14, f29]). She and WM jointly wrote Monroe: "May 'Poetry' continue though capitalism fall" (November 1, 1932 [RLC, PMP12–35]). Later poems continued radical themes, including "The Rose and the Skull," published in *transition* 27 (1938), and "Depositions for the Fatherland," in *P* 52, 4 (July 1938), 186–8: "The nominal lion and the lamb / Rehearsing to our times its names / Explode the trigger / Scatter in dreadful roar / The veritable war" (187).

50. Emphasis added. Irvin Ehrenpreis speculated, I think incorrectly, that WS was referring to "Waving Adieu, Adieu, Adieu" (*Wallace Stevens: A Critical Anthology*, ed. Ehrenpreis [Harmondsworth, Middlesex: Penguin, 1972], pp. 24, 99).

51. WS's choice of Brahms as emblematic of outmoded musicality also deliberately courted antiformalist disapproval. Such counterattacks continue to this day; see, for instance, Ira Sadoff's criticism of Robert Richman's "neo-formalist" anthology, *The Direction of Poetry: An Anthology of Rhymed and Metered Verse Written in the English Language since 1975* (Boston: Houghton Mifflin, 1988). Richman claims that his selection offers evidence that "musicality [i]s showing new vigor," to which Sadoff responds that neoformalism entails "a dangerous nostalgia"; he identifies Bishop, Wilbur, Kunitz, Walcott, and Justice, the "masters of received form," as "the Brahmses of this century" ("Neo-Formalism: A Dangerous Nostalgia," *American Poetry Review* 19, 1 [January–February 1990], 7).

52. "France and Italy," *NYT*, January 8, 1935, p. 20; and "Franco-Italian Cordiality," *HT*, January 9, 1935, p. 10. See also "France and Italy See Pact Delayed," *HT*, January 1, 1935, p. 3.

53. The later gloss reads in full: "Most people stand by the aid of philosophy, religion and one thing or another, but a strong spirit (Anglais, etc.) stands by its own strength. Even such a spirit is subject to degeneration. I suppose we have to consider new faiths with reference to states of helplessness or states of degeneration. If men have nothing external to them on which to rely, then, in the event of a collapse of their own spirit, they must naturally turn to the spirit of others. I don't mean conventions: police" (*L* 348).

54. KB was characterizing Italian cultural fascism, a new order that had introduced "the glorification of industrial and financial nationalism" (*Attitudes Toward History*, p. 32).

55. Joseph Carroll has observed that the Englishman is "haunted by his memory of the moon as a basic poetic element" (*Wallace Stevens' Supreme Fiction: A New Romanticism* [Baton Rouge: Louisiana State Univ. Press, p. 1987], p. 66).

56. Among them Litz, *Introspective Voyager*, pp. 186–7; Beckett, *Wallace Stevens*, p. 103; Carroll, *Stevens' Supreme Fiction*, p. 66; and Bloom, *The Poems of Our Climate* (Ithaca: Cornell Univ. Press, 1976), p. 113.

57. William Rose Benét, "Three Poets and a Few Opinions," *North American Review* 243, 1 (Spring 1937), 197.

58. Litz, *Introspective Voyager*, p. 230.

59. Taggard, "Silence in Mallorca," *Collected Poems, 1918–1938* (New York: Harper and Brothers, 1938), pp. 157–9.

60. MM, "Unanimity and Fortitude," *P* 49, 5 (February 1937), 268–72.

61. It was announced in "Book Notes," *NYT*, October 21, 1936, p. 25.

62. See, e.g., "The Shape of Things," *N* 143, 4 (July 25, 1936), 85–6; 143, 5 (August 1, 1936), 113; 143, 6 (August 8, 1936), 141.

63. Rolfe Humphries's translation of Lorca's "Song of the Little Death" clearly supported that policy and stands as the one notable exception (*N*, 143, 22 [November 28, 1936], 635).

64. The poem is set in an "ancient cupola'd capitol" suspiciously resembling St. Petersburg, where strikes have shut down the city. "The lately spat-on, become our tyrants," blood runs, and the ironies flowing from depictions of a once-radical society now requiring new radicalization are obvious: "Our new Caesar is crowned / By old newspapers. Look closely! You will see / His oppressive scepter has been rolled / From a revolutionary manifesto" (*N*, 143, 17 [October 24, 1936], 481).

65. Ben Belitt to AF, June 28, 1988.

66. From an interview conducted for *Contemporary Authors* (New Revision Series), vol. 7, p. 46.

67. Ben Belitt, *The Five-Fold Mesh* (New York: Alfred A. Knopf, 1938), "Prefatory Note," n.p.

68. Ben Belitt, "127,000,000 Poets, or the Muse's Guinea Pigs," *N* 142, 3698 (May 20, 1936), 648–9; Eda Lou Walton, "The Vanity Press Racket," *N* 142, 3700 (June 3, 1936), 722.

69. Calvin Bedient, "Ben Belitt and the High Jinks of the Elegiac," *Salmagundi* nos. 74–5 (Spring/Summer 1987), 131; William Matthias Robins, "Ben Belitt," *Dictionary of Literary Biography* (Detroit: Gale, 1980), vol. 5, p. 33.

70. Ben Belitt, *Possessions: New and Selected Poems (1938–1985)* (Boston: David R. Godine, 1985), p. 140.

71. Belitt, "The Violent Mind," *N* 143, 24 (December 12, 1936), 709.

72. Belitt to WM, February 2, 1937 (HRC, WM Papers).

73. Belitt, "The Violent Mind," 710.

74. James Baird noted, for example, that the poem was "inspired by the sacrifice of the Spanish Republicans" before it goes on to speak of life as the fulfillment of desire (*Dome and Rock*, p. 210).

75. Even Litz, whose praise for this poem is stronger than any other critic's, speaks of the death of the soldier as beyond ideology: the poem records "a simple and instinctive heroism which defies all theories" (*Introspective Voyager*, pp. 230–1)

76. Harold Rosenberg, "Spanish Epitaph," in *New Letters in America* 1 (New York, 1937), ed. HG, p. 106.

77. Samuel French Morse, "Man with Imagination," *Twentieth Century Verse* 8 (January–February 1938), 168.

78. Bates, *Mythology of Self*, p. 184. James Longenbach has agreed (*Plain Sense of Things*, p. 172).

79. Vendler, *Wallace Stevens: Words Chosen out of Desire* (Knoxville: Univ. of Tennessee Press, 1984), pp. 20–1.

80. Aaron, *Writers on the Left*, p. 157.

81. See Mariani, *William Carlos Williams: A New World Naked* (New York: McGraw-Hill, 1981), p. 401.

82. WCW, "Poets' Corner," *NR* 93 (November 17, 1937), 50.

83. Josephson provides an accessible descriptive chronology (*Infidel*, pp. 435–6). Only by 1938 did a sizable minority of Americans favor repeal of the embargo.

84. Belitt's mid-September letter to MZ confirms that he and other *N* staff members had already begun evaluating poems for the prize. "Things have been so fearfully congested here during the last week," he added (September 17, 1936 [RLC, MZ Papers, b1, f6]).

85. Neugass, "Headlines from Spain," *NM* 20 (August 4, 1936), 13. There are a few other immediate literary responses, but these were poets offering prose about Spain. Louis Untermeyer was among those contributing statements to "Viva España Libre!" in the August 18 *NM*. See also Muriel Rukeyser's "Barcelona on the Barricades" and Dorothy Canfield Fisher's "In Defense of a Free Spain," in the September 1 and September 8 issues of *NM* respectively.

86. Not, that is, like Rolfe's "City of Anguish," written in August 1937 about Madrid but "whose surreal violence . . . *recalls* Picasso's *Guernica*" (Nelson, *Repression and Recovery*, p. 113): "The headless body / stands strangely, totters for a second, falls."

87. Roy Campbell, *Talking Bronco* (London: Faber and Faber, 1946), p. 79.

88. Auden, introduction to *C. Day Lewis, The Poet Laureate: A Bibliography*, ed. Geoffrey Handley-Taylor and Timothy d'Arch Smith (Chicago: St. James Press, 1968), p. v.

89. Aaron, *Writers on the Left*, p. 157.

90. See Gabriel Jackson, *The Spanish Republic and the Civil War, 1931–1939* (Princeton: Princeton Univ. Press, 1965), p. 331. Picasso began the first sketches for *Guernica* on May 1, 1937.

91. Josephson, *Infidel*, p. 425.

92. Rexroth, "Requiem for the Spanish Dead," *The Collected Shorter Poems* (New York: New Directions, 1966), p. 86.

93. Jackson, *Spanish Republic*, p. 256; F. Jay Taylor, *The United States and the Spanish Civil War* (New York: Bookman Associates, 1956), pp. 57ff. On the ambivalent attitudes of leftist writers: Josephson recalls a discussion with Robert Cantwell, then "still an ardent fellow traveller," in which Cantwell argued that it was not worth endangering "the security of 180 million Russians . . . for the sake of a small country of 20 million like Spain" (*Infidel*, p. 408).

94. Josephson, *Infidel*, p. 408.

95. Arthur A. Ekrich, Jr., *Ideologies and Utopias: The Impact of the New Deal on American Thought* (Chicago: Quadrangle Books, 1969), p. 219.

96. "600 Dead in Battle on Way to Malaga," *NYT*, July 28, 1936, p. 2.
97. Robert G. De Pury, "Rebels Massacre Irun Defenders / Priests Crucified by Leftists," *HT*, September 4, 1936, p. 2; "Defenders of Irun Making Last Stand," *HT*, September 1, 1936, p. 1, "Prisoners in Irun Exposed to Bombs," *NYT*, September 1, 1936, p. 1. "Chained and shackled": "Spanish Govt. Would Blow Up 1700 Rebels," AP report carried by *HC*, September 2, 1936, p. 1. For more on Irun, see Jackson, *Spanish Republic*, p. 273.
98. Jackson, *Spanish Republic*, p. 313.
99. Ibid, pp. 283, 287, 298, 314.
100. Stephen Spender, introduction to *Voices against Tyranny: Writing of the Spanish Civil War*, ed. John Miller (New York: Scribner's, 1986), p. 7. He was describing the effect of Roy Campbell's accounts of the war. "At the time," Matthew Josephson wrote of the war's first weeks as viewed from the United States, "there were many reports of atrocities committed by Republican mobs as well as by the fascists" (*Infidel*, p. 425). For more on journalistic coverage of left terror, see Warren, *Liberals and Communism*, pp. 136–8.
101. Allen Guttmann has presented persuasive evidence that the communists and their pro-Republican supporters worked "to disguise and to de-emphasize . . . [their] very serious quarrel with the Church and to publish statements by Catholics who supported the Republic. . . . [F]or the most part, communists made backbreaking efforts to draw the line between the hierarchy's evil and the believers' good" (*The Wound in the Heart: America and the Spanish Civil War* [New York: Free Press of Glencoe/Macmillan, 1962], p. 77).
102. WS sensed, correctly, that the term "rebel" was itself already a cause for controversy. The American right complained that the term was in itself leftist propaganda, since to them the Spanish right fought for "world democracy." See John P. Delaney, "Call Not These Men Rebels," *America* 55 (August 22, 1936), 460. Guttmann's survey of conservative magazine and newspaper opinion found that the Hearst papers specialized in praising the Nationalist freedom-fighters by calling "rebel" and "rebellion" into doubt; "[t]he so-called rebellion" was the phrase Guttmann found typical (*Wound in the Heart*, p. 56).
103. For more on anticlerical passions, see Jackson, *Spanish Republic*, pp. 218 (170 churches destroyed by fire, 251 attempts at such arson), 286, 292 (up to 6000 priests and monks killed in the cities). See also Megan Laird, "A Diary of Revolution," *Atlantic Monthly*, November 1936, pp. 513–33 (after one church was set afire, priests emerged and were machine-gunned). Reasonable explanations of Republican fury against the Church were published immediately; Reinhold Niebuhr's "Arrogance in the Name of Christ," *Christian Century* 53, 36 (September 2, 1936), 1157–8, was among the earliest.
104. For an overview of the importance of Irun, I have relied upon G. L. Steer's *The Tree of Gernika: A Field Study of Modern War* (London: Hodder and Stoughton, 1938), pp. 21–53.
105. Pound was responding to a survey entitled "Authors Take Sides" (quoted in *Voices against Tyranny*, ed. Miller, p. 141).
106. Ibid.
107. For more on the poetic consequences of WS's isolationism, see AF, *Stevens and the Actual World*, pp. 3–28.

108. H. R. Hays, "Defenseless Spring," *P* 52, 4 (July 1938), 208; emphasis added.

109. Guttmann, *Wound in the Heart*, p. 57.

110. Quoted by Guttmann, *Wound in the Heart*, p. 56.

111. George Orwell, *Homage to Catalonia* (New York: Harcourt Brace Jovanovich, 1952), p. 65.

112. Frederick R. Benson, *Writers in Arms: The Literary Impact of the Spanish Civil War* (New York: New York Univ. Press, 1967), p. 222. Two contemporary conservative views of press distortion are John A. Toomey, "Press Propaganda Tinctures the News," *America* 58 (December 11, 1937), 225–6; and Fletcher Pratt, "Propaganda Captures the Newspapers," *American Mercury* 44, 176 (August 1938), 450–8; and for a liberal view, see J. S. Huxley, "Faking the Spanish News," *N* 143, 12 (September 19, 1936), 322.

113. André Malraux, *L'espoir* (New York/Paris: Editions Gallimard/Random House, 1937), p. 429.

114. Stephen Spender, introduction to *Voices against Tyranny*, ed. Miller, p. 3. One cannot help modifying this and similar statements in view of Spender's changing position. In *The Thirties and After*, he wrote: "[M]y own Thirties' generation ... never became so politicized as to disagree seriously with an older generation of writers who held views often described as 'reactionary,' fascistic even, but whom we admired this side of idolatry" – and he goes on to name Yeats, Lawrence, and "most of all" Eliot (*The Thirties and After: Poetry, Politics and People, 1933–1975* [London: Macmillan, 1978], pp. xiii, xiv).

115. Spender, "Thoughts During an Air Raid," *NR* 95 (May 18, 1938), 42.

116. HG, "One Writer's Position," *NM* 14, 7 (February 12, 1935), 20–1.

117. Edwin Seaver, "Another Writer's Position," *NM*, February 19, 1935, 21–2.

118. Rahv was reviewing Spender's *The Destructive Element* ("An Esthetic of Migration," *PR and Anvil* 3, 3 [April 1936], 28).

119. Campbell, *Talking Bronco*, p. 53.

120. Claud Cockburn, a follower of the party line, was later *critical* of those who believed their writing about Spain depended on physical involvement. "Quite a lot of the literary people of the '30s had an exaggerated idea of physical action," Cockburn said in 1965. Such a writer's "certainty was that *unless* he personally and physically fought he would cease to function fully as a writer" – a disposition the communists opposed. "A Conversation with Claud Cockburn," *The Review* 11/12 (1965), 51, 52.

121. The phrase is Edward Mendelson's, but he was somewhat critically summarizing the point of Valentine Cunningham's anthology *Spanish Front* ("Caught in War of Words," *Times Literary Supplement*, January 16, 1987, p. 63). A strong case for the special importance of the media in the civil war is made in Arthur Koestler's *Spanish Testament* (London: Victor Gollancz, 1937), pp. 17–19, 117–145.

122. "A Conversation with Claud Cockburn," 51, 52.

123. On Hemingway's sponsorship of Rolfe, see Allen Guttmann, "The Brief Embattled Course of Proletarian Poetry," in *Proletarian Writers of the Thirties*, ed. David Madden (Carbondale: Southern Illinois Univ. Press, 1968), pp. 266–7. "City of Anguish" was published in Rolfe's *First Love and Other Poems* (quoted by Guttmann, p. 266).

124. HG, "One Writer's Position," 20.
125. Luccock, *American Mirror*, p. 224; emphasis added.
126. HG, "One Writer's Position," 20.
127. The poem was first published in *Dynamo: A Journal of Revolutionary Poetry* 2, 1 (May–June 1935), 11–15.
128. Teres, in the forthcoming *Banners & Wings*, analyzes Rahv and Phillips in this way.
129. T. S. Eliot, "Dante," *The Sacred Wood* (1920; reprinted, New York: Methuen, 1980), pp. 170–1.
130. Bryher to HG, September 27, 1935 (ALS, HG Papers).

Chapter 2: The Poet and the Depression

1. Earl C. Henderson, "Social Security Act and Insurance Companies," *Metropolitan Hartford* 21, 6 (March 1936), 16.
2. Isidor Schneider, "Sunday Morning," *The Temptation of Anthony* (New York: Boni & Liveright, 1928), pp. 94–5.
3. Ettore Rella, "Sunday Morning," in *Social Poetry of the Thirties: A Selection*, ed. Jack Salzman and Leo Zanderer (New York: Burt Franklin, 1978), pp. 212–13.
4. O'Donnell to Samuel French Morse, June 29, 1938 (WUL, O'Donnell Papers).
5. Klaus Mann, *The Turning Point* (New York: L. B. Fischer Publishing Corp., 1942), pp. 294–5.
6. Alfred Kazin, *Starting Out in the Thirties* (Boston: Little, Brown, 1965), p. 15.
7. William Phillips and Philip Rahv, "Literature in a Political Decade," *New Letters in America* 1 (1937), 170.
8. Solon R. Barber, "Memory of Habana: a hot night," *The Left* 1, 1 (Spring 1931), 42.
9. HG, "Introduction," *New Letters in America* 1 (New York: Norton, 1937), 10.
10. In the 1932 election Bynner eventually voted for Roosevelt because, as he put it, the best way to move America toward socialism was to proceed "undercover" (Bynner to Arthur D. Ficke, August 23, 1932 [Beinecke, Ficke Papers]). For more on WS's relationship with Bynner, see Joan Richardson, *Wallace Stevens: The Early Years* (New York: William Morrow, 1986), pp. 200–2, 336–40, 456–8. Bynner and WS were back in touch in the early thirties (as letters at Houghton show).
11. Eastman, *The Literary Mind*, p. 92.
12. George Marion O'Donnell to Samuel French Morse, June 29, 1938 (WUL, O'Donnell Papers).
13. Taggard, *Collected Poems, 1918–1938*, pp. 64, 128–9.
14. Josephine Miles, "Interlude," *Collected Poems* (Urbana: Univ. of Illinois Press, 1983), p. 18.
15. [Joseph Freeman,] "Preface [to the poetry section]," *PLUS*, p. 145.
16. Maxwell Bodenheim, "To a Revolutionary Girl," *PLUS*, p. 147.
17. WM, "Journey and Return," *P* ("Federal Poets Number"), 52, 4 (July 1938), 211.

18. Hector Rella, "The Bone and the Body," *Dynamo* 1, 2 (March–April 1934), 10; emphasis added.

19. WS's critics have indeed had much to say about his hiatus in the mid- and late-twenties. Most helpful of all is Longenbach (*Plain Sense of Things*, especially pp. 105–19). Earlier, Bloom argued that the last major effort of the twenties, "The Comedian as the Letter C," was a crisis poem that failed to suggest a continuity for the "visionary capacity for response." Thus, he argues, WS's career was threatened until "the sun of March 1930 reillumined things for the master of evasions" (*Poems of Our Climate*, p. 87). Refuting Bloom's "Crossing of Solipsism" (p. 2), Sidney Feshbach is typical of others who cite Holly Stevens's explanation that the hiatus was caused by distractions in WS's life: the birth of his first and only child, Holly, in 1924; the noisiness and lack of space in the two-family house on Farmington Avenue, where the Stevenses lived until 1932; the fact that "his energy . . . went largely into his work at the insurance company" (*L* 242; "Communications," *WSJ* 2, 1–2 [Spring 1978], 44–5).

20. That summer it was rejected by *NR* (Ridgely Torrence to WS, July 14, 1922 [HL, WS Papers, WAS 2324]).

21. "New England Verses," *The Measure* 26 (April 1923), 3–7.

22. *The Collected Poems of William Carlos Williams*, ed. A. Walton Litz and Christopher MacGowan (New York: New Directions, 1986), vol. 1, pp. 321–2; I have quoted the first version of 1930.

23. *Collected Poems of Williams*, p. 371.

24. See John Gould Fletcher, "The Revival of Aestheticism," *Freeman* 8 (December 10, 1923), especially 355–6; Gorham Munson, "The Dandyism of Wallace Stevens," *Dial* 79 (1925), especially 413–17. Munson's judgment gained wider acceptance when his essay on WS's dandyism was included in *Destinations: A Canvass of American Literature since 1900* in 1928.

25. The scene was remembered by Albert Halper, and must thus be reckoned with a sense of Halper's hatred of the communists by the time he wrote his memoir (*Good-bye, Union Square: A Writer's Memoir of the Thirties* [Chicago: Quadrangle Books, 1970], p. 95).

26. H. R. Hays, "Laforgue and Wallace Stevens," *Romanic Review* 25 (July–September 1934), 243.

27. Here are the lines HG quotes in the review:
    One might in turn become less diffident,
    Out of such mildew plucking neater mould
    And spouting new orations of the cold.
    One might. One might. But time will not relent. (*CP* 96)
    ("Highly Polished Poetry," *NYHTB*, September 27, 1931, 28). For more on WS's revision of the poem, see *The Palm at the End of the Mind: Selected Poems and a Play*, ed. Holly Stevens (New York: Random House, 1971), p. 401; Litz, *Introspective Voyager*, pp. 98–9; and J. M. Edelstein, *Wallace Stevens: A Descriptive Bibliography* (Pittsburgh: Univ. of Pittsburgh Press, 1972), C65.

28. As of late April ("Fred" [F. W.] Dupee to HG, April 21, 1937 [ALS, HG Papers]).

29. WM to George Marion O'Donnell, July 6, 1937 (WUL, O'Donnell Papers).

30. For more on HG's row with *NM*, see Chapter 5, section 4.
31. HG, "Poetry in 1937," *NM* 25, 11 (December 7, 1937), "Literary Supplement," pp. 13–14, 12–13.
32. From McCarthy's "A Critic's Daybook," *Life and Letters* 9 (June 1933), 135; reprinted in *Sur Plusieurs Beaux Sujects [sic]: Wallace Stevens' Commonplace Book: A Facsimile and Transcription*, ed. Milton J. Bates (Stanford and San Marino: Stanford Univ. Press and Huntington Library, 1989), p. 29.
33. HG, "Highly Polished Poetry," 28.
34. I quote Alan Wald's paraphrase of the *H&H* rejoinder to Granville Hicks's attack in the spring of 1932. Wald's account of the controversy can be found in *Revolutionary Imagination*, pp. 98–9.
35. Joseph Freeman, *An American Testament* (New York: Farrar, 1936), p. 636.
36. Granville Hicks, "The Crisis in American Criticism," *NM* 8, 7 (February 1933), 5.
37. HG, "Introduction," *New Letters in America* 1 (1937), 13–14.
38. Writing of his friend KB (though the point characterizes HG's half-critical, half-hopeful sense of Stevens, and Wheelwright's of *H&H*), Jerre Mangione has written that it was nearly enough to use one's writing to "emphasize the negative aspects of life under capitalism, such as indolence [and] dissipation" (*An Ethnic at Large: A Memoir of American in the Thirties and Forties* [Philadelphia: Univ. of Pennsylvania Press, 1983; first published, 1978], p. 266). This supports the judgment of Irving Howe and Lewis Coser, who in the late fifties noted that communists in the early thirties, working with the so-called "Third Period" sectarian policy, "strove to create a picture of a capitalist world infinitely worse than it already was." Interestingly, this left noncommunist writers with the opportunity of providing descriptions of social "sickness" to the right of the communist policy, "emphasiz[ing] negative aspects" of American life, and yet able to claim comparative neutrality. Despite the communists' "picture" of capitalism actually "worse than it already was," Howe and Coser point out, "in 1930 and 1931 there could hardly be any point in exaggerating the sickness of American society" (*The American Communist Party: A Critical History (1919–1957)* [Boston: Beacon Hill Press, 1957], p. 189).
39. One of eight principles Johnson argued should guide leftist literary criticism entailed the politics of observation: "Fiction, considered as genuine art, may or may not, at any given time, have *propaganda* value . . . ; a novel giving an objective picture of a Methodist community in Tennessee – for instance – might be used, regardless of the author's intentions, in an anti-religious campaign" ("Pure Propaganda and Impure Art," *The Left* 1, 1 [Spring 1931], 32).
40. C. Day Lewis, "Aphorisms for Revolutionary Artists," *Direction* 1, 3 (April–June 1935), 144.
41. Louis Kronenberger, "Mail-Order Movie," *N* 145, 19 (November 6, 1937), 511.
42. In the late twenties Walton's efforts to put together an anthology of poetry about urban existence – "a kind of symphony of city life," she told *P*'s editors – gave her an opportunity to meet an array of "poverty stricken" urban poets who were otherwise inaccessible. She began urging Harriet

Monroe to publish poems by various proletarian protégés, such as one nine-teen-year-old "factory girl with almost no training" whose "emotions are fairly clear" because "[s]he is poverty stricken" (Eda Lou Walton to Harriet Monroe, August 2, 1928, January 6, 1932, March 16, 1932 [RLC, PMP12–35, b26, f7]). Richard Gillman and Michael Paul Novak, in the process of editing the letters of Rolfe Humphries, discerned Walton as a "left-wing activist" (*Poets, Poetics, and Politics: America's Literary Community Viewed from the Letters of Rolfe Humphries* [Lawrence: Univ. of Kansas Press, 1992], p. 122). As a witness for the government in a 1953 hearing before the Subversive Activities Control Board, excommunist Louis Budenz claimed that in the thirties and forties he had "constantly been informed officially of [Walton's] connection with the Communist Party" (*Official Report of Proceedings Before the Subversive Activities Control Board*, Docket No. 107–53, *Herbert Brownell, Attorney General of the U.S. v. The Jefferson School of Social Science*, December 10, 1953, pp. 720–1 [Hoover Institute Library, SACB Papers, Box 31]).

43. Eda Lou Walton, "Beyond the Wasteland," *N* 133, 3453 (September 9, 1931), 263–4. She was quoting from "Le Monocle de Mon Oncle": "I shall not play the flat historic scale" (*CP* 14).

44. Rexroth, *American Poetry in the Twentieth Century*, p. 96.

45. WM, "A Brief Statement," *P* 52, 4 (July 1938), 227–8.

46. One is "Speech from the Wings," which appeared in the May Day 1935 issue of *NR* (p. 212). "Anecdote: Lament for Abundance," dedicated to WCW, takes one of WCW's "proletarian portraits" a step further: A Depression-era still life is interrupted by "a thrust-up palm," followed by a voice: "Can you spare a dime, eh, Mister? / I'm *really* hungry" (*NR* 92, 1191 [September 29, 1937], 216).

47. Fearing, "Dirge," *Collected Poems of Kenneth Fearing* (New York: Random House, 1940), p. 60.

48. Patchen, *Before the Brave*, p. 61.

49. Herman Spector, "Timeclock," first published in *The Left* 1, 2 (Summer & Autumn 1931), 44–6. It has been reprinted in *Social Poetry of the 1930s*, pp. 284, 285, but I am quoting a version somewhat different from that appearing in *PLUS*.

50. Rukeyser, *Theory of Flight*, p. 77.

51. Larsson, "The Beau as Poet," *The Commonweal* 15, 23 (April 6, 1932), 640–1.

52. MZ, "Force as Criticism," *N* 149, 15 (October 7, 1939), 382.

53. MZ to Ben Belitt, October 21, 1936 (RLC, MZ Papers, b1, f6).

54. MZ, "The Harmonium of Wallace Stevens," 152.

55. KB, "Revolutionary Symbolism in America," in *American Writers' Congress*, ed. Henry Hart (New York: International Publishers, 1935), p. 92.

56. Cowley, in the original epilogue to *Exile's Return*, reprinted as "Art Tomorrow," in *Think Back on Us*, ed. Piper; I have quoted from pp. 57, 58.

57. "Left!," *The Left* 1, 1 (Spring 1931), 3.

58. I base this judgment on the material presented immediately below; on a comparison between Schneider's early and late poetry; and on SB's personal recollection (interview with AF and Teres). It's certain that Schneider, loyal to the party's cultural policy long after the Nazi-Soviet pact, would never

have admitted such discomfort in print; thus his unpublished letters to Granville Hicks (at ALS) are helpful. See also Cowley, *Golden Mountains*, p. 298.

59. Isidor Schneider to Hicks, June 26, 1936 (ALS, Hicks Papers).
60. Edwin Rolfe, "Poetry," *PR* 2, 7 (April–May 1935), 33.
61. WM to "Jay" [RLL], February 5, 1935 (RLC, RLL Papers). "Alcestis #2 carries a satire on the Soviet Union by one e. e. cummings (which, by the way, though it was magnificently done, I objected most violent to)" (WM to John Wheelwright, February 12, 1935 [JHB, Wheelwright Papers, b9, f2]).
62. Isidor Schneider, "Order Limited," *NM* 21, 5 (October 27, 1936), 24.
63. MM's use of "the form 'this, this, and this'" is lucidly described by Margaret Holley in *The Poetry of Marianne Moore: A Study in Voice and Value* (New York: Cambridge Univ. Press, 1987), pp. 64–5.
64. It is not clear from her praise of HG if MM knew that his poetry and criticism drew him leftward; it was, however, general knowledge. "I like Horace Gregory and am in sympathy with the trend of his tastes," she wrote, "and when HARMONIUM was reissued, thought his review one of the good ones" (MM to MZ, August 25, 1933 [RLC, RLL papers, f MM]). She later quoted HG's review to open her 1952 essay on WS, "A Bold Virtuoso" (*Complete Prose of Marianne Moore*, ed. Patricia C. Willis [New York: Viking, 1986]): "All voices fall to a whisper and the expression of the face is indicated in the lifting of the eyebrow" (p. 443). MM's poems have been quoted from *The Complete Poems of Marianne Moore* (New York: Macmillan, 1967), pp. 54, 55, 56.
65. For Samuel French Morse, WS's trips to Florida "sufficed to satisfy his recurrent need for poetry" as "the equivalent of Crispin's 'yearly sonnet to the spring.'" Poems in the early and mid-thirties thus come, in Morse's reading, in "response to all this" – "all this" being "'a vast amount of nature'" (*Poetry as Life*, pp. 140–1). For a persuasive corrective, see Longenbach, *Plain Sense of Things*, pp. 126–8.
66. WS to Elsie Stevens, February 28, 1931 (HL, WS Papers, WAS 2047).
67. Unpublished, untranscribed portion of Peter Brazeau's interview with Margaret Powers, July 1976 (HL, HM 53733).
68. The poem is "A Fish-Scale Sunrise" (*CP* 160–1). Margaret Powers explained the origin of this poem to Peter Brazeau (*WSR* 90–1). Her comments suggest 1933 as the date of the poem, which was not published until *Ideas of Order* of 1935.
69. WS to Elsie Stevens, March 5, 1931 (HL, WS Papers, WAS 2043).
70. "To Put Key West on Its Feet," *Digest* 118, 4 (July 28, 1934, 37), 37.
71. In his letters addressed to Elsie and his young daughter Holly, the trope of fecundity persists into the thirties, as nowhere else. See, e.g., the letter of February 28, 1931 (HL, WS Papers, WAS 2047).
72. Anderson, "Key West, Bottled in Bonds," 312.
73. J. P. Clark, "Key West's Year 1," *Survey Graphic* 24 (August 1935), 313.
74. WS to Elsie Stevens, February 28, 1931 (HL, WS Papers, WAS 2047). Part of the letter is printed in *L* 261. During their next contact Powers's youthful pride seemed to irritate WS further (WS to Elsie, March 5, 1931 [HL, WS Papers, WAS 2043]). The story was briefly recounted by Margaret Powers for

Peter Brazeau in 1976 (unpublished, transcribed portion of interview, HL, HM 53733).

75. Litz, *Introspective Voyager*, p. 187.

76. The poem had been published first in *The Left* 1, 2 (Summer/Autumn 1931), 20–1.

77. "This poet has *not* 'escaped.' He is here," a delighted Eda Lou Walton wrote, "taking part in America's radical thought. . . . [H]e can look deeply inward, but he never forgets the larger perspective of human history" ("No Frustration," *N* 136, 3535 [April 5, 1933], 378–9).

78. HG, *No Retreat*, pp. 4–5.

79. In an undated letter, RLL wrote WM that he had received the following poems for the first number of a new journal he was founding: "Wallace Stevens two long (as fine as he's ever done) & 2 short, yours [four poems by WM] . . . – I have 4 more Stevens but want to save them for a later issue." This certainly refers to "Lions in Sweden," one of eight poems RLL published in *Alcestis* 1. The letter, in the WM Papers at HRC, can be dated between late March and May 1934, given the context provided by other letters RLL wrote WM (at HRC) and WM's letters to RLL (RLC, RLL Papers). RLL, whom WM had known as Leippert, "the Editor of the Late LION & CROWN," reintroduced himself in a letter antedating WM's of March 20, 1934 (HRC). With his March 27 response (RLC), WM sent RLL a poem, the same work mentioned in the undated, handwritten letter containing the reference to the submission of WS's eight poems.

80. "What [National City Bank] was doing during the pre-depression years many another bank president was doing" ("The Week," *NR* 74, 953 [March 8, 1933], 87).

81. Reconstruction Finance Corporation (RFC) disbursements to banks in Connecticut alone amounted to $24.6 million (a figure unadjusted to present values).

82. A year before the trial, when the mess at National City Bank was first disclosed, the editors of *NR* had already drawn a radical conclusion shared by many observers then and throughout the spring of 1934 as the story caught on: "[T]hese operations are entirely consistent with the universal practices of business men under private capitalism. . . . If you don't like the[se] practices . . . the only answer is to dissociate banking operations entirely from the realm of private operation for profit" ("This Week," 87). The editors of *The World Tomorrow* wrote: "The National City Bank . . . is presenting the nation with an interesting case study in the ethics of American capitalism. . . . We wonder if it is really possible to read what [its officers] and all the 'good' and the 'bad' capitalists did in the heyday of American prosperity and still have any confidence in capitalism" ("The Morals of a Decadent Capitalism," *The World Tomorrow* 16, 10 [March 8, 1933], 219, 220).

83. *Collier's* 91, 13 (April 1, 1933), 50.

84. In 1929 insurance companies had been at $145.4 million (C. F. Roos, *NRA Economic Planning* [Bloomington: The Principia Press, 1937], p. 115).

85. "LETTERS FROM THE PEOPLE: Social Justice," *HT*, January 9, 1935, p. 10.

86. *Six Plays of Clifford Odets* (New York: The Modern Library, 1939), p. 20.

87. Vincent Pecora, *Wall Street Under Oath* (New York: Simon & Schuster, 1939), p. 127.

88. "Bank Management Assailed on Loans," *NYT*, March 23, 1934, p. 35. See "Stillman Praises City Bank Policies," *NYT*, April 11, 1934, p. 17. The Senate Banking Committee had learned a year earlier that just 5 percent of these loans were repaid ("This Week," 87).

89. "Swenson at Trial . . . Says Huge Amounts Were Well Earned," *NYT*, May 24, 1934, p. 17. The investigation conducted by Pecora and recounted in his sensational *Wall Street Under Oath* also discovered that National City had bought a block of Boeing Corporation stock at a low price, whereupon "a select list of 'officers, directors, key men, and special friends,' including Mr. Swenson" decided then that Boeing was too speculative for public offering and sold large blocks to themselves (p. 124).

90. Quoted in "Swenson at Trial," *NYT*, May 24, 1934, p. 17. See also "Perkins Defends City Bank Loans," *NYT*, March 24, 1934, p. 21.

91. Litz's suggestion about "icy Sweden" seems quite enough to explain the lineage of the images on which Swenson depends (*Introspective Voyager*, p. 188). If possibly Stevens concerned himself with Eric Swenson's Swedish origins – Svente Magnus Swenson was a famous Swedish immigrant – and thus the National City Bank's disproportionate financial interactions with Sweden (controversially in gold), the fact adds little to Stevens's poetic uses of Sweden in association with meteorological poverty, "the harsh reality" described much later (*CP* 506); see AF, *Stevens and the Actual World*, pp. 236–9.

92. On the same day Eric P. Swenson testified that he approved of the management fund because it made sense given the great jumps in the earnings of the bank between 1923 and 1929, largely due to the efforts of the officers now being aided, Arthur Anderson of Chicago was called by the defense to argue that "he did not regard the compensation to National City men as excessive because 'their success was phenomenal'" during boom years ("Swenson at Trial," 17).

93. "National City: Loans Were Made 'To Maintain Morale,'" *Newsweek* 3, 13 (March 31, 1934), 25.

94. "Perkins Defends," *NYT*, March 24, 1934, p. 21. This argument was made by the defendants time and time again. "Then the break came and there was an enormous strain placed upon these men. We considered it vital to keep the organization functioning at top speed, and to keep it functioning we had to see that the individuals who kept up the machinery were able to carry it on without worry" ("Bank's Aid to Staff in Crash Defended," *NYT*, March 27, 1934, p. 17).

95. "Mitchell's Bonus Held Spur to Aides," *NYT*, April 5, 1934, p. 29.

96. See John Rogers's version in *WSR* 59–61. The partly untranscribed, taped version of this interview (HL, HM 53893) contains details of "the famous coup" (Rogers's phrase) not in *WSR*. I have also relied on Brazeau's interview with Manning Heard, later The Hartford's general counsel (HL, HM 53894). J. Collins Lee was one of those who resigned; Heard describes "a tremendous amount of animosity between" WS and Lee.

97. *HA* 25, 9 (February 1934), 123.

98. Barrett Wendell to Oswald Garrison Villard, June 4, 1900 (Massachusetts, WS Papers).

99. Oswald Garrison Villard, "Issues and Men," N 136, 3532 (March 15, 1933), 279.

100. Rexford G. Tugwell, *The Battle for Democracy* (New York: Columbia Univ. Press, 1935); see Chapter 5. Proctor W. Hansl, *Years of Plunder: A Financial Chronicle of Our Times* (New York: Harrison Smith and Robert Haas, 1935).

101. "Dr. Bowie Assails Business Ethics," *NYT*, April 9, 1934, p. 3.

102. Typical of Garrett's official optimism is a letter of March 1908, written to boost his son's confidence in his business career: these letters spoke incessantly of "your readiness your energy and your success" (Dec. 8, 1907 [HL, WS Papers, WAS 2166]).

103. For such a reading, see AF, "Wallace Stevens and the Crisis of Authority," *American Literature* 58 (December 1984), 560–78.

104. Manning Heard, who was WS's assistant at the time of the 1934 promotion, told Brazeau that WS did not have "the slightest desire to go any further .... I don't think he would have accepted an overall executive position if it had been offered to him" (*WSR* 66).

105. See Arthur M. Schlesinger, Jr., *The Coming of the New Deal* (Boston: Houghton-Mifflin, 1959), p. 183.

106. Filene, "Relations between Business and Government," p. 97.

107. Linda Keller Brown, "Challenge and Response: The American Business Community and the New Deal, 1932–1934" (Ph.D. diss., Univ. of Pennsylvania, 1972), 169–76.

108. For many such observations, see *WSR* 3–93.

109. Here is a relevant excerpt from the essay:

> Out of the income we should be able, by the payment of a trivial premium, to protect ourselves, our families and our property against everything. The procedure would necessarily be simple: Probably the dropping of a penny each morning in a box at the corner nearest one's place of residence or on the way to one's place of employment. Each of us would have a personal or particular penny. What is the difference between a personal penny and a social security number? The circle just stated: income, insurance, the thing that happens and income again, would widen and soon become income, insurance, the thing that fails to happen and income again. (*OP* 234)

On "The Specter of Insecurity," see Abraham Epstein, *Insecurity: A Challenge to America* (New York: Smith and Haas, 1936), pp. 3–20.

110. Henderson, "The Social Security Act," 16.

111. A complaint summarized by Glenn Weaver, *Hartford: An Illustrated History of Connecticut's Capital* (Woodland Hills, CA: Connecticut Historical Society, 1982), p. 122.

112. John Band McNulty, *Older Than the Nation: The Story of the* Hartford Courant (Stonington, CT: Pequot Press, 1964), p. 180.

113. "Industry Out to Wage War on New Deal / Business Leaders Ratify Creed Built about Assertion American System Has Not Failed," *HC*, December 6, 1935, pp. 1, 4.

114. Howell Cheney quoted by Herbert F. Janick, Jr., *A Diverse People: Connecticut, 1914 to the Present* (Chester, CT: Pequot Press, 1975), pp. 48–9.

115. "Even if [social security] is considered from the view of the nationalization of the [insurance] business, it is not to be supposed that any government can maintain an entire population indefinitely at a loss. If private companies can continue to expand with profit, no question of nationalization, except in regulatory and certain social aspects, is likely to arise under our system" (*OP* 236). For a sampling of the radical argument in support of social security, see Mary van Kleek, "H.R. 7578 – A Debate on Social Insurance," *NM* 14, 1 (January 1, 1935), 28–34.

116. Maxwell S. Stewart, "Congress Discovers the Class Struggle," *N* 140, 3634 (February 27, 1935), 249.

117. "Choose Your Ism Now," *Redbook*, July 1934, 26; and *It's Up to Us* (New York: Knopf, 1934), p. 11.

118. Schlesinger, *Coming of the New Deal*, p. 160.

119. "Mitchell for Federal Control," *NYT*, February 23, 1933, p. 9.

120. "Map 5-Point Plan to Restore Prices," *NYT*, April 6, 1933, p. 27; "Uphold Roosevelt on his Gold Policy," *NYT*, November 18, 1933, p. 10. To be sure, the Committee eventually could not restrain its fears of bolshevism, supervising the publication of W. A. Wirt's pamphlet *America Must Lose*.

121. *HC*, December 9, 1934, sec. 5, p. 1.

122. "Insurance Ratings Based on Market," *NYT*, April 9, 1933, p. 7; "Banks, Insurance Companies Hope for 'Intrinsic Value' Rule," *Business Week*, July 6, 1932, 5.

123. James K. James, "Your Insurance – 'Thar She Blows!': America Approaches Major Crisis over Casualty and Indemnity Insurance Business," *New Outlook* 164, 1 (July 1934), 16.

124. Schlesinger, *Coming of the New Deal*, p. 96. This then-unusual position is typified by Montague's 1931 address before the American Manufacturers Export Association: "Public consciousness is becoming awakened to the folly of compelling . . . a competitive over-production" ("Price-Fixing Plan Urged to Aid Trade," *NYT*, May 29, 1931, p. 11).

125. Despite Holly Stevens's note signalling a correspondence "reveal[ing] a longstanding friendship" (*L* 443 n. 3), the few who have cited Montague mention only the letter WS wrote him in connection with the composition of *Notes toward a Supreme Fiction*, in *L* 443: Richardson cites the same published letter twice (*Early Years*, p. 74; and *Later Years*, p. 217).

126. The twenty-four letters from WS, among Montague's papers at New York Public (b6, f marked "General S" [New York Public, Montague-Collier Family Papers]), are undoubtedly a small surviving fraction of a fifty-five-year correspondence. Letters quoted are dated June 22, 1943 and January 29, 1945.

127. Respectively, b1, f marked "General B"; b2, f marked "Doc to Dy"; b3, f marked "Frankfurter"; b3, f marked "General F"; b4, f marked "General H[#2]"; b5, f marked "General P" (New York Public, Montague-Collier Family Papers).

128. B5, f marked "General R" (New York Public, Montague-Collier Family Papers); "Gilbert Montague," *NYT*, February 6, 1961, p. 23; Rexford Tugwell,

The Democratic Roosevelt (Garden City: Doubleday, 1957), p. 53n; *F.D.R., His Personal Letters: Early Years* (New York: Duell, Sloan, and Pearce, 1947), p. 460.

129. Rockefeller praised Montague's speeches on the NRA as "informing, to the point, convincing and valuable" (Rockefeller to Montague, April 3, 1934 [New York Public, Montague-Collier Family Papers]).

130. Sullivan to Montague, July 26, 1926 (New York Public, Montague-Collier Family Papers, b6, f marked "General S").

131. Gilbert Holland Montague, "Can Business Afford to Take a Chance on Sherman Act Revision?" *Magazine of Business* 55 (March 1929), 334.

132. "Fascism Offsets Told to Academy," *NYT*, April 7, 1935, p. 28.

133. Gilbert Montague, "Price Fixing, Lawful and Unlawful," *American Law Review* 62 (July 1928), 523. Later Hoover supported antitrust action that Montague criticized.

134. The phrase used by Ellis W. Hawley to characterize a group of people "on the business side," including Montague and other trade association lawyers like Benjamin Javits and David Podell ("The New Deal and Business," *The New Deal: The National Level*, ed. John Braeman et al. [Columbus: Ohio State Univ. Press, 1975], p. 59).

135. "Lawyers Aiding NRA Although Exempted," *NYT*, September 14, 1933, p. 4. For more on Montague's role in the formation of the NRA, see Robert F. Himmelberg, *The Origins of the National Recovery Administration: Business, Government, and the Trade Association Issue, 1921–1933* (New York: Fordham Univ. Press, 1976), pp. 32, 82, 125–7.

136. Montague, "Price Fixing," 505.

137. Ibid., 522–4.

138. Gilbert H. Montague, "Coronation of the Democratic Principle," delivered before the Colonial Dames of America in Washington on May 6, 1937, reprinted in *Vital Speeches* 3, 14 (May 1, 1937), 470–4.

139. Ibid., 472.

140. Ibid., 472, 471.

141. Ibid., 472.

142. "Insurance and Social Change" was first published in *HA* 29, 4 (October 1937).

143. The Hartford's official historian has defined insurance generally as "Act of insuring, or assuring, against loss or damage by a contingent event" (Hawthorne Daniel, *The Hartford of Hartford: An Insurance Company's Part in a Century and a Half of American History* [New York: Random House, 1960], p. 267). WS dealt regularly with forms of "contingent liability," "contingent commission" involving reinsurance, and "contingent business interruption insurance" covering one business whose losses resulted from the losses of major suppliers.

144. Russell Kirk, *The Conservative Mind* (Chicago: Henry Regnery, 1953), p. 325.

145. "New Field of Insurance," *NYT*, March 8, 1934, p. 35.

146. Daniel, *The Hartford of Hartford*, p. 268.

147. Partly transcribed, taped interview with Manning Heard conducted by Brazeau, September 1976 (HL, HM 53854).

148. "Deny Pressure on Ford: Hartford Insurance Men Say They Did Not Cover

Deposits" and "Ford's Bank Action Told," both *NYT*, February 15, 1933, p. 2. For an accessible narrative of this episode, see Carol W. Gelderman, *Henry Ford: The Wayward Capitalist* (New York: Dial Press, 1981), pp. 311–14.

149. "Dishonesty Insurance," *HA* 25, 5 (November 1933), 67.

150. J. Schmidt, Jr., "Loss Prevention Service," *HA* 25, 6 (December 1933), 84; emphasis added. For more on the Hartford's dishonesty insurance, see the transcription of Brazeau's taped interview with John Ladish (HL, HM 53863).

151. "Dishonesty Insurance," 67.

152. Daniel, *The Hartford of Hartford*, p. 228.

153. Henry Dawes, for example, once on the RFC's engineers advisory board, moved to Connecticut General in Hartford, to become an officer there. Directorships in insurance companies frequently went to ex-New Dealers, for instance Leo Wolman who had served on the Automobile Labor Board, hand-picked by Roosevelt (see Josephson, *Infidel*, p. 269).

154. "Where Insurance Companies Find Their Investments," *Business Week*, December 5, 1936, 42.

155. The experiment resulted in the formation of the Federal Crop Insurance Corporation in 1939.

156. Walter R. Whitford, "A '$220,000,000 Surety Bond,'" *HA* 29, 6 (November 1937), 103.

157. F. Robertson Jones, "Insurance and the Law," *HA* 27, 3 (September 1935), 66–8.

158. "Insurance Attack on Securities Act," *NYT*, April 26, 1934, p. 11.

159. John M. Holmes, "Check Up on Government's Public Works Program in Your Vicinity," *HA* 25, 6 (December 1933), 81–2.

160. *HA* 27, 4 (October 1935), 82–3.

161. WS to RLL, March 23, 1936 (RLC, RLL Papers).

162. *HA* 27, 11 (May 1936), 243.

163. "Granite, Too, Has Strength to Weather the Tests of Time," *HA* 27, 6 (December 1935), advertisement opposite p. 168. The WPA *American Guide* for Connecticut described the new building on Asylum Avenue, noting "the severity of its mass" (*Connecticut: A Guide to Its Roads, Lore, and People. . . .* [Boston: Houghton Mifflin Co., 1938], p. 186).

164. Fearing, "Dividends," *Dynamo* 1, 1 (January 1934), 13.

165. *HA* 25, 11 (May 1934), [15].

166. *L* 266–7. He was actually referring to a man "said to be a Russian refugee" – Holly Stevens's recollection – who "built a shack out of old boxes, tin cans, etc." on the dump toward which the declivity behind WS's house ran (*L* 266 n. 4).

167. Lechlitner, "Imagination as Reality," *NYHTB*, December 6, 1936, 40.

168. Genevieve Taggard, "Interior," *PLUS*, p. 197.

169. League of Professional Groups for Foster and Ford, *Culture and the Crisis: An Open Letter to the Writers, Artists, Teachers, Physicians, Engineers, Scientists, and Other Professional Workers of America* (New York: Workers Library Publishers, October 1932), p. 6.

170. James Neugass, "The Hour of Lateness," *Alcestis Quarterly* 4 (July 1935), [2].

171. Quoted in Beach, *Obsessive Images*, p. 261.

172. Lechlitner, "For Statisticians," *Tomorrow's Phoenix* (New York: Alcestis Press, 1937), p. 41.
173. E. T. Kennedy, "May Day Bombings Again Demonstrate Need for Adequate Riot and Civil Commotion Protection," *HA* 24, 10 (April 1933), 194; emphasis added.
174. Quoted by Schlesinger, *Coming of the New Deal*, p. 118.
175. Kazin, *Starting Out*, p. 15.
176. I am quoting from Frank Lentricchia's insightful paraphrase of KB's revisionism (*Criticism and Social Change* [Chicago: Univ. of Chicago Press, 1983]), pp. 27, 26. KB, "Revolutionary Symbolism in America," pp. 87–94.
177. Mary Heaton Vorse, *Labor's New Millions* (New York: Modern Age Books, 1938). The amply covered speech by Labor Secretary Frances Perkins championed the NRA, endorsed plans for passing the Social Security Act, and highlighted government's responsibility to protect workers from unfair business practices ("Text of Secretary Perkins's Labor Day Speech," *NYT*, September 4, 1934, p. 2).
178. *NYT*, September 2, 1934, sec. 8, p. 1.
179. "Danger Seen," *NYT*, September 1, 1934, p. 1.
180. "'Coldest of Cold Blood,'" *Time* 24, 13 (September 24, 1934), 57.
181. "Mayor LaGuardia's Address," *NYT*, September 4, 1934, p. 10.
182. *NYT*'s Hartford correspondent, evidently a little unnerved, noted that if the organized Hartford mills shut down it would mean nearly 40,000 "thrown out of employment," including non-union workers in related industries ("Hartford Prepares for Strikes," *NYT*, September 1, 1934, p. 5). *HT* reported tensions as follows: "New England observed Labor day with perhaps the most important and far-reaching strike in its history menacing its great textile industry." The story prepared readers for "[d]anger of violence and disorder tomorrow, the first working day when the strike would be in effect" ("New England Strike Effects to be Discussed Tomorrow," *HT*, September 3, 1934, p. 17).
183. For more on the 1934 textile strikes, see Samuel Yellen, *American Labor Struggles* (New York: Harcourt, Brace and Company, 1936), pp. 292–320; and Jeremy Brecher, *Strike!* (Boston: South End Press, 1973), pp. 150–79. Brecher (p. 174) gives a brief account of troubles in Connecticut. For a full sense of the strike's impact in Hartford, I have relied on daily accounts in *HT* and *HC*. See also Janick, *A Diverse People: Connecticut*, pp. 50–1.
184. "Labor Revives Parade Event; 8,000 in March / Unioned Workers Tread City Streets for First Time in Years," *HT*, September 3, 1934 (final edition only), p. 1.
185. *HT* described the parade as highlighted by "floats, costumes and uniforms. . . . One of the brightest features of the line was two floats. . . . The first carried a huge open book before which stood a man, ostensibly writing on the page, and the truck bore the legend 'Labor Laws.'" The other float bore a sign urging theatre managers to employ only union members and conveyed six "pretty girls in brilliant costumes" ("Labor Revives Parade," p. 1).
186. Rukeyser, "Cats and Cock," *Theory of Flight*, p. 81.
187. Howard Fast, "The Poet in Philadelphia," *Looking Forward*, ed. Alexander Trachtenberg (New York: International Publishers, 1954), p. 83.

188. Taggard, *Collected Poems, 1918–1938*, pp. 57, 52.
189. Jospehine Miles, "Local Habitation," *P* 44, 6 (September 1934), 304.
190. Patchen, *Before the Brave*, p. 68.
191. Cowley, *Golden Mountains*, p. 247.
192. "The Midwest John Reed Club" [a summary of the regional conference held at Chicago, August 5–7, 1933], *Left Front* 1, 2 (September–October 1933), 11.
193. Norman Macleod, "Communist Day Song," *Left Front* (September–October 1933), 3.
194. C. Day Lewis, "The Magnetic Mountain," *Collected Poems of C. Day Lewis* (London: Jonathan Cape/Hogarth Press, 1954), p. 81.
195. Charles I. Glicksberg, "Symbolism in Proletarian Poetry," *Prairie Schooner* 17, 3 (September 1943), 186.
196. J. Hillis Miller, *Poets of Reality: Six Twentieth-Century Writers* (Cambridge: Harvard Univ. Press, 1965), p. 252.
197. Ibid.
198. HG, "One Writer's Position," 20.
199. For more on the symbolism of the NRA eagle, see Schlesinger, *Coming of the New Deal*, pp. 114–15.
200. According to the September 1933 issue of *HA*, from that point The Hartford bore the NRA Member eagle seal, printed with "We Do Our Part."
201. Quoted by Schlesinger, *Coming of the New Deal*, p. 114.
202. Josephson, *Infidel*, p. 263.
203. Quoted in George Wolfskill and John A. Hudson, *All But the People: Franklin D. Roosevelt and his Critics, 1933–39* (London: Macmillan, 1969), p. 150. The communists called it "a blue buzzard for the workers" (quoted in Cowley, *Golden Mountains*, p. 209).
204. MZ to Harriet Monroe, January 2, 193[5] (RLC, PMP12-35, b28, f16).
205. WCW was here criticizing RLL, publisher of *Ideas of Order*, for including the poem in that book (WCW to RLL, August 19, 1935 [RLC, RLL Papers, f21]).
206. SB, "Wallace Stevens and the Statue," *Sewanee Review* 69 (1961), 363.
207. Arthur Powell to Hi Simons, April 8, 1940 (RLC, Simons Papers).
208. Milton Bates, introduction to *Sur Plusieurs Beaux Sujects*, p. 7.
209. Isidor Schneider, "Now," *The Temptation of Anthony* (New York: Boni & Liveright, 1928), p. 76.
210. Franklin Folsom, "These Days," *P* 44, 1 (April–September 1934), 8; this part of the poem is titled "Exploration."
211. Gold, "Wilder: Prophet of the Genteel Christ," *NR* 64, 829 (October 22, 1930), 266. For an account of the controversy this stirred, see *Years of Protest: A Collection of American Writings in the 1930's*, eds. Jack Salzman and Barry Wallenstein (New York: Pegasus, 1967), p. 233; and Aaron, *Writers on the Left*, pp. 241–3.
212. Isidor Schneider, "To the Museums," in *PLUS*, p. 191.
213. Rosenfeld, "Bread Lines and a Museum," *N* 132, 3423 (February 11, 1931), 160–3.
214. Ezra Pound, *Personae: Collected Shorter Poems* (New York: New Directions, 1971), pp. 96–7.

215. League of Professional Groups for Foster and Ford, *Culture and the Crisis*, p. 17; emphasis added.

216. This was Geoffrey Grigson's recollection of his published 1936 view (in *The Private Art: A Poetry Notebook* [London: Allison and Busby, 1982], p. 138). For more on Grigson's disparaging figure, see Chapter 6, Section 3.

217. WM, "Season for Action," *Alcestis Quarterly* 1, 4 (July 1935), [27].

218. WCW's "metal rose," eschewing the beautiful rose of traditional lyric practice ("The rose is obsolete"), may be found in *Spring and All* (1923; reprinted in *Imaginations* [New York: New Directions, 1970], p. 107).

219. Sol Funaroff, "What the Thunder Said: A Fire Sermon," first published in *NM* of August 1932, reprinted in *Social Poetry of the 1930s*, pp. 63–6.

220. Sol Funaroff, "American Worker," *The Left* 1, 2 (Summer/Autumn 1931), 82.

221. Jackson Lears, *No Place of Grace: Antimodernism and the Transformation of American Culture, 1880–1920* (New York: Pantheon, 1981). There was a degree to which the young Stevens was influenced by such conservative "antimodernism"; see AF, "Wallace Stevens and the Strength of the Harvard Reaction," *New England Quarterly* 58 (March 1985), 27–45.

222. Stephen Spender, *Forward from Liberalism* (London: Victor Gollancz, 1937), p. 36. In making his case against Marxists' critique of modernism, somewhat influenced by the Frankfurt School, Perry Anderson has described how "the energies and attractions of a new machine age were a powerful imaginative stimulus," noting Parisian cubism, Italian futurism, and Russian constructivism as each reflecting this attraction. "In no case," Anderson argues, "was capitalism as such ever exalted by any brand of 'modernism'" ("Modernity and Revolution," *New Left Review* 144 [March–April 1984], 105).

223. Rukeyser, "The Gyroscope," *Theory of Flight*, p. 35.

224. HG, "Dempsey, Dempsey," in *Poems 1930–1940* (New York: Harcourt, 1941), p. 21; first collected in 1930 and reprinted in *PLUS*, p. 161. See Nelson, *Repression and Recovery*, p. 153.

225. SB, "I, Jim Rogers," *NM*, March 12, 1935, 19–20; reprinted in *PLUS*, pp. 149–52.

226. "Industry Out To Wage War On New Deal," p. 1. The anti–New Deal counterattack coincided with the founding of the American Liberty League (1934–6).

227. The language of the provision included this: "[E]mployees shall have the right to organize and bargain collectively through representatives of their own choosing, and shall be free from the interference, restraint or coercion of employers" (quoted in Brecher, *Strike!*, p. 149).

228. The case received more attention, surely, for that fact that, "as the year 1934 drew to a close," it coincided with a general sense among *supporters* of the NRA "in business circles" that "priority now must be given to limiting or rolling back the power of a threatening, unpredictable, and potentially dangerous state bureaucracy" (Hawley, "The New Deal and Business," p. 65). On the disposition of the new Congress, see Irving Bernstein's *Turbulent Years: A History of the American Worker, 1933–1941* (Boston: Houghton Mifflin, 1970), pp. 322–3.

229. A plant in Buffalo had refused to comply with the collective bargaining

provision of the NRA; the government sued the company, setting up the first court test of the provision. Trade associations lined up with the Houde employers, and both sides acknowledged that the case was "the most important one on collective bargaining" to that point ("Houde Plant Sued," *NYT*, December 1, 1934, p. 1; "Houde to Court," *Time* 24, 24 [December 10, 1934], 14). For my sense of section 7a as integral to New Deal liberalism, I have relied on Stanley Vittoz, *New Deal Labor Policy and the American Industrial Economy* (Chapel Hill: Univ. of North Carolina Press, 1987), pp. 137–52. NRA Night in Hartford: it had taken place on Tuesday evening, September 19, 1933 (Weaver, *Hartford: An Illustrated History*, p. 122).

230. The number of charters issued by national and international unions, which had increased during 1933 and 1934, declined sharply in 1935. Between August 1934 and August 1935, 634 unions were disbanded in various ways (Vittoz, *New Deal Labor Policy*, p. 141).

231. Schlesinger, *Coming of the New Deal*, pp. 148, 147.

232. "Houde to Court," 12.

233. Winters, "Postcard," *Years of Protest*, p. 244.

234. Walton, "Portrait of an Old Man," *P* 36, 1 (April 1930), 30.

235. Walton, "Enigma," *P* 27, 3 (December 1925), 144.

236. Schneider, "Portrait of a False Revolutionist," *Dynamo* 1, 3 (Summer 1934), 12.

237. See "America – 1919," *P* 17, 1 (October 1920), 24–9.

238. A typescript of the poem is at RLC (PMP12–35, b21, f29).

Chapter 3: What Superb Mechanics

1. RLL to WM, undated [late 1934] (JHB, WM Papers).

2. Pound to Tyler, April 24, [1933?] (JHB, Tyler Papers).

3. Alfred McIntyre, "Birth Control for Books," *Publishers' Weekly* 120 (December 26, 1931), 2711–13. See the chapter "Depression and Celebration" in *One Hundred and Fifty Years of Publishing: Little, Brown and Company, 1837, 1987* (Boston: Little, Brown & Company, 1987), pp. 84–96, especially 84–5.

4. Among them Louis Untermeyer's *First Words Before Spring* (1933), Witter Bynner's *Against the Cold* (1933), Sara Teasdale's *A Country House* (1932), and Leonie Adams's *This Measure* (1933).

5. Knopf did publish his "Borzoi Chapbooks," for instance Frost's *The Lone Striker* (1933), a single poem of three pages, produced in an arrangement with the Plimpton Press.

6. John Crowe Ransom, "The Poets Go Along," *Portrait of a Publisher, 1915/1965*, vol. 2 (New York: The Typophiles, 1965), pp. 228, 230.

7. *One Hundred and Fifty Years of Publishing*, p. 85.

8. "Title Output Shows Sharp Drop," *Publishers' Weekly*, January 21, 1933, 191; Edward Weeks, "Hard Times and the Author," *Atlantic Monthly* 155 (May 1935), 551–62; see especially p. 555; "American Book Production, 1932," *Publishers' Weekly*, January 21, 1933, 192. The brief portrait of Knopf in the depression has been informed variously by Geoffrey T. Hellman, "Publisher," in three parts, *New Yorker*, November 20, November 27, December 4, 1948,

44–7, 36–52, 40–53; see, e.g., November 27, 37–9, December 4, 40–1; Alfred Knopf, "Book Publishing: The Changes I've Seen," *Atlantic* 200, 6 (December 1957), 155–6, 160. I am also grateful for information shared by Peter Prescott, author of a forthcoming biography of Knopf.

9. Quoted in Leonard Greenbaum, *The Hound & Horn: The History of a Literary Quarterly* (The Hague: Mouton, 1966), pp. 49–50.

10. Even at the bottom of the depression in 1933, three new small presses emerged and flourished: House of Books, The Cassowary Press, and Writers' Editions (the last founded by WS's friend, Alice Corbin Henderson in Santa Fe).

11. RLL to S. Foster Damon, October 10, 1935 (JHB, Damon Papers, b14, uncatalogued f marked "L").

12. Ruth Lechlitner to WM, September 4, 1937 (HRC, WM Papers).

13. WM to George Marion O'Donnell, January 4, 1938 (WUL, O'Donnell Papers).

14. Tate to Ashley Brown, July 19, 1977 (Ashley Brown).

15. W. Rothenstein to RLL, November 28, 1934 (RLC, RLL Papers).

16. RLL to WM, undated [early 1935?], undated [late January 1935] (HRC, WM Papers); WM to RLL, February 1, 1935 (RLC, RLL Papers). He attended the Albany Business School (Madeleine Leippert Hall, interview with AF, March 27, 1989).

17. According to the records of Our Lady of Angels Parish, in Albany, New York, James Leippert was received into the Third Order (Secular) of St. Francis of Assisi, on February 10, 1935, by Father John Murnane (Germain Williams, OFM. Conv. to AF, November 6, 1989). By his profession RLL lived "in the world . . . but not of the world," wearing a habit consisting of scapular and cord in private which is easily hidden under everyday clothes (Father Conan Lynch, OFM.Conv. to AF, November 11, 1989). "Unfortunately," RLL wrote WM, "complete monastic retirement from the world is impossible at this time but at the end of the year when I make my Profession I hope to enter the monastic branch of the Third Order. . . . One leads . . . a monastic life especially as regards renunciation of worldly luxuries and vanities – chastity and continence . . . are enjoined" (RLL to WM, undated [late January 1935], [HRC, WM Papers]). To WM this was "dynamite news," understandably: "business school to monasteries!" (WM to RLL, February 5, 1935 [RLC, RLL Papers]).

18. WM to RLL, January 21, 1934, May 27, 1934, June 26, 1935 (RLC, RLL Papers); RLL to WM, undated [early May 1934]; undated [1934]; undated [late March 1935] (HRC, WM Papers).

19. WM to RLL, January 4, 1935 (RLC, RLL Papers).

20. To George Lensing, RLL is "the most enigmatic of those individuals who figure prominently in Stevens's career" (Lensing, *Poet's Growth*, p. 122).

21. RLL to WM, undated [April 1934] (HRC, WM Papers).

22. RLL to WM, undated [mid-May 1935] (HRC, WM Papers).

23. Lew Ney to Allen Tate, May 6, 1936 (WUL, O'Donnell Papers).

24. S. Foster Damon to WM, June 1, 1935 (HRC, WM Papers).

25. WM to RLL, January 4, 1935 (RLC, RLL Papers).

26. Robert Fitzgerald to WM, May 11, 1934 (HRC, WM Papers).

27. Martin Jay to Sherwood Anderson, November 21, 1933 (Newberry, Anderson Papers).
28. Bynner to Leippert, June 4, 1933 (RLC, RLL Papers); see *L* 270.
29. Basil Bunting to Leippert, September 26, 1932; and October 30, 1932 (RLC, RLL Papers); Ezra Pound to RLL, March 26, 1935 (RLC, RLL Papers).
30. Fanya Foss to Milton [Abernethy], July 2[5?], 1933 (HRC, Contempo Papers).
31. RLL to WM, undated [early 1935] (HRC, WM Papers). According to a Columbia classmate, the poet and journalist Gerard Previn Meyer (later a reviewer of WS's *Transport to Summer*), RLL justified the name "Latimer" "on the grounds that the Blessed Martyr, Bishop Hugh Latimer, who died at the stake in Oxford during the reign of 'Bloody Mary' with two others . . . had been an ancestor of his" (Meyer, "Immortality in a Footnote," *Journal of the Long Island Book Collectors* 3 [1975], 62). James G. Leippert despised his Germanic surname, and took "Lane" – from his uncle Frederick Lane, his mother's brother and his one-time benefactor – in order to sever himself from his father's family (Madeleine Leippert Hall, interview with AF, March 27, 1989; Charles A. Robertson to AF, June 18, 1987; Gerard Previn Meyer to AF, November 2, 1987).
32. WM to George Marion O'Donnell, April 29, 1935 (WUL, O'Donnell Papers).
33. Bishop to RLL, March 6, 1936 (RLC, RLL Papers). Peter Monro Jack went to the proper address for Alcestis and was told that "there was no such Press there" (Jack to Ruth Lechlitner, January 23, 1937 [Iowa, Lechlitner Papers]).
34. Benét to "Miss Lane," October 31, 1936; Alcestis Press to Benét, November 27, 1936 (RLC, RLL Papers); WM to Sara Bard Field, August 14, 1937 (HL, C.E.S. Wood Papers, WD 166[20]). On WS's intercession: WS to RLL, November 6, 1936 (RLC, RLL Papers).
35. The manuscript of *The Mediterranean* was in the hands of Alcestis editors in June 1935, if not still earlier (WM to RLL, June 29, 1935 [RLC, RLL Papers]); it was not until the following July that Tate was sent proofs. See also Tate to RLL, March 26, 1936 (RLC, RLL Papers).
36. Tate to WM, May 13, 1936 (HRC, WM Papers); emphasis added.
37. WS to RLL, May 22, 1936; August 29, 1936; September 3, 1936 (RLC, RLL Papers); Willard J. Colling to AF, April 20, 1988 and February 3, 1989; Madeleine Leippert Hall, interview with AF.
38. See AF, *Stevens and the Actual World*, pp. 203–5.
39. WM to RLL, June 23, 1935 (RLC, RLL Papers); Madeleine Leippert Hall, interview with AF; WM to O'Donnell, November 26, 1937 (WUL, O'Donnell Papers).
40. RLL to S. Foster Damon, March 9, 1936 (JHB, Damon Papers, b14, f uncatalogued marked "L"); verso of WS to RLL, May 10, 1937 (RLC, RLL Papers); verso of WS to RLL, November 2, 1937 (RLC, RLL Papers); verso of Stevens' letter dated January 26, 1938 (RLC, RLL Papers).
41. WS to WM, February 4, 1937 (HRC, Stevens Papers).
42. WS to WM, February 4, 1937 (HRC, WM Papers).
43. He mailed one letter he had received from Leippert to Witter Bynner, dated

April 4, 1933, which Bynner later sold to the Houghton Library along with his own materials. Here is the text of the letter WS retained, bearing a Columbia University return address (which Bynner had copied and, presumably, returned to WS):

> Dear Mr. Stevens: / The mss. reached me safely, many thanks. It is quite legible and needs no rewriting. Am expecting H.D.'s mss. any day now & shall then proceed with getting out the first numbers (yours, H.D.'s[,] Ezra Pound's, and Marianne Moore's) though they won't be *published* till early in September. However, I'll let you know how things are progressing. I'd thought of having your copy bound in orange crushed levant and shall do so unless you object to that colour. If I don't hear from you regarding it I shall take it for granted that that will be satisfactory. / Sincerely yours, James G. Leippert.

Bynner jotted this somewhat misleading commentary for archival posterity:

> Note: This man Leippert whom, I think, none of us had met, wrote a number of poets in 1933: Archibald MacLeish, Frances Frost and Elizabeth Madox Roberts besides those mentioned in Stevens's letter [that is, in the letter from Leippert to WS] and myself, asking us to send him manuscript copies of poems to be luxuriously printed in reproduction. I believe that all of us responded with labor and mss. for him – none of which came to publication or as far as we could find later to any other use. W.B.

(WS to Bynner, with enclosures [Houghton, WS Papers].)

44. RLL saved WS's originals, carting them with him from place to place, job to job, and eventually sold them to the University of Chicago (RLL to M. Llewellyn Raney, April 5, 1940 [RLC: RLL Papers]). Fortunately, RLL drafted some of his letters to WS on the reverse of WS's letters to him, and these are preserved in the RLL Papers at RLC. As for the possibility that RLL's letters were destroyed at The Hartford after WS's death, as all but a few of Gilbert Montague's almost certainly were, it seems quite remote. As I have suggested, Montague's would normally have been filed with business correspondence; RLL's, handwritten, often with a calligraphy pen – and sometimes in alternating black and red ink – could not possibly have been mistaken for business letters.
45. WS to RLL, September 8, 1936 (RLC, RLL Papers).
46. RLL to WM, undated [March 1935] (HRC, WM Papers).
47. WS to RLL, November 2, 1936; April 22, 1937; April 27, 1937; October 13, 1937; and Knopf to WS, April 26, 1937 (RLC, RLL Papers).
48. WS to WM, February 4, 1937 (HRC, WS Papers).
49. WM, John Wheelwright, David DeJong (a poet associated with the journal *Smoke*), and RLL prepared written rankings of contemporary poets: RLL to WM, undated [early May 1934] (HRC, WM Papers); WM to RLL, May 9, 1934 (RLC, RLL Papers); DeJong to RLL, May 2, 1934 (RLC, RLL Papers).
50. RLL to Bishop, April 4, 1935 (Princeton, Bishop Papers b21, f18).
51. Martin Jay to WM, undated (JHB, WM Papers). The latter poem was "The Woman Who Blamed Life on a Spaniard," the former "Snow and Stars."
52. RLL to Bishop, April 4, 1935 (Princeton, Bishop Papers b21, f18).

53. These poets were published in the fall 1932 issue (unnumbered) and volume 1, number 2 (undated) of the *Lion and Crown*. Pound to Leippert, November 20, 1932; Basil Bunting to Leippert, January 4, 1933 (RLC, RLL Papers).

54. RLL to WCW, undated [October or November 1932] (Beinecke, WCW Papers, Za Williams, Misc. f marked "L").

55. Of the all-WCW number, RLL wrote WCW: "I hope to make it a really great issue" (Leippert to WCW, August 30, 1932 [Beinecke, WCW Papers, Za Williams, f marked "Misc. 'L'"]); see also WCW to Leippert, November 30, 1932 (RLC, RLL Papers).

56. WCW to RLL, January 8, 1935 (RLC, RLL Papers).

57. According to James Laughlin's letter to RLL, October 14, 1936 (RLC, RLL Papers).

58. WCW to RLL, February 6, 1936 (RLC, RLL Papers): "I have enough material for another book among the notes of the long poem, Paterson, which it has been my ambition to finish for several years. . . . When you are ready for a third book, that is to say, ready to print it, I'll have the script in condition for you to see." No Alcestis *Paterson* was ever published.

59. James G. Leippert to Tate, February 9, 1933; and March 18, 1933 (Princeton, Tate Papers b9, f25).

60. James G. J. Leippert to Fletcher, April 27, 1933; Macmillan Co. to Fletcher, June 5, 1933 (Arkansas, Fletcher Papers).

61. WS to Martin Jay, June 1, 1933 (RLC, RLL Papers). This is the earliest letter from WS to RLL extant. Moore's and Witter Bynner's submissions came at the same time (MM to J. Leippert, June 17, 1933 [Columbia, Frederick Coykendall Papers]; Bynner to Leippert, June 4, 1933 [RLC, RLL Papers]).

62. Leippert, now almost exclusively "Martin Jay," would co-edit the new magazine with Fanya Foss. Martin Jay to Milton Abernethy, undated (HRC, Contempo Papers); and Martin Jay to Sherwood Anderson, November 11, 1933 (Newberry, Anderson Papers). On *Flambeau*: Fanya Foss to Milton [Abernethy], July 2[5?], 1933 (HRC, Contempo Papers).

63. "I think you will like the issue," wrote RLL's associate Gerard Previn Meyer to John Gould Fletcher, "among the things to be in it are *five new poems by Wallace Stevens*, a new translation of LaForgue's HAMLET, and work by Erskine Caldwell, C[harles] E. Hudeburg, and Richard Thoma" (Meyer to Fletcher, August 17, 1933 [Arkansas, Fletcher Papers]). Three poems Fletcher had submitted were accepted, but they did not appear until the third number of *Alcestis* (Spring 1935). The earliest confirmation of RLL having all eight new WS poems, ones that would appear in the first *Alcestis*, is late March 1934: "Wallace Stevens," RLL informed WM of prospective contents for the first number of *Alcestis*, "two long [poems] (as fine as he's ever done) & 2 short. . . . I have four more Stevens but want to save them for a later issue" (RLL to WM, undated [late March or early April 1934] [HRC, WM Papers]).

64. Martin Jay to Sherwood Anderson, November 21, 1933 (Newberry, Anderson Papers). LeSueur had made O'Brien's "Roll of Honor" (*The Best Short Stories of 1932* [New York: Dodd, Mead, 1932], pp. 138–52, 285]).

65. RLL to WM, undated [mid-March 1934] (HRC, WM Papers); WM to RLL, March 20, 1934 (RLC, RLL Papers).

66. WM's poverty: Harriet Monroe to WM, December 18, 1932 and September 30, 1933 (HRC, WM Papers); WM to "Jannine" [?], December 10, 1937 [HRC, WM Papers, unidentified authors f]).

67. WM to RLL, March 27, 1934 (RLC, RLL Papers).

68. Enclosed with J. G. Leippert to [Milton] Abernethy, undated [1933]; Martin Jay to Abernethy, October 2, 1933 (HRC, Contempo Papers).

69. RLL to WM, undated [early March 1934] (HRC, WM Papers).

70. Enclosed with Martin Jay to Milton Abernethy, October 2, 1933 (HRC, Contempo Papers).

71. RLL to WM, undated [late March or early April 1934] (HRC, WM Papers); my dating of this important letter is determined by WM to RLL, March 27, 1934 (RLC, RLL Papers), to which RLL's letter is a direct reply.

72. WM to RLL, December 26, 1934 and March 5, 1935; H.D. to RLL, May 14, 1935 (RLC, RLL Papers); and RLL to WM, undated (JHB, WM Papers).

73. Basil Bunting to Leippert, September 26, 1932 (RLC, RLL Papers).

74. Pound to RLL, March 26, 1936 (RLC, RLL Papers): Pound took the offer seriously, declining, finally, because a "Collected Poems wd/ include too much inferior work."

75. Basil Bunting to Leippert, September 26, 1932 (RLC, RLL Papers).

76. Unpublished portion of WS to RLL, September 25, 1935 (RLC, RLL Papers).

77. RLL to WM, undated [internal evidence suggests early summer 1935] (JHB, WM Papers, f marked "Latimer, James R. L.").

78. The former published by Random House, the latter by International Publishers, both in 1935.

79. MM to RLL, October 3, 1935 (RLC, RLL Papers).

80. Ibid.

81. MM to RLL, October 7, 1935 (RLC, RLL Papers).

82. RLL to WM, undated [Spring 1934] (HRC, WM Papers); Madeleine Leippert Hall, interview with AF.

83. RLL to WM, undated [mid-May 1935] (HRC, WM Papers).

84. WM to RLL, June 23, 1935 (RLC, RLL Papers).

85. RLL to WM, undated [early summer 1935] (JHB, WM papers, f marked "Latimer, James R. L.").

86. WM to RLL, July 7, 1935 (RLC, RLL Papers).

87. RLL to Ruth Lechlitner, August 13, [1937] (Iowa, Lechlitner Papers); Lechlitner to WM, August 14, 1937 (HRC, WM Papers); and Paul Corey and Ruth Lechlitner to AF, June 27, 1987).

88. RLL, "And Three More," PR 4, 2 (January 1938), 63.

89. RLL's "Exhortation to My Brothers" begins: "Strong men, my brothers, the weak & crippled, / my brothers, also, who sit in the councils / through the hot nights and the cold nights / planning the day of justice & plenty.... / Be glad that the privilege is yours to awaken / the sleepers & yours to be the first in the battle / & yours the pain that will make you the stronger / to lift the gun & to lead the charge." One of the three poems is dated "August '37." There are a number of autograph corrections, and these are certainly in RLL's hand (RLC, RLL Papers).

90. Editor's statement, *Alcestis* 1, 1 (October 1934), [3].
91. WM to RLL, May 9, 1934 (RLC, RLL Papers).
92. WM to RLL, May 13, 1935 (RLC, RLL Papers).
93. WM to RLL, June 29, 1935 (RLC, RLL Papers).
94. RLL to S. Foster Damon, undated, postmarked October 19, 1936 (JHB, Damon Papers, b14, uncatalogued f marked "L").
95. WM to RLL, June 29, 1935; July 7, 1935 (RLC, RLL Papers).
96. Wheelwright to WM, undated (JHB, WM Papers).
97. E.g., WM to Lechlitner, November 24, 1935 (Iowa, Lechlitner Papers); here WM called Tate's and Bishop's work "Open Fascism and dull as hell."
98. "I agree absolutely with you," she wrote WM, "about Tate, Bishop, Warren, et al. Latimer's giving ear to these makes me hesitate to submit anything which I may have to him. Doesn't he know that that outfit is not only passe today – but absolutely bad-smelling even in conservative camps?" (Ruth Lechlitner to WM, November 26, 1935 [HRC, WM Papers]); also Lechlitner to WM, July 7, 1937 (HRC, WM Papers).
99. This was openly discussed (WM to RLL, July 16, 1935 [RLC, RLL Papers]). On Deutsch's literary politics, see "Meaning and Being," *P* 52, 3 (June 1938), 153–6: Poets "diverted by the noises of a panic-stricken crowd below" produced work that "employ[s] the facile vulgar style . . . [that] mak[es] an effort . . . at public speaking."
100. Ney to Tate, copy retyped by Tate for O'Donnell, May 6, 1936 (WUL, O'Donnell Papers); Tate to WM, May 6, 1936 (HRC, WM Papers); Tate to H. T. Stuart, with pencil notations in RLL's hand, July 7, 1935 (RLC, RLL Papers).
101. The book was published in August 1935. "Really *mon ami*," RLL wrote WM, "if all the left-wing writers were as charming as you, I'd publish none else" (undated [September 1935] [JHB, WM Papers]).
102. WM to Wheelwright, December 29, 1934 (JHB, Wheelwright Papers, b8, f23).
103. Damon to WM, October 31, 1934 (HRC, WM Papers).
104. WM to "Editor of Alcestis," November 1934 (RLC, RLL Papers).
105. WM to RLL, November 25, 1934 (RLC, RLL Papers).
106. WM to RLL, December 15, 1934 (RLC, RLL Papers).
107. In early 1937 WM was still calling WS's new work "wholly delightful" and "brilliant" ("A Crisis in Language," *NYHTB*, February 7, 1937, 14).
108. WS's first glimpse at WM's *Fire Testament* elicited a response of "Delightful," to which WM replied: "hot dickity-dog" (WM to RLL, June 29, 1935). Earlier WM's "Valediction at Repose" had appeared with WS's "Botanist On Alp" and "Hieroglyphica" in Kerker Quinn's *Direction* (Autumn 1934), 46, 12–13.
109. A now-lost letter from WS to WM is quoted by WM in WM to O'Donnell, January 20, 1937 (WUL, O'Donnell Papers). WM's application essay is filed with the WM Papers at HRC. See also *L* 319.
110. The letter has been lost; I quote WM quoting WS in a letter to Lechlitner (December 1, 1935 [Iowa, Lechlitner Papers]).
111. WS to RLL, August 11, 1937 (RLC, RLL Papers).

112. WM to RLL, July 7, 1935 (RLC, RLL papers): "I can just hear [John Gould] Fletcher and O'Donnell screaming."

113. Portions from NR and N reviews of WM's *Fire Testament* quoted from proofs of the Alcestis brochure (filed with other press prospectuses in the WM papers at JHB). The first was Philip Blair Rice's ("Affirmation," N 142, 3679 [January 8, 1936], 53) and the second Kerker Quinn's (untitled, NR 85, 1094 [November 20, 1935], 55). Quinn had actually written: "Every poem in 'Fire Testament' is alive, healthily created, more color-strewn than any verse since the Imagists, suggestive of Wallace Stevens' serenity (*without his wit*) and of W. C. Williams' gusto (without his concreteness)."

114. WM to RLL, May 13, 1935 (RLC, RLL Papers); emphasis added.

115. WM to Wheelwright, February 12, 1935 (JHB, Wheelwright Papers, b9, f3).

116. Harold Rosenberg to WM, December 28, 1934 (JHB, WM Papers).

117. Muriel Rukeyser, "Child and Mother," *Alcestis: A Poetry Quarterly* 1, 4 (July 1935), n.p.; reprinted in *The Collected Poems* (New York: McGraw-Hill, 1978), p. 52.

118. Ruth Lechlitner to WM, January 24, 1936 (HRC, WM Papers).

119. WCW to RLL, November 26, 1934; April 16, 1935; and December 28, 1935 (RLC, RLL Papers).

120. When RLL was "sending a copy of Tate to New Masses" it was because he wanted "to see what they do to it" (WM to Lechlitner, undated [late 1935] [Iowa, Lechlitner Papers]).

121. WM to RLL, July 7 and 8, 1935 (RLC, RLL Papers).

122. AF and Teres, "Interview with Stanley Burnshaw," 111.

123. WS to RLL, January 26, 1938 (RLC, RLL Papers).

124. WS to RLL, December 23, 1937 (RLC, RLL Papers).

125. RLL to WM, undated [March 1934] (HRC, WM Papers). The letter has been dated from information it contains that corresponds with the contributor's note in P 43, 6 (March 1934), 355.

126. WM to RLL, July 7, 1935 (RLC, RLL Papers).

127. Lechlitner to WM, January 24, 1936 (HRC, WM Papers). Lechlitner was responding to various questions WM posed her about the party line on certain poets and issues.

128. Lechlitner to WM, October 15, [1936] (HRC, WM Papers).

129. John Wheelwright to WM, undated (HRC, WM Papers).

130. WS to RLL, November 10, 1936 (RLC, RLL Papers).

131. James Laughlin to RLL, October 13, 1937 (RLC, RLL Papers). In response to Laughlin's complaint, RLL made gifts of WS's *Ideas of Order*, and the Warren, Bishop and Tate books (acknowledged in Laughlin to RLL, October 10, 1937 [RLC, RLL Papers]).

132. Laughlin to RLL, October 19, 1937 (RLC, RLL Papers); emphasis added.

133. WM to O'Donnell, July 6, 1937 (WUL, O'Donnell Papers).

134. Mariani, *A New World Naked*, p. 377; he cites, as one of his sources for this paraphrase of WCW's position, a letter to RLL, November 22, 1935 (RLC, RLL Papers). Mariani also refers to WCW's review of H. H. Lewis (written July 1936; published in NM in November 1937).

135. WCW to RLL, November 22, 1935 (RLC, RLL Papers).

136. Mariani, *A New World Naked*, p. 382.
137. The word is Mariani's (*A New World Naked*, p. 369).
138. WM to RLL, July 7, 1935 (RLC, RLL Papers); emphasis added.
139. MZ to WM summarized in WM to MZ, November 30, 1935 (RLC, MZ Papers, b2, f15).
140. SB to AK, August 28, 1935 (Virginia, AK Papers).
141. Henry Hart, *A Relevant Memoir: The Story of the Equinox Cooperative Press* (New York: Three Mountains Press, 1977); the description of Schneider's book appears on p. 66.
142. *NM* 14, 4 (January 22, 1935), 23. The book included pieces by Michael Gold, Earl Browder, Corliss Lamont, Langston Hughes, and Joseph North.
143. "Call for an American Writers Congress," *NM* 14, 4 (January 22, 1935), 20.
144. Lechlitner to WM, January 24, 1936 (HRC, WM Papers).
145. In fact, WM scoffed at the sectarian notion of "Artists in Uniform" (WM to RLL, June 24, 1935 [RLC, RLL Papers]).
146. Lincoln Steffens to Louis Birk, February 19, 1936 (ALS, Hicks Papers).
147. T. S. Eliot, "Introduction," *Selected Poems of Marianne Moore* (New York: Macmillan, 1935), p. vii.
148. Orrick Johns, "Marianne Moore and Eliot," *NM* 15, 10 (June 4, 1935), 24.
149. Tate to RLL, December 4, 1935 (RLC, RLL Papers).
150. Morse to MZ, January 15, 1937 (RLC, RLL Papers).
151. S. Foster Damon to WM, August 25, 1935 (HRC, WM Papers). Nor did reviewer Peter Monro Jack (Jack to Ruth Lechtliner, January 23, 1937 [Iowa, Lechlitner Papers]).
152. RLL to Damon, October 10, 1935 (JHB, Damon papers, b14, f uncatalogued marked "L").
153. RLL describing himself in a letter to WM, undated [early 1935?] (JHB, WM Papers).
154. WS to RLL, January 26, 1938 (RLC, RLL Papers).
155. "One neither writes nor publishes poetry with the idea of buying a new bassoon out of the proceeds," he once wrote (WS to RLL, March 18, 1936 [RLC, RLL Papers]).
156. WCW to RLL, May 1, 1936 (RLC, RLL Papers).
157. See, e.g., WS to RLL, August 29 and September 3, 1936 (RLC, RLL Papers).
158. These papers are recent acquisitions at Iowa.
159. Lechlitner to WM, July 25, 1937 (Iowa, Lechlitner Papers).
160. Lechlitner, *Tomorrow's Phoenix*, p. 3.
161. WS to RLL, August 11, 1937 (RLC, RLL Papers).
162. Jerome J. McGann, *Social Values and Poetic Acts: The Historical Judgment of Literary Work* (Cambridge: Harvard Univ. Press, 1988), p. 73.
163. WS to RLL, May 27, 1935 (RLC, RLL Papers).
164. Ibid.
165. WM to RLL, July 7, 1935 (RLC, RLL Papers).
166. Page proofs of *Ideas of Order* are in the WM Papers at JHB.
167. WM to RLL, July 16, 1935 (RLC, RLL Papers).
168. Hale Anderson, Jr., recalled for Brazeau WS's unusual and elaborate process of handling the huge accumulation of claims files (*WSR* 22), referred to

generally at The Hartford as WS's "freight-yard method" (according to Richard Sunbury, *WSR* 38). See also *WSR* 33.

169. WS to RLL, October 11, 1935 (RLC, RLL Papers).
170. WCW to RLL, July 20, 1935 (RLC, RLL Papers).
171. RLL to WCW, October 21, 1937 (Beinecke, WCW Papers).
172. RLL to WCW, January 20, 1938 (Buffalo, WCW Papers).
173. A typescript draft of "Guitar Blues" (Buffalo, WCW Papers, A2776).
174. Three distinct, typewritten versions, with typewritten deletions and holograph revisions, totalling nine leaves, are in the collection of the Houghton (MS Am1956 *47M-351 [2]).
175. WCW, "Poets' Corner," *NR* 93 (November 17, 1937), 50.

Chapter 4: The Rage for Order

1. Bishop to Anne Ford, dated January 8 and 20, 1964, and October 27, 1964 (WUL, Anne Ford Papers).
2. Johns, "Moore and Eliot," 24-5.
3. Quoted in Lensing, *Poet's Growth*, p. 169.
4. O'Connor, *The Shaping Spirit: A Study of Wallace Stevens* [Chicago: Henry Regnery, 1950), p. 45. The clearest readings of this incident are provided by Albert Gelpi, "Stevens and Williams: The Epistemology of Modernism," in *Wallace Stevens: The Poetics of Modernism*, ed. Gelpi (Cambridge: Cambridge Univ. Press, 1985), pp. 3-23, especially 10-15; A. Walton Litz, "Wallace Stevens' Defense of Poetry: *La poésie pure*, the New Romantic, and the Pressure of Reality," in *Romantic and Modern: Revaluations of Literary Tradition*, ed. George Bornstein (Pittsburgh: University of Pittsburgh Press, 1977), pp. 111-32, especially 125; and George Bornstein, *Transformations of Romanticism in Yeats, Eliot, and Stevens* (Chicago: Univ. of Chicago Press, 1976), especially pp. 163-80. Bornstein helpfully emphasizes WS's contradictions: "Stevens openly called for a new romanticism that in practice sometimes subverted the old" (p. 163).
5. The assumption here observes Gelpi's idea that "[t]he problem with WS' description of the romantic as idealistic solipsist in a shabby, commercialized society is that it befits him more than Williams" ("Stevens and Williams," p. 10).
6. The press was Rakosi's; Zukofsky had urged WCW to do the collection and oversaw the typescript; Oppen has been identified as "the angel" behind the venture; all three young poets were in regular contact with WCW when WCW received WS's introduction in early December 1933. See Mariani, *A New World Naked*, p. 339. Bruce Ahearn, working with the Zukofsky-Pound correspondence, deduces a missing letter "in late September or very early October" proposing a "Writers Extant" series to include a volume by WCW "with a preface by Wallace Stevens" (*Pound/Zukofsky: Selected Letters of Ezra Pound and Louis Zukofsky* [New York: New Directions, 1987], p. 154).
7. Patchen, *Before the Brave*, p. 17.
8. William Phillips and Philip Rahv, "Literature in a Political Decade," *New Letters in America* 1 (1937), 172-3.
9. Joseph Freeman, "Preface [to the poetry section]," *PLUS*, p. 145.

10. Harry Roskolenko, *Sequence on Violence* (New York: Signal Publishers, 1938), p. 57; emphasis added. By 1937 Roskolenko was a dues-paying member of the Socialist Workers Party (ALS, Roskolenko Papers, b10, Socialist Workers Party f).

11. H. R. Hays, "Nothing But the Truth," *H&H* 7, 4 (July–September 1934), 737; a review of books by WCW, Reznikoff, and Oppen, all works issued by the Objectivist Press.

12. Zukofsky to Pound, October 29, 1933; *Pound/Zukofsky*, p. 185. Zukofsky's comment came as a rejoinder to Pound's assumption that Zukofsky felt this way: "Well, if you mean . . . that I believe . . . in the possibility of matter to think . . . – then you're probably right."

13. The politics of objectivism is an extremely vexed question, and it is not my intention here to do more than hint at the radical *perception*, such as Hays's, of the objectivists as themselves radicalized respondents to imagism's anti-rhetorical stripping. If "[t]he first principle of objectivism [was] that 'associational or sentimental value is false'" and the second was "that the objectivist poet must have 'earthy tastes,'" then the combination was surely a poetics palatable to the poetic left, just as L. S. Dembo has suggested (*Conceptions of Reality in Modern American Poetry* [Berkeley: University of California Press, 1966], p. 57); note, then, that in Dembo's formulation, WS's 1934 preface not only violated a "first principle," but threatened to divert WCW's aesthetic convergence with leftism. For a brief, basic introduction to the question of Zukofsky's alignment with thirties radicalism, see Nelson, *Repression and Recovery*, pp. 175–7. Oppen's has been amply documented. The clearest communist denunciation of objectivism as an inadequate nominalism and a "rootless esotericism" was offered by Morris U. Schappes in a review of *The "Objectivists" Anthology* ("Historic and Contemporary Particulars," *P* 41, 6 [March 1933], 340–3). My own sense of the relationship has been enhanced by reading Kenneth Fearing's informal but incisive unpublished letters to Rakosi (HRC, Rakosi Papers); typical is Fearing's remark, "What do you mean [by saying that I am] 'on the right side for the wrong reasons'? I resent this . . ." (undated [early 1933]). The alliance between objectivists and communists, never fully tested, relied finally on a fundamental agreement about a poetic quality described by SB: "Clarity . . . directness . . . – these are in the direction of affirmation: and as such, in the direction of revolutionary poetry wishing to be concretely effective. . . . If we achieve clarity and directness we create a literature interesting not primarily to intellectuals, sophisticates, and specialists but to masses" ("Notes on Revolutionary Poetry," 22). As will be clear shortly, however, SB was not here speaking of objectivism; his response to the objectivist number of *P* was quite negative.

14. SB, "The February Number," *P* 38, 1 (April 1931), 55. It was in 1932 that SB realized that he was "perversely becom[ing] more red than ever!" (SB to AK, November 4, 1932 [Virginia, AK Papers, #6561, b1]).

15. While seeing radical potential in the objectivists' obsession with "fact," Hays named WS's analysis of sentimentality in then suggesting that Reznikoff's work showed him "less successful [than WCW] in his struggle with sentimentality" ("Nothing But the Truth," 738).

16. Charles Henry Newman, "How Objective Is Objectivism?," *Dynamo* 1, 3 (Summer 1934), 26.

17. Michael Davidson, "Dismantling 'Mantis': Reification and Objectivist Poetics," *American Literary History* 3, 3 (Fall 1991), 521.

18. *Pound/Zukofsky*, pp. 184–5.

19. Carl Rakosi, "A Journey Away," *H&H* 5, 4 (July–September 1932), 603; reprinted in *The Collected Poems of Carl Rakosi* (Orono, Maine: National Poetry Foundation, 1986), p. 450.

20. George Oppen, "Bad times," *Discrete Series* (with a preface by Ezra Pound) (New York: The Objectivist Press, 1934), p. 32. For more, see Eleanor Berry, "The Williams-Oppen Connection," *Sagetrieb* 3, 2 (Fall 1984), 99–117.

21. "Simplex Sigilum Veri," *Collected Poems of Williams*, p. 399.

22. *Collected Poems of Williams*, vol. 1, p. 325.

23. The phrase is from the sixth poem in Zukofsky's *A* (1930). In the introduction to *An "Objectivists" Anthology*, Zukofsky quoted the phrase programmatically ("'Recencies' in Poetry," *An "Objectivists" Anthology* [Le Beausset, France: To Publishers, 1932], p. 10).

24. Charles Altieri has made these helpful distinctions between the objectivist and symbolist modes ("The Objectivist Tradition," *Chicago Review* 30 [Winter 1979], 68).

25. We know that the objectivists were reading and were surprisingly influenced by WS; the evidence has been gathered and clearly assessed by Alan Golding, in "The 'Community of Elements' in Wallace Stevens and Louis Zukofsky," in *The Poetics of Modernism*, pp. 121–40. One letter WS wrote Zukofsky, in 1948, is in the Zukofsky collection at HRC, and was mentioned by Zukofsky himself in his 1971 Wallace Stevens Memorial Lecture (and briefly quoted by Golding [p. 137 n. 3]).

26. The words are Celia Zukofsky's in "A Commemorative Evening for Louis Zukofsky," *American Poetry Review* 9 (January-February 1980), 26.

27. From this we know that WS continued to read Rakosi, at least until the early forties (see the unpublished letter at the end of this chapter).

28. For a study of WS's relationship to the orientalist strain in imagism, see Robert Buttel, *The Making of Harmonium* (Princeton: Princeton Univ. Press, 1967), especially pp. 64–8, 70, 73–4, 84–5.

29. This entails Altieri's useful definition of modernist rhetoric: "[T]he term [among modernists] referred to various forms of self-delusion, especially those caused by a willingness to interpret and judge experience without being aware of its full complexity. This blindness was attributed to many sources – to Romantic sentimentalism [and] to Romantic expressionism which made subjective feelings the criteria for the truth of an experience" ("Objective Image and Act of Mind in Modern Poetry," *PMLA* 91, 1 [1976], 101).

30. And to the extent that they were criticized for the reduction, radical poets could include them in the ill-defined but powerful leftist project of stripping poetic rhetoric and returning somehow to a poetry of immediacy and presence; this was helped along by Zukofsky's willingness to vindicate *An "Objectivists" Anthology* as "proceed[ing] . . . very closely along the lines of revolutionary thinking." "The revolutionary aim," he wrote, "cannot become

apparent except as it is cognizant of all the intellectual and physical topography of which it is a consequence" (letter published in *P*, dated March 3, 1933, quoted from typescript version at RLC, PMP12–35, b41, f14). Nonetheless, radical writers, such as Schappes and HG, attacked the objectivists as romantics. HG felt that they "will die for lack of oxygen if they ignore the panorama of strictly American life" (quoted by Zukofsky in a letter to Monroe, February 11, 1931 [RLC, PMP12–35, b41, f14]). "There must be trees (particulars)," wrote Morris Schappes in *P*, "but you must be able to discern a wood; . . . good art needs both the trees and the wood" ("Historic and Contemporary Particulars," 341).

31. On WS's involvement with imagism, see Buttel, *The Making of Harmonium*, pp. 125–47; and Golding, "Stevens and Louis Zukofsky," *The Poetics of Modernism*, p. 132.

32. Spire: "Look at this woman, those roughened hands, that wrinkled neck, / Yellowish straggles of hair, reddened skin, distended stomach! / – Then praise, if still you dare to praise, / Motherhood, Toil, and the Sun!"

33. Morris Schappes, "André Spire as Poet and Socialist," *P* 44, 6 (September 1934), 348.

34. Ruth Lechlitner, "The Poetry of William Carlos Williams," *P* 54, 6 (September 1939), 329; emphasis added.

35. *Collected Poems of Williams*, vol. 1, p. 371.

36. Oppen, *Discrete Series*, p. 16.

37. MM, "Things Others Never Notice," *P* 44 (May 1934), 104, 106.

38. KB, referring to the excessively inclusive "Our Revolutionary Heritage," a lecture by Granville Hicks (statement in the "What Is Americanism?" symposium, *PR*, 3, 3 [April 1936], 10).

39. Eda Lou Walton, "'Beauty of Storm Disproportionately,'" *P* 51, 4 (January 1938), 209. Further evidence of Walton's alliance with the literary radicals may be found here (212).

40. KB, "What Is Americanism?" 10.

41. "'Memory and Desire'" was a review of *The Dark Land* by Kathleen Tankersley Young (*P* 42, 1 [April 1933], 50–2). TCW also reviewed Pound's *Draft of XXX Cantos* for *SRL* (July 1, 1933) and placed three poems and an essay in the August 1933 and January 1934 issues respectively.

42. "Gallant Chateau," "Polo Ponies Practicing" and "Gray Stones and Gray Pigeons" in *Westminster Magazine* 23, 3 (Autumn 1934), 186–7.

43. If I may judge from TCW's exchanges with MM (at RML), WS (HL), WCW (Buffalo and Beinecke), WM (HRC), HG (ALS), and Harriet Monroe (RLC).

44. *Westminster* 24, 1 (Spring/Summer 1935); the number was issued with *Bozart* (9, 1) as *Bozart-Westminster*. Pound wrote the foreword to the American section (21–2) of the special issue, which was given the title, "An Anthology of modern English and American poetry." For more on TCW's plans for the anthology, see TCW to Roy Cowden, January 31, 1935 (Michigan, Hopwood Room Collection) and Robert England to MZ, December 15, 1934 (RLC, MZ Papers, b1, f27); and *The Letters of Ezra Pound*, ed. D. D. Paige (New York: Harcourt, Brace, 1950), p. 250.

45. TCW to MM, July 16, 1934 (RML, MM Papers, V:78:04).

46. MM, "Lot in Sodom," *Close Up* 10, 4 (December 1933), 92-5.
47. MM to TCW, July 20, 1934 (RML, MM Papers, V:78:04).
48. TCW to MM, October 1, 1934 (RML, MM Papers, V:78:04).
49. TCW to MM, September 6, 1934 (RML, MM Papers, V:78:04).
50. Marjorie Perloff, in "Pound/Stevens: Whose Era?" (*New Literary History* 13, 3 [Spring 1982]), quotes an "unnecessarily dismissive" letter Pound wrote WCW in 1955: "it wd/ be highly improper for me to have opinions of yr/ opinion of a bloke I haven't read" (quoted on 486).
51. Pound to Zukofsky, October 14, 1933; *Zukofsky/Pound*, p. 154.
52. Pound to Parker Tyler, dated "14 February/[anno] XI" [1933] and "19 March" [1933] (JHB, Tyler Papers).
53. TCW to MM, January 12, 1935 (RML, MM Papers, V:78:04). TCW had published McCraig's poetry in *Westminster.*
54. *Collected Poems of Williams*, vol. 1, p. 540.
55. I am quoting from the early version, published in *Galaxy: An Anthology* (1934).
56. TCW to MM, January 12, 1935 (RML, MM Papers, V:78:04).
57. Surely Pound's association with the left-leaning objectivists in this period contributed to TCW's misunderstanding. It was known among poetry circles that The Objectivist Press was considering a scheme for the publication of Pound's collected prose in many volumes; so too, Pound's *Profile: An Anthology Collected in 1931*, poems "which may possibly define their epoch," included four by WCW, one by Zukofsky, and two groups taken from the communist *NM.* See Mary Oppen, *Meaning a Life: An Autobiography* (Santa Barbara: Black Sparrow Press, 1978), pp. 132-6.
58. MM to MZ, January 29, 19[35] [misdated "1934"] (RLC, MZ Papers, b2, f22); emphasis added.
59. When accepting "Irrealistic Verses" for *P*, Monroe wrote "Reality + view are good" on Ross's typescript (RLC, PMP12-35, b20, f18).
60. It remained in WS's library and is now part of the collection at HL (RB#440394).
61. MM to WS, January 3, 1933 (HL, WS Papers, WAS 42).
62. [W. W. E. Ross], *Sonnets of ER* (Toronto: The Heaton Publishing Co., 1932), p. 49.
63. *Collected Poems of Williams*, vol. 1, p. 269; emphasis added.
64. This was the basis of WCW's somewhat willful misreading of Pound's XXX *Cantos* as objectivist, in his essay, "Excerpts from a Critical Sketch: The XXX Cantos of Ezra Pound," *Symposium* 2, 2 (April 1931), 257-63.
65. This is how a reviewer of *We Gather Strength* described the "despair" of Spector, Kalar, Rolfe and Funaroff: "These poets are no apostles of defeatism – despair is bitter but a challenge to revolt" (Herbert Klein, "Comrade Poets," *Left Front* 1, 2 [September–October 1933], 15).
66. While otherwise *supporting* radicals' negotiation with modernist forms, the editors of *The Left* wrote in 1931, "The LEFT calls the intellectual and artist from his blind bourgeois psychology, his pathological introspection, his defeatism and futile liberalism" ("Left!" 3).
67. As late as 1933 John Gould Fletcher wrote: "I agree . . . that a revivified

romanticism would be much better for the present day than the – to me – dead and musty classicism of the Eliot school, but I by no means agree that all the manifestations of bygone romanticism were necessarily bad" (Fletcher to Lewis Mumford, August 5, 1933 [Arkansas, Fletcher Papers]).

68. Bernard Bandler, "The Treason of an Intellectual," *H&H* 2, 2 (January–March 1929), 173.

69. *Humanism and America: Essays on the Outlook of Modern Civilization*, ed. Norman Foerster (New York: Farrar and Rinehart, [1930]), p. 227.

70. Donald Stanford, then at Harvard, in recalling that he "talked quite a bit with R. P. Blackmur about WS – this was the fall of '33," confirms that immediately after "Examples of Wallace Stevens" Blackmur continued to wrestle with his not entirely favorable response to WS's new work. "I thought a little more highly of Stevens than Blackmur [did] at that time," Stanford remembered (unpublished, untranscribed portion of Brazeau's interview with Donald Stanford [HL, HM 53682]).

71. They seem to have been inspired by WS's February 1934 trip to Key West. The movement from North to South, from spare to fecund, in "Winter Bells" is underscored by a postcard WS wrote his seven-year-old daughter from Key West in late February: "This Church [depicted on the card] is nearby and we go there on Sunday mornings when we are here. The rector comes from Vermont, I believe" (WS to Holly Stevens, February 24, 1932 [HL, WS Papers, WAS 2225]). "Gray Stones and Gray Pigeons" was sent to TCW for *Westminster Magazine* in summer 1934 (WS to TCW, July 19, 1934 [Beinecke, TCW Papers]).

72. Babbitt, "Humanism, an Essay at Definition," in *Humanism and America*, pp. 26, 28–9.

73. Ramon Fernandez, "On Classicism," *The Symposium* 1, 1 (January 1930), 43; emphasis added.

74. Ibid., 38, 37.

75. When introducing himself to WS by mail, Blackmur mentioned that he had noticed WS's name on the list of subscribers (Blackmur to WS, April 13, 1929; cited in Greenbaum, *The Hound & Horn*, p. 39). WS's interest may have originated in the fact that *H&H* seemed altogether a journal in the Harvard matrix – edited by Harvard men (save Blackmur himself, actually), handling work by Eliot, Henry Adams, Babbitt, Cummings, Henry James, Santayana, and initially subtitled, "A Harvard Miscellany" (Greenbaum, *The Hound & Horn*, p. 37).

76. "New Magazine Ready Soon," *NYT*, November 24, 1929, p. 4. The merger fell through, but the *Symposium* ran Ramon Fernandez as announced in its first issue. *H&H* editors considered Fernandez well suited to their journal, and continued to seek translations of his essays, such as "A Humanist's Theory of Value," which one of the editors told T. S. Eliot "would have been an excellent instance" of the reason why Eliot's *Criterion* and the *H&H* should collaborate (Greenbaum, *The Hound & Horn*, pp. 47–8). Joseph Riddel, in offering a somewhat different reading of Fernandez' impact on WS, quotes WS's dismissal of the connection – "I used two everyday names [Ramon and Fernandez]. And I might have expected, they turned out to be an actual

name" – and concludes: "If Fernandez is unknown to Stevens, then we are witness to the most astounding instance of critical telepathy in literature" (Riddel, *Clairvoyant Eye*, p. 117).

77. Blackmur's letter to Tate, dated October 5, 1929 (Princeton, Blackmur Papers) reveals some of the debate between these two men on how precisely humanism ought to be qualified. Tate, "The Fallacy of Humanism," *H&H* 3, 2 (January–March 1930), 234–57.

78. Tate, "Poetry in the Laboratory," *NR* 61, 785 (December 18, 1929), 111–13.

79. Blackmur to Tate, February 16, 1932 (Princeton, Tate Papers, b12, f6).

80. John Crowe Ransom to Allen Tate, undated [1933] (Princeton, Tate Papers).

81. Blackmur to Tate, May 4, 1934 (Princeton, Tate Papers, b12, f6). Later Tate and Blackmur were mostly congenial colleagues in the Creative Writing Program at Princeton.

82. Blackmur to Cowley, April 27, 1934 (quoted by Aaron, *Writers on the Left*, p. 257). For more on Blackmur's approach to – or at least acceptance by – the poetic left, see HG, "Prologue as Epilogue," *P* 48, 2 (May 1936), 95.

83. F. W. Dupee to HG, April 14 [1937?] (ALS, HG Papers).

84. Blackmur to WS, November 11, 1931 (HL, WS Papers, WAS 200).

85. This letter, housed with the Blackmur Papers at Princeton (b8, f9), was not included in *L*. With it, WS sent "Autumn Refrain," though he does not say that the poem, "a scrap written a few weeks ago," had any relation to Blackmur's or his own ideas about ambiguity "as essential to poetry."

86. WCW, "The New Poetical Economy," *P* 44, 4 (July 1934), 223.

87. Rakosi, "William Carlos Williams," *Symposium* 4, 4 (October 1933), 439.

88. Robert von Hallberg, "The Politics of Description: W. C. Williams in the 'Thirties," *ELH* 45, 1 (Spring 1978), 142.

89. Blackmur to WS, December 2, 1931 (HL, WS Papers, WAS 201).

90. F. R. Leavis, "Dr. Richards, Bentham and Coleridge," *Scrutiny* 3, 4 (March 1935), 382–402; on experimental submission, see 399.

91. R. P. Blackmur, "Examples of Wallace Stevens" *H&H* 5, 2 (January–March 1932), 225; emphasis added.

92. Richards, *Principles of Literary Criticism* (London: Kegan Paul, Trench, Trubner, 1930; reprint New York: Harcourt Brace Jovanovich, 1985), p. 248. For more on inclusivity in Blackmur's sense of WS, see Melita Schaum, *Wallace Stevens and the Critical Schools* (Tuscaloosa: Univ. of Alabama Press, 1988), p. 69.

93. Denis Donoghue, *Ferocious Alphabets* (Boston: Little, Brown, 1981), p. 57.

94. Blackmur, "Examples," 226; emphasis added.

95. Ibid., 223.

96. Ibid., 230.

97. Ibid., 223.

98. Ibid., 223–4.

99. B. J. Leggett, working with the same materials, reads Richards's impact on later poems, in particular "Notes toward a Supreme Fiction"; some internal evidence suggests that Leggett is right to conclude that WS reread *Coleridge on Imagination* in preparation for writing "The Noble Rider and the Sound of Words" in 1941 and "Notes" in 1942. I have no doubt that WS's first reading came soon after the book appeared in 1934. See Leggett, *Wallace*

Stevens and Poetic Theory: Conceiving the Supreme Fiction (Chapel Hill: Univ. of North Carolina Press, 1987), pp. 17–41.

100. On "rightness," see Richards, *Principles*, p. 28.

101. Richards, *Coleridge on Imagination*, p. 125.

102. For a clear example of Richards's use of this term, see *Principles*, pp. 248–9.

103. Richards, *Coleridge on Imagination*, p. 128; emphasis added.

104. "Of an aesthetic tough, diverse, untamed / Incredible to prudes, the mint of dirt, / Green barbarism turning paradigm."

105. Simons to WS, July 5, 1941 (RLC, Hi Simons Papers). In a long letter to WS "concerning your 'system,'" Heringman told WS of his conclusion that "green *is* the synthesis of blue and gold. . . . Also, red, green's opposite, becomes 'red emptiness'" (Heringman to WS, May 3, 1949 [HL, WS Papers, WAS 865]).

106. See Frank Lentricchia, *After the New Criticism* (Chicago: Univ. of Chicago Press, 1980), p. 251.

107. Richards, *Coleridge on Imagination*, p. 77.

108. The poem has received virtually no critical attention, exceptions being Litz, *Introspective Voyager*, pp. 179–80; and Doggett, *Making of the Poem*, p. 4. Donoghue found this sort of WS poem "charming" but imbued with "a 'complacency of sense'"; he passingly mentioned "the jaunty rhythms" of "Table Talk" as displaying this manner "at its most provincial" ("Wallace Stevens and the Abstract," *Studies: An Irish Quarterly Review* 49 [Winter 1960], 390).

109. A typescript is at HL.

110. Richards, *Coleridge on Imagination*, pp. 198–9.

111. Richards, *Principles*, p. 88.

112. Ibid., p. 89.

113. Richards, *Coleridge on Imagination*, p. 157.

114. Richards, *Principles*, p. 120.

115. Ibid., p. 25.

116. William W. Herrick to WS, blood and urine test report enclosed, January 2, 1935 (HL, WS Papers, WAS 895). Dr. Herrick proposed a rigid diet of regular "fast days" consisting of plain milk for twenty-four hours and "nothing else," and another of one cup of coffee in morning with milk, broth and a piece of toast for lunch, afternoon tea with milk, and a dinner plate of thin soup; and final fast day entailed four bananas and a quart of skimmed milk. I am grateful to Dr. Kurt Albertine, Univeristy of Utah Medical School, for evaluating WS's blood test and urinalysis reports; Albertine notes that in addition to the toll obesity was taking on WS's cardiovascular system, there was a strong chance WS would develop a diabetic condition (his urine contained acetone and diacetic acid).

117. WS's letters to Philip May, written during and immediately after this trip (Houghton, bMS Am 1543), and May's later recollections, passed on to his son, Philip, Jr. (interview with AF, May 23, 1987), suggest that it was indeed a culinary debauch (the "green cocoanut ice cream" mentioned in *L* 274 being the least sign of it) — so much of a debauch, in fact, that when planning the 1936 trip, WS wrote May a series of elaborate descriptions of his diet, insisting that while in Florida he would "have to be rather fussy about

the diet." He planned then to keep his weekly "fast day." "The trouble is, Phil," he added, "that every time I go down to Florida, . . . I . . . always return feeling pretty much like a flagellant" (WS to May, January 27, 1936 [Houghton]).

118. "Man is not in any sense primarily an intelligence; he is a system of interests" (Richards, *Science and Poetry* [London: Trubner & Co., 1926], p. 21).

119. Richards, *Principles*, p. 47.

120. Hartman, "I. A. Richards and the Dream of Communication," in *The Fate of Reading and Other Essays* (Chicago: Univ. of Chicago Press, 1975), p. 22; emphasis added.

121. The point is made in *Principles* in the chapter entitled "The Normality of the Artist" (especially pp. 190, 194, 195).

122. KB, making this criticism, gives it a firm Marxist twist: if Richards is "'projecting' Coleridge's formulas into the contemporary scene," why not "also discuss their bearing upon our economic quandaries"? When society's "patterns are in disarray, how can the mind be wholly ordered, except by reference to some scheme of purposes and methods, still to be attained?" Richards should not have "so cursorily dismissed the 'propagandist' element in poetry today" (KB, "Coleridge Rephrased," *P* 47, 1 [October 1935], 54).

123. The phrase was Leavis's ("Dr. Richards, Bentham and Coleridge," 396).

124. Richards, *Coleridge on Imagination*, pp. 26, 145.

125. Richards, *Principles*, p. 131; emphasis added.

126. Coleridge to Robert Southey, August 7, 1803 (*Letters of Samuel Taylor Coleridge*, ed. Earl Leslie Greggs [Oxford: Clarendon Press, 1966], vol. 2, p. 510. Quoted in Richards, *Coleridge on Imagination*, p. 168.

127. Richards, *Principles*, p. 148.

128. George Bornstein speaks of WS's "where my spirit is I am" as "reaching back through Coleridge's definition of imagination as infinite repetition of 'the infinite I AM' to Hebrew definitions of God" (*Transformations of Romanticism*, p. 178).

129. Richards, *Coleridge on Imagination*, p. 86.

130. TCW to MM, April 9, 1935 (RML, MM Papers, V:78:04). It begins: "I am taking the liberty of quoting from Wallace Stevens' letter in regard to writing about your poems, for I think what he says would interest you, and I am sure that he would not object to my doing this."

131. TCW to MM, May 27, 1935 (RML, MM Papers, V:78:04).

132. Celeste Goodridge, *Hints & Disguises: Marianne Moore & Her Contemporaries* (Iowa City: Univ. of Iowa Press, 1989), p. 5.

133. KB, "Likings of an Observationalist," *P* 87, 4 (January 1956), 239–40.

134. Goodridge, *Moore & Her Contemporaries*, p. 5.

135. SB, "Mr. Tubbe's Morning Service (Homage to T. S. Eliot)," *NM* 13 (November 13, 1934), 19.

136. KB, *Attitudes Toward History*, p. 64. The harder line would hold, with Mike Gold, that "Masses are never pessimistic" (Irwin Granich [pseud.], "Towards Proletarian Art," *The Liberator* 4, 2 [February 1921], 22).

137. MM to WS, July 11, 1935 (HL, WS Papers, WAS 43). She continued: "I should add, however, since this sounds as if T. S. Eliot contributed an introduction that

I had discussed with Mr. Frank Morley who came to see me when in New York, the reprinting of some things T. S. Eliot had said about me in the Dial."

138. This is Alan Wald's characterization of Sherry Mangan's criticism of Eliot (*Revolutionary Imagination*, p. 139). Mangan's noncommunist "On the Somewhat Premature Apotheosis of Thomas Stearns Eliot," published with fanfare in *Pagany* (1, 2 [April–June 1930], see especially 23) and savored by Williams in his radical moment (see Mariani, *A New World Naked*, p. 305), is typical of such rejections.

139. TCW to MM, May 27, 1935 (RML, MM Papers, V:78:04); he was quoting from Eliot, "Introduction," *Selected Poems*, p. xi. "The first aspect in which Miss Moore's poetry is likely to strike the reader," Eliot wrote, "is that of minute detail rather than that of emotional unity" (p. x).

140. *Complete Prose of Moore*, p. 580.

141. MM to TCW, May 31, 1935 (RML, MM Papers, V:78:04).

142. This is confirmed and dated by MM to Eliot, October 4, 1935 (RML, MM Papers, V:17:26). "Stevens . . . seems to read what you write yourself," MM noted here.

143. TCW to MM, June 26, 1935 (RML, MM Papers, V:78:04).

144. TCW, "New Problems," *Trend* 3, 1 (March–April 1935), 9–10.

145. "A Bold Virtuoso," *Complete Prose of Moore*, p. 443.

146. HG, "Highly Polished Poetry," 28. ·

147. See Champion's "Poem" in the Objectivist number of *P* (37, 5 [February 1931], 265). SB made a point of doubting Champion's place among the objectivists ("The February Number," 54).

148. TCW, "Let Us Go No More to Museums," in *Trial Balances*, ed. Ann Winslow (pseudonym Verna Elizabeth Grubbs) (New York: Macmillan, [October] 1935), p. 169.

149. HG, "Toward New Horizons," *Trial Balances*, pp. 173, 171.

150. TCW, "New Problems," 9.

151. TCW reported to HG another's conversation "with Partisan nit-wits": "[T]hey told him that as a result of the vicious anticultural persecution by the Stalinists they were coming out and be out and out and out Trotskyites. What an excuse! Everybody knows that's what they intended to do all along" (TCW to HG, October 8, 1937 [ALS, HG Papers]). A month later he wrote that "[w]e must fight and expose the errors and viciousness of the Trotskyites" (TCW to HG, November 6, 1937 [ALS, HG Papers]). On Williams's choice of *NM*: TCW to HG, December 2, 1937 (ALS, HG Papers).

152. This plan is described in various letters exchanged between TCW and HG (Beinecke, TCW Papers).

153. Gregory reported to Jack Wheelwright that Latimer had asked TCW to do a book of poems with Alcestis (probably at Maas's urging), and took the occasion to blast Alcestis for having seen into print a "surprisingly too prolific and diluted Stevens," while attacking Latimer's fancy limited editions by likening Alcestis to "the 'album' racket of Lady Blessington's day." TCW, himself refusing Alcestis, "told them their high prices . . . were far in excess of value received" (HG to Wheelwright, August 4, 1936 [JHB, Wheelwright Papers, b9, f26]).

154. Spector, "Sadly They Perish," reprinted in *Social Poetry of the 1930s*, pp. 287–8.

155. Louise Bogan, *Achievement in American Poetry, 1900–1950* (Chicago: Henry Regnery Company, 1951), p. 85.

156. In fact, "his is the final word" on the Eliotic theme (Walton, "Beyond the Wasteland," 263).

157. A typescript of the essay was enclosed in TCW to HG, October 20, 1937 (ALS, HG Papers); it was written in response to a review by Granville Hicks of *New Letters*.

158. TCW, "Strong Enchantment," *Quarterly Review of Literature* 4, 2 (Summer 1948), [184].

159. *Harvard Advocate* 127 (December 1940), 31.

160. MM to TCW, July 5, 1935 (RML, MM Papers, V:78:04).

161. Bryher to HG, January 30, 1936 (ALS, HG Papers). TCW had not become an editor of this journal, as has been assumed. He later explained to WCW that he merely helped with publicity in the United States (TCW to WCW, July 6, 1938 [Buffalo, WCW Papers]).

162. Thus obscuring its very close relation to the poems written the previous spring.

163. Used twice at the beginning of the review to refer to MM's care with her lines, this word had been "fastidious" before WS asked TCW to change it (*L* 281).

164. In "The Irrational Element in Poetry" and "The Noble Rider and the Sound of Words" respectively.

165. Fearing, "Symbols of Survival," *PR* 2, 7 (April–May 1935), 91.

166. Rukeyser, "This House, This Country," in *Theory of Flight*, p. 30.

167. TCW to MM, October 22, 1935 (RML, MM Papers, V:78:04). I have silently normalized several incidental errors in TCW's prose.

168. MM to TCW, November 29, 1935 (RML, MM Papers, V:78:04).

169. WS had informed RLL about MM's review (*L* 287) and when MM sent a copy to RLL (now at RML) he immediately passed it along to WS (*L* 290).

170. KB, "Likings of an Observationalist," p. 127.

171. Much of Goodridge's study, including a splendid chapter on the MM-WS relationship, is devoted to describing the complex way in which MM "believe[d] that her reviews of Stevens, Pound, and Williams might counter the reactions of a potentially unreceptive public" (*Moore & Her Contemporaries*, p. 7).

172. Goodridge, *Moore & Her Contemporaries*, p. 19.

173. MM, "Ideas of Order," *The Criterion* 15 (January 1936), 309; emphasis added.

174. G[eoffrey] E. [Grigson], "A Stuffed Goldfinch," *New Verse* 19 (February–March 1936), 18–19.

175. *Scribner's* 93 (May 1933), 318, 320.

176. MM to WS, March 10, 1936 (HL, WS Papers, WAS 45).

177. Carbon of MM to WS, October 29, 1936 (RML, MM Papers, V:63:22).

178. In *Banners & Wings* (in press), Teres claims not only that "the politics of Eliot's early criticism (and by implication that of many modernist texts) has never been as transparent as many make it out to be," but also that Rahv and Phillips successfully involved Eliot's ideas about "sensibility" in their project of "remaking Marxist criticism."

179. Eastman, *The Literary Mind*, p. 20.
180. Geoffrey Grigson, "Letter from England," *P* 49, 2 (November 1936), 102.
181. Kenneth Fearing, "American Rhapsody (I)," *Collected Poems*, p. 43. Quoted by KB in "Two Kinds of Against," *NR* 83, 1073 (June 26, 1935), 199.
182. TCW, "New Problems," 9.
183. Johns, "Moore and Eliot," 24–5.
184. MM, "Unanimity and Fortitude," 268–72; on Eliot, see p. 269; on the "egress-negress" rhyme, see p. 268.
185. Morse to MZ, February 11, 1937 (RLC, MZ Papers, b2, f15).
186. Ibid.
187. Rolfe, "Poetry," *PR* 2, 7 (April–May 1935), 32.
188. MM's copy of *The Man with the Blue Guitar & Other Poems* is at RML. In the abridged version the poem was named "The Statue at the World's End"; but MM also owned the original Alcestis edition.
189. KB, "What Is Americanism?" 10.
190. WS to Rakosi, August 18, 1942 (HRC, Rakosi Papers).

Chapter 5: Turmoil in the Middle Ground

1. HG, "Introduction," *New Letters in America* 1 (1937), 14.
2. "What Is Americanism?" 11.
3. MZ, "Recent Magazines," *P* 45, 3 (December 1934), 172, 173.
4. He was evaluating the special "Federal Poets" number of *P* (Cowley to WM, July 8, 1938 [HRC, WM Papers]).
5. Kazin, *Starting Out*, p. 16. For more on Cowley's *NR* and its relation to cultural communism, see Paul Buhle, *Marxism in the United States* (London: Verso, 1967), pp. 178, 179. Not surprisingly, Howe and Coser see even stronger "Stalinist influence" there as well as at *N* (*The American Communist Party*, p. 314).
6. Lillian Symes, "Our Liberal Weeklies," as quoted and paraphrased by Aaron, *Writers on the Left*, p. 335; see Symes, 9.
7. Warren, in *Liberals and Communism*, describes this decision and its impact on the magazine (pp. 27–8). The editorial pronouncement came in "Liberalism Twenty Years After," *NR* 81 (January 23, 1935), 290–3.
8. The critic was H. A. Mason, writing in *Scrutiny*. Cowley decided that the article actually expressed the opinion of "the redoubtable Mr. Leavis." Mason, it should be pointed out, based his criticism on a survey of everything *NR* had published in 1931, though he was writing at the end of the decade ("'The New Republic' and the Ideal Weekly," *Scrutiny* 7, 3 [December 1938], 250–61). Cowley's reply, from which I have quoted, appeared as "Transatlantic View," *NR* 97, 1259 (January 18, 1939), 318–20.
9. Cowley did just this in rejecting a poem WM had submitted to *NR* (Cowley to WM, December 14, 1936 [HRC, WM Papers]).
10. Quoted by Peter M. Gareffa, "Malcolm Cowley," *Contemporary Authors*, new rev. series, vol. 3 (Detroit: Gale, 1981), p. 142; emphasis added.
11. William Phelps (pseudonym for Phillips), "Three Generations," *PR* 1 (September–October 1934), 51.

12. James Kempf, "Encountering the Avant-Garde: Malcolm Cowley in France, 1921–1922," *Southern Review* 20, 1 (January 1984), 12–28; MacLeod, *Stevens and Company*, pp. 86–7.

13. The Cowley papers at Newberry contain surprisingly little *NR* correspondence from the thirties; there is a file of miscellaneous editorial material in the Robert Morss Lovett collection at RLC (b3, f20); Lovett (b. 1870) was associate editor at *NR* from 1921 to 1941.

14. The letter does not survive, but we have Monroe's note on Cowley's letter to MZ, November 9, 1934 (RLC, MZ Papers, b1, f17).

15. Cowley to MZ, February 13, 1935 (RLC, MZ Papers, b1, f17).

16. Cowley to MZ, January 5, October 15, and October 22, 1934 (RLC, MZ Papers).

17. Cowley to MZ, May 4, 1934 (RLC, MZ Papers).

18. The first four pieces were written by editors, Calvin P. Richards, Constance Rourke, and William P. Mangold; Louis M. Hacker, reviewing Turner's massive elaboration of his sectionalist theory, *The United States: 1830–50: The Nation and Its Sections* (1935), titled his piece "Frederick Jackson Turner: Non-Economic Historian"; Cowley on Mead, "News from New Guinea" (107), was a review of *Sex and Temperament in Three Primitive Societies* (*NR* 83, 1070 [June 5, 1935], 90, 92–5, 101–2, 102–3, 108, 107).

19. Basso, "Radio Priest − in Person," *NR* 83, 1070 (June 5, 1935), 96–8; Stevens's poem was fitted directly beneath Basso's last column.

20. George Charney, *A Long Journey* (Chicago: Quadrangle Books, 1968), p. 17.

21. Cornwall, "Twilight at the House of Morgan," *NR* 83, 1072 (June 19, 1935), 157.

22. Miles, "For Futures," *NR* 83, 1070 (June 5, 1935), 99.

23. Kazin, *Starting Out*, p. 19.

24. Howard Baker, "Wallace Stevens and Other Poets," *Southern Review* 1 (Autumn 1935), 387, 373; emphasis added.

25. Untitled essay by SB in *PR* 2, 7 (April–May 1935), 47.

26. For SB, Millay was "[a]dept of naive ecstasy," but there was still a "prospect" for her on the left: she "[r]ebell[ed] against bourgeois conventions, [and] trumpeted woman's right to sexual equality" (SB, "A Prospect for Edna Millay," 14, 1 [January 1, 1935], 39). A little later HG was incensed that Granville Hicks would rather "try to 'win over' Miss Millay than to encourage a number of younger (and, I believe, clearer and better) writers," the latter including Muriel Rukeyser, David Wolff, Alfred Hayes, and TCW ("A Symposium – Horace Gregory," originally published in *NM*, October 12, 1937; reprinted in *Granville Hicks in the New Masses*, ed. Jack Alan Robbins [Port Washington, NY: Kennikat Press, 1974], p. 391).

27. In Albert Halper's bitter phrase (*Good-bye, Union Square*, p. 146).

28. WS to RLL, November 10, 1936 (RLC, RLL Papers).

29. Quoted from the untitled preface to the first *American Caravan* (New York: The Literary Guild of America, 1927), eds. Van Wyck Brooks, Lewis Mumford, Paul Rosenfeld, and AK, p. ix.

30. Of the forty-five writers represented in the collection, no fewer than seventeen were identifiable as communists or fellow-travelers at the time. Leftist

writers gratefully considered the *American Caravan* of the thirties, the fourth
and fifth issues, "a prime literary target" among the few relatively popular
venues open to them, knowing that to have a piece appearing there was a
career "break" (Halper, *Good-bye, Union Square*, p. 56). To be sure, SB recently described his own contribution as "Parnassan" (interview with AF
and Teres), and HG judged it at the time to be "a pathetic last tribute to the
America *that was*," presumably referring to the presence of work by nonleftists
known for twenties hilarity – Aiken, Cummings, Marsden Hartley, and Jean
Toomer (HG, "Firsts," *Story* 10, 54 [January 1937], 8).

31. "I predict a big rise in the Kreymborg star," SB added (SB to AK, undated
     [1934] [Virginia, AK Papers]).
32. The statement read: "The subject of Wallace Stevens' poem in this New
     Caravan arose from my review of his book which was printed in *The New
     Masses*" (*The New Caravan*, eds. AK, Lewis Mumford, and Paul Rosenfeld
     [New York: W. W. Norton, 1936], p. 656).
33. "I wouldn't want to do a poor article for the Caravan. You said there might
     be a chance for some poems. Poems would be, after all, the best 'reply' to
     Stevens that I could make . . ." (SB to AK, undated [February or early March
     1936] [Virginia, AK Papers]).
34. AF and Teres, "An Interview with Stanley Burnshaw," 112, 120.
35. Monroe, "Volume Forty," *P* 40, 1 (April 1932), 32.
36. Monroe to WS, August 8, 1932 (HL, WS Papers, WAS 35).
37. Monroe to WS, March 11, 1935 (HL, WS Papers, WAS 36).
38. See Ellen Williams, *Harriet Monroe and the Poetry Renaissance: The First Ten
     Years of Poetry, 1912–22* (Urbana: Univ. of Illinois Press, 1977), pp. 276–77.
39. Albert Edmund Trombly, "Enough to Be," *P* 48, 5 (August 1936), 260.
40. "A Word from Mr. Pound," *P* 47, 1 (October 1935), 55. HG, "The A.B.C. of
     Ezra Pound" (*P* 46, 5 [August 1935], 279–85) had connected Pound to Ital-
     ian fascism (in *The A.B.C. of Economics* HG hears the "fog-horn voice of
     Mussolini" [285]). Pound's rejoinder publicly accused HG and other leftists
     "bolshevikly ignorant of" fascist ideas of "crass stupidity" ("A Word," 55).
41. SB, interview with AF and Harvey Teres. Once the depression came and
     poets like Raymond Larsson were informing Monroe pitifully that "such
     sums [as one earns from appearing in *Poetry*] are my life, what life it is"
     (Larsson to Monroe, December 26, 1934 [RLC, MZ Papers, b2, f11]), she
     might break her own "strict rule" against paying in advance of publication –
     "since you seem to be so hard up," as she explained to WM, who was liter-
     ally going hungry (Monroe to WM, December 18, 1932 and September 30,
     1933 [HRC, WM Papers]). WM and Dorothe Bendon, with whom he was
     then living, reacted ecstatically to this financial deliverance (WM to Mon-
     roe, December 27, 1932 [RLC, PMP12–35]).
42. WM to Monroe, January 30, 1932 (RLC, PMP12–35).
43. Postcard from Monroe to WM, March 1, 1932 (JHB, WM Papers).
44. Monroe, "*Poetry's* Old Letters," *P* 47, 1 (October 1935), 38.
45. Monroe to HG, May 25, 1935 (ALS, HG Papers).
46. Monroe to HG, September 10, 1935 (ALS, HG Papers). When, doubtless in
     reply to Monroe's lack of enthusiasm, HG let the notion of an all-radical

issue of *P* lapse, Monroe jotted a grateful note to HG's wife, the poet Marya Zaturenska, asking that HG be told that "I am relieved he is giving up that proletarian number" (November 17, 1935 [ALS, HG Papers]). In fact the "proletarian number" did become the "Social Poets Number" (48, 2 [May 1936]).

47. Isidor Schneider, "Passerby," unpublished typescript (RLC, PMP12–35, b21, f29).
48. Monroe to Marya Zaturenska, April 11, 1934 (ALS, HG Papers).
49. Pound, "Small Magazines," *P*, August 1930, 691.
50. The corrected typescript remains at RLC in PMP12–35, b12, f14.
51. Johns to Monroe, November 21, 1931 (RLC, PMP12–35, b12, f14).
52. Johns to Monroe, undated on "National Committee for the Defense of Political Prisoners" stationery [Summer or Autumn 1932] (RLC, PMP12–35).
53. SB to Monroe, March 23, 1933 (RLC, PMP12–35). Monroe's rejection is noted and dated in her hand on this letter.
54. SB to Monroe, October 22, 1932 (RLC, PMP12–35).
55. SB to AK, May 5, 1934 (Virginia, AK Papers); emphasis added
56. Monroe, "Volume Forty," 30; Rose Henrikson to MZ, October 17, 1936 (RLC, MZ Papers, b2, f1).
57. Monroe, "Volume Forty," 30.
58. For WS's encouragements of Monroe during his own fallow years, see, e.g., *L* 243, 244, 260. From among a good deal of archival evidence of WS's support of MZ, one finds a very warm telephone message WS left for him at the *P* offices, dated February 5, 1934: "Wallace Stevens called – likes your work – left his regards. He says your tone & temper are in the mood of English critics, whom he likes better than Am. mostly" (RLC, MZ Papers, b3, f9).
59. Harriet Monroe, *A Poet's Life* (New York: Macmillan, 1938), pp. 342–3, 390–1.
60. A portion of the *Sun* article was quoted on the contents page of *P* 49, 3 (December 1936).
61. *PR* 2, 7 (April–May 1935), 47. Cowley wrote: "It is the fashion now to jeer at such phrases as 'poetry renaissance'" (untitled statement, *P* 49, 3 [December 1936]), 158).
62. Rolfe, "Poetry," *PR* 2, 7 (April–May 1935), 32, 33.
63. MZ, "Force as Criticism," 382.
64. MZ, "A Poetry of Beliefs," *NR* 83, 1072 (June 19, 1935), 173.
65. MZ, "The Harmonium of Wallace Stevens," 149, 152.
66. Undated memorandum [January or February 1935] (RLC, PMP12–35, b28, f16).
67. *P* had in fact published "Good Man, Bad Woman" in October 1932, but WS himself recognized this as a "scrap" (*L* 262), sending it to Monroe with skepticism and leaving it uncollected at his death.
68. MZ, "Recent Magazines," 174, 175; emphasis added.
69. MZ to Robert England, February 10, 1934 (RLC, MZ Papers, b1, f27).
70. Morse to MZ, January 6, 1937 (RLC, MZ Papers, b2, f15).
71. An undated, three-page memorandum from MZ to Monroe [1935] (RLC, PMP12–35, b28, f16).

72. Memorandum from MZ to Monroe, November 30, 1930 (RLC, MZ Papers, b2, f1).
73. At least this was the rumor O'Donnell reported to WM (October 28, 1937 [WUL, O'Donnell Papers]). See also WM to Sara Bard Field, January 14, 1938 (HL, C.E.S. Wood Papers, WD 166[23]).
74. George Dillon to Marjorie Allen Seiffert, October 3, 1938 (Colorado, Seiffert Papers).
75. On newsstand sales: Dillon to MZ, January 5, 1937; on Auden and Spender, of whom Dillon told MZ forthrightly he was "a keen admirer": Dillon to MZ, October [2]7, 1936 (RLC, MZ Papers, b1, f23). The negotiations for Dillon's assumption of editorship began in December 1936 (see MZ to Dillon, December 29, 1936 [ALS, Dillon Papers]). Astonishingly, from 1930 through the beginning of 1937, not a line of verse by Auden, Spender, or Day Lewis appeared in *Poetry*; in the next four years, Day Lewis's work appeared five times, Spender's ten, Auden's four.
76. Dillon to Jessica North, August 27, 193[7] (RLC, MZ Papers, b1, f22).
77. Ruth Lechlitner to George Dillon, December 5, 1938 (RLC, PMP36–53, b15, f2).
78. WM to Dillon, February 18 and 24, 1938; Dillon to WM, February 21, 1938 (RLC, PMP36–53); Cowley to WM, February 24, 1938; Ruth Lechlitner to WM, August 9, 1928 (HRC, WM Papers); "The Federal Poets Number," 276–83. The all-radical issue included poems by Van Ghent, Funaroff, Fearing, Rosenberg, Vincent McHugh, Larsson, Alfred Hayes, Harry Roskolenko, AK, and WM himself. *P*'s more conservative poets were certain Dillon was taking the magazine both leftward and downhill. "The WPA issue was bad," Samuel French Morse confided to O'Donnell, "but it is an indication of what is happening, it helps us to know what must be done. . . . It ought to be possible, I think, to have another Southern Number. . . . Dillon has no taste. . . . It is discouraging to see the magazine going to pieces. . . ." (Morse to O'Donnell, August 16, 1938 [WUL, O'Donnell Papers]).
79. In strongly endorsing the Coffee-Pepper Bill, which would have funded a permanent federal Bureau of Fine Arts, Dillon took *P* to its furthest left position. This really was a bold position: Even proponents of federal aid to the arts, such as George Biddle, feared that Coffee-Pepper would curtail artists' freedom from political control ("Art under Five Years of Federal Patronage," *American Scholar* 9 [Summer 1940], 327–38). Moreover, Dillon's rationale for supporting the bill was distinctly marked by leftist rhetoric (a point that would have been extremely clear to WM and other communists): "If it is defeated," Dillon wrote in *P*, "the reign of barbarism which is spreading in Europe *and which threatens America* will have won an advance victory" ("News Notes," *P* 51, 6 [March 1938], 350; emphasis added). Dillon was responding to WM's urging (WM to Dillon, February 18, 1938 [RLC, PMP36–53]; and from WM to Sara Bard Field, March 5, 1938 [HL, C.E.S. Wood Papers, WD 166(24)]).
80. Lechlitner to Dillon, August 16, 1938 (RLC, PMP36–53, b15, f2).
81. Lechlitner to Dillon, January 27, 1938 (RLC, PMP36–53).
82. Lewis to Dillon, with editorial notes by Dillon, April 1, 1938 (RLC, PMP36–

53, b15, f4); the typescript of the poem is in this file. It was published in *P*
52, 3 (June 1938), 115–17.

83. Dillon to Lewis, November 2, 1938 (RLC, PMP36–53, b15, f4).

84. WM to Dillon, February 18, 1938 (RLC, PMP36–53).

85. WM to Sara Bard Field, January 14, 1938 (HL, C.E.S. Wood Papers, WD 166[23]).

86. WM to Dillon, February 18, 1938 (RLC, PMP36–53).

87. That he was keeping up with *P*'s doings is the underlying assumption of WS to MZ, March 3, 1933; October 22, 1934; and MZ to WS, October 25, 1934 (RLC, MZ Papers, all b3, f9).

88. WM, "Four Young Revolutionists," *P* 54, 1 (April 1934), 51–3; emphasis added.

89. The phrase about Magil did not appear in the printed review, only in the typescript, which is now filed with other poems and reviews WM wrote for *P* (RLC, PMP12–35, b14, f29).

90. WM to Monroe, January 9, 1934 (RLC, PMP12–35).

91. SB to MZ, June 2, 1934 (RLC, MZ Papers, b1, f14).

92. His itinerary, advertised in *NM*, listed Hartford as one of his New England engagements ("A New Masses Editor Goes on Tour," *NM*, April 17, 1934, 2), but that stop was cancelled (interview with AF and Teres). "Too bad," SB wrote me recently, "for I think Stevens might have attended. You recall that he referred to himself in one of his letters as belonging to the left!!!!" (SB to AF, April 9, 1988). I am grateful to Paul Rogers for sharing with me his detailed recollections of SB's tour stop in Oberlin, Ohio (Rogers to AF, February 17, 1989).

93. SB to AK, May 5, 1934 (Virginia, AK Papers).

94. This sequence consisted of six poems, which might be characterized as the sort of aestheticism which the SB of 1933–4 might have criticized as "escapist" and the SB of 1935 might have upheld as "confused." "Restful Ground," typical of the group, begins:

> I have known solitudes, but none has been
> Such as I seek this hour: a place so still
> That the darkened grasses wake to no sound at all
> Nor float their shadowy fingers in a wind.

"Eartha," *P* 37, 6 [March 1931], 297–300. But it should be noted that when asked recently about the validity of Monroe's remark on his seemingly abrupt shift from nature poems to social realism, SB said, "You should look at my *later* book, *The Iron Land*, which appears in 1936 and contains *all* the poems that appeared in that 'Eartha' sequence" (interview with AF and Teres). Jack Salzman seems to support SB's view, and has included "Eartha" in his selection of "social poetry" (*Social Poetry of the 1930s*, pp. 17–20). A slightly revised version of "Restful Ground" was included in *The Iron Land* (p. 66).

95. John Drinkwater, *The Poet and Communication* (London: Watts & Co., 1923), p. 56.

96. Lola Ridge, *Dance of Fire* (New York: Harrison Smith & Robert Haas, 1935); the book was awarded the 1935 Shelley Memorial Award and won Ridge a Guggenheim fellowship.

97. Rolfe Humphries, "Discipline in Verse," 34.

98. Monroe, "Art and Propaganda," *P* 44, 4 (July 1934), 210–15.

99. Joseph Wood Krutch, "Literature and Utopia," *N* 137, 3563 (October 18, 1933), 442.

100. Paul Rosenfeld, "The Authors and Politics," *Scribner's* 93, 5 (May 1933), 318–20.

101. SB to AK, August 7, 1934 (Virginia, AK Papers).

102. His July 26 letter, addressed to Monroe but in part complaining about Zabel ("Mr. Zabel has been guilty of breaches in good breeding and common courtesy"), was answered not by Monroe but by Zabel (SB to Monroe on *NM* stationery, July 26, 1934 [RLC, PMP12–35, b3, f11]. A note in MZ's hand atop the first page of the letter reads: "ansd by MDZ July 25, '34."

103. SB, "The Poetry Camps Divide," *NM* 12, 5 (July 31, 1934), 21–3; "Stanley Burnshaw Protests," *P* 44, 6 (September 1934), 351–4.

104. Monroe, "Art and Propaganda," 213.

105. SB, "The Poetry Camps Divide," 22.

106. SB to Monroe, July 26, 1934 (RLC, PMP12–35, b3, f11).

107. That MacLeish's poem expressed hatred of "the Harrimans, Vanderbilts and Morgans who 'screwed america gaunt and scrawny with their seven year panics'" was not adequate if it did not at the same time stipulate "that the wealth of the nation be restored to the nation, the stock market plowed under for a truck farm" (Gold, "Out of the Fascist Unconscious," *NR* 73 [July 26, 1933], 295).

108. Calmer, "Portrait of the Artist," 3.

109. SB to Hicks, July 22, 1936 (ALS, Hicks Papers).

110. Louis Untermeyer, *Poetry: Its Appreciation and Enjoyment* (New York: Harcourt, Brace and Co., 1934), p. 293.

111. SB, "A New Untermeyer Product," *NM*, August 14, 1934, 26. Untermeyer *was* the "perfect liberal," among the first to advocate in print the cause of the Spanish Republic.

112. WM to RLL, December 15, 1934 (RLC, RLL Papers). WM understood fully the special expectations that communist reviewers had for poets of their own political stripe: "I am not at all sure that my book won't get the worse panning of all [the Alcestis Press books] since they [the *NM*] expect much from me in a revolutionary way" (WM to RLL, July 7, 1935 [RLC, RLL Papers]).

113. Selections from the MacLeish controversy are reprinted in *Years of Protest*, pp. 239–44. "McBosh": SB to AK, undated [1934] (Virginia, AK Papers).

114. HG, "One Writer's Position," 20.

115. Meridel LeSueur, "The Fetish of Being Outside," *NM* 14, 5 (January 26, 1935), 22. HG took his counter-response, "Revolution and the Individual Writer," to *PR* (2, 7 [April–May 1935], 52–8).

116. Howe and Coser, *The American Communist Party*, p. 190.

117. Herbert Solow "Minutiae of Left-Wing Literary History," *PR* 4, 4 (March 1938), 59. For a general, though implicitly partisan survey of the left-wing "Intellectual Merry-Go-Round" in this period, see Harvey Klehr, *The Heyday of American Communism: The Depression Decade* (New York: Basic Books, 1984), pp. 349–64.

118. I use the term "social poetry" sparingly and quite distinctly to refer to a broad category of poems generally aligned with the left, written by poets whose total output in the thirties may or may not have been so aligned. In this I am following Jack Salzman's indulgent definition guiding the selection in *Social Poetry of the 1930s*, pp. vii–ix. Salzman's notion that "Not all the *social poems* of the 1930s . . . came from poets who *were identified* with the Left" (never mind that they might have actually been loyal and active participants) suggests that the term is thus especially appropriate to my discussion of "passing aesthetic opportunities" and good timing.

119. SB to WM on *NM* stationery, June 11, 1934 (JHB, WM Papers). SB did encourage WM to send other poems.

120. "'The Anarchic Masque,' much as I enjoyed most of it (in fact probably more than the others), I feel to be counter-revolutionary in tone," WM wrote when rejecting Wheelwright's poem for *Alcestis*, "especially since this number is supposed to uphold revolutionary letters, and I really feel it would be somewhat ridiculous for me to publish a satire on many of the very people I shall publish in my issue" (WM to John Wheelwright, February 12, 1935 [JHB, Wheelwright Papers, MS 79.1]).

121. Characteristically, Wheelwright was including himself among "radicals" (Wheelwright to WM, undated [JHB, WM Papers]).

122. "V.B.W." to WM, undated [early 1935?] (HRC, WM Papers).

123. Howe and Coser, *The American Communist Party*, p. 286.

124. SB to Hicks, undated [early 1934] (ALS, Hicks Papers).

125. WM, "An Improvement," *NM* 11, 5 (May 1, 1934), 23.

126. George Wolfskill, "New Deal Critics: Did They Miss the Point," *Essays on the New Deal*, eds. Harold M. Hollingsworth and William F. Holmes (Austin: Univ. of Texas Press, 1969), p. 50.

127. Kazin, *Starting Out*, p. 73.

128. Freeman, *PLUS*, p. 28.

129. Calmer, "Portrait of the Artist," 14.

130. Serge Guilbaut, *How New York Stole the Idea of Modern Art: Abstract Expressionism, Freedom, and the Cold War*, trans. Arthur Goldhammer (Chicago: Univ. of Chicago Press, 1983), p. 18.

131. Paul Buhle, *Marxism in the U.S.*, p. 179.

132. William Z. Foster, "People's Front and People's Democracy," *Political Affairs* 29, 5 (June 1950), 15.

133. The figure is not arbitrary: Fearing called HG's "emotional confusion" a "malady" when he attacked the historical references in *Chorus for Survival* ("Symbols of Survival," *PR* 2, 7 [April–May 1935], 90).

134. In my view, then, the difference between the two hermeneutic procedures was neither of kind nor of degree. Yet because the later policy was inclusive in effect (though not necessarily by design), while the earlier was exclusive (in effect and by design), leftists like KB much preferred the later. It is also true that the main result of "the shift . . . from a fant[as]ized constituency to a real one," to quote Buhle's description (*Marxism in the U.S.*, p. 178), was that such a challenging, "real" readership had raised, not lowered, expectations. Yet, again, the very least that was expected of readers

and authors alike was basic sympathy, even if it had to be described as "unconscious."

135. Raymond Williams, *The Politics of Modernism: Against the New Conformists* (London: Verso, 1989), p. 59.

136. Isidor Schneider to Ruth Lechlitner, October 3, 1935 (Iowa, Lechlitner Papers).

137. Like the New Left claim that American communism grew from American roots, this assertion is controversial, and draws fire from Theodore Draper. That a "tactful and considerate attitude" toward bourgeois culture was being systematically advocated by communists well before 1935 is the main contention of James F. Murphy's *The Proletarian Moment: The Controversy over Leftism in Literature* (Urbana: Univ. of Illinois Press, 1991); see especially pp. 24, 27, 206.

138. Freeman, "The Tradition of American Revolutionary Literature," *NM*, May 5, 1935, 24; this ran with Cowley's "What the Revolutionary Movement Can Do For a Writer" (22) and Waldo Frank's "Values of the Revolutionary Writer" (20–2). There now began to appear in *NM* reviews frequent (and positive) mentions of especially well-known poets whom the left wanted to attract; Millay, Robinson and even Frost appeared sympathetically in Orrick Johns's otherwise scorching attack on MM (or, rather, on Eliot via MM).

139. Josephson, "Review and Comment: For a Literary United Front," *NM*, April 30, 1935, 22.

140. Dale Curran, "Only One Subject," *NM*, April 9, 1935, 21.

141. Norbert Guterman, "Towards Marxist Criticism," *NM*, April 2, 1935, 32; emphasis added. Matthew Josephson similarly dredged up Engels's appreciation of Balzac, long in disuse among Marxists, as "the best medium thus far developed for conveying social truths as literature" ("For a Literary United Front," 22). It was actually asserted that one must work to reverse the literary-critical trend at *NM*, where one unfortunately found the "frequent condemnation of the genuine revolutionary" works of literature "on the sole ground that they do not portray a true Communist" ("Towards Marxist Criticism," 32).

142. SB, "Middle-Ground Writers," *NM*, April 30, 1935, 19.

143. In a section called "Literary Buckshot," John Pyros accumulated these and many other examples of Gold's talent for skull-cracking (*Mike Gold: Dean of American Proletarian Literature* [New York: Dramatika Press, 1979], pp. 148–9).

144. SB, "Middle-Ground Writers," 20.

145. For some already sympathetic poets, such as Kenneth Rexroth, the latitudinarian inclusion of everyone worked in reverse. Rexroth was "not altogether nuts about the sort of thing the *New Masses* & *New Republic* have used in the last two years. They represent a sort of literary Popular Frontism, a definite attempt to reach and influence as large an audience as possible as quickly as possible. . . . [I]t seems to me that the poems of mine you [WM] refer to suffer from the suspicion of an 'emergency program'" (Rexroth to WM, March 8, [1938] [HRC, WM Papers]). Rexroth felt that what had been a distinct line based on substantive disagreements had been replaced by a position entirely based on strategy and without distinct substance.

146. WM, "An Improvement," 23.
147. Unpublished portion of interview with AF and Teres. At this point, Teres asked: "To what extent was *self*-censorship going on?" SB replied: "It's hard to know."
148. In 1937, she was an associate editor of *Pacific Weekly*, edited by Lincoln Steffens; Sara Bard Field and Carey McWilliams were other associates (ALS, Granville Hicks Papers, Box 69).
149. SB to WM, April 16, 1934 (HRC, WM Papers).
150. SB to WM, April 23, 1934 (HRC, WM Papers).
151. WM, unsigned review of Welch, *NM*, May 24, 1934, 28; emphasis added. Welch's political verse subsequently appeared in *NM*, e.g. "The Armed Multitude," 20, 4 (July 21, 1936), 17; and "Call It Your World," 20, 11 (September 8, 1936), 21.
152. WCW to Samuel French Morse, March 8, 1934, "Four Unpublished Letters from William Carlos Williams to Samuel French Morse," ed. Guy Rotella, *William Carlos Williams Review* 14, 2 (Fall 1988), 74.
153. Humphries, "Discipline in Verse," 34.
154. Lechlitner, *Tomorrow's Phoenix*, p. 13.
155. Harold Rosenberg, "The Bureaucrats," *New Letters in America* 1 (1937), 106–7.
156. David Wolff, "Remembering Hart Crane," *PLUS*, pp. 201–2.
157. Harvey Breit to Harry Roskolenko, May 5, 1938 (ALS, Roskolenko Papers). On "[r]evolutionary inadequacies" and more on Breit's political affiliations: Breit to Roskolenko, January 20, 1937 (ALS).
158. Anticommunist critics reanimated the term "sensibility" largely in reply to the left; the right, in other words, re-emphasized this particular distinction that had already somewhat lapsed in modernist theory. MZ, appalled that Bernard Smith would put "invisible but unmistakable inverted commas of ironic contempt" around the phrase "the quest of beauty," responded by countering what he saw as the Marxist attack on "sensibility": "Sensibility [i]s a critical instrument of infinitely greater importance to criticism than popular or political passions" ("Force as Criticism," 382).
159. SB, "Middle-Ground Writers," 19.
160. MM, "There Is a War That Never Ends," *Kenyon Review* 5 (Winter 1943), 145.
161. Belitt, "The Violent Mind," 710.
162. Fearing to Rakosi, undated [1935?] (HRC, Rakosi Papers). The Fearing-Rakosi letters at HRC are all undated, but a time frame can be inferred from one letter that mentions Albert Halper's *Union Square*, first published in 1933.
163. Belitt, "The Violent Mind," 710; emphasis added.
164. Herman Michelson to Granville Hicks, November 4, 1937; Hicks to Michelson [November 1937] (ALS, Hicks Papers). Hicks's review appeared in *NM* of November 23, 1937 (25, 9), 20–1.
165. "[N]umerous [critics] stated that form cannot be considered as separate from content, and let it go at that. I. A. Richards . . . tried to prove . . . that all of the elements in the response run together" (SB, "Notes on Revolutionary Poetry," 20).
166. Wallace Phelps [pseudonym], "Form and Content," *PR* 2, 6 (January–February 1935), 32. For a classic early-thirties condemnation of Richards, see

Max Eastman, *The Literary Mind*, pp. 297–317; Eastman did praise Richards for adhering to a scientific concept of art (pp. 57–8).

167. SB, "Notes on Revolutionary Poetry," 20, 21; emphasis added.

168. SB to AF, May 23, 1990.

169. Lechlitner to WM, [Summer 1935] (JHB, WM Papers).

170. WM to Sara Bard Field, August 14, 1937 (HL, C.E.S. Wood Papers, WD 166[20]).

171. Warren French, "The Thirties – Poetry," *The Thirties: Fiction, Poetry, Drama*, ed. Warren French (Deland, FL: Everett Edwards, Inc., 1967), p. 121; emphasis added.

172. Benét, "Three Poets and a Few Opinions," 196.

173. TCW to MM, May 27, 1935 (RML, MM Papers, V:78:04).

174. The book is in SB's possession (an unnumbered review copy, signed by WS and marked by RLL as "out of series").

175. Benét, "Three Poets and a Few Opinions," 196; he was quoting WS's "Academic Discourse at Havana" (*CP* 144). He added: "If the reader is inclined to shout 'Yes!' [in answer to the question "Is the function of the poet here mere sound?"] he is far too hasty." And yet he proceeded immediately to speak of "The Idea of Order at Key West," "one of the best" poems in *Ideas*, as "almost pure music" (196).

176. "Domination of Wallace Stevens (1925)," *Collected Poems of Carl Rakosi*, p. 471.

177. Untermeyer, "The New Poetry," *American Mercury* 36, 143 (November 1935), 378.

178. Roethke, untitled review, *NR* 87, 1128 (July 15, 1936), 305.

179. See KB, "The Vegetal Radicalism of Theodore Roethke," *Sewanee Review* 58 (1950), 68–108.

180. William Phillips's 1934 essay "Sensibility and Modern Poetry," published in the proletarian *Dynamo*, concluded with an appeal for the literary left to adopt his slogan, "Let sensibility takes its course": "For when a poet's sensibility is rooted in the proletariat *and adjusted to traditional poetry*, he has the equipment to produce good proletarian poetry" (Wallace Phelps, *Dynamo*, 1, 3 [Summer 1934], 25). There can be little doubt that Roethke's use of the term for WS had Phillips's revisionism in mind.

181. AK's *Our Singing Strength: An Outline of American Poetry (1620–1930)*, first published in 1929 ([New York]: Coward-McCann), went through several editions in the early thirties.

182. Belitt, "The Violent Mind," 710.

183. Gold, "Wilder: Prophet of the Genteel Christ," 267, 266. What became "The Gold-Wilder Controversy" (see *NR* 65, 834 [November 26, 1930], 49) would have been very hard to miss. Letters defended and excoriated Gold until mid-December ("The Final Round," *NR* 65, 837 [December 17, 1930], 141).

184. Kenneth Patchen, *Before the Brave*, p. 56.

185. Rukeyser, "Poem out of Childhood," *Theory of Flight*, p. 12.

186. E.g., in his book, *André Spire and His Poetry* (Philadelphia: Centaur Press, 1933).

187. SB to AK, undated [March or April 1936] (Virginia, AK Papers). This is not to suggest that no esteemed radical writers used or worked hard at tra-

ditional meters or subgenres; for more on this point, see Chapter 7, section 1.

188. Lola Ridge, "Russian Women," *Red Flag* (New York: Viking, 1927), p. 52.

189. Schneider, "Portrait of a False Revolutionist," *Dynamo* 1, 3 (Summer 1934), 12; emphasis added.

190. KB, *Attitudes Toward History*, p. 43.

191. A song from *Pins and Needles*, lyrics by Harold Rome, produced and presented collectively by the International Ladies Garment Workers' Union Players at the Labor Stage Theatre in New York, November 27, 1937.

192. In the same essay in which Dorothy Van Ghent criticized WS for "standing alone," she stretched popular-front categories of the "materialism" of modernist poetry to include MM: "It is, of course, a little shocking to suggest that the poetry of Marianne Moore, this poetic Audubon of jerboas and Egyptian pulled glass bottles, may have more to do with 'social reconstruction' than the poems one reads nowadays about strikers and the fascist threat." Van Ghent pointed out that MM might help "younger [radical] poets who have ignored or deliberately repudiated the tradition of her generation" ("Where Poets Stood Alone," 44).

193. MM, "The Labors of Hercules," *Selected Poems*, p. 59.

194. "Free thought, free art, free poetry have all produced this sort of tyranny" (*L* 574).

195. Notes on loose sheets removed from MM's copy of *Harmonium* (RML, MM Papers).

196. A hint of this view, expressed randomly in letters throughout the mid- and late-forties, can be found in WS, *The Necessary Angel: Essays on Reality and the Imagination* (New York: Knopf, 1951), p. 19.

197. Baird, *Dome and Rock*, p. 244.

198. Chambers, "October 21st, 1926," *P* 37, 5 (February 1931), 258.

199. Lechlitner, "Imagination as Reality," 40.

200. Bloom, *Poems of Our Climate*, p. 113.

201. SB, "Turmoil in the Middle Ground," *NM*, 17, 1 (October 1, 1935), 41.

202. Ibid., 42.

203. Ibid.

Chapter 6: Toward a Rhyming of Opposites

1. SB to AK, July 19, 1934 (Virginia, AK Papers).

2. Riddel, *Clairvoyant Eye*, p. 127. This reading of "Owl's Clover" is a revision of Riddel's 1958 essay, "'Poets' Politics' – Wallace Stevens' *Owl's Clover*"; the assertion quoted is not to be found in the earlier article.

3. Riddel, *Clairvoyant Eye*, p. 127; emphasis added.

4. Beckett, *Wallace Stevens*, p. 113.

5. For more on Draper's view, see notes 1 and 23 to the Introduction. Paul Buhle, in response to Draper's student Harvey Klehr, has written: "The most exciting and least understood truth of Communism in America lies in America above all. . . . The history of the Left never was separable from [American] communities" ("Historians and American Communism: An Agenda," *International Labor and Working Class History* 20 [Fall 1981], 44).

6. Nelson, *Repression and Recovery*, p. 164.

7. SB, "Wallace Stevens and the Statue," 356.

8. For SB's views on this matter, see AF and Teres, "An Interview with Stanley Burnshaw," 120. Frank Kermode's account of the SB episode (in *Wallace Stevens*, pp. 63–6), which SB felt was founded on a faulty or incomplete reading, was what prompted him to write an essay on the controversy for the *Sewanee Review* ("Wallace Stevens and the Statue"). I have also consulted Harry Levin to SB, September 22, 1961, which conveyed Kermode's response (HRC, SB Papers). SB wrote:

> Kermode . . . introduces the [WS-SB] affair by stating that the reviewer "criticized Stevens' apparent indifference to what was going on in the world," which is exactly what the review did not do. Mr. Kermode writes in England, where a 1935 issue of a foreign periodical may be a trouble to obtain; but can one write several pages of respectable first-hand criticism by referring only to what others have said? ("Wallace Stevens and the Statue," 356)

9. Cowley, "Thirty Years Later: Memories of the First American Writers' Congress," 498.

10. SB, "Turmoil in the Middle Ground," 364.

11. WS to RLL, April 15, 1936 (RLC, RLL Papers).

12. "When in the course of human events," *Before the Brave* (New York: Random House, 1936), p. 13.

13 SB, "New Youngfellow," *Dynamo* 1 (January 1934), 14–18; slightly revised for *The Iron Land: A Narrative by Stanley Burnshaw* (Philadelphia: Centaur Press, 1936), pp. 94–8.

14. AK, *Selected Poems (1912–1944)* (New York: E. P. Dutton, 1945), p. 233.

15. Isidor Schneider, "Jobhunt," *The Temptation of Anthony*, p. 115.

16. TCW, "Poem" in "There Comes An End," *P* 48, 2 (May 1936), 73. Other such poems are Miriam Kaplan's "City Scenes" (*P* 41, 5 [February 1933], 259), Sol Funaroff's "A Love Poem about Spring" (*NM* 8, 7 [April 1933], 20), and HG's "Men of Tree Ages" (*P*, 44, 5 [August 1934], 239–45).

17. Louis Lozowick, "Aspects of Soviet Art," *NM* 14, 5 (January 29, 1935), 18.

18. Merle E. Brown, *Wallace Stevens: The Poem as Act* (Detroit: Wayne State Univ. Press, 1970), p. 153.

19. Kermode, *Wallace Stevens*, p. 64.

20. Bloom, *Poems of Our Climate*, pp. 117, 113.

21. Riddel, *Clairvoyant Eye*, p. 121.

22. Ashbery's "prankster" *polyptoton* is discussed briefly by Douglas Crase, "The Prophetic Ashbery," in *Beyond Amazement*, ed. David Lehman (Ithaca: Cornell Univ. Press, 1980), pp. 45–6. I hope it is clear that I am pointing to a similarity between Stevens and Ashbery that goes well beyond Ashbery's first uses of "decorous diction, derived from Stevens" (in, for instance, Ashbery's poem "Some Trees") or the Stevensian tercets in early Ashbery (David Shapiro, *John Ashbery: An Introduction to the Poetry* [New York: Columbia Univ. Press, 1979], pp. 50, 44).

23. SB, "Notes on Revolutionary Poetry," 22.

24. Hi Simons to WS, August 3, 1940 (HL, WS Papers, WAS 90).

25. SB to AK, undated [February or early March 1936] (Virginia, AK Papers). The poem SB would send as his reply was then tentatively titled "Fragments of a Memorial." It was not, finally, the poem AK published; that was "Driving Song."

26. Wallace Phelps [pseudonym], "Eliot Takes His Stand," *PR* 1, 2 (April–May 1934), 54.

27. Quoted in Howe and Coser, *The American Communist Party*, p. 293.

28. Calmer, "Portrait of the Artist," 14.

29. KB, "What Is Americanism?" 10.

30. Holly Stevens, "Holidays in Reality," in *Wallace Stevens: A Celebration*, ed. Frank Doggett and Robert Buttel (Princeton: Princeton Univ. Press, 1980), p. 113.

31. See *Souvenirs and Prophecies: The Young Wallace Stevens* (New York: Knopf, 1977), ed. Holly Stevens, pp. 56–8.

32. See *Souvenirs and Prophecies*, ed. Holly Stevens, pp. 131–2, 132–3.

33. Holly Stevens, "Holidays in Reality," p. 113; emphasis added.

34. One hundred acres, named after Elizabeth, the wife of Charles M. Pond (d. 1894), originally constituting the Pond homestead on Prospect Avenue, became Elizabeth Park not long after Pond's will left the land and $189,000 to the city of Hartford in 1894. See *Souvenir of the Public Parks of Hartford, Conn., 1895–1905* (Hartford: [Hartford Park Commission], [1905]). For description and "use analysis" of Hartford's public parks, I have relied on Philip Laurence Buttrick, *Public and Semi-Public Lands of Connecticut* (Hartford: [Connecticut] State Geological and Natural History Survey, 1930), pp. 74–85, 136–9.

35. See Phoebe Cutler, *The Public Landscape of the New Deal* (New Haven: Yale Univ. Press, 1985), pp. 50–63 and *passim*. On parks and "social control," see Galen Cranz, *The Politics of Park Design* (Cambridge, Mass.: MIT Press, 1982), pp. 236–9, 253, 255, 295–6.

36. Cutler, *Public Landscape of the New Deal*, p. 82; see also Cranz, *Politics of Park Design*, pp. 110–11, 176–8.

37. Jesse Steiner, "Challenge of the New Leisure," *NYT Magazine*, September 24, 1933, 1–2, 16. On "calming and containing," see Cranz, *Politics of Park Design*, p. 116.

38. Enid Baird and H. B. Brinton, *Average General Relief Benefits, 1933–1938* (Washington, D.C.: U.S. Government Printing Office, 1940), p. 18. "Hartford Business Indicators," *Metropolitan Hartford* 21, 2 (November 1935), 18–19.

39. Steiner made the connection explicit: "The NRA has brought the problem of leisure prominently before the nation" ("Challenge of the New Leisure," 1). See also Peter J. Schmitt, *Back to Nature: The Arcadian Myth in Urban America* (New York: Oxford Univ. Press, 1969); the chapter "The Literary Commuter" informatively describes reactions against the recreation movement in the period immediately preceding the depression (pp. 20–32). On use of parks by the lower classes, I have relied on Cranz, *Politics of Park Design*, pp. 184–6. See also Perk Whitman, "Parks Which Serve the People," *Recreation* 27, 5 (August 1933), 228–9.

40. See Janick, *A Diverse People: Connecticut*, p. 43.

41. One of many such projects was the construction of a music shell in Bushnell

Park, an E.R.A. undertaking (William F. McDonald, *Federal Relief Administration and the Arts* [Columbus: Ohio State Univ. Press, 1969]), p. 78.
42. Robert E. Pawlowski, *How the Other Half Lived: An Ethnic History of the Old
East Side and South End of Hartford* (Robert E. Pawlowski, Hartford, 1973),
pp. 48–9, 50.
43. Elizabeth W. Gilboy, *Applicants for Work Relief* (Cambridge: Harvard Univ.
Press, 1940), pp. 208–9.
44. William Taylor, writing to *HT*, wrote: "Hartford is the city in Connecticut
that comes closest to the South today. It is the Alabama of New England. In
not one other city in Connecticut can we find more jim-crowism, segregation . . . than in Hartford." He found an "unconscious campaign against the
Negro," and noted that "white collar positions are closed to [blacks] entirely." In 1934 70–80% of Hartford's black citizens were unemployed (*HT*,
December 11, 1934, 14). Naaman Corn, a black "manservant" at The Hartford, frequently met Stevens in Hartford's Keney Park (*WSR* 55). For a brief
description of Hartford public works programs, see Weaver, *Hartford: An Illustrated History*, p. 122. On relations between East and West Hartford, and
Hartford proper – e.g., East Hartford residents owned half the autos owned
in West Hartford, though the populations were roughly the same – I have
relied on a comparison published in *Metropolitan Hartford* (21, 6 [March 1936],
35). On the modern history of "blacks as park users," see Cranz, *Politics of
Park Design*, pp. 119–202.
45. Steiner went so far as to suggest that "[a] strategic move of lasting benefit to
the nation would be the expansion of the functions of the National Recovery Administration to include responsibility for guiding the people in the
use of their new leisure" ("Challenge of the New Leisure," 2) and discussed
"[c]ities of the future" designed around existing and prospective parks
("America at Play: A Changing Panorama," *NYT Magazine*, June 2, 1933, 8).
46. "Housing Plan Upheld, Attacked at Hearing / Crowd Applauds Wildly," *HC*,
August 1, 1935, 1.
47. But see Aldon Lynn Nielson, *Reading Race: White American Poets and the Racial Discourse in the Twentieth Century* (Athens: Univ. of Georgia Press, 1988),
pp. 60–5.
48. Lensing, *Poet's Growth*, p. 187.
49. Unpublished portion of interview conducted in June 1976 (HL, HM 53893).
50. *Souvenirs and Prophecies*, ed. Holly Stevens, pp. 166–7.
51. See Cranz, *Politics of Park Design*, e.g. p. 229.
52. Hector Rella, "The Bone and the Baby," *Dynamo* 1, 2 (March–April 1934), 12.
53. George J. Fisher quoted in Whitman, "Parks Which Serve the People," 229.
54. Gold, "Out of the Fascist Unconscious," 295.
55. Turner's "common man," committed to sectionalist identity yet prepared for
unification through balances and compromises, was fully described in Turner's
posthumous *The United States, 1830–1850: The Nation and Its Sections* (1935),
the book reviewed in the issue of *NR* in which "Dance of the Macabre
Mice" appeared. On Turner's "undifferentiated American," see John Higham,
History: Professional Scholarship in America (Baltimore: Johns Hopkins Univ.
Press, 1965), p. 176.

56. The intellectual proximity of Boston's Immigration Restriction League to the Harvard of WS's years there can be fully deduced from Barbara Miller Solomon's *Ancestors and Immigrants, and Changing New England Tradition* (Cambridge: Harvard Univ. Press, 1956). I have described WS's possible intersections with this and other aspects of Harvard's illiberal, anti-modernist *fin de siècle* in "Wallace Stevens and the Strength of the Harvard Reaction," *New England Quarterly* 48, 1 (March 1985), 27–45.

57. It was rare that WS saved full runs of journals to which he subscribed, still rarer in the thirties; but he did just that in the case of Grigson's. The WS archive at Massachusetts includes numbers 1 through 31/32 of *New Verse*, old series, and the first two issues in the new series (beginning January 1939). By March 1936 WS was writing of Grigson's journal as the organ of a political "group" (*L* 309). Several years later, he wrote that "Grigson has his eye on the right values. However, he belongs to a group" (*L* 332).

58. In "Sensibility and Modern Poetry," Phillips mentioned Auden, Day Lewis, Spender, and HG as a "transition group," whose "sensibility" placed them in transit between traditional and proletarian verse (22). In noticing just this, Harvey Teres comments on the way in which the *PR* intellectuals were "[e]mploying language from Eliot" ("Remaking Marxist Criticism" in *Banners and Wings* [in press]).

59. Samuel French Morse to George Marion O'Donnell, May 13 and June 19, 1938 (WUL, O'Donnell Papers).

60. Adrian Caesar, *Dividing Lines: Poetry, Class and Ideology in the 1930s* (Manchester: Manchester Univ. Press, 1991), p. 27. Caesar has made a close study of Grigson and *New Verse* (pp. 107–20) and describes contemporary assumptions "that *New Verse* had left-wing pretensions" (p. 112).

61. Untitled review of Day Lewis, *A Hope for Poetry* in the *Criterion* 14, 55 (January 1935), 327.

62. "Politics: and a Request," *New Verse* 2 (March 1933), n.p.

63. Grigson, "A Letter from England," 103.

64. Quoted in Elizabeth Drew and John L. Sweeney, *Directions in Modern Poetry* (New York: W. W. Norton, 1940), p. 103; emphasis added.

65. W. H. Auden, "Song," *New Verse* 1, 1 (January 1933), 5.

66. Edgar Foxall, "The Politics of W. H. Auden," *The Bookman* 85 (October 1933–March 1934), 475.

67. Typical is the brief comment by Doggett, *The Making of the Poem*, pp. 122–3. Beckett seems to me entirely confused by Grigson's failure to fit the monolithic mold of Anglo-American Marxist rhetoric in the thirties; to her, Grigson's style suggests "the left-wing sledgehammer . . . garlanded with literary frills," as if Grigson and not she were the one metaphorically mixed (*Wallace Stevens*, p. 113). Joan Richardson, in an otherwise dense account of the stir caused by Stevens's engagement with radicalism – in her account, mostly "naive socialism" – identifies Grigson's position only through Stevens's assumption that he was just "interested in propaganda" (*Later Years*, p. 131). Yet Grigson many times published expressions of his hatred of propaganda.

68. Morse to George Marion O'Donnell, July 18, 1938 (WUL, O'Donnell Papers).

69. MM to WS, March 10, 1936 (HL, WS Papers, WAS 45).

70. Grigson, untitled review of MacNeice's *Poems* (London: Faber & Faber, 1935), in the *Criterion* 15, 54 (January 1936), 320, 322.

71. MZ, "Recent Magazines," 174; emphasis added.

72. *New Verse* 11 (October 1934), 15.

73. This was Edmund Wilson's critical characterization of the American cultural environment as gloomily rendered by Dos Passos at *NR* lunchtime discussions (quoted by Josephson, *Infidel*, p. 66)

74. The office records of Alfred A. Knopf, Inc., now in the collection at the Harry Ransom Humanities Research Center, include individual files on each WS book the firm published. Unfortunately, the earliest extant readers' reports date from March 1942, when WS submitted the manuscript of *Parts of a World*, his fourth collection with Knopf. The tenor of these later reports strongly suggests that by 1942 a long-term strategy of tolerating Stevens's evident detachment from reality was well in place. So well, in fact, that in writing a negative report, editor Paul Hoffman, who had come to Knopf from the Atlantic Monthly Press, knew that even his unqualified dissent was but a formality. Hoffman stressed that "one pretty much has to be . . . a Wallace Stevens fan . . . to 'get' him," and found the verse "harder to grasp" than any the house published. But Hoffman had been warned by a fellow editor, who was named in the report, "that Stevens is someone we're pretty sure to want to keep publishing," and understood fully that his report was merely for the record (reader report dated March 3, 1942 [HRC, Knopf Papers]). By 1950 the manuscript record card for WS would read "All that need be said is that Wallace Stevens is still Wallace Stevens" (Herbert Weinstock, under "By whom read," acceptance dated "AAK 1/10/50" [HRC, Knopf Papers]). I am grateful to Knopf's William Koshland for his help in identifying Paul Hoffman's responsibilities (Koshland to AF, December 9, 1987).

75. Geoffrey T. Hellman, "Publisher – The Pleasures, Prides, and Cream," *New Yorker* 24, 41 (December 4, 1948), 42.

76. For me Morse described the choice as "instinctive and somewhat going against aesthetic value" (interview with AF). On the "irrational commitment," see Nelson, *Repression and Recovery*, p. 192: "[T]here is a regrettable tendency for people to feel a volume of collected poems eliminates the need to go back and look at individual volumes."

77. The cuts have been listed by Riddel, "Poets' Politics," 132; and Litz, *Introspective Voyager*, pp. 317–19.

78. I am quoting TCW's critical redaction of Edmund Wilson's "The Canons of Poetry," *Atlantic Monthly* 153, 4 (April 1934), 455–62; see TCW, "The Muse and Edmund Wilson," *P* 52, 3 (June 1938), 150–1.

79. In early 1935 WM noted that Fitzgerald had "gone quite Auden-Spender," which made Fitzgerald's work "much more interesting" (WM to RLL, March 5, 1935 [RLC, RLL Papers). Indeed, Fitzgerald was to appear with the communist poets in the revolutionary number of *Alcestis*. Wheelwright felt that Fitzgerald "would make a good radical" (Wheelwright to WM, undated [JHB, WM Papers]). TCW put Fitzgerald with HG, Auden, Rukeyser, Day Lewis,

and the young John Cheever when describing writers "representative in style and ideology" (letter from TCW "To the Editors of the New Republic," [1937] [ALS, HG Papers]). Not surprisingly, poets still further left suspected Fitzgerald, as Ruth Lechlitner did, of being "too Hound-and-Hornish" (Lechlitner to WM, January 24, 1936 [HRC, WM Papers]).

80. Fitzgerald, "Thoughts Revolved," *P* 51, 3 (December 1937), 155.
81. TCW to HG and Marya Zaturenska, October 15, 1937 (ALS, HG Papers).

Chapter 7: A Million People on One String

1. Morse, "Man with Imagination," 168.
2. "Hanfstaengl Gets a Plea from Harvard for Gift," *NYT*, February 8, 1936 (all citations in this note refer to the year 1936), p. 7; "Harvard Rejects Hanfstaengl Gift," *NYT* February 12, p. 16; "Hanfstaengl Chides Harvard Courtesy," *NYT*, March 17, p. 11. "Says Harvard Students Hiss Newsreel Figures," March 1, p. 34; "Treasurer of Harvard Lampoon Says Editors of That Publication Raised Red Emblem," *NYT*, May 8, p. 25; "Harvard Will Act in Red Flag Incident," *NYT*, May 9, p. 17.
3. Charney, *A Long Journey*, p. 71.
4. Roger N. Baldwin and Corliss Lamont, "Harvard Heretics and Rebels," *Harvard Advocate* 122, 4 (March 1936), 6.
5. "Harvard Commencement Speakers Assail Teachers' Oath Law, Peril to Freedom Seen at Harvard," *NYT*, June 19, 1936, p. 12.
6. Thomas Dorgan as quoted by Cornelius Dalton, John Wirkkala, and Anne Thomas, *Leading the Way: A History of the Massachusetts General Court, 1627–1980* ([Boston]: Office of the Massachusetts Secretary of State, 1984), p. 260.
7. "Harvard Seniors Mark Class Day," *Boston Globe*, June 17, 1936, p. 1. The orator was Roy Winsauer ('36); his target, Representative Dorgan, answered with additional charges of subversion (see "Dorgan Hits Back at Harvard Orator," *Boston Globe*, June 18, 1936, p. 14).
8. Such as Samuel Eliot Morison, whose commencement talk suggested that "many well-intentioned people even take so distorted a view of academic freedom as to regard it ... a shield for political plots against the state" ("Fate of Universities 'Depends on Harvard,'" *Boston Globe*, June 18, 1936, p. 18).
9. A transcript of Roosevelt's Harvard speech was reprinted in full under the headline "Roosevelt Recalls Fears Voiced for Nation in Past," *Boston Globe*, September 19, 1936, p. 6.
10. Porter Sargent, *A Handbook of Private Schools: An Annual Survey, 1936–37* (Boston: Porter Sargent, 1937; 21st ed.), pp. 57, 59.
11. Porter Sargent, *Between Two Wars: The Failure of Education, 1920–1940* (Boston: Porter Sargent, 1941), p. 319.
12. "28 Harvard Alumni Revive Sacco Case," *Boston Evening Globe*, September 1936, p. 24; "Assail Dr. Lowell on Sacco Decision," *NYT*, September 19, 1936, p. 6; "Harvard Men Ask Pamphlet Inquiry," October 1, 1936, p. 52; Sargent, *Between Two Wars*, p. 328.
13. Hermann Hagedorn, "Harvard, What of the Light?" reprinted in the *Harvard Advocate* 123, 2 (November 1936), 9.

14. A letter from Sargent to WS suggests that Sargent, a few years WS's and Witter Bynner's senior, had known them fairly well at Harvard (April 24, 1950 [HL, WS Papers, WAS 1696]). Sargent saw Bynner regularly when that mutual friend made trips East from Santa Fe. The letter of 1950 makes it clear that Sargent was writing in reply to a note from WS, but the HL collection includes nothing from Stevens to Sargent, nor does the Sargent file at the Harvard University Archives.

15. "Porter Sargent," *NYT*, March 28, 1951, 29.

16. Porter Sargent, *The New Immoralities: Clearing the Way for a New Ethics* (Boston: [Porter Sargent], 1935).

17. See Robert Keen Lamb, "Harvard Starves the Social Sciences," *N* 144, 20 (May 15, 1937), 561-2. Porter Sargent quoted an article later appearing in the *Harvard Progressive*: the two fired instructors "were not only good teachers, they represented a school of economic thought which the overwhelming conservatism of the Harvard economics department is slowly stifling" (*Between Two Wars*, p. 386).

18. Porter Sargent to John Wheelwright, July 9, 1937 (JHB, Wheelwright Papers, b10, f7). For more on the allegedly political firings of economics instructors Walsh and Sweezy, see "Dr. Conant Denies Ban on Liberals," *NYT*, April 13, 1937, p. 14. A conservative's brief view of the Harvard economics department at just this moment is offered by Henry Regnery in *Memoirs of a Dissident Publisher* (New York: Harcourt Brace Jovanovich, 1979), pp. 16-17. For this incident, and generally for a sense of the Harvard left, I have relied on Zachery Robinson, "The Progressive Student Heritage," in *How Harvard Rules: Reason in the Service of Empire*, ed. John Trumpbour (Boston: South End Press, 1989), especially pp. 383-9.

19. A. M. Schlesinger, Jr., "Harvard Today," *Harvard Advocate* 123, 1 (September 1936), 20, 21, 22.

20. William Bentinck-Smith and Hume Dowe, "More Matter with Less Art: Harvard's Student Union," *Harvard Advocate* 123, 3 (December 1936), 55.

21. "[T]he Harvard Student would never have been born without the Communists' willingness to cooperate" (Joseph E. Forbes, "The Future Veterans and the Future Revolution," *Harvard Advocate* 122, 6 [June 1936], 12). The Harvard Union itself undertook the publication of Malraux's *The Fascist Threat to Culture* (issued in 1937). For more on the thirties student left, see Susan Stout Baker, *Radical Beginnings: Richard Hofstadter and the 1930s* (Westport, CT: Greenwood Press, 1985), pp. 28-36.

22. Hermann Hagedorn, "The Oxford Group and the World Crisis," *Harvard Advocate* 123, 3 (December 1936), 23-6, 51-2; Howe and Coser, *The American Communist Party*, pp. 202-3. The figure for the 1936 strike was arrived at by reducing the students' claim of 1 million by press reports of five hundred thousand.

23. Hagedorn, "The Oxford Group and the World Crisis," 23.

24. WS, *The Necessary Angel*, p. 30.

25. This, at any rate, is the contention of AF, *Stevens and the Actual World*, pp. 3-28.

26. AF, *Stevens and the Actual World*, pp. 3-9.

27. HG, "Firsts," 103.

28. HG, "Introduction," *New Letters in America*, 10. HG shrewdly did admit that "what seems clear to one generation is obscure to the next" (10).

29. In a speech at the first American Writers' Congress, quoted by Cowley, *Golden Mountains*, p. 246.

30. Helen Davis, "Come Words Our Tools," *Cambridge Left* 1, 3 (Spring 1934), [1].

31. Marvin Klein, "Sonnet to Disintegration," *The Left* 1, 1 (Spring 1931), 91. Joseph Freeman, one of the most influential figures on the literary left, who had come intellectually of age before modernism, continued to advise young revolutionary poets to "Stop thinking of yourselves as poets who are also revolutionists or as revolutionists who are also poets. Remember that you are *revolutionary poets*. Then work hard at your poetry." For a sampling of Freeman's elaborate sonnets, see "In this black room" and "Mankind looks forward, but the hurt look back," in "Four Poems," *PR* 1, 1 (February–March 1934), 44–5. Millay, of course, wrote classical sonnets on political themes throughout the thirties, most extraordinarily in *Wine from These Grapes* (1934), but her choice of diction clearly indicates her sense of what alterations the form requires in such practice, e.g. in the first of "Two Sonnets in Memory" of Sacco and Vanzetti:

> we alone remain
> To break a fist against the lying mouth
> Of any man who says this was not so:
> Though she be dead now, as indeed we know. (p. 43)

32. AK, "American Jeremiad," *PLUS*, p. 171.

33. Michael Gold, "Examples of Worker Correspondence," *PLUS*, p. 160.

34. When reprinting one poem from Gold's "Workers' Correspondence" series in *Mike Gold: A Literary Anthology* (New York: International Publishers, 1972), Michael Folsom noted "a few minor changes which Gold pencilled in on a clipping of the original [letters] column after it appeared" (p. 215). Folsom meant to suggest that in copying such letters from the rank-and-file Gold was acting more as reproducer than writer; my point is that such an assessment neglects to account for the great changes occurring in verse lineation.

35. It was a borrowing American intellectuals in all fields made as they moved toward historicist analysis from left as often as from right. David Marcell has described Charles Beard's shift from a reliance on economic determinism to an interest in ideological forces ("Charles Beard: Civilization and the Revolt Against Empiricism," *American Quarterly* 21 [Spring 1969], 65–86). That shift caused literary communists to deem Beard one "who makes a general economic interpretation of history but does not accept the class struggle" (Isidor Schneider to Granville Hicks, June 26, 1936 [ALS, Hicks Papers]).

36. Roosevelt's margin in Cambridge was 62.6 percent to Landon's 37.4 percent; in Boston it was 69.9 percent to 30.1 percent (table 5, p. 171 in Alec Barbrook, *God Save the Commonwealth: An Electoral History of Massachusetts* [Amherst: Univ. of Massachusetts Press, 1973]). Harold Gorvine has shown that what was so stunning about FDR's overwhelming popularity in Massachusetts was the completeness with which he gained new adherents there;

his totals for the 1936 election more than doubled the victorious margin in 1932. If WS was judging from results in Hartford, his statement is even more remarkable: In 1932 Hartford County, which included Stevens's suburban West Hartford, favored Hoover by 300 votes; in 1936 the county went for Roosevelt by 38,000 (Edgar Robinson, *They Voted for Roosevelt* [New York: Octagon Books, 1970], p. 70). The statewide margin has been termed "astounding" by an otherwise solemn chronicler of Connecticut politics, John W. Jeffries (*Testing the Roosevelt Coalition* [Knoxville: Univ. of Tennessee Press, 1979], p. 27).

37. Granville Hicks, "Sinclair Lewis – Anti-Fascist," reprinted in *Granville Hicks in the New Masses*, p. 94.

38. Hallie Flanagan, *Arena: The History of the Federal Theater* (New York: Benjamin Blom, Inc., 1940), pp. 120–1.

39. Brooks Atkinson, "It Can't Happen Here," *NYT*, October 28, 1936, p. 30; "'It Can't Happen' Opens on 21 Stages," *NYT*, November 8, 1936, sec. 10, p. 1.

40. Mark Sullivan, "It Can't Happen Here," *HC*, October 23, 1935, p. 20; emphasis added. Only "protests and resistances" against New Deal legislation that causes the American people to worship the state "will help to make sure that it can't happen here" (20). For a sampling of New Dealers' reply to Sullivan's attacks on central planning, see Hugh S. Johnson, *The Blue Eagle from Egg to Earth* (Garden City, NY: Doubleday, Doran & Co., 1935), pp. 276, 309.

41. This was WS's own estimate, offered to RLL several days after the occasion (WS to RLL, December 9, 1936 [RLC, RLL Papers]).

42. *WSR* 164; unpublished, untranscribed portions of interview with Arthur Berger conducted by Peter Brazeau in November 1976 (Hm 53685).

43. Frank Lentricchia, *Criticism and Social Change*, p. 15.

44. KB, *Counter-Statement*, p. 71.

45. Riddel, *Clairvoyant Eye*, p. 136.

46. KB, *Attitudes Toward History*, p. [1]; this was KB's way of elaborating the title of his book.

47. A holograph of the poem is at Buffalo. Bates, in his new edition of *OP*, notes that vii and xxxii are not part of the holograph manuscript (322); it is almost certain that they were added when the poem was typewritten, which for Stevens was a late stage of composition.

48. For more on the particular surrealism of "Blue Guitar," see Glen MacLeod, "Stevens and Surrealism: The Genesis of 'The Man with the Blue Guitar,'" *American Literature* 59, 3 (October 1987), 359–77.

49. Riddel, *Clairvoyant Eye*, p. 135.

50. Krutch, "Literature and Utopia," 441–3.

51. Philip Rahv, "How the Waste Land Became a Flower Garden," *PR* 1, 4 (September–October 1934), 37–42.

52. Harold Rosenberg, "A Specter Haunts Mr. Krutch," *PR* 2, 7 (April–May 1935), 82–4.

53. Charles I. Glicksberg, "Joseph Wood Krutch, Critic of Despair," *Sewanee Review* 44, 1 (January–March 1936), 77–93.

54. Krutch, "Literature and Utopia," 441.

55. E.g. to *CP* 59. On WS's interest in Vaihinger's "as-if" philosophy, see Bates, *Mythology of Self*, pp. 201–2, 247; and Frank Doggett, *Stevens's Poetry of Thought* (Baltimore: Johns Hopkins Press, 1966), pp. 99n, 100n, 105–6, 185.

56. Georgi Dimitrov, *Selected Works in Three Volumes*, trans. Spass Roussinov (Sofia: Sofia Press, 1972), vol. 2, p. 22.

57. Simons to WS, August 3, 1940 (HL, WS Papers, WAS 90).

58. Morse, *Poetry as Life*, p. 159. In spite of this later conclusion, Morse's earlier one was: "Stevens has so constructed the whole that he goes progressively forward to a conclusion" (Morse, "Man with Imagination," 169).

59. Morse, *Poetry as Life*, p. 188. Susan Brown Weston has seen "the extraordinarily stylistic development" of "Blue Guitar" dependent on "Stevens's dissatisfaction with *Owl's Clover*," reading the Harvard lecture as an expression of the break between the two works ("The Artist as Guitarist: Stevens and Picasso," *Criticism* 17, 2 [Spring 1975], 111). For Louis Martz, parts of "Blue Guitar" take readers "as far as we can get from puzzled ruminative ebb and flow of *Owl's Clover*" ("Wallace Stevens: The World as Meditation," 527).

60. Krutch, "Literature and Utopia," 442.

61. Krutch, "Literature and Utopia," 441.

62. KB, "Two Kinds of Against," 198.

63. Rexroth, "Poem," *PR & Anvil* 3, 5 (June 1936), 11. In the volume *In What Hour* (New York: Macmillan, 1940) the poem was given the title "March 18, 1871–1921"; still later, in *Collected Shorter Poems* (New Directions, 1956), it appears as "From the Paris Commune to the Kronstadt Rebellion."

64. Lola Ridge, *Dance of Fire*, p. 103.

65. Taggard, *Collected Poems, 1918–1938*, p. 121.

66. The next line: "How to conceive in the name of a column of marchers?" (MacLeish, "Invocation to the Social Muse," *Collected Poems, 1917–1952* [Boston: Houghton Mifflin, 1952], p. 95.

67. Quoted derisively by HG in "Le Front Rouge," 284.

68. SB, interview with AF and Harvey Teres.

69. Quoted in Aaron, *Writers on the Left*, p. 209; emphasis added.

70. James Neugass, "A Landscape of Variations," *P* 44, 1 (April 1934), 14.

71. Cora G. Cormier, "A Little Patient Explaining," *NM* 18, 13 (March 24, 1936), 20.

72. "I always read [*Partisan*]," WS told a visitor. "The only exception to the dreary scene" (*WSR* 130). See AF, *Stevens and the Actual World*, pp. 102, 302 n.62.

73. Leon Trotsky, *Literature and Revolution*, trans. Rose Strunsky (New York: International Publishers, 1925), p. 48; the chapter is entitled "Pre-Revolutionary Art." I have quoted from Whitman's preface to the 1855 edition of *Leaves of Grass*, ed. Malcolm Cowley (New York: Viking, 1960), p. 24. For more on the American communists' Whitman, see Gold, "Towards Proletarian Art," 22–3.

74. Walton, "Wallace Stevens's Two Worlds," *NYT*, October 24, 1937, sec. 7, p. 3.

75. G. W. Pierson, *Yale: the University College, 1921–1937* (New Haven: Yale Univ. Press), pp. 302–5.

76. Charles Seymour, "Wallace Stevens: A Study in Contemporary Minor Poetry," *Harkness Hoot* 4 (November 1933), 26; illustration on 27.

77. WS, "Two Poems," *Twentieth Century Verse* 3 (April–May 1937), [3].
78. Quoted in Glicksberg, "Symbolism in Proletarian Poetry," 183.
79. Josephine Miles, "Physiologus," *P* 44, 6 (September 1934), 307.
80. Soon Picasso would address the American Artist's Congress. And in *Guernica*, as Picasso himself put it, he will make "a deliberate appeal to people, a deliberate sense of propaganda" (quoted in Patricia Leighten, *Re-ordering the Universe: Picasso & Anarchism, 1897–1914* [Princeton: Princeton Univ. Press, 1989], p. 146). See also Jay Peterson, "Picasso as a Spaniard," *NM* 25, 13 (December 21, 1937), 7.
81. AK, *Scarlet and Mellow* (New York: Boni & Liveright, 1926), p. 27.
82. TCW to HG and Marya Zaturenska, November 6, 1937 (ALS, HG Papers).
83. TCW to MM, June 26, 1935 (RML, MM Papers, V:78:04).
84. Rukeyser, "The Lynching of Jesus," *Theory of Flight*, pp. 42–3.
85. KB, *Attitudes Toward History*, p. 262.
86. Rolfe, "Poetry," 40–1.
87. KB, *Attitudes Toward History*, p. 328.
88. Bernard Smith, *Forces in American Criticism*, p. 379.
89. Rukeyser, *Theory of Flight*, p. 45.
90. Baird, *Dome and Rock*, p. 114.
91. Oppen, *Discrete Series*, p. 33.
92. Deutsch, "Meaning and Being," 153.
93. Perlis, *World of Transforming Shapes*, p. 43.
94. Fitzgerald, "Thoughts Revolved," 155.
95. Fredric R. Jameson, "The Symbolic Inference; or, Kenneth Burke and Ideological Analysis," *Critical Inquiry* 4, 3 (Spring 1978), 512.
96. Morse to MZ, undated [1937] (RLC, MZ Papers).
97. Beckett, *Wallace Stevens*, pp. 115, 120.
98. Ibid, p. 115.
99. Morse, "Man with Imagination," 169.
100. Morse to WM, September 7, 1938 (HRC, WM Papers); emphasis added.
101. WCW, "Poets' Corner," 50.
102. Fitzgerald, "Thoughts Revolved," 157.
103. Walton, "Two Worlds," p. 3.
104. Herman Michelson, another *NM* editor, expressed doubts about HG privately, even as the latter was working as poetry editor: "As I see it [HG] has suddenly awakened to the fact that he is in great danger of assuming a definite political position and is hastily withdrawing his big toe from the deep water in which he can't swim and beating it for the ivory tower" (Michelson to Granville Hicks, November 26, [1937] [ALS, Hicks Papers]).
105. HG, "Poetry in 1937," 14, 13; emphasis added.
106. Paul Corey to Granville Hicks, August 3, 1937 (ALS, Hicks Papers).
107. Paul Corey has described his and Ruth Lechlitner's association with leftwing politics in "Lurching toward Liberalism: Political and Literary Reminiscences," *Books at Iowa* 49 (1988), especially 64–5.
108. Paul Corey to AF, July 19, 1990.
109. And we know that WS and Lechlitner had at least one personal meeting (Paul Corey and Ruth Lechlitner to AF, June 27, 1987). "You have never met

Stevens, I suppose? That'll be an amusing encounter," WCW wrote RLL
after himself agreeing to come to "your party for Ruth" (WCW to RLL,
November 16, 1936 [RLC, RLL Papers]).

110. Paul Corey to AF, July 19, 1990; evidence of editorial tampering was given
in Lechlitner to WM, May 1, 1936 (HRC, WM Papers).

111. Like Walton, the reviewer for *HT*, Martha Spencer, was taken in completely
by the guitarist's position. Under the headline, "*Blue Guitar* Shows Values
'Mid Chaos," she concluded that WS was "keenly aware of the present world
of constantly changing confusions" and she somehow read canto iv as *up-
holding* the detractors. WS, according to Spencer, showed "that the millions
twanging one string of manners are demonstrating one way of individual
expression, en masse" (*HT*, October 2, 1937, p. 7).

112. HG, "Prologue as Epilogue," *P* 48, 2 (May 1936), 98. "Didacticism is an ugly
word, but to deny the existence of its quality in the new poetry is to deny a
fact so evident that it is mere cowardice to escape from its reality" (98).

113. Josephine Miles, "Imperative," *P* 44, 6 (September 1934), 306-7.

114. Harold Rosenberg, "New Poetry," *PR and Anvil* 3, 3 (April 1936), 29. SB,
"Invocation to the Unrisen," *The Iron Land*, p. 115.

115. In RLC's *P* Papers, ALS's HG or Dillon Papers, or Newberry's MZ Papers.

116. The untitled typescript, numbered "III," is at RLC in the MZ Papers, b3,
f9. A question mark in pencil appears at the top.

117. Stanzas that become xxi and xxvi are dated January and February respectively (see *OP* 322).

118. Mark Sullivan, "Dictatorship Trend Seen by Sullivan / Agrees with Miss
Thompson that First Steps Being Taken Toward Different Government," *HC*,
April 6, 1937, p. 7. See also William H. Felt, "Centralization: This Trend in
Federal Government Can Be Carried Too Far," *HC*, April 4, 1937, sec. A, p.
2. Sullivan quoted Dorothy Thompson as follows: "If any President wanted
to establish a dictatorship, and do so with all the appearance of legality, this
is the way he would take" (p. 7). For an earlier version of the charge of
"dictatorial spirit," see Walter Lippmann, *Interpretations, 1933–1935*, ed. Allan
Nevins (New York: Macmillan, 1936), p. 98.

119. Felix Morley, *Freedom and Federalism* (Chicago: Regnery and Co., 1959), p.
123.

120. "Gay Throng Ready for Inaugural," *HC*, January 20, 1937, p. 1; "Inaugurated in Pelting Rain, President Promises Aid to Millions of Unfortunates
. . . Refuses to Ride in Closed Car," January 21, 1937, pp. 1–2 (photograph
on p. 2 bears the caption: "President and Wife in Open Car Brave Rain at
Inaugural . . . He is shown with Mrs. Roosevelt in the open car they used").

121. The text of the address was reprinted in full in *HC*, January 21, 1937, p. 5.
Looking Forward had been first published in 1933, and was used in the 1936
elections.

122. Ruth Lechlitner, *We Are the Rising Wing*, in *New Directions in Prose and Poetry,
1938*, ed. James Laughlin IV (Norfolk, Conn.: New Directions, [1938]), p.
46. The play was written in 1937 (Lechlitner to WM, September 4, 1937
[HRC, WM Papers]).

123. This response was described for me (Paul Corey to AF, August 8, 1990).

124. Eastman, *The Literary Mind*, pp. 78, 92; emphasis added.
125. MM, "Unanimity and Fortitude," 272.
126. The passage is to be found in Jacques Maritain, *The Degrees of Knowledge*, trans. Bernard Wall and Margot R. Adamson (London: G. Bles, Centenary Press, 1937), p. 4; reproduced in *Sur Plusieurs Beaux Sujects*, pp. 58–9.
127. Edward Dorn, "Strumming Language," *Talking Poetics from Naropa Institute: Annals of the Jack Kerouac School of Disembodied Poetics*, ed. Anne Waldman and Marilyn Webb (Boulder: Shambhala, 1978), vol. 1, pp. 86, 90. I have quoted the first line of a "journal poem" that "comes from a visit to Safeway"; the next line is "So the work of our non-existent critics is unnecessary" (p. 90).

Index

Entries under "Stevens, Wallace" primarily give information not found elsewhere in the index.

Continued from the front of the book

DATE DUE